ACKNOWLEDGEMENTS

My sincere thanks to all those who contributed to the successful publication of this book, in particular the many people who took the time and trouble to read and comment on the draft versions, including Graeme Dargi, Yolande Pierce-Holmes, Alan Allebone, Ron & Pat Scarborough, Joe Laredo, John Holmes, James Burton, Dianne Rodgers, Eugene Benham, Louise Stapleton, Pam Miller, Charles King, Adèle Kelham and everyone else who contributed in any way and whom I have omitted to mention. Also a special thank you to Jim Watson (who's a genius) for the superb cover, wonderful cartoons, illustrations, maps, etc.

By the same author:

Buying a Home Abroad
Buying a Home in Florida
Buying a Home in France
Buying a Home in Portugal
Buying a Home in Spain
Living and Working in America
Living and Working in Britain
Living and Working in France
Living and Working in Spain
Living and Working in Switzerland

Order your copies today by phone, fax, mail or e-mail from: Survival Books, PO Box 146, Wetherby, West Yorks. LS23 6XZ, United Kingdom (tel/fax: 44-1937-843523, e-mail: survivalbooks@computronx.com, internet: computronx.com/survivalbooks). See order form on page 511.

What Readers and Reviewers Have Said About Survival Books

When you buy a model plane for your child, a video recorder, or some new computer gizmo, you get with it a leaflet or booklet pleading 'Read Me First', or bearing large friendly letters or bold type saying 'IMPORTANT - follow the instructions carefully'. This book should be similarly supplied to all those entering France with anything more durable than a 5-day return ticket. — It is worth reading even if you are just visiting briefly, or if you have lived here for years and feel totally knowledgeable and secure. But if you need to find out how France works then it is indispensable. Native French people probably have a less thorough understanding of how their country functions. — Where it is most essential, the book is most up to the minute.

Living France

We would like to congratulate you on this work: it is really super! We hand it out to our expatriates and they read it with great interest and pleasure.

ICI (Switzerland) AG

Rarely has a 'survival guide' contained such useful advice — This book dispels doubts for first-time travellers, yet is also useful for seasoned globetrotters — In a word, if you're planning to move to the USA or go there for a long-term stay, then buy this book both for general reading and as a ready-reference.

American Citizens Abroad

It's everything you always wanted to ask but didn't for fear of the contemptuous put down — The best English-language guide — Its pages are stuffed with practical information on everyday subjects and are designed to complement the traditional guidebook.

Swiss News

A complete revelation to me — I found it both enlightening and interesting, not to mention amusing.

Carole Clark

Let's say it at once. David Hampshire's *Living and Working in France* is the best handbook ever produced for visitors and foreign residents in this country; indeed, my discussion with locals showed that it has much to teach even those born and bred in *l'Hexagone*. — It is Hampshire's meticulous detail which lifts his work way beyond the range of other books with similar titles. Often you think of a supplementary question and search for the answer in vain. With Hampshire this is rarely the case. — He writes with great clarity (and gives French equivalents of all key terms), a touch of humor and a ready eye for the odd (and often illuminating) fact. — This book is absolutely indispensable.

The Riviera Reporter

The ultimate reference book — Every conceivable subject imaginable is exhaustively explained in simple terms — An excellent introduction to fully enjoy all that this fine country has to offer and save time and money in the process.

American Club of Zurich

What Readers and Reviewers Have Said About Survival Books

What a great work, wealth of useful information, well-balanced wording and accuracy in details. My compliments!

Thomas Müller

This handbook has all the practical information one needs to set up home in the UK — The sheer volume of information is almost daunting — Highly recommended for anyone moving to the UK.

American Citizens Abroad

A very good book which has answered so many questions and even some I hadn't thought of — I would certainly recommend it.

Brian Fairman

A mine of information — I might have avoided some embarrassments and frights if I had read it prior to my first Swiss encounters — Deserves an honoured place on any newcomer's bookshelf.

English Teachers Association, Switzerland

Covers just about all the things you want to know on the subject — In answer to the desert island question about *the one* how-to book on France, this book would be it — Almost 500 pages of solid accurate reading — This book is about enjoyment as much as survival.

The Recorder

It's so funny — I love it and definitely need a copy of my own — Thanks very much for having written such a humourous and helpful book.

Heidi Guiliani

A must for all foreigners coming to Switzerland.

Antoinette O'Donoghue

A comprehensive guide to all things French, written in a highly readable and amusing style, for anyone planning to live, work or retire in France.

The Times

A concise, thorough account of the DO's and DON'Ts for a foreigner in Switzerland — Crammed with useful information and lightened with humourous quips which make the facts more readable.

American Citizens Abroad

Covers every conceivable question that might be asked concerning everyday life — I know of no other book that could take the place of this one.

France in Print

Hats off to Living and Working in Switzerland!

Ronnie Almeida

CONTENTS

12. HEALTH 273

13. INSURANCE 295

IMPORTANT NOTE

A ustralia is a diverse country with many faces; a plethora of ethnic groups, religions and customs; and continuously changing rules, regulations (particularly regarding social security, Medicare, education and taxes) and prices. Note that a change of government in Australia, which can occur every three years, can have far-reaching repercussions for many important aspects of daily life in Australia.

I cannot recommend too strongly that you always check with an official and reliable source (not always the same) before making any major decisions, or taking an irreversible course of action. However, don't believe everything you're told or read (even, dare I say it, herein). Useful addresses and references to other sources of information are included in all chapters and in **Appendices A and B**, to help you obtain further information and verify details with official sources. Important points have been emphasised, **in bold print**, some of which it would be expensive, or even dangerous, to disregard. **Ignore them at your peril or cost.** Unless specifically stated, the reference to any company, organisation or product in this book doesn't constitute an endorsement or recommendation. Any reference to any place or person (living or dead) is purely coincidental. There's no such place as Wogga Wogga.

AUTHOR'S NOTES

- The federal or Commonwealth government refers to the Australian national government which has its seat in Canberra (Australian Capital Territory). The term 'state government' applies to the government of a particular state (such as New South Wales) or territory (such as the Northern Territory). Unless otherwise noted, the term 'state' also applies to territories. Note that the term 'state capital' refers to the capital of an Australian state, e.g. the capital of New South Wales is Sydney, while the capital of the Commonwealth of Australia is Canberra.

- The following (official) abbreviations for the Australian states and territories are used in this book: Australian Capital Territory (ACT), New South Wales (NSW), Northern Territory (NT), Queensland (QLD), South Australia (SA), Tasmania (TAS), Victoria (VIC) and Western Australia (WA).

- All times are shown using am (ante meridiem) for before noon and pm (post meridiem) for after noon. Most Australians don't use the 24-hour clock. All times are local, so always check the time difference when making inter-state or international telephone calls (see **Time Difference** on page 461).

- All prices shown are in Australian dollars unless otherwise noted (e.g. £ = £sterling). **Prices should be taken as estimates only, although they were mostly correct at the time of publication.**

- His/he/him also means her/she/her (please forgive me ladies). This is done to make life easier for both the reader and (in particular) the author, and *isn't* intended to be sexist.

- Most spelling is (or should be) English, although a few words (e.g. program) are shown using American spelling in the local style.

- Warnings and important points are shown in **bold** type.

- Lists of Useful Addresses and Further Reading are contained in **Appendices A** and **B** respectively.

- For those unfamiliar with the metric system of weights and measures, Imperial conversion tables are shown in **Appendix C**.

- A map of Australia is contained in **Appendix D**.

- A **Glossary** of Australian words and slang is shown in **Appendix E**.

INTRODUCTION

Whether you're already living or working in Australia or only thinking about it — this is **THE BOOK** for you. Forget about all those glossy guide books, excellent though they are for tourists, this amazing book was written especially with you in mind and is worth its weight in gold (and *not* fool's gold). *Living and Working in Australia* is designed to meet the needs of anyone wishing to know the essentials of Australian life including immigrants, temporary workers, businessmen, students, retirees, long-stay tourists, holiday home owners and even extra terrestrials. However long your intended stay in Australia, you'll find the information contained in this book invaluable.

General information isn't difficult to find in Australia, where a multitude of books are published on every conceivable subject. However, reliable and up-to-date information specifically intended for foreigners *Living and Working in Australia*, isn't so easy to find, least of all in one volume. My aim in writing this book was to help fill this void and provide the comprehensive *practical* information necessary for a relatively trouble-free life. You may have visited Australia as a tourist, but living and working there is a different matter altogether. Adjusting to a different environment and culture, and making a home in any foreign country can be a traumatic and stressful experience, and Australia is no exception.

You need to adapt to new customs and traditions, and discover the Australian way of doing things, for example finding a home, paying bills and obtaining insurance. For most foreigners in Australia, finding out how to overcome the everyday obstacles of life has previously been a case of pot luck. **But no more!** With a copy of *Living and Working in Australia* to hand, you'll have a wealth of information at your fingertips. Information derived from a variety of sources, both official and unofficial, not least the hard won personal experiences of the author, his family, friends, colleagues and acquaintants. *Living and Working in Australia* is a comprehensive handbook on a wide range of everyday subjects and represents the most up-to-date source of general information available to foreigners in Australia. It isn't, however, simply a monologue of dry facts and figures, but a practical and entertaining look at life in Australia.

Adapting to life in a new country is a continuous process and although this book will help reduce your learner's phase and minimise the frustrations, it doesn't contain all the answers (most of us don't even know the right questions). What it *will* do is help you make informed decisions and calculated judgments, instead of uneducated guesses and costly mistakes. **Most important of all it will help you save time, trouble and money, and repay your investment many times over!**

Although you may find some of the information a bit daunting, don't be discouraged. Most problems occur once only and fade into insignificance after a short time (as you face the next half a dozen). The majority of foreigners in Australia would agree that, all things considered, they love living there. A period spent in Australia is a wonderful way to enrich your life, broaden your horizons, and hopefully please your bank manager. I trust this book will help you avoid the pitfalls of life in Australia and smooth your way to a happy and rewarding future in your new home.

Good luck!

David Hampshire
February 1998

1.

FINDING A JOB

Finding a job in Australia may be easier than you expect, despite the relatively high unemployment rate, as there are vacancies for skilled tradesmen and professionals throughout the country. However, if you don't automatically qualify to live or work in Australia (for example as a citizen of New Zealand), obtaining a visa is likely to be more difficult than finding a job. Australia is no longer the legendary 'land of opportunity' or 'the lucky country', at least not for the hundreds of thousands of migrants it previously welcomed; it now hopes to become 'the clever country' through the importation of highly-educated and skilled workers. Not surprisingly it's a popular destination among prospective migrants and few countries offer such an attractive lifestyle, high standard of living, and good business and employment prospects.

Immigration: Australia is a country of immigrants and is second only to Israel as the most polyglot, multicultural nation in the world, with huge ethnic communities and migrants from over 125 nations. Before WWII, Australian migrants were predominantly from Britain and Ireland and even 40 years ago Britain dominated Australia's migrant intake, when Australia would take virtually anyone and even offered a £10 assisted passage scheme. Britain has provided over 2m migrants since 1945 and over 7m in total. However, today only some 10 per cent of new migrants are British, although Britain still remains the largest source of skilled migrants (and second overall to New Zealand).

Since the war there has also been an influx of migrants from continental Europe, including large numbers of Greeks and Italians, plus Lebanese, Turks, Yugoslavs and various others. All major cities contain suburbs with predominantly ethnic communities and atmospheres including Chinese, Greek, Italian, Lebanese and Yugoslav. Sydney is home to more New Zealanders than most cities in New Zealand and Melbourne's Greek population is the third-largest in the world (after Athens and Thessalonica). Since the end of the official 'white-Australia' policy in 1975, Australia has admitted large numbers of Asian immigrants, including many refugees from Indochina. There are also large numbers of immigrants from the Pacific, Middle East, southern Europe, Central and South America, and South Africa. In 1997, over 90 per cent of the population was of European descent, 5 per cent Asian and 1.5 per cent Aboriginals. Over 60 per cent of the some 4m immigrants who were born overseas came from a non English-speaking country and immigration accounts for a sizeable portion of the country's population growth. Immigrants make up around a quarter of the labour force.

Today Australia has a multicultural migration policy and settlers are encouraged to retain their ethnic languages, lifestyles and artistic traditions. Many immigrants now originate from Asia, which is the fastest growing ethnic group and expected to outnumber immigrants from Britain in the next decade. However, some Australians are alarmed about what they call the 'Asianisation' of Australia's immigration policy — within the next 50 years around 25 per cent of Australia's population is likely to be of Asian origin. Nevertheless, it isn't all one-way traffic and around 30,000 people leave Australia each year and many immigrants return home after a relatively short period (around 20 per cent of new arrivals in the last decade have left again). Around 5 to 10 per cent of Australians have also emigrated to other countries.

Migrant numbers have fallen dramatically in recent years, from around 140,000 a year in the '80s to a quota of just 68,000 in 1997-98 (there has been a fall of 20 per cent in the last two years alone). Australian embassies and consulates receive around a million enquiries a year, of whom some 400,000 make applications. Of those accepted, over half have family in Australia, around 25 per cent are professionals or skilled workers, and some 15 per cent are refugees. In recent years debate has centred on how migration affects employment, with those claiming it increases unemployment in the ascendancy. However, many analysts believe it's a knee-jerk reaction to make migrants the scapegoats for Australia's economic woes and that no link has been established between migration and high unemployment. Indeed, in the USA it has been calculated that immigration boosts the economy by $billions a year.

Employment Prospects: Australia has a small labour force of around 8.5m people, some three-quarters of whom are employed full-time, and relatively high unemployment at around 8.5 per cent in late 1997 (although falling). You shouldn't plan on obtaining immediate employment in Australia unless you have a firm job offer or special qualifications and experience for which there's a strong local demand. If you want a good job you must usually be well qualified and speak fluent English (if you're an independent migrant you won't be accepted without these qualifications). Unemployment is high among non-English speaking adult migrants, particularly those from North Africa, the Middle East and the Indian subcontinent. This mostly applies to those who come to Australia under the family reunion program (although two-thirds have professional qualifications), many of whom wish they had never come to Australia and believe that they were better off at home.

It's important to obtain the latest information concerning jobs (official information sometimes lags behind the real situation) and if possible, try to secure a position before your arrival. Most states publish data on current job prospects, indicating occupations with shortages or surpluses of experienced workers. It's advantageous to make a fact-finding visit to Australia to check your job prospects at first hand, although this may not be feasible (a research trip would also help you to judge more accurately whether you're likely to enjoy the Australian way of life). This may also help you find a prospective employer willing to sponsor you, which will make the task of obtaining a visa much easier. If you plan to arrive in Australia without a job, you should have a detailed plan for finding employment on arrival and try to make some contacts before you arrive.

The Australian job market changed dramatically in the '90s, during which most new jobs shifted from manufacturing, construction and finance, to the property, communications and service industries (e.g. retailing and computing). There has been huge jobs growth in the white-collar services sector in recent years (the growth industry of the '90s), particularly in property and business support services, which now employ some 80 per cent of the workforce and are responsible for 20 per cent of export earnings. Agriculture (including horticulture, fishing, forestry, horses and the service industries to agriculture and agribusiness) has also created over 20,000 jobs in the last few years. Retailing is the largest source of jobs in Australia with some 1.3m workers and a further 1.1m are employed in manufacturing, although its share of national employment has halved to below 15 per cent since the mid-'60s. In recent years most new jobs have been created in Queensland and Western Australia.

Australian manufacturers and the Australian labour market have been slow to embrace new technology and to adjust to the rapidly changing world economy. Many companies depend on (declining) assistance (worth $4 billion a year) through tariffs on imports, production bounties and export incentives, rather than improving productivity, reducing costs and eradicating restrictive working practices. Australian productivity is the lowest of 12 developed countries (including Belgium, Canada, France, Germany, Japan, the Netherlands, Sweden, the UK and the USA) and just half that of the US and some 60 per cent of the average in many developed countries. Like most western countries, Australia has found it increasingly difficult to compete with cheap imports from countries (e.g. Asian) who pay their employees peanuts.

The information technology age has spawned a new class of low skilled, low paid, part-time and casual workers, and trade unions fear that new technology is creating an underclass and dumping thousands of people on the job scrap heap. Banks have shed some 30,000 jobs in the last five years and the water, electricity and gas utilities have also lost around a quarter of their workforce in the last few years. However, although new technology is putting people out of work in some industries, it's credited with creating jobs overall. Australia's job market, like that of most western countries, has been dramatically transformed in the '90s and it's vital for workers to keep their skills up to date in order to stay ahead of the pack.

Although it isn't as easy to find work as in the '80s, there's a steady demand for skilled workers in most regions and a shortage in some areas, which has been exacerbated by a sharp reduction in apprenticeships and training in recent years. If you have a choice, compare the job or business opportunities in all states and territories before deciding where to live, as job prospects vary considerably from city to city and state to state (as does the lifestyle, culture and to a lesser extent, the weather). Some states (such as South Australia) have a shortage of skilled workers and offer incentives to migrants such as job matching schemes, subsidised accommodation and low-interest loans. It's also easier to qualify for immigration if you're willing to settle outside the major cites in a 'designated' low-growth area (in recent years job prospects have grown faster in regional centres than in state capitals).

Changing Workforce: The jobs lost in recent years have generally been well-paid skilled and semi-skilled manufacturing jobs, which have often been replaced by low-paid, part-time or temporary jobs with few benefits (which it's estimated will comprise some 40 per cent of all jobs in Australia by the year 2000). Labour experts believe that the era of secure full-time employment with comprehensive employee benefits and lifetime guarantees has gone forever (not just in Australia, but worldwide). Today there's a new psychological contract between employers and employees, where job security isn't part of the deal. In the last few decades the country has gone from boom to bust, with the prosperous '80s followed by the worst recession (which hit Australia earlier than most other western countries) since the great depression of the 1930s. In recent years Australia has undergone an economic revolution, during which many sacred cows have gone (or are going) to the wall including protectionism, state ownership, the welfare state and the power of the unions. Today employees must be flexible with diverse and up-to-date, saleable skills, constantly renewed through further education and training. Australia has a highly mobile labour force (a quarter of Australia's workforce changed jobs in 1995), particularly among the young, and even managers and executives often need to change careers or move to another city to find a job. Nowadays an increasing number of people are 'tele-working' (working from home via telephone, fax and computer), either from choice or because their employers have closed offices to reduce costs. There are over a third of a million home-based workers in Australia, which is growing at three times the rate of overall employment and it's estimated will increase to 25 per cent of the workforce in the next decade.

Industrial relations: Industrial relations have historically been poor in Australia, although there has been a huge reduction in strikes during the last 15 years, due to the 'accord' between unions and employers instigated by the Labor Party when they came to power in the early '80s. This altered the constant cycle of confrontation between workers, management and the government, and heralded an era of relative industrial peace. In place of demands for higher wages, workers were given better working conditions and benefits, which helped put a brake on runaway inflation and strengthened the economy. Between 1981 and 1990 the number of days lost to strikes fell from some 800 per thousand employees to just over 200. However, the reduction in strikes was also influenced by the recession and the consequent sharp rise in unemployment.

For many years Australian workers were blessed with falling working hours, high wages (which kept pace with or exceeded inflation) and extensive employee protection. However, this was won at the cost of higher unemployment, low productivity and reduced competitiveness in international markets. Many observers expect industrial relations to deteriorate rapidly in the coming years as a result of the end of the accord between the Liberal government (which won power in 1996) and trade unions, and the introduction of controversial labour-relations' reforms. Signs of increasing industrial unrest were already evident in 1997 with strikes in a number of key industries and the public sector (including the post office, mining, hospitals, dockers, construction, public transport and education), with lost working days the highest since 1992.

Unemployment: As Australia approaches the new millennium, unemployment is the biggest problem facing the nation. During the early '90s, Australian workers were hit by a combination of recession and 'restructuring', with many companies slashing their staff in order to become 'lean and mean' and compete more effectively. Companies quickly realised that they could operate with smaller workforces and today Australia's largest employers are continually reducing their staff, and have become ruthless in making employees redundant. Downsizing by government (the number of federal employees has halved in the last 10 years) and businesses has retrenched over 3m full-time workers in the last decade. Increasing competition (at home and overseas), new technology and greater automation have all exacerbated the problem, and have led to relatively high levels of unemployment, particularly for a country that has traditionally enjoyed low unemployment compared with the rest of the world.

However, after peaking at 11.3 per cent in 1992, the number of jobless has fallen slowly in recent years and at the end of 1997 stood at around 8.5 per cent (over 800,000 people, 250,000 of whom are long-term unemployed, i.e. out of work for a year or longer). Unemployment is highest in Tasmania and South Australia, and lowest in New South Wales and Western Australia. It's also much higher in rural than metropolitan areas, which is why most migrants head for the cities. Unskilled and semi-skilled workers have been hardest hit by the downturn, as have the young and the older age groups (most long-term unemployed are under 25 or over 45). Age discrimination is widespread in Australia (although it's illegal to specify age in job advertisements in some states) and the older you are, the more difficult it is to find a job. Unemployment is, not surprisingly, much higher than average among migrants who don't speak fluent English. In recent years many migrants who have been unable to find a job have experienced great hardship as they can no longer claim social security during their first two years in Australia (although some migrants have successfully challenged the new law). Working holidaymakers no longer find it easy to find work, as unemployed young Australians are snapping up the temporary and casual low-paid jobs which were once the preserve of the itinerant 'backpacker'. In the last few years the government has introduced a number of job creation schemes, such as Job Search and New Start (see page 300), in an effort to boost employment, particularly among the young and long-term unemployed.

Work Ethic: Australians aren't renowned for their work ethic ('sickies' — days off work for no reason — are widespread) and Australian industry is noted for its low productivity. However, Australians believe in working (and playing) hard, and they generally work as hard and efficiently as workers in other western countries. Don't be misled by the informality and casual atmosphere and dress in many companies, as Australian employers can be ruthless when it comes to the bottom line. Although the usual working week is just 35 to 40 hours for most wage earners, overtime is normally available and is usually considered a bonus. Twelve-hour days aren't uncommon among managerial and professional staff. In fact, the higher you climb up the ladder of success, the harder you're expected to work (burn-out is common among managers and executives). Redundancies and cost-cutting in recent years have increased the pressure on all employees, particularly white-collar workers, many of whom now do the work of a number of people. Job dissatisfaction is rife in Australia, with one survey showing that (incredibly) over 60 per cent of employees would like a new job.

Further Information: There are numerous books written for those seeking a job in Australia including *How to Get a Job in Australia* by Nick Vandome (How To Books), *Universal's Job Guide* (Universal Consumer Guides), the *Australia & New Zealand Contact Directory* (Expat Network Ltd., tel UK 0181-760 0469) and *Looking for a Job* published by the Graduate Careers Council of Australia, PO Box 28, Parkville, Victoria. A range of reports and information is available at Australian missions including *Australian Jobs Review*, *Job Futures* and *Introduction to Skills Recognition*. A monthly Skill Vacancy Survey (SVS) index is published by the Department of Employment, Education, Training and Youth Affairs (DEETYA). DEETYA also projects employment trends for the next 10 years in a wide range of industries, trades and professions, and publishes a number of booklets including *Australia's Workforce in the Year 2001*. The Australian Bureau of Statistics (ABS) also publishes job figures and employment forecasts. Finally, a wealth of job information can be found via the internet (e.g. www.employment.com.au).

QUALIFICATIONS

The most important qualification for working in Australia is the ability to speak English fluently (see page 44). If you have a degree or a certificate from a recognised educational establishment in an English-speaking country, language usually presents no problems. However, applicants from non English-speaking countries or backgrounds must usually pass an English test and possibly also an occupational English examination, where the pass mark depends on your profession or trade. The failure rate is high.

Once you have overcome this hurdle you should establish whether your trade or professional qualifications and experience are recognised in Australia. While you may be well qualified in your own country, you may need to pass professional examinations or trade tests to satisfy Australian standards (overseas trained doctors recently went on hunger-strike claiming that they were denied the right to practise by discriminatory qualification tests). If you aren't experienced, Australian employers will expect your studies to be in a relevant discipline and to have included work experience. Professional or trade qualifications are required to work in many fields in Australia. The points system (see page 84), on which most immigration is based, depends to a large extent on the skills and qualifications of applicants. Points are awarded for skill levels based on your current or previous employment and whether your qualifications are adequate, including formal qualifications, occupational on-the-job training and experience. Theoretically, qualifications recognised by professional and trade bodies overseas should be recognised in Australia. However, recognition varies depending on the country and in some cases foreign qualifications aren't recognised by Australian employers or professional and trade associations. All academic qualifications should also be recognised, although they may be given less prominence than equivalent Australian qualifications, depending on the particular country and the educational institution.

To practise a profession or trade in Australia you require evidence of an appropriate level of education and practical experience; the usual minimum number of years' experience is three and can be much higher for some jobs. To work in Australia as a licensed tradesman your qualifications must be assessed by a 'Vocational Training Board' or similar state organisation, and you may also need a special licence to work in some states, trades or professions (or pass an examination). Trades Recognition Australia (TRA) provides a trades assessment service and assesses migrants' trade qualifications, skills and experience against comparable standards in Australia. For example the metal and electrical trades have a system whereby the qualifications of overseas-trained tradesmen are recognised in Australia by an 'Australian Recognised Tradesman's Certificate'.

The recognition of professional qualifications is usually the responsibility of the relevant professional body, which migrants are normally required to join to practise in Australia. Note, however, that a favourable assessment isn't a guarantee that you will be professionally recognised or be able to gain employment in your field of expertise, as some professional bodies require overseas practitioners to pass examinations conducted or supervised by themselves. In some cases it's necessary for foreign professionals to work under the supervision of a registered professional Australian for a period, e.g. one year, or to undertake further training. Medical practitioners must have studied medicine in Australia or New Zealand to work in some states, e.g. NSW, and foreign doctors cannot work for Medicare (the state health scheme).

The Australian government no longer lists the skills and qualifications necessary for occupations. However, you can check the qualifications required for a particular job in the *Australian Standard Classification of Occupations (ASCO)* dictionary, available for reference at Australian High Commission offices and other Australian government offices overseas, and at offices of the Department of Immigration and Ethnic Affairs in Australia. Additional information can be obtained from the National Council of Overseas Skills Recognition (NCOSR), PO Box 1407, Canberra City, ACT 2601 (tel. (02) 6276 8111).

Whatever kind of job you're looking for in Australia, whether temporary or permanent, part or full-time, always take proof of your qualifications, training and experience with you, plus copies of references and an up-to-date *curriculum vitae* (see page 36).

EMPLOYMENT NATIONAL & CENTRELINK

Until 1997, the Commonwealth Employment Service (CES) was the federal government employment agency in Australia. However, in September 1997 the government created a new statutory authority named Centrelink and the CES was renamed Employment National and now competes with private agencies to find people jobs (see below). Centrelink offices provide a range of customer services which were previously provided by the departments of employment, education, training and youth affairs; social security; health and family services; and primary industries and energy. Centrelink offices now provide many of the services formerly provided by CES offices, including registration and acceptance of new applicants for income support and employment assistance; self-help job facilities, including computer access to a national job vacancies database; advice and information regarding the government Jobs, Education and Training (JET) program; and specialist labour market assistance services for disadvantaged groups including Aboriginals and Torres Strait Islanders, sole parents, people with disabilities, migrants and young people.

Employment National (which formally took over from the CES on 30th April 1998) is a government-owned company run on market lines (it's expected to retain some 20 per cent of the job placement market). It competes head on with a host of community-based 'job brokers' including community job centres (such as Work Ventures and Work Solutions in Sydney), employer organisations, local councils and job search private companies, which have contracts with the government and are paid by results, i.e.

getting people jobs. However, due to the structure of the new system, the length of contracts and the relatively low commission offered, many of Australia's major recruitment companies have declined to bid for contracts. According to some reports the awarding of contracts has been a shambles, with the jobless being 'sold to the lowest bidder' with no regard given to previous experience.

It's hoped that becoming a customer-oriented operation and paying agencies to find the unemployed jobs will help reduce unemployment, although it's feared that the long-term unemployed and 'difficult' cases will be ignored by placement companies. A fee is paid to job placement companies for finding permanent employment for 15 hours a week over five consecutive working days and agencies will be paid a bonus when a person remains employed for more than 13 weeks. Australia is the first industrialised country to try to privatise its government employment agency and the 'experiment' is being followed with interest by other countries.

PRIVATE EMPLOYMENT AGENCIES

Private employment agencies abound in all major cities and towns in Australia and are big business. Many large companies are happy to engage agents and consultants to recruit employees, particularly executives, managers, professional employees and temporary staff. There are four main types of employment agencies in Australia: personnel consultants, employment agencies, labour hire contractors and student employment services. Personnel consultants (head-hunters) handle mostly executive, managerial and professional positions (lawyers are in demand, so if you're feeling unloved in your home country, you can go to Australia and be unloved there too), although there's some overlap with 'general' employment agencies. Labour hire contractors handle jobs for skilled, semi-skilled and unskilled manual blue-collar workers, and tend to be located in industrial areas rather than the main streets of major cities.

The largest number of agencies simply come under the generic term 'employment agencies' and specialise in particular fields or industries including accounting; agriculture; au pairs and nannies; banking; carers; computing; engineering and technical; hospitality; industrial and manual work; legal; medical and nursing; mining; outback jobs; sales; secretarial; resort work; and tourism, while others deal with a range of industries and professions. Some agencies deal exclusively with temporary workers in a variety of occupations including office staff, baby-sitting, housekeeping, cooks, gardeners, chauffeurs, hairdressing, security, cleaners, labourers and industrial workers. Nursing, nanny and care agencies are common and usually cover the whole gamut of nursing services. Many agencies handle both permanent and temporary positions.

There are a plethora of employment agencies in Australia, many operating nationally with offices in all major cities, while others operate in one or two cities only. Among the largest agencies operating nationwide or in most major cities are Accountancy Placements, ADIA, Alfred Marks, BDS Challenge International, Brook Street, Centacom, Computer People Pty Ltd, Dial-an-Angel, Drake Personnel, Ecco Personnel, Forstaff, Julia Ross Personnel, Kelly Services, Key People, Manpower, Metier Personnel, Morgan & Banks, Select Appointments, Skilled Work Force, Temporary Solutions, Templine and Western Staff Services. Check the yellow pages for local offices of these and other agencies. If you're travelling around Australia and plan to work in a number of major cities, you may find it advantageous to work for an national agency with offices nationwide.

Agencies are usually prohibited from charging a fee to job applicants as they receive their fees from clients, although in some states they may charge a registration fee (check first). For permanent staff, the fee paid by the employer is a percentage of the annual salary (e.g. 10 per cent) and for temporary, hourly-paid staff they take a percentage of the hourly rate paid by employers. If you take a temporary job through an agency you will be paid by the agency, usually weekly or fortnightly, which may include paid public and annual holidays after a qualifying period. Always obtain a contract and ensure that you know exactly how much and when you will be paid, and the conditions relating to the termination of a job.

Agencies must deduct income tax from gross pay and you're required to give an agency your tax file number (see page 321) within a few weeks of starting work, otherwise they must deduct tax at the highest marginal tax rate. Salaries vary considerably depending on the type of job, but most secretarial jobs pay between $10 and $15 an hour or $300 to $450 a week net (after tax). You usually receive extra pay (loading) for weekend and night work, and there are allowances (called tropical loading or a remote area allowance) for jobs in remote areas of the Northern Territory and Western Australia (above the 26th parallel 'Tropic of Capricorn').

When visiting employment agencies, you should dress appropriately for the type of job you're seeking, and take your passport (with a visa if applicable), tax file number (TFN), *curriculum vitae (CV)*, references and your bank details (if you want to get paid!) with you. Office staff may be given a typing or literacy test (if applicable) and some agencies have in-house training programs for secretarial staff. It's advisable to register with a number of agencies to maximise your chances of finding work. Keep in close contact and try to provide a telephone number where you can be contacted, otherwise you should ring in every day.

Employment agencies earn a great deal of money from finding people jobs, so providing you have something to offer they'll be keen to help you (if you're an experienced accountant, nurse or secretary you may get trampled in the rush). If they cannot help you, they'll usually tell you immediately and won't waste your time. To find local agencies, look in the yellow pages under 'Employment Agencies' and in local newspapers. Employment agencies are increasingly using the internet to advertise job vacancies, which speeds up the response and processing of job applications. Many Australian agencies employing temporary staff advertise overseas in publications (see **Appendix A**) targeted at those with working holidaymaker visas. A list of agencies specialising in particular jobs or fields is contained in *Live, Work & Play in Australia* by Sharyn McCullum (Kangaroo Press).

CONTRACT JOBS

Contract or freelance jobs are available through specialist employment agencies in Australia. Contracts are usually full-time and for a fixed period, although they may be open-ended. There's a thin dividing line between contract and temporary jobs (see page 28), which are often one and the same. In recent years many companies have been shifting from full-time employees to contract workers and contracting out jobs such as cleaning, building maintenance, catering, construction work, introducing new computer systems and even parts of the manufacturing process.

Many contract positions are for specialists in a wide range of fields including accountancy, computing, engineering, electronics and mining, although there's also a strong market in providing cleaning, catering, maintenance and manual workers. Rates vary considerably, e.g. from around $12 an hour for a clerk up to $100 or more an hour for a computer specialist. Contractors may work at home or on a client's or contract company's premises. There used to be a lucrative market in contract jobs in Australia, particularly for information technology specialists, although the recession in the '90s paid to many jobs. Consultant companies (also called bodyshops) in Australia specialise in supplying contract staff to major companies. Employees of many Australian consultant companies are permanent company employees, although they often work full-time for another 'client' company on a contract basis. Note that the usual visa regulations apply to contract workers, unless they're employed to work overseas (outside Australia).

PART-TIME JOBS

Part-time jobs are available in most industries and professions in Australia, and are most common in offices, pubs, shops, factories, cafes and restaurants. In the last few years the number of part-time workers in Australia has risen considerably, particularly among women, and now totals around 3m. Part-time employment increased from 18 to 25 per cent of total employment between 1990 and 1995. Over 75 per cent of part-time jobs in larger workplaces (with a minimum of 20 staff) are in the retail, accommodation, cafe and restaurant, education, health and community service sectors. Part-time jobs apply to all levels (from executives to clerks) and all businesses, with many turning to it for lifestyle, health or family reasons. Job satisfaction is generally higher among part-time workers than those in full-time employment (wouldn't you be happier working fewer hours?).

A part-time job is generally defined as less than 20 hours a week. Part-time workers are usually paid on an hourly basis and don't have the same rights as full time workers, but pay awards normally contain provisions to protect part-time workers' rights. They don't, however, usually receive annual leave, sick pay, maternity leave or other entitlements that full-time workers get, although this imbalance is being redressed in various industries. Part-time workers are also generally poorly paid compared to full time employees. Many jobs listed below under **Temporary & Casual Jobs** are also available on a permanent part-time basis. Part-time jobs may be advertised in Employment National offices (see page 25).

TEMPORARY & CASUAL JOBS

Temporary and casual jobs differ from part-time jobs in that they are usually for a limited (fixed) period only, e.g. from a few hours to a few months, or even intermittent. Most Australian companies employ temporary or casual staff at some time or other (around 50 per cent on a regular basis), particularly in clerical positions when staff are sick or on holiday, for special projects and to supplement permanent employees. The casual job market has grown considerably in recent years, particularly in the food, beverage and manufacturing sectors. The temporary job market was hard hit during the recession in the early '90s, although there has been a huge increase in demand in the last few years, particularly in the major cities. Downsizing and the cost of retrenching full-time employees (and unfair dismissal claims) has led many companies to employ an army of temporary employees, which is often more time-efficient and cost-effective.

Many people choose to make careers in temporary and contract work, which provides them with maximum flexibility when it comes to travel, working hours, time off and holidays. Although there's less security than with a full-time job and you don't usually receive any benefits, you're generally compensated by a higher hourly rate of pay. Temporary work also offers an opportunity to try your hand at a range of jobs which you would otherwise probably never do. The easiest way to find temporary work in the major cities is through an employment agency (see page 26), when, providing you have a marketable skill (e.g. accountancy, computing or nursing), it's relatively easy to find well-paid temporary work. Hourly rates range from around $12 an hour for clerical staff to over $100 for IT professionals.

Working Holidaymakers: Temporary work particularly applies to foreigners with working holidaymaker visas, which permit you to work for any one employer for a maximum of three months only. Note that it isn't easy to find temporary or casual work in many areas and you often need to hustle to get a job and may require experience or qualifications. It's important to ensure that you have sufficient funds to tide you over until you can find work. The easiest work to find is on farms, usually picking fruit or vegetables (see below). Note that you should be prepared to splash out on some smart clothes if a job requires them (or arrange in advance to have them sent to you from overseas).

During university holiday periods, you will have stiff competition from students, so if you're planning to work in a major city try to get there before the local students break for their holidays. Most holiday jobs are available in retailing, fast food, harvesting and hospitality. Recruiting is often done a few months prior to holiday periods, e.g. companies hire in August to October for the summer period from December to February. Well-known department and chain stores are generally the best employers. Avoid jobs offering unpaid 'trial' periods, which is illegal and is usually simply a con trick to get you to work for nothing. You should also avoid door-to-door selling requiring advance payment (e.g. $200) for sample kits (selling them is how some companies make their money) and jobs which pay commission only.

You will usually have better job prospects if you plan to stay put for a number of months rather than just a few weeks. Note that you may be entitled to a tax rebate when you leave Australia, although claiming it may be more trouble than it's worth. A good source of information for working holidaymakers is *Live, Work & Play in Australia* by Sharyn McCullum (Kangaroo Press) and the TNT *Australia & New Zealand Travel Planner* (see address in **Appendix A**), which contains advice on finding casual and temporary work. The British Universities North America Club (BUNAC, 16 Bowling Green Lane, London EC1R 0BD, UK, tel. 0171-251 3472) has a 'Work Australia' program which helps graduates with working holidaymaker visas find temporary work.

Farm Work: One of the most common forms of temporary work in Australia is fruit and vegetable picking, which can be done somewhere in Australia throughout the year (many people manage to stay in work all year round). Pay varies considerably (from excellent to poor) and is either an hourly rate or (more usually) piece work, where the more you pick the more you earn. Doing peace work you can earn around $100 a day, although you will need to work between 50 and 80 hours a week, possibly seven days a week. You should expect to earn from around $300 a week after tax from most harvesting jobs. Always establish your hours, conditions and pay in advance, as there are unscrupulous employers around who will happily take advantage of you given half a chance.

Farming is a rough and ready experience and involves hard, often dirty work — definitely not for softies and bludgers. You must usually provide a tent or vehicle to sleep in, although some employers provide basic accommodation and food (there may be a charge), but it's usually terrible and it's better to provide your own. It pays to have your own transport as farms are generally situated in remote areas (there aren't too many in downtown Sydney). Note that large farms are sometimes targeted by immigration officials, resulting in deportation for illegal workers. The government publication, *Harvest Table*, carries job advertisements from local fruit-growers' associations and there are harvest labour offices in many country areas. A state by state harvest guide is also included in *Go Australia* (see **Appendix A**) and, *A Traveller's Guide to the Australian Fruit and Vegetable Harvest*, an excellent source of information for temporary workers (available from Mark Taylor, PO Box 420, Gymea, NSW 2227, who also publishes a newsletter).

Salary & Tax: Employers or agencies require your tax file number (see page 321) and when you leave an employer you should receive a group certificate (for tax purposes). If you don't provide a tax file number, your employer must deduct tax at the highest marginal tax rate (49 per cent). If you earn over $450 a week, your employer must pay 4 per cent of your salary into a superannuation fund. This is intended to be rolled over from employer to employer until you reach retirement age, but if it amounts to less than $500 it's usually paid to you in cash. Many employers illegally pay temporary staff in cash without making any deductions for tax (see **Working Illegally** on page 43). Rates of pay for temporary jobs are often higher than for permanent jobs as there's no entitlement to holiday or sick pay or other benefits, and no notice period may be required by either party.

Casual Work: Casual workers are usually employed on a daily, first come, first served basis. The work often entails heavy labouring and is therefore more suitable for men, although if you're a female weightlifter there's no bar against the fairer sex. Pay for casual work is usually low (from $5 an hour) and is usually paid cash in hand. Temporary and casual work includes the following:

- Office and secretarial work is available throughout Australia for qualified people. It's usually well paid and the easiest work to find in cities due to the large number of temporary secretarial and office staff agencies (see page 26).

- Work in the building trade, which can be found through industrial employment agencies and by applying direct to builders and building sites.

- Work at exhibitions, shows, fairs and circuses, such as setting up stands, catering (waiting and bar staff), and loading and unloading jobs.

- Jobs teaching English are available in the major towns and cities, where qualified teachers can earn between $10 and $20 an hour.

- Jobs as sports instructors including scuba diving, para-gliding, hang-gliding, snorkeling, sailing and surfing are available in beach resorts throughout Australia for qualified people.

- Jobs looking after children and elderly people, which may be live-in or live-out positions. Although desirable, experience may be unnecessary.

- A wide range of jobs are available on farms and cattle and sheep stations, including work as a jackaroo or jillaroo, stockman, rouseabout, mechanic, welder, governess, teacher, cook, home-help, driver or pilot. It's an advantage if you can ride a horse or motorbike (or pilot a plane or helicopter).

- Hospitality work, which applies to a host of jobs in the tourist industry including most staff in hotels, bars and restaurants. This is the most common source of temporary work in coastal resorts, particularly in Queensland.

- Work in ski resorts in NSW and Victoria. Note that the number of jobs is limited and you must arrive early in the season and have experience to get the best paid jobs.

- Good cooks (females preferred) and chefs are in high demand throughout Australia, from outback cattle stations, mining camps and road stations, to a wealth of bars, cafes and restaurants in cities and resorts. Experienced chefs are in high demand in the major cities.

● A number of jobs are available in the mining industry, which is one of the best paid in Australia, although the work is hard (often seven days a week) and in remote areas where there's often little to do (on the rare occasions when you aren't working). However, you're adequately compensated and can earn $1,000 or more a week with allowances and overtime. Experience is preferred, although there are a number of unskilled jobs available (for both men and women).

● Work is available on fishing vessels out of major ports such as Broome, Cairns, Carnarvon, Darwin, Karumba and Townsville.

● Selling jobs can be found in the major cities, although many pay commission only and are best avoided (unless you're a super salesperson).

● Hostels may offer free accommodation in return for cleaning work and there may also be a variety of other temporary jobs available. Hostel notice boards are also a good source of information about temporary jobs.

● Jobs in stores over Christmas, during sales periods and during the peak season in resorts.

● Gardening jobs, both in private gardens and public parks. Jobs may be advertised in local newspapers, on bulletin boards and in magazines. Local landscape gardeners and garden centres often need extra staff, particularly in spring and summer.

● Market research, which entails asking people personal questions, either in the street or house to house (ideal job for nosy parkers). Tele-marketing work (selling by phone) is also relatively easy to find in Australian cities.

● Collecting for charities.

● Modelling at art colleges (paid 'flashing'); both sexes are usually required and not *just* the body beautiful.

● Security work (although it consists of long hours for low pay).

● Nursing and auxiliary nursing staff in hospitals, clinics and nursing homes, who are usually employed through nursing agencies, although you can apply directly to large hospitals to be included in their casual pools. Note that to be employed as a Registered Nurse (RN) in Australia you must be registered in the state where you plan to work. Once you're registered to work in one state, it's relatively easy to be registered in most other states. Nurses with specialist skills such as theatre, critical and intensive care, and midwifery are in high demand.

● Newspaper and magazine distribution.

● Courier work (own transport required, e.g. motorcycle, car or van) and driving jobs including coach and truck drivers, and ferrying cars for manufacturers and car hire companies.

● Miscellaneous jobs as cleaners, baby-sitters and labourers, are available from a number of agencies specialising in temporary work, e.g. Manpower.

Temporary jobs may also be advertised in Employment National offices (see page 27). See also **Employment Agencies** on page 28.

VOLUNTARY WORK

The minimum age limit for voluntary work in Australia is usually 18 and most organisations require good or fluent English to be spoken. No special qualifications are required and the minimum length of service varies from one month to one year (often there's no maximum length of service). Handicapped volunteers are also welcomed by many organisations. Voluntary work (not surprisingly) is unpaid, although meals and accommodation are usually provided and some organisations also pay pocket money. However, this is usually insufficient for your out-of-pocket living expenses (entertainment, drinks, etc.), so make sure that you bring sufficient money with you. Unemployed persons aged over 50 receiving unemployment benefits can do voluntary work with an approved organisation, subject to a minimum of 32 hours every two weeks.

It's essential before planning to come to Australia to do voluntary work, that you check whether you're eligible and will be permitted to enter Australia under the immigration and employment regulations. The usual visitor's visa regulations apply to voluntary workers, but you don't require a special visa for unpaid work. Volunteers are usually required to pay a registration fee, pay for their own travel to and from a workcamp, and may also be expected to contribute towards the cost of their board and lodging.

One of the largest voluntary organisations in Australia is the World Traveller's Network which offers a work and travel package (Echidna), a six-week conservation program costing applicants around $1,000. You can choose the state where you wish to work, which may consist of tree planting; erosion and salinity control; collecting seeds from indigenous plants; building and maintaining bushwalking tracks; endangered flora and fauna protection surveys; and habitat restoration. Work sites vary from inner city parks and reserves, to rural farming and the outback. The program is open to all age groups, although most volunteers are aged 18 to 25. For information apply to the World Traveller's Network, Head Office, 3 Orwell Street, Potts Point, Sydney, NSW 2011 (tel. (02) 9357 4477) or to the World Traveller's Network, European Administration Office, Travel Active Program, PO Box 107, 5800 AC Venray, The Netherlands (tel. (31) 4780 88074). Other Australian voluntary organisations include:

- The Involvement Volunteers (PO Box 218, Port Melbourne, Victoria 3207), who maintain a register of voluntary positions and offer some paid work, e.g. on farms.

- The Australian Trust for Conservation Volunteers (ATCV, PO Box 423, Ballarat, Victoria 3353, tel. freecall 1800-032501 or (03) 5332 7490) has projects such as tree planting, track conservation, and flora and fauna surveys. Most projects are for a weekend or a week only and all accommodation, food and transport is provided in return for a small contribution (e.g. $20 a day) to help defray costs.

- The Australia & New Zealand Scientific Exploration Society (PO Box 174, Albert Park, Victoria 3206, tel. (03) 9690 5455) is a non-profit organisation that undertakes scientific expeditions into wilderness areas of Australia. Volunteers are sent into the field under the guidance of an experienced leader.

- The international organisation, Willing Workers on Organic Farms (WWOOF), Mt Murrindal Co-Op, Gelantipy Road, Buchan, 3885 Victoria (tel. (03) 5155 0235/0218), has around 500 participating farms in Australia (a booklet is available listing all members). You receive food, accommodation and experience, but no pay. Membership costs $25 for a single person and $30 for couples.

- The Wilderness Society (1st Floor, 263 Broadway, Glebe, NSW 2037) also requires a constant supply of volunteers.

Many other organisations require voluntary workers including the Red Cross Society, the Salvation Army and the St. John's Ambulance Association.

WORKING WOMEN

Some 55 per cent of Australian women work, comprising around 45 per cent of the total Australian workforce including 35 per cent of full-time employees and 75 per cent of part-time workers (half of all women in paid employment work part-time). A woman doing the same or broadly similar work to a man and employed by the same employer is legally entitled to the same pay and terms of employment as a man ('equal pay for work of equal value'). However, as in most western countries, although there's no *official* discrimination, in practice this often isn't the case. Despite equal pay legislation (enshrined in the Sex Discrimination Act of 1984), women have found it impossible to close the pay gap between themselves and men, and in the mid-'90s men's wages were increasing at around twice the rate of women's. Women are disadvantaged in terms of pay scales at all levels of employment in all industries and professions, and most employers pay only lip service to equal pay.

Women receive an average of around two-thirds of men's wages and although this is influenced by the fact that more women do menial jobs than men, the percentage of female executives and managers is low and women are consistently paid less for doing the same work. Careers in which women predominate such as nursery and primary school teaching; speech and occupational therapy; nursing; and librarianship, are comparatively poorly paid compared with those where men dominate. The concentration of women in part-time work and the failure of award wages to keep pace with enterprise agreements is also widening the gap between male and female earnings. Women working full-time are likely to be paid less than men and are less likely to have had a recent pay rise or to receive bonuses.

In recent years women have been moving into male-dominated professions in increasing numbers including accountancy, auditing and mathematics. However, although women are breaking into the professions in increasing numbers, they don't usually reach the top, where the 'old-boy' network thrives. The main discrimination among women professionals isn't in salary or title, but in promotion opportunities, as many companies and organisations are loathe to elevate women to important positions (ostensibly due to fears that they may leave and start a family or at least take long breaks from work — in 1997, only around 2,000 men took leave from work for family reasons compared with some 85,000 women). This invisible barrier is known as the 'glass ceiling'. Although 'the best man for the job is often a woman', this is seldom acknowledged by Australian employers, who mostly prefer male candidates. Male chauvinism is alive and positively thriving in Australia, where women employees also face the additional hazard of sexual harassment.

Although the glass ceiling is less of an obstacle to success than previously (cracks have been appearing in recent years), men are four times more likely than women to be managers and administrators. Women are almost non-existent among the directors of major companies, and although 25 per cent of the representatives on government authorities and boards are officially supposed to be women (a figure which should rise to 50 per cent in the long term), in reality it's much lower. Just 6 per cent of company directors and 10 per cent of top management positions are held by women. Most successful businesswomen are forced to put their career before their family (most don't have children) and personal life, with most female executives working over 50 hours a week. Employers are (not surprisingly) wary of female employees becoming pregnant, as after one year's employment they are entitled to 12 months' unpaid maternity leave, after which they have the right to return to the same job with the same pay.

Self-employment is the best bet for women who want to get to the top and not surprisingly it has increased steadily during the last decade, despite the fact that banks and other financial institutions are usually loathe to lend women money. See also **Discrimination** on page 49.

JOB HUNTING

When looking for a job in Australia (or anywhere for that matter), it isn't advisable to put all your eggs in one basket, as the more job applications you make the better your chances of success. Contact as many prospective employers and employment agencies as possible, either by writing, telephoning or calling on them in person. Whatever job you're looking for, it's important to market yourself correctly and appropriately, which depends on the type of job you're seeking. For example, the recruitment of executives and senior managers in Australia is usually handled by consultants, who advertise in the Australian national press (and also overseas) and interview all applicants prior to presenting clients with a shortlist. At the other end of the scale, manual jobs requiring no previous experience may be advertised at local Employment National offices, in local newspapers or even in shop windows, where the first suitable able-bodied applicant may be offered the job on the spot.

When writing for a job, address your letter to the personnel director or manager (try to obtain his name) and include your *curriculum vitae (CV)*. Note, however, that writing for jobs from overseas is usually a hit and miss affair and is probably the least successful method of securing employment (although it can be successful for those seeking 'temporary' jobs for up to four years). If you're applying from overseas and are planning to visit Australia, you should tell prospective employers when you will be available for interview and should arrange as many interviews as you can fit into your timetable (companies may wish to see a copy of your visa before interviewing you). Note that visiting Australia for an interview usually impresses prospective employers of you're commitment. Your method of job hunting obviously depends on your particular circumstances, qualifications and experience, and the sort of job you're looking for, and may include the following:

- Visit local Employment National offices in Australia (see page 27). This is mainly for non-professional skilled and unskilled jobs.

- Check the TV teletext job service, internet (which is increasingly being used by Australian agencies and headhunters) and other bulletin boards.

- Contact private recruitment consultants and employment agencies (see page 28).

- Obtain copies of Australian daily newspapers (see page 427), all of which contain 'positions vacant' sections (the Saturday editions are best) including job advertisements dedicated to particular industries or professions on certain days. Most local and national newspapers are available in the reading rooms of local libraries in Australia, so you don't usually need to buy them. Jobs are also advertised in industry and trade newspapers and magazines. Australian newspapers are available in some countries from international news agencies; Australian embassies and consulates; Australian trade and commercial centres; and Australian social clubs (although they don't always contain the 'situations vacant' sections).

In Britain, single copies of the major Australian newspapers can be purchased from Smyth, International Media Representatives, 1 Torrington Park, London N12 9GG, UK (tel. 0181-446 6400). Subscriptions to Australian newspapers are available from TNT Express World, Unit 6, Spitfire Way, Spitfire Estate, Hounslow, Middx. TW5 9NW (tel. 0181-561 2345), but are expensive. **The 'jobs vacant' sections of major Australian newspapers can also be perused via the internet (a useful resource for anyone who isn't in Australia).**

- Networking (basically getting together with like-minded people to discuss business) is a popular way of making business and professional contacts in Australia. It can be particularly successful for executives, managers and professionals when job hunting.

- If you have a professional qualification that's recognised in Australia, you can write to an Australian professional organisation for information and advice (addresses are obtainable from Australian chambers of commerce overseas), membership of which may be obligatory to work in Australia. All associations publish journals containing 'positions vacant' advertisements, where members can also offer their services to prospective employers.

- Apply to international and national recruiting agencies acting for Australian companies. Agencies mainly recruit executives and key managerial and technical staff, and some have offices overseas, e.g. in Britain.

- Apply to foreign multi-national companies with offices or subsidiaries in Australia and make written applications directly to Australian companies. You can obtain a list of companies working in a particular field from trade directories, copies of which are available at reference libraries in Australia (they can also be consulted at Australian missions and chambers of commerce overseas).

- Information about specific professions, trades and industries, particularly job opportunities in individual states, cities or areas, can be obtained from local chambers of commerce in Australia.

- Place an advertisement in the 'Situations Wanted' section of a national newspaper in Australia or a local newspaper in the area where you wish to work. If you're a member of a recognised profession or trade, you could place an advertisement in a newspaper or magazine dedicated to your profession or a particular industry.

- Ask relatives, friends or acquaintances working in Australia whether they know of an employer looking for someone with your experience and qualifications.

- If you're already in Australia, contact or join expatriate social clubs, churches, societies and professional organisations, particularly your country's chamber of commerce.

- Students can use the internet to contact prospective employers via Gradlink, established by the Graduate Careers Council of Australia.

- Apply in person to Australian companies (see **Personal Applications** below).

Always obtain a job offer in writing and a contract, and steer clear of an employer who won't provide them. An official job entitles you to accident insurance, unemployment benefit, state pension and superannuation, redundancy payments and official protection from exploitation, among other benefits (see also **Working Illegally** on page 43).

Personal Applications

Your best chance of obtaining some jobs (particularly temporary jobs) in Australia is to apply in person, when success is often simply a matter of being in the right place at the right time. When looking for a job for which no special qualifications or experience are required, it isn't necessarily *what* you know, but *who* you know. Many companies don't advertise but rely on attracting workers by word of mouth and their own vacancy boards. Always leave your name and address with a prospective employer and (if possible) a telephone number where you can be contacted, particularly if a job may become vacant at short notice. Advertise the fact that you're looking for a job with friends, relatives and acquaintances, and anyone you come into contact with who may be able to help. You can give lady luck a helping hand by your persistence and enterprise by:

- cold calling on prospective employers;
- checking wanted boards;
- looking in local newspapers;
- checking notice and bulletin boards in large companies, shopping centres, embassies, clubs, sports centres, stores, universities, churches and hostels;
- ask friends, acquaintances (etc.) and other temporary workers.

When leaving a job in Australia, it's advisable to ask for a written reference (one isn't usually provided automatically), particularly if you intend to look for further work in Australia or you think your work experience will help you obtain employment overseas.

CURRICULA VITAES & INTERVIEWS

Curricula vitaes (CVs) are important in Australia when looking for a job, particularly when jobs are thin on the ground. Don't forget that the purpose of your CV is to obtain an interview, not a job, and it must be written with this in mind. This means that your CV must be individually tailored to every job application. If you aren't up to writing a good CV, you can employ a professional writer who should be able to turn your boring working life into something which Indiana Jones would be proud of. A good CV should be brief (four pages or less); typed/printed on white A4-sized sheets (one side only); without strange fonts or bizarre layouts; word perfect and user-friendly; plus no ego, verbosity, salary demands or unexplained gaps in employment. Include a paragraph on your achievements. Your covering letter also needs to be word perfect and to grab the reader's attention. **The standard of most CVs in Australia is abysmal, so if yours is exceptional you're way ahead of the pack already.**

Job interviews shouldn't be taken lightly, as making a good impression can make the difference between being on the ladder of success or in the dole queue. Although dress rules in Australia aren't as strict as in some other countries, you should always dress smartly and appropriately when applying for a job (i.e. shorts and thongs are out). The secret of success is in your preparation, so do your homework on prospective employers and try to anticipate every conceivable question (and then some) that you may be asked, and rehearse your answers. Be prepared to answer questions about why you came to Australia and what you think of the country and its people. Questions may be blunt and to the point and answers should be positive — you should avoid criticising your home country and former employers (or, needless to say, Australia!).

In recent years Australian employers and recruitment agencies have been increasingly using psychology and personality tests to select staff. Some employers also require prospective employees to complete aptitude and other written tests. In addition to a CV, employers may also require the names of a number of personal or professional referees, whom they may contact. You should take evidence of your educational, trade and professional qualifications, and references from former employers. You may also be required to produce your passport and visa entitling you to live and work in Australia (if already issued), plus your driving licence.

SALARY

It can be difficult to determine the salary you should command in Australia, as they aren't always listed in job advertisements, except for public sector employees (who are paid according to fixed grades). Salaries may vary considerably for the same job in different parts of Australia. In general, wages are highest in New South Wales (particularly Sydney, which has the highest cost of living in Australia) and Canberra, and lowest in Queensland and South Australia. However, salary variations aren't uniform across Australia and people living in areas with a low cost of living can sometimes earn as much as those in cities with a much higher cost of living. Australia generally has a lower cost of living (see page 357) than most European countries (similar to the USA). However, although Australians have traditionally been highly paid, some analysts believe that Australia's future may be low-tech, low-pay (compared with other OECD countries Australia is going backwards).

There isn't a national statutory minimum wage in Australia, where minimum 'award wages' are set for different industries, trades and professions through a unique award system, decided at the federal or state level by national pay agreements between unions and employers. There are some 5,000 federal and state awards, each with six to eight wage classifications, making a total of around 35,000 different 'minimum wages'. Minimum wage 'award' rates (which employers are obliged to pay) cover over 80 per cent of Australian workers, although many employers pay above the award rate. Small businesses are more likely to pay above award wages than big companies (over two-thirds of small companies pay above award wages compared with around 50 per cent of large companies). Overtime rates are usually one and a half times the normal hourly award rate, but can be twice the normal rate for weekend work.

Employees not on awards often receive the federal minimum wage, which in 1997 was $359.40 a week (equal to a minimum hourly rate of $9.45 for a 38-hour week). The ACTU would like the wages of Australia's lowest-paid workers to increase to $380 a week from April 1998 and to $418 in April 1999. Many analysts think that the relatively high minimum wage is partly responsible for high unemployment, although it's effectively cut by employers hiring part-time and casual workers (many employers, particularly restaurants, pay below the legal rate of pay). Many people believe that there should be a lower minimum wage for unskilled labour, who are currently priced out of jobs. Government surveys of average weekly earnings are published regularly for a wide range of trades and professions, both nationally and for individual states and cities. There are also a number of books which detail wages in different occupations including *What Jobs Pay* by Rod Tilson.

In 1997, the average weekly wage for adult males in full-time employment was around $725 ($780 with overtime) and $600 ($615 with overtime) for women. A third of employees earn less than $400 a week (many migrants from non-English speaking countries earn below $300 a week), while around 10 per cent earn over $1,000 a week.

Average weekly wages have been increasing more slowly in recent years than in the '80s, although they're usually ahead of inflation. However, real wages for many workers fell over the last decade and many families receive social security payments (e.g. the additional family payment) to top up their incomes. Government employees earn more on average than employees in the private sector and receive higher wage increases. The highest paid jobs are usually in mining, finance and insurance, while the lowest paid are in retailing, catering and tourism. Under a scheme called 'leave loading', full-time employees are paid an extra 17.5 per cent of their normal wage when they're on holiday (usually paid in December).

In 1997, the average starting salary for graduates was around $30,000 for men and $28,500 for women (the gap is narrowing). At the other end of the scale, managing directors earn between $300,000 and $500,000 a year in Sydney (it isn't unusual for companies to pay executives 10 to 25 per cent more when they move to Sydney) compared with $175,000 to $350,000 in Melbourne and $125,000 to $200,000 in Perth. Executive salaries in Australia are catching up fast with the rest of the world and expatriate American bosses of top Australian companies earn $millions a year (including tens of $millions in bonuses in the form of share incentives/options and performance-related bonuses).

Usually salaries are negotiable and it's up to you to ensure that you receive the level of salary and benefits commensurate with your qualifications and experience (or as much as you can get!). If you have friends or acquaintances working in Australia or who have worked there, ask them what an average or good salary is for your particular trade or profession. Salaries paid by some foreign companies (e.g. American or Japanese) may be higher on average than those paid by Australian companies, particularly for executives and managers imported from overseas. Your working hours (see page 56) in Australia may differ from those in other countries and will vary depending on your profession and where you work. The standard working week is between 37 and 40 hours, although many employees work up to 10 hours a week overtime. Hourly paid workers are paid overtime for extra hours and higher 'penalty' rates for night, shift and weekend work. In contrast, executives, professionals and managers often work over 50 hours a week without extra pay. There are allowances (called 'tropical loading' or a 'remote area allowance') for work in remote areas of the Northern Territory and Western Australia (above the 26th parallel 'Tropic of Capricorn').

Women have fallen behind in the pay stakes in recent years, particularly those employed in part-time and temporary jobs, where wage growth has been minimal. Pay increases are often linked to improved productivity and performance, and pay generally rises faster than inflation. The 'accord' between workers, management and the former Labor government (from 1983 to 1996) generally heralded the end of massive pay rises for workers in return for better working conditions and fringe benefits. In 1997, average pay rises were around 4.5 per cent (or twice the rate of inflation), although at the bottom of the scale those without industrial clout and working outside the formal award system received little or nothing at all.

For many employees, particularly executives and senior managers, their 'salary' is much more than what they receive in their weekly or monthly pay packets. Many companies offer a number of fringe benefits (or perks) for executives and managers, which may even continue into retirement. These include company cars used for private purposes, private health insurance, children's private education and expense accounts (see also **Managerial & Executive Positions** on page 53). However, fringe benefits have declined considerably in recent years due to the introduction of a fringe benefits tax (FBT), which is levied at 48.4 per cent on the taxable value of employee fringe benefits. There has also been a tax crackdown on executive pay packages, particularly 'salary sacrifice' schemes, where executives sacrifice part of their pay in return for higher superannuation payments and other benefits.

The most common forms of fringe benefits are subsidised company restaurants or canteens, allowances for living away from home, and superannuation (which is compulsory), all of which are covered by union awards and aren't liable to FBT. Under the mandatory Superannuation Guarantee (introduced on 1st July 1992), employers must pay a percentage of your salary into a superannuation fund (see page 303). Most employees consider fringe benefits to be important, particularly superannuation, income protection insurance, flexi-days, life insurance, company cars, staff discounts and child care on business premises. The opportunity to work overtime is also seen as an important 'fringe benefit' by most hourly paid workers, many of whom earn around a quarter of their wages from overtime. Always check whether a quoted salary is salary only or the total salary package including for example superannuation and a company car.

SELF-EMPLOYMENT & STARTING A BUSINESS

Anyone who's an Australian citizen or a permanent resident can work in a self-employed capacity in Australia, which includes sole proprietors, partnerships, co-operatives, franchises and private limited companies. There are numerous opportunities for entrepreneurs in Australia, where everyone (or at least most people) has equal opportunity and is judged on his merits. However, if you're planning to enter Australia as a business migrant, you need to have considerable financial resources and pass a points test (see page 84). Business migrants in the past three years brought in over $500,000 each and created around 4,000 jobs (each migrant created an average of seven jobs).

Although new businesses have a high failure rate within the first few years, working for yourself is still the best way to become (and remain) rich in Australia (and most other countries). There's considerable red tape for those wishing to start a business in Australia (although it isn't as restrictive as in many other countries), where the average small businessman spends around four hours a week on government paperwork. Much of the fall in unemployment in recent years has been as a result of self-employment or jobs created by small companies. Redundancy (and the difficulty in finding full-time employment) is often the spur for over 45s to start their own business and around 20 per cent of retrenched employees turn to self-employment. **However, it isn't a panacea for unemployment.**

Research: For many people, starting a business is one of the quickest routes to bankruptcy known to mankind. In fact, many people who start businesses would be better off investing in lottery tickets — at least they would then have a chance of getting a return on their investment! **If you're going to work for yourself you must be prepared to fail (despite your best efforts) as almost two out of three new businesses fail within three to five years.** The key to starting or buying a successful business is research, research and yet more research (plus innovation, value for money and service). Bear in mind that choosing the location for a business is vital. Always thoroughly investigate an existing or proposed business (including the location, catchment area, competition and history) before investing a cent. Generally speaking it isn't advisable to run a business in a field in which you have no experience, although obviously this isn't always practical (and some businesses require little experience, specialist knowledge or training). When experience or training is necessary, it's often wise to work for someone else in the same line of business to gain experience, rather than jump in at the deep end. Assistance (including hands-on training) from the seller could be made part of a purchase contract. **Like most countries, Australia isn't a place for amateur entrepreneurs, particularly**

**those who don't do their homework and are unfamiliar with Australians and the
Australian way of doing business.**

Business Structure: There are three main types of business structure you can choose
if you're self-employed: a sole proprietorship, partnership or a limited company, which
can be public or proprietary (which means private). Due to the ever-changing and
complex Australian tax laws, you should consult a tax expert before deciding on the best
one for you. You must also decide whether to buy an established business, a franchise or
start a new business from scratch. Note that although franchises have a higher success
rate than other start-up businesses, it may take years to make a profit (often the only one
to get rich is the franchise company). A *Franchisees Guide* can be obtained from the
Franchisers Association of Australia and New Zealand, Unit 9, 2-6 Hunter Street,
Parramatta, NSW 2150 (tel. (02) 9891 4933).

Buying A Business: Businesses for sale are advertised in magazines such as
Australian Business for Sale News (PO Box 586, Darlinghurst, NSW 2010, tel. (02) 9281
4599) and some daily newspapers. There are also business migration agents in Australia
and overseas who can help you buy or establish a company in Australia, although their
fees can be high. Note that the purchase of a business *must* always be conditional on
obtaining visas, licenses, permits, loans and other necessary funding, and anything else
that's vital to its successful establishment. While it's easier to buy an existing business
(which gives you an immediate cash flow) than start a new one, you must thoroughly
investigate the financial status, turnover and value of a business (*always* obtain an
independent valuation). It's important to engage an accountant and lawyer at the earliest
opportunity. Note that a lawyer should be acting solely for you and not for any other
parties in a transaction, and shouldn't be receiving commissions from anyone involved.
Take care as there are crooks around who prey on innocent foreigners!

Finance & Cash Flow: Most people are far too optimistic about the prospects for a
new business and over-estimate income levels (it often takes years to make a profit). Be
realistic or even pessimistic when estimating your income and overestimate the costs and
underestimate the revenue (then reduce it by up to 50 per cent!). While hoping for the
best, you should plan for the worst and have sufficient funds to last until you're established
and profitable. New projects are rarely, if ever, completed within budget. Make sure you
have sufficient working capital and that you can survive until a business takes off.
Australian banks are wary of lending to new businesses, especially those run by new
immigrants. If you wish to borrow money for a business venture in Australia, you should
carefully consider where and how you plan to raise it. Under-capitalisation is the main
reason for small business failures and isn't helped by cash-flow problems caused by late
payers. See also **Loans** on page 335.

Grants & Incentives: The Australian government welcomes successful business
people and investors to apply for residence in Australia, although applicants are generally
required to invest at least $500,000 in a business (see page 89). The Australian Business
Migration scheme provides prospective migrants with a link to professional and
commercial advisors who provide specialist advice and other services. Compare your
business prospects in all states and territories, all of which compete to attract foreign
investors and business people with incentives such as tax rebates, free counselling, cash
grants and loan guarantees. Some state governments publish lists of business
opportunities for migrants. For information about government backed finance, contact
the Australian Trade Commission (AUSTRADE), AIDC Tower, Maritime Centre, 201
Kent Street, Sydney, NSW 2000 (tel. (02) 9390 2000).

Information & Professional Advice: A wealth of free advice and information for
budding entrepreneurs is available from Australian embassies and high commissions;

federal government and state agencies; chambers of commerce; professional associations; trade unions; and local councils. The Office of Small Business is a government agency with offices in all major cities, offering free advice and assistance to those planning to start their own business. It publishes a wealth of information and publications, particularly concerning raising finance for a new business. The government publishes a 'Jobhunt' booklet entitled *Be Your Own Boss* (available from Employment National and Centrelink offices) and the Australian Government Publishing Service publishes many books for those planning to start a business including *Checklist for Starting a Business, Buying or Selling a Small Business* and *Sources of Finance for Small Business*. There are Business Enterprise Centres (BECs) in some states and territories (e.g. NSW and the ACT) where you can obtain free advice and support on a wide range of business-related subjects.

Most international firms of accountants have offices in major cities in Australia (and in many other countries) and are an invaluable source of information (in English and other languages) on a wide range of subjects including forming a company, company law, taxation and social security. Many publish free books about doing business in Australia including *Doing Business in Australia* (Ernst & Young *and* Price Waterhouse) and *Establishing a Business in Australia* (Minter Ellison). Information about starting a small business in Australian can also be obtained from the Department of Business and Regional Development, Office of Small Business, 3rd Floor, Enterprise House, 1 Fitzwilliam Street, Parramatta, NSW 2150 (tel. (02) 9895 0555), the Australian Small Business Association, 28 Mary Road, Auburn, NSW 2144 (tel. (02) 9649 8298) and Australian Small Business & Investing, 180 Bourke Street, Alexandria, NSW 2015 (tel. (02) 9353 6666). Australia's major banks have small business centres providing free banking, financial and other advice to new businesses. The Australian Tax Office publishes a *Tax Guide for New Small Businesses* and a *Guide to Keeping Your Business Records*. There are a number of journals published for prospective business buyers including *Business and Properties FOR SALE* (Pacific O'Brien Publications Pty. Ltd., PO Box 2170, Southport, QLD 4215, tel. (07) 5571 1103), which is also available on the internet (www.peg.apc/-abson).

Local Information: There are many state and local government agencies and departments providing information and advice about starting and running a business. All states operate business advisory, development, investment, industry and technology corporations or departments. One of the best places to start is your local chamber of commerce, which is a mine of information about every aspect of business and relocation to particular towns or areas (many produce relocation and business information packages). Libraries are also an excellent source of information about starting a business.

Wealth Warning: Whatever people may tell you, working for yourself isn't easy (otherwise most of us would be doing it). It requires a lot of hard work (self-employed people generally work much longer hours than employees); usually a sizeable investment and sufficient operating funds (most business failures are due to a lack of capital); good organization (e.g. bookkeeping, planning and research); excellent customer relations (the customer is always right, even when he's wrong!); and a measure of luck (although generally the harder you work, the more 'luck' you will have). Don't be seduced by the apparent laid-back way of life in Australia — if you want to be a success in business you cannot play at it. Note that the self-employed must provide their own health and pension plans, and don't qualify for unemployment insurance or workers' compensation.

AU PAIRS

Single females aged between 17 and 27 (usually referred to as 'girls') are eligible for a job as an au pair in Australia. The au pair system provides you with an excellent opportunity to travel, improve your English and generally broaden your education by living and working in Australia. Au pairs are usually contracted to work for a minimum of three to six months and a maximum of two years, although shorter assignments may be available. You may work as an au pair on a number of separate occasions, providing the total period doesn't exceed two years. You require a visa to enter Australia to work as an au pair.

It isn't necessary for au pairs to come to Australia to learn the language and a good basic knowledge of English is expected of all au pairs, although English classes (see page 210) are available at language schools and colleges in most towns in Australia. When applying, you should state whether you wish to attend English classes, so that you can be placed with a family living within a reasonable distance of a language school. As an au pair, you receive free meals and accommodation and have your own room. You're usually required to pay your own fare to and from Australia, although some families may pay towards the fare home for au pairs staying six months or longer. In some families, au pairs holiday with the family or may be free to take holidays at home or with friends. Check in advance.

Most families prefer non-smokers (smokers aren't popular and aren't accepted by some families) and girls with a driving licence (so you can take little Bruce or Sheila to school, sports events, etc.). Working hours are officially limited to 30 a week, five hours a day (morning or afternoon), six days a week, plus a maximum of three evenings' baby-sitting. You should have at least one full day and three evenings free of household responsibilities each week, and should be free to attend religious services if you wish. Au pairs are paid the 'princessly' sum of between $125 and $200 'pocket money' a week (rates are highest in the major cities), which means you stand little chance of getting rich unless you marry a wealthy Australian.

Au pairs are usually placed in families with children. Duties consist of light housework including simple cooking for children; clothes washing (with a machine) and ironing (for children only); washing up and drying dishes; making beds; dusting; vacuum cleaning; and other light jobs around the home. In order to endure (or possibly even enjoy) the work, you should be used to helping around the house and working with children. You aren't a general servant or cook (although extra services are often taken for granted) and shouldn't be expected to look after physically or mentally handicapped children. Unfortunately abuses of the au pair system are common (in all countries) and you may be expected to work long hours and spend many evenings baby-sitting, while the family are out enjoying themselves.

Some families may also expect you to act as an unpaid language teacher for members of the family, which you should refuse (unless they offer you lots of money!). On the other hand, you shouldn't expect the family to teach you English, although most are only too willing to help. If you have any questions or complaints about your duties, you should refer them to the agency which found you your position (if applicable). Make sure you have a return ticket (or the money to buy one), so that if you're faced with an intolerable situation, you can at least go home (some agencies will find you another family). You're usually required to give notice if you wish to go home before the end of your agreement, although this won't apply if the family has abused the arrangement. If you're ill or have an accident during your stay in Australia, you can obtain treatment under the Medicare national health scheme (see page 277).

Au pair positions must be arranged privately, either directly with a family or through a private agency (there's no official government agency). There are dozens of agencies who specialise in finding au pair positions (both in Australia and overseas) and au pair positions can also be found through magazines and newspapers in Australia, but you're usually better off going through an agency. The best agencies vet families in advance, make periodic checks on your welfare and help you overcome any problems you may have (either personal or with your family).

Some agencies offer a two-week trial period, after which either the au pair or the family can terminate the arrangement if they wish without notice. If the arrangement is terminated after the trial period the agency will usually try to find you another family. Write to a number of agencies and compare the conditions and pocket money offered. Agencies must provide a letter of invitation clearly stating your duties, hours, free time and pocket money (which must be shown to the immigration officer on arrival in Australia). Most agencies provide you with a list of other au pair girls in your area and may also put you in touch with local youth and social centres. **Au pair agencies aren't permitted to charge au pairs a fee, which is paid by the family.**

Agencies will send you an application form (questionnaire) and usually ask you to provide character references, a medical certificate, a number of photographs, a letter written to a prospective family and possibly a number of international reply coupons. You can choose a particular city or area, although most agencies prefer applicants who are willing to be located anywhere (however, take care, or they may send you to Kalgoorlie or Wagga Wagga). When completing the form, be careful with your answers and get help if there's anything you don't understand, e.g. when asked if you have any allergies, it wouldn't be advisable to write 'children'. A useful book for prospective au pairs planning to work in Australia is the *Au Pair and Nanny's Guide to Working Abroad* by Susan Griffith & Sharon Legg (Vacation Work).

WORKING ILLEGALLY

An estimated 50,000 people live illegally in Australia, some 60 per cent of whom also work illegally. The illegal labour market (usually called the black economy) thrives in Australia and is estimated to cost the government up to $15 billion in lost tax revenue annually. Most illegal workers are young people who overstay their working holiday visas or who arrive as tourists and stay on. The vast majority are employed on farms (e.g. fruit picking) and in factories and restaurants. Many unscrupulous employers use illegal labour in order to pay low wages for long hours and poor working conditions, particularly in the farming industry. However, there has been a crackdown in recent years and immigration officials link tax file numbers with immigration details, and make routine swoops on fruit farms and other suspect employers.

It's strictly illegal to work in Australia without a valid visa. If you're tempted to work illegally, you should be aware of the consequences as the black economy is a risky business for both employers and employees. When someone is discovered working illegally they're usually given the choice of voluntary rapid departure from the country or face deportation (around 7,500 people are deported annually). A foreigner caught working illegally is usually fined and deported, and may be barred from entering Australia for one to three years. Fines of up to $4,000 and suspended prison sentences of up to six months can also be imposed. Persons deported for criminal or security reasons are permanently excluded.

Employees without a valid visa permitting them to work in Australia have no entitlement to state or company pensions, unemployment benefits, accident insurance at work and no legal job protection.

LANGUAGE

English is the most important and most widely spoken language in the world and is spoken by some 1.4 billion people as their first or second language. It's the world's *lingua franca* and is the language of the United Nations antechamber, international peacekeeping, world banking and commerce, air traffic control, academic research, computers, the internet, space travel, scientific discovery, news gathering and world entertainment. If you're planning to live or work in Australia you'll need to speak, read and write English well enough to find your way around the country, e.g. dealing with government officials, public transport and shopping, and to understand and hold conversations with the people you meet. Independent migrants from non-English speaking backgrounds may need to take an English test. Your chances of obtaining a good job (or any job) in Australia are greatly diminished if you don't speak English fluently and many immigrants from non-English speaking backgrounds are unemployed because their lack of English would endanger other employees and reduce workplace efficiency. English proficiency is also important if you have a job requiring a lot of contact with others or which involves speaking on the telephone or dealing with other foreigners, many of whom speak their own 'dialect' of English.

Surprisingly an estimated one million migrants cannot speak English, a huge number in a country of less than 18 million people, and some 2.5 million residents (around 15 per cent of the population) speak a language other than English at home. Sydney is Australia's most multicultural city (closely followed by Melbourne), where four out of six people in some suburbs speak a language other than English at home (overall some 30 per cent of the population in Sydney doesn't speak English at home). Sydney and Melbourne are home to around 65 per cent of all non English-speaking migrants, who speak a total of some 240 foreign languages. Many migrants predominantly use their mother tongue (e.g. Arabic, Cantonese, German, Greek, Hindi, Italian, Korean, Lebanese, Serbo-Croat, Spanish, Turkish or Vietnamese) on a day-to-day basis and have only a smattering of English. Australia's failure to train migrants in English is handicapping them in respect of social, economic and political life, and real ghettos are emerging where Australian-born children don't speak fluent English. There's a thriving ethnic radio and TV broadcasting network, the Special Broadcasting Service (SBS), which was established in 1978 and broadcasts in the main cities.

It's particularly important for students (unless they are studying English) to have a high standard of English, as they must be able to follow lectures and take part in discussions in the course of their studies. This may also require a much wider and more technical or specialised vocabulary. For this reason, most universities and colleges don't accept students who aren't fluent in English and many require a formal qualification or require students to take a written test. Whether you speak British English, American English or some other variety is irrelevant, although some foreigners have a problem understanding the natives (even Americans and Britons occasionally have problems understanding Australians).

Australian English is similar to British English with their own colourful vernacular speech, called 'strine' (from the way 'Australian' is pronounced with a heavy Australian accent), thrown in for good measure. Strine (also called Ozspeak) is Australia's greatest creative form and is full of abbreviations, word-tweaking, profanities, hyperbole and vulgar expressions (or flash, filth and fun). Strine is the language of a rebellious subculture and has its origins in the Cockney (English) and Irish slang of the early convicts. The use of strine and slang words varies depending of the state or region and the Australian language also includes many words adopted from Aboriginal languages.

There are slight regional variations in the Australian accent, although foreigners usually find it difficult to detect them. Accents are broader in isolated country areas than among the middle class city dwellers, many of whom are of British ancestry. Newcomers have difficulty distinguishing between Australians and New Zealanders (who, like Americans and Canadians, don't take kindly to being confused with the other lot). Australians tend to speak through their noses (not moving your lips when talking keeps the flies out) with a broad nasal drawl, which although acceptable or even attractive for a man is considered by many to be unpleasant for a woman. The use of expletives is widespread, many of which are used as a sign of familiarity and even affection (bloody is in everyday use and no longer considered a swear word in Australia). Aussies believe in calling a spade a spade and to hell with the consequences! Absurd comparisons are frequently used for emphasis such as 'busy as a bricklayer in Beirut' (idle), 'as useful as a wether at a ram sale' (useless) and "as straight as a dog's hind leg' (bent).

Australians often cannot decide whether to use American or British spelling (e.g. program/programme, labor/labour, etc.) and consequently misspellings abound. In everyday use many words have a completely different meaning in Australia than they do in other English-speaking countries such as crook (ill), game (brave), globe (light bulb), knock (criticise), ringer (a top performer), shout (a round of drinks) and tube (a can of beer). Everything and anything is abbreviated in Australia, often by shortening any word with more than two syllables and adding the vowel e or o on the end of it as in derro (derelict), garbo (dustman), reffo (refugee) and rego (car registration), or adding a suffix such as 'ie', 'y' or 'i'. Common Ozspeak includes, chrissy (Christmas), barbie (barbecue), brickie (bricklayer), postie (postperson), mozzie (mosquito), cossie (swimming costume), truckie (truck driver), blowie (blowfly), tinny (can of beer), Aussie (Australian) and footy (football).

Australian English occupies its own special niche in the English-speaking world and many books have been written about Australian vernacular speech including *The Australian Language* by Bill Horpadge (Cassell), *Let's Stalk Strine* by Afferbeck Lauder, *The Dinkum Aussie Dictionary* (National) and the *Australian Phrasebook* (Lonely Planet). The standard Australian English dictionary is the Macquarie Dictionary (compiled by the Macquarie University, Sydney), the bible of Aussie English (2,500 pages!).

Aboriginal Languages: Australian Aboriginal (literally meaning 'indigenous') society has the longest unbroken cultural history in the world, dating back 70,000 years to the ice age. When the First Fleet arrived in Australia in 1788 there were estimated to be around 250 separate Australian languages (all believed to have evolved from a single language family) comprising some 700 dialects (although the British didn't do any surveys before massacring the natives). Of the original 250 or so languages, only around 20 survive and are spoken regularly and taught in schools. Kriol, spoken mostly in northern Australia, is the most widely used Aboriginal language and the native language of many young Aboriginals. It contains many English words but the meanings are often different and the spelling is phonetic.

If you wish to improve your English before starting work or a course of study in Australia, there are English-language schools throughout the country where you can enrol in a part or full-time course lasting from a few weeks to a year or longer (see **Language Schools** on page 210). See also the **Glossary** on page 491.

2.

WORKING CONDITIONS

Working conditions in Australia are among the best in the western world and are decided for most fields of employment at the federal or state level, where legislation covers such matters as annual and public holidays; long service leave; workers' compensation; occupational health and safety; discrimination; and redundancy procedures and payment. Working conditions and wages in Australia aren't usually determined by the free market, but are subject to industrial law and decided in negotiations between the unions and employers, and are subject to approval by the Australian Industrial Relations Commission. The end result of this process is termed the 'award' for a particular job or industry. It sets minimum wages and 'penalty' rates of pay for overtime and unsociable hours, and includes such matters as working hours, holiday entitlement, sick leave, redundancy and termination of employment. Many employers' pay and conditions are more generous than the statutory minimum decided under industry awards. Employees in Australia are also protected by a comprehensive federal social security (welfare) system which includes pensions, unemployment benefits, sickness and disability allowances, and family payments (see page 298).

From the mid-'80s until 1996, pay and working conditions were based on the 1983 Prices and Income Accord between the Labor government and unions, whereby basic pay and conditions for most employees were decided collectively. Industrial disputes in Australia are usually resolved by arbitration, with all parties agreeing to abide by the final decision of the Conciliation and Arbitration Commission, the highest legal authority within the Australian industrial system. In recent years many trades and industries have been encouraged to enter into enterprise working agreements and decentralised bargaining with individual employees and groups of employees, which are eating into the unions' traditional authority in the workplace. The Liberal/National coalition government (which came to power in 1996) plans to replace the 'award' system with a system of Australian Workplace Agreements (AWAs) setting out minimum working conditions. Under these agreements workers usually give up certain rights (such as agreeing to a longer working week at ordinary time or giving up high penalty rates for overtime) and restrictive practices in return for increased wages or bonuses. However, some analysts believe that the only way for Australia to reduce unemployment is to introduce a US-style deregulated labour market. This would mean removing or lowering minimum wages (which ensure that many unskilled people remain unemployed), taking unions out of the industrial process and reducing the dole (unemployment benefit) or making it more difficult to obtain.

Workers are generally well paid in Australia with extensive fringe benefits, especially in professional and executive positions, where 'perks' constitute a sizeable slice of pay packets. However, despite relatively high salaries and generally good working conditions, employees in Australia are becoming increasingly dissatisfied with their lot including pay and conditions; workplace-related stress; long hours and high workload; poor treatment by management; job insecurity; and the balance between work and family life. Many people work too hard and too many hours, and it has been estimated that as many as one in four employees has taken time off work in connection with workplace-related stress.

Information about employment conditions and workers' rights can be obtained from the Australian Industrial Relations Commission, 80 William Street, East Sydney, NSW 2001 (tel. (02) 9282 0888) and the Department of Industrial Relations, Employment, Training & Further Education, 1 Oxford Street, Darlinghurst, NSW 2010 (tel. (02) 9266 8111).

DISCRIMINATION

It's illegal under the Racial Discrimination Act (1975) and Sex Discrimination Act (1984) to discriminate against an employee because of sex (unless a person's sex is an essential qualification for a job), because he is married or because of his race, nationality, colour, sexual orientation, or ethnic or national origin. It's also illegal to discriminate against an employee because he does or doesn't wish to join a trade union. A woman doing the same or broadly similar work to a man or work of equal value, is legally entitled to the same salary and other terms of employment as a man (see **Working Women** on page 33). Discrimination applies to selection, appointment, training, promotion and dismissal. Note that discrimination is particularly rife where young employees are concerned, most of whom are unaware of their rights. Some companies have a policy of employing disabled or handicapped applicants whenever possible (or at least not discriminating against them), taking into account their ability, safety and comfort.

Note, however, that employers may discriminate against smokers and over three-quarters of Australia's top companies restrict smoking (and the consumption of alcohol) in the workplace. Around half of all companies have a total ban on smoking at work and a third have designated areas where employees are permitted to smoke. It's legal for employers to specify in job advertisements whether they will hire smokers (employers are fearful of law suits from non-smokers regarding 'passive' smoking). Smoking breaks (called a 'smoko') in Australia are estimated to cost business $billions a year!

It's difficult to prove discrimination on the grounds of sex and almost impossible on the grounds of race, although it's acknowledged that discrimination is widespread. If you're subjected to sexual harassment (which can happen to both women *and* men) you should report it to your supervisor or manager, as many companies have internal procedures to deal with such matters. However, if you don't receive satisfaction you can report it to your union or the police and take legal advice. The Human Rights and Equal Opportunities Commission (HREOC) handles sexual harassment and discrimination cases in the utmost confidence and can advise you whether you have legal grounds for a complaint (which must be submitted in writing). The HREOC's national office is in Sydney (GPO Box 5218, Level 24, American Express Building, 388 George Street, Sydney, NSW 2000, tel. (02) 9229 7600) and it has regional offices in Brisbane, Darwin and Hobart. Complaints in NSW are handled by the NSW Anti-Discrimination Board and in other states by Equal Opportunity Commissioners.

Note, however, that victims of discrimination who win compensation payments are often left frustrated and empty-handed by employers. Rulings by the HREOC aren't legally enforceable and compensation ordered by it is rarely paid without victims being forced to take further legal action (many just give up). This has lead to claims that Australia's discrimination laws are merely symbolic and a sham.

TERMS OF EMPLOYMENT

Negotiating an appropriate salary is only one aspect of your remuneration, which, for many employees, consists of much more than what they receive in their pay packets. When negotiating your terms of employment for a job in Australia, the checklists on the following pages should prove helpful. The points listed under **General Positions** below apply to most jobs, while those listed under **Managerial & Executive Positions** (on page 53) usually apply to executive and top managerial appointments only. Many companies offer a number of benefits (often referred to as perks) for executives, managers and key personnel, and it isn't unusual for the perks of board members to comprise as much as half their total remuneration. Note, however, that since the introduction of fringe benefits tax (FBT), employees must pay tax on fringe benefits and you should therefore check their real cash value (see page 352). Employees being relocated to Australia by their overseas employers are exempt from paying tax on some fringe benefits.

General Positions

- Salary:
  - is the total salary adequate, taking into account the cost of living in Australia (see page 357)? Is it index-linked?
  - does it include an allowance for working (and living) in an expensive (e.g. Sydney) or remote area?
  - how often is the salary reviewed?
  - does the salary include commission and bonuses (see page 56)?
  - does the employer offer profit-sharing, share options or share-save schemes?
  - is overtime paid or time off given in lieu of extra hours worked?
  - is a 'golden hello' paid (i.e. a 'signing on' fee)?
  - is the total salary (including expenses) paid in Australian dollars or is it paid in another country (in a different currency) with expenses for living in Australia?
- Relocation expenses:
  - are relocation expenses or a relocation allowance paid?
  - do the relocation expenses include travelling expenses for all family members?
  - is there a maximum limit, and if so, is it adequate?
  - are you required to repay your relocation expenses (or a percentage) if you resign before a certain period has elapsed?
  - are you required to pay for your relocation expenses in advance (which could run into many thousands of dollars)?
  - if employment is for a fixed period only, are your relocation expenses paid when you leave Australia?
  - if you aren't shipping household goods and furniture to Australia, is there an allowance for buying furniture locally?
  - do relocation expenses include legal and estate agent's fees incurred when moving home?
  - does the employer use the services of a relocation consultant (see page 115)?
- Accommodation:
  - will the employer pay for an hotel (or pay a lodging allowance) until you find permanent accommodation?
  - is subsidised or free, temporary or permanent accommodation provided? If so, is it furnished or unfurnished?
  - must you pay for utilities such as electricity, gas and water?
  - if accommodation isn't provided by the employer, is assistance in finding suitable accommodation given? What does it consist of?

- what will accommodation cost?
- while living in temporary accommodation, will the employer pay your travelling expenses to your permanent home? How far is it from your place of employment?
- are your expenses paid while looking for accommodation?

• Working Hours:
  - what are the weekly or monthly working hours?
  - does the employer operate a flexi-time system (see page 57)? If so, what are the fixed (core time) working hours? How early must you start? Can you carry forward extra hours worked and take time off at a later date (or carry forward a deficit and make it up later)?
  - are you required to clock in and out of work?
  - can you choose either to take time off in lieu of overtime worked or to be paid for it?

• Part-Time or Periodic Working:
  - is part-time or school term-time working permitted?
  - are working hours flexible or is part-time working from home permitted?
  - does the employer have a job-sharing scheme?
  - are extended career breaks permitted with no loss of seniority, grade or salary?

• Leave entitlement:
  - what is the annual leave entitlement? Does it increase with age?
  - what are the paid public holidays?
  - is free air travel to your home country or elsewhere provided for you and your family, and if so, how often? Are other holiday travel discounts provided?
  - is maternity/paternity leave provided?

• Insurance:
  - is health insurance or regular health screening provided for you *and* your family? If so, what does it include (see page 306)?
  - is free life assurance provided?
  - is accident or any special insurance provided by the employer?
  - for how long is your salary paid if you're ill or have an accident?

• Company pension (superannuation):
  - is there a company superannuation (super) fund (see page 303)?
  - can you pay a lump sum(s) into the super fund in order to receive a full or higher pension?
  - what are the rules regarding early retirement?
  - is the pension index-linked and based on your final salary?
  - do the pension rules apply equally to full *and* part-time employees?

• Employer:
  - what is the employer's future prospects?
  - is his profitability and growth rate favourable?
  - does he have a good reputation?

- does he have a high staff turnover?
- Women:
  - what is the employer's policy regarding equal opportunities for women?
  - how many women hold positions in middle and senior management or at board level (if the percentage is low in relation to the number of women employees, perhaps you should be wary if you're a career woman)?
  - is paid maternity leave provided, and if so, for how many weeks?
- Training:
  - what initial or career training does the employer provide?
  - is training provided in-house or externally and will the employer pay for training or education overseas, if necessary?
  - does the employer have an on-going training program for employees in your trade or profession (e.g. technical, management or language)? Is the employer's training recognised for its excellence (or otherwise)?
  - will the employer pay for a part or the total cost of non-essential education, e.g. a computer or language course?
  - will the employer allow paid day release for you to attend a degree course or other studies?
- What are the promotion prospects?
- Does the employer provide a free nursery or crèche for children below school age, or a day care centre for the elderly?
- Are free or subsidised English language lessons provided for you and your spouse (if necessary)?
- Is a free or subsidised employee restaurant provided? If not, is a lunch allowance paid? Is any provision made for shift workers, i.e. breakfast or evening meals?
- Is a travelling allowance paid from your Australian home to your place of work?
- If the job involves a lot of air travel, are you entitled to claim frequent flyer points?
- Is free or subsidised parking provided at your place of work?
- Are free work clothes, overalls or a uniform provided? Does the employer pay for the cleaning of work clothes?
- Does the employer offer inexpensive or interest-free home loans or mortgage assistance? Note that an inexpensive home loan can be worth $thousands a year.
- Is a company car provided? What sort of car? Can it be used privately, and if so, does the employer pay for petrol?
- Does the employer provide fringe benefits such as subsidised in-house banking services, a car discount scheme, cheap petrol, travel discounts, employees' discount shop, product discounts, sports and social facilities, or subsidised tickets for social and sports events?
- Do you have a written list of your job responsibilities?
- Have the employment conditions been confirmed in writing?
- If a dispute arises over your salary or working conditions, under the law of which country will your contract be interpreted?

Managerial & Executive Positions

* Is a 'golden hello' paid, i.e. a payment for signing a contract?

* Is private schooling paid for or subsidised by the employer? If necessary or desired, will the employer pay for a boarding school in Australia or another country?

* Is the salary index-linked or protected against devaluation and cost of living increases? This is particularly important if you're paid in a foreign currency that fluctuates wildly or could be devalued. Are you paid an overseas allowance for working in Australia?

* Is there an executive superannuation scheme? Note that the Australian Taxation Office has clamped down on salary sacrifice packages, whereby executives and other highly-paid employees sacrifice a large part of their salaries in return for higher superannuation payments (see page 303).

* Is a housing allowance paid or a rent-free house or apartment provided?

* Are paid holidays (perhaps in a company owned house or apartment) or 'business' conferences in exotic places provided?

* Are the costs incurred by a move to Australia reimbursed? For example, the cost of selling your home, employing an agent to let it for you or storing household effects.

* Will the employer pay for domestic help or towards the cost of a servant or cook?

* Is a car provided (possibly with a chauffeur)?

* Are you entitled to any miscellaneous benefits such as private club membership, free credit cards, or tickets for sports events and shows?

* Is there an entertainment allowance?

* Is extra compensation paid if you're made redundant or fired? Redundancy or severance payments (see page 67) are compulsory for all employees in Australia (subject to length of service), but executives often receive a generous 'golden handshake' if they're made redundant, e.g. after a takeover.

CONTRACT OF EMPLOYMENT

Under Australian law a contract of employment exists as soon as an employee proves his acceptance of an employer's terms and conditions of employment, e.g. by starting work, after which both employer and employee are bound by the terms offered and agreed. A contract isn't always in writing (it can be verbal and sealed by a handshake), although a company must usually provide employees who are normally employed in Australia with a written statement containing certain important terms of employment and additional notes, e.g. regarding discipline and grievance procedures. A written contract of employment usually contains all the terms and conditions agreed between the employer and employee. Note that employees have the right to review a contract for 14 days before signing it.

Under the Workplace Relations Act (1996), which came into effect on 1st January 1997, employers have increasingly been offering employees individual contracts, i.e. non-union certified agreements and Australian Workplace Agreements (AWAs). AWAs are valid for a maximum of three years and are effectively fixed-term contracts for three years. A non-union certified agreement must be approved by the Industrial Relations Commission, although only a majority of workers need to vote in favour and individual workers aren't required (or even entitled) to sign or veto an agreement. Contracts are subject to a no-disadvantage test and must meet seven minimum conditions, including no reduction in pay when compared with awards. However, in some cases employers have been permitted to offer non-union employment agreements that reduce living standards, if they can show that the deals increase job security.

Under AWAs many companies reserve the right to use contractors, part-time, casual and temporary workers as required; recruit, transfer or retrench on the basis of merit rather than prior agreement from industry or seniority; and use staff, production or engineering employees to perform any task within their competence, thus breaking down existing demarcations. Employees may also be required to work shifts of up to 12.5 hours. In return workers usually receive guaranteed annual pay rises, performance bonuses and a guarantee that AWA pay rates will equal or outstrip wages under any certified agreement negotiated with unions. In many cases employees with individual contracts are worse off, as contracts seek to cash out sick leave and other leave entitlements and allowances for employees in skilled trades; cut penalty rates, leave loading and overtime, and tailor working hours to meet peaks and troughs in demand; and undermine restrictive work practices in heavily unionised industries. Around 10 per cent of employees have signed individual contracts, which have become a potent and damaging weapon against the union movement and have reduced the cost of labour. However, many workers are rejecting the agreements and staying with collective agreements negotiated through their union.

Contracts may consist of a simple sheet of paper or be comprehensive multi-page documents, e.g. from a multi-national company. You should usually receive some form of contract, even for part-time and temporary jobs, although you won't usually receive a contract for casual work such as fruit picking (but you should get written confirmation of your wages and hours). A contract for a temporary position must state the period of the contract and should guarantee you compensation in the event that employment is terminated without notice. Note that either party can sue for breach of contract.

You usually receive two copies of your contract of employment (which may be called a 'statement of terms and conditions' or an 'offer letter'), both of which you should sign and date. One copy must be returned to your prospective employer, assuming you agree with the terms and want the job, and the other is for your own records. There are usually no hidden surprises or traps for the unwary in an Australian contract of employment, although as with any contract you should know exactly what it contains before signing it. If your knowledge of the English language is poor, you should ask someone to explain anything you don't understand in simple English (Australian companies rarely provide foreigners with contracts in a language other than English). Your contract of employment usually contains the following details:

- name of the employer and employee;
- date employment begins and whether employment with a previous employer counts as part of the employee's continuous period of employment;
- job title;
- salary details, including overtime pay and piece-rates, commission, bonuses and agreed salary increases or review dates;
- when the salary is to be paid, e.g. weekly, fortnightly or monthly;
- hours of work;
- annual and public holiday entitlements and pay;
- sickness and accident benefits;
- pension (superannuation) scheme details;

- probationary and notice periods (or the expiry date, if employment is for a limited period);
- disciplinary and grievance procedures (which may be contained in a separate document).

If there are no agreed terms under one or more of the above headings, this may be stated in the contract. Any special arrangements or conditions you have agreed with an employer should also be contained in the contract. If all or any of the above particulars are contained in a collective agreement, an employer may refer employees to a copy of this, including other documents such as work rules or handbooks, wage regulation orders, sick pay and superannuation scheme conditions, and the rules relating to flexible working hours and company holidays. Before signing your contract of employment, you should obtain a copy of any general employment conditions (see below) or documents referred to in the contract and ensure that you understand them.

Your employment is usually subject to satisfactory references being received from your previous employer(s) and/or character references. In the case of a school-leaver or student, a reference may be required from the principal of your last school, college or university. For certain jobs, a pre-employment medical examination is required and periodic examinations may be a condition of employment, e.g. where good health is vital to the safe performance of your duties. If you require a visa to work in Australia, your contract may contain a clause stating that 'the contract is subject to a visa being granted by the authorities'. Employees must usually be notified in writing of any changes in their terms and conditions of employment, e.g. within one month of their introduction.

EMPLOYMENT CONDITIONS

The term employment conditions (as used here) refers to an employer's general employment terms and conditions (including benefits, rules and regulations) that apply to all employees, unless otherwise stated in individual contracts of employment. General employment conditions are usually referred to in employment contracts and employees normally receive a copy on starting employment (or in some cases beforehand). Employment conditions are explained in this chapter or a reference is made to the chapter where the subject is covered in more detail.

Validity & Applicability

Employment conditions usually contain a paragraph stating the date from which they are valid and to whom they apply.

Place of Work

Unless there's a clause in your contract stating otherwise, your employer cannot change your place of work without your agreement. Note that the place of work usually refers to a town or area of a large city, rather than a different office or new building across the street. If applicable, a contract may state that you can occasionally be required to work at other company locations.

Salary & Benefits

Your salary is stated in your contract of employment and salary reviews, overtime rates, piece and bonus rates, planned increases and cost of living rises may also be included. Only general points, such as the payment of your salary into a bank or other account, and the date of salary payments are usually included in employment conditions. You should usually receive an itemised pay statement (or wage slip), either with your salary (if it's paid weekly or fortnightly in cash) or separately (when your salary is paid monthly into a bank account). **Always ensure that you receive a pay slip containing the legally-required information, as it's almost impossible to dispute pay claims without one.**

Salaries in Australia are generally reviewed annually, although the salaries of professional employees and all employees in some businesses may be reviewed every six months. The salaries of new employees may also be reviewed after six months. A percentage of your annual salary increase is usually to compensate for a rise in the cost of living, although some employees receive pay rises below the annual rate of inflation. Annual increases may be negotiated separately by employees on individual contracts, by an independent pay review board or by a union (or unions), when an industry is covered by an award (see **Salary** on page 37). Employees not on awards often receive the federal minimum wage, which in 1997 was $359.40 a week (equal to a minimum hourly rate of $9.45 for a 38-hour week).

Commission & Bonuses

Your salary may include commission or bonus payments, calculated on your individual performance (e.g. based on sales) or the company's performance as a whole, which may be paid regularly (e.g. monthly or annually) or irregularly. Some employers pay employees a special annual bonus (not to be confused with a general award holiday pay bonus) at the end of the year, although this isn't normal practice in Australia. When a bonus is paid it may be stated in your contract of employment, in which case it's obligatory. If applicable, an annual bonus is usually paid pro rata if you don't work a full calendar year, e.g. in your first and last years of employment with a company. CEOs in Australia typically receive a bonus averaging 25 to 30 per cent of their gross salary.

Some employers operate an annual voluntary bonus scheme, based on each employee's individual performance or the company's profits (a profit-sharing scheme), although this may apply only to senior managers and executives. Profit-sharing schemes aren't common in Australia, although performance-related bonuses or commissions are common in the finance industry. In some companies, employees are offered company shares at a favourable price, usually well below the market price. If you're employed on a contract basis for a fixed period, you may also be paid an end-of-contract bonus. When discussing your salary with a prospective employer, always take into account the total salary package including commission, bonuses and fringe benefits such as a company car or a low-interest home loan. In industry, particularly in small firms, blue-collar workers are often paid bonus or 'piece-work' rates based on their individual productivity.

Working Hours

Working hours in Australia vary depending on your employer, your position and the type of industry in which you're employed. A national 38-hour working week was introduced in 1981, since reduced to 37 hours. However, many people work longer hours, particularly employees in factories who often work 10 or more hours overtime a week.

A recent survey showed that average working hours increased from around 40 to 44 hours between 1990 and 1995. A standard working day (without overtime) for a blue-collar worker is from 7 or 8am to 3.30 or 4.30pm, while working hours in most offices and shops are from 8.30 or 9.30am until 4.30 or 5.30pm, with an hour's break for lunch.

Most employees work a five-day week, although over 25 per cent of men work weekends and some 20 per cent work shifts. In the last few years many companies have switched from eight-hour to 12-hour shifts, which means working 11 or 12 days a month only or 10 days in a three-week roster. Twelve hour shifts are common in enterprise deals where the advantage for employers is that they mean no overtime payments. Employees also gain as they earn around the same as previously (when they worked overtime) and have much more leisure time. Most workers prefer 12-hour shifts after having tried them, although there's a safety risk, particularly in factories, where it's estimated that there's double the risk of accidents due to fatigue.

Hourly paid workers are usually paid overtime (see below) for extra hours and higher 'penalty' rates for night, shift and weekend work. On the other hand, executives, professionals, managers (and an increasing number of non-union workers) often work overtime without extra pay. Many people work much longer hours now than they did in the '70s and '80s, and stress and illness from overwork is a constant threat for managers and executives. Tea or coffee breaks (often referred to as a 'smoko' or smoke break) may be scheduled at set times during mid-morning and mid-afternoon, particularly in factories (employers usually provide free tea or coffee and many also provide biscuits). Tea and coffee breaks are estimated to cost around $12 billion a year. Long business lunches (two hours or more) are becoming less common, although it's still customary to find employees finishing their lunch late in the afternoon on Thursdays and Fridays.

Your working hours may not be increased above the hours stated in your employment conditions without compensation or overtime being paid. Similarly, if you have a guaranteed working week, your hours cannot be reduced (i.e. short-time working) or changed without your agreement, unless there's a clause (sometimes referred to as a 'mobility clause') in your contract. In reality an employer is unlikely to change or reduce your hours without agreement if he wants to retain your goodwill and services. If you refuse short-time working and are subsequently dismissed, you can usually regard yourself as being retrenched (see page 67), in which case you should receive compensation. Some employers operate a system of flexible working hours and may also permit employees to take part in job-sharing (where two people share a job), voluntary reduced hours and working part of the time at home. Around a third of Australian workers (usually blue-collar) are required to sign-on or clock in and out of work (employees caught cheating may be summarily dismissed).

Days Off & Flexi-Time Rules

Many Australian companies operate flexi-time working hours or a system of rostered days off (RDO). The conditions and rules relating to flexi-time and RDO schemes vary depending on your employer (they are most common in public service) and are more likely to apply to those in managerial, administrative and professional occupations. At their peak, RDOs applied to almost a third of wage and salary earners, although they are now being lost through enterprise bargaining. RDOs are usually taken on a Monday so that they provide a long weekend, but this has proved disruptive to companies' operations. In recent years employers have been cutting back on RDOs, e.g. from 12 to six a year; converting them to annual or special accrued leave; swapping them for superannuation payments; or replacing them with time off in lieu spread over different days.

Many employees can work flexible hours if they need to and working parents are usually permitted to leave work for up to an hour at any time for personal reasons. A flexi-time system usually requires all employees to be present between certain hours, known as the core or block time. For example 9 to 11.30am and from 1.30 to 4pm. Employees may make up their required working hours by starting earlier than the required core time, reducing their lunch break or by working later. Many business premises are open from around 7am until 6pm or later, and smaller companies may allow employees to work as late as they wish, providing they don't exceed the safe maximum permitted daily working hours.

Overtime & Time Off

The opportunity to work overtime is seen as a lucrative fringe benefit by most blue-collar workers, many of whom earn around a quarter of their wages from overtime. In some industries there's an ingrained 'overtime culture', although for many workers overtime is a matter of economic necessity, without which many families would find it difficult to pay their bills. Of the some 6m people in full-time employment, almost half regularly work overtime and some 25 per cent of men work over 50 hours a week. Overtime is generally paid at time-and-a-half for the first three hours and double-time thereafter (plus Sundays and public holidays), or as detailed in the award for the trade or industry (workers in some industries receive 2.5 times the day shift rate for Sundays). Penalty rates of pay are paid for regular night, shift and weekend work, and there are allowances (called 'tropical loading' or a 'remote area allowance') for work in remote areas of the Northern Territory and Western Australia (above the 26th parallel 'Tropic of Capricorn').

However, in order to reduce overtime costs, many companies have been extending the normal working week and changing to 12-hour shifts. In non-union agreements, workers are three times more likely to have a standard working week longer than 38 hours and overtime may be paid at the standard rate (more likely in non-union workplaces). As much as half of all overtime worked is unpaid and fewer than 40 per cent of workers work standard hours. Many enterprise agreements stipulate that employees work longer hours at ordinary time (e.g. up to 50 a week) in return for higher wages and bonuses. Some companies pay overtime only when work is urgent and officially approved, and many prefer salaried (i.e. monthly paid) employees to take time off in lieu of overtime worked or expect them to work unpaid overtime. Working hours for employees who work a flexi-time system (see above) are usually calculated on a monthly basis, with employees being permitted to carry forward extra hours worked and take time off at a later date, or carry forward a deficit and make it up later.

Travel & Relocation Expenses

Your travel and relocation expenses to Australia (or to a new job in another region of Australia) depend on your agreement with your employer and are usually detailed in your contract of employment or conditions. If you're hired from outside Australia, your air ticket (or other travel costs) to Australia is usually booked and paid for by your employer. You can usually also claim any additional travel costs, for example the cost of transport to and from airports.

Australian employers may also pay your relocation expenses to Australia up to a specified amount. This may be paid as a percentage of your salary, a block allowance or specific expenses only, such as removal, legal and estate agent's fees. The allowance should be sufficient to move the contents of an average house (castles aren't usually catered for) and you must normally pay any excess costs yourself. A company may ask you to obtain two or three removal estimates when they are liable for the total cost of removal. If you don't want to bring your furniture to Australia or have only a few belongings to ship, you may be given an allowance to purchase furniture locally (check with your employer). Generally you're required to organise and pay for the removal yourself. Your employer usually reimburses the equivalent amount in Australian dollars *after* you have paid the bill, although it may be possible to get him to pay the bill directly or make an advance payment. If you change jobs within Australia, your new employer may pay your relocation expenses when it's necessary for you to move home. Don't forget to ask, as he may not offer to pay (it may depend on how desperate he is to employ you). See also **Relocation Consultants** on page 115.

Social Security

The Australian social security system is non-contributory and funded out of general taxation, with the exception of a Medicare levy of 1.5 per cent of gross taxable income (above $13,127 a year). For information see page 277.

Medical Examination

Many Australian companies require prospective employees to have a pre-employment medical examination, which is performed by a company doctor (or a doctor nominated by the employer). An offer of employment is usually subject to you being given a clean bill of health. This may be required for employees over a certain age (e.g. 40) or for those in particular jobs only, e.g. where good health is of paramount importance for reasons of safety. Thereafter a medical examination may be required periodically (e.g. every one or two years) or when requested by your employer. Medical examinations may be required as a condition of membership of a company health, pension or life insurance scheme. Some companies insist on key employees having regular health screening, particularly senior managers and executives.

Company Cars & Driving Licences

Many Australian employers provide senior employees such as directors, senior managers and professionals with a company car as a fringe benefit, in addition to employees who need a car to do their job (e.g. sales' reps.). Most companies provide executives with a luxury car (worth over $55,134) under a novated lease arrangement, which allows the employer to claim fringe benefits tax on cars provided as part of employee packages. Note that with a novated lease, although the company provides the car, if you leave for any reason you're responsible for the balance of the finance. If you're provided with a company car, you usually receive full details regarding its use and your obligations on starting employment. If you lose your licence (e.g. through drunken driving) and are unable to fulfill the requirements of your job, your employment may be terminated (i.e. you'll be fired), and you may not be entitled to any compensation. If a company car is provided, check what sort of car it is and whether you'll be permitted to use it privately. Note that employees are required to pay fringe benefit tax (FBT) on the value of a company car that's used privately (see page 352). Many companies allow employees to buy secondhand company cars at favourable prices.

Superannuation

A compulsory superannuation (or company pension) was introduced in 1992 to help persuade trade unions to accept moderate pay rises (the rules have since been extended to include part-time workers and those who leave the workforce for up to two years). Employers must contribute from 6 per cent (1997-98), depending on the size of their payroll, of an employee's monthly salary (which is usually paid into an approved superannuation fund). The prescribed minimum percentage is set to increase annually until the year 2002/03 when it will be 9 per cent for all employees. For further information see page 303.

Accident Insurance

All employers in Australia are required to have occupational accident insurance (called workers' compensation liability or WorkCover) for employees working on their premises, whether in a factory, office, shop, warehouse or residential accommodation. Schemes are financed by a levy on salaries, e.g. 2.8 per cent in NSW and 1.8 per cent in Victoria. Some states (such as Victoria) have attempted to overhaul their workers' compensation schemes in recent years (many of which operate at a loss), although the proposed changes in Victoria were met with massive opposition culminating in widespread strikes. Victoria wants to introduce a new scheme to exclude common law, as in schemes operated by South Australia, the Northern Territory and the Commonwealth government.

In order to reduce accidents, employees must obey all safety regulations such as no-smoking regulations; the use of safety equipment and clothes such as hard hats, steel-capped boots and goggles; securing long hair or ties; and the wearing of jewellery. However, unless an employee is grossly negligent and recklessly ignores safety rules and regulations, an employee is invariably deemed to be entitled to compensation. A worker is paid compensation (commonly called 'compo') if he is injured or sick as the result of an accident in the workplace, or when travelling to or from work or on company business. Compensation covers medical and other expenses and loss of earnings, and a workers' dependants are entitled to compensation if he's killed on the job. Note that Australians tend to claim compo for the slightest injury at work. However, although bogus claims are rife, particularly concerning the health effects of workplace-related stress, making a claim for compo often carries a stigma and many workers therefore try to avoid it (particularly those on contracts).

Occupational health and safety is dealt with by both federal and state governments, and at the federal level is determined by the National Occupational Health and Safety Commission. The conditions of payment and the amount of compensation payable is laid down in various state acts, although in some states Workers' Compensation Boards decide on individual claims. If a claim is rejected a worker can take his case to his union and it will be decided by a workers' compensation commission.

Sick Pay

Most employees are entitled to take up to two weeks' paid sick leave each year, depending on the award for the trade or industry. Because there's an allowance for sick days (called a 'sickie'), many employees feel that they should take them whether they are sick or not (poor health is usually the last reason why employees take sickies), particularly those in the public sector. It's estimated that around 15 per cent of companies with five or more employees have between 10 and 25 per cent of their workers absent 'sick' each day. Some

40m working days (or an average of 5 per cent of the total) are lost to sickies each year, costing employers $billions.

Usually you must have been employed for a minimum period before you're entitled to sick pay, e.g. three or six months, which may coincide with your probationary period. If you're sick during this 'probationary' period your pay will be docked, but when you've completed three or six month's service you may be reimbursed. A doctor's certificate isn't required for sick days taken within your annual allowance, although a certificate is required for additional sick days (for which you may not be paid), which are apparently easy to obtain even if you aren't sick. An employee cannot usually be dismissed when he's sick, although this depends on the period and the frequency of sick days and should be stated in your employment contract. In some states (e.g. NSW) up to five days of an employee's sick leave can be used to care for a partner (even same sex partners) or family member. Some employers have an occupational sick pay (OSP) scheme, under which you receive your full salary for a number of months (depending on your length of service) in the event of sickness or after an accident. OSP may be provided by your employer as part of a company pension scheme.

Miscellaneous Insurance

Other insurance provided by your employer is usually detailed in your employment conditions. This may include free life and health insurance, which also covers travel overseas on company business. Some companies provide free membership of a private health insurance scheme, although this may apply to executives, managers and key personnel only. Where applicable, check whether health insurance includes your family. Companies may also operate a contributory group health insurance scheme, offering reduced subscriptions for individual members.

Notification of Sickness or Accident

You're usually required to notify your employer as soon as possible of sickness or an accident that prevents you from working, i.e. within a few hours of your normal starting time. Failure to do so may result in you not being paid for that day's absence. You're required to keep your boss or manager informed about your illness and when you expect to return to work. For sick days that fall within your annual entitlement (see **Sick Pay** above) you aren't required to provide a doctor's certificate, although one is required for additional sick days.

Annual Holidays

All permanent employees in Australia are entitled to at least four weeks' annual holiday and many receive up to six weeks, depending on the award for their trade or industry. Many employers offer four weeks in the first year of employment and six weeks thereafter, and employees in some industries and professions receive as many as eight or nine weeks' paid annual holiday. Under a scheme called holiday or leave 'loading', full-time employees are paid an extra 17.5 per cent of their normal wage (a sort of booze allowance) when they take their annual holidays, although this is increasingly being eliminated by AWAs. Some companies pay leave loading only to employees below a certain salary level, e.g. $50,000. In some industries and professions (e.g. teaching), employees are required to take compulsory paid holidays at certain times (what a hardship!).

Holiday entitlement is calculated on a pro rata basis (per completed calendar month of service) if you don't work a full calendar year. Part-time staff may also be entitled to paid holidays on a pro rata basis. Holidays must usually be taken within the year in which they are earned, although many companies allow employees to carry any outstanding annual holiday entitlement over to the next year. Employers may also allow employees to take their total annual holiday entitlement in one block rather than split it into periods throughout the year.

Before starting a new job, check that any planned holidays will be approved by your new employer. This is particularly important if they fall within your probationary period (usually the first three months/13 weeks), when holidays may not be permitted. Holidays may usually only be taken with the prior permission of your manager or boss, and in many companies must be booked up to one year in advance. If you resign your position or are given notice, most employers will pay you in lieu of any outstanding holidays, although this isn't an entitlement and you may be obliged to take the holiday at your employer's convenience.

Public Holidays

The number of statutory public holidays a year in Australia varies from state to state and is usually between 10 and 12. There are eight national public holidays plus two to four state public holidays, the dates of which vary depending on the state or territory (some companies and industries also have special holidays such as a company outing or a union picnic day). All states also celebrate Labour Day (in addition to those shown below), although the date varies from state to state. Schools, banks, businesses and most shops are closed on public holidays. The following days are public holidays throughout Australia:

Date	Holiday
1st January	New Year's Day
26th January	Australia Day (the actual date varies from state to state and is usually on the Monday following the 26th if it doesn't fall on a Monday)
March/April	Good Friday (the date changes each year)
"	Easter Monday (the Monday after Good Friday)
25th April	Anzac Day (in memory of those who died in the two world wars)
June	2nd Monday - Queen's birthday (except Western Australia, which celebrates the Queen's Birthday in September)
25th December	Christmas Day
26th December	Boxing Day (called Proclamation Day in South Australia)

If a public holiday falls on a weekend, there's usually a substitute holiday on the following Monday (but not always). Some companies close during Christmas and New Year, e.g. from close of work on the 24th December until the 2nd January. To compensate for this shutdown and perhaps other extra holidays during the year, employees may be required to work extra hours throughout the year, or may be required to take part of their annual holiday entitlement. Part-time staff may be paid for a public holiday only when it falls on a day when they would normally be working.

You aren't required to work on public holidays unless otherwise stated in your contract of employment. When it's necessary to work on public holidays, you normally receive the same or a higher rate of pay than is paid for working on a Sunday (e.g. double the normal rate) and/or time off in lieu. When a job involves working at weekends and on public holidays (e.g. shift working), you usually receive a higher 'penalty' rate or are paid a shift allowance.

Compassionate & Special Leave of Absence

Whether or not you're paid for time off work or time lost through unavoidable circumstances (e.g. public transport strikes or car breakdowns) depends on your employer; whether you're paid weekly or monthly (e.g. with an hourly rate of pay); and not least, whether you're required to punch a clock. The attitude to paid time off may also depend on your status and position. Executives and managers (who often work much longer hours than officially required) have much more leeway regarding time off than a factory worker. All employees are allowed (by law) to take time off work for the following reasons:

- An expectant mother is entitled to 'reasonable' paid time off work for ante-natal care.

- A trade union official is entitled to paid time off for trade union duties and training for such duties, and employees may also be paid to attend union meetings during working hours. Similarly, a safety representative is allowed paid time off in connection with his safety duties.

- Time off for public duties such as service as a juror or court witness, councillor or school governor, or as a member of a statutory tribunal or authority, although your employer isn't usually required to pay you.

- If you're made redundant, you're entitled to take one day off each week to look for a new job or to arrange training in connection with a new job.

Many Australian companies also provide paid compassionate or special leave on certain occasions, which may include your own or a family marriage, birth of a child, or the death of a family member or close relative. Many employers allow special leave including long service leave, family leave, carers' leave and unpaid leave. However, only some 25 per cent of employees have the right to specific family or carers' leave and only around 20 per cent of enterprise agreements contain specific provisions addressing work and family issues (e.g. through special leave provisions). Women are far more likely to take leave for family reasons than men and in 1996 some 85,000 women took leave compared to only around 2,000 men. After 10 or 15 years' continuous service with an employer, you may be entitled to long service leave of up to six months on full or half pay. Some employers also permit unpaid career breaks (sabbaticals) of up to three years. The terms and conditions for special leave vary considerably depending on the employer and, where applicable, should be detailed in your employment conditions.

Paid Expenses

Expenses paid by your employer are usually listed in your employment conditions. These may include travel costs from your home to your place of work, which (if applicable) may consist of a bus or rail season ticket or the equivalent in cash (paid monthly with your salary). Companies without a company restaurant or canteen may pay employees a lunch allowance or provide luncheon vouchers. Expenses paid for travel on company business or for training courses may be detailed in your employment conditions or listed in a separate document. Most companies pay a 'km' allowance to staff who are authorised to use their private motor vehicles on company business (but ensure that business use is covered by your car insurance).

Probationary & Notice Periods

For most jobs there's a probationary period, which may vary from two weeks for weekly paid employees to three months (13 weeks) for permanent staff employees. Your notice period normally depends on your method of salary payment, your employer, your profession and your length of service, and is detailed in your contract of employment and employment conditions. Note that probationary and notice periods apply equally to employers and employees. The notice period for weekly paid workers is usually as follows:

Length of Service	Notice Period (weeks)
less than 1 year	1
1 to 3 years	2
3 to 5 years	3
over 5 years	4

Employees aged over 45 with more than two years' service are entitled to an extra week's notice or pay in lieu of notice. Most monthly paid employees have a one-month (or four-week) notice period, which takes effect after any probationary period. The notice period may be longer for executive or key employees, e.g. three or six months, or may be extended after a number of years' service (in which case it will be noted in your employment conditions).

If an employer doesn't give you the required notice in writing, he's liable to pay you in full for the period of official notice (see **Discipline & Dismissal** on page 66). If you resign your job, you must usually do so in writing. If you resign or are given notice, your company may not require you to work your notice period, particularly if you're joining a competitor or your boss feels that you may be a disruptive influence on your colleagues. However, if he doesn't want you to work your notice, he must pay you in full for the notice period, plus any outstanding overtime or holiday entitlement.

If an employer goes bankrupt and cannot pay you, you can terminate your employment without notice, but your employer cannot legally do this. Other valid reasons for an employee *not* to give notice are assault or abuse on him or a colleague by the employer, and failure to pay or persistent delay in paying his wages. Nevertheless, employees can usually leave a job without giving notice and the chances of an employer having any legal rights worth enforcing are negligible. However, you may lose any bonuses or other monies owed to you, plus any possibility of receiving a reference.

Education & Training

Education and training provided by your employer may be stated in your employment conditions. It's in your own interest to investigate courses of study, seminars and lectures which you feel will be of direct benefit to you and your employer. Most employers give reasonable consideration to a request to attend a course during working time, providing you don't make it a full-time occupation. In addition to relevant education and training, employers must also provide the essential tools and equipment for a job (although this is open to interpretation). It's compulsory for companies to provide appropriate and adequate safety and health training for all employees. However, Australian employers are notoriously bad when it comes to providing adequate training and only around half the workforce receives education or training during a year (which may be on the job or in formal courses). To encourage employers to improve the quantity and quality of their training programs, an Industry Training Levy was introduced in 1990 requiring employers to pay a penalty when specified minimum training levels aren't met.

If you need to improve your English, language classes may be paid for by your employer. If it's necessary to learn a foreign language (other than English) in order to perform your job, the cost of language study should be paid by your employer. An allowance may be paid for personal education or hobbies (e.g. flower arranging, kite flying or break-dancing) which aren't work related or of direct benefit to your employer (unless he's in the flower, kite or dance business).

Pregnancy & Confinement

Time off work for sickness in connection with a pregnancy is usually given without question, but it may not be paid unless authorised by a doctor if it exceeds your annual sick leave allocation. Depending on the industry or sector in which they're employed, most female employees are entitled to 12 months' unpaid maternity leave and those in the public sector are entitled to 12 weeks' paid maternity leave (pregnant fathers aren't entitled to anything, but may qualify for the Nobel prize for medicine!). Very few employees in the private sector receive paid maternity leave (Australia is one of the few countries in the world that has no laws requiring paid benefits in the private sector), although some employers give employees with 12 months' continuous service six weeks' paid maternity leave. Paid maternity leave is available in some 35 per cent of workplaces, although companies are increasingly scrapping it and it's also under threat from the out-sourcing of jobs. Part-time employees may be entitled to pro rata maternity leave and pay. A women usually has the right to return to her job with the same pay within 12 months of giving birth. Around 20 per cent of employers provide paid paternity leave for fathers and most employers allow fathers to take unpaid leave when their partner gives birth.

Part-Time Job Restrictions

Restrictions on part-time employment for an employer other than your regular employer may be detailed in your employment conditions. Many Australian companies don't allow full-time employees to work part-time (i.e. moonlight) for another employer, particularly one in the same line of business. You may, however, be permitted to take a part-time teaching job or similar part-time employment (or you can write a book).

Confidentiality & Changing Jobs

If you disclose any confidential company information, either in Australia or overseas (particularly to competitors), you may be liable to instant dismissal and may also have legal action taken against you. You may not steal any secrets or confidential information (e.g. customer mailing lists) from a previous employer, but you may use any skills, know-how, knowledge and contacts acquired during his employ. If you make any inventions while an employee, they remain your property unless you sell them or a licence to your employer; the invention was made as part of your 'normal duties'; or you were specifically employed to invent, e.g. in research and development.

You may not compete against a former employer if there's a valid, binding restraint clause in your contract of employment. Your contract may also contain a clause defining the sort of information that the employer considers to be confidential, such as customer and supplier relationships and details of business plans. If there's a confidentiality or restraint clause in your contract that's unfair, e.g. it inhibits you from changing jobs, it will probably be invalid in law and therefore unenforceable. If you're in doubt, consult a solicitor (who's an expert in company law) about your rights. If you're a key employee, you may have a legal binding contract preventing you from joining a competitor or starting a company in the same line of business as your employer for a period, and in particular, enticing your former colleagues to join your company. However, such a clause is usually valid for a limited period, e.g. one year.

Acceptance of Gifts

With the exception of those employed in the public sector, employees are normally permitted to accept gifts of a limited value from customers or suppliers, e.g. bottles of wine or spirits or other small gifts at Christmas. Generally any gifts given and received openly and above board aren't considered a bribe or unlawful (although if you give your business to someone else in the following year, don't expect a 'bribe' next Christmas). You should declare any gifts received to your immediate superior, who will decide what is to be done with them. Most bosses pool gifts and divide them among all employees. (If you accept a real bribe, make sure it's a big one and that you have a secret Swiss bank account.)

Long Service Awards

Most large companies present their employees with long service awards after a number of years, e.g. 15, 20 or 25 years. These are usually in the form of a gift such as a watch or clock (so you can count the hours to your retirement), presented to individuals by senior management. Periods of absence on maternity leave may count as continuous employment when calculating your length of service.

Retirement

Your employment contract may be valid until the official state retirement age only, currently 61 for women (although it's gradually being increased to 65) and 65 for men. In many large companies, early retirement is possible from the age of 55. If you wish to continue working after you have reached retirement age, you may need to negotiate a new contract of employment (you should also seek psychiatric help). If your employer has a compulsory retirement age, usually 65, he isn't required to give you notice. Many companies present employees with a gift on reaching retirement age (e.g. the key to your ball and chain), the value of which usually depends on your number of years' service. See page 301 for more information.

Discipline & Dismissal

Most large and medium size companies have comprehensive grievance and disciplinary procedures, which must usually be followed before an employee can be suspended or dismissed. Some employers have disciplinary procedures whereby employees can be suspended with or without pay, e.g. for breaches of contract. Employees can also be suspended (usually with pay) pending investigation into an alleged offence or impropriety. Disciplinary procedures usually include both verbal and official written warnings, e.g. first verbal warning, second verbal warning, first written warning, second written warning, interview with board, etc., and official records must be kept by your employer. These procedures are both to protect employees from unfair dismissal and to ensure that dismissed employees cannot sue their employer. If you have a grievance or complaint against a colleague or your boss, there may be an official procedure to be followed in order to obtain redress. If an official grievance procedure exists, it will usually be detailed in your employment conditions.

It's illegal to dismiss employees on grounds other than those detailed in government and union agreements. In instances where employment was terminated on unjustified grounds, there may be a review by an industrial court and wrongful dismissal can result in a claim for damages. There has been a massive increase in unfair dismissal claims in recent years (almost 11,000 claims were lodged in 1996) due to the government's tightening of federal industrial relations laws. However, employees dismissed for 'serious misconduct' such as disobedience of management decisions, fraud or any other illegal activity aren't entitled to notice or benefits. If you believe that you've been unfairly dismissed, you can take your case to the Conciliation and Arbitration Commission. There's a $50 filing fee for a claim for unfair dismissal and provisions allowing costs to be awarded against employees who make frivolous claims. Those earning over $66,200 a year are excluded from claiming for unfair dismissal, along with casuals on short-term arrangements, those on probation for three months or less, and apprentices.

Redundancy

Redundancy (called retrenchment in Australia) has become a common occurrence in recent years, particularly during the recession in the early '90s. Retrenchment is defined as 'where an employer has made a definite decision that he no longer wishes the job that an employee has been doing to be done by anyone, and this is not due to the ordinary and customary turnover of labour'. Retrenched workers are entitled to severance pay under the Termination Change and Redundancy (TCR) case in 1984. The rules governing severance pay and periods of notice for those employed under federal awards depend on the length of service of an employee, as shown below:

Length of Service	Severance Pay (weeks)
less than 1 year	0
1 to 2 years	4
2 to 3 years	6
3 to 4 years	7
over 4 years	8

Employees aged over 45 with over two years' service are entitled to an extra week's notice or pay in lieu of notice. Severance pay is higher in some states, e.g. 16 weeks in NSW plus an extra 25 per cent for those aged over 45. Many enterprise agreements allow for three or four weeks' pay for each year of service when an employee takes forced redundancy. Severance pay cannot exceed the amount an employee would have earned had he remained in employment until his normal retirement date and is paid at ordinary time rates for the standard working week. If an employee receives a superannuation payment (see page 303), the amount is generally deducted from his entitlement to severance pay.

The average severance pay for executives is usually around six months, although some executives, managers and key personnel have a clause in their contract whereby they receive a generous 'golden handshake' if they are retrenched, e.g. after a takeover. Employers have no unfettered right to dismiss executives and must safeguard themselves against compensation claims by executives they sack. This applies even if they obtain an indemnifying deed of release, which is supposed to protect employers from further suits, claims or demands when an employee accepts a redundancy package.

When an employee has been notified of his retrenchment, he's permitted to take a day off each week with pay to look for another job. Employers must contact a Centrelink office and inform them of the number of proposed retrenchments, the category of employees affected, and the period over which the retrenchments will be made. Some companies provide 'outplacement' consultancy or agency services for employees who are retrenched. This includes advice and counselling on future job prospects, job hunting, state benefits, retirement, retraining, setting up in business, and financial advice for employees who receive large redundancy payments.

Australia has no unemployment benefit scheme, but unemployed people receive social security payments under either the Jobsearch or Newstart schemes (see page 300). Retrenched employees are entitled to a 'statement of employment' (reference). It's also possible for employees to take voluntary redundancy or early retirement and receive an early pension, e.g. in the event of ill health.

References

In Australia, an employer isn't legally obliged to provide an employee with a written reference or 'statement of employment', except in the case of retrenchment. However, if you leave an employer on good terms, he'll usually provide a written reference on request. If your employer refuses to give you a written reference or gives you an unwarranted 'bad' reference, it's advisable to ask your immediate boss or a colleague for a personal reference. In Australia, prospective employers may contact your previous employer (or employers) directly for a reference, either orally or written. This can be bad news for employees, as you have no idea what has been said about you and whether it's true or false. An employer is under no obligation (except perhaps morally) to provide a reference, but if he does, he cannot (legally) maliciously defame you, although should he do so verbally, it's almost impossible to successfully sue him.

Trade Union Membership

Trade unions have been active in Australia since the mid-19th century, when many professional agitators were deported from Britain and Ireland. Australia has a long tradition of supporting workers' rights, better working conditions and improved pay, all of which unions have fought hard for over the years. However, the unions earned themselves a terrible reputation during the '60s and '70s, when the country and the economy was frequently crippled by strikes. This was brought to an end in the mid-'80s with the accord between employers, unions and government, brokered by the Labor government elected in 1983 (the unions have traditionally had strong links with the Australian Labor Party). In recent years there has been a series of confrontations between the (Liberal/National coalition) government and the unions, after the government brought in tougher 'anti-union' laws, which included anti-strike provisions and tough sanctions against some primary and secondary boycotts. This has led to some bitter disputes between employers wishing to end outdated restrictive work practices (and the resulting low productivity), which are rampant in industries with strong unions such as mining and the docks.

Today there are over 300 trade unions in Australia, around half of which are affiliated to the Australian Council of Trade Unions (245 Chalmers Road, Redfern, NSW 2016, tel. (02) 9690 1022). Union membership in Australia is among the highest in the world at around 30 per cent of the workforce (some 2.1m people), although in the last few decades they have been losing ground in their areas of traditional strength and have largely failed to recruit young workers, women, workers in small businesses and those in growth industries. There was a net loss of 600,000 union members between 1990 and 1995 and some 60 per cent of workers believe unions are no longer relevant to them (a survey in 1997 found that non-union members are more likely to be satisfied at work, have more positive attitudes to management and feel more secure than those in unions).

Nevertheless, despite their reduced membership, unions have a great deal of influence, particularly in companies and industries which previously had 'closed shop' agreements, where all employees needed to join a union (the Workplace Relations Act 1996 abolished compulsory union membership). However, although union membership isn't compulsory, some union representatives or trades put a lot of pressure on employees to join. The public sector is the most heavily unionised with around 55 per cent of employees being members, although membership in the private sector is below 25 per cent. Large companies with over 100 employees have the highest rates of unionisation and small businesses with less than 10 employees the lowest (unions are now active in less than 20 per cent of workplaces).

Whether you're better off as a member of a trade union will depend on the industry in which you're employed. There are benefits to be gained from union membership and, in addition to negotiating better pay and conditions for members, unions also offer members legal and medical assistance in work-related disputes. In most industries which recognise trade unions, members pay and conditions are decided by collective bargaining between employers and trade unions. Employers aren't allowed to discriminate against an employee in selection, promotion, transfer, training or dismissal because he belongs (or wishes to belong) to a trade union.

Sanity Clause

Does the contract of employment include a sanity clause? This is particularly important if you have young children. Some people, however, don't believe in sanity clause (particularly scrooges).

3.

PERMITS & VISAS

Before making any plans to live or work in (or even travel to) Australia, you *must* ensure that you have the appropriate visa, without which you will be refused permission to enter the country. With the exception of citizens of New Zealand, anyone wishing to enter Australia as a visitor, or for any other purpose, requires a visa. Australia is a nation of migrants and only the 1.5 per cent Aboriginals represent the indigenous population; everyone else is an immigrant or descended from an immigrant. After the second world war Australia instituted a mass immigration policy ('populate or perish') and accepted virtually anybody who applied, even providing assisted passages where migrants paid only a small sum (e.g. £10 in Britain) towards their fare to Australia. However, immigration policy has altered dramatically since then and Australia's entry qualifications for independent migrants (those without family in Australia) are now among the most stringent in the world. In the '60s, Australia accepted around 140,000 migrants a year, peaking at 172,000 in 1988, although in recent years the quota allocation has been reduced considerably (to just 68,000 in 1997-98). However, serious doubts were being raised in 1998 that the quotas are now too low, particularly regarding skilled migrants, and could stifle economic growth.

Immigration is a sensitive subject in Australia, where the majority of people are against large-scale immigration (although many also believe that it provides real benefits for the country and stimulates economic growth). Migrants bring $billions into Australia each year and migration is the country's third-largest, foreign-currency earner after tourism and agriculture (to say nothing of the wealth created by migrants). However, not everybody welcomes immigrants and issues such as over-crowding and over-population, and protecting Australia's environment, culture and economy, are arguments frequently cited by those opposed to large-scale immigration. Despite its vast size, Australia has a relatively small population (around 18m) and is actually considered by many Australians to be over-populated due to its lack of productive land, shortage of water and generally over-crowded cities. Many Australians feel that migrants are a strain on the economy and take jobs away from 'real' Australians, a view which has become more prominent in recent years (fuelled by high unemployment and anti-immigration sentiment whipped up by Pauline Hanson and her One Nation Party). The ethnic background of migrants is also a thorny issue and although race and ethnic origin aren't officially an immigration issue, almost half of all Australians believe that the country accepts too many Asians and some would also like fewer migrants from the Middle East (settlers from Asia, Africa and the Middle East have borne the brunt of the government's recent cuts in immigration).

Note that there's a huge unsatisfied demand for emigration to Australia, which is much more difficult than emigrating to the USA, Canada, New Zealand or South Africa (the regulations are designed to keep people out rather than let then in). It's becoming increasingly difficult to obtain a visa as an independent migrant and it's also more difficult (or impossible) for immigrants who don't speak fluent English. Australian missions receive over a million enquiries a year and 400,000 applicants, of which around 70,000 who are accepted for emigration. Over half of those accepted already have family in Australia, around 25 per cent are professionals or skilled workers and as many as 15 to 20 per cent are refugees.

Applying for a visa as a migrant (permanent residence) is time consuming, confusing, difficult and expensive, and has spawned a wealth of migration consultants and keeps thousands of civil servants in 'employment'. The Australian government is constantly changing the rules and sometimes introduces retrospective changes that apply to applications already lodged (but not processed). Before making an application, *always* check the latest regulations and criteria for visa applications. Note that even when new requirements have been announced, they may not be introduced for many months or even years, and could even be rejected by the upper house (Senate) of the Australian parliament after being passed by the lower house (as happened in 1996). Application fees for migrant visas are high and aren't refundable, so you should ensure that you have a *very* good chance of being accepted before making an application (otherwise you would be better off spending your money on lottery tickets!). **Note that a two-year waiting period has been introduced in recent years before most migrants can claim social security, which has caused many unemployed migrants to become destitute and homeless (particularly those from third world countries with little money).**

Permanent foreign residents of Australia don't receive the same rights as Australian citizens with regard to their freedom to leave and enter Australia. Migrants are generally allowed to come and go as they please for the first three years after their initial entry. After three years, if you choose not to apply for Australian citizenship, you must obtain a 'resident return visa' (RRV) before leaving the country. Whether the visa is granted depends on how long you have spent in Australia during the previous three years. This visa allows you to return to Australia within three years of your departure, after which your status as a permanent resident expires. An RRV cannot be extended.

If it expires, you must apply for a new one and the amount of time you have spent outside Australia in the three years immediately prior to your application will determine whether you're eligible for a new visa, and if so, what type. For example if you have lived in Australia for at least two years within the last five years, you will probably be eligible for an RRV which gives you the right to remain outside Australia for up to five years. If you have been resident for less than 12 months in the last three years, you may not be eligible for a new visa at all. If you choose to return to Australia just before your visa expires, you will be obliged to remain there for at least 12 months before you're eligible for another RRV. If you need to leave due to an emergency during this period, you will allowed to do so once only.

Note that information in this chapter is intended as a guide only and that the rules and regulations concerning visas change frequently. It's imperative to check the latest rules and regulations with an Australian mission before making a visa application and, if necessary, obtain professional advice.

VISAS

With the exception of New Zealanders and members of the British Royal Family, anyone wishing to enter Australia requires a visa, which must be obtained before arrival in the country. New Zealanders receive a special category visa on arrival and nothing is stamped in their passports. There are no formalities and they can live and work in Australia for as long as they wish. **If you need a visa and arrive without one, you'll be sent back to your home country at your own expense.** The type of visa issued depends on the reason for your planned trip to Australia, which may be anything from a few weeks' holiday or a short business trip to permanent residence.

There are three main categories of visas: migration, temporary residence and visitors. Multiple-entry visas are issued to those who need to visit Australia frequently over a long period, such as businessmen, the parents of children living there, entertainers and sportsmen. Note that there are fees for anything other than a three-month visitor's visa, which have been increased considerably in recent years (to discourage applicants?). The processing of Visa applications in some categories can take a considerable time in some countries due to the large number of applications to be processed, and approval can take anything from a few weeks to a number of years.

Information about visas, charges and forms can be obtained from offices of the Department of Immigration and Multicultural Affairs (DIMA) in Australia and Australian missions overseas. General information about visa applications is contained in *making and processing Visa applications* (form 1025i). It's important to obtain and complete the correct form, pay the correct fee and satisfy other requirements such as being inside or outside Australia, as required. You must be careful to indicate the visa class under which you wish to be considered, as your application cannot be considered under any class other than the one shown on your application form. An *Application for Migration to Australia* form (47) must be completed by all applicants wishing to travel to Australia to live **permanently** and applications must be sent or delivered to a DIMA office or an Australian mission overseas, with all relevant documentation and the fee.

Family members who apply at the same time can usually apply on the same form and pay just one fee (a child born after an application is made, but before it's decided, will be included in the parents' application). In certain circumstances, a spouse or dependant child can be added to an application. Applications for some visas, such as visitors' visas, may be decided while you wait. In this case, if you're granted a visa you're usually given a visa label in your passport. If your application for a visitors' visa is refused, you will be given a notice of refusal. For all other visas, you're notified of the decision by letter. If you're refused a visa, you will be notified why and, if applicable, where you can apply for a review of the decision and the time limit for doing so.

If you plan to travel to or from Australia while your visa application is being considered (assuming this is possible), you should inform the DIMA, as a visa will be refused if you're in the 'wrong place' when a decision is made. For most visas where an application is made overseas, you must be outside Australia when a decision is made and for visa applications in Australia, you must be in Australia when the decision is made. If you make a visa application in Australia, you must ensure that you have a visa to return *before* leaving the country, otherwise if you're application is refused you may have no right of review. If you apply for a visa in Australia, you will usually be granted a bridging visa to remain within the law if your current visa expires while a decision is being made on your application.

Extensions, Conditions & Expiry: If you wish to stay longer than your visa allows, you should apply for another visa. If your visa expires while you're in Australia and you haven't applied for an extension, you're committing a criminal offence and can be fined up to $4,000, given a suspended prison sentence of up to six months or deported. If you're deported, you will usually be barred from entering Australia for one to three years. Persons deported for criminal or security reasons are permanently excluded. If a visa is granted subject to certain conditions, e.g. restrictions on work or study, you must abide by those conditions or your visa may be cancelled. If you wish to change your visa status, e.g. from a visitor to a student, you must leave the country and make a new application while overseas.

Migration Agents: Some people use a migration agent to make a visa application on their behalf, although this can be *very* expensive and doesn't guarantee success. There have been a number of cases where migration agents have charged large fees and lodged applications on behalf of clients who had no chance of ever being approved for immigration. Agents levy high fees for their services (which must be paid in addition to official application fees) and few agents ever give refunds, even when they have been negligent (despite 'guarantees'). Before paying any fees you should ask yourself whether this isn't something you can do yourself and what exactly you will receive for your money. Many people who use migration agents could easily make their own applications, e.g.

professional people. **It should be noted that agents cannot influence the DIMA in their decision to accept or reject an application.**

There are a number of unqualified 'cowboy' agents operating in some countries (e.g. Britain) and there's usually no regulation of agents outside Australia (although moves are afoot to introduce some form of voluntary regulation). An added problem is that agents occasionally go bankrupt, with clients losing their fees. If you plan to use an agent, you should choose one who's a member of a professional association or organisation which sets standards and a code of ethics for the industry. In Australia all agents must pass exams and be registered with the Migration Agents Registration Board, PO Box 25, Belconnen, ACT 2616 (tel. (02) 6264 4683). Most agents offer a free or inexpensive assessment to prospective migrants.

In the opinion of the Australian Department of Immigration, Local Government and Ethnic Affairs, there's no need for most people to use an agent and the vast majority of applicants from around the world don't. There's no particular advantage in having a migration agent lodge your application for you and they have no greater chance of success than an individual lodging his own paperwork (despite what they may tell you). However, if your English isn't good or you have difficulty filling in forms, then it may be worthwhile, although it will be much cheaper to get a friend to help you. If you don't lodge all the information necessary to judge your case it will take longer to assess, but it won't automatically be refused. Your case officer will contact you and explain exactly what it is that he needs (a service which is included in the lodgement fee).

Waiting Period: Note that it can take a long time to receive a migrant visa. However, if you're really keen to go and meet the criteria for the category of visa for which you're applying, you will usually get your visa in the end. You must usually be prepared for a long wait (e.g. a number of years) and possibly a lot of questions and demands for additional paperwork from immigration officials. If your application is pooled (which applies to visas in categories subject to a 'points test') or if the processing of the class of visa is suspended, your application will be delayed indefinitely and may eventually be refused. The processing time for migration applications varies depending on the country where you're applying and the number of applicants. Family migrants are given priority. In certain circumstances, e.g. for compassionate reasons, an application can be expedited, although no guarantees are given.

Visa Validity: If you're accepted for immigration you will be asked to send your passport to the embassy or consulate and a visa will be stamped in it. You must usually arrive in Australia within six months of the date stamped in your passport. Note that if you don't enter Australia by the 'initial entry' date of your visa, it will expire and you will need to re-apply for migration. If you enter Australia by the initial entry date you will have used (or validated) your migrant visa and by doing so will have become a permanent resident (if applicable).

MIGRATION

To be accepted for migration to Australia you must meet the personal and occupational requirements of the category for which you're applying, and be of good health and character. The Australian migration program is divided into four main visa categories: family; skill; refugee, humanitarian and special assistance; and interdependent migrants, each of which have their own eligibility requirements.

• **Family Migrants** must have a relative in Australia who can sponsor them.

- **Skill Migrants** must have skills or abilities that will benefit Australia.

- **Refugee, Humanitarian and Special Assistance Migrants** — see page 83 and information form 964i (*Refugee and Humanitarian Entry*).

- **Interdependent Migrants** must have an interdependent relationship with an Australian citizen, permanent resident or eligible New Zealand citizen.

The above migration categories are explained in detail in this chapter. In addition to the above, former Australians who have lost their Australian citizenship and former residents who have spent most of their life before the age of 18 in Australia and who have maintained ties with Australia, are also eligible for migration. Dependants of New Zealand citizens who have settled or intend to settle in Australia are also allowed entry into Australia. In general, applicants must apply for residence while outside Australia, although applications can be made while in Australia in exceptional circumstances, e.g. when a visitor's family overseas has died while he's in Australia, when he has met an Australian and plans to marry, or when a return to his country could result in political persecution.

The Department of Immigration and Multicultural Affairs (DIMA) has an enquiry telephone service in Australia (tel. 13 1881 — calls are charged at local call rates from anywhere in Australia). In most countries the local Australian embassy or consulate has a recorded message information service (e.g. tel. 0891-600 333 in Britain), although it's usually difficult to get through and numbers are often expensive premium rate lines. The form, *Migrating to Australia - Who can migrate?* (957i), contains general information about migration and the various categories. An *Application for Migration to Australia* form (47) must be completed by all applicants wishing to travel to Australia to live permanently. There's a charge (e.g. £6 in Britain) for this form and the information package. If you wish to inquire about an application it must be made in writing, quoting your DIMA file number, although you may telephone the DIMA and enquire about the progress of your application (but this can delay its processing).

Never make any firm plans or arrangements (such as travel arrangements, selling your home or resigning your employment) in the expectation that your visa application will be granted. Even when an application appears to be going smoothly it can still be delayed or even rejected at the last minute, e.g. on health grounds.

Visa Quotas

The Australian migration year runs from 1st July to 30th June (the same as the Australian financial year) and each year the federal government announces the quotas for the coming year. All applications for categories where a quota (or capping) applies are processed on a 'first-come, first-served' basis. When a cap is reached for the current immigration year, the granting of visas is suspended, although processing continues and applicants are granted visas when the new immigration year commences (and a new quota is allocated). The following quotas were announced for 1997-98:

Category/Component	Quota
Family:	
Preferential Family	32,000
Total Family	32,000

Skill:

Skilled—Australian-linked*	8,000
Employer Nominated (ENS/RSMS)	5,800
Business Skills	6,000
Special Talents	260
Independents	14,700
1st November	500
Total Skill	**35,260**
Special Eligibility	740
Total 1997-98	**68,000**

* In the 1997-98 program, the Concessional Family category was renamed the Skilled—Australian-linked (SAL) category and moved from the family to the skilled component.

Migration planning figures can never be exact because while some categories (e.g. independent and SAL) attract fixed quotas, others are demand-driven. There's no upper limit placed on the number of migrants who can qualify in demand-driven categories, where, if you meet the criteria, you're accepted.

Health & Character Checks

Applicants for migration visas must pass health and character checks before they are granted a visa.

Medical Examination: All applicants (and their family members) for permanent or long-term temporary residence (over 12 months), plus short-term temporary applicants if their health is of 'special significance', are required to undergo a medical examination. This includes an x-ray for those aged 16 or older and an HIV/AIDS test for those aged 15 or over. TB screening is part of the medical examination for all those aged 16 or over (and for those aged under 16 if it's suspected that they have or have had TB). Visitors to Australia are required to sign a declaration stating that they "have never had tuberculosis or any serious condition likely to endanger or be a cost to Australia". Pregnancy must be declared by prospective migrants. Note that a long term or serious illness or condition suffered by you or a dependant could void your application, e.g. if you have a child who requires special schooling. Results of the examination are sent to the Department of Health in Australia and can take around six weeks to be assessed. Your case officer will provide you with instructions and forms for undergoing your medical examination after you have lodged your application and during its processing.

Statement of Good Character: One of the requirements for entry into Australia is that you must be of good character. Applicants aged 16 to 65 who have resided in their present country for over 12 months in the last 10 years must obtain a 'police certificate' detailing any criminal convictions against them. This is required regardless of whether or not you have had any criminal convictions. The police certificate can be obtained as soon as you decide to apply for migration to Australia and if you receive it before making your visa application it should be included with it. The procedure for obtaining a police certificate varies from country to country, e.g. in Britain a 'certificate' can be obtained by visiting your local police station and requesting a 'Personal Record of Prosecution/Criminal History' from the National Identification Service, Subject Access Office, Room 31, New Scotland Yard, Broadway, London SW1H 0BG (fee £10). In Australia a certificate of 'no criminal record' (fee $19) can be obtained from the Australian Federal Police, Criminal History Branch, Locked Bag 1, Weston, ACT 2611. Note that if you have a criminal record it may jeopardise your application (stringent efforts have been made in recent years to prevent the entry of convicted criminals and other undesirables). Further information is provided in *Character requirement: police certificates* (form 47P).

Medical and police clearances are valid for 12 months only, and therefore you're required to make your initial entry into Australia within 12 months of your medical or police clearance date, whichever occurs first.

Documentation & Interviews

All application forms must be completed in English and you must provide originals or certified copies of all documents (as requested).

Documentation: You must usually provide certified copies of documents such as educational and trade qualifications, training courses and experience, employer references, and birth and marriage certificates. All documents must be certified by a legal professional, a Justice of the Peace or other person authorised to witness statutory declarations (e.g. a Commissioner for Declarations in Australia), who must state that the photocopy is a true copy of the original. **Original documents mustn't be sent unless specifically requested.** Additional information concerning your application can be provided at any time (and will be taken into account) prior to a decision being made on your application. You must keep the DIMA informed of any change in your circumstances if they relate to information already provided that's no longer correct. Note that if you provide incorrect information or documents, your application or visa can be cancelled.

Trade & Professional Qualifications: Assessments of some qualifications can usually be done fairly quickly, although if they must be referred to Australian professional bodies it can take up to six months.

Interviews: If you meet the criteria for migration to Australia, you and your family members (if applicable) will be invited to attend an interview with an officer of the Department of Immigration and Ethnic Affairs. If for some reason you fail to attend a scheduled interview your application won't automatically be refused and a decision may be made on the basis of the information already provided. If you're invited to an interview, take care how your answer seemingly innocuous questions such as "Why do you wish to emigrate to Australia?" It's advisable to always answer positively and rehearse your answers to potential tricky questions.

FAMILY MIGRATION

There's now only one category of family migration called 'preferential family', as the former category of 'concessional family' was moved to the skilled component on 1st July 1997 and renamed Skilled—Australian-linked (SAL). There's a strict quota for family migration, which in 1997-98 was 32,000. Of these places, 25,600 were reserved for spouses of Australians, 1,800 for fiancés, 2,000 for children, 400 for adopted children,

1,000 for parents, 1,000 for other dependants and special need relatives, and 200 for interdependent relatives (mainly sane sex partners). The allocation for parents was slashed from 6,000 in 1996/97 to just 1,000 in 1997-98, which in effect means that the government has virtually stopped the immigration of mostly aged people to join their family members already in Australia.

Applicants in the preferential family category must be sponsored by a relative who must be aged at least 18 and a settled Australian resident (which is generally accepted to be the case after two years continual employment). However, in spouse and parent classes, a minor child can act as a sponsor under certain special circumstances. Your relative in Australia must undertake to assist you financially and with accommodation during your first two years in Australia (and with attendance at English-language classes, if necessary). Migrants aren't usually eligible to receive unemployment and other welfare benefits for a period of two years or longer, so sponsors must be prepared to accept a possible significant cost. For more information see the form entitled *Sponsorship* (961i).

Family Migration Classes

You can be sponsored as a family migrant in one of the following visa classes:

- **Spouse (class 100):** A husband, wife or *de facto* partner who has been living with the sponsor for at least one year.

- **Dependant Child (101):** A natural or adopted child of the sponsor who's dependent on the sponsor. A child who's married or engaged to be married isn't eligible.

- **Adoption (102):** A child under 18 coming to Australia for adoption, where the adoption is supported by the appropriate state or territory welfare authorities in Australia, or a child under 18 who was adopted by Australian citizens or permanent residents while they were genuinely resident overseas for at least 12 months at the time of the application.

- **Parent (103):** A parent of the sponsor in Australia. Parents must meet the 'balance of family' criteria outlined in the information *Sponsorship* form (961i). The sponsor must have lived in Australia for at least two years before lodging the application.

- **Orphan Relative (104):** An orphan under 18 who's unmarried and a relative of the sponsor.

- **Special Need Relative (104):** A relative capable of providing substantial and continuing help to an Australian citizen, permanent resident or eligible New Zealand citizen living in Australia, who's in need of permanent or long-term help which cannot be provided by a relative in Australia or obtained from local welfare, hospital, nursing or community services.

- **Aged Dependant Relative (104):** A relative who's old enough to be granted an old age pension under the *Social Security Act 1991*, isn't married and is dependent on the sponsor in Australia. The sponsor is expected to have lived in Australia for at least two years before lodging the application.

- **Remaining Relative (104):** The sponsor's last brother or sister or non-dependant child outside Australia. You and your spouse must not have a parent or sibling or non-dependant child (or step relative within the same degree of relationship) living in the same country or have more than three relatives outside Australia. You must also have had no ongoing contact with such relatives for a reasonable period. The sponsor is expected to have lived in Australia for at least two year years before lodging the application.

• **Prospective Marriage (300):** A prospective spouse planning to marry a sponsor in Australia receives a temporary visa to stay in Australia for up to nine months. You must marry your sponsor and apply to remain permanently within this period, after which you will be granted a two-year provisional (temporary) visa if all the requirements are met. If the relationship is still ongoing at the end of the two-year period, you will be granted a permanent visa.

Assurance of Support

An assurance of support is mandatory for some categories of family migration, where the sponsoring relative in Australia must undertake to provide financial support (should it be necessary) to the migrant. It's a legal commitment by the assurer to repay the Australian Government if certain welfare benefits are paid to the migrant during his first two years in Australia. Where applicable, a refundable bond and a migration 'health services' charge is payable (a bond isn't required for orphan relatives). The points test (see page 84) doesn't apply to family applicants. An assurance of support may be requested in other family visa classes, but neither the bond nor the migration health services charge are applicable.

The Assurance of Support bond is $3,500 for the first applicant and $1,500 for each other person over 18 included in the application). The bond now applies to a wide range of family categories including spouses and fiancés, and is a legally binding guarantee that none of those being sponsored will seek to obtain certain social security benefits within their first two years in Australia. Financial institutions providing the assurance of bond service charge a fee of around $200 (a list is available from Australian missions). The bond is refundable after two years.

There's also a migration health services charge of around $900 for most applicants who require an assurance of support. This charge offsets the cost to the health budget arising from the health needs of migrants covered by the assurance of support in their first two years' residence in Australia. The charge applies to each person included in the application regardless of age and must be paid before the application can be approved. The charge is refunded if the applicant withdraws his application or decides not to travel to Australia after payment has been made.

Under current policy, children sponsoring their parents as immediate family must arrange an assurance of support to care for their parents for 10 years. An assurance is sought when the parent is within 10 years of retirement (currently age 51 for a woman and 55 for a man). This means that any special benefit paid to the parent becomes a debt payable by the assurer, although assurances aren't currently enforced when the parent becomes a citizen. However, due to rising welfare costs, the government has revised the scope of the assurances, which will remain in force for five years even when the parent becomes a citizen. Any unemployment benefit paid to the parent during this period will also be recoverable from the assurer. An assurance of support is required if you sponsor:

• a parent who meets the balance of family test applying to stay in Australia;

• an aged parent who meets the balance of family test applying to stay in Australia;

• an orphaned unmarried relative under 18;

• a relative who's willing and capable of providing support to an Australian resident who's in special need of assistance on a permanent or long-term basis;

- an aged relative who's dependent on you;
- a last remaining brother or sister or non-dependant child outside Australia;
- a relative assessed by the Department of Immigration as being at risk of becoming a charge on the social welfare budget if approved to settle or remain in Australia.

For more information see the *Assurance of Support* form (960i).

SKILLED MIGRATION

The skilled migration category is intended to contribute to Australia's economic growth and to be accepted there must be a demand in Australia for your skills, outstanding talent or business skills. Some states offer financial assistance and other help to migrants, for example in 1997 South Australia was offering skilled migrants financial assistance for up to two years after their arrival (Tasmania also plans to lure more skilled migrants). The skilled migration visa classes are skilled—Australian-linked (previously called 'concessional family'); labour agreement; employer nomination; distinguished talent; independent; and business skills, each of which is described in more detail below:

- The **skilled—Australian-linked (SAL)** migration category provides migration for non-dependant children; parents of working age (who don't meet the 'balance of family' test); brothers and sisters; and nieces and nephews. Those planning to migrate in this visa category must be sponsored by a relative in Australia and meet health and character requirements. There are two subclasses, Skilled—Australian-linked (SAL) and regional linked, under which all applicants are assessed.

    Applicants in the **skilled—Australian-linked** subclass must be of working age and pass a 'points test' (see page 84). Points are awarded for skill, age, relationship to sponsor, citizenship of the sponsor, the capability of the sponsor to provide settlement support, and the residential location of the sponsor in Australia. Points are awarded for English language ability in the SAL category.

    Applicants in the **regional linked — skilled migration** subclass must be aged under 45, have at least functional English and hold a qualification equivalent to an Australian diploma or higher, which is relevant to their usual occupation. In addition, their sponsor must have lived in a designated area (see page 89) of Australia for at least one year and must not have received certain social security benefits for more than two weeks during this period. Further details of both subclasses are provided in forms *Skilled—Australian-linked* (958iS) and *Regional linked - skilled migration* (958iR).

    If you have relatives who are able to sponsor you under the SAL category, you should ask them to obtain a form *Sponsorship for Migration to Australia* (M40) from their local office of the Department of Immigration, Local Government and Ethnic Affairs in Australia. When they have completed the sponsorship form they should send it to you and you should then obtain a copy of the *Application for Migration* kit from your nearest Australian mission.

- **Labour Agreement:** Allows the entry of people with skills, qualifications and experience required by a labour agreement or a regional headquarters agreement. Applicants must be nominated by an employer or organisation with which an agreement exists and the terms and conditions of that agreement must be met.

- **Employer Nomination:** Allows the migration of highly skilled people, nominated by employers in Australia who have been unable to find or train workers in Australia. The **Employer Nomination Scheme (ENS)** allows employers anywhere in Australia to sponsor overseas employees when they cannot find suitable applicants in Australia. Employers must have advertised vacancies both locally and nationally and must have a good training record. Nominations are valid for 12 months only and the scheme is subject to annual quotas (5,800 in 1997-98, including RSMS below).

  The **Regional Sponsored Migration Scheme (RSMS)** was established in 1995 and provides a mechanism for employers in regional Australia to nominate skilled workers for permanent entry to Australia. Note that, even when you're sponsored by an employer, it's important to assess your prospects of future employment in Australia should you need or wish to change jobs. You should also bear in mind that ENS/RSMS applicants are tied by contract to work for an employer for a certain period, so you won't be able to leave after a short period to work for another employer or become self-employed. Applicants should be aged under 45 and must have functional English skills and possess qualifications and/or job training equivalent to at least Australian diploma level.

  Skill matching is designed to help migrants find employment in regional Australia if their particular skills and abilities are in demand. Applicants under the independent migration category who intend to settle in a city or area of Australia other than Sydney, Melbourne, Brisbane, Perth, the Gold Coast or the Sunshine Coast, and haven't yet decided where they wish to settle, can apply to have their skills matched with an employer seeking someone with their skills. The core requirements for skill matching are the same as the requirements under RSMS.

- **Distinguished Talent:** Allows the migration of people with outstanding records in an occupation, the arts or sport. Applicants must show they will be an asset to the Australian community.

- **Independent:** This class covers the entry of highly skilled people whose education, skills and employability will contribute to the Australian economy. Applicants must be of working age and pass the 'points test' (see page 84) under which points are awarded for skills, age and English-language ability. Applicants whose job is on the 'occupations requiring English' list must demonstrate a high standard of English language ability. Further details are provided in the information form *Independent skilled migration* (958iI). Applications are made using form 47 (*Application for Migration to Australia*) and additional information is provided in form 47N (*Explanatory notes - Application for migration to Australia*).

  The quota for independent migrants in 1997-98 was 14,700, although the category is usually suspended well before the end of the immigration year. The new Liberal/National coalition government elected in 1996 has tightened the immigration criteria and doing more rigorous investigation, and successful applicants can now expect to wait up to two years for a visa.

- **Business Skills:** Provides for migration on the basis of established skills in business and/or investment. Applicants must have recent experience running a successful business or a substantial investment portfolio as an owner or part-owner, or have been a senior executive in a large company. They must be committed to managing a business and/or investment in Australia in which they have substantial ownership. Further information is provided in the *Business Skills Migration - Requirements* form (962i).

REFUGEE & HUMANITARIAN MIGRANTS

Australia is committed to supporting international humanitarian and refugee programs, and per capita takes in more refugees than any country in the world. It has become home to some 600,000 refugees since 1945 (over 100,000 from southeast Asia since 1975) including large numbers of Afghans, Cambodians, Chileans, Chinese, Czechs, Hungarians, Lebanese, Soviet Jews, Timorese, Vietnamese, White Russians and Yugoslavs. In the 1997-98 immigration year, 12,000 places were allocated to refugee and humanitarian migrants (4,000 for refugees, 2,800 for the special humanitarian component, 3,200 for the special assistance category and 2,000 for onshore protection visas). These aren't included in the immigration quotas for 1997-98. Note, however, that illegal immigrants (such as boat people) may be 'interned' for years to discourage others and refugees often have a *very* difficult time finding work. Under new laws proposed by the government, humanitarian refugees may be denied social security for up to six years.

The only people who don't need to apply for refugee status on arrival in Australia are those whose status has already been decided overseas under the terms of the United Nations convention. Otherwise you'll be granted refugee status in Australia, only if you can prove that you have 'a well-founded fear of persecution in your own country for reasons of race, religion, nationality, or membership of a particular social group or political opinion'.

INTERDEPENDENT MIGRANTS

Interdependent migrants include people who are married to or in a *de facto* marriage with their partners and those planning to marry their sponsors in Australia. There was a quota of 1,800 for this visa category in 1997-98. A *de facto* partner must have been living with the sponsor for at least one year. Dependent members of a family, such as children or aged relatives of the applicant, can be included in the application. Spouses and prospective spouses must be sponsored by an Australian citizen, permanent resident or eligible New Zealand citizen, with whom they have an interdependent relationship. This relationship must be ongoing, involve a mutual commitment to a shared life together and a fiancé must be genuinely known to the sponsor and must not be coming to Australia for an arranged marriage. As with most migrants, prospective partners must be assessed for good health and character (see page 77). An 'assurance of support' isn't required from the sponsor. Applicants must complete form 914 (*Application for Entry for Temporary Residence in Australia on the Grounds of Interdependency*) and the sponsor is required to complete the 'sponsorship' section of this form.

If you're sponsoring a spouse or fiancé, you can sponsor only a total of two people a minimum of two years apart, and if you were sponsored to Australia as a spouse or fiancé, you cannot sponsor a spouse or fiancé yourself for five years after the date you were sponsored. Exceptions are if your previous spouse/partner has died or abandoned the relationship leaving children, or if you have formed a new relationship which is long-standing or which has produced children.

Spouse applications are processed in two stages. In the first stage a prospective spouse receives a temporary visa (subclass 300) to stay in Australia for up to nine months, during which period he must marry his sponsor and apply to remain permanently. After marriage you will be granted a two-year temporary visa (subclass 820) providing all the requirements are met. The second stage begins around two years after the application for a provisional visa, when, providing the relationship is still ongoing, you will be granted a permanent visa. A prospective spouse is permitted to work in Australia.

Note that the DIMA requires declarations from both partners and two other people that a marriage is genuine and ongoing, evidence to support your claim and an Australian police clearance if you have lived in Australia for over one year. A non-resident who has a long-term relationship with an Australian resident or citizen and who overstays his visa by more than 28 days can now make an application for residency in Australia (previously you had to leave Australia and apply overseas). Further information is contained in the form *Migrating to Australia as a spouse or prospective spouse* (1093i).

POINTS TEST

A points test applies to certain categories of migrants including skilled—Australian-linked applicants, independent migrants and business migrants. Some factors apply to skilled—Australian-linked applicants only and some just to business migration applicants. The points test aims to ensure that the principal applicant has the skills and other attributes necessary to allow him to quickly enter the Australian workforce, and support himself and his family without relying on the Australian government. Note that only one spouse is assessed and either partner can be considered a principal applicant for the points test, so couples should choose the partner with the best prospects of scoring sufficient points. The principal applicant for **independent migration** (see page 85) is assessed under the following factors only:

- **Skill:** qualifications and experience in his occupation;
- **Age:** at the date the application is lodged;
- **Language Skills:** English language skills, which may be tested before points are allocated.

Applicants for **skilled—Australian-linked** skilled migration (see page 81) are assessed under the following factors in addition to the above:

- **Relationship:** relationship of principal applicant to sponsor;
- **Citizenship:** citizenship of sponsor;
- **Location:** location of sponsor in Australia;
- **Settlement:** settlement of sponsor (i.e. whether they are self-supporting).

Business migrants (see page 89) are assessed under a range of factors including business attributes (turnover, labour cost, assets, sponsorship and investment), age, language and capital.

Information forms for the above categories contain a do-it-yourself points test. However, you shouldn't be too optimistic and unless you're certain that you qualify for a skills category you should err on the conservative side. **Note that your score will depend on whether your trade or professional qualifications are accepted in Australia.** If you have qualifications in a field in which you don't work and have no current experience, they won't be taken into account when assessing your points total. Applicants for trade skills' assessments are classified against the relevant Australian occupations on the basis of their training and employment experience, and the specific duties of individual trades' classifications in Australia. Skilled tradesmen may be given additional points if they're willing to settle in Australia's major regional cities or in the larger outback towns, i.e. outside the country's capital cities. Some two-thirds of migrants currently settle in Sydney or Melbourne.

When you lodge your application at an Australian mission, a provisional score is made, although in many cases the final assessment depends on checking your skills and qualifications in Australia or confirming certain details. This can take some time. Note that if your circumstances change after you have made an application which would increase your score, you cannot make any changes and must make a new application and pay an additional fee. Therefore any imminent changes in your situation should be taken into account before making an application.

In 1992 a 'pool system' was reintroduced, giving prospective migrants a second opportunity to gain acceptance for migration. If you gain insufficient points to pass but attain the pool mark, your application will be held in the pool for 12 months in case a newer, lower pass mark is set. **Note, however, that your likelihood of being accepted for migration after joining the pool are almost non-existent, as pass marks are usually raised rather than lowered.** If your score doesn't reach the pool mark it's automatically refused.

In managing the migration program, the Australian government periodically changes the pass and pool marks of the points test, and applies limits (caps) on the number of visas granted in certain categories. Changes to pass and pool marks affect applications in the pool as well as applications which have been lodged and not yet assessed. When the cap has been reached, applications continue to be processed in the order in which they are lodged, up to the visa approval stage. However, visas aren't granted until places become available in the next 'immigration' year (when a new quota is allocated). **Note that when a change is made to the points test between the time an application is lodged and before it's assessed, the change will apply to that application.**

Independent Migration

The score required for independent migrants, i.e. migrants who aren't applying for skilled—Australian-linked or business migration, is 115 points to pass and 100 points to join the pool. Your score is calculated on employability, skills, age and language skills criteria as shown below. Note that applicants for independent visas have no right of appeal, even when an obvious error has been made. Only Australians who have been affected by an adverse decision can seek a review of a decision, e.g. when an Australian employer or an individual citizen sponsors someone (in any case very few applications are approved after a review). Under a new rule, skilled migrants must prove that they have at least $40,000 to provide for themselves and their families in the event that they cannot find work in Australia.

Employability Factor: The qualifications and experience listed in this factor relate to the qualifications and experience necessary to work in your usual occupation in Australia. Your usual occupation is a job in which you have worked for a continuous period of at least six months during the two-year period immediately prior to lodging your application. If you have held more than one occupation which fits this description, you will be assessed against each occupation and will be given your best score. If you do a skilled job but don't have the required training or qualifications, you won't get top marks as a skilled tradesman. Note that since 3rd July 1995, medical practitioners (e.g. doctors) have received a 25-point skill factor **penalty** (i.e. 25 points are deducted from their score), because Australia has a surfeit of medical practitioners. For information see form 1062i, *Medical doctors (Including specialists)*.

Points for skills are awarded for your usual occupation and the acceptability of your qualifications, based on what's necessary to follow your occupation in Australia. The requirements may involve a combination of a number of factors such as the possession of formal qualifications, a period of job training and/or work experience, plus membership of a professional association or an industry body. Currently the only occupations which will score sufficient points for you to be successful as an independent migrant are those for which the skill level in Australia requires a trade certificate, degree, diploma or an associate diploma. General information about individual occupations and the required skill levels can be obtained from the Australian Standard Classification of Occupations (ASCO) dictionary, available for reference at Australian missions overseas and offices of the Department of Immigration, Local Government and Ethnic Affairs in Australia. Graduates who have obtained their qualification in the five years prior to application are awarded 40 points for their skills and are required to demonstrate that they have worked continuously for at least six months in the last two years.

To achieve the points set out below, your qualifications must be assessed as equivalent to the Australian qualification level listed below and must be relevant to your usual occupation. Note that an applicant in the independent migration category must score at least 50 points for skill to achieve the necessary points to be accepted for the pool.

Points Criteria:

80   Occupations which require a trade certificate or degree *and* which are included on the Priority Occupation List (POL). **Note that these points apply only when the POL is in operation.** Qualifications must have been obtained at least three years prior to the application, you must have at least three years post-qualification work experience and have been working in the occupation for at least two of the three years prior to application;

70   The criteria are the same as for 80 points, but without the requirement of the occupation being listed on the POL.

60   Occupations which require a trade certificate or degree, but without all the experience in that occupation listed above (for 80 points)

55   Occupations which require a diploma or associate diploma. Qualifications and experience are as listed above for 80 points.

50   Occupations which require a diploma or associate diploma, but without all the experience in that occupation listed above for 80 points.

30   Applicants who have qualifications that require minor upgrading and who were working in the occupation three years prior to their application.

25   Applicants with qualifications that aren't accepted by the appropriate authority in Australia or the skill level for the occupation requires an acceptable certificate or advanced certificate in the occupation and four to six years' secondary education, that applicants are able to meet.

20   The skill level in Australia for the occupation requires 12 years of primary and secondary education and applicants are able to meet these requirements.

The points scores of from 20 to 30 shown above apply to applicants in the Skilled—Australian-linked category only (see page 81).

Age: Age is one of the most important criteria for gaining acceptance as a migrant. For example, in the independent category even if you have a university degree and a decade of experience in a related field you won't attain the 115 points necessary (assuming POL isn't in operation) unless you're under 35 years old. Note that age is frozen on application, so it's therefore important to apply before your age puts you into a higher age bracket (giving fewer points), particularly if this would give you too few points to qualify. Points are allocated for age as follows:

Age	Points
18 to 29	30
30 to 34	25
35 to 39	15
40 to 44	10
45 to 49	5
under 18/over 50	0

Language Skills: Language skills apply to migrants in the independent, skilled—Australian-linked and regional linked categories. The English test applies to around 115 occupations and was expanded to include most skilled occupations from 1st July 1997. An Occupations Requiring English (ORE) list is published and prospective migrants whose occupations are listed on the ORE must demonstrate that they have vocational level English (and must score at least 15 points in the 'language skills sub-factor), irrespective of any other attributes they may have.

Families with a spouse or adult dependants aged 18 or over with less than functional English must pay an 'English Education Charge' (EEC) to cover the cost of English language classes in Australia. Under this scheme applicants must pay from $1,020 to $4,080 for English lessons, e.g. a primary applicant seeking a visa under the employer nomination scheme who doesn't have functional English must pay $4,080 and a spouse or adult dependant must pay $2,040 each in fees, in return for which migrants receive up to 510 hours of English tuition.

Applications for residence made in Australia are exempt from the English education charge, although overseas applicants in certain migration categories are liable for the charge if they don't have functional English. For further information see forms *Migrating to Australia: English language assessment* (9661) and *Fees* (990i). The following points are awarded for English language skills:

Points	Language Skills
20	Able to communicate effectively in English in a range of situations, in the four skills of reading, speaking, understanding and writing;
15	Able to communicate effectively in English in a range of situations, in three of the four skills of reading, speaking, understanding and writing;
10	Able to communicate in English on everyday, familiar topics;
5	Able to handle basic communication in English in familiar everyday topics or fluent in at least two languages other than English;
0	Familiar with only a few common English words and phrases.

The maximum 20 points may be awarded:

• Without testing if you hold a degree, higher degree, diploma or trade certificate which required at least three years' full time study and all instruction was conducted in English;

• If you have passed an Occupational English Test as part of an assessment of your qualifications;

• If you have achieved an Australian Assessment of Communicative English Skills (AACES) test score of at least five on each of the four test components (total score at least 20);

- If you have achieved an International English Language Testing System (IELTS) test score of at least 6.0 on each of the four test components.

15 points may be awarded:

- Without testing if you hold a degree, higher degree, diploma or trade certificate which required at least two years' full time study and all instruction was conducted in English;
- If you have achieved an AACES test score of at least 16 taking into account only the three best scores of the four test components;
- If you have achieved an IELTS test score of at least 6.0 taking into account only the three best scores of the four test components;

10 points may be awarded:

- Without testing if you have completed either all primary and three years' secondary schooling or five years' secondary schooling at educational establishments in which all instruction was conducted in English;
- If you have achieved an AACES test score of at least 15 taking into account only the three best scores of the four test components;
- If you have achieved an IELTS average band score of at least 5.0 based on the four test components;

5 points may be awarded:

- Without testing if you have completed either all primary and two years' secondary schooling or three years' secondary schooling at educational establishments in which all instruction was conducted in English;
- If you have achieved an AACES test score of at least 12 based on the four test components;
- If you have achieved an IELTS average band score of at least 4.0 based on the four test components;
- If you're fluent in two languages other than English.

Skilled—Australian-linked Migration

The pass mark for skilled—Australian-linked migration is 115 points and the pool mark is 110 points. Note that a husband and wife can combine their skills and age points to pass the points test under the skilled—Australian-linked class. Skilled—Australian-linked migration applicants are also assessed under skill and age (shown under **Independent Migration** on page 85), but not English language skills, plus family relationship, citizenship of sponsor, location of sponsor and settlement factors, as shown below:

Family Relationship:

Points	Relationship of applicant to sponsor
15	Parent
10	Brother, sister or self-supporting child
5	nephew or niece

Citizenship:

Points	If the sponsor has been an Australian citizen:
10	for five years or more
5	for less than five years

Location Factor:

If your sponsor has lived in a state or territory designated (i.e. outside the main cities) area for the last two years you can add five points. These include Queensland (except urban Brisbane and the Sunshine and Gold Coasts), Western Australia (except the Perth Metropolitan area), South Australia, the Northern Territory, Tasmania, the Australia Capital Territory or Victoria (except the Melbourne region). Note that nowhere in NSW is a designated area. A list of post codes of designated areas is provided. There's an increased allocation for skilled—Australian-linked category for regional migration. A bond (e.g. $10,000 to $30,000) may be payable by migrants who settle in regional areas and will be forfeited if they move to a state capital city.

Settlement:

If your sponsor has been resident in Australia for the last two years and your sponsor (or the spouse of your sponsor) has been in employment (including self-employment) or is financially independent (such as a self-supporting retiree) in Australia for the last two years, you can add 10 points. Note, however, that no points will be awarded if the sponsor has received jobsearch allowance, newstart allowance, or special benefit for more than four weeks in total in the last two years, or if they are currently receiving any form of social security benefit, allowance or pension, other than the age or war veterans' pension, family allowance and family allowance supplement.

Business Migrants

The Business Migration Program (BMP) seeks to attract successful business people planning to establish a new business venture in Australia or to become an owner or part-owner of an existing business in Australia and to actively participate in the enterprise. Note that the application fee is high (e.g. £1,310 in Britain) and therefore you must ensure that you qualify under the current rules before making an application. Business migrants who pass the points test and establish a business in Australia are closely monitored for the first three years of business operation. Under the Business Migration Points Test, applicants must pass a similar points test to other migrant categories and score at least 105 points from the factors of business attributes, age, language and capital, outlined below:

Business Attributes:

Owner/part-owner (subclass 127): An owner/part-owner business is defined as one in which you (or you and your spouse) have had at least a 10 per cent shareholding equity in not less than two of the four years preceding the application, plus a day-to-day management role responsible for overall direction and performance. In addition, you must have employed not less than five full time or equivalent employees. A maximum of two businesses may be combined for the purpose of calculating points under this factor and some part-time employees, consultants and contractors may be counted pro-rata as employees.

Turnover: Business attributes relate to the turnover of an existing principal business in not less than two of the four years preceding the application, for which points are awarded as shown below:

Turnover	Points
$5,000,000	60
$3,000,000	55
$1,500,000	50
$750,000	40
$500.000	35

Labour Costs: Additional points are awarded for annual labour costs and/or total assets. If the main business had annual labour costs in two of the four financial years preceding the application of not less than $250,000 or $500,000, the following points are awarded:

Amount	Points
$500,000	10
$250,000	5

Assets: If the main business had total assets in two of the four financial years before application of not less than $750,000 or $1.5m, the following points are awarded:

Amount	Points
$1.5m	10
$750,000	5

Sponsorship: If you have been offered sponsorship by a state or territory government, you receive an additional 15 points, which are awarded in addition to any gained as an owner/part owner. State or territory sponsored owner/part owner applicants apply under visa subclass 129.

Senior executive in a major business (subclass 128): A major business is defined as one which had an annual turnover of at least $50m in two of the four years preceding the application. Sponsorship by a state or territory government has the effect of redefining a major business as one which has had an annual turnover of at least $10m in two of the four years preceding the application. State-sponsored senior executive applicants apply under visa subclass 130, which earns 65 points.

Established business in Australia (subclass 845): If the following conditions applied for the 12 months prior to application, 60 points are awarded:

- the main business employed three legal permanent residents (who weren't members of your family) in direct full time employment or its equivalent AND
- had a minimum turnover of at least $200,000 a year OR
- had exports with a minimum value of $100,000 a year.

Investment-linked migration (subclass 131): The following points are awarded when an applicant has deposited the sums listed below for a minimum three-year term in a designated investment:

Amount	Points
$2m	80
$1.5m	70
$1m	65
$750,000	60

Points scored from factor four (net assets) are not applicable to this visa class.

Age: The following points are awarded to business migrants for age:

Age	Points
30 to 45	30
45 to 50	25
25 to 30	20
50 to 55	10
under 25/over 55	0

Language: The following points are awarded to business migrants for English language ability:

Points	Standard
30	better than functional
20	functional
10	less than functional but bilingual in two or more other languages
5	Limited
0	None

These point scores apply to all visas apart from Investment-Linked Migration, for which all levels of language ability attract an additional five points. The exception is 'no ability in English' which scores no points.

Capital: The following points are awarded to business migrants for the capital factor, which includes the net assets of the applicant and spouse:

Amount	Points
$2,500,000 or more	15
$1,500,000 to $2,500,000	10
$500,000 to $1,500,000	5
less than $500,000	0

You may include personal and business assets, but only if these assets are available for transfer to Australia within two years. Note that this isn't applicable to Investment-Linked Migration.

VISA FEES

There are fees (which have increased considerably in recent years) for all visas other than a three-month visitor's visa. Application fees for migrant visas are particularly high (£455 in Britain) and aren't refundable, so you should ensure that you have a *very* good chance of being accepted before making an application. Fees are supposedly intended to cover the costs incurred by the Australian government and aren't refunded if your application is unsuccessful (although many applications must be rejected in minutes, particularly those where the points test applies). Applicants adversely affected by a change of rules prior to an application being assessed, such as an increase in the number of points required under the points test, aren't entitled to a refund of fees.

Fees can be paid in cash or by cheque or postal order payable to the 'Commonwealth of Australia'. The temporary business entry (TBE) visa may be paid by credit card (e.g. American Express, Diners Club, Mastercard or Visa). Applications for visitors' visas can be made by post, in person or through an authorised travel agent. The fees shown below are those which applied in Britain on 1st January 1998 and are similar in other countries (**N.B. fees depend on the prevailing exchange rate and are liable to change at short notice**).

Type of Application	Fee
Migration Australia Forms Package	£6
Sponsorship for entry for Temporary Residence	£95
Resident return Visa - Lodged Overseas	£35
Migration to Australia	£455
Declaratory Certificate of Australian Citizenship	£24
Registration of Australian Citizenship by descent	£48
Additional children registered at the same time	£37
Grant of Australian Citizenship	£52
Evidentiary certificate of Australian Citizenship	£24
Resumption of Australian Citizenship	£28
Temporary Resident	£65
Working Holidaymaker	£65
Occupational Trainee	£65
Student	£125
Visitor Visa (max. six months, valid 4 years)	£20
Re-Evidencing of Resident return visa	£30
Business Migration Program	£1,310
Temporary Business Sponsorship	£1,310
Temporary Business Nomination	£95
Declaratory visa (adult)	£97
Declaratory visa (under 18)	£74
Temporary Business Entry (short stay)	£20
Temporary Business Entry (long stay)	£65

TEMPORARY RESIDENCE

Temporary residence includes people coming to live or work in Australia for periods of from three months to four years. Applicants are expected to stay for the full period of their planned stay. There are no set quotas for visas for most temporary workers which are open to a wide range of people including executive, technical and professional people;

academic staff; medical practitioners; foreign government officials; sports people; entertainers; media and film staff; working holidaymakers; religious personnel; domestic staff; retirees; and occupational trainees (a full list is given below). Applications for temporary residence visas are made using a form 147 *'Application for a temporary residence visa (non-business)'*. Applicants may be required to have a medical examination and chest x-ray before a visa is granted, although this isn't usual when the intended stay is 12 months or less. In most cases, temporary residents are granted a multiple entry visa for the period of their approved stay.

Sponsors: Many temporary residents must be sponsored (or require a nomination, written invitation or a sponsor's undertaking to support an application), e.g. by a prospective employer or organisation, as shown in the table below. Sponsoring employers must have a satisfactory record of training staff and show that there's no resident person available with the required skills. The sponsor must be willing to accept financial and legal responsibility for the temporary resident and is responsible for his welfare and accommodation. If the sponsor is an employer, any salary paid must be guaranteed and must fall within the industry pay awards for the job. Temporary residence subclass visa groups include the following:

Number	Visa Type	Fee	Sponsorship
410	Retirement	Yes	No
411	Skill Exchange	No	No
415	Foreign Government Agency	Yes	Yes*
416	Special Program	Yes	No
417	Working Holiday	Yes	No
418	Educational/Research	Yes	Yes*
419	Visiting Academic	Yes	No
420	Entertainment	Yes	Yes
421	Sport	Yes**	Yes*
422	Medical Practitioner	Yes	Yes
423	Media and Film Staff	Yes	Yes*
424	Public Lecturer	Yes	Yes*
425	Family Relationship	No	No
426	Domestic Worker (Diplomatic/Consular)	Yes	No
427	Domestic Worker (Overseas Executive)	Yes	Yes***
428	Religious Worker	Yes	Yes
430	Supported Dependant	Yes	No
432	Expatriate	Yes	No
442	Occupational Trainee	Yes	No
456	Business (Short Stay)	Yes	No
457	Independent Executive	Yes	Yes
956/977	Business (Short Stay) ETA	Yes	No

* Formal sponsorship is required if the stay in Australia exceeds three months.

** Fee applies to professional sportspersons only.

***Must have been included in sponsorship of an overseas executive.

Temporary Workers: Certain categories of skilled workers and professionals are permitted to enter Australia for a fixed period (e.g. the duration of a contract) to take up employment where it can be shown that a job cannot be filled by a resident. Temporary workers seeking to work in Australia for longer than four months must be sponsored by their prospective employer. The sponsor must lodge a *Sponsorship for Entry to Australia for Temporary Residents* form. Applications for temporary residence for employees are granted for a period of up to four years providing:

• the prospective employer will provide sponsorship and pay the fees;

• the required skills are shown to be unavailable in Australia;

• the job is full time;

• the pay and conditions aren't less than the normal pay and conditions for such a job in Australia;

• the employment of a temporary resident isn't a substitute for training Australian or permanent residents for such a position;

• the position isn't for an unskilled or semi-skilled job;

• the normal health and character requirements are met.

If you receive a temporary resident visa permitting you to work in Australia and your spouse is named on the application as your dependant, then he or she will also be permitted to work in Australia. A temporary residence visa isn't automatically renewable and no change of job or sponsor is allowed after entry into Australia. Note that anyone in Australia for less than six months must have private health insurance unless their country of citizenship has a reciprocal health agreement with Australia (see page 292). Information about non-business temporary residence visas is provided in *Temporary residence in Australia - non-business — general guide* (form 986i).

Business

Temporary business people can work in Australia for from three months to four years and there's no market testing for personnel coming to undertake key activities. Regular employers of overseas personnel can seek ongoing sponsorship status as pre-qualified sponsors and don't need to establish their sponsorship credentials each time they wish to sponsor personnel from overseas. Standard sponsorship status is available to employers wishing to sponsor a fixed number of personnel on a one-off basis. Most visas don't allow workers to change their employer or occupation without prior permission. Note that it's no longer possible to obtain a temporary business visa in Australia when you arrived as a tourist, because many people with temporary business visas granted in Australia were found to be working illegally. The temporary business class visa includes the following subclasses:

• **Exchange:** Skilled people wishing to come to Australia to broaden their work experience and skills under reciprocal arrangements which allow Australian residents similar opportunities overseas. It includes people seeking entry under certain bilateral exchange agreements.

- **Independent Executive:** People wishing to establish a business in Australia using their own capital (usually a minimum of $250,000).

- **Executive (Overseas):** Senior management personnel and staff for executive positions covered by a Regional Headquarters (RHQ) agreement.

- **Specialist:** Workers with trade, technical or professional skills who have been recruited by an Australian employer for a limited period. It also applies to staff for a specialist position covered by a Regional Headquarters (RHQ) agreement.

- **Medical Practitioner:** Suitably qualified foreign medical practitioners where the relevant state or territory health authority endorses the need to meet specific requirements from overseas.

Cultural & Social

The cultural and social class visa includes the following subclasses:

- **Special Program:** People coming to Australia under approved programs to broaden their work experience and skills (generally youth exchanges). It includes young people coming to Australia under a Churchill Fellowship to broaden their experience and understanding of the country, generally in the context of a youth exchange program or to take part in a community based program of cultural enrichment or community benefit. You may not change your employer or occupation without prior permission.

- **Entertainment:** People involved in a wide range of social and cultural events and activities, taking into account the need to protect employment of Australians in the industry. You may not change your employer or change the times or places of engagements in Australia without prior permission.

- **Sport:** Amateur or professional sports people coming to Australia to engage in competition with Australian residents and to improve general sporting standards through high calibre competition and training. Sports people coming to Australia for periods of less than four months to participate in specific events don't require a sponsor, but they must have an invitation from the organisers of the event or evidence of acceptance of a nomination to participate in specific events or contests. They must sign a declaration that on arrival in Australia they will have a return or onward ticket and sufficient funds to support themselves (and any family members accompanying them) for the duration of their stay.

- **Media and Film Staff:** Correspondents and other professional media staff members posted to Australia by overseas news organisations, and photographers and film and TV crews making documentaries or commercials for overseas consumption.

- **Public Lecturer:** Professional lecturers or subject experts invited to make public presentations.

- **Religious Workers:** Religious workers, including ministers, priests and spiritual leaders to serve the spiritual needs of people of their faith in Australia.

Domestic Workers

The domestic workers class visa includes the following two subclasses:

- **Domestic Workers (Diplomatic/Consular):** Domestic staff for diplomats and consular staff posted to Australia. Written approval is required from the Department of Foreign Affairs and Trade (DFAT).
- **Domestic Workers (Overseas Executive):** Domestic staff of holders of visas in subclass 412 (Independent Executive) and subclass 413 (Executive/Overseas). A visa in this class may be granted only if it can be shown that the entry of domestic staff is necessary for the proper discharge of the executive's representational duties. Domestic workers may not change employers or remain in Australia after the permanent departure of their employer.

Educational

The educational class visa includes the following subclasses:

- **Foreign Government Agency:** Foreign government officials to conduct official business on behalf of their government when the officials don't have diplomatic or official status in Australia.
- **Educational:** Full-time staff for educational and research institutions or organisations to fill academic, teaching and research positions unable to be filled from within the Australian labour market.
- **Visiting Academic:** People whose presence in Australia will contribute to the sharing of research knowledge. They may not receive a salary from the host institution in Australia.
- **Occupational Trainee:** Persons undergoing training in Australia compatible with their employment history. The training should be to upgrade existing skills and be readily usable on return to the applicant's home country. They may not work in Australia other than in relation to their course of training.

Expatriate

The expatriate class visa allows for the temporary stay of certain spouses or dependants of persons employed by international companies in remote locations in Southeast Asia, the South Pacific or Papua New Guinea. They may not perform any work in Australia.

Family Relationship

The family relationship class visa allows the temporary stay of unmarried young people under the age of 18 for an extended holiday with relatives or close family friends who are Australian citizens or residents. They may not perform any work in Australia.

Retirement

The retirement class visa provides an extended temporary stay for those wishing to retire to Australia. Note, however, that it allows 'temporary' residence only, albeit indefinitely (although it can be revoked at any time), and there's no provision for retirees to apply for permanent residence at a later date. Retirees who apply to enter Australia under this visa category can be either single people or couples (either married or in a *de facto* relationship), who must meet the following criteria:

- be at least 55 years of age (your spouse may be any age);
- have no dependants other than their spouse;
- satisfy the funds transfer requirements (see below);
- have no intention of entering the workforce;
- must take out private medical insurance while in Australia or make arrangements for medical cover in their own country (retirees aren't covered by Medicare, Australia's national health care system);
- meet health and character requirements.

At the date that you apply to settle in Australia, you must have sufficient funds to maintain yourself while in the country, which should consist of either a capital transfer of at least $500,000 or a capital transfer of at least $150,000 plus a pension or income, or further capital providing an annual income of at least $35,000. The income can come from any source, a pension or dividends from investments. If you receive a British state pension you should be aware that the amount you receive will be frozen when you leave Britain and you won't be entitled to any annual cost of living increases (see page 357). For more information see *Summary of Funds Available for Transfer.*

Note that you must be able to meet the funds criteria on the day that you lodge your application. If you need to sell a house or other assets to meet these requirements, the sale must be completed within 12 months of the date of your application. Once accepted you will receive a visa allowing you to make multiple entries during the first six months after the date when the visa was issued. When you arrive during this six month period, you will receive an entry permit allowing you to stay in Australia for four years. The multiple entry visa expires six months after your visa is issued. If you then need to leave Australia for a temporary period you *must* obtain another visa to allow you to return to Australia. Once in Australia you can apply for an extension of stay after four years and, providing you still meet the criteria for a retirement visa, you will be granted a further stay of two years.

Note that if you have relatives in Australia who can sponsor you (see page 78 and 80) you may be able to retire to Australia under the family migrant scheme.

Supported Dependant

The supported dependant class visa allows the temporary stay of certain dependants of persons entitled to remain permanently in Australia. The supporter must complete a Declaration of Support with documentary evidence of the family relationship.

Working Holiday

The working holiday class visa includes just one subclass: Working Holiday, which is the largest visa category for temporary residents and accounts for over 45 per cent of the total. Concerns have been voiced in Australia over jobs being taken from Australians by working holidaymakers; however, the farming industry, particularly fruit and vegetable picking, relies to a large extent on working holidaymakers to harvest their crops. In 1997, a parliamentary committee decided that visitors on working holiday visas take jobs from young Australians (despite evidence to the contrary showing that they take jobs where Australians either lack the necessary skills, are unwilling to take jobs or local labour isn't available). Statistics also show that those on working holiday visas inject almost $500m a year into the economy and many businesses in the tourist industry would be hard hit without them (creating yet more unemployment). There's a cap on the number of working holiday visas issued, which was 55,000 for 1997-98. Individual countries also have a quota.

Eligibility: Working holiday visas are available to single people and childless couples between the ages of 18 and 25, although in certain cases those aged from 26 to 30 may also qualify. The purpose of the working holiday visa is to allow young people the opportunity to visit Australia and supplement their travels through casual employment. Those eligible for a working holiday visa include nationals of Canada, Denmark, France, Germany, Greece, Ireland, Italy, Japan, South Korea, Malta, the Netherlands, Spain and the UK. If you hold a British, Canadian, Dutch or Irish passport you may apply in any country; others must apply in the country of their nationality. Note that you can obtain a working holiday visa once only. Applicants must satisfy the following criteria:

- the prime purpose of the visit is a temporary stay in Australia and permanent residence isn't intended;
- employment is incidental to the holiday and is to be used to supplement the money that you bring with you;
- employment mustn't be arranged in advance except on a private basis and on your own initiative;
- there must be a reasonable prospect of you obtaining temporary employment to supplement your funds;
- you must show that you have reasonable funds to support yourself for some of your time in Australia and pay for your return air fare. The minimum amount required is £2,000 in Britain, although it isn't necessary to have a return ticket at the time of your entry into Australia. It helps to have relatives or friends in Australia who can provide extra funds if necessary;
- you must meet normal character requirements and health standards, where necessary;
- full time employment should not be taken for over three months with one employer;
- you must leave Australia when your working holiday visa has expired;
- the maximum stay is 12 months;
- you must sign a declaration not to undertake any studies in Australia apart from a short-term English language course of a maximum of 10 weeks' duration.

Applications must be made to an Australian mission in your home country (or the country where you're resident) with the following:

- a completed application form 147 (if your application form isn't completed correctly it will be returned);
- three recent passport photographs signed on the reverse;
- evidence of funds for the duration of your stay, which must be confirmed by a bank statement or other evidence. If you don't have sufficient funds at the time of your application you could borrow some and repay it after obtaining a bank statement. However, it isn't advisable to arrive in Australia with insufficient funds, as you may need to prove you have access to funds on arrival and if you don't you could be refused entry.

- a valid passport, which should be valid for three months *after* your proposed departure date from Australia (if your passport doesn't comply with this, you must obtain a new one);
- a cheque payable to the 'Commonwealth of Australia' for the sum of £65;
- a stamped addressed envelope for the return of your passport.

Applications can be made in person or by post (preferred). You should apply for a working holiday visa at least one month before your intended departure date and if you're applying by post, you should send documents by recorded delivery. If your application is approved, your visa will be valid for 13 months from the date of issue. If your first arrival date in Australia won't allow you to have your full 12 months there, you can apply for an extension, although there's a hefty fee. If you plan to apply for an extension, you should apply around two months before the expiry of your temporary entry permit. An extension of stay beyond 12 months after your first entry isn't possible.

VISITORS

A visitor's visa is valid for stays of up to three months (visa valid 12 months) or for stays of up to six months (visa valid four years or the life of your passport, whichever is shorter). A visitor's visa is also required by those coming to Australia to conduct business of a short-term nature and for someone visiting Australia for medical treatment (see below), although a different form must be completed. Visas can be obtained on-the-spot from travel agents (for nationals of selected countries, see ETA below) and at Australian missions (if you're applying by post you should allow a minimum of three weeks in most countries). Many travel agents and companies provide a visa service for visitors, although there's usually a fee (in addition to any visa fee levied by the Australian government).

There's no fee for a visitor's visa valid for stays of up to three months, but a fee (£20 in Britain) applies to a visitor's visa valid for stays of up to six months (or for a visa valid for four years for short stays of up to three months). If applicable, ensure that your visa allows multiple entries within its period of validity, when it should be marked 'multiple travel'. If you're applying for a six-month visa, you must be able to show that you have access to adequate funds, although this will be less if you will be staying with friends or family in Australia. The retired parents of an Australian citizen can obtain a visitor's visa valid for 12 months. It isn't necessary to make a separate application for a child who's included on a parent's passport. Note that your passport must be valid for the period of your proposed stay in Australia.

Australia has one of the most efficient visa processing systems in the world for visitors planning to spend up to three months there, called Electronic Travel Authority (ETA). Under the ETA system travellers can be pre-cleared for travel at the same time as they make their travel arrangements. Travel agents using the ETA system simply enter your passport number into a computer system linked to the Australian immigration database and receive a confirmation within seconds. No stamp is placed in your passport. Note that to qualify you must travel to Australia on a participating airline (includes most major airlines) or a cruise ship. ETA is eventually intended to replace visa application forms and labels or stamps in passports, although if you require a passport stamp you must complete an *Application to visit Australia for tourism* (form 48). An ETA visa is issued free of charge (although agents may levy a fee) and is valid for a single entry into Australia within one year. Citizens of the following countries are eligible for an ETA visa: Andorra, Austria, Belgium, Brunei, Canada, Denmark, Finland, Germany, Greece, Iceland,

Ireland, Italy, Japan, Liechtenstein, Luxembourg, Malaysia, Monaco, the Netherlands, Norway, Singapore, South Korea, Sweden, Switzerland, the United Kingdom and the USA.

The ETA system builds on the Advanced Passenger Clearance (APC) system whereby Qantas passengers arriving at Sydney airport can be cleared in as little as 20 seconds. It's designed to fast-track passengers at airports through immigration and customs processing, and has substantially reduced the time taken to process passengers. It also allows passengers on certain flights to Australia to complete their immigration and customs processing while in the air. On arrival, electronic cards containing passenger details are simply 'swiped' through an immigration card reader.

It's possible to obtain an extension for a visitor's visa under certain circumstances, although you must apply before your visa expires and must have a good reason. However, a stay totalling more than six months in a calendar year isn't usually permitted. Note that it's expensive (currently $145) to extend a three-month visitor's visa to a six-month visa in Australia, therefore if there's any likelihood of you wishing to stay longer than three months you should obtain a six-month visa. Note that visitors extending their stay in Australia must produce evidence of health insurance.

There are plans to scrap tourist visas for visitors from 'low risk' countries, i.e. rich countries such as Canada, Japan and the USA whose nationals have little intention of overstaying their permitted period in Australia. **Note that visitors aren't permitted to engage in any type of employment or formal study.** Visitors may, however, undertake non-formal study involving short-term courses of up to three months which are recreational or 'personal-enrichment' in nature, and aren't subsidised by any government.

Business Visitors

A visitor's visa is also required by someone coming to Australia to conduct business of a short-term nature, i.e. business agreed to by the Australian Government Office. A business visa allows you to visit Australia to look for business opportunities, assess business conditions, act as a consultant, attend meetings and sign contracts. Nationals of eligible countries (see the list above) can obtain a business ETA valid for the life of your passport, otherwise you must complete form 456, *Application for a temporary business entry visa (for a stay of up to 3 months)*. A visa allowing a stay of up to one month with a single entry valid for one month from the date of issue is issued free of charge. A temporary business entry (TBE) visa valid for stays of up to three months (with multiple entries valid for five years or the life of your passport, i.e. up to 10 years) costs £20 in Britain and a long stay visa valid for four years and stays of up to six months costs £65. There are plans to issue business visitors with an Australian Business Access (ABA) card, which will facilitate and speed their arrival in (and departure from) Australia at international airports.

Medical Treatment

A visitor's visa is also required by someone coming to Australia for medical treatment, when form 48ME (*Application to Visit Australia for Medical Treatment*) must be completed. Medical treatment includes either elective or emergency treatment for either a short or a long stay. Those coming to Australia for medical treatment must fulfill the following conditions:

• you must provide documentary evidence that you can pay for medical treatment;

- arrangements must be made for hospital accommodation and treatment in advance;
- treatment must not be available in your home country;
- you must receive significant benefit from such treatment in Australia;
- you must not pose a public health risk, e.g. because of a contagious disease.

If you're applying for an extension of stay for medical treatment, you will need to meet the criteria and present evidence that:

- arrangements have been made with a doctor and/or hospital to provide you with medical and/or hospital care, i.e. a firm date for treatment has been made;
- arrangements have been made to pay the full unsubsidised cost of treatment and you can demonstrate you have the means to pay;
- if treatment is in a public hospital, the state or territory medical authorities must have agreed to your admission and treatment.

If you're providing comfort and support to a person seeking medical treatment and that's the purpose of your stay in Australia, then you should also apply for a medical treatment visa.

STUDENTS

Foreign students require a student visa (costing around £125 in Britain), which is issued after acceptance on a course and payment of at least half of the first year's annual fees. Students must have the financial resources to meet tuition fees (scholarships are available), return fares to Australia and day-to-day living expenses for the duration of their course. Courses that qualify for a student visa include tertiary level studies at universities or colleges; courses at Technical and Further Education (TAFE) colleges; English-language courses; occupational or religious training; business study or training, e.g. secretarial and business courses; short courses at universities or colleges of advanced education; and study exchange arrangements between Australian and overseas educational establishments. Secondary-level applicants for non-government schools must first obtain an offer of a place, which must be confirmed by a letter from the school. Full fee-paying students from so called 'gazetted' countries (with a lower risk of students overstaying their visas) should lodge their application for a visa *after* they have enrolled and obtained an *Acceptance Advice Form* (AAF). Full fee-paying students from non-gazetted countries should lodge their application for a visa *before* paying tuition fees, confirming enrolment and obtaining an AAF.

Students must usually be attending full-time courses, but are permitted to take part-time jobs of up to 20 hours a week to help cover their living costs, plus a full-time holiday job during the summer break. The spouse of a post-graduate student may be permitted to work full time and other dependants up to 20 hours a week. In order to retain a student visa you must have a satisfactory attendance and academic results' record. On completion of your course you must leave Australia when your visa expires, for which an undertaking must be given in writing. Private health insurance is required by all students, e.g. through the Medicare Private Overseas Student Health Cover facility. Note that it isn't possible to switch from a visitor's visa to a student visa while in Australia.

Information about student visas is provided in *Student entry to Australia—(form 981i)* and *Application for a Student (Temporary) Visa* (forms 157Y/157W).

4.

ARRIVAL

On arrival in Australia, your first task will be to negotiate immigration and customs, which fortunately for most people presents no problems. Australian customs and immigration officials are usually polite and efficient, although they may occasionally be a 'trifle overzealous' in their attempts to deter smugglers and those planning to remain or work illegally. You may find it more convenient to arrive in Australia on a weekday rather than during the weekend, when offices and banks are closed. If you arrive in Australia by ship, customs' and immigration officials may board the vessel to carry out their checks. Small boats must dock at a 'proclaimed point of entry' (which includes various ports throughout Australia) and you should notify officials a few hours in advance of your arrival. Note that with the exception of New Zealanders, all persons wishing to enter Australia require a visa (see **Chapter 3** for information). **If you arrive in Australia without one, you will be refused entry.**

There are also a number of tasks that should be completed on arrival, which are also described in this chapter, plus suggestions for finding local help and information.

IMMIGRATION

All arrivals must complete an 'Incoming Passenger Card' (one per person) and a 'Traveller's Statement' (one per family), which are distributed by airlines and shipping companies, before their arrival in Australia. The incoming passenger card contains your personal details such as name, address, date of birth and passport number, and is used by immigration to record the reason for your visit. The traveller's statement is for customs and quarantine purposes and contains questions concerning illegal plants and animals, and whether you have exceeded the duty-free allowances. A married couple and their children under 18 years need complete one statement only. Note that if you (or any person over 12 months of age who's travelling with you) have visited a yellow fever infected country or area (e.g. Africa or South America) in the 14 days prior to your arrival in Australia, a yellow fever vaccination certificate is required.

When you disembark you proceed to the 'Entry Control Point' where you present your passport, passenger card and traveller's statement. You may be asked to verify the reason for your visit and provide evidence that you have sufficient funds for your trip and a return or onward ticket. Your traveller's statement' is returned to you and must be presented when you arrive at the customs' checkpoint (see below). Australia operates an Advanced Passenger Clearance (APC) system at some airports (e.g. Sydney) where passengers can be cleared in as little as 20 seconds. It's designed to fast-track passengers through immigration and customs' processing and substantially reduces the time taken to process passengers. It also allows passengers on certain flights (e.g. Qantas) to complete their immigration and customs' processing while in the air, where a card containing a passenger's details is simply passed through an immigration card reader on arrival.

When you receive your visa from an Australian mission overseas, you usually get a stamp in your passport stating that the visa is valid 'subject to entry permit on arrival.' This means that you must satisfy the immigration official that you won't infringe the terms of your visa. If you have a visitor's visa, you should present it along with evidence that you have sufficient funds (or access to funds) to last you throughout your stay (e.g. $1,000 a month) and enable you to leave Australia when your visa expires. Cash, travellers' cheques, credit cards, bank statements and an airline ticket will all help convince immigration officials. If you have friends or relatives in Australia with whom you will be staying, you will usually require less funds. Note, however, that the immigration officer may check with them to verify your statement. Generally the onus is on anyone visiting Australia to *prove* that he's a genuine visitor and won't infringe the immigration laws. The immigration authorities aren't required to establish that you will violate the immigration laws and in extreme cases where they believe that you plan to work illegally or will overstay your visa, they can refuse you entry or restrict your entry to a shorter period than that permitted by your visa.

The treatment of foreigners by immigration officers varies, but some people complain of harassment and have trouble convincing officials that they are genuine visitors. Young people may also be liable to close scrutiny, particularly those travelling light and 'scruffily' dressed or coming from the more notorious drug areas of Asia or South America. As with most visitors, it's advisable to carry evidence of your funds (or access to funds) and proof of why you're entering Australia and why you will need to leave (e.g. to return to work or study overseas). Be careful how you answer seemingly innocent questions (immigration officials *never* ask innocent questions) from immigration officials as you could find yourself being refused entry if you give incriminating answers. Whatever the question, never imply that you may remain in Australia longer than the period permitted or for a purpose other than that for which you have been granted permission. For example, if you aren't permitted to work in Australia you could be asked: "Would you like to work in Australia?" If you reply "Yes", even if you have no intention of doing so, you could be refused entry.

When all is in order and the immigration official is satisfied, he will stamp your passport with the official entry permit stating the period that you're permitted to remain in the country. If you decide that this isn't long enough, some visas (e.g. visitor's) can be extended, but it's an expensive procedure and you will need to convince the authorities that you should be granted an extension. You may find that it's easier to leave the country, e.g. by travelling to New Zealand or Indonesia, and reapplying for a new visa from there.

CUSTOMS

After you have cleared immigration, you proceed to the baggage claim area to collect your bags. After you have all your bags you go to the customs' checkpoint, where you hand your Traveller's Statement to a customs' officer. All airports in Australia use a system of red and green 'channels'. Red means you have something to declare and green means that you have nothing to declare, i.e. no more than the duty or tax-free allowances, no goods to sell, and no prohibited or restricted goods. **If you're certain that you have nothing to declare go through the 'green channel', otherwise go through the red channel.** Customs' officers make random checks on people going through both red and green channels and there are stiff penalties for smuggling.

When you enter Australia to take up temporary or permanent residence, you can usually import your personal belongings duty and tax free. However, any duty or tax payable may depend on where you came from, where you purchased the goods, how long you have owned them, and whether duty and tax has already been paid in another country. Personal and household goods that you have owned and used overseas for over 12 months can be imported free of duty and sales tax, although proof of length of ownership may be required and this concession doesn't apply to motor vehicles, alcohol or tobacco products. Any goods not owned and used overseas for over 12 months may be subject to duty and tax at varying rates. If you need to pay duty or tax, it must be paid at the time the goods are brought into the country; payment may be made in cash, by travellers' cheque in Australian currency, or by American Express, Bankcard, Diners Club Card, Mastercard or Visa.

There's no limit to the amount of Australian or foreign currency (banknotes and coins, not travellers' cheques or other monetary instruments) that can be brought into Australia, but amounts of $10,000 or more (or the equivalent in foreign currency) must be declared on arrival. **Note that if you're caught trying to smuggle any goods into Australia they can be confiscated and if you attempt to import prohibited items (see page 107) you may be liable to criminal charges and/or deportation.**

Australian Customs publish a variety of information for travellers including a booklet entitled *Customs Information for Travellers*, available from Australian Customs' offices (see **Appendix A** for a list). General enquiries should be directed to the Australian Customs Service, GPO Box 148, Fyshwick, ACT 2609 (tel. (02) 6275 5041). For information regarding:

* duty-free allowances (e.g. alcohol and tobacco), see page 432;
* the importation of motor vehicles, see page 236;
* the importation of yachts and leisure craft, see page 408;
* the importation of pets, see page 454.

Temporary Residents & Visitors

In addition to the usual duty-free concessions (see page 432), temporary residents and visitors coming to Australia for a limited period may bring most articles into the country duty and tax free, providing customs is satisfied that they are for your personal use and will be taken out of Australia on your departure. However, you may be required to lodge a cash or bank security with customs to the value of the duty and tax otherwise payable. Customs will determine the form of security acceptable in each case and if you don't take the articles with you when you leave Australia, you will need to pay the duty and tax assessed. Before shipping any articles to Australia which you think will qualify for this concession, you should contact a customs' office for advice (see **Appendix A**). This concession isn't available if you're migrating to Australia or a returning resident.

Tourists and temporary residents may bring a motor vehicle, caravan, trailer, yacht or other craft to Australia for up to 12 months (or longer under certain circumstances) without paying duty or tax on them. However, you may be required to lodge a cash or bank security with customs equal to the amount of duty or tax otherwise payable.

Migrants & Returning Residents

If you're a migrant coming to Australia to take up permanent residence for the first time or a person returning to resume permanent residence, you may import duty and tax free personal belongings, furniture and household articles, which you have owned and used overseas for at least 12 months before your departure for Australia. Migrants may also bring machinery, plant and other equipment to Australia duty and tax free providing certain conditions are met. Commercial equipment imported tax and duty free mustn't be sold, hired, mortgaged, or otherwise disposed of during your first two years in Australia.

Unaccompanied Effects: The Australian customs' service is responsible for the clearance of all unaccompanied effects from overseas. Unaccompanied personal effects can be cleared by the owner, a nominee appointed by the owner or a customs' broker (a list of brokers, who charge a fee for their services, is published in the yellow pages). If you don't use a broker, you will need to contact the local state or territory customs' office to arrange clearance, and must produce your passport and complete an *Unaccompanied Effects Statement* (form B534). Your effects can be cleared through customs prior to your arrival, providing you will arrive in Australia within six months after the arrival of your belongings. If you employ an international removal company (see page 137), they will handle the associated paperwork and customs' clearance for you. Household effects are inspected on arrival in Australia for possible illegal and quarantine risk items. A list of all the items you're importing is required if you pack the goods yourself. Note that duty-free concessions don't apply to goods arriving in Australia as unaccompanied effects. Australian customs publish an *Unaccompanied Effects* leaflet.

Prohibited & Restricted Goods

There are strict laws prohibiting or restricting the entry of drugs, steroids, weapons, firearms and certain articles subject to quarantine into Australia. If you're carrying any goods which you think may fall into any of the following categories, you must declare them to customs on your arrival in Australia.

Drugs of Dependence: If you're carrying any prescribed drugs of dependence, including medicines containing narcotics, hallucinogens, amphetamines, barbiturates or tranquilisers, you must declare them to customs on arrival. It's advisable to carry a doctor's prescription with you. If you're uncertain about any drugs or medicines which you're carrying, check with the customs' officer on your arrival. **Note that penalties for drug offences in Australia are severe and can result in imprisonment** (see **Crime** on page 442).

Other Substances: The importation of anabolic steroids, androgenic substances, natural and manufactured growth hormones, and certain other pharmaceutical substances is prohibited unless prior written approval has been obtained from the Drug Safety and Evaluation Branch of the Therapeutic Goods Administration, Department of Health and Family Services, Canberra (tel. (02) 6289 1555).

Weapons/Firearms: Many weapons and firearms are prohibited in Australia while others require a permit and safety testing to import them. You should contact Australian customs before you travel if you intend to import any weapons or firearms. Note that there are strict rules about carrying firearms and dangerous goods such as fireworks, flammable liquids, etc. in aircraft. If you wish to do so, contact your airline for advice before you travel.

Quarantine: Australia is free from many of the world's worst animal and vegetable diseases and pests that afflict many other regions of the world, and it has strict quarantine regulations to ensure that it remains that way. **All food or goods of plant or animal origin must be declared on your Traveller's Statement.** This includes gifts and souvenirs that are made from plants or animals, or that contain plant or animal material (such as seeds, skin or feathers). If you have prohibited or unwanted items that you don't wish to declare, you can drop them in the quarantine bin on the way to collect your baggage. Food includes any fresh or cooked, dried, packaged, bottled or tinned food products, e.g. meat and meat products, milk and dairy products, egg and egg products, honey and bee products, beans, nuts, confectionery, herbs and spices, jams, sauces, herbal medicines, or teas and beverages. Any food from meals you were served on the aircraft or ship must be left on board or put in the quarantine bin. Animal products include rawhide, bee products, skins and hides, feathers, bones, wool and animal hair, shells or hunting trophies. Plants and plant products includes wood carvings, bamboo, cane and rattan items, straw objects such as corn dollies, fresh and dried flowers, potpourri, seeds, pine cones and ornamental wreaths. Live animals can be imported only with prior permission and a valid import permit (see page 454). Note that there are also restrictions on taking fruit and vegetables (produced in Australia) between certain states. Declared goods won't automatically be confiscated and in most cases they are simply inspected by a quarantine officer and returned to you, although some items may require treatment (e.g. fumigation) before they are returned. Quarantine inspections have been strengthened in recent years and on-the-spot fines of up to $250 are imposed for minor offences. For further information contact the Australian Quarantine Inspection Service (AQIS), GPO Box 858, Canberra, ACT 2601 (tel. (02) 6272 3933 or call the quarantine enquiry line freecall 1800-020504). AQIS publish an information leaflet, *What Can I Take Into Australia - A Quarantine guide for people entering Australia*.

Protected Wildlife: Australia has laws which strictly regulate the import and export of wildlife and products made from the skins, feathers, bones, shells, etc. of protected species. Wildlife or any clothing, accessories, handbags, shoes, trophies, ornaments, souvenirs, etc. made from protected species will be seized by customs on arrival. Travellers are particularly warned of restrictions on items made from hard corals (including black coral); giant clam shells; orchids (including live orchids); turtles, alligators and crocodiles (including gavials and caiman); cats (leopards, tigers, jaguars, etc.); elephants (especially ivory and hide products); snakes, lizards and monitors (goannas); rhinoceros; whales; and zebras. Some overseas retailers provide certificates and other guarantees stating that their products are made from protected animals specially bred in captivity and legally farmed for by-products, such as their skins. Such certificates aren't recognised by Australia and the only document recognised by customs is an import permit from the Australian Nature Conservation Agency (ANCA), GPO Box 636, Canberra, ACT 2601 (tel. (02) 6250 0300). Import permits may be issued by ANCA providing that export approval has been obtained from the relevant wildlife authority in the country where you made the purchase and where Australian wildlife import requirements have been met.

Telephones & CB Radios: The importation of cordless telephones and citizenband (CB) radios is prohibited unless they are approved by the Australian Spectrum Management Agency (SMA). Only importers authorised by the SMA and the Australian Telecommunications Authority (AUSTEL) who comply with strict conditions may bring cordless telephones into Australia. Approved cordless telephones must display an approval number and an AUSTEL 'permit to connect' authorisation number. Cellular mobile telephones and facsimile machines can be imported.

EMBASSY REGISTRATION

Nationals of some countries are required to register with their local embassy or consulate as soon as possible after arrival in Australia. Registration isn't usually mandatory, although most embassies like to keep a record of their nationals resident in Australia (if only to help justify their existence) and it may help to expedite passport renewal or replacement.

FINDING HELP

One of the biggest difficulties facing new arrivals in Australia is how and where to obtain help with day to day problems. For example, finding a home, schools, insurance requirements and so on. This book was written in response to this need. However, in addition to the comprehensive information provided herein, you'll also require detailed local information. How successful you are in finding help will depend on your employer, the town or area where you live (e.g. those who live and work in a major city are much better served than those living in rural areas), your nationality, English proficiency and your sex. Note that many people find their first few weeks or months in Australia stressful, so it helps if you're prepared for a turbulent time. The British newspaper, *Australian News* (see **Appendix A**), has a pen-pals page through which prospective migrants can make contact with recent migrants already in Australia.

Obtaining information isn't a problem as there's a wealth of information available in Australia on every conceivable subject (from astronomy to zoology). The problem is sorting the truths from the half truths, comparing the options available and making the right decisions. Much information isn't intended for foreigners and their particular needs. You may find that your friends, colleagues and acquaintances can help, as they are often able to proffer advice based on their own experiences and mistakes. **But beware!** Although they mean well, you're likely to receive as much false and conflicting information as you are accurate (not always wrong, but possibly invalid for your particular area or situation).

The Department of Immigration, Local Government and Ethnic Affairs provides some basic post-arrival facilities and there are a wealth of settlement programs for migrants in Australia. A limited number of hostels (in Melbourne and Sydney) and self-contained apartments are provided for immigrants with nowhere to stay on arrival, although they are drab, depressing places mostly used nowadays by refugees. Some states offer extra help to immigrants, for example South Australia provides skilled migrants with financial assistance for up to two years after their arrival and employer groups also take part in this scheme. Government programs for immigrants include migrant resource centres, telephone interpreter services, translation services, an adult migrant English program, welfare assistance and a grant-in-aid scheme (mainly for refugees). Migrant resource centres (over 30) are located in all major cities and towns, and provide newcomers with counselling and contacts to help them overcome any initial problems.

Telephone interpreter services are available 24 hours a day throughout the country for the cost of a local phone call (tel. 13 1450). Operators speak a wide range of languages and can provide information on accommodation, education, health, insurance, legal and police matters, social welfare and a wide range of other topics. There are also translation units in Sydney, Melbourne and Canberra, and translations can also be done via the telephone interpreter service (a fee may be charged for documents other than migrant settlement documents).

Local council offices, libraries, tourist offices and Citizen's Advice Bureaus (CABs) are excellent sources of reliable information on a wide range of subjects. Some companies may have a department or staff whose job is to help new arrivals or they may contract this job out to a local company. If a woman lives in or near a major town, she's able to turn to many women's clubs and organisations for help (single men aren't so well served). There are numerous expatriate associations, clubs and organisations in Australia's major cities and large towns (including 'settlers' or 'friendship' associations) for immigrants from just about every country, providing detailed local information regarding all aspects of life in Australia including housing costs, schools, health services, shopping and much more. Many organisations produce data sheets, booklets and newsletters; operate libraries; and organise a variety of social events which may include day and evening classes ranging from cooking to English-language classes. For a list of local clubs, look under 'Clubs and Associations' in your local yellow pages. The Department of Immigration can put you in touch with clubs and societies in the city or area where you plan to live in Australia.

Most embassies and consulates provide information bulletin boards (jobs, accommodation, travel, etc.) and keep lists of social clubs and societies for their nationals, and many businesses (e.g. banks and building societies) produce books and leaflets containing useful information for newcomers. Local libraries and bookshops usually have books about the local area (see also **Appendix B**).

CHECKLISTS

Before Arrival

The following checklist contains a summary of the tasks that should (if possible) be completed before your arrival in Australia:

- Obtain a visa (if applicable) for all your family members (see **Chapter 3**). Obviously this *must* be done before arrival in Australia.
- If possible, visit Australia prior to your move to find a job, compare communities and schools, and arrange schooling for your children (see **Chapter 9**).
- Arrange temporary or permanent accommodation (see page 114).
- Arrange for the shipment of your personal effects to Australia (see page 137).
- Arrange health insurance for your family (see page 306). This is essential if you won't be covered by Medicare on your arrival in Australia (see page 277).
- Open a bank account in Australia and transfer some funds (you can open an account with most Australian banks from overseas). It's advisable to obtain some Australian currency before your arrival in Australia as this will save you having to change money immediately on arrival.
- Obtain an international driver's licence, if necessary.
- Obtain an international credit card (or two), which will prove invaluable during your first few months in Australia.
- Collect and update your personal records including those relating to your family's medical, dental, educational (schools), insurance (e.g. car insurance), professional and employment (including job references) history.

Don't forget to bring all the above documents with you including birth certificates, driver's licenses, marriage certificate, divorce papers, death certificate (if a widow or widower), educational diplomas and professional certificates, employment references, student ID cards, medical and dental records, bank account and credit card details, insurance policies, and receipts for any valuables you're bringing with you. You will also need any documents which were necessary to obtain your visa (see **Chapter 3**), plus numerous passport-size photographs.

After Arrival

The following checklist contains a summary of tasks to be completed after your arrival in Australia (if not done before arrival):

- On arrival at an Australian airport or port, have your visa cancelled and passport stamped, as applicable.
- If you don't own a car, you may wish to rent one for a week or two until you buy one locally (see page 266). Note that it's *very* difficult or impossible to get around in rural areas without a car.

- Register with your local embassy or consulate (see page 108).

- If you plan to work in Australia, obtain a tax file number as soon as possible (see page 321). This is necessary to open a bank account and before (or soon after) starting work.

- Open a bank account at a local bank and give the details to your employer (see page 327). This should be done within six weeks of arrival, during which period your passport is sufficient identification (after six weeks other proof of identification is necessary). If you don't have a permanent address, you can pay to use a 'travellers' contact point' which provides mail holding and electronic mail (e-mail) services.

- Do the following within the next few weeks:

  – apply for a Medicare Card at a Medicare office. This also applies to temporary residents if their country of nationality has a reciprocal agreement with Australia.

  – arrange schooling for your children (see **Chapter 9**);

  – find a local doctor and dentist (see **Chapter 12**);

  – arrange whatever insurance is necessary (see **Chapter 13**) including:

    * health insurance (see page 306);

    * car insurance (see page 246);

    * home-contents insurance (see page 312);

    * personal liability insurance (see page 314).

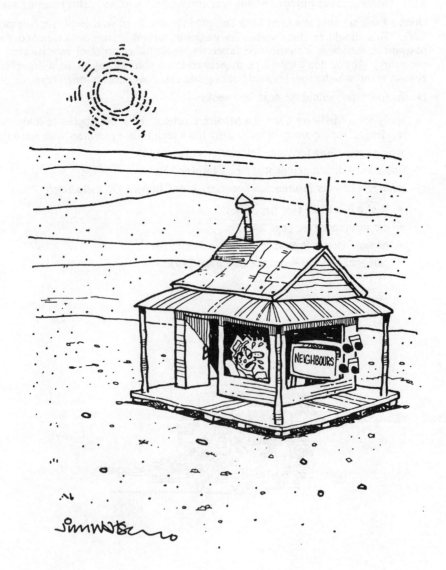

5.

ACCOMMODATION

In most cities and regions of Australia there's a wealth of property for sale, although finding decent rental accommodation isn't so easy, particularly in cities such as Sydney and Melbourne. In Sydney, property at affordable prices is in high demand and short supply, and rents are high and expected to soar even higher in the run up to the Olympics in the year 2000. Particularly hard hit are those on low incomes, students and the young, the unemployed, pensioners and single parents, some of whom spend half of their wages on rent. Accommodation usually accounts for around 30 per cent of the average Australian family's budget, but can rise to as much as 50 per cent for tenants and those buying in major cities (renters generally pay a higher proportion of their income in rent than homebuyers do in mortgage payments). Around 18 per cent of Australians move house every year and the average person has 11 addresses during his lifetime.

Home ownership in Australia is, at around 70 per cent (40 per cent owned outright), one of the highest rates in the world and higher than both Britain and the USA. Most Australians expect to be buying their own homes by the time they are in their 30s, although in recent years more people have been renting and many people aged under 35 have dropped out of the home ownership market altogether. Australia is a highly urbanised society with over 70 per cent of the population living in the main cities situated on or near the coast including Adelaide, Brisbane, Canberra, Darwin, Melbourne, Perth and Sydney, all of which have their own character and particular attractions. Only some 15 per cent of Australians live in rural areas. The vast majority of Australians live in detached bungalows on individual plots of land, although apartments (called 'units' or 'home units') are common in inner cities and coastal areas, and townhouses are also popular in the suburbs.

Oversupply generated by a building boom in the '80s followed by a severe recession in the early '90s led to a slump in house prices and the worst market for 20 years, which left many people in negative equity (where their mortgage was more than the value of their homes). However, prices have recovered in the last few years in most regions and the market is healthier than it has been for some years in the major cities, where spacious quality properties are in particularly high demand. In 1997 the average house price in Australia was around $150,000, although it's much higher in the major cities, particularly anywhere within easy travelling distance of the central business district (CBD).

Homelessness is a big problem in Australia where soaring rents and a critical shortage of public housing have led to tens of thousands of people being forced to live in cars, caravans, private hotels, rooming houses and Salvation Army hostels. In major cities, people with mental health, drug and alcohol problems make up most of the homeless, although an increasing number of families and unemployed people find themselves in the same predicament. Public housing is provided by state governments and is available to those on low and moderate incomes (applicants are means tested), although there are long waiting lists (over 200,000 nationwide) usually comprising a number of years. Homelessness is set to worsen as a consequence of government cutbacks in public housing in recent years.

TEMPORARY ACCOMMODATION

On arrival in Australia you may find it necessary to stay in temporary accommodation for a few weeks (or even a few months), before moving into permanent accommodation or while waiting for your personal effects and furniture to arrive from overseas. In most large towns and cities, apartments or holiday apartments are available, which are fully self-contained furnished apartments with their own bathroom and kitchen. They are cheaper (e.g. 25 to 50 per cent cheaper than a standard hotel double room), have over twice the space and are more convenient than hotels, particularly for families. Service apartments are usually rented on a weekly basis. Single people and married couples (without children) may be able to find temporary accommodation in hostels (see page 368). There are a limited number of government hostels (in Melbourne and Sydney) and self-contained apartments for migrants with nowhere to stay on arrival, although these are usually drab, depressing places and are mostly used by refugees nowadays. For information about hotels, bed and breakfast, self-catering and hostels see **Chapter 15**.

RELOCATION COMPANIES

If you're fortunate enough to have your move to (or within) Australia paid for by your employer, he may arrange for a relocation company to handle the details. Relocation companies in Australia generally specialise in corporate relocations rather than acting for individuals. In addition to housing, education and employment services, many relocation companies will also find business premises in Australia and relocate complete companies, including plant and machinery. There are relocation companies in all major cities in Australia, most of which provide the following services:

House Hunting: This is usually the main service provided by relocation companies and includes both rental and purchase properties. Services usually include locating a number of properties matching your requirements and specifications, and arranging a visit to Australia to view them. You should usually allow at least two months between your initial visit and moving into a purchased property. Rental properties can usually be found in two to four weeks, depending on the location and your requirements.

Negotiations: Companies will usually help and advise with all aspects of house rental or purchase and may conduct negotiations on your behalf, organise finance (including bridging loans), arrange surveys and insurance, organise your removal to Australia and even arrange quarantine for your pets (see page 454).

Schools: Consultants usually provide a special report on local schools (both state and private) for families with children. If required the report can also include private boarding schools.

Local Information: Most companies provide a comprehensive information package for a chosen area including information about employment prospects, state and private health services, local schools (state and private), estate agents, shopping facilities, public transport, amenities and services, sports and social facilities, and communications.

Miscellaneous Services: Companies may provide advice and support (particularly for non-working spouses) both before and after a move; orientation visits for spouses; counselling for domestic and personal problems; help in finding jobs for spouses; and even marriage counselling (moving to another country puts a lot of strain on relationships). A relocation company may also find you a suitable car if one isn't provided by your employer.

Although you may consider a relocation company's services expensive, particularly if you're footing the bill yourself, most companies and individuals consider it money well spent. You can find a relocation company through the Relocation Group in Australia and the International Relocation Association (TIRA) or look in your local yellow pages under 'Relocators'. One relocation company with offices throughout Australia is Australiawide Relocations Pty Ltd., PO Box 111, 19-23 Bridge Street, Pymble, NSW 2073 (tel. (02) 9488 9444).

If you just wish to look at properties for rent or sale in a particular area, you can make appointments to view properties through estate agents in the area where you plan to live and arrange your own trip to Australia. However, you must make *absolutely certain* that estate agents (see page 129) know exactly what you're looking for and obtain property lists in advance. It's also possible to view properties over the internet, e.g. via the Real Estate Display Centre (realestatecentre.com.au). Most agents will also send you details of properties by fax or e-mail.

BUYING PROPERTY

Buying a house or apartment in Australia has traditionally been a good long-term investment, although this was severely tested during the recession in the early '90s. However, most people still find buying preferable to renting, depending of course on how long you're planning to stay in Australia and where you're planning to live. If you're staying short term only, say less than two or three years, then you may be better off renting. For those staying longer than two or three years or indefinitely, buying is the better option, particularly as buying a house or apartment is generally no more expensive (or cheaper) than renting and you could make a profit. Some market analysts have forecast that property prices in Australia's major cities (particularly Sydney and Melbourne) will soar in the next five years. It's also more difficult to rent than buy a good property in most cities.

However, if you're a migrant, you should seriously consider renting for a period before buying, particularly if you're unsure of where you want to live or work; there's a possibility that you may change jobs or states within your first year or two in Australia; or, as many people do, you may even decide that Australia isn't for you and return home within a few years.

The secret of successfully buying a home in Australia (or anywhere else for that matter) is research, research and more research, preferably before you even set foot there. You may be fortunate and buy the first property you see without doing any homework and live happily ever after. However, a successful purchase is much more likely if you thoroughly investigate the towns and suburbs in your chosen area; compare the range and prices of properties and their relative values; and study the procedure for buying property. It's a wise or lucky person who gets his choice absolutely right first time, but there's a much better chance if you do your homework thoroughly. There's a huge choice of homes in Australia including apartments, townhouses and a wide range of 'standard' and individually-designed, detached homes. Apartments (called 'units' or 'home units') are common in inner cities and coastal areas, and townhouses (or row houses) are also common in cities and their suburbs. Villa units are low-rise properties separated by a garage or small courtyard (garden) and similar to a townhouse. Outside the major cities, most people have a home built to a standard (or their own) design on their own plot of land, although package deals including a plot of land and a house are also common.

Information: Magazines are published by local real estate associations in major cities and states. Most banks, building societies and credit unions publish free booklets for homebuyers, most of which contain excellent (usually unbiased) advice, and the Home Purchase Assistance Authority (tel. freecall 1800-806 653) publish a free booklet, *The A-Z of Home Purchase*. The Saturday editions of major newspapers are the best for home advertisements, most of which have a 'Property' section. Note, however, that sometimes the advertised price is for the plot of land only and the building is extra. The measurements of rooms are usually stated in feet and inches (not metres or square metres) and aren't usually included in ads. The size of a plot may be stated in square metres or acres and the size of a house in squares, where one square equals 100 square feet (9.29m2).

Non-Residents: All proposed acquisitions of urban real estate by non-resident foreigners must be approved by the Australian authorities. Retirees and other 'temporary' residents must obtain permission from the Foreign Investment Board, Department of the Treasury, Parkes Place, ACT 2600 (tel. (02) 6263 3795) to buy property in Australia. Minter Ellison (tel. UK 171-831 7871) publish a free booklet entitled *Investing in Australian Property*.

See also **Mortgages** on page 336.

Australian Homes

Don't be in too much of a hurry to buy a home in Australia until you've had a good look around; have a clear idea of the relative prices and types of properties available; *and* know exactly what you're looking for. For example, do you want a house with a garden or an apartment, with perhaps higher security and lower heating bills? Do you want an older house with character and space, or a modern townhouse or apartment with all mod cons? There are a huge variety of homes to choose from in Australia including modern detached homes, apartments, townhouses, old period homes and mobile homes.

Modern Homes: Over three-quarters of Australia's 8m homes are traditional free-standing detached houses, some 15 per cent are apartments, and around 10 per cent are townhouses, semi-detached, row or terrace homes. The most common Australian family home is a detached, single-storey bungalow (ranch style) on a quarter or third of an acre plot. It has three or four bedrooms, a combined lounge/dining room, kitchen (possibly eat-in), bathroom (or two), separate toilet, laundry room, possibly a family or rumpus room (which may be an extension of the kitchen), and a garage or car port. Bathrooms usually include a bath and separate shower and there may also be a separate shower room. Larger houses, e.g. from four bedrooms, have two or more bathrooms, with the master bedroom having an *en suite* bathroom or shower. Larger homes may also have a study and other rooms. The mild climate allows year-round, outdoor living and most detached homes have terraces or patios with a barbecue, and around half have a swimming pool (which must be completely fenced off and childproof).

The quality of modern Australian homes is generally excellent. Construction varies from brick (most expensive and generally reserved for luxury homes), brick veneer (a timber inner-frame structure lined with plasterboard), weatherboard and asbestos/fibre cement known as fibro (cheapest). Brick veneer is the most popular and has the outward appearance of a full brick home, except that the inner frame structure is made of timber and the inside is lined with plaster board or similar material. It costs less than a full brick home and is particularly suited to Australia's climate. A fibro house is basically a timber frame covered with asbestos cement on the outside and plasterboard on the inside. Roofs are generally made of terracotta or cement tiles, although galvanised colour bond steel decking or corrugated fibre/asbestos cement sheeting is often used in contemporary style homes. In remote country areas (e.g. the outback and the bush) running water, sewerage, mains electricity and telephones are a luxury, and septic tanks, rain water tanks, generators and dirt roads are common. Houses are raised on stilts in some tropical areas or those subject to flooding, where the garage may be located below the living area.

When you buy a new home, kitchen and bathroom fittings, fitted carpets, curtains and light fittings are usually included in the price. Bedrooms have built-in wardrobes and kitchens are fully fitted with a cooker and possibly even a dishwasher. Fly screens are common on external doors and all windows, and allow you to leave the doors and windows open without inviting insects in. Good insulation helps keep homes cool in summer and warm in winter, and in the southern states homes may have a fireplace or a heating unit in the lounge. Air-conditioning may be fitted as standard in up-market homes. Interior walls are generally painted and wallpaper is rare in Australia. In major cities there are home display villages where you can view the latest designs from Australia's largest builders. New properties come with a builder's warranty.

Apartments: Apartments (flats), called units or home units in Australia, are common in inner city and beachside areas because of the high cost of land, although they aren't as widespread as in European cities. Apartment blocks are usually purpose-built with up to 20 storeys and are rarely conversions of old large houses. Blocks may contain split-level apartments and penthouses (which traditionally occupy the whole top floor of a high-rise building) and usually have underground parking. Many modern apartment blocks have communal pools and other facilities such as tennis courts, saunas and gymnasiums. Queensland's Gold Coast is popular among retirees who buy apartments in retirement villages which include swimming pools, bowling greens, tennis courts, croquet lawns, billiards' rooms and village buses. Units in Australia are sold freehold under the Strata Titles Act (see page 123). Note that apartments, particularly older apartments, aren't usually built or designed to the high standards found in North America or many European countries. Many older apartments are tiny with poor storage, inadequate parking, and lacking in quality fixtures and fittings.

Period & Older Homes: There are many old period homes in the inner city suburbs of the major cities, most of which have been modernised and are now relatively (or very) expensive. Terraced housing is found in some older inner-city suburbs, e.g. in Sydney, where decorative lace wrought ironwork is a feature of early homes, particularly in inner-city suburbs such as Paddington and Darlinghurst. Federation (early 19th century) houses made of wood and sandstone are also attractive and highly prized. In Queensland there are elevated timber and iron houses with balustrades and verandas (known appropriately as 'Queenslanders'), which allow cooling breezes to permeate the house. However, there's also a vast amount of housing stock with no architectural merit or heritage value. Many of the homes built in the '50s and '60s building boom reflect the less sophisticated and enlightened ideas of that era, and are entirely unsuited to today's lifestyle. In many cases the plots they occupy represent prime real estate and are worth much more than the value of the properties built on them. If you need to modernise or renovate a property, you should expect to pay at least 20 per cent more than your original budget. Note also that many old homes have problems such as damp, electricity faults and insect infestations (see **Inspections & Surveys** on page 128).

Mobile Homes: Mobile homes (also called transportable homes) are popular in Australia particularly among retirees, where they are called manufactured homes because they are factory built in two or more sections and erected on site (usually in around six weeks). Many mobile homes look like conventional homes and include features such as bay windows, skylights, verandas, built-in wardrobes and even brick finishes. They cost between $50,000 and $110,000 and at the top end of the market there isn't a huge saving over a conventional home. Note also that mobile homes are likely to depreciate in value over the years, rather than appreciate in value like a conventional home. They are usually sited in caravan parks and in specially built manufactured home estates, although sites must usually be leased, e.g. on a weekly or monthly basis, and owners must also be wary of spiralling rents which are an issue in most states (although some parks have rent controls). There are also a range of restrictions in parks, e.g. overnight fees for guests, and in some states owners even require the permission of park owners to sell. For further information contact the Manufactured Housing Industry Association, PO Box H114, Harris Park, NSW 2150 (tel. (02) 633 9377), which publishes an informative booklet.

Cost

Property prices vary considerably throughout the country and in the various suburbs of the major cities. Not surprisingly, the further you are from a town or city, the lower the cost of land and property. Two-bedroom apartments (of around 75 square metres) start at around $80,000 in outer city suburbs and rise to over double this in a central or popular beach location. For many buyers it's a choice between a small apartment in an inner city and a large detached family home in the outer suburbs (in recent years the average 'Aussie battler' has had to move further and further into the outer suburbs of major cities in order to find affordable accommodation).

A two or three bedroom single-storey home in most city outer suburbs costs between $50,000 and $90,000, and four bedroom two-storey homes cost from around $60,000 to $150,000. On the other hand, waterfront properties in Sydney are astronomically expensive and a reasonable two-bedroom apartment in a nice building with water views can cost around $500,000 (million dollar homes are commonplace in Sydney and to a lesser extent in Melbourne). You usually pay a premium for a home with water views. There's a high demand for waterfront properties, which are generally an excellent investment, particularly in NSW where the government plans to preserve the coastline from further development (canal developments are already banned).

Average house prices in the capital cities in late 1997 were around $250,000 in Sydney, $180,000 in Darwin, $175,000 in Melbourne, $150,000 in Canberra, $140,000 in Brisbane, $135,000 in Perth, $125,000 in Adelaide and $110,000 in Hobart. Units and townhouses are some 20 to 30 per cent cheaper than detached houses. Average prices for apartments in Adelaide, Canberra, Hobart and Perth have remained stagnant in recent years, while prices have been escalating in Brisbane, Melbourne and Sydney. Sydney has the most expensive real estate in Australia, while South Australia is the cheapest state for homes for typical first-time buyers.

With the exception of Brisbane, Melbourne and Sydney, 1997 was a buyers' market in most cities and regions. In some areas, homes were selling for prices far below the cost of construction around three or four years ago, due to an over-supply of new housing and builders 'dumping' new houses for little profit. Interest rate cuts in the last few years mean that although prices have risen, homes were some 25 per cent more affordable than two years previously. However, although low interest rates and rising prices meant that in 1997 there had never been a better time to buy, it's feared that many people could find themselves in severe financial difficulties if interest rates were to rise sharply.

In 1997, buyers were flocking back to inner cities (i.e. up to around 10km/6mi from the centre), which led to a huge increase in prices as demand outstripped supply (penthouses are in particular demand). Buying 'off plan' is usually necessary when buying a new apartment in a city centre. Not surprisingly, selling at auction is particularly popular when prices are rising. Around 25 to 30 per cent of homes in Melbourne are put to auction compared with around 20 per cent in Sydney, around 15 per cent in Brisbane and 10 to 15 per cent in Adelaide. High demand in 1997 led to houses in the inner suburbs of Melbourne and Sydney selling at auction for between $50,000 and $100,000 above their guide prices. The difference between inner suburb house prices in Sydney and Melbourne are considerable, with a $250,000 house in Melbourne costing as much as twice the price for a similar house in a similar suburb in Sydney.

Note that a few kilometres can make a huge difference to the price, with apartments in central areas up to $2,000 a square metre higher than those in harbourside developments a few kilometres further out. The average cost of a Sydney house increased by around 25 per cent in 1997, with the biggest price rises among homes valued at over $500,000.

As with most things, higher priced houses (e.g. over $200,000) generally provide better value for money than cheaper houses, e.g. a much larger built area and plot, better build quality, and superior fixtures and fittings. Most semi-detached and detached houses have single or double garages included in the price.

Land prices reduce considerably from around 15km/9mi outside a city and are at their lowest around 25km/16mi from cities. The cost of land varies from as little as $20,000 for an average size suburban building block over 25km/16mi from cities such as Adelaide, Hobart and Perth to over $150,000 for a building block within 15km/9mi of central Sydney (if you can find one). The cost of building a home varies depending on the location, quality and the materials used, e.g. brick (most expensive), brick veneer, weatherboard and fibre cement (cheapest). Brick veneer is the most popular and costs from around $400 to $700 per metre, depending on the location. For up-to-date prices obtain a free copy of the *Cost of Living and Housing Survey Book* published by the Commonwealth Bank of Australia.

There are few bargains when it comes to buying property and although you may be able to negotiate a reduction of 5 or possibly 10 per cent (particularly if a seller is looking for a quick sale in a buyer's market), there's usually a good reason when a property is substantially cheaper than other similar properties. Although it's sometimes inadvisable to look a gift horse in the mouth, you should generally be suspicious of a bargain. On the other hand, most sellers and estate agents price properties higher than the market price or the price they expect to receive, knowing that buyers will try to drive the price down, so always haggle over the price asked (even if you think it's a bargain). This is, in fact, one of the few occasions in Australia when you're expected to bargain over the price, although you should try to avoid insulting an owner by offering a derisory price.

If you're buying a home for a limited period or as an investment, you should buy one that will hopefully sell quickly and at a profit. Homes that sell best are exceptional period houses of character with lots of original features, plus water and beach-front homes (particularly in Queensland), which are in high demand and can be let for most of the year to holidaymakers if required. Water-front homes are generally in short supply and are considered a particularly good investment. Luxury units in central Brisbane, Melbourne and Sydney are also a good investment (prices in Sydney are expected to soar in the next few years during the run up to the Olympics in the year 2000). Note, however, that buying property in Australia is usually a long term investment and isn't advisable for those seeking a short term gain. You must pay capital gains tax on the profit made on the sale of an investment property (see page 120).

You can find out the price of homes in any Sydney suburb through the *Sydney Morning Herald Home Price Guide* which lists all the sales' results (both auction and private treaty) in Sydney suburbs for the last 12 months (it can be ordered via the internet from apm.com.au). A similar service is provided by newspapers in other major cities and you can also peruse property ads. in a wide number of publications via the internet.

Fees

The fees associated with buying a home in Australia usually total 4 to 5 per cent of the purchase price, which is lower than in many other countries. Most fees are calculated as a percentage of the value of the property you're buying, therefore the more expensive the property, the higher the fees. Even removal costs will be higher if you have a large house (unless you have a lot of empty rooms). If you're buying *and* selling, you must consider the cost of both transactions.

- **Stamp Duty:** Stamp duty varies depending on the state or territory and is an average of around $1,000 ($50,000 property), $2,300 ($100,000 property) and $7,000 ($200,000 property). On moderate priced properties (up to $100,000), it's lowest in Western Australia and highest in the Northern Territory and South Australia. Stamp duty is lower in some states for first-time buyers and some states also waive all or part of the stamp duty for first-time buyers.

- **Land Transfer Registration:** This is payable each time a property is purchased and is to pay for recording the change of owner at the Land Titles Office. It's either a flat fee (ACT, NSW, NT, QLD and TAS) or a variable fee based on the actual price paid (SA, VIC and WA). The fee on a $100,000 property varies from $55 in New South Wales (fixed fee) to $345 in South Australia ($765 on a $200,000 property).

- **Legal Fees:** Legal fees are usually 1 to 2 per cent of the purchase price, but may be based on the actual work involved. Legal fees and stamp duty vary considerably from state to state, e.g. from $400 in Adelaide, Perth and Hobart to around $1,500 in Brisbane for a property costing over $100,000. The fees in most states are within the $500 to $750 range.

- **Solicitor's or Conveyancer's Fees:** These are the fees for the documentation necessary to allow a property purchase to go ahead (see **Conveyancing** on page 127). There isn't a fixed charge and the cost of conveyancing can range from around $300 to $900.

- **Government Taxes:** There are federal and state taxes on financial transactions, which vary depending on the state or territory.

- **Mortgage Fees:** A range of fees are associated with mortgages including a mortgage application and establishment fee, valuation fee, stamp duty, mortgage registration and indemnity insurance (for information see page 339).

- **Termite & Pest Inspection:** This is compulsory in some states, while in others it's sufficient to simply certify that a property is free of termites and pests. However, a termite inspection is always advisable, whether required by law or not. The inspection costs around $100 and may be paid by the vendor or buyer or shared.

- **Strata Inspection:** When you're buying an apartment (unit), it's wise to have a strata inspection which will tell you whether there have been any structural problems in the building and highlight any administration problems.

- **Inspection or Survey Fee:** Although it isn't compulsory to have a building inspection or a structural survey carried out, it's often wise, particularly when you're buying an old detached house (see **Inspections & Surveys** on page 128). You should allow around $500 for a structural survey.

- **Buildings Insurance:** It's a condition of lenders that properties are fully insured against structural and other damage (see page 311). Note that it may be necessary to insure a property from the day you sign the purchase contract.

- **Miscellaneous Costs:** If you're buying a new home you may need to pay an architect and other fees. You will also usually need to pay utility connection, reconnection, registration or transfer fees for gas, electricity, water and telephone. Although not a fee as such, removal costs must also be taken into account. In addition to the fees associated with buying a property, you must also consider the running costs which include local property taxes (rates) and possibly land tax (see page 340); building and contents insurance (see page 311 and 312); standing charges for utilities (electricity, gas, telephone, water); community fees for a unit or other community property (see page 123); garden and pool maintenance; and a caretaker's or management fees if you leave a home empty or let it. Annual running costs usually average around 2 to 3 per cent of the cost of a property.

Building Your Own Home

Building a new home or having a new home built is common in Australia and usually takes from four to 12 months. It's generally cheaper and better to have a new home built than to buy and renovate an older home, and you don't need to make compromises for old building standards, and the existing dimensions or plot restrictions. You also don't need to match new work to old or make good any damage to existing structures. New homes are generally built to much higher standard that older homes. Many Australians design and even build their own homes and if you're up to it you can even do much of the work yourself, although plumbing and electrical work can be done only by qualified tradesmen. **Note, that building a home isn't for the faint-hearted as it's fraught with problems.** Alternatively you can buy a plot and hire a builder to build a home or purchase a plot from a builder/developer with exclusive rights to develop a particular estate (called project or estate homes). Builders' project homes are cheaper than building a home to your own design and land and house packages are cost effective. All builders maintain show homes which can usually be visited without an appointment on weekends.

The cost of building per square metre depends on the type of construction and the location; full brick $450 to $750, brick veneer $400 to $750, weatherboard $350 to $650, fibre cement $400 to $700. Brick veneer is the most popular, while full brick is reserved for luxury homes, and weatherboard or fibre cement are rarely used nowadays. Timber cladding is popular in some cities, e.g. Brisbane. Note that the quality of fixtures and fittings make a huge difference to the price.

Land: The cost of land varies considerably depending on the city or region and the distance from a city centre. For example a plot around eight to 15km/9mi from Sydney centre will cost at least $200,000, while a similar plot in Perth will cost from around $50,000. Plots over 30km/19mi from city centres range from a high of around $65,000 in Sydney to around $25,000 in Adelaide and Perth. Most land and property in Australia is owned freehold, the only exception being the Australian Capital Territory (ACT), where land is sold on a 99-year lease (the ACT government is considering extending leases to 999 years when renewals begin to come up early next century). Residential blocks are released by the government and sold at public auction and any unsold sites are available for sale at the Land Sales Office. Plots up to 30km/19mi from the city cost from around $40,000 to $130,000. Reserve prices (average $60,000) are set at 80 per cent of the assessed market value and lessees must start work on building within 12 months and complete properties within two years. All sites are provided with services such as water, electricity, sewerage and sealed roads.

New properties built by a professional builder are always covered by a warranty (most lenders won't make a loan on a new house without a warranty). A standard contract for a new home usually provides that the builder rectifies any defects notified by the purchaser for a limited period, e.g. three months. Note that it's important to choose your builder carefully, as building disputes are common and can be expensive if you need to seek legal redress.

Community Properties

Apartments (called units in Australia) and other properties with common elements (whether a building, amenities or land) shared with other properties are owned through a system of co-ownership or community ownership, similar to owning a condominium in the USA or an apartment in most European countries. Community owned properties in Australia include apartments, townhouses, and single-family (detached) homes on a private estate with communal areas and facilities. It may apply to residential properties and mixed residential, commercial and industrial sites, and retirement villages. In general, the only properties that don't belong to a community are detached houses on individual plots in public streets or on rural land. The most common forms of community ownership in Australia are strata title and company title.

Strata Title: A strata title is a document showing ownership of part of a parcel of land or of a 'piece of air' (stratum), which usually applies to home units (apartments). Under the Strata Titles Act each unit or property has a separate freehold and owners have a share in the land surface and the building built on it. Owners not only own their homes, but also a share of the common elements of a building or development which may include foyers, hallways, lifts, patios, gardens, roads, and leisure and sports facilities. Each owner of a unit has a copy of the strata title and is a member of the owners' corporation which manages the building. If you have a **stratum title**, you own your own unit or a larger property and are also a shareholder in the company that manages the common area (not just a member).

Company Title: Company title is when a company owns land or property, usually consisting of units, and the buyer acquires shares in the company equal to the value of his unit (the same as a co-operative apartment in the USA). Owners pay expenses for the building's mortgage, rates, employee salaries and expenses for the upkeep of the building, proportionate to the number of shares they own. A managing agent and staff are hired to run and secure the safety of the building and its units, and a board of directors is elected by tenants to supervise and control the management of the corporation. Apart from the difference in how a property is owned, there's little difference between a strata title and company title property under Australian law, and many of the statutory provisions are the same. Strata title ownership is much more common than company title ownership.

Management: In an apartment block with a strata title, property is administered and maintained by an owners' corporation (previously called the body corporate) consisting of a number of owners. Owners are required to attend an annual general meeting to discuss the annual fees and to elect the president and committee members, although they can name someone to represent and vote for them by proxy. Voting proxies are limited to 12 months or two consecutive annual general meetings. Owners' corporations must have minimum public liability insurance of $10m.

Rules or By-Laws: Maintenance of common areas is the responsibility of all title holders and subject to 'fair and reasonable' rules or by-laws (which are enforceable by law), a copy of which is given to all owners. Developers can customise the rules to attract young families by having common areas devoted to children's playgrounds, or allowing residents to keep pets (such as cats and dogs), removing many of the unwieldy regulations imposed by the previous compulsory by-laws. Guide or hearing dogs are permitted and there are no restrictions on occupation by children aged under 18. However, all residents must be treated equally and the owners' corporation cannot discriminate against tenants. Under the Strata Schemes Management Act, there are fines of up to $5,000 for breaches of by-laws. Owners are also liable to a fine of $500 if they don't inform the owners' corporation of a leasing arrangement.

Community Fees: Owners of community properties must pay strata fees or maintenance costs for the upkeep of communal areas and for communal services. Charges are calculated according to each owner's share of the development (his 'unit entitlement') or apartment building and *not* whether they are temporary or permanent residents. Shares are calculated according to the actual size of properties, e.g. 10 properties of equal size would each pay 10 per cent of community fees. The percentage to be paid is detailed in the property deed. Shares not only determine the share of fees to be paid, but also voting rights at general meetings.

Fees go towards road cleaning; green zone maintenance (including communal gardens); cleaning, decoration and maintenance of buildings; porterage or concierge; communal lighting in buildings and grounds; water supply (e.g. swimming pools, gardens); insurance; administration fees; rates; and maintenance of radio and TV aerials. Always check the level of general and any special charges before buying a community property. If you're buying an apartment from a previous owner, ask to see a copy of the service charges for previous years and the minutes of the last annual general meeting, as owners may be 'economical with the truth' when stating service charges, particularly if they are high. Fees are usually paid by a quarterly levy and owners' corporations may offer a 10 per cent discount for early payment. Community fees vary considerably depending on the size of a property and the communal facilities provided, from a few hundred dollars a year to $1,000 a week. High fees aren't necessarily a negative point (assuming you can afford them), providing that you receive value for money and the community is well managed and maintained. The value of a community property depends to a large extent on how well the development is maintained and managed.

Pre-Purchase Checks: While it isn't usual to have a survey or structural inspection on an apartment, you should have a strata inspection carried out which will tell you whether there are any structural problems in the building and highlight any administration problems. Owners' corporations maintain 'sinking funds' to cover future needs, although (if necessary) owners can be charged a special levy to make up any shortfall of funds for maintenance or repair work. You should check the condition of the common areas (including all amenities) in an older development and whether any major maintenance or capital expense is planned for which you could be assessed. Beware of bargain units in buildings requiring a lot of maintenance work or refurbishment.

Advantages: The advantages of owning a community property include increased security; lower property and land taxes than detached homes; a range of community sports and leisure facilities; community living with lots of social contacts and the companionship of close neighbours; no garden, lawn or pool maintenance; fewer of the responsibilities of home ownership; ease of maintenance; and they are often situated in locations where owning a single-family home would be prohibitively expensive, e.g. a beach-front or town centre.

Disadvantages: The disadvantages of community properties may include excessively high maintenance fees (owners may have no control over increases); restrictive rules and regulations (e.g. regarding pets, children and washing lines); a confining living and social environment and possible lack of privacy; noisy neighbours (particularly if neighbouring apartments are let to holiday-makers); limited living and storage space; parking problems; and acrimonious owners' meetings, where factions may try to push through unpopular proposals (sometimes using proxy votes).

Before buying a community property it's advisable to ask current owners about the community. For example do they like living there; what are the fees and restrictions; how noisy are other residents; are the recreational facilities easy to access; would they buy there again (why or why not); and, most importantly, is the community well managed.

You may also wish to check on your prospective neighbours. If you're planning to buy an apartment above the ground floor, you may also want to ensure that the building has a lift. Note that upper floor apartments are both colder in winter and warmer in summer and may incur extra charges for the use of lifts. They do, however, offer more security than ground floor apartments. Note that an apartment that has other apartments above and below it will generally be more noisy than a ground or top floor apartment.

Retirement Homes & Sheltered Housing

For those who are retired or nearing retirement age (e.g. over 55), purpose-built retirement homes and sheltered housing are available in most areas of Australia, where there are over 2,300 retirement villages. Villages vary in size and offer differing levels of accommodation, from self-contained independent living apartments, townhouses or cottages, to serviced apartments, hostel and nursing-home care. Most villages offer a luxurious lifestyle; a supportive environment; safety and security; and some are more like country estates or luxury hotels with prices starting at well over $300,000. Before buying a retirement home, you should visit a number of villages and talk to residents, as they vary enormously in the quality and variety of housing, amenities and cost. Note that there's a huge demand for homes in retirement developments and villages, and they usually sell quickly.

Retirement homes offer special features, facilities and convenience for the elderly and retired (most residents are in their late 60s or older), including guest suites that can be booked for visitors. Facilities may include a heated outdoor or indoor swimming pool, spa complex, bowling green, tennis courts, croquet lawn, landscaped gardens, restaurant, lounge/dining area, open fire, billiard room, craft room, library service, sun room, private bar, lifts, garage and private gardens. Some villages include all home cleaning and may also provide meals (called 'assisted living'). One of the most important features of retirement homes is that help is on hand 24-hours a day, either from a live-in warden or caretaker, or via an alarm system linked to a control centre. A nurse and maintenance man are usually on call and there are visiting doctors and dentists. Many villages provide 24-hour, seven days a week emergency care and some also have their own nursing homes.

Most villages are **resident funded**, where each resident purchases a unit through a tenancy arrangement. Some villages are **donor funded** run by a charitable or non-profit organisation and operated on a loan and licence arrangement, which reserve places for retirees who are unable to make a donation. A **strata or unit title** is the same as buying a unit in the normal way (see **Community Properties** on page 123). Strata title arrangements in retirement villages also usually include a management agreement for the provision of services and facilities tailored to the needs of residents, as well as a possible deferred management fee. Strata title provides the highest level of security of tenure, the ability to borrow against the equity in your home, and retention of any appreciation in its value.

Under **leasehold title** you purchase a long-term lease rather than full ownership of a property, which is a common tenancy arrangement in retirement villages. Leases are usually for 99 or 199 years and buying a leasehold property is cheaper than a strata title, although stamp duty is still quite high. Note that leases are transferable, but there's no capital appreciation if the lease is transferred. A **company-share title** involves buying a share in the company that owns the village which includes the right to tenancy. However, shares can be difficult to resell. A **loan and licence** arrangement usually applies to donor-funded villages, where you pay the sponsor/developer a sum (donation) plus an interest-free loan, which buys you the right to occupy a unit and use the facilities of a village.

Initial (ingoing) costs include the purchase of a unit or lease, fees such as stamp duty and legal fees, and costs associated with agreements or contracts. Running (ongoing) costs include weekly/monthly fees for maintenance, insurance, rates, services and facilities. A deferred management fee may be payable on leaving a retirement village, which is usually a percentage of the original purchase price. Note that when a unit or lease is to be sold, fees must usually be paid until it's sold. This leaves owners (or their families) open to abuse and some retirement villages deliberately allow units to lie empty so that they can charge fees (of up to $1,000 a month!) without providing any services. Other common problems include financial issues, access to services, quality of management, dispute resolution, and compliance with the mandatory code of practice.

State governments oversee the retirement village industry and most have a code of practice that aims to regulate the promotion, development and operation of villages. Check with the state authorities and the state retirement Village Residents Association. All states also have a Council of the Aging (COTA) which provides information and advice about retirement villages.

Contracts

Once a suitable property has been found and a price has been agreed, the real estate agent will complete a Contract of Sale which is signed by both parties. Contracts are published in standard form by the Law Society and the Real Estate Institute. **Note, however, that you should never sign a contract without having it checked by your legal adviser.** It's important to check that a property's particulars are complete in every detail and have been entered correctly, and that the terms of sale are correct including any changes made to the standard terms. A deposit (typically 10 per cent of the purchase price) is paid by the buyer to the agent and deposited in the agent's 'trust account' (escrow) until completion, which is usually around one month later. **Note that the deposit is forfeited if you pull out of a purchase after signing a contract, when you aren't covered by a clause in the contract.** However, a holding deposit paid before signing a contract (as a sign of 'good faith') is refundable if you change your mind. Only after the contract has been signed do the searches and checks (see **Conveyancing** below) take place, and when all the searches have been satisfactorily completed the sale is completed.

After signing and exchanging contracts, called simply 'exchange', both parties are legally obliged to go through with the deal, subject to cooling-off rights in NSW, the NT, SA and Victoria of from two to five business days. For example buyers in NSW have a cooling-off period from the day of exchange until 5pm on the fifth business day following, during which they can withdraw from the purchase without penalty other than forfeiting an amount equal to 0.25 per cent of the purchase price. Note that cooling-off rights don't apply when buying at public auction. Any conditions attached to a sale must either be dealt with before the exchange or during the cooling-off period, otherwise they *must* be included as a specific provision (conditional clause) in the contract. Note that vendors sometimes refuse to sell unless a certificate waiving the cooling-off period is signed.

Conditional Clauses: Contracts often contain conditional clauses, such as the sale being conditional on a clear survey or smoke test. Conditions usually apply to events out of control of the vendor or buyer, although almost anything agreed between the buyer and vendor can be included in a contract. If any of the conditions aren't met, the contract can be suspended or declared null and void, and the deposit returned. However, if you fail to go through with a purchase and aren't covered by a clause in the contract, you will forfeit your deposit or could even be compelled to complete a purchase. Note that if you're buying anything from the vendor such as carpets, curtains or furniture which are included in the purchase price, you should have them listed and attached as an addendum to the contract. Any fixtures and fittings present in a property when you view it (and agree to buy it) should still be there when you take possession, unless otherwise stated in the contract.

When signing a contract to buy a home or land on which you require a loan, you should complete the clause regarding your ability to obtain finance. This makes the contract 'subject to finance' and if you cannot obtain finance within the time specified in the contract, e.g. seven to 14 days, it will then become null and void and you won't have to proceed. Without a finance clause you could be sued by the vendor for failing to buy the property. If you cannot arrange finance in the specified time, you can ask for an extension to the settlement date.

Most properties in Australia are owned freehold, where the owner receives a copy of the certificate of title (deeds) or the strata title for a community property (see page 123). A certificate of title is usually issued by the state lands title office (land registry), where land and property ownership is recorded. Mortgages are also recorded at the lands title office.

Conveyancing

Conveyancing is the legal term for the process of buying and selling properties and transferring the deeds of ownership. A conveyance is a deed (legal document) which conveys a house from the vendor to the buyer, thereby transferring ownership. There are two main stages when your conveyancer will become involved. The first stage will take you up to the exchange of contracts and the second will lead to the completion of the sale, when you become the new owner.

Conveyancing includes ensuring that a proper title is obtained; arranging the necessary registration of the title; checking whether the land has been registered and the existence of any restrictive covenants; enquiring about any planned developments that may affect the value of the property (like a new airport runway or highway at the bottom of your garden); and drawing up a contract of sale. Note, however, that conveyancing duties and laws in Australia vary depending on the state or territory where the property is situated. Searches should include an identifications survey, zoning certificate, drainage or sewerage service diagram, property certificate, building inspection report, pest certificate, technical report, strata records search (for a strata title unit), and enquiries with the local council and utility companies as to whether the property is clear of any debts. Note that land tax, council and water rates are a charge on the property, and if they aren't paid by the previous owner, the new owner must pay them.

Property conveyancing in Australia is usually done by a solicitor (lawyer) or a conveyancer (although you can also do it yourself). In the ACT, Queensland and Tasmania, solicitors have a monopoly on conveyancing and in Victoria a conveyancer must work with a solicitor, but in other states you can engage a conveyancer. In some states (such as South Australia and Western Australia) the majority of settlements are handled by conveyancers (also called settlement agents, land brokers and land agents), which helps reduce costs. Some lenders carry out conveyancing as a free service to borrowers. Separate conveyancing fees are usually paid by both the buyer and the vendor (in some states the buyer's costs are higher as there's more work involved).

There isn't a fixed fee for conveyancing, which can range from around $300 to $900. Shop around for the lowest rate (some solicitors and conveyancers will negotiate).

Conveyancing companies are generally cheaper than solicitors and usually levy fixed fees with no hidden charges. Always check what is included in the fees and whether a quoted fee is 'full and binding' or just an estimate. A low basic rate may be supplemented by much more expensive 'extras' (called disbursements). Ask your friends, neighbours and colleagues if they can recommend a solicitor or conveyancer, and try to obtain a binding quotation in writing. **It isn't wise to use a solicitor or conveyancer who's acting for both the borrower and the lender, as potential conflicts of interest could arise.**

It's possible and perfectly legal to do your own conveyancing and there are a number of DIY kits available. However, you'll need to do at least 10 hours work and you require a good grasp of details plus a good measure of patience. **It isn't recommended for most people, as it's complex, time-consuming and can be risky.** If you miss a mistake in the lease, you could be left with an unsalable property — if a solicitor or licensed conveyancer is at fault, you can at least sue him!

Inspections & Surveys

Only a small percentage of buyers have a building inspection or a full structural survey when buying a property in Australia, despite the fact that many properties are discovered to have major faults such as damp or dry rot (serious defects are even found in properties less than 10 years old). Many older properties were built with inferior materials and common problems include rusting lead water pipes; asbestos; poor wiring; defective plumbing and drains; lead-based paint (which is poisonous and now banned); rising damp; dry and wet rot; uneven flooring; collapsing facades; subsidence; woodworm and termites; bulging walls; and cracked internal and external walls. In fact it isn't unusual for brand new houses to have problems. Note that a vendor in Australia has no legal obligation to inform prospective buyers about any defects that might exist in a property.

One of the problems with the home-buying system in Australia is that prospective buyers must have a survey done before making an offer on a property, and even if an offer is accepted, there's no guarantee that the sale will be completed (sellers are allowed to pull out of a sale at any time up to the signing of a contract). It can be an expensive business if a sale falls through (as many do) after paying for a survey costing hundreds of dollars. Some people delay having a survey done until both parties are ready to exchange contracts (or have it done during the cooling-off period), as it's expensive having a report done for every house in which you're interested. Many experts believe that houses should be sold with a 'certificate of quality' or that there should be a compulsory seller's survey.

When engaging a surveyor, you should put your instructions in writing and include anything you particularly want inspected, plus details of any major work you're planning to have done after buying. A survey can include a termite and pest inspection in states where it isn't compulsory. Find out exactly what you will receive for your money and obtain a written estimate including all expenses. Note that it's important to engage a surveyor you can trust to do a good job, as a bad survey can be just as expensive as none at all (as many buyers have found out to their cost). The conditions and contents of a report are usually a matter of negotiation between you and the surveyor. If you want a detailed survey, make sure that the seller will allow your surveyor free access to the property, e.g. to the roofspace (loft), and allow him to pull up carpets to examine floorboards. A structural survey can save buyers a lot of money and heartache and is generally well worth the cost, if only for the peace of mind it affords.

A surveyor can also tell you whether you should have a smoke test, which is primarily to ensure that the storm water run-off isn't illegally connected to the sewer. If illegal connections have been made they can be expensive to rectify, so it should be clarified before agreeing the purchase price and exchanging contracts. If the storm water run-off is illegal, obtain an estimate of the cost of rectifying it and negotiate a price reduction with the vendor. A smoke test can be arranged before or after the exchange of contracts, but is best done before exchange or during the cooling-off period following exchange (if applicable), so that any defects are identified before making the final commitment to buy. Note, however, that unless the contract has a specific provision that the sale is conditional on a clear smoke test, any defects disclosed by the test would not entitle you to withdraw.

Sometimes an inspection or survey shows that a property is in poor condition, or that there are structural faults or other problems such as dry rot, woodworm or rising damp. If the poor condition isn't already reflected in the purchase price, you should be able to negotiate a reduction to cover the cost of repairs or improvements. Note, however, that your lender may not provide a mortgage on a property in a bad condition. If your new home turns out to have damp, dry rot or to be infested with termites which your surveyor has failed to discover, you can usually successfully sue him for damages (although it's always advisable to give a surveyor written instructions in respect to these and other possible problem areas).

ESTATE AGENTS

Most property in Australia is bought and sold through estate agents who sell property on commission for owners. When buying property in Australia, always use a licensed agent. The Real Estate and Business Agents Act imposes obligations and requirements on licensed agents, which protect both buyers and sellers by creating a source of legal redress in the event of error, negligence, misrepresentation or loss. However, the act doesn't apply to private sales where no agent is involved. The act protects deposits paid by purchasers and prevents conduct which could be misleading or prejudicial to buyers, and is backed by disciplinary procedures and a Fidelity Guarantee Fund.

Each state has its own real estate organisation, e.g. the Real Estate Institute of New South Wales, and you should check that an agent is a member. Members must adhere to a code of ethics (of which you can request a copy) and must have mandatory professional indemnity insurance cover. There's a multi-listing service in all states where your home is advertised in real estate offices throughout the state, which costs vendors nothing until their home is sold. However, some agents may only show you, or at least try to push, properties for which they have an exclusive listing (when they don't need to share the commission with anyone else).

Estate agents usually act for the seller and it's their job to obtain the highest price they can for a property, so don't expect impartial advice if you're a buyer. If they offer to make a considerable reduction on the advertised price, it probably means that it's overpriced and has been on their books for a long time. An estate agent will usually try to get you to view as many properties as possible (irrespective of whether they fit your requirements or price range), as this shows sellers that he's doing a good job. You should try to sort out the possibles from the improbables before making any appointments to view, and if you're shown properties that don't meet your specifications, tell the agent immediately. You can also help the agent narrow the field by telling him exactly what's wrong with the properties you reject.

Don't see too many properties in one day, however anxious you are to find somewhere, as it's easy to become confused as to the merits of each property. Many homes for sale hold an 'open house' at weekends (possibly with a 'home open' sign outside), although the total inspection period may be as little as one hour. Otherwise it's essential to make an appointment with an owner or agent to inspect a property. Note that it's possible to inspect Australian properties via the internet from anywhere in the world. Agents, builders and developers are increasingly using computers to find, buy, design, build, furnish and decorate homes to buyers' tastes.

Buying at Auction: An alternative to buying from an agent is to buy a property at an auction, although this method generally applies to properties at the upper end of the market. This method of selling has become increasingly popular in the last few years, as sellers can sell quickly and buyers can usually save money (it's most common in Melbourne and Sydney). Note, however, that it's absolutely vital to do your homework before buying at auction, particularly regarding the market value of properties. Many agents will quote a price 10 or 20 per cent below a property's expected sale price in order to attract more interest at auctions. Note that in a sellers' market, many properties sell at auction for up to $50,000 to $100,000 above the reserve price. Property auctions are advertised in local newspapers and may be held on site.

You can engage a buyer's representative to find a house, bid for it at auction and negotiate the sale. Agents may charge from as little as a few hundred dollars to bid at an auction or up to 1 to 3 per cent of the price if they conduct a search and secure a property. However this can save you a lot of time, trouble and money. It's advisable not to bid yourself unless you know the ropes and are confident of what you're doing. It's necessary to have your finances in place in advance when buying at auction, as you will be required to pay the deposit on the spot (usually 10 per cent) and close within a reasonable period. Note that cooling-off rights (see page 126) don't apply when buying at auction.

Publications: Many estate agents produce free newspapers and magazines containing details of both old and new houses, and colour prospectuses for new property developments. There are a number of free real estate magazines in Australia including *The Homebuyer* (Published by the Real Estate Institute of Western Australia), *Multilist Realtor* (the official magazine of the Estate Agents Co-operative Ltd., 274 Miller Road, Villawood, NSW 2163, tel. (02) 9724 6999) and the *Owners' Own Real Estate Catalogue* in which properties are advertised directly by owners.

SELLING PROPERTY

Most property sold in Australia is sold through estate agents (see above), although an increasing number of people sell their homes at auctions and it's also possible to sell your own home. Before offering your home for sale you should consider smartening it up by giving it a fresh coat of paint (inside and outside, as necessary); repairing or replacing anything that's damaged; cleaning the carpets, curtains, tiles, timber floors, windows, porcelain, (etc.); tidying the garden; and uncluttering the rooms. Note, however, that doing expensive renovations such as adding a new bedroom or putting in a swimming pool doesn't usually help, and you could easily end up losing money.

You should take particular care when selecting an agent as they vary considerably in their professionalism, expertise and experience (the best way to select one is by posing as a buyer). It's often advisable to use the same agent through which you purchased a property (if applicable) as he will already be familiar with it. The commission charged by agents varies and depends on whether you have an exclusive authority or a multiple listing (see below). You may be able to negotiate a lower rate of commission when the market is flat.

Before an agent can offer a home for sale he must obtain written authority from the owner. This can take a number of forms including an *open listing* where any agent can sell the property and you can also sell it yourself; a *multiple or conjunction listing* where the property is listed with agents throughout Australia and the listing agent shares the commission with the agent who finds the buyer; and an *exclusive authority*, where a single agent has the authority to sell a property. An authority usually runs for three months, but can be for any period. Note that with an *exclusive authority*, you must still pay a commission to the agent even if you find your own buyer (during the period of the authority).

It's important to bear in mind that, like everything, property has a market price and the best way of ensuring a quick sale is to ask a realistic price. However, don't tell the agent your lowest price, as he may pass it on to a buyer in the hope of making a quick sale. Note that some agents discourage higher offers or keep the price low by telling buyers how much to offer. Both are illegal as agents are required by law to obtain the best deal they can for the seller. Check the contract and make sure that you understand what you're signing. It may be possible to reduce your estate agent fees through a flat fee deal, where you agree to pay a flat fee for a standard estate agency package. The fee is usually non-returnable and you must pay it regardless of whether the agent sells your property.

Vendor Survey: One way to lure buyers is to have a structural survey (see page 128) completed prior to putting a property on the market. This can usually be charged to the buyer (with his agreement) and paid at the exchange of contracts. This is particularly advisable when selling an 'old' property, when buyers may be deterred by the thought of finding hidden defects later. It isn't just attractive to buyers but reduces time and costs for both parties. Make sure that your surveyor will allow prospective buyers to question him, otherwise they may suspect that you have a 'pet' surveyor who has produced a doctored report (buyers are a suspicious lot).

Selling Your Own Home: One alternative to using an estate agent is to sell your own home, or at least try. The first thing you will need to do is to value your home, which most agents will do free of charge, otherwise you will need to pay a surveyor. You can put a big 'for sale' sign in your garden like that of estate agents with your telephone number. Take care to make a professional looking signboard, as success can save you thousands of dollars. Do some market research into the best newspapers for your area and type of property, and place an advertisement in those that look most promising. You can have an advertising leaflet printed extolling the virtues of your property, which you could drop in local letter boxes or have distributed with a local free newspaper (most people buy a new home within the immediate vicinity of their present homes). You could also couple this with a finder's fee for anyone who finds you a buyer. Lastly, don't omit to advertise your home around local companies, schools and other establishments, particularly if they have a lot of itinerant employees. Set yourself a realistic time limit to sell your home, after which (if you have no success) you can engage an estate agent. The more expensive your property, the more it will pay you to sell it yourself.

Selling at Auction: If you own an unusual property or a home in an area that's much in demand, you could try selling it at auction, which may help increase the price (particularly when prices are rising and there's a dearth of properties for sale). Note, however, that it may be no cheaper to sell at auction than through an agent after the auctioneer's fees have been taken into account. Always check an auctioneer's track record, as some sell a lot more properties than others. See also page 130.

Swapping Your House: An alternative to selling is to swap your house with someone else. If you decide to swap with a more expensive property than your present home, you pay the difference. House swaps often involve more than two houses. Before going through with a swap, it's important to have a structural survey carried out on your prospective new home. If you're buying a new property from a builder or developer, he may offer to purchase your house.

Gazundering: Sellers should beware of the 'gazunderer', i.e. a buyer who agrees a price and then starts to complain in order to drive the price down when the sale is going through and other buyers have evaporated (usually after you have found a new house and are desperate for the sale to go through). Some unscrupulous buyers even go so far as to arbitrarily reduce the price by 10 to 15 per cent in the final contract without even telling the seller, in the expectation that the seller will be forced to go through with the sale. If this happens to you and you feel compelled to complete the sale, the very least you should do is strip the house and the gardens bare of anything that isn't specifically included in the sale, such as fixtures and fittings, carpets, plants, shrubs and even the turf from the lawns!

See also **Buying Property** on page 116, **Estate Agents** on page 129 and **Capital Gains Tax** on page 355.

RENTED ACCOMMODATION

Renting rather than buying a home is usually the best choice for anyone who's staying in Australia for a few years or less, when buying isn't usually practical, and for those who don't want the expense and restrictions involved in buying and owning a home. If you're a migrant, it's also advisable to rent for a period before buying, particularly if you're unsure of where you will live or work. There's also a likelihood that you will change jobs or states within your first few years in Australia (a common occurrence), or even decide to return home (many migrants decide Australia isn't for them and return home within a few years). Renting also allows you to become familiar with the weather, the people and the local neighbourhood, before deciding whether you want to live there permanently.

There's isn't a strong rental market in Australia (although it's becoming more popular in the major cities), where most people own their own homes and renters are often made to feel like second-class citizens. Rented accommodation is scarce in most major cities, particularly the inner suburbs of Sydney and Melbourne, where houses are scarce and you may have to settle for an apartment or house in an unpopular outer suburb. Furnished accommodation is more expensive than unfurnished and is even more difficult to find, which can be a problem if you're waiting for your furniture to arrive from overseas. Short term holiday rentals (see page 368) can usually be arranged before arrival, although it isn't advisable to rent a property long-term sight unseen. If you're planning to rent for more than a few weeks, it's wise to investigate the rental market in your chosen area before arriving in Australia, e.g. by studying the advertisements in Australian newspapers, which can be done via the internet, and contacting agents. Note that some landlords don't allow pets or smokers, so check what restrictions apply in advance.

Finding a Rental Property

Your success or failure in finding a suitable rental property depends on many factors, not least the type of property you're looking for (a one-bedroom apartment is easier to find than a four-bedroom detached house), how much you want to pay and the area where you wish to live. Good rental accommodation is in short supply in major cities, particularly Sydney and Melbourne, with the possible exception of luxury homes with astronomical rents. There are often 20 to 30 applicants for each vacant property in popular suburbs, particularly homes with three or more bedrooms, and you may have to take what you can get. Most people settle for something in the outer suburbs and commute to work. Note, however, that if you need to travel into a city centre (particularly Sydney) each day, you should be prepared to spend at least an hour or longer travelling each way from the outer suburbs. There are a number of ways to find a rental property, including the following:

- Ask your friends, relatives and acquaintances to help spread the word, particularly if you're looking in the area where you already live. A lot of rental properties are found by word of mouth, particularly in Sydney and Melbourne, where it's almost impossible to find somewhere with a reasonable rent unless you have connections (many rental properties change tenants without coming onto the market).

- Check the advertisements in local newspapers and magazines (see below). The best days for advertisements are Saturdays.

- Visit real estate and letting agents. All cities and large towns have estate agents who also act as letting agents for owners (look under *Real Estate Agents* in the yellow pages). Obtain rental lists from agents during the week or have them faxed to you at your place of work.

- Look for advertisements in shop windows and on notice boards in shopping centres, supermarkets, universities and colleges, and company offices.

- Check newsletters published by churches, clubs and expatriate organisations, and their notice boards.

To find accommodation through advertisements in local newspapers you must usually be quick off the mark, particularly in the cities. Buy the newspapers as soon as they are published, if possible the night before, and start phoning 'at the crack of dawn' (even then you're likely to find a queue when you arrive to view a property in Sydney or Melbourne). You must be available to inspect properties immediately or at any time. Finding a property to rent in Sydney is similar to the situation in London and New York, where the best properties are usually found through personal contacts. Some people will go to any length to rent a property including offering to pay above the asking price (bidding wars sometimes break out), pay six months' rent in advance and sign a contract for two or three years.

Most properties in Australian cities are let through agents, whose main task is to vet prospective tenants. Always dress smartly when visiting agents in order to create a good impression. When registering with an agent, you will need two forms of identification (e.g. drivers's licence and passport), written references from your employer and/or previous landlord, and character references. Agents usually contact all referees and may ask why you left your previous accommodation. If you have a pet, you may need a reference from your previous landlord stating that it was clean and well-behaved. Note that animals aren't usually permitted in rental apartments. You will need to complete a registration form and should ensure that it's complete and correct in every detail, otherwise you will jeopardise your chances. Young people, students, the unemployed and single parents have a tough time finding anywhere at an affordable rent, and if you're on a low income or are unemployed you will need to prove how you can pay the rent. If you're acceptable, you may be given the keys to view a property in return for a $50 deposit and proof of identity (e.g. your driver's licence).

Rental Costs

Rental costs vary considerably depending on the size (number of bedrooms) and quality of a property, its age and the facilities provided. Not least, rents depend on the region, city and neighbourhood. Rents are also lower in rural (country) than urban (city) areas.

As a general rule, the further a property is from a large city or town, public transport or other facilities, the cheaper it will be (obvious really, isn't it?). The average renter spends around $150 a week on housing, although in recent years rents have increased at a much faster rate than house prices in most major cities. A typical three bedroom house will cost you between around $150 and $175 a week in most cities with the exception of Sydney, where you will pay over $300 a week. Sydney rents are around twice as high as in other cities and are expected to rise even higher in the run up to the Olympic Games in the year 2000 (when rents for luxury homes are expected to reach up to $17,500 a week!). Rents may also increase considerably in Sydney in 1998, as owners are hit by higher land tax. Approximate weekly rents for unfurnished properties are shown below:

Type of Property	Weekly Rent ($)
studio/bedsit	75-100
1 bedroom apartment	100-150
2 bedroom apartment	125-200
3 bedroom apartment	150-300
2 bedroom house	125-250
3 bedroom house	150-350
4 bedroom house	200-500 +++

The lower rents quoted above apply to modest to average homes in the less expensive outer suburbs of cities such as Adelaide and Perth. The upper bracket applies to outer suburbs in more expensive cities such as Sydney, Melbourne, Brisbane and Darwin. They don't include properties located in the central business district (CBD) of major cities or in exclusive residential areas, for which the sky's the limit. It may be possible to find cheaper, older apartments and houses for rent, but they are rare, generally small and don't contain the standard 'fixtures and fittings' of a modern home.

Most rented property is let through letting agencies or estate agents, who usually charge tenants a fee of two weeks' rent for a one-year lease and one week's rent for a six-month lease, which are legal maximums. Usually you're expected to pay one month's rent in advance, depending on the type of property and the rental agreement, plus a bond (see below) which is held against damages. Tenants must also pay a fee for the lease document, plus a deposit for electricity and gas. Beware of hidden extras such as a fee for connecting the gas, electricity or telephone (or a refundable deposit).

Bond: When renting property in Australia, a bond (deposit) equal to four (usual) to eight weeks' rent must be paid in advance. The bond is usually higher for furnished than unfurnished properties and can be as much as six months' rent for a luxury furnished property, e.g. the bond is unlimited in NSW on fully furnished properties costing over $250 a week. It's lodged with the Rental Bond Board together with a copy of the inspection (condition) report which details the condition of the home plus an inventory. The inspection and inventory must usually be done within seven days of taking possession and tenants receive a copy which is signed by both the tenant and the agent. The property is re-inspected when you leave and, if necessary, deductions are made for cleaning and repairs, although there's no deduction for ordinary wear and tear. Disputes regarding bond money are handled by the appropriate tribunal.

It's advisable to pay your rent by cheque or standing order, for which you should (by law) receive a receipt from your landlord. Rents are controlled in some states, although it doesn't usually extend to new properties or tenancies after a certain date. Your contract may include details of when your rent will be reviewed or increased, if applicable (the rent for a fixed-term tenancy can be increased only when provision for an increase is included in the lease contract). You must be given notice in writing of any rent increases and a rent tribunal can review excessive rent increases and the existing rent if services are reduced.

Rental Contracts

When you find a suitable house or apartment to rent, you should insist on a written contract with the owner or agent, which is called a tenancy agreement. In some states such as NSW and Victoria, a standard agreement form must be used by law and in others there are usually minimum conditions which cannot be reduced by landlords. The Agreement for Tenancy states the responsibilities of both parties and provides a fair balance between the landlord and tenant, although you should read it carefully before signing it. Apart from self-catering holiday accommodation (see page 368), renting a house or apartment usually requires a commitment of at least six months and possibly longer. During the recession in the early '90s it was common to have five or even ten-year contracts with a fixed rent. However, in recent years the most common rental contract has been a one or two-year lease with an option to renew.

The owner is responsible for property rates (property taxes) and unit service charges, and the tenant for utility costs, unless otherwise agreed. Tenants must take good care of a property, although the landlord is required to maintain the property in good and habitable condition, and ensure that basic services such as water and sewerage are in order. If a landlord refuses to carry out urgent and necessary repairs within a reasonable period of time, you can arrange to have them done and send him the bill, although you mustn't deduct the cost from the rent. If you rent a house, garden and swimming pool, maintenance costs may be included in the rent.

If you wish to vacate a property before your lease expires, you're liable to pay the rent up to the end of your lease period, although you may be able to find someone to take over the lease and repay your bond (check whether this is possible with your agent or landlord). If you give the landlord adequate notice of termination (usually 21 days), he should try to minimise his loss by advertising and re-letting the property. If you have a verbal contract (termed a periodic tenancy) on a weekly or monthly basis, then a week's or a month's notice is sufficient. If you're a tenant with a verbal or written agreement, you cannot be evicted or be forced to leave unless your landlord obtains an eviction order. In order to be evicted you must be in breach of your lease, e.g. by failing to pay the rent, damaging the property, sub-letting or renovating without permission, or refusing the landlord entry. The landlord may also repossess a property for his own use or to sell with vacant possession. A landlord cannot evict you illegally by removing your belongings and changing the locks or forcing you to leave by cutting off services. At the end of a fixed-term residential tenancy agreement, the landlord can terminate the agreement by giving 60 days notice before the end of the agreement. He isn't required to have a valid reason, although there may be grounds for the tenant to appeal to the local Residential Tenancy Tribunal, e.g. age, poor health or lack of alternative accommodation.

A renting guide is available from real estate agents explaining the rights and responsibilities of tenants and landlords. Some people (e.g. Asians, coloureds and students) may encounter discrimination, although it's illegal under the Federal Discrimination Act. Most states have a Residential Tenancy Tribunal to investigate complaints by landlords and tenants, such as disputes over bonds, excessive rents, repairs and evictions. You can also obtain advice at a tenants' advice centre, community legal centre, consumer affairs office, citizens advice bureau or the legal aid commission. Most large cities also have a tenants' union hotline. The local Department of Fair Trading in many states publishes a *Renting Guide* or *Tenants' Rights Manual*.

Single Accommodation

Finding accommodation that doesn't break the bank is a huge problem for young single people and students (and anyone not earning a fortune). For many the solution is a bedsit, lodgings or sharing accommodation with others. If you're seeking inexpensive accommodation, you may find it more difficult in cities when the new term starts and students are looking for accommodation. Single accommodation covers a broad spectrum, including hostels, guest houses, lodgings, bed & breakfast and inexpensive hotels, although these usually provide temporary accommodation only. Don't expect any luxuries in inexpensive single accommodation, as the standard is generally poor and is usually at its worst in areas with high demand. You must be over 18 to hold a tenancy agreement and young people usually find it harder to find a rental property than more mature people, due to the usual arguments that the young are unreliable, noisy, poor, itinerant and untidy (etc.).

There's a huge (largely unfilled) demand for student accommodation (often from overseas students) in the major cities, particularly in Sydney and Melbourne. In some cities, students have saturated the rental market and foreign students who are prepared to pay more for accommodation than Australian students have helped drive up rents and have created problems for others (although Asian students were hard hit by the currency crisis in 1997).

Bedsits: If you prefer to live on your own but don't want to pay a lot of rent (who does?), the solution may be a bedsit or studio apartment. A bedsit usually consists of a furnished room in an old house, where you live, eat, sleep and sometimes cook. If separate cooking facilities are provided, you must usually share them with someone else (or a number of people). You must also usually share a bathroom and toilet, provide your own linen (sheets, blankets and towels), and do your own laundry and cleaning. Bedsits offer plenty of privacy but can be lonely and depressing. A single bedsit costs from around $75 a week for singles and from $100 a week for doubles. Slightly up market from a bedsit is a flatlet or studio flat, which may have its own bath or shower and toilet, and sometimes a separate kitchen or kitchenette (a tiny kitchen). The rent for a studio apartment is around 50 per cent more than for a bedsit.

Lodgings: Another possibility is to find lodgings in a private home, which is becoming increasingly common as many people have been forced to take in lodgers to pay their mortgages. This is similar to bed and breakfast accommodation (see page 367), except that you're usually treated as a member of the family and your rent normally includes half-board (breakfast and an evening meal). In lodgings you have less freedom than a bedsit and are required to eat at fixed times, but will at least have some company. Lodgings are often arranged by schools and colleges for foreign students. A boarding house is similar to lodgings, where the owner takes in a number of lodgers and may provide half-board or cooking facilities. The rent is around the same as for bedsits. Note that a border, paying guest or lodger is termed a 'licensee' in law and has fewer rights than a tenant, although it may be difficult to make a distinction. This applies to anyone lodging with the owner and sharing the bathroom and kitchen. If you're a 'licensee', your landlord cannot increase your rent without your consent, although he can ask you to leave at any time (but must give you adequate time to pack and remove your belongings).

Sharing accommodation is another answer to high rents, particularly in major towns and cities, and is popular among students and the young. Sharing usually involves sharing the kitchen, bathroom, living room and dining room, and may also include sharing a bedroom. Sharing usually means sharing all bills (in addition to the rent) including electricity, gas and telephone, and may also include the sharing of food bills and cooking. Some landlords may include electricity, gas and water in the rent. The cleaning and the general upkeep of the house or apartment is also usually shared. As always when living with others, there are advantages and disadvantages of shared accommodation, and its success depends on the participants' ability to live and work together. If you rent a property with the intention of sharing, make sure that it's permitted in your contract. The law regarding flatsharing is complicated and it's simpler when one person is the tenant and sub-lets to the others, which must be permitted by the tenant's agreement. It's possible for all sharers to be joint tenants with one tenancy agreement, or individual tenants with individual tenancy agreements. Whatever the agreement, you should have one rent book only and pay the rent in a lump sum. It's usually the occupants' responsibility to replace flatmates who leave during the tenancy. If you're seeking long-term accommodation, check the duration of the lease.

The cost of sharing a furnished apartment varies considerably depending on the size, location and amenities. A rough guide is from around $75 (single) to $100 (double) a week with your own bedroom, or up to $150 or $200 with your own bathroom. Note that often you will be sharing with the owners, which can sometimes be a bit inhibiting, as many couples buy a three-bedroom house and let one or two bedrooms to help pay the mortgage. Flatsharing is particularly common in major cities, where many newspapers and magazines contain advertisements for flatsharers, e.g. the *Sydney Morning Herald* and the *Melbourne Age*. Note, however, that 'broad-minded girl/guy' is usually code for 'we are lesbian or homosexual'. There are also agents in major cities where you pay a $100 to $150 registration fee and sharers are matched to others with similar interests.

GARAGE OR PARKING SPACE

A garage or parking space may not be provided when you rent or buy an apartment, although most modern houses have a single or double garage and sometimes room for further parking in the driveway. New houses and blocks of apartments are likely to have adequate parking for both residents and visitors. Note that when buying a property, the cost will almost always include the garage or garage space if a property has one, i.e. it won't be sold separately as in some other countries. If you live in a town or city it's often difficult to find an apartment or house with a garage or parking space, although it may be possible to rent a parking space in a private car park or a lock-up garage locally. A garage is useful, particularly in areas with a high incidence of car theft (anywhere in most cities).

Free on-street parking is often difficult or impossible to find in cities and large towns, although you may be able to obtain a resident's parking permit for on-street parking. In general, off-street parking in Australia is in short supply, particularly in cities and older residential areas, where houses were built without garages or off-street parking areas.

MOVING HOUSE

Shipping your belongings to Australia takes just a few weeks from Europe or North America, although it can take two to three months from the time your belongings are collected and arrive at your new home in Australia. Unless you plan well in advance, you will almost certainly arrive in Australia before your belongings. Obtain at least three written quotes before choosing a shipper and check what the extra cost will be if you need to increase the load later, as it isn't unknown for original estimates to spiral wildly. Note that some companies routinely increase the price after everything has been packed, ostensibly because more was included than was included in the estimate. A removal company (called a removalist in Australia) will usually send a representative to carry out a detailed inspection and provide an estimate. There are numerous advertisements from shipping companies in newspapers published specifically for migrants such as *Australian News* and *Australian Outlook* in the UK (see **Appendix A**).

If possible always use an international removal company that's a member of an international association such as the International Federation of Furniture Removers (FIDI), the Overseas Moving Network International (OMNI) or the Association of International Removers Ltd. (AIR). Members usually subscribe to a payment guarantee bonding scheme providing a guarantee. If a member company fails to fulfill its commitments to a customer, the removal will be completed at the agreed cost by another company or you will receive a full refund. Removal companies will also pack your belongings and provide packing cases and special containers, although this is naturally more expensive than doing it yourself (ask how they pack fragile and valuable items). Check whether the cost of packing cases, materials and insurance are included in a quote.

You can send your effects by full container load (FCL) or part load (groupage), which is cheaper but takes longer to be delivered. FCL shipments are loaded into an individual container holding around 28 cubic metres (1,000 cubic feet). A shipment of around 800 cubic feet (22.6m3) is cheaper to send as groupage. Obtain a separate quotation for any excess items which won't fit into the container. If the destination in Australia isn't within 30 miles of the port of arrival you may need to pay an extra charge for door to door delivery. There may also be extra charges in Australia such as storage, quarantine (if necessary) and demurrage. Ask about possible extra charges in advance. Note that most international removers expect to be paid before your household goods are shipped, although some allow you to pay when you take delivery in Australia. The cost of moving your house contents from your previous country of residence to Australia may be paid for by your Australian employer.

Before shipping any household articles to Australia, check whether they are worth taking, e.g. many people take a lot of furniture and electrical apparatus which are incompatible (e.g. TVs), unsuitable or simply aren't needed in their new home. It isn't worthwhile taking TVs (see page 178), refrigerators (which are usually too small), cookers (provided) and wardrobes (which are built-in in most homes). If you're moving from a country with a cold climate, bear in mind that furniture and furnishings must be suitable for a hot climate (unless you're heading for Tasmania). You should carefully consider the cost of packing and shipping large items to Australia, as it may be cheaper to sell them and buy new items after you arrive. Generally you should take possessions with you if it's cheaper than buying them in Australia, taking into account the cost of shipping large items. Good quality furniture and antiques are worth taking, as are small electrical appliance if the voltage is the same as Australia (240v).

If you pack your belongings yourself, you will need to provide an inventory for Australian customs. If you do your own packing don't use straw but wood wool or paper and don't include any prohibited or illegal items (see page 107), as customs' and quarantine checks can be rigorous and penalties severe. Most shippers provide special cartons and packing materials. On the day of the move, make sure there's room for the removal van or truck to park, if necessary by asking the police to cordon off an area outside your home. Give the shipping company a telephone number and an address in

Australia through which you can be contacted and try to get a relative or friend to handle any problems in the country from which your belongings are being shipped.

Be sure to fully insure your household contents during removal with a well established insurance company (you aren't required to use the one recommended by the removal company, but it may be advisable to avoid a dispute between the remover and insurer). You should have an all risks marine insurance policy from domicile to domicile, which is underwritten by an established and solid insurance company. It's advisable to make a photographic or video record of any valuables for insurance purposes. If you need to make a claim, be sure to read the small print, as all companies require you to make claims within a limited period. Send a claim by registered mail. **If you need to put your household effects into storage, it's imperative to have them fully insured as warehouses have been known to burn down.** Don't forget to insure your home contents from the day you move in (see page 312).

Although most people wouldn't consider doing their own house move, if you have only personal effects to transport locally within Australia you can hire a van by the hour, half-day, or day (small local rental companies are cheapest). Many removal companies sell packing boxes in numerous sizes and hire or sell removal equipment (trolleys, straps, etc.) for those who feel up to doing their own house move. See also the checklists contained in **Chapter 20**.

INVENTORY

When moving into a property you have purchased, you should check that the previous owners haven't absconded with anything that was included in the purchase as part of the fixtures and fittings or anything which you specifically paid for, e.g. carpets, light fittings, curtains, fitted cupboards, kitchen appliances or doors. One of the most important tasks on moving into a rented house or apartment is to complete an inventory of the contents and an inspection report on its condition. This includes the condition of fixtures and fittings, the state of furniture and carpets (if furnished), the cleanliness and state of the decoration, and anything missing or in need of repair. A rental property should be spotless when you move in, as this is what your landlord will expect when you move out.

An inventory is provided by your landlord or a letting agent which may include every single item in a furnished property (down to the number of teaspoons). The inspection and inventory must usually be done within seven days of taking possession and you will receive a copy which is signed by both you and the agent or landlord. A copy is also lodged with the Rental Bond Board (see page 135) and the property is re-inspected when you leave and, if necessary, deductions are made from the bond for cleaning and repairs, although there's no deduction for ordinary wear and tear.

Note the reading on your meters (electricity, gas, water) and check that you aren't overcharged on your first bill. The meters should be read by the relevant authorities before you move in, which you may need to organise yourself.

HOME SECURITY

House-breaking and burglary are endemic in Australia's major cities, where many homes are broken into a number of times a year, often within a short space of time. If your home is broken into, it's imperative to protect your property from further thefts. When moving into a new home, it's advisable to replace the locks (or barrels) and fit high security locks, as you have no idea how many keys are in circulation for the existing locks. Note that if you change the locks in a rented property, you may need to obtain approval from your landlord or agent and must also give him a copy of all keys. In addition to new locks, you may wish to install an alarm, window locks, window shutters, window grilles, security lights and other deterrents. According to crime statistics, entry in around 40 per cent of home burglaries is via an unlocked door or window, so always ensure that they are locked, even when vacating your home for a short period (doors should be locked even when your home is occupied). Don't let anyone into your home unless you're sure who they are, particularly at night. External doors can be fitted with a spy-hole, so that you can check a visitor's identity before opening the door. **Remember, prevention is better than cure, as people who are burgled rarely recover their property.**

A good alarm system is probably the best way to frighten away burglars or housebreakers and it may also reduce your home contents insurance (see page 312). Some security companies provide home security systems connected to a Central Monitoring Station (CMS). When a sensor (e.g. smoke or forced entry) detects an emergency or a panic button is pushed, a signal is sent automatically to the CMS which is manned 24-hours a day. Always choose a system that's tailored to suit your house and requirements.

Some properties are fitted with special high security door locks which are individually numbered and for which extra keys cannot be cut at a local store. Make sure you have full details from the previous owner or your landlord so that you can get additional keys cut or change the lock barrels. No matter how good your door and window locks, a thief can usually break in if he's determined enough, often by simply breaking a window (although you can fit steel security blinds) or if he's really determined, by punching a hole in a wall or the roof in remote areas. Try to deter thieves by ensuring your house is always well lit, particularly when nobody is at home, when it's also advisable to leave a TV or radio on (a timer switch can be used to randomly switch on and off radios, TVs and lights). **It's always advisable to give the impression that a house is occupied, particularly when it isn't!** Some people keep a large dog (a miniature poodle isn't much good as a deterrent) to guard their homes when they're out. The Australian Consumers Association (see page 434) publish an excellent book entitled *Safe and Secure - A Guide to Household and Car Security* by Richard Upton.

Smoke Alarms: An important aspect of home security is making sure that you have early warning of a fire, which is done by installing smoke detectors. A battery-operated smoke detector costs from around $10 and they may be fitted as standard equipment in new houses. One should be fitted on each floor, but not in kitchens or bathrooms. Only a small percentage of Australian homes are fitted with smoke detectors, although it has been estimated that the death toll from fires could be reduced by half (plus a drastic reduction in the number of injuries) if all homes had them. Smoke alarms should be tested weekly to ensure that the batteries aren't exhausted. You can also install a gas detector which activates an alarm when a gas leak is detected.

UTILITIES

Utilities is the collective name given to electricity, gas and water companies. Electricity and gas are used for cooking and heating in cities and towns throughout Australia, and it's common for homes to have both electricity and gas. Each state and territory has its own Energy Commission for electricity and gas, which have traditionally been owned and administered by local governments. However, in recent years Victoria has deregulated and privatised its electricity industry (total deregulation of retail electricity prices is scheduled for the year 2000) and NSW and South Australia have plans to follow suit. Privatisation has enabled business users to shop around for electricity (and save $millions a year), even from distributors in neighbouring states connected to the same grid system (Tasmania, Western Australia and the Northern Territory aren't linked in a grid with the rest of the country or neighbouring states). There are a number of electricity generating and distribution companies in most states. Note that Australia has a non-nuclear policy and has no nuclear power stations (despite being a major producer of uranium).

Electricity

The electricity supply in Australia is 240/250 volts AC, with a frequency of 50 hertz (cycles). If you move into a new home in Australia, the electricity supply may have been turned off by the local electricity company. To have the electricity reconnected and the meter read, for which you should allow at least two days, you must contact your local electricity company and complete a registration form. There's usually a charge for connection and a security deposit, e.g. around $100. You must contact your electricity company to get a final reading when you vacate your home. Power cuts are rare in most parts of Australia, although some areas experience an above average number a year.

Power Rating: Electrical equipment rated at 110 volts AC (for example, from the USA) requires a converter or a step-down transformer to convert it to 240 volts AC, although some electrical appliances (e.g. electric razors and hair dryers) are fitted with a 110/240 volt switch. Check for the switch, which may be located inside the casing, and make sure it's switched to 240 volts *before* connecting it to the power supply. Converters can be used for heating appliances but transformers, which are available from most electrical retailers, are required for motorised appliances (they can also be purchased secondhand). Total the wattage of the devices you intend to connect to a transformer and make sure its power rating *exceeds* this sum.

Generally all small, high-wattage, electrical appliances, such as kettles, toasters, heaters and irons, need large transformers. Motors in large appliances such as cookers, refrigerators, washing machines, driers and dishwashers, will need replacing or fitting with a large transformer. In most cases it's simpler to buy new appliances in Australia, which are of good quality and reasonably priced, and sell them when you leave if you don't want to take them with you. Note also that the dimensions of Australian cookers, microwave ovens, refrigerators, washing machines, driers and dishwashers, differ from those in some other countries. All electrical goods sold in Australia must conform to Australian safety standards. If you wish to buy electrical appliances, such as a cooker or refrigerator, you should shop around as prices vary considerably (choose those that have a high energy efficiency rating, which are cheaper to run). Refrigerators/freezers in Australia are normally 'tropicised' or fan assisted to cope with the high average temperatures, which is why it isn't usually worthwhile bringing one with you.

Frequency Rating: A problem with some electrical equipment is the frequency rating, which in some countries, e.g. the USA, is designed to run at 60 Hertz and not Australia's 50 Hertz. Electrical equipment *without* a motor is generally unaffected by the drop in frequency to 50 Hz (except TVs, see page 178). Equipment with a motor may run okay with a 20 per cent drop in speed, however, automatic washing machines, cookers, electric clocks, record players and tape recorders are unusable in Australia, if they aren't designed for 50 cycle operation. To find out, look at the label on the back of the equipment. If it says 50/60 Hertz, it should be okay. If it says 60 Hz, you might try it anyway, **but first ensure the voltage is correct as outlined above.** If the equipment runs too slowly, seek advice from the manufacturer or the retailer. For example, you may be able to obtain a special pulley for a tape deck or turntable to compensate for the drop in speed. Bear in mind that the transformers and motors of electrical devices designed to run at 60 Hz will run hotter at 50 Hz, so make sure that equipment has sufficient space around it for cooling.

Fuses: Most apartments and all houses have their own fuse boxes, which are usually of the circuit breaker type in modern homes. When a circuit is overloaded the circuit breaker trips to the OFF position. When replacing or repairing fuses of any kind, if the same fuse continues to blow, contact an electrician and **never attempt to fit a fuse of a higher rating than specified, even as a temporary measure.** When replacing fuses, don't rely on the blown fuse as a guide, as it may have been wrong. If you use an electric lawn-mower or power tools outside your home or in your garage, you should have a Residual Current Device (RCD) installed. This can detect current changes of as little as a thousandth of an amp and in the event of a fault (or the cable being cut), will switch off the power in around 0.04 seconds.

Plugs: Unless you have come from New Zealand, all your plugs will require changing, or a lot of expensive adapters will be required. Australian (and New Zealand) plugs have three pins: two diagonally slanting flat pins above one straight (earth) pin, which are unique. Plugs aren't fused. Some electrical appliances are earthed and have a three-core flex — you must *never* use a two-pin plug with a three-core flex. **Always make sure that a plug is correctly and securely wired as bad wiring can prove fatal.** Note that for maximum safety, electrical appliances should be turned off at the main wall point when not in use.

Bulbs: Electric light bulbs (called globes in Australia) are of the Edison type with a bayonet not a screw fitting. To insert a bulb you push it in and turn it clockwise around 5mm. Low-energy light bulbs are also available and are more expensive than ordinary bulbs, although they save money by their longer life and reduced energy consumption. Bulbs for non-standard electrical appliances (i.e. appliances not made for the Australian market) such as refrigerators, lamps and sewing machines, may not be available in Australia (so bring extras with you). Plug adaptors for imported lamps and other electrical items can be difficult to find in Australia, so it's advisable to bring a number of adapters and extension cords with you, which can be fitted with Australian plugs.

Safety: Only a qualified electrician should install electrical wiring and fittings, particularly in connection with fuse boxes. Always ask for a quotation for any work in advance and check the identity of anyone claiming to be an electricity company employee (or any kind of 'serviceman') by asking to see an identity card and checking with his office. Special controls can be fitted to many appliances to make their use easier for the disabled and the blind or partially sighted (e.g. studded or braille controls).

Cost & Bills: Electricity charges vary considerably depending on the state and local competition, e.g. Energy Australia (Sydney) charge 10.15¢ per kilowatt hour (kWh), plus a standard service charge (e.g. $15 to $20 a quarter). Some companies offer a range of tariffs which may include peak, off-peak and weekend rates (some tariffs require a special meter to be installed). The biggest savings can be made when using a night rate with electric storage water heaters. Many metropolitan households use gas for cooking and heating and some 5 per cent (300,000) of Australian homes use solar energy (see page 145) for heating water. Bills usually show meter readings, the kWh used, charges and a daily energy/cost comparison. There's no tax on electricity bills in Australia. Customers are billed quarterly and payment can be made at post offices, certain banks, by phone (with a credit/EFTPOS card) and by mail (by cheque).

Gas

Australia has vast natural gas reserves and it's available in all of Australia's major cities from companies such as Australian Gas Limited (AGL). Gas is popular for cooking (it costs less than electricity) in Australia, although it's less commonly used to provide heating and hot water (although gas heaters are becoming increasingly popular). Note that there may be no gas supply in older homes and modern houses may also be all electric. If you're looking for a rental property and want to cook by gas, make sure it already has a gas supply (some houses have an unused gas service pipe). In country areas without piped gas, you can buy a 'bottled gas' cooker. If you buy a house without a gas supply, you can arrange with your local gas company to install a line between your home and a nearby gas main (providing there's one within a reasonable distance, otherwise the cost will be prohibitive).

If a home already has a gas supply, simply contact your local gas company to have the gas supply reconnected or transferred to your name (there's a connection charge). Usually a security deposit (e.g. $100) is payable and there may also be a payment to establish an account (e.g. $20). You must contact your local gas company to get a final reading when vacating a property. If you need to purchase gas appliances, such as a gas cooker or fire, you should shop around as prices vary considerably. Note that special controls can be fitted to many appliances to make them easier to use by the disabled and the blind or partially sighted (studded or braille controls). Gas tariffs vary but are around 6¢ per unit, per day for the first 10 units, after which there's usually a reduced rate, e.g. around 4¢ per unit, per day. Rates vary from city to city (or even the suburb) and region to region, and are more expensive in remote areas. There's also usually a daily supply (service) charge which works out at around $8 to $10 a quarter. There's no tax on gas bills in Australia. Customers are billed quarterly and payment can be made at post offices, certain banks, by phone (with a credit/EFTPOS card) and by mail (by cheque).

Gas central heating boilers, water heaters and fires should be checked annually. Always ask for a quotation for any work in advance and check the identity of anyone claiming to be a gas company employee (or any kind of 'serviceman') by asking to see an identity card and checking with his office. **Note that gas installations and appliances can leak and cause explosions or kill you while you sleep. If you suspect a gas leak, first check to see if a gas tap has been left on or a pilot light has gone out.** If not, then there's probably a leak, either in your home or in a nearby gas pipeline. Ring your local gas service centre immediately and **vacate your home as quickly as possible.** Gas leaks are extremely rare and explosions caused by leaks even rarer (although often spectacular and therefore widely reported). Nevertheless, it pays to be careful. You can buy an electric-powered gas detector which activates an alarm when a gas leak is detected.

Water

In Australia each city and major region has a water board operated by the local government. Water, or rather the lack of it, is a major concern in Australia and the price paid for all those sunny days. Australia is the world's driest continent and country areas are hit by frequent droughts. Many country homes have a bore (well) that comes in handy when there are water restrictions, which may restrict homeowners to watering their gardens once every three days before dawn or after dusk (to reduce evaporation). Many homes also have rain water tanks that can be used to water gardens and also for baths and showers. In some states there are often water restrictions such as sprinkler bans during the day, e.g. between 9am and 6pm or from 8am until 8pm in Western Australia, although there may be no restriction on hand held hoses. To reduce water consumption, many people plant mainly native Australian plants requiring little water, and use wood chips and gravel as an alternatives to lawns. A government evaluation of Australia's water resources is being carried out and will be completed by the year 2000. **In Australia water is a precious resource and not something simply to pour down the drain!**

When moving into a new home you should enquire where the main stopvalve or stopcock is, so that you can turn off the water supply in an emergency. If the water stops running for any reason, you should turn off the supply to prevent flooding from an open tap when the supply starts again. Contact your local water company if you have a problem reconnecting your water supply, as it could have been turned off by them. If you need a plumber, e.g. as a result of a burst pipe, you may be able to get a recommendation or a list of names from your local water company. Before calling a plumber always ask the minimum call out charge. Note that the changes in some states (e.g. Victoria) mean that water companies no longer inspect work carried out by plumbers, who self-certify their own work. Plumbers must be licensed and have indemnity insurance, and work valued at over $500 must have a certificate of compliance. New sewerage systems have been installed in many areas, with the bulk of the cost being paid by residents, irrespective of whether they want or need the improvements.

Charges & Bills: There was traditionally a fixed charge for water in Australia based on the gross rental or rateable value of a property. However, water is now metered in metropolitan areas where most households pay for their actual consumption, rather than a flat fee. When consumption is based on a meter reading you may be charged around 60¢ to 80¢ per 1,000 litres (kl). Bills also contain a water service charge, e.g. $20 a quarter. Water bills include water, sewerage and drainage and may show your average daily use in litres. Bills can usually be paid in a number of instalments, e.g. two or four a year, and can be paid at post offices and certain banks (in cash or by cheque), by phone (with a credit/EFTPOS card) and by mail (by cheque).

Quality: Although Australian drinking water is among the cleanest and safest in the world, the quality varies and it can taste terrible in areas with high mineral deposits. It's possible to have a water purifier fitted to a drinking water tap to improve the taste. Fluoride is added to water in some cities. Australian water doesn't usually contain limescale, so it isn't necessary to use a decalcification liquid to keep your kettle, iron and other apparatus and utensils clean. Contaminated water in garden hoses and domestic swimming pools can cause amoebic meningitis (not nice) and it's therefore important to clean pools and hoses thoroughly and often.

HEATING & AIR-CONDITIONING

Heating: Central heating isn't common in northern, eastern and western Australia as the climate doesn't usually warrant it. In these regions a portable electric fan heater, fire or radiator/column heater, or a gas fire is sufficient to heat most rooms during the wet or winter seasons. Both gas and electric heaters and hot water systems have an energy efficiency rating. Central heating, double glazing and good insulation are more common in new homes in southern states, where many people consider them essential. Central heating systems may be powered by oil, gas, electricity or solid fuel (e.g. coal or wood) and luxury homes may have a combined, thermostatically controlled, heating and cooling (air-conditioning) system. Many homes have storage heaters which store heat from electricity supplied at a cheaper, off-peak rate over night, and release it to heat a home during the day. In country and remote areas, solid fuels such as coal and wood are commonly used, where open fires, stoves and solid-fuel fireplaces are fairly common (and may also provide hot water). Whatever form of heating you use, you should ensure that your home has good insulation, without which up to 60 per cent of heat goes straight through the walls and roof.

Solar Heating: Solar heating is popular in Australia and is most commonly used to provide hot water, although dual solar hot water and heating systems (with a hot-air solar radiator) are available. These are usually combined with an electric booster or gas heating system, as solar energy cannot be relied upon year-round for hot water and heating requirements, e.g. on overcast days or when demand is high. The use of solar energy is most common in remote areas. Some 5 per cent of Australian homes (300,000) use solar energy for heating water including around 25 per cent of homes in WA and 60 per cent in the Northern territory (average savings are around $200 a year compared with electricity). Although currently relatively expensive to install, breakthroughs in solar cell technology are set to increase its efficiency and reduce the cost dramatically in the next decade. Employing passive design principles, solar energy can meet up to 90 per cent of normal household space heating needs.

Humidity: Note that central heating dries the air and may cause your family to develop coughs and other ailments. Those who find the dry air unpleasant can increase the relative humidity by adding moisture to the air with a humidifier, vaporizer, steam generator or even a water container made of porous ceramic. These range from simple water containers hung from radiators to expensive electric or battery-operated devices. Humidifiers that don't generate steam should be disinfected occasionally with a special liquid available from pharmacies (to prevent nasty diseases). In regions where high humidity is a problem, you can buy a dehumidifier to recirculate room air and reduce the relative humidity.

Air-Conditioning: In most regions of Australia, air-conditioning is a blessed relief in summer, while in northern and western Australia it's considered mandatory at almost any time of the year (also in cars). It's still considered something of a luxury in southern temperate states such as Victoria and New South Wales, where it's usually confined to luxury properties, although you won't consider it a luxury when the temperature soars above 40°C (104°F)! Most business premises are air-conditioned throughout Australia. Modern homes in tropical areas often have a ducted air-conditioning system powered by electricity. You can choose between a huge variety of air-conditioners, fixed or moveable, indoor or outdoor installations, with high or low power. An air-conditioning system with a heat pump provides cooling in summer and heating in winter.

Most window-mounted air-conditioning units have a choice of fan speeds and the fan can usually be switched on separately from the cooling system. The cooling system can be adjusted for temperature and units often have a vent that can be opened to allow air into the room when they aren't in use. When using air-conditioning, all windows and outside doors should obviously be closed. Note that if you suffer from asthma or respiratory problems, air-conditioning can exacerbate your condition. Many homes have electric pedestal and/or ceiling fans to provide cooling during the summer.

You can have a study made of your home's heating and cooling requirements and the cost, taking into account the climate and the current insulation and equipment installed. An engineer will produce a report detailing the most-effective means of insulating, heating and cooling your home, and provide a number of cost estimates. The Australian Consumers Association (see page 434) publish an excellent book entitled *Warm House Cool House* by Nick Hollo.

6.

POST OFFICE SERVICES

Australia Post (AP) handles over four billion articles of mail a year (11m a day, a large percentage of which is junk mail, in which Australia is a world leader) and provides one of the best postal services in the world in terms of cost, speed and reliability. AP underwent deregulation in 1994 when parts of the mail business were opened to private competitors. However, it has since gone from strength to strength and is a highly profitable and well-run business. A review in 1998 is likely to open AP to further competition and all mail services could be completely deregulated by 1999 (Australia mail favours 2002), although this brings into question the future of the standard letter rate of 45¢ across Australia, which is heavily subsidised in remote areas.

There's a post office or post office agency in most towns in Australia (a total of over 4,000), offering a wide range of services, most of which are described in this chapter. In country and outback towns, postal services are provided by an Australia Post agency (at a general store, petrol station or cafe/restaurant) licensed by the post office, which provides most of the services offered by a main post office. The post office provides a wide range of services, which, in addition to the usual services provided in most countries, include a number of unique services. Services include stamps, poste restante mail, telegrams, faxpost, money orders, giroPost, bill payment, passport applications, stationery sales and gifts (e.g. at Christmas by AP Shops or mail order).

Australia Post sells stationery and office products (they publish a catalogue) and orders with a minimum value of $50 are delivered free of charge almost anywhere in Australia. It operates the country's largest over-the-counter bill payment service (Telstra, income tax, gas, electricity, council rates, water rates, Medibank and insurance) and some 20 per cent of consumer bills are paid at Australia Post's retail outlets. AP handles over 130m financial transactions a year through its electronic retail network and provides one of the country's largest banking services (giroPost). Credit cards can be used to pay for purchases costing over $10.

Post boxes in Australia are red with a white stripe and modern mailboxes look like litter bins, although there are still some Victorian 'receiving pillars' around. In cities and large towns there are express 'gold' post boxes (see page 151). However, postboxes are scarce in rural areas and you may need to take your post to a post office or agency. In 1997, special festive Santa post boxes were set up at post offices to facilitate the sorting of letters to Santa — letters are answered by post office staff in their spare time (who said post offices don't have a heart?). In major towns and metropolitan areas there are mail deliveries once a day, Monday to Friday, while in remote areas deliveries may be restricted to once a week only (although a twice-weekly service has been introduced in some areas). In remote areas, deliveries can be affected by the weather as mail is usually delivered by air. In the outback, mail must usually be collected from a local post office or agency. There are no weekend deliveries anywhere in Australia.

The post office parcel delivery and courier services have been privatised in recent years, although AP maintains a monopoly on letters weighing up to 250g. Private operators must also charge a minimum of $1.80, which is four times the AP rate for a standard letter. However, there's a thriving courier business in Australia, particularly in the major cities, where 24-hour domestic and international courier services are provided by many companies including Allied Express, Ansett Courier, DHL, FedEx, Mayne Nickless and TNT. AP also operates a domestic courier service, Australia Air Express, with Qantas. Many more companies (such as Salmat and Streetfile) just deliver locally, e.g. within a particular city. In major cities there are companies such as Mail Boxes Etc. providing a wide range of mail (e.g. mail boxes), courier, fax, telephone and business services.

The post office produces a wealth of free brochures regarding postal rates and special services, most of which are available from any post office. A general *Post Charges* booklet contains details of most services and rates, and a comprehensive *Post Guide* ($50) is available for businesses. Information about Australia Post's services is also available via the internet (www.auspost.com.au).

BUSINESS HOURS

Post office business hours in Australia are usually from 9am to 5pm, Monday to Friday, and from 9am to 12am on Saturdays. In major cities, general post offices may have slightly longer business hours, e.g. Sydney general post office is open from 8.15am to 5.30pm Monday to Friday and from 8.30am to noon on Saturday. Post offices in major towns don't close at lunchtime. In country and outback areas, Australia Post agencies basically keep the same hours as post offices, but may close for an hour during lunch or close earlier. They usually open on Saturday mornings and have extended opening hours on some evenings.

LETTER POST

AP provides a single domestic mail service, where there has been a price freeze at 45¢ for standard (small) letters since January 1992. Domestic mail charges also apply to Christmas island (Indian Ocean), Cocos (Keeling) Islands, the Australian Antarctic Territories and Norfolk Island. Domestic mail is sent by air between states or to remote areas within Australia. Domestic Christmas greeting cards posted in November and December are charged at a reduced rate of 40¢.

Australia post delivers over 93 per cent of metropolitan letters the next day and over 98 per cent one day later. Local mail is usually delivered the next day and interstate mail to major towns and cities in one to two days. However, the post office has a worse record for deliveries to country locations, which officially take two days in the same state and up to four days interstate. The airmail service is fast and reliable with airmail letters taking a maximum of seven or eight days to most destinations (e.g. three to five days to Britain and six to seven days to the USA), depending on where they are posted and the destination. Compensation (at AP's discretion) up to $50 is paid for loss or damage of mail upon production of a receipt or other proof of lodgement.

The cost of posting a letter or postcard in Australia is as follows:

Domestic Mail:*

Small letters#	45¢
Large letters:#	
up to 50g	70/75¢
from 50g-125g	85/95¢
from 125g-250g	$1.25/1.50
from 250g-500g	$2.00/2.65

Air Mail   **International Zones****

	1	2	3	4	5
letter up to 20g	70/75¢	80/85¢	85/95¢	90¢/$1.05	$1.00/1.20
letter 20g to 50g	$1/1.10	$1.10/1.20	$1.20/1.30	$1.30/1.50	$1.40/1.70
postcards	65/70¢	70/80¢	75/90¢	80/95¢	85¢/$1
Sea Mail:					
letter up to 50g	90¢	90¢	90¢	$1.00	$1.00

*   There are two rates for domestic letters sent by ordinary post: same state (first rate shown above) and other states (second rate shown above). Over 500g, parcel post rates apply (see page 154).

**   Australia divides international mail into five zones as follows: Zone 1 includes New Caledonia, New Zealand, Papua New Guinea, Solomon islands and Vanuatu; Zone 2 includes Brunei, Fiji, Indonesia, Malaysia and Singapore; Zone 3 includes Bangladesh, Cambodia, China, Hong Kong, India, Japan, Korea, Pakistan, the Philippines, Taiwan, Thailand and Vietnam; Zone 4 includes the USA, Canada, Mexico and the Middle East; Zone 5 includes Europe, Africa, Central and South America. The two prices shown in the table above are for economy air (first price) and normal airmail.

\#   Small letters (previous page) sent by ordinary post must be rectangular in shape with the length at least 1.414 times the width; a maximum size of 122mm x 237mm; a maximum thickness of 5mm; and a maximum weight of 250g. Large letters sent by ordinary post must be rectangular in shape; a maximum size of 260mm x 360mm; a maximum thickness of 20mm; and a maximum weight of 500g.

Inland Mail

The following points apply to inland mail services:

• In addition to post offices, stamps can be purchased at hotels, motels, stores, newsagents and from vending machines. Most machines issue fixed-value stamps, although new electronic machines print gummed postage 'labels' to the exact value required. Peel and stick stamps (no licking) at 45¢, the cost of a standard letter in Australia sent by ordinary post, are available in booklets of 10 ($4.50), 100 ($45) and 200 ($90). No surcharge is levied by private stamp vendors in Australia.

• Pre-paid envelopes are available in various sizes: DL and C6 (maximum 5mm thick) cost 55¢ each or $5.25 for a pack of 10, C5 (max. 20mm thick) $1.10 ($10.45 for 10), C4 (20mm) $2.20 ($20.90 for 10) and B4 (20mm) $2.75 ($26.15 for 10). The maximum weight for DL and C6 envelopes is 250g and for all other sizes it's 500g.

• AP provides an express domestic post service with guaranteed next day delivery. No paperwork or forms need be completed as items are sent in pre-paid envelopes or 'satchels'. There are three sizes of pre-paid envelopes: C5 ($3), B4 ($4) and DL (only available with window faced envelopes in business packs of 50), which can be used for letters and documents weighing up to 500g and up to 20mm thick. In addition, express post satchels are available in two sizes (items can be any thickness): up to 500g ($5) and up to 3kg ($8). Items weighing from 3kg to 20kg or too large for an express post satchel must be sent by express post parcels (see page 154). All sizes of envelopes and satchels are available in packs of 10.

Pre-paid envelopes and satchels can be handed in at post offices or posted in express 'gold' post boxes in cities and major towns. Items must be presented at a post office before close of business or the mail closing time in some provincial centres. Items posted by 6pm (earlier in Perth and some provincial centres) Monday to Friday are guaranteed next day delivery to Australia's capital cities and some major provincial centres. The express service also operates within states between the capital city and major provincial centres. Outside these areas the fastest possible delivery is provided, but there are no guarantees. The cost is refunded if items aren't delivered the next working day (where applicable). Express post must not be used to send cash, gold, jewellery, precious stones, negotiable securities or other valuables, which should be sent by registered post (see page 156).

- Domestic mail, including parcels and registered packets, can be sent Cash on Delivery (COD), where the addressee pays a specified amount to the postman on delivery. The fee is $3.20 in addition to postage and includes insurance cover up to $100 (additional insurance is available for $1 per $100 insured).

- There are reduced rates for bulk local deliveries of a minimum of 50 letters (10 in a small community). The post office also provides a 'print post' service for periodical publications within Australia.

- If you send a letter with insufficient postage it will usually be delivered, although the addressee will be charged $1 plus the deficient postage (also applies to parcels). If the post office is unable to deliver a letter it's returned to the sender with a note giving the reason why it couldn't be delivered.

- Most mail in Australia is sorted by machine, which is facilitated by the use of full and correct postal addresses (omitting all punctuation). All items of mail should have a four-digit postcode (zip code) after the town and state or territory. In major cities, codes indicate whether the town is a suburb of a major city, e.g. 2000 is the central business district (CBD) of Sydney and all other 2000 postcodes are suburbs. A locked or private bag is the same as a post office box number (written as 'PO Box' or 'GPO Box'). All addresses must contain the name of the state or territory, which are abbreviated as follows:

State/Territory	Abbrev.	First Digit
Australian Capital Territory	ACT	2
New South Wales	NSW	2
Northern Territory	NT	5
Queensland	QLD	4
South Australia	SA	5
Tasmania	TAS	7
Victoria	VIC	3
Western Australia	WA	6

Postcodes are listed at the back of the white pages. You can buy envelopes with pre-printed squares for the postcode. A typical Australian address is shown below:

Ned & Sheila Kelly
99A Waltzing Matilda Street
Wooloowollongong
Sydney
NSW 2005
Australia

Note that you should always put your address on the back of mail so that it can be returned to you if it cannot be undelivered.

* Domestic mail for the blind weighing up to 7kg is delivered free of charge. International sea mail for the blind weighing up to 7kg is delivered free of charge and airmail up to 7kg costs 9¢ per 50g or part thereof. Items must have the special 'blind' symbol on the address side or 'MATERIALS FOR THE USE OF THE BLIND' or similar words.

* You can receive mail via post offices throughout Australia through the international *poste restante* service, where mail is addressed to a main post office. Mail sent to a poste restante address is returned to the sender if unclaimed after 14 days or one month if sent from overseas. Identification is necessary for collection, e.g. a passport. Mail should be addressed as follows: Your Name, c/o Poste Restante, Chief Post Office, Sydney, NSW 2000. Note that some poste restante desks in main cities are hectic and it's often better to send mail to a smaller town or a suburb (where you may be able to check whether you have any mail by phone). Some general post offices (e.g. Martin Place in Sydney) provide a list of addressees of poste restante mail on a computer. Poste restante mail can be redirected to a suburban post office from a main office for $5 a month.

   Most hostels and hotels will hold mail for you and there are also private mail and message holding and forwarding services in Australia, e.g. travel agencies, which charge a monthly or annual fee. When using a mail holding service you can telephone from anywhere in Australia to see if there's any mail for you and have it redirected. If you have an American Express card or use American Express travellers cheques, you can have mail sent to an American Express office in Australia. Standard letters are held free of charge, while registered letters and packages aren't accepted. Mail, which should be marked 'client mail service', is kept for 30 days before being returned to the sender. Mail can be forwarded to another office or address, for which there's a charge. Other companies also provide mail holding services for customers, e.g. Thomas Cook and Western Union.

* Like many countries, Australia provides a range of special services for philatelists. In addition to Australia, AP also produces stamps for the Australian Antarctic Territory, Christmas island and the Cocos (Keeling) Islands. AP publishes a free *Stamp Bulletin* magazine (five issues a year) which is available from Reply Paid 64, Australian Stamp Bulletin, Locked Bag 8, South Melbourne VIC 3205. Australia Post also operates a Stamp Explorers Club for children aged six to 13 years. Members receive a membership card entitling them to special discounts and benefits and the Stamp Explorer magazine (four issues a year). To join the Stamp Explorers write to Reply Paid 14, Australian Stamp Bulletin, PO Box 511, South Melbourne VIC 3205.

Finally, carefully check all your mail and don't throw anything away unless you're certain that it's junk mail (e.g. unsolicited direct mail, circulars and free newspapers). It isn't unknown for newcomers to throw away important correspondence during their first few weeks in Australia (hopefully a few bills will be included!). Look for 'real' letters among your junk mail.

International Mail

AP provides four services for international mail: express post international, ordinary air mail, economy air and sea mail.

- **Express Post:** AP provides an express post international service to over 140 countries. The service offers two sizes of pre-paid envelopes, C5 ($9.80) and B4 ($14.80), which can be used to send letters and documents up to 500g. Envelopes are also available in packs of 10 at a discount. As with domestic express mail, items can be posted in special express mail 'gold' posting boxes. Air despatch from Australia is guaranteed the next day from capital cities and other specified areas subject to the availability of flights (otherwise your envelope will be replaced free of charge).

- The fastest way to send mail overseas via a post office is by **EMS International Courier** (see page 154), AP's premium door-to-door express courier service.

- **Air Mail:** All airmail letters (including letters for European destinations) should have a blue airmail label affixed to the top left hand corner, available from post offices, or 'PAR AVION - BY AIR MAIL' should be written or stamped on items. Aerogrammes (pre-printed airmail letters) are available and cost 75¢ to all destinations. They are also sold in packs of 10 ($7). International postage pre-paid envelopes are available in three sizes: DL ($1.35), C5 ($3.35) and B4 ($6), and can be purchased in packs of 10 at a small discount. Airmail letters, documents and parcels are limited to 20kg for most countries (some countries have a lower limit, e.g. 10kg).

- **Economy Air:** For non-urgent international mail, AP provides an economy air mail service where the main part of the journey is made by air. Mail takes between 10 and 28 days to most destinations, e.g. 10 to 14 days to Britain and 14 to 21 days to the USA. Note, however, that for most mail it's hardly worthwhile as the savings are insignificant unless you're sending a heavy parcel (see page 154).

- **Sea Mail:** Sea mail is the cheapest service and allows delivery to almost any country. It's ideal for heavier items when speed is not critical, i.e. fast delivery is of absolutely no consequence! Average sea mail delivery times are: zones 1 and 2, one to two months, and zones 3, 4 and 5 (including Britain and the USA), up to three months or longer (much, much, longer to some countries).

- The latest date for sending international Christmas cards is around four weeks before Christmas. Leaflets are published in September listing the latest mail posting dates for Christmas for surface and airmail, which are sometime between the beginning of October (e.g. 6th October for the UK and 8th October for the USA for sea mail) and the end of November, depending on the country.

- If you want to increase your chances of receiving a reply or simply wish to save a correspondent money, you can send them an **international reply coupon** ($2). These are exchangeable at post offices overseas for postage stamps equivalent to the basic air mail rate anywhere in the world for a letter weighing up to 20g.

PARCEL POST

Standard parcels are usually delivered the next working day within the metropolitan area of capital cities and certain large country towns in the same state, and within two working days to other locations in the same state. Interstate parcels are delivered within two to six working days, depending on the destination. Note, however, that AP has a poor reputation for deliveries to country locations. AP provides five services for international parcels (in order of speed and cost): EMS international courier, express, air mail, economy air and sea mail.

Domestic Parcels: The cost of domestic parcels varies considerably depending on where they are sent from and the destination (based on the postcode). A parcel weighing up to 250g costs up to $2.10 anywhere in Australia outside the local area; between 500g and 1kg the price is from $3 to $8.35 (i.e. from NSW to WA); from 5kg to 6kg the cost is $3 to $17.75; from 10kg to 11kg it's from $3 to $31.85; and from 19kg to 20kg it costs from $3 to $53. Note that large letters (see page 150) weighing up to 500g can be sent by letter mail. Important parcels can be sent by registered post which provide a signature on delivery and insurance cover of up to $100. Parcels can also be sent cash on delivery. AP provides special satchels for sending articles anywhere in Australia in two sizes: Up to 500g ($3.50) and up to 3kg ($6.50). Local parcels cost $1.35 up to 500g and a flat rate of $3 from 500g up to the maximum weight of 20kg (there's also a flat rate for airmail parcels of $10). AP also operates a small parcel service costing $2.10 for parcels weighing up to 250g and $3.10 for parcels weighing from 250g to 500g for deliveries throughout the country. Regular parcels weighing over 500g cost $4.60 for deliveries within 50km/31mi.

EMS International Courier Service: The fastest way to send international parcels is via the EMS international courier service (serving over 180 countries). As with all international mail, rates are calculated according to a five-zone system. A parcel weighing up to 500g costs from $21 to $27 ($25 to the USA and Canada and $27 to Europe) and between $33 and $57 for parcels weighing between 1.5 and 2kg. Above 2kg, each additional 500g costs between $4 and $10 depending on the zone, up to a maximum of 20kg. Although relatively expensive, EMS rates are usually lower than other international courier services. EMS parcels are guaranteed to arrive at their destination within a certain number of days, e.g. two to four days to Britain and four to five days to the USA.

Express Parcels: AP provides a domestic and international express post parcel service. For domestic express parcels there's guaranteed next day delivery between Australia's capital cities (except Darwin) and some other major centres (you can claim a refund if a parcel isn't delivered next day). The service also operates within states between the capital city and major provincial centres. Outside these areas the fastest possible delivery is provided, but there are no delivery guarantees. The maximum permitted weight is 20kg, maximum length 105cm and maximum girth 140cm. Parcels must be presented at a post office before close of business or mail closing time in some provincial centres. There's a standard charge of $5.50 for parcels weighing up to 500g and $8 for parcels weighing from 500g up to 20kg, plus a distance charge per kilogramme (or part) calculated using the origin and destination zones, e.g. for a parcel going from Sydney (zone 2000) to Adelaide (zone 5000) the charge is $2.65 per kg. Note that for parcels weighing over 1kg where a distance charge applies, the charge may be calculated on the 'cubic' weight (based on a parcel's measurements) rather than the actual weight, whichever is the greater.

Air Mail: The airmail service is fast and reliable with airmail letters taking a maximum of seven or eight days to most destinations (e.g. three to five days to Britain and six to seven days to the USA), depending on where they are posted and the destination.

Economy Air: For non-urgent international parcels, AP provides an economy air mail service. The main part of the journey is made by air and items take between 10 and 28 days to most destinations, e.g. 10 to 14 days to Britain and 14 to 21 days to the USA. Note that while the maximum weight limit for economy air is 20kg to Britain and the USA, to many countries it's just 500g. Note that the saving over regular air mail is insignificant unless you're sending a parcel weighing over 1 or 2kg.

Sea Mail: Sea mail is the cheapest way to send parcels and allows delivery to almost any country. It's ideal for heavier items when speed is of no importance. Average sea mail delivery times are one to two months to zones 1 and 2 and two to three months (or longer) to zones 3, 4 and 5 (which include Britain and the USA).

Customs Declaration: Parcels and small packets sent to international addresses must be accompanied by a customs declaration form available from post offices. No customs form is required for small and large letters and express post international. A *Customs/Douane* form CN22 (C1) must be completed for items weighing up to 2kg and up to $500 in value and an *International Post - Customs Declaration* (form C231/CP72) for items weighing above 2kg and over $500 in value. Insured articles other than EMS articles (see above) require form C233. Press firmly when completing forms, some of which have six copies! Gifts posted to Australia up to the value of A$200 are duty-free, except for alcohol and tobacco products. For gifts exceeding A$200, duty is calculated on the value in excess of the A$200 limit. The value of packages that are part of a larger consignment will be totalled for customs purposes. Note that there are restrictions on the sort of goods that can be posted to Australia (see below). Dangerous goods must not be sent through the mail and senders of parcels and satchels must sign a Dangerous Goods Declaration.

Wrapping Parcels: A leaflet entitled *Packaging Hints* is available from post offices, which describes how to pack goods for sending through the mail. When sending drawings, large photographs, paintings, or anything which will be damaged if bent, **always sandwich them between stiff cardboard.** Postpak packaging products including boxes (plus gift boxes), padded bags, tough bags, mailing tubes and accessories are available from Australia Post Shops and stationery stores. You can send quite large objects by parcel post, but it's advisable to enquire before packaging your mother-in-law for shipment to Outer Mongolia (just to make sure she arrives safely and *isn't* returned). All parcels must be securely wrapped and clearly addressed and if they aren't you may be asked to wrap them again. **Note that international parcels must be very securely wrapped, otherwise they will be shredded in transit to some countries.**

Restricted Articles: A dangerous goods brochure, *Some Things Were Never Meant To Be Posted*, is available from post offices and lists what *cannot* be sent through the mail. This includes anything that's radioactive, flammable, explosive, corrosive, an oxidising material, a compressed gas (such as an aerosol can), alive, or likely to deteriorate during its journey through the post. Many overseas countries have restrictions on certain items such as medicines and alcohol.

IMPORTANT DOCUMENTS & VALUABLES

The post office provides a number of services for the delivery of important documents and valuables:

Registered Mail: If you're sending money, jewellery or valuable documents then you should use registered mail. Domestic pre-paid envelopes which include postage and the registered post fee are available in two sizes: small or DLE (130 x 240mm, 5mm thick) which cost $2.20 each ($21 for 10) and large or B4 (353mm x 250mm, 20mm thick) costing $3.20 each ($31 for 10). Domestic registered post labels are also available in boxes of 50 ($77.50). Registered post for single articles costs $1.80. International registered post is available for letters and documents only and costs $8 for DLE size (130 x 240mm) and $14 for B4 size (353 x 240mm). You receive a receipt for registered mail, which must be signed for on delivery (although the signatory doesn't need to be the addressee). Delivery of domestic registered post can be confirmed (fee $1.40) by completing a delivery confirmation card and sending it with your registered post article. There's also a person-to-person option (fee $4) where a registered article must be signed for by the person to whom it's addressed.

Insurance: International insurance is available for EMS international courier (see page 154), letter and parcel post articles. The basic fee is $3 plus $2 for each $100 (or part thereof) insured up to a maximum of $5,000 (a lower limit applies to some countries). Domestic and international registered mail is 'insured' for $100 against loss or damage and additional insurance up to $5,000 is available for domestic registered mail for $1 per $100 insured. Additional insurance cannot be purchased for international registered mail.

Delivery Confirmation: Delivery confirmation is available with registered post, insured articles and, for some countries, parcel post. International delivery confirmation costs $2 per article plus postage. Delivery confirmation costs an additional $1.40 per article for registered post and $4 for person-to-person delivery. Proof of delivery must be requested at the time of posting. Signed evidence of delivery is returned to the sender, but not from a named individual.

MISCELLANEOUS SERVICES

The following miscellaneous services are provided by Australia Post:

Payment of Bills: AP provides a bill payment service from all post offices and post agencies. A total of some 160 organisations offer their customers the option of paying their bills at post offices including telephone bills, tax payments, credit card bills, electricity, gas, council rates, water rates and insurance premiums. Simply present your account slip and invoice together with payment by cash or cheque. A receipt is provided.

Money Orders: Money orders offer a convenient, safe and economical way to pay bills, transfer cash and pay for mail-order purchases if you or the recipient doesn't have a cheque account. Money orders can be purchased for 5¢ amounts up to $1,000 and cost $2, so they aren't cost effective for small amounts. Express money orders up to the value of $10,000 cost $20 and can be transferred across Australia from post office to post office within one business hour. There's an additional 10¢ stamp duty in Western Australia. Money orders can be cashed at post offices (identification is required for values above $20) or paid into a bank account.

American Express International Money Orders: AP is the Australian agent for American Express International Money Orders. These $US money orders are recognised and accepted in over 120 countries and sold at larger post offices throughout Australia. They can be purchased for values up to $US1,000 for a fixed fee of A$6 (plus 10¢ stamp duty in Western Australia), irrespective of their value. They must be cashed at an American Express bank or travel service office or paid into a bank account.

GIROPOST

GiroPost (written giroPost) is the Australia Post banking service, available to the customers of leading banks and other financial institutions, and offering retail banking services at over 2,000 post offices throughout Australia (displaying the giroPost symbol). Participating banks include Adelaide Bank, Advance Bank, Bank of Melbourne, Bendigo Bank, Challenge Bank, Citibank, Commonwealth Bank, Hongkong Bank and Metway Bank.

GiroPost allows customers holding accounts with participating banks and financial institutions to use their credit and debit cards at the post office, and undertake a variety of transactions such as deposits, withdrawals, account balance enquiries, paying credit card bills and opening accounts. In regional and rural areas, giroPost provides vital local banking facilities that otherwise would not be available, and it also provides a valuable service for interstate travellers and tourists.

CHANGE OF ADDRESS

When moving house within Australia you should obtain a 'Change of Address Kit' from a post office containing a 'Change of Address Request' form, a brochure describing the service, a moving home checklist, and six post cards to inform your relatives and friends about your move. The change can be permanent or temporary and mail can also be held at your local post office or be collected from a nominated post office. Proof of identity must be provided when lodging the form and a minimum of three business days' notice is required. There's a monthly fee of $30 for business and government, and $5 for others (there's no charge for certain pensioners and sickness beneficiaries). There's an additional charge for the redirection of parcels.

AP provides a 'priority address notification' service which saves time and effort in informing organisations of your address. Upon receipt of your 'Change of Address Form', AP will send you a list of companies which you may wish to notify of your new address. If you're a customer of any of the companies listed on the form, you need simply tick the box beside the company's name and AP will inform them of your change of address free of charge.

If you receive mail for the previous occupants of your home or any mail that isn't addressed to you, you have two choices what to do with it (the third is to throw it away, which is illegal!). If known, you can send it on to the addressee by crossing out the address, writing the new or correct address and dropping it in a post box without a stamp. If you don't know the addressee's new address, you can cross out the address and write 'Address Unknown' and drop it in a post box.

7.

TELEPHONE

A lmost all Australian homes (some 97 per cent) have a telephone and Australia also has one of the highest (per capita) numbers of mobile phones in the world. Due to its huge size, communications in Australia have always been a priority and today it has one of the highest standards of communications in the world, employing the latest digital technology, broadband cable, fibre optics and satellite systems. Wireless and radio-based communication is used in rural and remote areas, where residents will in future receive their telecommunications' services via satellite links and enjoy the same services that are available in metropolitan centres. There are also solar-powered public phone boxes in outback areas requiring no mains electricity. The Australian telecommunications market was deregulated in 1997 and consumers are now able to choose from a number of companies in most regions and major cities. Thanks to recent technological advances, it will soon be possible to have a single number for your home, office and mobile phones.

The telecommunications industry in Australia is regulated by the Australian Telecommunications Industry (Austel), PO Box 7443, St. Kilda Road, Melbourne, VIC 3004 and has its own ombudsman (tel. freecall 1800-062 058). The ombudsman attempts to resolve complaints concerning telecommunications' issues, but only after consumers have attempted to settle them with the company or carrier concerned.

Note that Australia has been introducing a new numbering system in the last few years and all telephone numbers will have an eight-digit subscriber number plus a two digit area code by November 1998, e.g. from August 1997 all 06 codes (ACT) became 02 and a 6 was added before the old 7-digit number. For information call the freecall hotline (1800-888 888) between 8am and midnight. Telstra also operates a 'changed number information service' on 12554. **The general emergency telephone number throughout Australia is 000.**

TELEPHONE COMPANIES

The Australian telecommunications market was deregulated on 1st July 1997, although it's still dominated by the duopoly of Telstra (formerly Telecom Australia and two-thirds government-owned) and to a much lesser extent, Optus. Telstra has an overall market share of around 75 per cent (9m customers), including 60 per cent of long-distance business. Its main rival Optus (established in 1992 and owned by Cable & Wireless) has around 15 per cent of the market (over 2.5m customers, including fixed and mobile phones). AAPT is Australia's third-largest communications company, although prior to July 1997 it served mainly business customers. Not surprisingly the lack of competition (prior to deregulation) led to Australians paying some of the highest telephone charges in the world, with Telstra and Optus charging an average of five times the cost of providing international call services.

However, since deregulation many new companies have entered the market including BT Australasia, GlobalOne, International PrimeCall, Pacific Star, Primus/Axicorp, Satellite Cowboys and WorldxChange, and users can now choose from a number of companies when making long-distance and international calls. Long-distance phone charges have been slashed by up to 70 per cent and the price of mobile phone calls are expected to fall by 50 per cent and local calls by up to 25 per cent in the next three years (some new companies even offer free local calls). In the first six months of deregulation there were tens of thousands of defections from Telstra and Optus. However, despite the increased competition, deregulation has failed to deliver the expected benefits to consumers.

New companies are restricted by the price Telstra charges for access to its local network and the absence of local number portability (LNP), which would allow users to switch between phone companies without changing their number. This is a major point of conflict between Telstra and Optus, and led to Optus filing a $900 million claim against Telstra for anti-competitive behaviour in the local call market. Telstra has a virtual monopoly on local telephone services worth $4 billion a year, although LNP is expected to be introduced some time in 1998. Other matters restricting competition include non-code access, wholesale tariffs, access pricing and spectrum allocation.

Before signing up with a telephone company, check the competition and compare rates. If you make a lot of long-distance and international calls you can save a lot of money by using one of the new companies whose call rates are often well below those charged by Telstra and Optus. However, you should continually monitor the market as new deals are constantly being introduced and what was the best offer last month (or week) is unlikely to remain so for long. Many companies offer a range of services which may include local and long-distance telephone services, pay TV, and high speed access to on-line and interactive services such as the internet. This may be beneficial, as many companies offer attractive package deals if you buy two or more services (such as telephone and pay TV).

INSTALLATION & REGISTRATION

Before moving into a new home, check whether there's a telephone line and that the number of lines or telephone points is adequate (most homes already have phone lines and points in a number of rooms). If a property has a cable system or other phone network, you don't require a Telstra phone line. However, if you move into a house or apartment where you aren't the first resident, a telephone line will almost certainly already be installed, although there will usually be no phone. If you're moving into a house or apartment without a phone connection, e.g. a new house, you must usually apply to Telstra for a line to be installed or connected.

To have a telephone line installed or re-connected, call at any Telstra shop or dial the Telstra Customer Service Centre (tel. 13 2200) between 8am and 5pm, Monday to Friday. Telstra will arrange a suitable date and time with you to connect your phone service. If you live in a metropolitan area, your phone should be connected within seven days at the latest. Connection often takes longer if you live in a rural or remote area, e.g. from two weeks to two months. If you simply need an existing Telstra service reconnected, this can usually be done on the day and time requested or within a maximum of three working days. If you're moving home within the same exchange area and same call-charging zone, you may retain your old number, otherwise your old number is typically re-allocated to the incoming customer at your old address. You may request an unlisted number ('silent line') for which an unlisted number fee applies.

Line installation costs $216, although this depends on the amount of work involved, and you're required to pay an advance of $300 from which the fee is deducted. If a line already exists, connection costs $50, which is deducted from an advance payment of $150. Credit assessments are made for all customers and your billing period may depend on your credit assessment. Payment of a security bond may be required or you may be given restricted access only, e.g. no international calls. Interest is paid on a bond which is generally repaid after 12 months when you have established a satisfactory payment record. Generally a $250 deposit is necessary if you wish to make interstate calls and a $500 deposit if you want to make international calls.

If your phone or line has a fault, you need to report it to Telstra on 13 2203 (international 1221). If your life, health, safety or shelter may be at risk without a phone, you can register for a priority repair service (24 hours, seven days a week). You can take out a maintenance contract with Telstra to maintain equipment and cabling. Under a new customer service guarantee introduced in 1998, if your phone isn't fixed within one working day you will receive a free month's line rental for each extra day it takes, and if the repairer is over 15 minutes late for an appointment, you will also receive a free month's rent. Telstra publish a booklet, *Guide to Using Telstra's Telephone Services for Residential & Business Customers*, available from Telstra shops or by calling 13 2200. If you need help with using a Telstra product or service, dial 13 2125.

CHOOSING A PHONE

You aren't required to rent a phone from Telstra and can purchase a phone from a wide range offered by Telstra and other retailers. Note that renting a phone from Telstra doesn't pay, as in one year you'll have paid for the price of a basic (but adequate) telephone. The only advantage of renting a Telstra phone is that they will fix it free of charge if it's faulty and you can change phones as often as you wish. On the other hand, if a inexpensive private phone has a fault, it may be cheaper to throw it away than have it repaired. **Before buying a phone, be careful to check prices and features, which vary considerably.**

The price of a phone usually depends on its quality, country of origin and not least its features. A basic, one-piece phone (with the keys on the handset) costs around $20, while an all-singing, all-dancing model costs between $60 and $80. Typical features include a built-in loudspeaker (so you can talk and listen without using the handset); on-hook dialling; number memory facility; last number re-dial; mute button; LCD display (so you can check the digits entered); hands-free operation; timer or call cost counter; lock; and an intercom system. You can even buy a videophone which allows two callers using them to see each other on a small screen.

Cordless phones are popular and can be operated at between 50 and 150 metres from their base station (the batteries last for from a few days to around 60 days when the handset hasn't been recharged). If you're thinking of buying a cordless phone, note that many rely solely on mains power and therefore are useless if there's a power failure. The latest cordless phones have a battery backup and should prevent calls being overheard and calls being made on your number with another handset (via a security code). Despite the battery backup of some phones, it's unwise to rely solely on a cordless phone. Other features may include a battery low indicator, paging and intercom facilities. Note that all cordless phones sold in Australia must have an Austel permit shown by a sticker and the importation of cordless phones and (citizenband radios) without it are prohibited. Most cordless phones cost between $100 and $250 (Panasonic make some of the best).

You might also consider a telephone with a built-in answering machine. Answering machines (like all electronic equipment) are becoming increasingly sophisticated and the latest machines offer a variety of features including fast erase, monitoring/screening, two-way conversation recording, cue and review, answer only, paging, logging of time and date, digital talking diary, call screening, music, memo facility; and remote message retrieval (which allows you to listen to your messages from almost anywhere in the world, simply by ringing your home or business number). Machines with two tapes are best (one for announcements and one for messages).

For those with special needs, a variety of special phones and attachments are available. If you live or work in a noisy environment, a headset can be purchased allowing hands-free operation. Special handsets are available for the blind (with a nodule on the figure 5) and extra large key pads for the partially blind. Phones fitted with a flashing light, loud ring, a built-in amplifier or magnetic coupling (for use with hearing aids) are available for the hard of hearing (e.g. politicians).

You can try the latest Telstra phones at your local Telstra shop (see your phone book), where advice and demonstrations are available. Telstra publish a wide range of booklets and leaflets including a catalogue of their products and services (for information tel. freecall 1800-359 048). There are over 80 Telstra shops in Australia for general enquiries; information about Telstra's products and services; product demonstrations and sales; and telephone bill payments. Shops are open from 9am to 4.30pm Monday to Friday or longer in many locations. Telstra also has telephone Customer Service Centres in all major cities and towns, open from 8am to 5pm, Monday to Friday. However, you should also compare phones and other equipment from high street shops, and if possible, test them before buying. See also **Mobile Telephones** on page 170.

USING THE TELEPHONE

Using the telephone in Australia is much the same as in any other country, with a few local eccentricities thrown in for good measure. When dialling a number within your own exchange area, dial the number only, e.g. if you live in Sydney and wish to dial another subscriber in Sydney. When dialling anywhere else, the area code must be dialled before the subscriber's number. When telephone numbers are printed, the area code is usually shown in brackets, e.g. (02) 1234 5678. When dialling a number in Australia from overseas, you dial the international access code of the country from which you're calling (e.g. 00), followed by Australia's international code (61), the area national code *without* the first 0 (e.g. 2 for Sydney) and the subscriber's number. For example, to call Sydney 1234 5678 from the UK you would dial 00-61-2-1234 5678. Note that because of the huge time difference between Australia and many other countries, you should always check the local time when making international calls. For operator assistance dial 1234.

In some remote areas there are still manual exchanges, where you must call the local operator to make a call. Some outback areas in Western Australia and the Northern Territory have radio telephones, where numbers are prefixed by R/T. Calls to R/T numbers can be made via the national network and radio telephone exchanges, although they are expensive. A radio telephone is like using a two-way radio and only one person can speak at a time (you need to say over when you finish speaking and cannot interrupt the other person). Party lines (shared by two or more homes) are common in the outback.

New Codes & Numbers: Australia has been introducing a new numbering system in the last few years and all telephone (and fax) numbers will have eight digits and a two digit area code by November 1998. For example from August 1997 all existing ACT phone numbers (which previously had an area code of 06) had a 6 added before the 7-digit number and the area code became 02. In regional areas, generally the last two digits of the current area code have been added to the front of the local number to form a new eight-digit number, although a small percentage of numbers have undergone two changes. During the six-month change-over period, both the old and new numbers are accessible followed by a further three-month period, when a recorded message refers callers to the white pages for information. If you have a problem obtaining a number, check that it's correct in the white pages or by calling directory enquiries (information) on 1223 (local and national) or 1225 (international). For general information about new numbers, call the freecall hotline 1800-888 888. The area codes for states and their capital cities are listed below:

State/Territory	Capital	Code
Australian Capital Ter.	Canberra	02 (old code 06)
New South Wales	Sydney	02
Northern Territory	Darwin	08
Queensland	Brisbane	07
South Australia	Adelaide	08
Tasmania	Hobart	03
Victoria	Melbourne	03
Western Australia	Perth	08 (old code 09)

Free Numbers: Toll-free numbers, called freecall in Australia, have a prefix of 1800 and are usually provided by businesses who are trying to sell you something or having sold you something, provide a free telephone support service. Note that mobile phone carriers usually charge for 1800 calls. As in most countries, freecall numbers leave you on hold for ages during which time you have to suffer the torment of muzak. You can obtain a personal freecall 1800 number called 'homelink 1800', which allows your family and friends to phone your home free of charge (so don't give it to telephone sales' persons!). There's a 10¢ surcharge for domestic each homelink call ($3 for an international homelink call).

Reduced Rate Service numbers with the prefix 13 or 1300 are usually charged at the local call rate from anywhere in Australia (although some 13 or 1300 numbers may be restricted to callers within a city or state).

Operator Assisted Calls: There's an extra charge for operator assisted calls which include reverse charge (collect) calls, person-to-person calls, ring back price, or a wake up or reminder call. The minimum charge period for all operator-assisted calls is three minutes. You can use Telstra Call Connect (dial 12456) when you don't know the number for a local or national call (a service fee of 50¢ applies). For operator-assisted domestic calls, dial 011. The following operator-connected services are also available:

Ring Back Price: A call can be timed and the charge given at the end of the call. If you want to know the cost of an national or international call dial 1222 before the number and the cost is telephoned back to you (for a fee) at the end of your call. Although useful when you aren't using your own phone and must pay for a call, using ring back price is expensive.

Particular Person Call: You can make an international particular person call (called a personal or person-to-person call in most other countries), where you start paying for the call only when the person required comes on the line. Note that it may be cheaper to make a brief call to find out whether the person you wish to speak to is available.

Reverse Charge & Third Party Charge Call: A reverse charge, transferred or collect call, is where the person called agrees to pay for the call. Useful when you've no change, the payphone won't accept your coins or when you're calling your mother-in-law. Note that making a reverse charge call from overseas to Australia is *very* expensive, as it's charged at the operator connected call rate. For reverse charge and third party charge calls, dial 12550. Note that reverse charge calls cannot be made to mobile phones.

Wake-Up Calls: To book a wake up or reminder call, dial 12454. Booking and call-back fees apply.

Line Faults: You can report line faults 24-hour a day to Telstra on 1100 (for residential customers), 13 2999 (for business customers) or 018 018 111 (for mobile phones). Telstra aims to repair telephone services within one working day in urban areas, two days in rural areas and three days in remote areas. If you suspect that your phone is faulty, test the line with another phone if you have one or test your phone on another line, e.g. that of a friend or neighbour. A priority repair service is provided for non-commercial emergency and essential service organisations, and to individuals whose life, health, safety or shelter would be at risk without a telephone.

Telstra Telecard: IDD and non-IDD calls (via the international operator) can be made with a free Telstra Telecard to over 200 countries and to Australia *from* over 50 countries using the Australia Direct service. Direct-dialled Telecard calls are 5 per cent cheaper than payphone rates, although if you call via the operator there's an additional service charge. Calls from payphones are charged at payphone rates (see page 168). Telecards can be used to dial direct from any tone phone, which includes all payphones and most private phones, although they cannot be used from mobile phones. When using a Telecard overseas you may be charged an astronomical sum. If Telecard calls need to be made via the operator, they are always dearer than making a direct-dialled call. Telecards are also prone to security risks, both in Australia and overseas. Although they offer convenience, it comes at a high price, which is fine **providing someone else picks up the tab**.

SPECIAL SERVICES

A number of special services (termed 'Easycall' features by Telstra) are available to subscribers with a tone phone connected to a digital exchange. You can buy or rent a special phone from Telstra (e.g. the Telstra *Touchfone* 400) that allows you to select certain Easycall services by simply pressing a button. Easycall services include the following:

Caller Number Display (CND) allows you to see the number of callers and decide whether you wish to speak to them. In order to use Caller Display you need to buy or rent a special phone with an LCD that displays and stores the numbers of callers. Users can opt out of the CND scheme and have their number blocked (from being displayed) by Telstra. Note, however, that Telstra initially took eons to do this and don't allow users to do it themselves (at least at the time of writing). CND costs $5 a month ($60 a year).

Call Forward allows you to automatically divert calls from your own phone to another number where you (or a colleague) can be reached, e.g. from home to office or to a mobile phone. There are three call forward options: immediate, no answer and busy.

Call Waiting tells you (via two beeps every five seconds) if another call is trying to get through to you when you're already on the phone and allows you to swap between calls.

Enquiry/Conference allows you to put a caller on hold and to make another (enquiry) call to a third person and, if you wish, hold a three-way conversation (conference).

MessageBank is an automatic answering service (with your own recorded message) that allows you to check your messages remotely using any touch-tone phone from almost anywhere in the world.

For information about Telstra's Easycall features dial 13 2200.

INFORMATION & ENTERTAINMENT NUMBERS

The use of premium rate information and entertainment numbers has increased considerably in recent years and includes numbers with the prefixes 0055, 0051, 065 and 190. Numbers with the prefix 0055 and 0051 provide recorded information services and are charged in multiples of 25¢ (40¢ from public phones). Rates are set by the service provider, e.g. 75¢ a minute at premium rate, 60¢ a minute at value rate and 40¢ a minute at budget rate. Most 'bulletins' last around three minutes. The same tariffs apply throughout Australia irrespective of the time of day or the day of the week. You can check whether a phone has access to 0055 services by dialling 0055 10055. Note that after 30th August 1998, 0055 services will change to InfoCall 190 numbers. InfoCall 190 numbers are also 'information' services, but are charged at either a timed fee (e.g. 35¢ to $5 a minute) or a fixed rate, e.g. from 35¢ to $30 per call. To check whether a phone has access to InfoCall services ring 1900 909 000. For information about InfoCall services, phone freecall 1800-035 055.

Information numbers offer a wide range of recorded information on practically any subject including astrology/horoscopes, comedy/entertainment, cricket, lotteries, keno and pools, news, sport, stock market information, telechat, tides, time, weather, snow reports, soccer results, racing, international flights, games, computer help, dating services, sex lines, legal and medical advice, and weather. You can also obtain personal (live) advice on finance, computers, study, legal matters and gardening. Most information service companies provide a free directory of their services. Information and entertainment numbers are huge money-spinners for the companies and are beloved by TV and radio competitions, which although the prizes may look attractive, are nothing compared to the revenue generated by the phone lines. **Note that if you use these numbers frequently you can go bankrupt!** Some people have received huge telephone bills which include calls to national and international sex lines that they haven't made. It's extremely difficult to prove that you (or a family member) didn't make these calls, even if you can show that you were out of the country at the time! To prevent this happening you can instruct Telstra (tel. freecall 1800-035 055) to bar calls to information services from your number.

DOMESTIC CALL RATES

In most towns and cities in Australia, local calls can be made only through Telstra, as other telephone companies don't have access to Telstra's local network, although some such as Optus are (very slowly) building their own local network. However, most users have a choice of companies for domestic long-distance calls. Telstra charges for all local calls (users don't receive a certain number of free calls per billing period) and levies a quarterly service and equipment charge, which is around $40 to $50 for a residential line.

Local Calls: Local calls (within a given distance of any city or region) from a private telephone cost 25¢ (40¢ from payphones) regardless of the length of the call. So-called 'community calls' (metro) are low cost calls made in and around a (state) capital city and its suburbs and surrounding towns. The boundaries for local and community calls are shown on a map in your white pages directory. Standard local calls are untimed calls between standard (fixed-line) telephones. Other local calls are charged in 3min blocks from 8am to 8pm Monday to Friday and in 4.5min blocks at other times. Note that calls within the same area code aren't all classed as local calls, e.g. all numbers in the Northern Territory have the code 08, but calls from Darwin to Alice Springs (a distance of 2,103km/1,307 miles) are charged at long-distance rates. Note that local calls made from a standard telephone to a mobile phone are charged at varying rates, depending on the time of day and the distance called.

Long-Distance Calls: You can use Telstra or another carrier or service provider (e.g. Optus) for your long distance (or subscriber trunk dialling/STD) calls. Customers with a choice of carriers need to dial a code before the area code, e.g. to choose Telstra you must dial 1411 before the area or country code. In future customers will be able to pre-select their preferred long-distance carrier and all calls will automatically be switched to their lines. The cheapest calls are available from Northgate (95¢ for an untimed long-distance call) and OzEmail's Internet Phone. You can find out the cost of Telstra national and international calls by dialling 1222 before dialling the number.

Long-distance STD calls are timed and charged according to the distance, time of day and the day of the week. STD calls are charged by the second and are itemised on your telephone bill. Note that long-distance call rates vary considerably and if you make a lot of calls you should shop around for the lowest rate.

Telstra Charge Rates: Telstra have three charge rates for self-dialled, domestic calls from ordinary lines (not payphones or mobile phones), depending on the time and day:

Rate	Time/Day	Cost
Day	8am to 6pm M-F	full rate
Evening	6pm to 8pm M-F	at least 14 per cent below the day rate
Economy*	8pm to 8am M-F	at least 55 per cent below the day rate

* The economy rate also applies from 8pm on Fridays until 8am on Mondays.

Special Tariffs: Telstra and other telephone companies (see page 160) offer a range of tariffs and discounts, although it's difficult to compare their value for money. For example Telstra's Smart Saver Flexi-Plan offers savings of 15 per cent on all Telstra STD and international calls when you spend a minimum of $15 a month.

INTERNATIONAL CALLS

International telephone, fax, and telex links are provided by the Overseas Telecommunications Commission (OTC) using undersea cables and satellites (Australia has telephone connections with around 200 countries via Intelsat). All private telephones in Australia are on International Direct Dialling (IDD), allowing calls to be dialled direct to some 200 countries. To make an International call, dial 0011, the country code, the area code *without* the first zero, and the subscriber's number. Dial 0101 for the international operator (0107 from payphones) to make non-IDD calls, credit card calls, person-to-person and reverse charge calls (which aren't accepted by all countries). Dial 1225 for international directory enquiries. The international code for most countries is listed at the back of the white pages under 'Telstra 0011 International and Telstra Faxstream 0015 International' and includes the time difference (one sure way to upset most people is to wake them at 3am). You can also obtain dialling codes, world time information and a time converter for over 220 countries via the internet.

Choosing the Carrier: Since the deregulation of telephone services in 1997, customers in most regions and major cities have been able to choose the carrier they use for international calls. This has resulted in a huge reduction in the cost of calls and it's now possible to telephone Britain and New Zealand for less than 40¢ a minute, with no connection fee (around one third of the cost before deregulation). Note, however, that if you make a lot of international calls it may be advisable to sign up with a number of companies and 'cherry pick', using the one that offers the lowest rate to the country you're calling. To use a particular carrier you must open an account with them and may be required to dial an access code before an STD or overseas number. In future customers will be able to pre-select their carrier.

Telstra off-peak rates for international calls are from 6pm to 9am Monday to Friday and from 6pm Friday to 9am Monday. Optus has three time bands: peak (8am-6pm Monday to Friday), weekend (midnight Friday to midnight Sunday) and off-peak (other times). Note, however, that many carriers charge a flat rate 24 hours a day, which is usually much lower than both Telstra's and Optus' peak rates. You can find out the cost of Telstra international calls by dialling 1222 before dialling the number.

Country or Australia Direct: Australia subscribes to a Country Direct service which allows you to make reverse charge (collect) or credit card (e.g. Telstra Telecard) calls to around 50 countries, including Britain and the USA. Codes are listed under the 'Operator Assisted Calls' section at the back of the white pages directory and further information can be obtained by dialling freecall 1800-801 800. You can also make reverse charge and credit card calls to Australia from over 50 countries using the Australia Direct service, which gives you direct and free access to an operator in Australia. Note, however, that using Country or Australia Direct is an expensive way to make a call.

TELEPHONE BILLS

Most residential customers in Australia are billed quarterly or bi-monthly for line rental, phone rental (if applicable) and calls. Business customers usually receive their bills monthly, although both business and residential customers may be able to choose to be billed monthly, bi-monthly or quarterly. Telstra also provides a Telstra payment card which allows you to pay your account in advance instalments. Where applicable, the telephone connection fee is included in your first bill. Telstra's billing is spread over a number of different systems and has been widely criticised. Itemised billing is being introduced and includes local calls, STD calls, international calls, telephone information services, operator-connected calls, calls to mobile phones, telecard calls, homelink 1800 calls, and line and equipment charges, all of which are itemised separately. Telstra also provides e-mail delivery of customer bills and an internet website where customers can check the current status of their account. Optus has an all-in-one billing service with a single bill for all services including local and long-distance calls, mobile phones, pay TV and internet services.

Telstra bills can be paid at any post office; by mail to 'Telstra, GPO Box 9901' in all capital cities; at Telstra shops (cash, cheques, credit/charge/EFTPOS cards); with a Telstra payment card; by electronic telephone banking; and by phone (with a credit/EFTPOS card). Telstra accepts American Express, Bankcard, Mastercard, Redicard, Diners Club and Visa credit cards. If you have any queries about your Telstra telephone bill, call the Telstra Customer Service Centre (tel. 13 2200 for residential services) between 8am and 5pm, Monday to Friday. If you believe that your bill is wrong, Telstra will monitor your line and equipment for faults and if you dispute the amount owed, you need only pay the amount that isn't in dispute while your query is being investigated. If you fail to pay your bill, a reminder or a disconnection notice will be issued. If you still fail to pay, your service will be disconnected and reconnection will take place only after payment of the account in full plus a reconnection fee.

PUBLIC TELEPHONES

Public telephones (or payphones) are provided in all cities and towns in Australia in public streets; inside and outside post offices; at airports, bus and railway stations; and in hotels, pubs, restaurants, service stations, shopping centres, and in other private and public buildings. Note that making non-local calls from hotels is expensive, although free local calls can often be made from phones in an hotel lobby. Payphones accept a range of payment options including coins, Phonecards, PhoneAway cards, Homelink services, Telstra Telecards, Optus Calling Cards, credit cards, and reverse charge and third party charge calls. A Telstra Telecard or Optus Calling Card allows you to make calls from virtually any phone and have them charged automatically to your home or business account. Locals calls cost 40¢ from a payphone for an unlimited period, although users are requested to limit calls to three minutes when there are people waiting. Modern pushbutton payphones accept 10¢, 20¢, 50¢ and $1 coins. Some 30,000 payphones also accept phone cards and some also accept credit cards. Telstra are installing new payphones that accept microchip smart cards. Calls to the 000 emergency service are free from payphones.

All payphones in Australia (some 85,000) are operated by Telstra (including around 300 solar-powered satellite payphones in remote outback areas), an estimated 95 per cent of which are claimed to be in working order at any given time (although it isn't uncommon to find vandalised or out-of-order payphones in some areas). Most are modern, digital, tone phones, although there are antiquated payphones in country and remote areas. In addition to these, there's an additional 40,000 payphones operated by private businesses in the form of Redphones or Goldphones. Around 1,000 multi-access payphones have been modified so that they can be used by the disabled including those in wheelchairs and the visually impaired. Some payphones also have hearing aid couplers, special volume controls and hands-free operation. There are also teletypewriter payphones at Telstra Payphone Centres in major capital cities and regional payphone centres for those with speech and hearing impediments (freecall 1800-066 456 for information). Telstra Payphone Centres in major cities are usually open from around 9am to 6pm, Monday to Friday, and from 10am to 4pm on Saturdays. Various types of payphones are found in Australia, including the following:

Greenphones (which are actually grey-green) are old phones with Subscriber Trunk Dialling (STD) and can be used to make domestic calls and calls to New Zealand and some South Pacific islands only. You can insert a maximum of seven coins (or $7) which can be replenished as they are used. Coins are visible and drop into the coin box automatically as they are used. Unused whole coins are returned at the end of the call, although no change is given if you insert large coins, so it's advisable to insert 10¢ or 20¢ coins rather than 50¢ or $1. To make international calls (apart from to New Zealand) from a green phone you must call the international operator (0107).

Redphones are modern pushbutton phones commonly found in shops, restaurants, pubs, shopping centres and other private businesses. They can be used only for local calls and accept only 10¢ and 20¢ coins.

Goldphones are pushbutton payphones (similar to red phones) and are installed in the same sort of locations. They allow both domestic and international calls and accept 10¢, 20¢, 50¢ and $1 coins.

Phonecards: Telstra phonecards are available in denominations of $5, $10, $20 and $50 and are available from over 15,000 retail outlets nationally (displaying a 'Phonecard Sold Here' sign) including newsagents, stores, pharmacies and kiosks. An audible signal is given when a phonecard is nearing the end of its value. Note that when making an international call you should insert at least $3 in coins or a phonecard with $3 credit. Phonecards can store and automatically dial telephone numbers through the use of Autocall features. They are produced in a number of designs and topical themes and (as in other countries) have become collectibles. Since their introduction in 1990 many are already fetching high prices among collectors and Telstra issues a bi-monthly newsletter and catalogue.

International Calls: Not all payphones in Australia can be used to make international calls. Payphones allowing international calls are marked ISD (International Subscriber Dialling), or IDD (International Direct Dialling). These include all gold phones. You can check by dialling 001100 (free). If it's an ISD phone you will hear the message 'congratulations, you're connected to ISD' and if not there will be no reply. International calls can also be made from Telstra telephone centres in the major cities and public telephone booths at major post offices. Calls made from a payphone are more expensive than from a private phone and they don't accept incoming calls.

When using a payphone, partly used coins are lost, but wholly unused coins are returned when you hang up the receiver. Payphones also have a 'follow on call' button; if you still have unused coins in credit, you can press this button and make another call using the remaining credit. If the display flashes, insert more coins until the flashing stops. It's advisable to insert relatively small coins unless you're calling long distance. Instructions for using modern pushbutton payphones are as follows:

1. Lift the handset and wait for the dialling tone. If you don't hear a dialling tone, the telephone is out of order.

2. Insert the minimum call charge of 40¢ (or more for long distance calls), a phonecard or a credit card. When you have inserted at least 40¢ the credit display will show how much you have in credit. If you're using a Phonecard or credit card, you'll be instructed when to dial.

3. Dial the number required.

4. When your credit is almost exhausted, there's an audible (a short burst of pips on the line) and visible warning (a flashing red light) 10 seconds before your time is about to expire. **Immediately insert more coins (or a new Phonecard) or the call will be disconnected.**

5. Replace the handset and any completely unused coins will be returned. If you still have credit for partly used coins, you can press the 'follow on call' button and make another call using the remaining credit. Otherwise any credit will be lost, so it pays not to insert too many $1 coins. If you're using a Phonecard or a credit card, **don't forget to take it with you.**

If you have difficulties phone the operator on 1234.

Credit Card Payphones: Some phones accept credit cards only (e.g. American Express, Diners Club, Mastercard and Visa), Telstra and Optus account cards, and EFTPOS cards. Credit card phones are predominantly located in major airports and other transport hubs and large shopping centres. To use a credit card phone you swipe the magnetic strip of your card through the phone's card reader, key in your PIN number and dial when you hear the dialling tone. Note that there's a high minimum charge of $1.20 when using a credit card payphone and therefore they should be used only in an 'emergency'.

MOBILE TELEPHONES

Mobile phones were introduced in Australia in 1987 and by 1997 it had the fourth-highest number of mobile phones per capita in the world after Sweden, Finland and Denmark. In 1997, over 5m Australians had a mobile phone (almost 30 per cent of the population), around half of which were analogue and half digital phones. The booming market shows no signs of slowing and mobile phones are expected to rise to 8m by the year 2000. **Before buying or using a mobile phone, you should be aware that health fears have been raised in some countries over the effects of the electromagnetic fields generated by them.** On the other hand, a mobile phone could save your life in an emergency!

Mobile phone services are operated by Telstra (over 60 per cent of the market), Optus (over 30 per cent), and Vodaphone (less than 5 per cent), who are expected to be joined by others following deregulation in 1997. Australia has both analogue (covering 95 per cent of the population) and digital networks, although the analogue network is due to be phased out by 1st January 2000 (however, phones in some rural areas without a digital service will still have access to the analogue service after this date). Digital mobile phone network covers some 90 per cent of the population, although it should be stressed that cover is restricted to the major population centres and corridors (all operators provide coverage maps). However, this will change when satellite mobile services go into operation in September 1998.

In addition to services in the major metropolitan areas, Telstra mobile satellite & radio services provide mobile communications to the marine, remote land mobile and aeronautical markets. MobileSat allows you to plug a computer, fax machine or satellite navigation equipment into a Mobilesat terminal in a car, boat or aircraft and receive crystal clear communication wherever you are in Australia or up to 200km/124mi off the coast. Australia subscribes to the GSM digital network which allows the same phone to be used in over 20 countries worldwide including most of western Europe, Asia, the Pacific, central and South Africa, and the Middle East (referred to as international roaming).

Buying a mobile phone is a mine-field, as not only are there three networks from which to choose but numerous tariffs, connection fees, monthly subscriptions, insurance and call charges. Before buying a cellular phone, shop around and compare phone prices and features; installation and connection charges; rental charges; and charge rates. **Most importantly, if you live in a remote area, make sure that a company's coverage includes the area where you live or do business.** Phones are sold by retail outlets such as Telstra shops, specialist dealers, and department and chain stores, who have arrangements with service providers or networks to sell airtime contracts (along with phones). Don't rely on getting good or impartial advice from retail staff, some of whom know little or nothing about phones and networks (it's said that the difference between Clint Eastwood and a mobile phone seller is that Clint isn't a real cowboy). Retailers advertise in magazines and newspapers, where a wide range of special offers are promoted. There are dozens of mobile phones on the market priced from around $400 for an average phone to over $700 for a top model. Secondhand phones can be purchased from around $150. Some car manufacturers fit car phones as standard equipment, particularly to attract women drivers (some of whom are born with phones attached to their ears).

Before buying a phone, compare battery life, memory number capacity, weight (now down to around 100g for the lightest models), size and features. Features may include alphanumeric store, automatic call back, unanswered call store, call timer, minute minder, lock facility, call barring, mailbox, messaging services, internet web-surfing and e-mail. New technology includes the personal handy phone system (PHS) currently available in Japan which operates as a cordless phone in the home (using your home fixed-line number) and a mobile phone elsewhere. Note that when you sign up with a service provider, the cost of a phone is subsidised (and remains the property of the service provider) and retailers and network providers recoup the cost through line rentals and call charges. You can sign up for as little as $100, although the minimum cost over 18 months is usually around $400 and often much more.

The most important point is where you're going to use a phone, followed by when, how often, and whether you will make mostly local, long-distance or international calls. Don't be influenced by an inexpensive phone when the real costs lie in high call and line rental charges. Generally the higher the connection and line rental charges, the lower the cost of calls. If you make a lot of calls, select a tariff with low call charges. Conversely, if you make few calls or need a phone mostly for incoming calls, choose a tariff with low monthly costs. Note that calls to and from mobile phones, including calls made from a fixed-line phone, are much more expensive than calls between fixed-line phones, and calls to freecall 1800 numbers aren't free from mobile phones. Telephone numbers with the prefixes 014, 015, 017, 018, 019 and 041 (analogue) are mobile phones. You can obtain pre-paid cards (e.g. $50 or $100) which avoid the need to sign a long-term contract or produce a credit card required for a contract. Note that if you have a phone with a pre-paid card, there's no charge for receiving calls, and it's an ideal solution for someone who wants a phone mostly for incoming calls and makes very few calls.

Security: Theft of mobile phones is a huge problem and stolen mobile phones are usually reprogramed (cloned) to make free calls overseas. Mobile phones should never be left in cars. It's advisable to insure a phone for its real value, as if a rented phone is stolen you will be billed for its replacement cost, not what you paid for it. All phones are provided with a unique serial number which allows their use to be blocked if they're stolen and digital phones can be programed to stop users making certain calls, e.g. international calls. New clone-proof digital mobile phones are being introduced and all mobile phones are expected to be digital within five years.

Free booklets, *Hold the phone — read this before you buy a mobile* and *Mobile phone etiquette for Australia*, are available from the office of the telecommunications industry ombudsman (tel. freecall 1800-062 058).

One spin-off of the mobile phone explosion is that they have created a new breed of 'cellular Samaritans' who report emergencies, accidents, crimes, traffic jams and other problems.

DIRECTORIES

Australian telephone subscribers, both business and private, are listed in directories (also called phone books) which may be subdivided into white and yellow pages. In most areas white and yellow pages are contained in the same volume, while in major cities such as Sydney there are separate volumes. White pages contain a list of subscribers in alphabetical order and yellow pages a list of businesses listed by business type. If you don't have the latest local phone book when you move into a new home, you can get one free from your local post office. You can order other directories (freecall 1800-011 843) for which there's a $5 delivery charge plus 80¢ for each directory in each consignment. You can also buy a CD-Rom ($49.95) containing all 55 Australian directories with over 7.5m names and phone numbers. White and yellow pages are also available on the internet, including versions of the white pages in German, Indonesian and Italian. New editions of phone books are delivered free to subscribers' homes. Directories can also be viewed at post offices, international telephone directory reference libraries and public libraries. Telstra recommend that you recycle your old telephone books (special bins are provided in major cities when new books are issued).

An entry containing your name, address and telephone number is automatically listed in the white pages directory covering your area. You may also purchase an extra entry, e.g. when two people share a telephone, or enhance your listing in **bold** type. Business customers may also list an occupation. You can request an unlisted number or ex-directory number (called a 'silent number'), for which there's a fee of $32 a year. In this case your name and number won't appear in any directories and won't be made available by directory assistance (1223). Elements of your address such as your street and house number can also be suppressed (e.g. just your name and suburb is listed), for which an annual fee of $30 applies. Around 10 per cent of Australians have silent numbers.

A wealth of information is contained in the white pages including translating and interpreting service (TIS), 24-hour emergency numbers, Telstra information and services, local and community calls, call information, international calls, operator assisted calls, directory information, services for the disabled and aged, community help and welfare services, abbreviations of place names (used in directories), telephone prefixes and place names, and telephone information services (0055 and 190 numbers).

Yellow Pages: In addition to subscriber phone books, business directories called *yellow pages* are published for all regions of Australia. Yellow pages include such information as emergency and useful local numbers, local government numbers, calendar of events, entertainment seating guide, public transport, inner city and surrounds maps, and getting about. Subscribers are listed under a business or service heading (in alphabetical order) for the area covered. If you don't have the latest local yellow pages when you move into a new home, you can obtain a free copy from your local post office. New editions of yellow pages are delivered to subscribers' homes. All phone books and yellow pages are available in public reference libraries and public telephone booths may also contain local directories. There are separate business directories in the major cities such as the Business Information Guide (BIG) in Melbourne.

Directory Enquiries: There are various numbers for directory enquiries (called 'directory assistance' in Australia). Usually you dial 013 for the area covered by your local telephone book, 0175 for other areas within Australia and 0103 for overseas directory enquiries. All directory assistance calls are free. Telstra wanted to impose a 50¢ levy on all 013 calls (which cost them over $200m a year), which would have been offset by a reduction in line rental costs. However, there's a government ban on 013 charges and (at least for the time being) a charge isn't being contemplated. If you want directory enquiries to find a number for you, you must know the town or city of the person or business whose number you require. Telephone numbers for most subscribers in major international cities can be obtained from directories in central reference libraries in major towns and cities.

EMERGENCY NUMBERS

There's only one national emergency number in Australia, the 000 service, which is for police, fire and ambulance emergencies, plus coastguard, cave and mountain rescue services. Emergency 000 calls are free from all telephones, including payphones. When you dial 000 the operator will ask you which emergency service you require ("Emergency, which service please?") and you'll immediately be switched through to that service. You must state clearly your name, location and give a brief description of the emergency.

A list of other '24-hour Emergency Numbers' or 'Personal Emergency & Help Services' is included at the front of the white pages telephone directory and inside the front cover of the yellow pages. These include maritime rescue, aviation search and rescue, chemist emergency prescriptions, child abuse, child protection, crime stoppers, crisis centre, customs coastwatch, dentists, distress call, doctors, domestic violence, drug intelligence, electricity, gas, water, hospitals, kids help line, lifeline, Mindwise (mental health), poison information, rape crisis, youth line, city missions, state emergency service, translating and interpreting service, veterinary surgeons and counselling for victims of crime. **Lifeline** (13 1114) provides a confidential, 24-hour counselling service in times of personal crisis throughout Australia for the cost of a local call. See also **Emergencies** on page 276 and **Counselling** on page 288.

INTERNET

Australia has the highest number of internet users per capita outside the USA (around 1.6m regular users) and enjoys the world's second lowest (after the USA) internet access charges thanks largely to Telstra's untimed local calls. This means that for a one-time charge of 25¢ subscribers can stay on the internet for as long as they wish. This is expected to continue, although timed local calls may be introduced if the telephone network is degraded by internet users. The speed of access is expected to increase dramatically in future, as high speed lines and cable modems are introduced. There are internet service providers in all capital cities and also in many regional cities, where the most popular providers are OzEmail, Access One and Telstra. Competition has driven down fees in recent years and you should shop around for the best deal. Users pay a monthly fee, e.g. $20, which includes a number of hours free access.

The success of the internet is built on the ability to collect information from computers around the world by connecting to a nearby service for the cost of a local phone call. However, if you have correspondents or friends who are connected to the internet, you can also make long-distance and international 'calls' for the price of a local phone call. Internet users can buy software from companies such as Quarterdeck and Vodaltec (costing around $100) that effectively turns their personal computer into a voice-based telephone (both parties must have compatible software). You also need a sound card, speakers, a microphone and a modem, and access to a local internet provider. While the quality of communication isn't as good as using a telephone (it's similar to using a CB radio) and you need to arrange call times in advance (e.g. by e-mail), making international 'calls' costs virtually nothing. All you pay is the cost of a local call to your internet provider. Even this call is free in some areas where cable phone companies provide free local calls. Once on the internet there are no other charges, no matter how much distance is covered or time is spent online. The internet can also be used to send electronic mail (e-mail) messages and letters written with a word processor.

TELEGRAMS, TELEX & FAX

Telegrams (cables) can be sent by phone or from any post office in Australia. There are three rates: urgent (two to four hour delivery), ordinary (four to six hours) and letter (24 hours), although in some remote areas of Australia deliveries are made just once a week by air. The cost depends on where it's being sent from, the destination and the speed required.

Fax: When sending an international fax dial 0015 (FaxStream) instead of 0011, followed by the country code, area code and fax number. FaxStream is a network of specially selected lines which provide optimum quality for international fax calls. Australia Post provides a public fax and delivery service (Faxpost) which allows faxes to be sent to virtually anyone in Australia or overseas, irrespective of whether you or the recipient has a fax machine. Faxpost allows delivery of faxed documents to all major centres in Australia within two hours or alternatively a same day service, plus fast delivery overseas. To fax a document via FaxPost to someone in Australia without a fax machine, you fax the document to the Fax Centre Post Office nearest the addressee (there are around

1,500 throughout Australia), which is then delivered within two hours, the same day or by mail, depending on your instructions.

Alternatively if you don't have a fax machine, but the addressee does, you need to deliver your document to the nearest Fax Centre from where it will be faxed to the addressee. A document can also be sent to someone when neither party has a fax machine, in which case the document is delivered to the nearest Fax Centre and faxed to the Fax Centre Post Office nearest the addressee, from where it's delivered. International faxes can be transmitted to over 90 countries and to any fax machine in the world, providing IDD phone access is available. Messages can be delivered to overseas addressee's without a fax machine by courier messenger, often on the same day, or can be delivered next day by mail. The cost for domestic faxes is $4 for the first page and $1 for additional pages, and $10 for the first page and $4 for additional pages to international numbers. Faxes can also be sent from hotels, business offices, and Telstra phone centres in major towns and cities.

Mobile phone and portable computer users can use a portable fax, which allows fax transmissions to be made from virtually anywhere in Australia and overseas. ISDN (integrated services digital network) lines allow you to send data, such as information held on computers, on a phone line at high speed and virtually error free, e.g. an A4 fax takes around four seconds to send.

Telex is the largest dedicated text message network in the world, with over two million subscribers worldwide in over 200 countries. There are public telex bureaux at all capital city chief telegraph offices and at Telstra offices in many towns.

8.

TELEVISION & RADIO

Australian television (the 'electric goldfish bowl') is among the best in the world and much better than the rubbish dished up in many other countries (i.e. better quality than American TV — what isn't? — but not as good as British TV). However, over half the programs are purchased from Britain and the USA, with most local content consisting of sports, soaps, current affairs and game shows. Free-to-air (or terrestrial) TV includes both government-owned and commercial stations. In addition to free-to-air TV, pay (cable) TV is provided in most major cities, and satellite TV is also available in country and outback areas. WebTV is expected to be introduced in 1998, where customers can purchase a set-top box (for around $200) with a built-in modem for internet access (no computer is required), a pay-TV decoder and a CD-ROM drive for games. Digital TV is expected to be available by the year 2000, which will allow hundreds of channels to be transmitted by satellite and cable. Australian radio includes both state-owned ABC and commercial stations and is generally excellent.

Australians are avid TV viewers and almost all homes have a colour TV (over half have two or more) and 80 per cent have a VCR, which has spawned a nation of couch potatoes. Children spend up to one-third of their leisure time watching TV (as in most western countries), which has been attacked as providing a mixture of 'mindless junk', violence and sex, detrimental to the education of children. In households where TV reigns supreme, the idiot box is far more influential with children than parents. The poor quality of some programs in Australia is offset by some of the best and funniest advertisements in the world (which they should be, considering they cost more to produce than many programs). There's no TV or radio licence (which were abolished in 1974), so at least the rubbish is 'free'!

TV programs are listed in daily newspapers (Saturday newspapers also include Sunday programs) and weekly guides such as *TV Week*, which is produced in separate editions for each state or territory (because of local time differences). Many Saturday and Sunday newspapers also provide free weekly TV guides. However, few if any pay TV programs are listed in most publications. Free weekly TV and radio guides are also provided with the weekend editions of major daily newspapers. Programs can also be displayed via the TV teletext. Note that the time difference between the states (see page 460) means that nationwide programs are broadcast at different times depending on where you live in Australia.

STANDARDS

The standards for TV reception in Australia aren't the same as in many other countries. TVs and video recorders manufactured for use in North America (NTSC Standard) and for the European PAL B/G or PAL-I systems, won't function in Australia due to different transmission standards. Some foreign TVs can be converted to operate under Australia's PAL-D system, although it usually isn't worth the trouble and expense of shipping a TV (or VCR) to Australia. The cost of a TV varies considerably depending on its make, screen size, features and, not least, the retailer (shop around). The cost of a quality TV ranges from around $300 for a 36cm (14in) portable TV to $600 for a state-of-the-art 63cm (24in) TV. Video recorders start at around $500.

TVs are becoming ever more sophisticated and many offer a wide array of features, including on-screen displays of volume and picture controls, and picture-in-picture, which allows you to superimpose on the screen a small picture of what's showing on other channels by pressing a button on the remote control. TV addicts can add dolby surround sound (with a Dolby pro logic amplifier with decoder and separate speakers) and create cinema sound effects. Other recent innovations include LaserDisc, Digital Video Disc

(DVD) and Video CD systems, although these are expensive when compared with VHS video and a waste of money for most people. When buying a TV in Australia you will find it advantageous to buy one with teletext, which apart from allowing you to display forthcoming program listings, also provides a wealth of useful and interesting information including news, weather, sport, travel, financial, consumer and entertainment. Teletext also provides subtitles for selected programs for people with hearing problems, which are usually indicated in program listings. Pay TV and satellite stations also provide teletext services. Note that whatever you buy, in a year's time (or less) it will be superceded by a new model.

There's an active market in secondhand TVs and videos (and most other things) in Australia, so should you wish to sell your old TV to buy one with all the latest bells and whistles (or because you're leaving Australia), you'll have no problem. Secondhand colour TVs can be purchased from retailers, rental companies and through advertisements in local newspapers from as little as $100. Some retailers offer to part exchange your old TV for a new one, although they may offer you less than its market value. TV rental is fairly common in Australia and is mostly offered by specialist national rental companies (such as Rentlo), although some local TV and radio shops also rent. It's always cheaper to buy than rent a TV or video, particularly over a long period. Some people are tempted to rent by the ever-changing technology, although you should bear in mind that rental TVs are rarely the latest models and the minimum rental period is usually 12 or 18 months. Renting a TV is a habit carried over from the '50s and '60s when few people could afford to buy a TV outright. **Today renting hardly ever makes economic sense.**

FREE-TO-AIR STATIONS

There are five national free-to-air (terrestrial) networks in Australia: ABC, Seven, Nine, Ten and SBS. ABC (Australian Broadcasting Corporation) and SBS (Special Broadcasting Service) are government owned, while Seven, Nine and Ten are commercial networks. There are also a number of regional commercial stations (including Capital, NBN, Northern, Prime, Seven Queensland, Southern Cross and Win), Imparja Television (an Aboriginal commercial station), plus local, community and student TV. Not all cities receive all the national networks and most capital cities can receive between three and five, while in some remote areas the ABC may be the only free-to-air station you can receive. The regional stations are affiliated to the national commercial networks: Seven (affiliated stations include Prime, Seven Queensland and Southern Cross), Nine (affiliated stations include NBN and WIN) and Ten (affiliated stations include Capital Television). Overall control of Australia's TV and radio services is exercised by the Australian Broadcasting Authority (ABA).

Programs: Australian TV is famous for its soaps, although some have terrible scripts and even worse 'acting'. The most popular Australian soaps include Neighbours, Home and Away, A Country Practice and Flying Doctor, which are sold worldwide and are particularly popular in Britain. British comedy, drama and soaps are also popular in Australia, as are the better American programs. The choice of films on free-to-air TV is usually terrible and you need to subscribe to pay TV to see the latest films. Australian TV isn't as paranoid about nudity as American TV, but you're unlikely to see any explicit sex (except perhaps on pay or satellite TV). News and current affairs programs are popular, although news tends to be parochial and doesn't include much world news. There are good weather forecasts on all channels.

Australian TV, particularly commercial stations, shows a surfeit of live sports, particularly at weekends. Cover includes both local and international events including tennis, soccer, cricket, rugby, Australian rules football, American football, baseball, basketball, motor racing and athletics. To protect significant sporting and cultural events currently covered by free-to-air (FTA) TV from being bought up by pay TV, the government introduced an 'anti-siphoning' list of events (11 sports plus the Olympic and Commonwealth Games) which should be available to be televised free to the general public. However, over half the events on the anti-siphoning list have never been shown at all on FTA TV and less than a third have been shown live on FTA. Pay TV operators are pushing to have the list reduced or to be permitted to show live sports and events that have been rejected by the FTA stations.

Commercial TV: Australia has three commercial networks: Seven, Nine and Ten, which are available in major cities and offer 24-hour programing. Nine Network has been the leading station for over 10 years, although it's closely rivalled by Seven Network. Nine is unashamedly populist and produces good lifestyle programs, game shows, and news and current affairs programs, but isn't so good at comedy and drama. However, its forte is sport, which dominates programing, and hit imports. Seven Network is the second-highest rated network (by viewing figures) after Nine and is strong on comedy and drama, and more likely to show non-commercial programs. Its most popular programs include *Home and Away* and *Blue Heelers*. Seven Network has weaker news and current affairs than the Nine Network. Ten Network has given up trying to compete with Nine and Seven for the mainstream market, and concentrates on screening popular American shows (*Seinfeld, The Simpsons, 90210, Melrose Place, X-Files*) for the under 40s. It isn't strong on local programs, although it did come up with *Neighbours* and *Heartbreak High*. Breakfast TV is popular on all commercial stations. **Imparja Television** is an aboriginal owned and run commercial TV station operating out of Alice Springs. It covers one-third of the country mainly in the Northern Territory, South Australia and western NSW. Broadcasts range from soap operas to programs made especially for Aboriginal people.

The quality of programs on commercial TV varies from terrible to excellent. The competition to buy foreign (e.g. British and American) programs and exclusive rights to sporting events is fierce, particularly with the increased competition from pay TV. It's hoped that this will result in the networks producing more of their own programs, which, apart from being superior to a lot of the imported drivel, are also a lucrative export earner. Commercial TV networks currently produce less than half their programs, which is due to be increased to 55 per cent in 1998. Ads. on commercial TV are frequent and irritating, particularly when you're trying to watch a film or sport. Some sports events are ruined by commercial breaks and ads. are sometimes even screened during play at the bottom of the screen. Breaks tend to be more frequent and last longer than in many other countries and even exceed some American stations (i.e. where the ads. seem to last longer than the programs). The maximum permitted advertising is 13 minutes an hour (although it sometimes seems that this is the time allotted to programs), but when the promotion of stations (and their proprietors) and upcoming programs are included it's much longer. Commercial stations are huge money-spinners and regularly change owners.

ABC: The Australian Broadcasting Corporation (ABC), affectionately known as 'Aunty' after the British Broadcasting Corporation (BBC) on which it's modelled, is government owned and operates both TV and radio (see page 184) stations throughout Australia. It's financed by the government and carries no advertising. The name of the local ABC station changes depending on the state, e.g. it's called ABN in NSW (the N is for NSW) and ABV in Melbourne (V for Victoria), although it's usually found on channel two. Being non-commercial, it holds the moral high ground with regard to quality programing (almost nothing American is aired) and its output contains a large percentage of locally produced programs with the emphasis on comedy, drama, natural history (mostly about Australia), news and current affairs. Comedy and drama programs are often imported from Britain. The ABC also operates Australia Television, an international satellite TV service broadcasting to over 30 countries and territories in Asia and the Pacific.

SBS: The Special Broadcasting Service (SBS) is a government sponsored, multicultural TV station, established in 1978 to provide multi-lingual radio and TV services that inform, educate and entertain all Australians, and reflect Australia's multicultural society. SBS is available in all major cities and a number of regional areas, reaching around 16m people. It's similar to PBS in America or Channel 4 in Britain, although it screens a large percentage of programs in foreign languages with sub-titles, in addition to English-language programs. It doesn't show advertising and is funded by the government. It's usually found on channel eight, although you need a special receiver in some areas. It has its critics, although most viewers appreciate that it provides foreign 'culture' unavailable on other channels and excellent world news coverage (e.g. 6.30pm eastern time) which is superior to the more parochial output of the ABC and commercial stations. It also shows foreign sport (e.g. European soccer) that isn't found on commercial TV and is the traditional host channel of the (soccer) World Cup. It is, however, sometimes criticised as being insensitive to community needs and although it exports its few home-produced programs, it also shows a lot of 'trashy' foreign movies. SBS has a relatively small but dedicated following.

Community or Local TV: There are around five or six community or local TV stations in all major cities which give everyone in the community access to TV. Community TV stations include ACE-TV (Adelaide), Briz31 (Brisbane), CATV (Canberra), MCT-31 (Melbourne), CTVP 31 (Perth) and CTS (Sydney). There's also student TV in some cities such as RMITV in Melbourne.

PAY TELEVISION

Pay TV (also called cable TV in other countries) was introduced in Australia in 1995 and shouldn't be confused with pay-per-view, where subscribers pay on a per program basis (e.g. for a live concert or sports event). With pay TV, viewers pay a monthly fee for a package of stations, delivered via cable or satellite. There are two major pay TV operators in Australia: Foxtel and Optus Vision. However, Galaxy TV was Australia's first pay TV service (it commenced broadcasting in January 1995 in Melbourne and Sydney) which is available via both cable and satellite,

The installation of cables for pay TV in Australia was one of the largest and fastest cable installation programs undertaken anywhere in the world. Both Telstra and Optus laid their cables in the same streets in Sydney, Melbourne and Brisbane, afraid that their rivals would steal a march on them (Optus laid its cables above ground, to the revulsion of residents, rather than burying then as Telstra did). Cable currently reaches around 3m homes or around 40 per cent of the total, mostly in major cities (with a few exceptions). Most homes in Brisbane, Melbourne and Sydney are cabled, plus around half of Adelaide and a small part of Perth. The broadband cable is used to deliver pay TV, FM radio, telephone, high-speed internet access, and other interactive services such as community information systems. It also enables operators to offer pay-per-view films and other broadcasts on demand.

Some 15 per cent of households in Melbourne and Sydney subscribe to pay TV, although it isn't very popular (the biggest fans are children) and many families have tried it and quit. Unlike satellite and cable TV in Europe and North America, pay TV in

Australia doesn't have sufficient big exclusive sports or entertainment specials to attract the average viewer (the climate also means that many people have better things to do than watch TV). Foxtel provides some 30 channels including world news, the cartoon network, the world movie channel, Fox Sports, Fox Children's network and BBC World. Optus Vision provides around 25 channels including news, general entertainment, education, sport, films, music and community broadcasts. However, critics claim that most output consists of old films, minor sports, boring documentaries and banal local news. Pay TV operators have been allowed to broadcast advertisements since 1st July 1997.

As with the rest of the media business in Australia, pay TV is a battle between the press moguls Kerry Packer (aligned with Optus Vision) and Rupert Murdoch (Foxtel in partnership with Telstra), with (so far) both coming out losers. To date pay TV has been a financial disaster, with combined losses for Optus Vision and Foxtel totalling over $3 billion in less than four years. Neither Foxtel or Optus Vision publish subscriber figures (which confirms that both are doing badly!), although it's estimated that there are a total of well under 1m subscribers. Many analysts believe that the market isn't large enough for two pay TV operators (it's yet to be proved whether it's large enough for one!) and the two companies have been slugging it out in the courts and on the streets of Australia for the last few years. Due to its high losses, Telstra terminated the cable roll-out of its broadband cable network at 2.5m homes, some 40 per cent short of its original target of 4m.

Foxtel and Optus both charge an installation fee of around $30 (which may be higher for homes with difficult access) and a monthly subscription of between around $30 and $60 depending on the program package (you can choose from a range of packages depending on your preferred viewing, e.g. sport or films). Subscriptions can be paid by direct debit, cash (at an ANZ branch or post office), by cheque, money order or credit card. Some cable companies offer inexpensive phone services, possibly including free local off-peak calls, and it's possible to save enough money on your phone bill to pay for your cable TV. Optus offers customers who use its pay TV and long-distance telephone services a 10 per cent discount on their monthly TV bill, or an equal discount on their long-distance phone bill.

Although Melbourne, Sydney and Brisbane are taken by Optus and Telstra, the rest of the country is wide open and being exploited by small companies (such as Northgate in Ballarat and Neighbourhood Cable in Mildura) who plan to steal Telstra's market share by offering telephone, TV and internet services at lower prices. For example, Northgate Communications provide a 25-channel pay TV service in Ballarat for $14.95 a month, which is reduced if customers also rent a telephone line. Subscribers usually receive free monthly program guides, which are also available from newsstands. Note, however, that most Australian newspapers and TV guides virtually ignore pay TV and don't list any programs, while some list selected channels only (e.g. Showtime and Foxtel highlights).

VIDEOS

In the last decade or so there has been an explosion in the number of video rental outlets in Australia, which reached saturation point some years ago (they total over 3,000 with an annual turnover of over $600m). Some 80 per cent of households (over 5m) have at least one VCR and around 60 per cent of households rent at least one video a month. There's also a thriving video sales market. Many video shops are open until between 8pm and 10pm, seven days a week. To rent a video you must usually be a member, for which shops insist on proof of address and verification of your signature. If you're under

18, a parent is required to stand as a guarantor. Some video shops have a children's membership scheme with special deals for kids and cheap rental rates for children's films (although most kids are more interested in video nasties than *The Jungle Book*!). The latest releases can be rented from around $5 a night and older films can be rented for up to a week for as little as $2. Rental outlets usually have special offers for film buffs such as a free old movie with each new release rented, or seven old movies for a week for $10.

Members are issued with a membership card which must be shown when hiring videos. Usually you can take out up to three or four films at any time, which must be returned at any time (or up to two hours before closing time) the following day. If you're late returning a film, you're charged an extra day's rental for each day overdue. Note that if you lose or damage a film, you'll be expected to pay for a replacement at retail price. Videos can also be rented from some public libraries. Most video shops also sell secondhand video films at reduced prices and older videos which are on general sale.

RADIO

Radio reception in Australia is excellent in most parts of the country, including stereo reception, which is clear in all but the most remote or 'mountainous' areas (not that Australia has many mountains). Radio is extremely popular, particularly among the young — three out of four teenagers listen daily to the radio. Local stations broadcast on FM wave band in stereo or on the medium wave (MW) band. High-quality FM radio can also be received via cable or satellite links, which provides dozens of stations. The shortwave (SW) band is useful for receiving foreign radio stations. There's an overheated market for commercial FM stations (which change hands for huge sums) and a pent-up demand for licences in the major cities (new licences are due to be issued in 1998). The largest radio station networks in Australia are owned by DMG Radio Australia, Austereo and the Australian Radio Network. Digital radio is due to be introduced in the next few years and will allow stations to transmit several channels of sound simultaneously, as well as text and pictures to a small screen attached to receivers. Australian radio is regulated by the Australian Broadcasting Authority (ABA) and there are no radio licence fees in Australia.

There are literally hundreds of radio stations in Australia including ABC, commercial, ethnic, community and university-based stations (operated on a shoe-string and run by volunteers). In the last few decades, dozens of public (community) radio stations have sprung up around Australia, supported by the government and various educational institutions. They often have a limited transmission range and cater for specific community groups within their areas, e.g. there are some 16 public radio stations in Sydney, which although amateurish are diverse and original.

Commercial Radio: Commercial radio is hugely popular in Australia and includes large city stations with vast budgets and hundreds of thousands of listeners. Stations provide a comprehensive service of music and other entertainment, local news and information, education, consumer advice, traffic information and local events. There are also 'talk-back' stations (such as Melbourne's top-rated 3AW station) which intersperse music with phone-in discussions providing listeners with the opportunity to air their views. Many stations have 'star' presenters whose 'fame- (infamy) is often due to their outrageous and insulting behaviour towards their listeners (sports' commentators can also be extremely rude about players' performances). The location of a station can be determined by its call sign, the first number of which is the same as a state or territory's postcode, e.g. 2UE is a Sydney station and 3CR is in Melbourne.

Stations cater for every musical taste (e.g. pop/rock, easy listening, classical, jazz), although pop stations are the most popular and cater mostly for mainstream tastes. Some stations even change their output (e.g. from easy listening to hard rock or vice versa) at the drop of a hat if their audience figures fall dramatically. Music is usually blended with news updates, traffic and weather reports, although some stations have taken to playing less music and telling jokes, which apparently receive a higher rating than music. Radio stations employ real 'comedians', not just DJs trying to raise a chuckle (termed comedy jocks), with a down-to-earth sense of humour where anything goes and nothing is sacred. As in other countries, radio stations scour the country (world?) to find brainless, incoherent, banal dimwits whom they can instantly turn into wallies of the radio waves, known as disc jockeys.

ABC: The Australian Broadcasting Corporation (ABC) is government funded and operates both TV (see page 180) and radio stations throughout Australia. It operates metropolitan radio stations in nine cities and 39 regional stations, including Radio National, ABC Classic FM, and the Triple-J youth radio network. ABC metropolitan radio includes 2BL (Sydney) and 3LO (Melbourne). It also operates the 24-hour Parliamentary & News Network (PNN), a parliamentary radio service broadcast to all capital cities except Darwin (lucky them!), and to Newcastle. The ABC is also responsible for Radio Australia, an international radio service broadcast via shortwave and satellite (in English and eight other languages) to the Asia-Pacific regions and worldwide (although services have been reduced in recent years and remain under threat from budget cuts).

ABC Radio National provides excellent news coverage (international news is sent by satellite from the BBC in London) and is broadcast nationwide on both AM and FM. However, in general, ABC stations aren't as popular as commercial stations (Triple-J is one exception) and is regarded as the thinking person's radio station. Triple-J (JJJ) is the ABC's youth FM radio station and is a good place to hear new music outside the main pop stream and plug into Australia's youth culture. There's no advertising on ABC radio stations, although it's the main source of income for commercial radio stations.

Ethnic Radio: Australians can tune into local radio broadcasts in over 50 languages, including Aboriginal radio in outback regions. The Special Broadcasting Service (SBS) was established in 1994 and like SBS TV (see on page 181) broadcasts in many languages. It's available in all state and territory capital cities plus some regional cities.

BBC World Service: The BBC World Service (the insomniac's station) broadcasts worldwide, in English and around 37 other languages, with a total output of over 750 hours a week (a *very* long week). The BBC World Service is the most famous and highly respected international radio service in the world, with regular listeners estimated at some 120 million (give or take a few). The main aims are to provide unbiased news, project British opinion, and reflect British life, culture and developments in science and industry. News bulletins, current affairs, political commentaries and topical magazine programs form the bulk of its output, supported by a comprehensive sports service, music, drama and general entertainment. For program and frequency information write to BBC World Service Publicity, PO Box 76, Bush House, Strand, London WC2B 4PH, UK. A BBC monthly magazine, *London Calling*, is available on subscription.

PUBLISHED SUMMER 1998

9.

EDUCATION

A ustralian educational institutions generally have a good international reputation, particularly universities and tertiary-level colleges, which enrol over 50,000 foreign students a year from all corners of the globe (plus a further 100,000 foreign students in vocational institutions, English-language colleges and other schools). Australian schools have a high standard of teaching and good academic results, and the country has a proud record of academic and scientific achievement. In international surveys, Australian students score highly in mathematics and science (ahead of most other western countries), but lag behind some Asian countries.

Full-time education is compulsory from the age of six until age 16 and has been compulsory in New South Wales for over 100 years. Around 75 per cent of pupils complete 12 years of schooling, although it varies depending on the state or territory. Primary education lasts for six or seven years up to the age of 12 or 13 and secondary school for five or six years until around age 18, making a total of 12 years. Students are encouraged to remain at school until the completion of their 12th year (around the age of 18), although this may depend on the local job market. The government has cut unemployment benefits for young people in recent years to encourage them to stay on at school or take up training, rather than leave school and search for non-existent jobs. This has led to overcrowding in many high schools with classes bulging with students who don't want to be there. A 13th year at a senior college or an extra buffer year at university is being considered by the federal government as an alternative to the current university entrance examination, to bring Australia in line with western Europe and the USA and reduce stress on year 12 students.

Education in Australia is mainly the responsibility of state and territory governments, each of which has its own education system. Australia has around 10,000 primary and secondary schools, some 30 per cent of which are private schools (mostly Catholic church schools with some Church of England and other parochial schools). Most public (i.e. state) schools are coeducational (mixed) day schools, with the exception of a few secondary schools that accept boarders. Private schools include both day and boarding schools, many of which are single-sex, particularly at the secondary level. It's generally considered that private schools are superior to public institutions, although there's little difference between the best public and private schools. However, it's true that the worst-performing private schools are generally streets ahead of the worst public schools, and school-leavers from the public system are much more likely to end up on the dole than those educated at private school. Your choice of local public and private schools will vary considerably depending on where you live.

Education at public schools is free, although parents must pay for books, uniforms, outings, caps and special programs. Independent (private) schools are also partially government funded, although they also charge fees, some of which are very high. Admission to a public school for foreign children is dependent on the type and duration of the visa (see **Chapter 3**) granted to their parents, and attendance may not be possible. With the exception of those studying and boarding at private fee-paying schools, only nationals of Papua New Guinea and certain South Pacific states can apply for entry to study at junior secondary public schools in Australia. Senior secondary-level students of any nationality can attend public and private schools, but must pay full fees (called the Overseas Students' Charge).

Note that there's no legal obligation for parents in Australia to educate their children at school and they may educate them themselves or employ private tutors (in future it's expected that the internet will make it possible for teachers to teach pupils almost exclusively from home). In Victoria, parents aren't even required to inform the Education Department of their decision. Parents educating their children at home don't require a teaching qualification, although they must satisfy the local education authority that a child is receiving full-time education appropriate to his or her age, abilities and aptitudes (they will check and may test your child). Information can be obtained from the Alternative Education Resources Group in most states.

Literacy: A national literacy survey in 1997 found that a third of students in primary years three and five cannot read or write adequately, branded a 'national disgrace' by the federal schools minister. New targets have been set for literacy for all pupils within four years of entering school and in future pupils will be tested for literacy skills every two years in school years 3, 5, 7 and 9 or 10. Some states (such as South Australia) have introduced mandatory literacy lessons in all schools for around 90 minutes a day. The problem of illiteracy is exacerbated by the thousands of migrant families who don't speak English or where English isn't spoken at home. Aboriginal children also have a low rate of literacy, generally three to four years behind other students. It's estimated that half of all Australians aged 15 to 74 (over 6m people) have poor or very poor literacy skills, with just 2m people (15 per cent) having good literacy skills and a mere 300,000 with very good skills. Adults with the poorest skills are (not surprisingly) mostly from non-English speaking backgrounds. The federal government also plans to introduce national standards and testing in numeracy.

Further Information: There are many books and magazines for parents faced with choosing a primary or secondary school including *Choosing a School* magazine (published in separate editions for the Sydney, Melbourne and Canberra areas), available from Universal Magazines, Private Bag 154, North Ryde, NSW 2113 (tel (02) 9887 0339). In addition to a detailed look at public and private education, this chapter also contains information about higher and further education and language schools.

PUBLIC OR PRIVATE SCHOOL?

If you're able to choose between public and private education, the following checklist will help you decide:

- How long are you planning to stay in Australia? If you're uncertain then it's probably better to assume a long stay. Due to language and other integration problems, enrolling a child in an Australian school with an Australian syllabus (public or private) is advisable only for a minimum of one year, particularly for teenage children.

- Bear in mind that the area in which you choose to live will affect your choice of public school(s). Although it isn't always necessary to send your children to the public school nearest your home, you may have difficulty obtaining admission to a public school if you don't live within its catchment area.

- If your stay in Australia will be for a limited period only, do you know where you're going after Australia? This may be an important consideration with regard to your children's schooling in Australia. How old are your children and what age will they be when you plan to leave Australia? What future plans do you have for their education and in which country?

- What age are your children and how will they fit into a private school or the Australian public school system? The younger they are, the easier it will be to place them in a suitable school.

- If your children aren't English-speaking, how do they view the thought of studying in English? Is teaching available in Australia in their mother tongue (and more importantly, is it advisable)?

- Will your children require your help with their studies? Will you be able to help them, particularly with the English language (if it isn't their mother tongue)? Is extra English tuition available at local schools?

- What are the school hours? What are the school holiday periods? How will the school hours and holidays influence your (and your spouse's) work and leisure activities?

- Is religion an important consideration in your choice of school? In public schools, religion isn't taught as a compulsory subject. However, most private schools are church-sponsored (e.g. Catholic) and religion is an important part of the curriculum.

- How large are the classes? What is the teacher-pupil ratio? What specialist staff does the school employ?

- Do you want your children to go to a co-educational (mixed) school? Public schools are usually co-educational, while private schools are often single sex.

- Should you send your children to a boarding school? If so, should it be in Australia or in another country?

- What are the secondary and further education prospects for your children in Australia or another country? Are Australian examinations recognised in your home country or the country where you plan to live after leaving Australia?

- Does the school have a good academic record? All schools can provide exam pass rate statistics (e.g. HSC) and a prospectus (which they may mail to you). Note, however, that public schools in some states aren't permitted to publish the results of their performance regarding university entrance ranking results (TER).

- Do students participate in decision-making?

- How much homework and what kind is expected at the various age levels?

- How are students selected? Is there a waiting list?

- Are uniforms worn and if so, are they compulsory?

- What are the facilities for art and science subjects, for example, arts and crafts, music, computer studies (how many computers?), science, hobbies, drama, cookery and photography? Does the school have an extensive library of up-to-date books (a good library is usually an excellent sign)? Obtain a school's prospectus or handbook, where this information should be listed.

- What is the general consensus in the local community about a school? Why do people feel the way they do? What are a school's aims and philosophies?

- Are parents actively involved in the school? Do you have the time or enthusiasm to get involved?

- Do the children and teachers seem happy? Is there a genuine warmth between pupils and teachers? Is there are sense of achievement, challenge and purpose?

Obtain the opinions and advice of others who have been faced with the same decisions and problems as you, and collect as much information from as many different sources as possible before making a decision. If possible, attend a school open day and speak to teachers, parents and students. Most parents find it helpful to discuss the alternatives with their children before making a decision (if it isn't already too late, you could always decide against children and save yourself a lot of trouble!).

Many schools have special programs for children with learning difficulties and for gifted children, and there are also special hospital schools, schools for children with learning difficulties, schools for gifted children, and schools for blind and deaf children. However, whenever possible children with disabilities attend regular schools in which support is provided for them. Parents can obtain information from the Australian Remedial Education Association (AREA) and the Special Learning Difficulties Association (SPELD). See also **Choosing a Private School** on page 200.

PUBLIC SCHOOLS

The term 'public school' refers to a non fee-paying school funded wholly from state and federal government budgets. The state and territorial governments have the major responsibility for education and provide most funding, supported by the federal government. States administer their own primary and secondary schools and are also responsible for technical and further education. The federal government is responsible for tertiary education and provides supplementary funding for schools and for technical and further education. It's also responsible for education in the Australian territories of Norfolk Island, Christmas Island and the Cocos Islands. The government is keen to foster links between schools, particularly technology high schools and TAFE colleges, and industry. Local businesses also provide sponsorship and extra funding for schools, plus practical work experience, share resources such as computers and other equipment, and help in creating specialised science courses.

However, in recent years many primary schools have been forced to cut back on computer classes due to a lack of resources. Spending on public schools varies from state to state and is a hotly debated subject. In 1996, the national average was $4,165 per student in primary schools and $5,772 in secondary schools. Education expenditure by the federal government exceeds $6 billion and has grown at around 10 per cent a year in recent years. A great number of public schools are modern institutions, having been built in the last decade, particularly in the outer suburbs of capital cities. However, budget restrictions have resulted in school closures and have driven more families to send their children to private schools. In recent years there has been an unprecedented exodus of students from public to private schools, making it difficult for governments to provide quality public education in some areas (some public schools have closed due to falling enrollments). The government plans to impose restrictions on the establishment of new private schools to stem the flow of students from public schools and avoid the over-supply of classes in some areas. Public school classes number between 30 and 35 pupils in metropolitan areas, less in rural areas, and are slowly being reduced in most states (classes are generally much smaller in private schools).

Most students attend schools near to their homes, although in country areas a long journey may be involved, particularly to secondary school. Usually primary and secondary schools are separate institutions, but in some country areas there are combined primary and secondary (area or central) schools. School buses may be provided for children in rural areas, while in remote outback regions children do their lessons by correspondence or via the 'school of the air', where lessons are given over the Flying Doctor radio network throughout Australia (both public and private schools participate in programs). Correspondence lessons use video and audio tapes and are usually supervised by a member of the family and administered by a correspondence school in state capital cities.   Public schools don't have canteens or restaurants and school 'tuckshops' sell snacks, sandwiches and soft drinks at break and lunchtimes.

P&C Committees: Parents play a vital role in education in Australia, where each school has a committee comprised of teachers, parents and student representatives, called a Parents and Citizens (P&C) committee. Parents can influence decisions such as the design and wearing of uniforms, discipline, homework and the curriculum. P&C committees (a third of which must comprise parents) also raise funds for school outings and equipment, and assist in running certain aspects of the school such as administration, classroom assistance and school shops. An enthusiastic and flourishing P&C committee is usually the sign of a good school. Note that in recent years some state schools have been increasingly turning to voluntary levies to raise funds (usually to pay for additional materials) as state and federal funding has been cut. In some states, 'free' public education is fast becoming a misnomer, with many parents being forced to pay $1,000 to $2,000 a year.

Curriculum: The curriculum contains eight key learning areas: English; mathematics; science; technology; human society and the environment; creative and practical arts; health and physical education; and foreign languages. Although states have a large degree of autonomy in setting their own curriculums, they are broadly similar and follow guidelines laid down by the federal government. Generally individual schools have a large degree of autonomy and can determine their own teaching and learning approaches within the guidelines provided, and offer options within the resources available. Some schools specialise in languages and place greater emphasis on foreign language study, with special programs and innovative teaching methods.   Where necessary, students from non-English speaking countries are given extra English classes and English as a Second Language (ESL) programs are provided in schools with significant numbers of children from non-English speaking backgrounds.   Children generally experience few problems when moving from one state to another.

Computer technology is an increasingly important aspect of teaching in Australian schools at all levels right across the curriculum, where computers are used in language development, to access databases, student-centred learning, desktop publishing and distance learning. Some schools excel in their use of computers, although the ratio of computers to students is low in most public schools, many of which buy computers (and other equipment) with money raised by parents and sponsors. Extra-curricular activities are common in Australia and include sports (an important feature of Australian school life), arts and crafts, camps, excursions and social events such as discos and barbecues. School bands, orchestras, choirs, dance troupes and dramatic societies are also common.

School homework varies considerably, with some children doing too little and others doing more than is healthy; only around a quarter of schools/pupils strike a healthy balance between study and recreation. A maximum of two or three hours each school day is recommended for students in their 11th and 12th years of secondary school, although many do over 20 hours a week. The maximum classroom teaching hours are around 20 hours in secondary schools and 22.5 in primary schools. Exam stress is a problem at secondary schools and universities.

Choosing a School: The quality of public schools, their teaching staff and the education they provide, varies considerably depending on the state or territory; region, town or city; suburb or individual school. If you want your children to have a good education, it's absolutely essential to get them into a good school, even if it means moving house and changing your job. Children have the right to attend their local public school, although they may attend any other public school (in the state or territory where they live) where there's a vacancy. However, priority at any school goes to local children. It's important to research the best schools in a given area and to ensure that your child will be accepted at your chosen school, **before buying or renting a home**. There's an education under-class in some deprived areas, particularly those with high unemployment and a large percentage of families living on income support. Some high schools (usually in the poorer and more disadvantaged areas) have discipline, drug and violence problems, and have installed video cameras and taken other measures to identify offenders. Obviously these schools are best avoided if at all possible.

Problems: The public school system has been in a state of almost constant flux in recent years, during which there has been criticism of the quality of teacher selection, and training and teaching methods (added to which there's expected to be an acute shortage of teachers early in the next century). Many teachers in public schools are demoralised and according to some reports around half would give up teaching if they could. Their complaints include falling pay compared with other professionals (although teachers are generally well paid); long teaching hours; a lack of resources; low professional standing; an overcrowded curriculum; overcrowded classes; violence and discipline problems (corporal punishment is forbidden in public schools); children with little or no English; and poor working conditions (e.g. teaching in portable classrooms in temperatures over 40°C/104°F!).

Admissions

You should address enquiries about admissions (enrolment) in public schools to the headmaster or principal of the school of your choice. Enquiries should be made well in advance of taking up residence in a new area. Most children go to the school nearest their home, particularly at primary level. All children are guaranteed a place at their local public high school, but parents have the option of applying to up to four non-local high schools. Placement outside the local area depends on the availability of places and if daily travel isn't feasible, accommodation at the school. Buses are provided for children who have a long journey to school. If possible, all schools prefer children to start at the beginning of a new term (see below). When visiting a school you should take your child's reports, references and certificates from previous schools. New pupils are assessed and admitted to the appropriate class for their age and educational level, although it's unusual for a child to be placed with children of more than one year's age difference.

Starting ages for primary and secondary schools vary depending on the state or territory and there are at least six different school entry ages across Australia, although the terms are similar. This causes problems when children move to a new state and the federal government has proposed a plan which would ensure that all children start school at the same age in all states. Most schools like parents to apply for entry in October for children starting school the following year. The normal intake is in January/February, although some states operate a mid-year intake as well. Although starting ages differ by only a few months between states, the differences can create problems. In South Australia and the Northern Territory there's a continuous intake and children may begin school when they turn five years of age. However, in Western Australia children born after 30th June aren't able to start school until the year they turn seven, and in Victoria they must be aged five by 30th April of the year of enrolment.

Although it isn't mandatory, most Australians believe that full immunisation (against diseases such as whooping couch, measles and rubella) may be made compulsory for all children before starting school (see page 275).

School Holidays & Hours

Australia's academic year follows the calendar year from January to December, and is usually divided into four terms of around 10 weeks' duration (depending on the state or territory), which are separated by holidays. There may also be breaks for public holidays. Most holidays are of two weeks' duration with the exception of the summer break which is six weeks. The length and dates of school holidays vary considerably depending on the state or territory. Public primary and secondary (high) schools in NSW had the following holidays in 1998 (all dates are inclusive):

Holiday	Dates (start/end)
Autumn	10th April to 24th April
Winter	6th July to 17th July
Spring	28th September to 9th October
Summer	21st December to 26th January 1999 (Eastern Division)
	21st December to 2nd February 1999 (Western Division)

School holiday dates are published by schools well in advance, thus allowing you plenty of time to schedule family holidays during official school holidays. Normally parents aren't permitted to withdraw children from classes during the school term, except for visits to a doctor or dentist, when the teacher should be informed in advance (if possible).

Classes start at around 9am and continue until 4pm with breaks for meals and mid-morning and mid-afternoon recesses. Some children may need to work longer hours if they need extra tuition, for example in English. Many schools provide care and recreational facilities outside school hours for children whose parents are working, seeking work or studying, for which a fee is levied. Supervision may include before and after school care and care during school holidays. Children being looked after may spend up to 25 hours a week in care, in addition to normal school hours. Fees vary from almost nothing to $60 a week for before and after school care, rising to $75 for two children and $90 for three.

Provisions & Uniforms

Most schools encourage pupils to wear school uniform and they are compulsory at some state and most private schools (although tracksuits or jeans may be permitted during winter). Uniforms are usually optional in primary school and can be expensive (with different uniforms for summer and winter), as each school usually has its own embroidered jumpers, socks, caps or blazers which means that they must be specially made in small quantities. Uniforms can sometimes be purchased secondhand from school shops. Hats are an integral part of school uniforms and are designed to protect pupils from the sun. High protection sunscreen is also provided free to pre-school and primary year one pupils in many states and most schools have a 'hot weather' policy where all children must wear sunhats (with a peak and 'legionnaire' flap to protect the back of the neck) and suncream at playtime. Students at some colleges are being encouraged to wear sunglasses with UV400 polycarbonate lenses to protect against eye cancer and other eye problems caused by the sun. In addition to uniforms, parents can expect to pay for some or all of the following:

- additional clothing items such as sportswear and gym shoes, and bags or satchels in which to carry them;

- transportation to and from school (local transport authorities may provide concessionary or free travel in some areas);

- textbooks, notebooks, writing paper, pens, pencils, calculators, etc., and arts, crafts and manual work materials. Some states provide free books for primary school students and their cost may also be subsidised for secondary school students. Many secondary schools operate a text book loan or rental scheme, whereby a refundable deposit is paid by each student at the beginning of secondary schooling. Text books can also be purchased secondhand.

- fees for libraries, sport facilities, excursions and sports team fees;

The estimated minimum cost of equipping a child is around $500 a year in primary school and up to $1,000 a year for senior secondary school. Parents of children in the last two years (11 and 12) of secondary school can apply for a means-tested grant from Austudy, see page 204).

Kindergarten & Pre-School

Attendance at a pre-school or kindergarten for children under five years of age isn't compulsory in Australia. However, for the over 30 per cent of Australian working mothers with children aged four or below, finding a day care centre or pre-school is usually essential, and can be particularly difficult in cities and urban areas. Attendance fees aren't usually charged in states where pre-schools are government run, but in others fees are payable to private or voluntary organisations. Federal government cuts have resulted in the closure of many non-profit, community-based, child-minding centres in recent years (those that have remained open have sharply increased their fees). This has meant a return of 'latch-key' kids who are forced to return to empty homes after school. Fees are around $15 a day at a public day care centre but may depend on the parents' income, with better off parents asked to contribute more and low income families exempt. However, fees at commercially run city centres are $200 a week or more for each child.

Most pre-schools are conducted on a session basis, with sessions of two to three hours for two to five days a week. Children can usually attend from 9am to 12noon or from 1pm to 3pm Monday to Friday. Many children attend public pre-school centres on a voluntary, part-time basis for around four half days a week during the year preceding primary school at age four (or from the beginning of the year in which they turn five). Free, although there may be a voluntary levy, public pre-schools (also called child-parent centres) are often located at primary schools and open during school hours. Pre-schools are also termed kindergarten in the year prior to starting primary school.

Programs usually follow the free play approach, with the emphasis on social and emotional development through creative activities. Pre-school doesn't generally provide education (just educational games) for under five-year-olds, although research has shown that children who attend pre-school are generally brighter and usually progress at a faster rate than those who don't. It's highly recommended, particularly if a child or his parents aren't of English mother-tongue. After one or two years in pre-school a child is integrated into the local community and is well prepared for primary school.

Primary School

Primary education in Australia begins at five or six years of age depending on the state or territory and is almost always co-educational (mixed). Some primary schools also provide nursery or pre-school classes for children under five and in some states (such as

Queensland) children can start primary school at four years of age at certain schools under a trial program (pupils are evaluated to see whether they are 'suitable' for early enrolment). Primary education isn't, however, compulsory until age six and lasts for six or seven years (school years one to six or seven) up to the age of 12 or 13, depending on the particular state or territory. Children generally start primary school with a kindergarten or preparatory year.

Pupils receive a thorough grounding in literacy and numeracy, and all schools must meet broad curriculum and standards' guidelines developed by the Board of Studies. In primary education, the main emphasis is on the development of basic language and literacy skills; simple arithmetic; moral and social education; health training; and some creative activities. In the higher primary years, lessons include English; mathematics; science; technology and computer studies; social studies (e.g. studies of society and environment); music, art and craft; health and physical education. Optional subjects may include religious instruction, community and foreign languages (called a 'language other than English' or LOTE), and instrumental music. Note that in some states (e.g. Victoria) foreign languages are compulsory. Schools can also develop their own programs to suit local needs and priorities within government guidelines. Swimming lessons are provided, usually at public swimming pools, as public schools don't usually have their own pools. Sex education is also taught.

Parent-teacher interviews are conducted once or twice a year and provide an opportunity for parents to discuss their child's progress. Children are continually assessed and parents periodically receive written reports, e.g. twice a year in Victoria. In some states, students are assessed against state-wide standards at two important stages during primary school (known as the 'Learning Assessment Project' in Victoria), which ties in with new Curriculum and Standards' programs. Assessment results are usually confidential and are used to identify pupils' special needs, such as those who need extra help with their English.

Primary education almost always takes place in the district where pupils live. The school day is generally divided into three or four sessions, with daily instruction lasting for around five hours and consisting of 20 or 30-minute lessons. Pupils in primary schools usually have one teacher for most (if not all) subjects and are promoted each year on the basis of completing the previous year, rather than achievement. In large schools, pupils are graded according to age, while in country areas a primary 'school' may consist of no more than a couple of portable classrooms and two teachers teaching 15 to 30 pupils in all subjects. Some primary schools have adopted open-plan learning, where team teaching (more than one teacher to a class) and multi-age grouping of students is occasionally practised. Many new primary schools are also designed on the 'open plan' concept which allows two or more teachers to supervise up to 70 pupils, although they are divided into small groups for separate activities, including individual study. Children progress to a secondary (high) school at school year seven or eight.

Secondary School

Secondary school (called high school in Australia) is for children aged from 12 or 13 until age 17 or 18 (from school years seven or eight to year 12). High school lasts for a maximum of five or six years, depending on the state or territory. All secondary students complete year 10 (until age 16) and the majority stay on at school until year 12 (age 18). Completion of year 12 is usually necessary to attend an institution of higher education, such as a university or college of advanced education.

The most common state secondary school is the comprehensive or multi-purpose high school. High schools are usually coeducational, although there are some single-sex schools in capital cities. In some states there are separate high schools for technical, agricultural and commercial subjects, where general academic subjects are combined with practical training, and selective high and grammar schools which provide a more challenging environment for academically-gifted students (competition for places is stiff). Some high schools are further classified as technology or language high schools, or as centres of excellence in certain subjects. The fifth and sixth years (11 and 12) are usually taken at separate colleges offering a range of subjects studied by adults as well as senior students. Agricultural high schools usually cater for boarders and some country state schools have hostels for children who are unable to travel to school daily. Technology high schools are generally for the less-academically gifted and put the emphasis on science and technology. Most states and territories also provide schools for academically gifted children, where admission is subject to test and school reports.

Students in secondary schools generally have a different teacher for each subject, although variations may occur where open-plan or more flexible teaching methods have been adopted. Promotion to the next year is generally automatic on completion of the previous year, although students may be grouped according to ability (streamed) in some subjects after an initial period in unstreamed classes. However, classes aren't streamed in academic or technically oriented subjects. In most states the first one or two years consist of a general program which is followed by all students, although there may be some choice of lessons (electives). In the last two years a basic core of subjects is retained with students able to select additional optional subjects, although in some states students select optional subjects from the start of high school.

The core subjects in all schools comprise the eight key learning areas of English, mathematics, science, technology, studies of society and the environment, the arts, health, and foreign languages. Optional subjects may include an additional foreign language, history, geography, a further humanities or social science subject, computer studies, commerce, art, crafts, music, theatre, home economics, a manual arts subject, agriculture and physical education. Some schools also offer optional courses in subjects such as consumer education, conversational foreign languages, word processing, commerce, driver education, drama and leisure-time studies. Note that in some schools, all students (regardless of their sex) may be required to study subjects such as cooking, sewing, woodwork and metalwork.

Most secondary schools have modern facilities for teaching commercial subjects, home economics, manual crafts and other technical subjects. Distance education (correspondence) courses may be available to students wishing to study a subject not generally offered (or which may clash with other subjects on the timetable) and Saturday schools may offer language studies that aren't available in a student's own school. A wider range of options is usually available in larger schools and there's an increasing trend towards encouraging individual schools to develop courses suited to the needs and interests of their students. For example, Victoria has a 'Schools of the Future' program, where schools are self-managing and control their own finances and develop their own teaching programs to reflect the aspirations of the school community, the interests and abilities of students, and the knowledge and skills of teachers. A school charter describes a school's specific educational philosophy and core purpose. In recent years there has been more emphasis on the incorporation of vocational training into the senior secondary curriculum. Under the Australian Vocational Training System, students may obtain vocational education and training sector certificates as part of their senior study, and undertake some of their programs in the workplace.

Students attaining the minimum school leaving age of 16 may leave school and seek employment, or enrol in a vocational course in a TAFE institution (see page 209) or a private business college. Completion of year 10 of secondary school is the minimum entry requirement for many TAFE courses. Those who continue to year 12 have a choice of options for further study in TAFE institutions, higher education institutions and other post-school institutions. A student's eligibility for entry to higher (tertiary) education is assessed during or at the end of the final two years in secondary schooling. Most states use various combinations of school assessment and public examinations (see below).

Examinations

Individual states and territories set their own examinations, although in most states students take the School Certificate (SC) at age 16 (the end of their 10th year) and the Higher School Certificate (HSC) at age 18 (at the end of the 12th year). Most states issue students with certificates after they have completed their compulsory education at age 16 and the majority of students who leave at this age go on to do an apprenticeship or other trade training. The school certificate (replaced by a junior or achievement certificate in some states) is based on school assessment as well as state-wide reference tests in English and mathematics. The HSC (replaced by a senior certificate, matriculation certificate or the tertiary admission examination/certificate of education in some states) is necessary in order to gain entrance to an Australian university. However, a few universities (in NSW) have waived the HSC requirement if families can afford fees of at least $8,000 for a year at a private college undergoing a 'foundation' course. Some schools also offer the International Baccalaureate (IB) plus additional courses with state or TAFE accreditation. Senior high schools offer tertiary courses such as Open University or TAFE off-campus.

The HSC is based on an external examination held in October or November of school year 12 in addition to school assessment based on a student's last two years' work. More emphasis is placed on course work and continuous assessment, rather than end of year or final examinations. This is so as not to disadvantage children who suffer from exam nerves and to reduce cramming and stress. In NSW, future HSC students will be assessed against a new set of standards, rather than against each other, as part of a radical change in measuring performance in the final years of schooling. Students will receive detailed information about their performance in each subject, detailing the skills they have mastered, and their results will more accurately reflect the actual score they achieve in schoolwork and exams.

PRIVATE SCHOOLS

Around 30 per cent (over 35 per cent in years 11 and 12) of Australian children attend some 2,500 private non-government schools (officially referred to as independent schools) in Australia, which include all educational establishments that aren't state run. They range from nursery (kindergarten) schools to large day and boarding schools, from traditional-style schools to those offering 'alternative' education such as Montessori and Rudolf Steiner schools (both of which are highly rated and have schools in many countries). They include schools sponsored by churches and religious groups (parochial), schools for students with learning or physical disabilities, and schools for gifted children. In addition to mainstream parochial (e.g. Catholic) schools, there are also schools for religious and ethnic minorities, for example Muslims, where there's a strict code regarding the segregation of boys and girls. Most private schools are single sex, although some have become co-educational in recent years. There are also boarding schools in

Australia, although few schools accept boarders only and many accommodate both day students and boarders. Children who board usually do so because they live too far from school to travel every day or because their parents are working overseas.

The Catholic church operates by far the largest number of private schools and there are relatively few other parochial schools. A total of over 600,000 children attend some 1,700 Catholic schools in Australia or two-thirds of all private school students and 20 per cent of the nationwide total. Most Catholic schools are part of a system administered by the Catholic Education Office and fees are usually much lower than for traditional independent schools. The federal and state governments fund 75 per cent of the cost of running the schools. Clergy account for almost all teachers in Catholic schools, which (not surprisingly) devote an above average amount of time to religious subjects. Catholic systemic high schools accept children from other religious backgrounds, but priority is given to Catholics.

Traditional private schools are often based on English public schools and generally use the same terminology as them. For example, years are called forms, with the first form at high school being equivalent to the public school year seven or eight at age 12 or 13, while final year students are referred to as sixth formers. Some private primary schools are called preparatory (prep) schools. However, there's no snobbery attached to attending a private school in Australia — what is important is a school's academic standing and how well your children perform. Some parents switch their children from a public to a private school when they progress to secondary school. The quality of secondary education is crucial in gaining access to a good university course and a child's subsequent career.

Fees vary considerably depending on a variety of factors including the age of students, the reputation and quality of the school, and its location (schools in major cities are usually the most expensive). Day school fees vary from as little as $1,250 to $1,500 a year for a parochial (e.g. Anglican, Uniting Church or Christian community schools) primary school and $2,000 to $3,000 a year for a high school. However, fees at non-denominational schools are up to $7,000 a year for primary and over $10,000 a year for 'elite' high schools (fees have risen considerably in recent years). Fees at boarding schools can top $20,000 a year, with boarding fees from around $6,000 to $10,000. Note that some schools publish fees per term (usually four a year), particularly if they are high, while others are per school year. Some schools offer reduced fees to parents with two or more children attending a school. To the fees must be added another $2,000 or so a year for uniforms, books, building levies, special equipment (e.g. for sports), excursion charges, computers and assorted surcharges.

Schools are funded partly by the federal government on a 12-point sliding scale with wealthy schools funded at the lowest level (one) and poor schools at the highest level (12). Students at most private schools receive more public funding than those in public schools and there's controversy over the public funding of elite and wealthy private schools, where affluent parents are subsidised from the public purse. Most private schools provide scholarships for bright or talented pupils, which vary in value from full fees to a small percentage only. Scholarships are awarded as a result of competitive examination, individual talents or skills, and need.

Most private schools provide a similar curriculum to public schools and set the same examinations. However, some private schools offer the International Baccalaureate (IB) examination, an internationally recognised university entrance qualification, which may be an important consideration if you intend to remain in Australia for a limited period only. The advantages of private schools are manyfold, not least their excellent academic record, which is generally much better than those of public schools. Don't, however, send your child to a school with high academic standards unless you're sure that he will be able to handle the pressure. Many private schools have resolutely embraced new technology, and the use of computers and the internet to teach pupils is widespread. Don't assume, however, that all private schools are excellent or that they all offer a better education than public schools, which manifestly isn't true.

Private schools place the emphasis on traditional teaching including hard work, good manners, consideration for others, responsibility, and not least, a sense of discipline (values which are sadly lacking in some public schools). They provide a broad-based education (aimed at developing a pupil's character) and generally provide a more varied approach to sport, music, drama, art and a wider choice of academic subjects than public schools. Their aim is more the development of the child as an individual and the encouragement of his unique talents, rather than teaching on a production-line system. This is made possible by small classes (an average of around 15 to 20 pupils or as little as half that of many public schools) which allows teachers to provide pupils with individually tailored lessons and tuition. Private schools are also able to cater for special needs including gifted children; slow learners or those who suffer from dyslexia; those who benefit from a single-sex school; those requiring boarding facilities; and children whose parents want them to be educated in the customs of a particular religious belief.

Make applications to private schools as far in advance as possible (before conception for the best schools). Obviously if you have just arrived in Australia, you won't be able to apply one or two years in advance, which is generally considered to be the best time to book a place. However, if you plan to send your children to private school, you should start planning well in advance, if possible long before arriving in Australia. The best and most popular schools have a demanding selection procedure and long waiting lists (perhaps many years), and parents register a child for entry at birth at some schools. Don't rely on enrolling your child in a particular school and neglect the alternatives, particularly if the chosen school has a rigourous entrance examination. When applying you're usually requested to send previous school reports, exam results and records. Before enrolling your child in a private school, make sure that you understand the withdrawal conditions in the school contract.

Choosing a Private School

The following checklist is designed to help you choose an appropriate and reputable private school in Australia.

- Does the school have a good reputation? Does it belong to a recognised body for private schools? How long has it been established? Is it financially secure?

- Does the school have a good academic record? For example what percentage of pupils obtain good examination passes or go on to good universities? What subjects do pupils do best in? All private schools provide exam pass rate statistics.

- What does the curriculum include (a broad and well-balanced curriculum is best)? Ask to see a typical pupil timetable to check the ratio of academic to non-academic subjects. Check the number of free study periods and whether they are supervised.

- Do you wish to send your children to a single-sex or a co-educational school? Some children make better progress without the distractions of the opposite sex (although their sex education may be neglected).

- Day or boarding school? If you're considering a day school, what are the school hours? Does the school provide transport for pupils to and from your home? Many schools offer weekly boarding which allows pupils to return home at weekends.

- Do you intend to send your children to a private primary or high school only or both?

- How many children attend the school and what is the average class size? What is the ratio of teachers to pupils? Are pupil numbers increasing or decreasing? Check that class sizes are in fact what it says they are in the prospectus. Has the number of pupils increased dramatically in the last few years (which could be a good *or* a bad sign)?

- What are the qualification requirements for teachers? What nationality are the majority of teachers? What is the teacher turnover? A high teacher turnover is a bad sign and usually suggests under-paid teachers and poor working conditions.

- What extras will you be required to pay? For example optional lessons (e.g. music, dancing and sports), lunches, art supplies, sports equipment, school trips, phone calls, clothing (most schools have obligatory uniforms, which can be *very* expensive), insurance, textbooks and stationery. Most schools charge parents for every little thing.

- Is religion an important consideration in your choice of school? What religious education is provided, if any?

- Are special English classes provided for children whose English doesn't meet the required standard? Usually if a child is under nine years of age it doesn't matter if his English is weak. However, children over this age may not be accepted unless they can read English fluently (as printed in text books for their age). Some schools provide intensive English tuition for foreign students.

- If you have decided on a boarding school, what standard and type of accommodation is provided? What is the quality and variety of food provided? What is the dining room like? Does the school have a dietitian?

- What languages does the school teach as obligatory or optional subjects? Does the school have a language laboratory?

- What is the student turnover?

- What are the school terms and holiday periods? Private school holidays may be longer than those at public schools and the dates may vary considerably (which could be a problem if you have children at both private and public schools).

- What are the withdrawal conditions, should you need or wish to remove your child? A term's notice is usual.

- What examinations are set? In which subjects? How do they fit in with your future education plans for your child?

- What sports instruction and facilities are provided?

- What are the facilities for art and science subjects, for example, arts and crafts, music, computer studies (how many computers?), science, hobbies, drama, cookery and photography?

- What sort of outings and holidays does the school organise?

- What medical facilities does the school provide, e.g. infirmary, resident doctor or nurse? Is health and accident insurance included in the fees?

- What sort of discipline and punishments are imposed and are restrictions relaxed as children get older? Note that corporal punishment is permitted in private schools in

Australia, but is forbidden in public schools. Schools should provide a copy of their discipline policy.

• What reports are provided for parents and how often? How much contact does the school have with parents?

• **Last, but not least, unless someone else is paying, what are the fees?**

Draw up a shortlist of possible schools and obtain a prospectus (some schools provide a video prospectus). If possible, obtain a copy of the school magazine (if applicable). Before making a final choice, it's important to visit the schools on your shortlist during term time and talk to teachers and students, and if possible, former students and their parents. **Where possible, check the answers to the above questions in person and don't rely on a school's prospectus to provide the information.** If you aren't satisfied with the answers, look elsewhere. Having made your choice, keep a check on your child's progress, listen to his complaints and compare notes with other parents. If something doesn't seem right, try to establish whether the complaint is founded or not, and if it is, take action to have the problem resolved. Don't forget that you (or possibly your employer) is paying a lot of money for your child's education and you should demand value for money. See also **Public or Private School?** on page 189.

HIGHER EDUCATION

Post-school education in Australia is generally divided into higher and further education. Higher education, called tertiary education in Australia, is usually defined as advanced courses of a standard higher than HSC (see page 198) or equivalent and usually refers only to first degree courses. Courses may be full-time, part-time or a sandwich course, which is nothing to do with food, but a course which combines periods of full-time study with periods of full-time training and paid work in industry and commerce. Australian universities are both teaching and research institutions, and many have world-renowned research programs funded by industry in the applied science and technology fields. The individual states and territories are responsible for higher education, but the federal government provides the funding. The number of students in higher education has increased considerably in the last decade and now totals some 600,000.

Degree level courses are offered by around 40 universities ('unis'), including former Colleges of Advanced Education (CAE) and Institutes of Technology (IT), which became universities in the late '80s. Australia has one of the highest ratios of universities to population in the world. The oldest universities are Sydney and Melbourne (established in the 1850s), which together with the universities of Adelaide, Queensland, Tasmania and Western Australia, form the traditional 'sandstone' universities (the Australian equivalent of America's ivy league). Note that degrees from 'new' universities aren't rated as highly as those from the old 'sandstone' universities, 'corporate' universities (UNSW and Monash) and the universities of technology (UTs).

Australia also has a number of specialist higher education establishments which include the Australian College of Physical Education (Sydney), the Australian Defence Force Academy, the Australian Institute of Music (Sydney), the Australian International Hotel School (Canberra), Avondale College (Cooranbong, NSW), the Christian Heritage College (Brisbane), Engineering Education Australia (distance education), the International College of Hotel Management (Adelaide), KvB College of Visual Communication (Sydney) and Macleay College (Sydney) and the National Institute of Dramatic Art (Sydney, NSW).

The age of admission to university is usually 18 (although most admit exceptional students at a younger age) and courses are usually for three years, although some last for four years. This is seen as a big advantage for foreign students from countries where courses often last much longer and helps Australian universities attract a large number of overseas students. Over a quarter of university students are 'mature' students aged over 30, two-thirds of whom are women. Most Australian universities have between 5,000 and 15,000 students, and the largest over 40,000 (Monash), although they are usually dispersed over a number of campuses. Most older universities follow British or American traditions and óffer a wide range of courses. Many universities have a multi-campus structure with each campus specialising in a particular discipline, e.g. an agricultural science college linked to the main campus.

Australia rates highly in the percentage of students accepted at its higher education establishments and its number of graduates (which are highest in natural sciences but low in engineering). However, disadvantaged students (which include women, those from non-English-speaking backgrounds, Aboriginals and Torres Strait Islanders, rural dwellers, the disabled and the poor) are under-represented at universities, particularly in the elite institutions. Many prospective students cannot afford the high fees, which have led to student protests in the form of occupations and sit-ins of university buildings in recent years. Universities have been struggling with funding cuts and many have been forced to axe places, cut research budgets and reduce postgraduate courses. Competition for students is fierce and universities have resorted to innovative advertising to lure school leavers and some have even lowered TER entrance scores to attract more students. Many universities deliberately over-enrol, partly in order to receive higher government grants, and offer places to students with low entrance grades. This has lead to an increase in student-staff ratios and fears of a reduction in the quality of teaching. In order to compete with private colleges and other degree-level public institutions, many universities have introduced associate degree courses in fields such as management, dance, applied science, dental therapy, electrical and electronic engineering, and others.

Overseas Students: All Australian universities accept overseas students and many spend $millions on overseas marketing and student recruitment (Australia's top eight sandstone universities established their own overseas marketing arm in 1997). There are no quotas for foreign students, but all non-resident students must pay full fees (although grants are available). Overseas students, mostly from Asia, are a major source of income for universities, contributing over $3 billion to the Australian economy. Many universities also have thousands of 'offshore' students at facilities in Asian countries and in New Zealand. Australian universities enrolled around 55,000 foreign students in 1996 and the number is expected to increase considerably in the next few years. When students at secondary schools and private colleges are included, the total number of foreign students studying in Australia numbers some 150,000. However, there were fears that the number of overseas students from Southeast Asia would fall dramatically in 1998 as a result of the currency crisis that erupted in late 1997.

Overseas students require a student visa, which is issued after acceptance on a course and payment of at least half the first year's fees. Students must have the financial resources to meet tuition fees, return fares to Australia and day-to-day living expenses for the duration of their course. Foreign students must have an adequate knowledge of English (unless studying English!). If English isn't your mother tongue or the language in which you gained your previous qualifications, you must take the Short Selection Test (SST). Private health insurance is required by all students, e.g. through the Medibank Private Overseas Student Health Cover facility (see page 309). Students must be attending full-time courses, but are permitted to take part-time jobs of up to 20 hours a week to help cover their living costs. In order to retain a visa, students must have satisfactory attendance and academic results' records. On completion of their courses, overseas students must leave Australia when their visas expire (an undertaking must be given in writing). Note that it isn't possible to switch from a visitor's visa to a student visa while in Australia.

Austudy Grants: Resident students studying an approved course at an approved educational establishment may be eligible for a government grant, called Austudy (a form of income support). A booklet explaining eligibility for Austudy grants is sent to all Australian applicants who are offered a place at university. Whether you receive a grant will depend on your income and assets (and those of your parents and spouse), and your age and living circumstances. The rules are complicated and the application contains a questionnaire with up to 320 questions! When applying you need your original birth certificate or passport; your tax file number, taxation notice of assessment and the tax file number of your parents or spouse (if applicable), plus other documents depending on your personal situation. Full details of the documentation required is listed on the Austudy application form. Applications should be made within 28 days of starting a course of 30 weeks or less; your birthday if you turn 16 or 17 during the year; or when you become eligible because your situation has changed.

Note that if you apply late you will receive your grant only from the date your application is filed. Once your form is received you will receive your Notice of Assessment (usually within 21 days) detailing your eligibility and payments. Payments are made directly into your bank, building society or credit union account every two weeks. In 1997-98 the following Austudy grants were available to qualified students:

Age/Status	Austudy Grant Standard	Away	Income Limits Standard	Away
under 18	$145.41	$240.07	$34,473	$44,305
over 18	$174.90	$265.39	$37,529	$46,957
Special Groups	$214.56	$322.42		

The 'standard' rate applies when a student lives with his parents and the 'away' rate when he has to live away from home. There are higher Austudy grants for some families with two or more students living away from home. 'Special groups' refers to single students aged 21 or over transferring from long term receipt of social security pension or benefits. In order to qualify for Austudy allowances, parental incomes mustn't exceed those shown above, although higher income levels are set for families with more than one eligible student. Students granted Austudy aid can earn up to $6,000 a year without affecting their grant. An Austudy supplement is available offering students the option of 'trading in' part of their Austudy grant in order to receive double the amount in the form of an interest-free loan. Repayment is required when income exceeds a certain level (the same as for HECS described below). Note that migrants aren't eligible for Austudy grants for two years after their arrival in Australia. Students who have been permanent residents for over three years and don't have Australian citizenship will no longer qualify for Austudy grants and will also be required to pay HECS fees in advance.

Other Grants: Special grants (awards) are available for those undertaking a masters degree by research/course work or a PhD. For details write to the Student Assistance centre, Locked Bag 1010, Civic Square, ACT 2608. There are special programs (e.g. Abstudy) for Aboriginal students from low-income families which provide for living allowances, extra student places and other support. A range of scholarships are also available and students may receive regular tax-free scholarship payments of around

$10,000 a year. Full information is provided in *Scholarships Australia: the Directory of Scholarships and Grants for Study in Australia and Overseas* (New Hobsons Press).

Cost of Living: The 1997-98 annual living costs for students (excluding course fees) are estimated to be a minimum of $15,000 a year plus a further $7,500 for each dependant (possibly less outside the major cities). Many students find it increasingly difficult to survive on their grants and some are forced to choose a university, not on course preference, but on where they can more easily survive on their meagre resources. Many students work part-time during terms and in their holidays to supplement their income, and around half live with their parents to save costs.

Course Fees: University tuition fees for Australian students were introduced in 1990 (prior to which tuition was free) under the Higher Education Contribution Scheme (HECS). There's a deferred payment option which makes the HECS charge an interest-free loan which is repaid weekly when a graduate's income exceeds $20,594 a year. The average student is expected to take five to eight years to pay off his HECS fees (depending on the subject taken). New higher fees were introduced in 1997 (prior to which all courses were charged at $2,487 per student year), to reflect both the actual cost of tuition and the future income of graduates. The fees payable depend on the subject(s) being studied:

- **Band 1:** Arts, humanities, social studies/behavioural science, visual/performing arts, education and nursing carry an HECS fee of $3,300 a year. Some 35 per cent of students study theses subjects.

- **Band 2:** Mathematics, computing, certain health sciences, agriculture, renewable resources, built environment/architecture, sciences, engineering, processing and administration, business and economics cost $4,700 a year.

- **Band 3:** Law, justice, legal studies, medicine, medical science, dentistry, dental services and veterinary science cost $5,500 a year.

If the units taken for a degree course fall into different fee bands, then the student pays a proportion of each band, depending on the number of units in each band. Students can choose to pay the HECS fee before graduation in a lump sum, in which case they qualify for a reduction of 25 per cent. For example an arts degree costs $3,300 a year, reducing to $2,475 a year if paid up front, a saving of around $2,000 over the three years of an undergraduate course. Paying in advance has an even bigger impact for students enrolled in the most expensive band 3 courses which cost $5,500 a year, where a 25 per cent reduction saves around $7,000 over five or six years. The 25 per cent discount applies to up-front payments of $500 or more made after 1st January 1998 and also applies to partial payments, although only one payment per semester attracts the discount. Voluntary payments of $500 or more made in respect of a deferred HECS liability attract a 15 per cent bonus. Students who choose to complete an optional honours year or a higher degree may be exempted from paying HECS fees for that year through an HECS scholarship or government or university funding. In addition to tuition fees, students can expect to pay between $500 and $1,000 on text books (although they can be purchased secondhand).

Grants are repaid after graduation when the graduate's income reaches a certain level as follows:

Salary	Per Cent
below $20,594	0
$20,594 to $28,494	2.0
$28,495 to $30,049	3.0
$30,050 to $32,381	3.5
$32,382 to $37,563	4.0
$37,564 to $45,335	4.5
$45,336 to $47,718	5.0
$47,719 to $51,292	5.5
over $51,292	6.0

In recent years many universities have increased the number of places allocated to full fee-paying Australian graduates, for students who aren't offered a government-funded place.

Overseas' Student's Fees: Overseas' students must pay the full cost of their tuition, which depends on the course and the particular university. The government sets minimum fees, although individual institutions can charge higher fees (which many do). The minimum fees are $7,500 to $10,000 a year for arts' courses; $11,000 to $15,000 a year for engineering, law and science courses; and between $15,000 and $26,000 a year for dentistry and medicine. Various scholarships are available which cover tuition fees and living costs or tuition fees only. These are administered by the Australian International Development Assistance Bureau (AIDAB) and the Department of Employment, Education and Training (DEET). Information can be obtained from Australian embassies and High Commissions overseas.

Entrance Qualifications: Admission to Australian universities for Australian students is usually based on their exam results in the Higher School Certificate (HSC) or equivalent taken in their final year of high school. However, some universities in NSW have waived the HSC requirement if families can afford fees of at least $8,000 for a year at a private college doing a 'foundation' course. This option has been available to overseas students for years, but is now also offered to local students.

University admission systems vary considerably and each state has its own system of ranking students for entry to universities within the state. New South Wales, the Australian Capital Territory and Victoria use a form of Tertiary Entrance Rank (TER) scores generated by the Tertiary Admissions Centre, which are issued to all students applying for a university course. The TER score (expressed as a percentage) determines whether a student will gain acceptance to a particular university or course and is based on exam results compared with other students and not against a set of standards (although changes are planned). Queensland uses the Overall Position (OP), which ranks students on a scale of 1 to 25 (out-of-state students are ranked 1 to 100) and South Australia uses a ranking system of 0 to 90. Western Australia uses the Tertiary Entrance Score (TES), which isn't a ranking, and the Northern Territory and Tasmania (which have only one university each) work on an institution basis. All universities accept students from other states, when a complicated system of converting marks is employed. There are plans to introduce a nationwide system of university entrance marks, although it's expected to be some years before this is instituted (like may things in Australia, most states think that their way of doing things is best).

Generally the better the university (or the better the reputation) and the more popular the course, the higher the entrance qualifications. The minimum entrance requirements are set by individual universities and colleges and vary considerably. Some universities have been forced to lower entrance requirements in recent years due to falling student numbers. Note that no university excels in all subjects and it's important to choose a university on the strength of it's teaching excellence in your particular subject. Obtain a prospectus from the universities on your shortlist. There are also a number of excellent guides available to help you make your choice (see page 209).

Generally overseas students' qualifications which would admit them to a university in their own country are taken into consideration. Whatever your qualifications, each application is considered on its merits. All foreign students require a thorough knowledge of English, which will usually be examined unless a certificate is provided. Australian universities accept the international baccalaureate (IB) certificate as an entrance qualification, but an American high school diploma isn't usually accepted. Contact individual universities for detailed information. Overseas students can obtain general information from the Overseas Students Branch, Department of Employment, Education and Training, PO Box 25, Woden, ACT 2606.

Applications: To apply for a place at university you should begin by writing to the Tertiary Admissions Centre (TAC) in the state of your choice. There's now a common deadline for applications of 27th September. Each state TAC allows you to make one application on which you list a number of preferences. Acceptance depends on Tertiary Entrance (TE) examination scores (see above) and how many places are available. You should make sure that you spread your preferences to include some courses on which you're almost certain to gain acceptance. It's possible to change preferences once you know your TE score, e.g. if you score considerably higher or lower than anticipated. Alternatively you can re-sit your exams or take a year off and re-apply the following year. Most universities operate special adult entry admission schemes which allow mature applicants over a certain age admittance on the basis of work experience and qualifications other than academic.

Semesters and Courses: The university academic year follows the calendar year with courses taking place from February until November or December. The year commences with an orientation week (O-week), during which enrolment takes place for new students. The year is usually divided into two semesters of around 14 weeks, with a recess of around two weeks in mid-semester and a six to eight week summer break, with examinations in November or December. Note, however, that most universities now offer summer semesters which allow students to catch up on failed or missed subjects. Students study a main subject plus one or two subsidiary subjects and specialise in their main subject for the first one or two years. In some universities it's possible for students to design their own degree courses. Many students choose a sandwich course, which includes a period spent working in industry or commerce. Timetables may be flexible and usually include less than 10 hours of classes a week in order to maximise individual reading and research time. Class sizes are usually very large with some lectures attracting as many as 500 students. Most courses are taught through lectures and tutorials, with students being assessed on their work in essays, assignments, practicals and examinations (annual and finals).

Degrees: A diploma is bestowed on students who successfully complete a course of at least two years, either full time or the equivalent period part-time. The most common degrees awarded in Australia are a Bachelor of Arts (BA) and a Bachelor of Science (BSc). Bachelor's degrees are given a classification, the highest of which is an 'honours' degree, which is granted to students who have undertaken an extra year of specialised study after a three-year pass degree, or is awarded to students who perform outstandingly well in a four-year degree course. The highest pass is a first-class degree, which is quite rare. Second-class degrees are average, while a third-class degree is poor. The lowest classification is a 'pass'. Students can request special consideration and be given a second chance by sitting another exam, or, if their pass work is of a sufficiently high standard, be granted a conceded pass. Second (postgraduate) degrees are usually a Master of Arts (MA) or a Master of Science (MSc), which are awarded to Bachelors' for a one-year course in a subject other than their undergraduate subjects. Students who do post-graduate work in the same subject(s) as their undergraduate work usually undertake a three-year Doctor of Philosophy (PhD) research program.

In 1995, a new national system was established for the recognition of qualifications, called the Australia Qualifications Framework, with the aim of linking the education system so that courses and former training can be easily classified. This will allow students to move more easily between TAFE (see page 209), private colleges and universities, and have their studies and experience recognised. Courses will exist under both the old and the new systems until 1999, when the new system comes into being. A new advanced diploma will be roughly equivalent to an old diploma and a new diploma will be around the same as an old associate diploma. The new qualifications will consist of diploma, advanced diploma, bachelors degree, graduate certificate, graduate diploma, masters degree and a doctorate.

Accommodation: Following acceptance at university, students are advised to apply for a place in a hall of residence or other college accommodation, such as self-catering houses and apartments. However, such accommodation is limited and in high demand, and many universities don't provide student accommodation at all. Students should write as soon as possible after acceptance to the accommodation or housing officer, whose job is to help students find suitable accommodation (both college and private). There's a huge (largely unfilled) demand for student accommodation (often from overseas students) in the major cities, particularly Sydney and Melbourne, and many universities are looking at ways of providing more student accommodation. The cost of accommodation in halls of residence range from around $75 a week for self-catering to around $150 full board. Overseas students are usually given priority for housing, although you should investigate the availability and cost of local accommodation before accepting a place at a university. The Coordinating Committee for Overseas Students helps overseas students find accommodation.

A large number of students rent privately owned apartments or houses, which are shared with other students, although in many areas this kind of accommodation is difficult to find and expensive (from around $75 a week for a single room and $100 for a double). Sharing a room with a fellow student costs from around $50 a week. Another alternative is to find lodgings where you rent a room in a private house with meals included (see also **Single Accommodation** on page 136). It's generally considered that students shouldn't spend more than 30 per cent of their income on accommodation.

Student Bodies: All universities have a huge variety of clubs, societies and organisations, many organised by the students association or union, which is the centre of social activities. Most campuses are members of the National Union of Students (NUS), which represents students at state and national levels. Most universities also have excellent sports facilities and all have bars and canteens. Most clubs fall into the categories of cultural, sporting, recreational, political and department-based. During orientation week, most clubs and societies are represented and compete to sign up new members. Fees are payable although there are a large number of benefits and facilities, many specifically for overseas students. All universities levy a student amenities or general service fee (anything from $100 to $400), which helps finance sports associations, the student union and the representative council.

Further Reading: A wealth of books are published for university students including *Study and Travel in Australia* (also available on CD-ROM) and *A Guide to Australian Universities*, both published by Magabook Pty Ltd, PO Box 44, Rockdale, NSW 2216 (tel. (2) 9567 5300). New Hobsons Press (Level 4, 2 Elizabeth Plaza, North Sydney, NSW 2060, tel. (02) 9936 8630) publish a wide range of books for students including *Australian Study Opportunities, The Directory of Higher Education Courses* and *The Student Companion*, a guide to Australian university life containing university profiles. The *Good Universities Guide* by Dean Ashenden and Sandra Milligan (available from Reply Paid 95, Good Universities Guide, 19 Olive Street, Subiaco, WA 6008 (tel. freecall 1800-682133) also makes interesting reading (although it has been criticised by some universities). A Higher Education supplement is published in the Wednesday edition of *The Australian* newspaper.

FURTHER EDUCATION

Further education generally embraces everything except first degree courses taken at universities and colleges of higher education, although the distinction between further and higher education (see page 202) is often blurred. Further education courses may be full or part-time and are provided at universities, Technical and Further Education (TAFE) colleges, technical colleges, evening colleges, the Adult Migrant Education Service, the Council of Adult Education, the Workers' Education Association and by numerous 'open learning' institutions such as the Open Training and Education Network (OTEN). Qualifications which can be earned through further education include the school certificate (SC), the higher school certificate (HSC), the international baccalaureate, trade certificates, bachelors and masters degrees, MBA degrees, and a range of internationally recognised certificates and diplomas. Around four out of five Australians take a further education course at some time during their lives.

TAFE Colleges: By far the largest organisation offering further education courses in Australia are Technical and Further Education (TAFE) colleges, which have over 1m students studying at some 200 colleges throughout Australia, many with a number of campuses and training centres (including some universities). Many courses have a strong vocational focus and are noted for their practical, hands-on emphasis. The majority of TAFE courses are at the certificate, diploma and advanced diploma levels, although some degree level courses are offered and courses can be used as entry to a full-time degree course at university. TAFE courses include apprenticeships, trade, post-trade and technician courses, plus commercial and general courses to certificate level. Some states have technical schools where high school students learn a trade and go on to a TAFE college. TAFE courses are also used to supplement apprenticeships and on-the-job training. Most courses last for around two years and can be undertaken on a part-time or full-time basis and can also be combined with a job when the employer allows time off to attend classes.

TAFE colleges offer hundreds of courses, including all major skills in a wide range of industrial, commercial, artistic and domestic occupations. Many courses are specifically designed for school leavers to upgrade their skills and for adults wishing to get back into the workforce. Courses span everything from semi-skilled trade training to professional subjects and include correspondence courses and special programs for disadvantaged groups. Courses for apprentices cover dozens of different trades including building, vehicle, metal, electrical, automotive, electronics, plumbing, printing, food, gardening, farming, fashion, hairdressing, textiles, jewellery and watchmaking industries, to name but a few. Pre-apprenticeship courses allow young people to undertake a substantial part of a trade course before taking up an apprenticeship with advanced standing. Fees vary depending on the state or territory, each of which sets its own fees. The average cost of a full-time course is $500 to $600 a year, although some states wave fees for school-leavers who enrol directly in TAFE courses on leaving school. Fees can be paid in instalments and there are concessionary rates (or no fees) for low-income earners. Students are also eligible for Austudy grants (see page 204).

Open Learning: Open (or distance) learning means studying at a time and place that suits you, which in Australia is coordinated by Open Learning Australia (OLA) and offered by around 30 universities and TAFE colleges. Flexibility is provided by OLA through four 13-week study periods a year, with students being able to choose the study period in which they start and how many periods they study each year. Students can also choose how many units they wish to study within a study period. Anyone can enrol and there are no pre-requisites for study, no quotas and no residential requirements. Courses are suitable for secondary students who were unable to gain a suitable university place or are unable to study full-time because of work or other commitments. OLA is also ideal for anyone wishing to study one or more university subjects without enrolling for a degree. Qualifications gained via OLA can also be used to gain admission to a university as a full-time student. Most units are broadcast twice a year on ABC TV and are supplemented by radio broadcasts, telephone tutorials, handbooks, and audio tapes. Fees are modest and some students can pay via a similar scheme to the HECS (see page 205). For information contact Open Learning Australia, 30 Collins Street, Melbourne, VIC 3000 (tel. freecall 1800-813666).

Private Colleges: Private colleges also offer vocational training and are closely aligned to the industries for which they prepare students. Many private colleges offer training in courses such as hospitality, secretarial, business and computer studies. Prospective students should check whether a course has been accredited by contacting the Australian Council for Private Education and Training (tel. (03) 9723 9271), which is the regulating body of private colleges and assures the quality of the tuition provided. Some institutions offer distance learning Master of Business Administration (MBA) courses for those who cannot (or don't wish to) study on a full or part-time, locally taught basis. Around 40 universities, business schools and professional organisations offer MBA courses in subjects such as banking, business administration, communications, economics, European languages, information systems, management, marketing, public relations, and social and political studies.

LANGUAGE SCHOOLS

If you don't speak English fluently (or you wish to learn another language) you can enrol in a language course offered by numerous language schools in Australia. Some 140 languages are spoken in Australia, so there's plenty of opportunity to learn and practice foreign languages. Obtaining a working knowledge or becoming fluent in English (or strine) while living in Australia is relatively easy, as you'll be constantly immersed in the English language and will have the maximum opportunity to practise. However, if you wish to speak or write English fluently, you'll probably need to attend a language school or find a private tutor. Many thousands of foreign students (mostly from Asian countries) come to Australia each year to learn English, thus ensuring that English-language schools are big business (although they will be hit hard by the Asian economic crisis in 1998). Note that it's usually necessary to have a recognised qualification in English to be accepted at a college of higher or further education in Australia.

English-language courses are offered at all levels by universities; language schools; migrant education colleges; foreign and international organizations; local associations and clubs; private colleges; Technical and Further Education (TAFE) colleges; open learning institutions; and private teachers. Classes range from language courses for complete beginners, through specialised business or cultural courses, to university-level seminars leading to recognised diplomas. The Department of Multicultural Affairs supports Settlement English courses for some migrants and the cost may be funded by the department. There are English-language schools in all cities and large towns in Australia, many equipped with computers, language laboratories, video studios, libraries and bookshops.

Most language schools offer a variety of classes depending on your current language ability, how many hours you wish to study a week, how much money you want to spend and how quickly you wish to learn. Full-time, part-time and evening courses are offered by most schools, and many also offer residential courses or accommodation with local families (highly recommended to accelerate learning). Courses that include accommodation (often half board, consisting of breakfast and an evening meal) usually offer good value for money. Bear in mind that if you need to find your own accommodation, particularly in Sydney or Melbourne, it can be difficult and expensive. Language classes generally fall into the following categories:

Category	No. hours a week
compact	10 to 20
intensive	20 to 30
total immersion	30 to 40+

Most schools offer compact or intensive courses and also provide special English courses for businessmen and professionals (among others), and a wide variety of examinations, most of which are recognised internationally. Course fees vary considerably and are usually calculated on a weekly basis. Fees depend on the number of hours tuition per week, the type of course, and the location and reputation of the school. Expect to pay up to $500 a week for an intensive course providing 20 to 30 hours of language study per week and around $300 a week for a compact course.

Total immersion or executive courses are provided by many schools and usually consist of private lessons for a minimum of 30 to 40 hours a week. Fees can run to $2,000 or more a week and not everyone is suited to learning at such a fast rate (or has the financial resources). Whatever language you're learning, don't expect to become fluent in a short period unless you have a particular flair for languages or already have a good command of a language. Unless you desperately need to learn a language quickly, it's better to arrange your lessons over a long period. Don't commit yourself to a long course of study (particularly an expensive one) before ensuring that it's the correct one. Most schools offer a free introductory lesson and free tests to help you find your appropriate level. Many language schools offer private and small group lessons. **It's important to choose the right course, particularly if you're studying English in order to continue with full-time education in Australia and need to reach a minimum standard or gain a particular qualification.**

For information about English courses for overseas students contact English Language Intensive Courses for Overseas Students (ELICOS), PO Box 30, 43 Murray Street, Pyrmont, NSW 2009 (tel. (02) 9660 6455). For an introduction to language in Australia see page 44.

10.

PUBLIC TRANSPORT

Public transport in Australia varies from region to region and town to town. In most cities and large towns services are good to excellent and relatively inexpensive, although some suburbs and areas are poorly served. Most Australian cities have a relatively small suburban rail network and many regions aren't served by trains at all, which is one of the reasons most Australians are so attached to their cars (only Americans are more devoted to their cars than Australians). However, it isn't *always* essential to own a car in Australia, particularly if you live in a city (where parking is often impossible). On the other hand, if you live in the country or a suburb off the main rail and bus routes, it's usually essential to have your own transport. Bus and rail services in most areas are also severely curtailed on Sundays and possibly also on Saturdays.

Bear in mind when travelling interstate that Australia is a huge country, nearly as big as Europe or the USA (and over 30 times the size of Britain), with vast distances between the capital cities. Flying will save you a lot of time and the loss of sleep associated with long-distance bus and train journeys, although you will see little of Australia while flying around the country. Book early if you plan to travel long distance on public holidays or at the beginning or end of school holidays (see page 194). Despite the vast distances involved in travelling in Australia, most Australians prefer to travel by private car.

Most cities have an integrated public transport system and tickets usually allow transfers between buses, trains, trams and ferries (as applicable), with fares calculated on a zone system (e.g. travelpasses in Sydney). Buses and trams carry around 65 per cent of passengers in the major cities, where there's a range of daily, weekly, monthly, quarterly and annual tickets, plus discounted books of 10 tickets offering savings on single fares. Many cities have free downtown shuttle buses. Note that passengers discovered travelling without tickets can be fined up to $200.

Sydney has an integrated service which includes buses, ferries and Cityrail's 'underground' system (not actually an underground 'metro' railway, but a conventional railway that runs underground part of the way) and suburban trains. Sydney also has a monorail, although it's expensive (particularly considering that it doesn't actually go anywhere) and is mainly a novelty for tourists, rather than a serious mode of public transport. It has the most expensive public transport of any Australian city, but is still relatively cheap by international standards. Trams were reintroduced in 1997 after 36 years absence and a new underground railway linking the airport to the city centre is under construction and due for completion in the year 2000 for the Olympics. There are also plans for a light rail network to service the northern beaches and western suburbs. A New South Wales state transit directory is available and a comprehensive Sydney & Suburbs *Bus-Rail-Ferry Guide* ($2.50).

Melbourne has a inexpensive and efficient public transport network consisting of buses, trains and trams. Trams form the backbone of the public transport system and the city's network is the most extensive in the world and the only one remaining in Australia (unlike Sydney, Melbourne was wise enough to retain its trams). The network covers 325km/202mi and is served by some 750 trams (only St. Petersberg has more) operating up to 20km/12mi outside the city centre. The Melbourne public transport system is called the 'Met', which is the collective name for bus, rail and tram services (a free 'Get around on the Met' map is available). Tickets can be purchased at train stations, on board buses and trams, and from retail outlets such as newsagents and cafés (an automated 'Metcard' ticketing system is being introduced).

Other Australian cities also have an adequate or good public transport service consisting mainly of buses and a limited suburban rail network, supported by a few ferries, and in Adelaide, a single tram line. Apart from New South Wales, few states have an extensive rail network.

Students visiting or living in Australia should obtain an International Student Identity Card (ISIC), which offer a range of travel discounts. STA Travel is the biggest nationwide travel agency and can provide tickets for all domestic and international travel. A number of guides are available for handicapped passengers including the *Smooth Ride Guide to Australia & New Zealand* by July Ramsay (FT Publishing), a guide to access for wheelchairs, and *Easy Access Australia - A Travel Guide to Australia.*

TRAINS

In the mid-19th century when the first Australian railways were built, the states were independent colonies and governed from London; consequently Australia's rail network grew piecemeal without any consultation between states. When the Australian federation was formed in 1901 the original six colonies all incredibly had different gauge lines to their neighbours! This resulted in passengers having to change trains at the state borders, often in the middle of the night, which continued until the early '60s when standard gauge lines (1,435mm) were introduced on some main lines. However, Australia still has three different railway gauges: 1,067mm, 1,435mm (standard) and 1,600mm, although the main interstate lines now run on standard gauge lines. This has meant that the development of rail travel has been stifled and it's only in the last few years that much thought has been given to expanding and updating the rail network, which by European standards is antiquated and severely limited. Most Australian cities have only a sparse suburban rail network and many areas of the country aren't served by trains at all.

Australian trains are more comfortable, leisurely and sociable than buses, but slower (Australian long-distance trains are God's way of telling you to slow down!), more expensive and sometimes difficult to book. You need to reserve well in advance for the most popular long-distance trains, particularly during the peak holiday season. Some trains have wheelchair access including the V/Line 'Sprinter' trains in Victoria and the Countrylink 'XPT' (an abbreviation for 'Express Passenger Train') and 'Xplorer' trains operating in NSW, Queensland and between Sydney and Melbourne (at speeds of up to 160kph/100mph).

Until recently most Australian railways were owned and operated by state or federal governments, although the federal government sold off its remaining lines in 1997. There are also a few small private railways serving mainly agricultural and industrial areas, e.g. the iron-ore mining developments in the northwest of Western Australia and an extensive tramway network in Queensland connecting the sugar cane fields to the mills in sugar-producing areas. Rail Australia consists of four state owned rail companies (Countrylink, Queensland Rail, V-Line and Westrail) and the Great Southern Railway (GSR), which was created when the *Ghan*, *Indian Pacific* and *Overland* services were sold by the federal government in 1997. Some states (such as Victoria) are planning to privatise their railways. Like the USA, the main task of Australian railways is to haul long-distance freight, bulk minerals (particularly coal in NSW and Queensland), grain and petroleum products.

There's an interstate railway service serving all states except Tasmania and the Northern Territory. There are no regular passenger railways in Tasmania, although there's a freight rail service throughout the island and several steam railways for tourists (e.g. Ida Bay to Deep Hole). With the exception of Alice Springs (which is connected to Adelaide), the Northern Territory (including Darwin) has no rail services, although there have been 'plans' to extend the line from Alice Springs to Darwin for around a century (this may at long last become a reality — but don't hold your breath).

Interstate Trains: Australia has some of the best long-distance rail journeys in the world, although the unchanging scenery in some regions can begin to pall after a few hours. Interstate rail travel has been overtaken by the age of air travel and (apart from suburban services in the major cities) are mainly of interest to tourists and travellers with plenty of time on their hands (the average speed of Australian trains is around 65kph/40mph). All long-distance trains are air-conditioned and don't stop at all intermediate stations, e.g. those within a few hours of major terminals. Long-distance trains have evocative names such as the *Spirit of the Outback* (Brisbane-Longreach), the *Ghan* (Adelaide-Alice Springs), the *Prospector* (Perth-Kalgoorlie), the *Indian Pacific* (Sydney-Adelaide-Perth) and the *Sunlander* (Brisbane-Cairns). The *Prospector* (Perth-Kalgoorlie) provides first-class, air-conditioned accommodation only, and maintains the fastest average speed (around 110kph/68mph) of any train in Australia, taking 7.5 hours for the 655km/407mi journey.

The *Indian Pacific* crosses Australia and takes it name from its route from the Pacific Ocean (Sydney) to the Indian Ocean (Perth), a journey of 4,348km/2,700mi taking around 65 hours. It includes the longest stretch of straight track (478km/300miles) in the world across the Nullabor Plain in Western Australia. The *Indian Pacific* is one of the world's longest trains with up to 25 carriages, plus an observation lounge, restaurant, bar and music room with piano. The Great Southern Railway has plans to turn the *Ghan* (which takes its name from the Afghanistan or Ghan camel drivers who opened up the interior of the country) into 'a five-start hotel on wheels' and become Australia's answer to Europe's Orient Express. Cars are carried on the *Queenslander*, the *Spirit of the Outback* and between Adelaide and Alice Springs, Melbourne and Perth, and on the Melbourne-Mildura goods line.

Accommodation: Long-distance trains offer a range of accommodation which may include de luxe, first, holiday and economy class sleeping berths, and first and economy class seats. Sleeping berths are available on overnight services (for a surcharge) and are well worth the extra charge on long journeys. In first class there are twinette cabins with seats that fold into two sleeping berths and shared facilities with adjacent cabins. First class single roomettes have a private toilet and wash basin, and first class cabins a shower, toilet, wash basin, hot and cold water, and an outlet for an electric shaver. Deluxe cabins and family units are available on the *Ghan* and *Indian Pacific* trains, where meals are included with first class sleeping berths. In Queensland, economy class sleepers have three sleeping berths and each carriage has communal showers and toilets. Where sleeping berths are unavailable, there are reclining seats. Two-berth 'holiday class' cabins are available on *The Ghan* and the *Indian Pacific* trains. Coach class cars have reclining seats and on trains to Perth, Alice Springs and Cairns, coach and economy class sitting cars include showers.

Vintage Trains: There are a number of vintage trains in Australia, e.g. from Cairns to Kuranda, which takes 90 minutes to travel 33km (20mi), and there are also vintage and tramway museums in all states where you can enjoy excursions on restored steam trains. These include the Puffing Billy in the Dandenongs Ranges in Victoria, the Ida Bay Railway in Tasmania and the New South Wales Railway Museum (at Thirlmere near Picton). On the first Sunday of the month from March to November, a steam train leaves Sydney Central station for Thirlmere. The Hotham Valley Tourist Railway in WA operates 'Explorer' trains to various destinations and restored locomotives operate on short excursions from Alice Springs.

Sydney has the most extensive suburban rail network in Australia, although even here many suburbs have no rail services. In cities, trains are much faster than buses, particularly during rush hours, even where new faster roads have been built. Most routes are served by old mostly double-decker trains (Sydney was the first country in the world to introduce double-decker electric trains) on which seats can usually be reversed to face in either direction (these are being replaced by ultra-modern Tangara trains). Yellow stripes on platforms indicate where half-length, four-carriage trains stop (you must stand behind the yellow line on platforms). Doors open and close automatically, although the doors on old trains are rarely closed during hot weather, so keep clear of the doors (or hold on tight). Trains operate from around 5am until midnight — violence, although rare, has caused the cancellation of trains after midnight on some suburban routes. After dark there are special 'Night Safe' areas (marked on the platform in blue) where you can wait for trains. After 8pm, only two carriages are in use (next to the guard's compartment, indicated by a blue light) and a help button is positioned near the door which can be used to alert the guard or driver.

The NSW Countrylink network operates the most comprehensive state rail service in Australia using Xplorer trains, on which seats must be booked in advance. There are commuter trains between Sydney and Wollongong, Katoomba, Lithgow, Newcastle and Goulburn. NSW State Rail has been plagued by problems in recent years and is starved of cash. Many trains run late and the failure of a new timetable introduced in 1996 meant that it had to revert to its previous timetable.

Canberra is served by the main Sydney-Melbourne line which passes through Goulburn around an hour northeast of Canberra (you must disembark here to get to Canberra). There are no connecting buses and most trains are very slow. It's usually advisable to take a bus or fly when travelling to Canberra. The main rail station is on Wentworth Avenue in the suburb of Kingston. However, there are advanced plans for a 'very fast train' (VFT) link between Sydney and Canberra, travelling at speeds of up to 300kph (186mph), although like most of Australia's rail modernisation plans, the idea has been around for some time (and will take eons to come to fruition — if ever).

Melbourne: The Victorian State Railway, V/Line, operates all rail (and associated coach routes) within Victoria, including day and overnight, high-speed XPT services to Sydney (Melbourne-Sydney during the day and Sydney-Melbourne overnight) taking 13 hours. The Canberra Link involves taking a train to Wodonga on the border with NSW and a bus from there to Canberra. There are *Overland* daily night services to Adelaide taking 12 hours (change to the *Indian Pacific* in Adelaide for Perth). The city centre 'City Loop' forms an underground railway around the centre. V/Line supersaver fares offer a 30 per cent discount when travelling off-peak, which entails travelling on Tuesday, Wednesday or Thursday and arriving in Melbourne after 9.30am, and leaving Melbourne at any time except between 4pm and 6pm. In recent years new air-conditioned, 'high-speed' Sprinter trains have been introduced on some routes.

Adelaide: Long-distance trains stop at the Adelaide Rail Passenger Terminal in Keswick, 2km southwest of the city centre. There's an overnight service to Melbourne taking around 13 hours and a day coach/train service taking 11 hours. The *Ghan* to Alice Springs (22 hours) leave at 2pm on Thursdays with an additional service on Mondays in winter. There are five weekly trains to Perth (none on Tuesdays and Thursdays) taking around 41 hours, possibly requiring a change of train at Port Pirie. There's a small network of suburban trains in Adelaide operated by the State Transport Authority. Note that tickets must be purchased before entering platforms or mounting trains.

Perth: Perth to Sydney on the *Indian Pacific* takes 64 hours and runs three times a week on Sundays, Mondays and Thursdays. The cheapest fare is around $220. Perth-Adelaide on the *Trans-Australian* takes 38 hours and departs on Wednesdays and Saturdays (fare from around $165). There are also suburban lines (operated by Westrail) from Perth to Armadale, Currambine, Fremantle, Joondalup and Midland. Western

Australia has no rail services outside Perth with the exception of the Perth-Bunbury line, the Perth-Kalgoorlie route operated by the *Prospector* and the main line to the east. Note that tickets should be purchased from vending machines at train stations before boarding. Multi-ride tickets can be validated at stations. Seven-day advance purchase fares are available in the low season offering a 30 per cent discount. A car train service is available between Adelaide and Perth.

Alice Springs: The station in Alice is a 15-minute walk from the edge of the town (taxis meet trains). Alice is served by the *Ghan* which departs from Adelaide at 2pm on Mondays and Thursdays and arrives in Alice at 12.30pm the following day (the journey time is 23 hours). The return leaves Alice at 5.10pm and arrives in Adelaide at 4.30pm the next day (although it's often early). The fare is from $125 one-way.

Queensland: Trains in Queensland are operated by Queensland Rail. Queensland has the most extensive rail network of any Australian state covering over 10,000km/6,200mi of lines on narrow gauge tracks (1,067mm). There's also a network of electric suburban trains in Brisbane and the 640km/398mi stretch between Brisbane and Rockhampton is electrified and served by modern tilt trains. Seat or sleeper reservations are compulsory on long-distance trains. The only rail link from outside the state is from NSW (served by XPT trains), on which northbound trains run overnight and southbound trains during the day. Main, long-distance trains are known as 'Traveltrains'. Note than many trains stop at small stations on request and some trains are mixed freight and passenger trains (usually mainly freight with one passenger car). There are 'plans' for a regional rail line on the Sunshine Coast (the existing track is sited 20km/12mi inland from the heavily-populated coastal area).

Local 'tourist' trains includes the *Spirit of the Outback*, the *Gulflander*, the *Savannahlander* and the Kuranda Scenic Railway. The *Spirit of the Tropics*, designed for budget travellers and incorporating a non-stop disco car (Club Loco), and the *Sunlander* (with restored colonial 'theme' carriages) operate on the Brisbane-Cairns route. The *Spirit of Capricorn* runs daily from Brisbane to Rockhampton. The *Queenslander* is Queensland Rail's 'flagship' luxury train (all passengers travel first class with sleeping berths), taking a leisurely 32 hours between Brisbane and Cairns. The *Westlander* operates from Brisbane to Charlesville (777km/482mi taking 16 hours) and the *Inlander* links Townsville with Mount Isa. Vehicles can be transported on the *Queenslander* and the *Spirit of the Outback* services. Cars can be transported by rail between Adelaide and Alice Springs, Melbourne, Perth and Sydney, and on the Melbourne-Mildura line.

Most services are air-conditioned and provide sleeping cars and sitting cars with bar and meal services. The vintage *Gulflander* train operates between Normanton and Croydon in the west of the state. Sunshine rail passes offer unlimited economy class travel on most routes (including the Brisbane suburban network). Ordinary one-way tickets allow unlimited stopovers and 14 days to reach your destination, while return tickets are valid for two months. Stop offs must be stated when buying tickets and reservations made for all journeys. You can change you travel plans, but a re-booking fee may be charged. Trains in Queensland are slower than buses due to the narrow gauge. There's a fast Citytrain service in Brisbane with seven lines. Day rover tickets in Brisbane cost $8.50 and are valid after 9am and at weekends.

For further information about Australian railways contact Rail Australia, 1 Richmond Road, Keswick, SA 5035 (tel. (08) 8217 4321). Rail Australia has agents in many countries including Canada, Denmark, France, Germany, Hong Kong, Japan, Korea, the Netherlands, New Zealand, Singapore, South Africa, Sweden, the United Kingdom and the USA. They publish a brochure, *Australia By Rail*, which describes the long-distance routes and trains. Bookings can also be made through Thomas Cook offices in many countries and Austrailpasses (see page 231) can be purchased from Qantas and Jetabout Tours' offices worldwide. An indispensable book for train buffs is *Australia & New Zealand by Rail* by Colin Taylor (Bradt Publications).

General Information

* Interstate train passengers are permitted up to 50kg/110lbs of luggage (two items not exceeding 25kg/55lbs each and within a maximum of 180cm in circumference). Medium-sized suitcases and hand baggage can be placed in compartments, but larger luggage should be booked in at the luggage desk not less than 30 minutes prior to departure. Note that booked luggage is carried in the baggage car and isn't accessible during the journey. There's also luggage storage space at the ends of passenger compartments.

* Luggage can be sent unaccompanied and can be insured. Many stations and airports have luggage lockers (from $2 for up to 24-hours), left luggage offices and luggage trolleys. When using a luggage locker insert the correct money to release the key. Note the number of the locker in case you lose the key.

* Snacks are served on long-distance, in-state trains (such as XPT and Xplorer trains) and all interstate trains have dining cars offering both *à la carte* dining and light meals. There are also lounge and club cars on most services. Railway food is generally good and can be excellent on famous 'tourist' trains such as the *Ghan, Indian Pacific* and *Queenslander.* Note that there are no bar facilities for economy passengers on some long-distance services (e.g. from Adelaide to Melbourne) and there may be a large fine (e.g. $100) for consuming your own alcohol! However, taking your own picnic onto a train isn't prohibited, but may be frowned upon. There are restaurants and snack bars at main stations, and food and drink machines are provided at many smaller stations.

* Public payphones (which accept Telecards) are available on long-distance train services.

* There's generally no smoking on Countrylink, Queensland Rail, V-Line and Westrail trains. There are designated smoking areas on national long-distance trains. You can be fined for smoking in a non-smoking carriage or area.

* Toilets are provided on trains on all but the shortest distance services (but shouldn't be used when a train is in a station).

* In most cities, bicycles can be transported on suburban trains free of charge or for a small fee during off-peak times, although a special permit may be required during peak periods (e.g. 6 to 9am and 3 to 6pm on weekdays) or it may be impossible.

* Banks or autobanks (ATMs) are located at the main railway stations in Brisbane and Melbourne (but surprisingly not in Adelaide, Perth or Sydney).

Tickets

Rail tickets in Australia can be purchased from station ticket offices, automatic ticket machines, newsagents (in major cities) and from state transit sales outlets. Most long-distance and main line trains have both first class and standard (economy) seating, although there's little difference between seats on some trains, e.g. XPT trains operating in NSW, Queensland and Victoria. The Perth-Bunbury line in Western Australia, most trains in outback Queensland, and all suburban lines have no first class accommodation. Children under the age of four travel free, unless they are occupying a separate seat or a sleeping berth on an interstate train (when the under 16 fare applies). Those aged from four to 15 travel at a discount (usually half-fare), as do students (e.g. at university) and pensioners (which may depend on your state of residence). Low season is from 1st February to 30th June and the normal season from 1st July to the 31st January. Low season and normal fares are the same when travelling in economy class seats or for travel on *Overland* trains between Adelaide and Melbourne.

Many ticket offices in Sydney and other NSW towns have restricted opening hours of only a few hours a day during rush hours, although passengers can buy tickets from automatic ticket machines. Many stations are unmanned for at least half the day during the week and all day at weekends. Tickets can be paid for with major credit cards (e.g. Mastercard and Visa) subject to a $10 minimum charge. Fare evasion is endemic in Australia, particularly in the major cities, where an estimated 3 per cent of passengers travel without tickets (over 5,000 culprits were discovered in a three-week blitz on Sydney's city loop). Fare evaders face fines of up to $100 and Sydneysiders may soon face a fine of $200.

Ticket Machines: Automatic ticket machines have been introduced in recent years, although there have been a 'few' teething troubles, particularly in Melbourne (where the first machines ate your money, chewed up your tickets and stole your change). You usually select your destination, choose the type of ticket (e,g, single or return), insert the fare (machines accept both coins and notes), and if you're lucky a ticket will be ejected with your change. You must get a ticket validated (stamped with the date and time) in a special machine, without which it's invalid, and you must validate a multiple-ride ticket each time you travel. In some cities you insert your ticket in a ticket barrier with a green arrow (not a red cross) in the direction of the arrow shown on your ticket when leaving a station. A return ticket or multi-day pass will be returned if you're on the outward journey, otherwise the ticket will be retained.

Reservations: Reservations are advisable (at least two months in advance) on all long-distance trains, many of which are booked out months in advance in the summer season and during school holidays. There's no reservation fee and bookings are accepted up to nine months in advance on major routes and six months in advance on other long-distance routes. However, if a booking is altered or cancelled there's a fee of $5, 30 days prior to travel, 10 per cent of the fare less than 30 days prior to travel and 20 per cent of the fare within seven days of travel. There are no refunds for unused tickets after the departure time and date shown on the ticket. For reservations telephone (02) 6249 8159 for the ACT, 300211 in Tasmania and 13 2232 in other states and territories.

Australia Rail uses a computerised booking system called the Customer Advance Purchase Excursion Rail (CAPER). Tickets can be booked for any journey throughout the country (apart from local suburban trains) and must be made and paid for at least seven days in advance. The outward journey must start on the date stamped on tickets and journeys must be completed within the validity of the ticket. Journeys can usually be broken, although a break of journey is usually prohibited with discount fares.

Discounts & Commuter Tickets: On some main routes there are discounts of up to 40 per cent for advance purchase tickets (e.g. seven days), although these aren't applied to the cheapest regular fares (and therefore may not be the cheapest travel option). Note that only a limited number of discounted seats may be available. Standby fares are available on some routes. In major cities, off-peak suburban fares are available after 9am on weekdays and any time at weekends, offering savings of up to 60 per cent on return journeys. In Sydney you can buy a Sydney Pass for three, five or seven days ($60, $80 and $90 respectively) which is valid for suburban trains, city buses and ferries. There are also a range of season tickets (weekly, quarterly and annual) for commuters, providing large discounts over standard fares, which may include travel on suburban trains/trams, buses and ferries (e.g. in Sydney). Weekly passes usually cost around eight times the single fare. A photograph is normally required for a season ticket.

BUSES & TRAMS

There are comprehensive bus services in Australia's major cities and an extensive network of long-distance interstate buses, usually referred to as coaches. Bus services in rural areas are less frequent and it may be necessary to have your own transport if you live in the country. Melbourne is the only Australian city with an extensive tram network, although Sydney reintroduced trams in 1997 after 36 years absence and other cities are also planning new tram lines.

Buses are the cheapest form of public transport in Australia, both within cities and long distance, and provide a far more comprehensive network than the railways, encompassing almost every corner of Australia. Each city and region of Australia has its own local bus companies providing town and country services. In large towns and cities, most bus services start and terminate at a central bus station, which is generally modern and clean. Most are equipped with toilets, showers, luggage lockers or a left luggage office, shops, and a snack bar or restaurant. They bear little relation to the seedy places inhabited by a surfeit of drunks, drug addicts and assorted derelicts, found in many other countries. Smoking is prohibited on all buses and trams in Australia.

If you need assistance, ask at the bus station information office. Most bus companies provide free timetables and route maps, and in some cities comprehensive timetables and maps are available which include all bus services operating within their boundaries. A night bus service operates in the major cities. See also **Timetables & Maps** on page 226 and **Visitors' Tickets** on page 231.

City and Country Buses

In most cities in Australia there are a number of local bus companies, sometimes operated by the local rail company or the state or city authorities. There's a comprehensive bus network in all Australian cities and services are frequent, including a night bus service in the major cities. Buses are slow but fairly frequent in most cities, where they are often the only option for getting to most suburbs. Major cities usually have an integrated public transport system with the same ticket being valid on buses, suburban trains, trams (Melbourne) and ferries (Sydney). In stark contrast to the cities, in country areas there's usually only one bus company and services are sparse and infrequent. In remote areas there may only be school buses, which usually carry other passengers but aren't obliged to.

Buses on most routes operate from around 6am until 11pm or midnight (but possibly only until 7pm on Sundays). Buses run frequently during the weekday rush hours, e.g. every 10 or 15 minutes on the main routes. Outside of rush hours, there's usually a half hour service on most routes during weekdays, although services are often severely restricted at weekends and on public holidays (there may be no service at all on some routes on Sundays and public holidays). In major cities there's usually an express bus service (called 'rockets' in some cities) operating between the outer suburbs and the major centres on routes to city centres (express bus numbers are usually prefixed with an 'X'). Night services are operated in the major cities from around midnight until 6am, some of which have radio links with taxi operators, so that you can arrange to have a taxi meet you at your destination (very civilised). There are free buses in most major cities covering a circular (loop) route within city centres.

It's usual to mount a bus via the front door and disembark from the centre doors. You must normally ring a bell to inform the driver that you want him to stop at the next stop (a buzzer sounds in the cab) and stand by the centre door. When the bus stops, a green light is illuminated which signals that you must push the handle or press a button to open the door, which doesn't usually open automatically. In most cities, bus stops have a number, which are often quoted by people when giving directions, and they may be colour-coded. Buses also display their route number, although in some cities numbers may vary depending on whether they are running to or from the city centre. All bus companies publish route maps and there are comprehensive city travel guides in most cities and state bus directories in some states.

Tickets: In the major cities journeys are based on a zonal system, where the bus network is divided into a number of zones (the central business district and inner suburbs are usually designated zone one). Tickets are valid for travel within a single zone or a number of zones, and may be colour coded corresponding to the zones (and modes of transport) for which they are valid. Tickets are usually valid for up to two hours with unlimited transfers during this time and 'single' tickets usually allow a return trip if it's completed within two hours. You must start your final journey and time stamp your ticket before the two-hour period has elapsed. Tickets may be valid for longer after a certain time, for example in Melbourne tickets are valid for six hours after 7pm.

Tickets can be purchased from bus stations, on board buses and trams, and also from retail outlets such as newsagents and cafés in some cities. Automatic ticket machines are also provided in some cities, but they may gobble your money and refuse to give you a ticket. You can usually buy a ticket from the driver or conductor on boarding a bus, which must then be validated in a machine (to the right of the driver) which dates and time stamps your ticket and prints the time of expiry. If you have a multi-ride ticket, you must validate it each time you travel.

All bus companies offer day passes and weekly, monthly and annual tickets for commuters. A monthly ticket may allow you to take an additional adult with you free of charge on weekends. There are also off-peak, reduced fare tickets which allow you to travel outside rush hours (e.g. between 9am and 3pm or 3.30pm Monday to Friday) and at weekends. In most cities you can buy a book of 10 tickets (e.g. a TravelTen in Sydney) at a saving of up to 40 per cent compared with buying single tickets. There are concessionary fares for children and pensioners, which are usually half the adult fare. A day 'rover' ticket is available for around $5 in most cities and allows unlimited bus travel for a whole day, and may also include travel on other modes of city public transport. Fares may be higher for travel during rush hours, at nights and at weekends. Note that there are fines of up to $100 for anyone discovered travelling without a ticket.

Long-Distance Buses

Long-distance interstate buses are generally cheaper, faster and easier to book than trains and there's a more comprehensive network. However, they are also less comfortable and more restrictive than trains, and time consuming due to the vast distances involved. Long-distance buses are particularly popular among independent travellers (e.g. backpackers), 80 per cent of whom use them almost exclusively. Travelling by bus is around one-third of the cost of travelling by air. There are numerous daily departures on the most popular routes, although some services operate only a few times a week and in the Northern Territory, northern Queensland and northern parts of Western Australia, some routes are interrupted for weeks at a time during the wet season (November to May).

Companies: The major long-distance bus company in Australia with the most extensive national route network (some 900 destinations daily) is Greyhound Pioneer Australia (tel. 13 2030), formed when Greyhound, Pioneer and Bus Australia merged. The other major national bus operator is McCafferty's, which covers most main routes except for Western Australia and Tasmania, and has over 1,000 regular scheduled services a week. The main bus operator in the southern part of Western Australia is the state rail company, Westrail, and Tasmanian Redline Coaches provides express services throughout Tasmania.

Reservations: Reservations can be made through travel agents or direct with bus companies; telephone 132030 (local call rate from anywhere in Australia) for Greyhound Pioneer and (076) 909888 for McCafferty's. There are also many booking agents in major cities including YHA travel offices, some of which allow you to book tickets by phone and pay with a credit card. Long-distance bus tickets are similar to airline tickets, with destinations shown by a code such as SYD for Sydney and MEL for Melbourne. When checking your baggage, make sure that the baggage code matches that of your destination (otherwise you may end up in Cairns and you baggage in Perth!).

Buses: Buses are usually equipped with air-conditioning, reclining seats, toilets, TV and videos with stereo sound, individual reading lights, panoramic windows and water fountains. It's advisable to get a seat near the front away from the toilet and on the left-hand side away from the lights of approaching traffic at night. Long-distance journeys are tiring and you shouldn't expect to get much (any) sleep if you're travelling overnight. Frequent stops are made for food, drinks, toilets and showers. There are strict rules concerning what you can eat and drink on buses. Note that no alcohol may be consumed (maximum fine $500) and smoking is prohibited on all services. Interstate buses don't cater for those in wheelchairs.

Fares: There's lively competition between the major long-distance bus companies and many independent and inter-state competitors, which helps reduce fares. Discounts abound and you should always shop around for the best deal (generally, the more popular the route, the lower the fares). Some companies offer discounts to backpackers on certain services and there are also discounts for students, although the biggest discounts are usually offered on last-minute bookings. Note that there are unsociable arrival hours on some long-distance routes. Visitors can purchase bus passes (see page 231) overseas in many countries, although you may get a better deal in Australia. Note that bus passes aren't valid on some local services and a surcharge is usually payable on routes in remote areas.

It's always cheaper to buy a through ticket for a long journey, rather than separate tickets for short stretches and most tickets allow unlimited stop-overs. You can cancel tickets providing you give 24 hours notice, but there's a cancellation fee of around $10 (refunds aren't possible if you give less than 24 hours notice). A 25 per cent discount is provided for students and children on most services. There's fierce competition on the most popular routes, e.g. Melbourne-Sydney, where fares can be below $50, although off the main inter-city routes fares can be high. The main express routes served by Greyhound Pioneer Australia include the following (times and prices are approximate only):

Route	Journey Time (Hours)	Approx. Fare One Way ($)
Sydney-Adelaide	25	100
Sydney-Canberra	5	35
Sydney-Melbourne (inland)	15	65
Canberra-Melbourne	10	50
Melbourne-Adelaide	10	60
Adelaide-Alice Springs	18	150
Adelaide-Perth	35	200
Adelaide-Brisbane	30	150
Darwin-Alice Springs	20	150
Darwin-Kakadu	4	30
Alice Springs-Ayers Rock	6	80
Cairns-Brisbane	25	150
Cairns-Darwin	40	300
Brisbane-Sydney	17	70
Brisbane-Melbourne	30	125
Perth-Darwin	55	350

Tours: Numerous coach companies offer tours which include accommodation (e.g. hotel, motel, bungalow, cabin or camping) and most meals, ranging from a few days to a few months. On camping tours, meals are usually cooked by a travelling cook and prices include meals, tents, sleeping bags and other equipment. Passengers aren't required to erect tents. Some tour companies cater for backpackers, which although they usually offer a more 'rough and ready' service, are good value for money.

FERRIES & SHIPS

Before the '60s the traditional method of travel to Australia was by ship, although most people now arrive by air, which is cheaper and takes just a day or so compared with weeks by ship. However, it's still possible to travel to Australia by ship (e.g. from Britain and the west coast of the USA) if you have lots of time (around five weeks from Britain) and money. Many container ships and freighters carry a limited number of fare-paying passengers, costing from around £2,000 one way (which isn't so expensive when you consider that it includes accommodation and all meals). Many cruise ships stop in Australia as part of their world cruise itineraries, departing from Europe in January or February and arriving in Australia in March or April. Shipping companies include CTC Lines, Cunard Lines and P&O Cruises. Contact your travel agent for information. For information about ships from Britain contact the Strand Cruise and Travel Centre (tel. UK 0171-836 6363) or P&O Containers, Fleet Operations (tel. UK 0171-441 1472).

Tasmania: The only regular maritime passenger service in Australia is the car ferry operating between Melbourne and Devonport on the north coast of Tasmania. It's served by the *Spirit of Tasmania*, a luxury 467-cabin cruise ship of 31,356 tonnes with a capacity of around 1,200 passengers plus vehicles. The trip is often rough, so poor sailors should take seasickness pills (or a plane). In fact, the ferry crossing isn't much cheaper than the air fare and takes around 14 hours compared with less than an hour by air from Melbourne to Hobart. Ferries run three times weekly in either direction on Mondays, Wednesdays and Fridays from Melbourne's Station Pier, and on Tuesdays, Thursdays and Saturdays from Devonport (although there are seasonal variations). Departures are at 6pm in both directions, arriving at 8.30am the following morning. Cabins and hostel-style accommodation are available.

Fares vary depending on the season (touring or holiday) and are from around $100 including an evening buffet dinner and continental breakfast. There are three fare rates depending on the time of year: bargain (late April to mid-September), holiday (Christmas to March) and shoulder (the rest of the year). There's a 25 per cent discount for students and occasional mid-week discounts also. Vehicles are carried for between $125 and $175 (depending on the season) one way. There's also a Seacat service between George Town (east of Devonport) and Port Welshpool 200km/124mi from Melbourne. The journey takes just four and a half hours but passengers are more prone to seasickness than on the ferry service. For information about ferries contact the TT Line, Station Pier, Port Melbourne, Vic 3000 (tel. freecall 1800-030344).

Sydney: Travelling by ferry is one of the joys of living in Sydney, where many people use them to commute to work. The city has eight main ferry routes and 33 ferry wharfs all served from the main Circular Quay ferry terminal. In addition to regular (slow) ferries, there's also a catamaran (RiverCat) service from Circular Quay to Parramatta (via the Parramatta River) and to Manly (JetCat). Most ferries run from around 6am until midnight, although times vary depending on the route, and services are restricted at weekends when ferries may not stop at all wharfs. Most services run every 50 minutes during the day and more often during rush hours, e.g. every 15 or 20 minutes. Regular commuters can buy a book of 10 tickets (called a 'FerryTen') and weekly, quarterly and annual commuter tickets, which offer even greater savings, and can be combined with other modes of public transport such as buses and suburban trains. Special tickets are available for trips to major attractions (such as Taronga Zoo) which include the return ferry trip from Circular Quay and the entrance fee, and are cheaper than buying separate tickets. Special ferries are also available to follow sailing races such as the famous Sydney-Hobart race which starts on Boxing Day (26th December).

Other Ferries: Ferries in Victoria (south of Melbourne) operate between Cowes on Philip Island and Stony Point on the Mornington Peninsula, from Stony Point to Tankerton on French Island, and from Sorrento to Queenscliff. Brisbane has a fast and efficient ferry service along and across the Brisbane river operating every 10 to 15 minutes from dawn until around 11pm, Monday to Saturday (operating hours are reduced on Sundays). In Perth there's a ferry service across the Swan River from Barrack Street jetty to the Mends Street jetty. Ferries also operate from Fremantle to Rottnest Island. Darwin harbour ferries make daily crossings to Mandorah on the Cox peninsula. A ferry service also operates from Woodbridge on the southeast coast of Tasmania to Roberts Point on Bruny Island.

Cruises: All major cities offer sightseeing trips and cruises on local waterways, which may include coffee, lunch and dinner cruises (often including a show). Longer cruises are also available including trips to the Great Barrier Reef from ports in northern Queensland, many of which use glass-bottomed boats to view the marine life. There are paddle-wheelers at Echuca-Moama in Victoria and paddle steamers in Mildura in northwestern Victoria.

Note that one of the first things you should do after boarding a ferry or ship is to study the safety procedures (e.g. what to do when it sinks!).

TIMETABLES & MAPS

All public transport companies in Australia produce comprehensive timetables, route maps and guides. At major airports and railway stations, arrivals and departures are shown on electronic boards and computer screens. Note that most transport companies use am (before noon) and pm (after noon) in timetables, rather than the 24-hour clock used in most countries. When am and pm isn't indicated, the general practice is that times printed in light type are before noon (am) and times printed in **bold** type are after noon (pm). When travelling from east to west (or vice versa), bear in mind the local time differences, which are usually announced by the conductor. There's a 30-minute time zone change between the eastern states and South Australia and one of 90 minutes out in the Nullabor Plain (see **Time Difference** on page 460).

Rail: Always check and double check the departure (and arrival) time of a train (particularly in the outback when the next train may be a week next Thursday and be fully booked), especially when you need to make a flight connection. Some journeys may necessitate part of the journey to be undertaken by air or bus to link up with a connecting train. Note that schedules are liable to change at short notice, particularly at weekends and during holiday periods. It's also important to check that a train actually stops where you want to go, as long-distance trains usually make few stops. Most long-distance trains operate throughout the year, but local and in-state trains may not run on public holidays, which vary depending on the state (see page 62). Schedules are liable to change at weekends and during public holiday periods (both national and local), and many local trains don't operate on holidays such as Christmas Day, Good Friday and ANZAC Day (25th April). Interstate and long-distance trains operate throughout the year.

The state rail authorities and the Great Southern Railway all publish their own free timetables and Rail Australia also publishes a summary of major long-distance services. Suburban timetables are published separately and leaflets are available about particular services from stations. The *Thomas Cook Overseas Timetable* is the nearest thing Australia has to an Australia-wide rail timetable. On long-distance timetables +1, +2 and +3 indicates that the train arrives the following, second or third day (after departure) respectively. **However, bear in mind that rail timetables in Australia are usually works of fiction and bear little relation to 'real' time.** Note that state capital cities have more than one railway station, although long-distance trains always arrive and depart from the main interstate station, e.g. Central Station in Sydney and Spencer Street Station in Melbourne. There are rail enquiry numbers in all states which can usually be reached by dialling 13 2232 (no area code is required), although it's often difficult to get through (lines seem to be continually engaged). It's usually easier to visit a rail information office or a station to obtain train information.

Bus: Bus timetables may be for individual routes, all routes operated by a particular company, or all routes serving a city, town or region. Bus timetables, which include all local bus company services, are often published by local councils and are available free (or for a nominal price) from bus companies, libraries and tourist information centres. Many councils publish excellent public transport guides and maps (available from libraries, tourist centres, newsagents and council offices), which include all bus, rail and ferry transport services operating within a city or region.

TAXIS

There are two kinds of taxis in Australia, licensed taxis or cabs (abbr. of cabriolet) and private radio taxis. The main difference from the passenger's point of view, is that licensed taxis (which are usually white or yellow) can be hailed in the street and radio taxis can only be booked in advance by phone. Taxis can be 'officially' shared in some states, e.g. in Darwin there are shared 'multi-ride' taxis with 12 seats which pick up passengers en route. Wheelchair accessible taxis are available in most major cities. There are also water taxis in Sydney operating from Circular Quay to most areas on the harbour, which are a novel (but expensive) way of getting around the harbour. The fare depends on the time of day and the number of passengers.

Licensed taxis can ply for hire anywhere within their fare area and can be hailed on the streets, hired from taxi ranks (special waiting places for taxis), railway stations, airports and hotels, or can be ordered by telephone. There are free courtesy phones outside main hotels. Taxis for hire display a 'Vacant' or 'For Hire' sign or light on the roof. It's usually fairly easy to get a taxi in a city late at night as there are many 'night' taxis, although they can be difficult to find just after the pubs close due to the strict drink-driving laws in Australia (and between midnight and 6am on Sundays in major cities). Taxi drivers run a high risk of being mugged in some areas of major cities (e.g. Sydney), which has led to some suburbs being officially classified as 'no-go' areas. Since 1997, taxis in Sydney have been fitted with a protection screen between the passenger compartment and the driver, and a satellite tracking system is installed in taxis to monitor their position and speed (taxis in Melbourne are being fitted with video cameras).

Taxis are relatively inexpensive in Australia and rates vary little from city to city. In Sydney there's a standing charge (flagfall) of $3 plus $1 per km. There are a number of surcharges including a charge of $1 when a taxi is called by telephone and an extra $1.50 when a bridge toll (e.g. Sydney Harbour Bridge) is included in the journey. There's usually a surcharge for journeys at night and at weekends (in some cities there are three daytime rates). There's usually also a small charge for luggage carried in the boot (trunk). Outside city limits you must pay a higher 'country' rate and possibly a surcharge ('befouling fee') of $15 if the taxi gets dirty! Many taxis accept credit cards for fares over $5.

Tipping isn't necessary and although most people round the fare up to the nearest dollar, drivers may actually round the fare down rather than give change and may even refuse tips (Americans will be horrified at this 'anti-tipping' attitude, which is obviously a Commie plot to undermine the free world!). Australian taxi drivers are generally honest and helpful (unlike those in many others countries) and are a blot on the taxi driver's bad name! Complaints about service or hire charges can be made to the local taxi licensing office. Make a note of the taxi's license number and the date and time of the incident, and if you think you have been overcharged, obtain a receipt.

In addition to taxi services, many taxi companies operate private hire (e.g. weddings, sightseeing), chauffeur and courier services, and provide contract and account services, e.g. to take children to and from school. A two passenger bicycle taxi (pedi-cab) can be hired in Adelaide for $20 an hour.

AIRLINE SERVICES

Air travel is the best and fastest way to get around Australia and 80 per cent of domestic long-distance trips are made by air. Australian airlines are strict about safety and it's one of the safest places in the world to fly (Qantas was recently rated the safest airline in the world by IATA). Australia is served by around 50 international airlines operating scheduled passenger services. Australia's national airline is Qantas (Queensland and Northern Territory Aerial Service), formed in 1922 (only KLM is older) and privatised in 1995. It's one of the best (noted for the excellence of its food and wines) and most profitable airlines in the world, and in 1995 was voted airline of the year by the industry magazine, Air Transport World. Qantas has a fleet of around 100 aircraft and carries over 16m passengers a year (including over 3m on international routes) to 40 destinations in 26 countries (although services to some Asian countries were slashed in 1998 as a result of the Asian economic crisis). It has partnership agreements with seven other international airlines including American Airlines and British Airways, whereby partners can buy seats on Qantas flights and vice versa. There are Qantas Club lounges at all major airports in Australia and shared lounges in many other countries.

Australia's second airline is Ansett, which serves over 70 towns and cities in Australia and also operates flights to New Zealand and a number of Asian destinations including Bali, Hong Kong and Malaysia. Ansett has 12 international partners including Singapore Airlines and Air New Zealand, and provides an extensive network of domestic flights through its subsidiaries Ansett Express, Ansett Airlines of South Australia, Ansett WA, Ansett NT, East-West and Air Queensland. Both Ansett and Qantas have their own terminals at Australia's major airports and both cater for disabled passengers and passengers in wheelchairs. Note that smoking is prohibited on all flights operated by Australian airlines, both domestic and international, with a maximum $500 fine for offenders (so don't get caught smoking in the toilet!).

Air travel is (not surprisingly) the most popular form of transport for journeys within Australia, where domestic airlines carry some 15m passengers a year. Flying times between Sydney and other state capitals are: Canberra (236km/147mi) 30 minutes; Brisbane (746km/464mi) and Melbourne (708km/440mi) around one hour 15 minutes; Adelaide (1,166km/725mi) and Hobart (1,039km/646mi) around two hours; and Perth (3,284km/2,041mi) around five hours (600km/372mi equals around one hour's flying time). As with international flights, the major domestic airlines are Qantas (50 destinations) and Ansett Australia (all major cities plus the most popular tourist destinations). There are also five regional airlines and around 25 smaller commuter airlines in Australia (many owned by or linked with Ansett or Qantas), which mainly fly in-state routes and provide access to remote areas, islands and tourist destinations.

There are many flights a day between Australia's major cities (although some journeys require a number of stops), but on less travelled routes there are just one or two flights a week. It's always advisable to book a domestic flight as far in advance as possible, particularly during holiday periods (this will also allow you to take maximum advantage of reduced fares). Many regional and local airlines operate small aircraft which are generally booked well in advance, and consequently don't offer discounts or low fares. Many domestic airlines also offer a variety of air tours lasting from two to 14 days.

Baggage: The baggage allowance in economy (tourist) class on flights from Europe depends on whether you travel east or west. On easterly flights (via Asia) the baggage allowance is 20kg/44lbs (one piece) and on westerly flights (via North America) it's two pieces. The maximum permitted weight of any single item is 32kg (70lbs) in both directions. Never pack electronic equipment such as personal computers and transistorised music systems in your hold baggage, but keep them in your hand baggage. If you have a portable computer, it's wise to have it checked by hand, as data could be erased or corrupted by powerful X-ray machines. Passengers are requested not to leave baggage unattended at any time at airports, as it may be stolen or taken away by security staff. Always obtain a check-in stub for your baggage, as without it you cannot claim for compensation if it's lost or stolen. **Keep any valuables in your hand baggage and ensure that it's fully insured.**

Passengers are limited to one piece of hand baggage per person such as a briefcase measuring up to 34cm x 23cm x 48cm or a soft frame garment bag measuring up to 60cm x 114cm x 11cm, plus a handbag and personal belongings such as a coat or camera. Hand baggage rules are strictly enforced and if you try to take too many items or too large an item on board it may be confiscated and put on a later flight. The baggage allowance on Qantas domestic flights is three bags for first class passengers, two bags for business class passengers and one for economy class passengers. The economy baggage allowance is 30kg (66lbs), but frequent flyers (Ansett and Qantas) and Qantas Club members receive an additional 10kg (22lbs) allowance. Check-in time is 90 minutes before departure for international flights and one hour for domestic flights (times may be less for first and business class passengers). Most airports have 24-hour luggage lockers, although you should note that after 24 hours lockers may be sealed to ensure that you pay the excess due. Some airline baggage enquiry offices allow passengers to leave bags free of charge for up to 24 hours.

Airports

The main airports in Australia are Adelaide, Brisbane, Cairns, Darwin, Melbourne, Perth, Port Hedland, Sydney and Townsville. Sydney and Melbourne are Australia's two major international airports, and Adelaide, Brisbane, Cairns, Darwin, Hobart, Perth and Townsville also have international airports. The capital, Canberra, doesn't have an international airport and is served by domestic flights from other Australian cities (Sydney is only half an hour away by air). Most of Australia's major airports are owned and controlled by the Federal Airports Corporation (FAC), although they are gradually being privatised. When minor airports and country landing strips are included, Australia has a total of over 400 'airports'. Most Australian airports are deserted much of the time and come to life for a few hours a day only, when international flights arrive and depart. Terminals may open for only a few hours before arrivals or departures and close for the day after the last flight has arrived or left. International terminals are usually separate from domestic buildings and they may be located some distance apart. There are bus and taxi services from all major airports to city centres.

Sydney: Sydney's international airport is named Kingsford-Smith (after Australia's pioneering aviator) and is located in the suburb of Mascot, 10km/6mi south of the city centre. The international and domestic terminals are located 4km/2.5mi apart on either side of the runway. It's Australia's busiest airport and handles around 6m passengers a year (three times the number of Melbourne and Brisbane airports). It's due to be refurbished and modernised in 1998 in time for the 2000 Olympics, which includes an underground railway link to the city centre. A second Sydney airport is planned, although the state government is finding it difficult to find a suitable site due to concerns over aircraft noise (anywhere but in my back yard).

Melbourne: Melbourne's Tullamarine airport is located 23km/14mi northwest of the city centre and is Australia's second-largest airport (after Sydney), although third in terms of international traffic after Sydney and Brisbane. It's the only airport in Australia operating 24 hours a day. Melbourne has tried (with some success) to lure airlines to Melbourne by reducing airport charges and now serves many more international destinations than previously. There are plans to build a rail link from the airport to the city. Melbourne has a second airport at Essendon between the city and Tullamarine, which operates local flights within Victoria and to Tasmania.

Brisbane: Brisbane airport is 10km/6mi from the city centre and has separate international and domestic terminals some 12 minutes apart by road. There are international flights to New Zealand, Europe, North America, Japan, Singapore and Papua New Guinea.

Adelaide airport is just 6km/4mi southwest of the city centre and has both international and domestic terminals five minutes walk apart. Only two airlines, Qantas and Singapore International, have direct international flights to Adelaide, although many airlines provide free connecting flights to Melbourne, Sydney or even Singapore in order to attract passengers to Adelaide.

Perth airport (21km/13mi east of the city centre) is a gateway for services from Asia and Europe. It has international and domestic terminals located on opposite sides of the runway some 10km/6mi apart by road. Changing flights can be a burden, although many international flights arrive after midnight when there are no connecting domestic flights anyway. Fares to Europe are lower from Perth than elsewhere in Australia and there's a lively market in international tickets.

Darwin airport (located 8km/5mi south of the city centre) has the longest runway in the country and operates international flights to Singapore, Kuala Lumpur, Bali, Kupang, Timor and Borneo. There are domestic flights (from the same terminal as international flights) to most major cities once a day or less.

Other Airports: **Alice Springs** airport is 7km/4mi south of the town centre, from where most flights are to Darwin or Adelaide. **Cairns** and **Townsville** also have international airports which are connected to Brisbane and other major cities by regular domestic flights. **Tasmania** has three main airports: Hobart, Lauceston, and Devenport & Wynyard (Burnie), served by domestic flights from the mainland. The only international flights are from Hobart to New Zealand (Christchurch).

Fares

The Australian airline industry was deregulated in 1990, prior to which there was a duopoly operated by Qantas and Ansett who charged the same (very high) fares and offered virtually the same services. Deregulation heralded the arrival of a number of new domestic carriers who quickly forced Qantas and Ansett to reduce fares, e.g. the cost of a Sydney-Perth ticket was immediately halved! Random discounting is now common on domestic flights, although there are often conditions such as advance booking, flying on weekends only or between fixed dates. A variety of discount fares are available when flying to Australia from some countries (e.g. Britain), although Australia's isolated position in the world means that international travel is expensive. Domestic air travel is also relatively expensive because of the long distances involved. **If you're migrating to Australia, you should book as far ahead as possible (but never before you have received your visa!).**

International Fares: Air fares are high from most countries to Australia, as there's a relatively low volume of traffic on most routes and little competition. The main exception is between Britain and Australia (the 'kangaroo route'), which is one of the most competitive routes in the world. The low season return fare is around £550 from London to Sydney (£325 single) between April and June, rising to £1,000 during the high season of December to January (when fares vary little between airlines). Fares during the shoulder season of July to November and February to March are usually between £650 and £750. Fares From London to Melbourne or Brisbane are usually more expensive than to Sydney. From Europe, fares vary depending on whether you're flying east via

Asia or west via North America. It's usually cheaper to fly via America from November to February, rather than via Asia.

Note that flights in the weeks immediately prior to Christmas are usually fully booked months in advance and delaying your flight a few days until after the Christmas period can mean a considerable saving. Expect to pay £100 to £200 or more for return flights with British Airways, Qantas or Singapore Airlines, which may be worthwhile if you take advantage of their domestic fare deals (see **Visitors' Tickets** below). Fares are higher if you break the journey, although most travellers find that it's worthwhile taking advantage of stopover deals and it also helps avoid or reduce jet lag.

Fares from the USA aren't as good value as from Europe, although excursion and promotional fares are available which are much lower than full-fares, e.g. apex and promotional return fares from Los Angeles to Sydney/Melbourne are around US$1,000 in the low season and US$1,300 in the high season. Regular tickets are valid for 12 months, so it may pay to buy your ticket well in advance of your trip. There's not a lot of choice from the USA, from where only five airlines fly non-stop to Australia: Air New Zealand, Canadian Airlines, Continental, Qantas and United Airlines. Most other airlines stop at Honolulu (not a great hardship as a stopover), Papeete or Auckland or more than one of these. When flying from Sydney to Los Angeles, you leave Sydney in the afternoon and arrive in LA in the morning of the same day! (After crossing the international date line.) An open-jaw ticket (flying into one airport and out of another) is usually no more expensive than an ordinary return.

Charter flights are also available from Britain to Australia (with Britannia Airways and Airtours) between November and April. Flights cost from around £400 return. Note, however, that charter flights have severe restrictions including no stopovers, a minimum stay of two weeks and a maximum of eight. Major airlines offer economy, business and first class fares. Full fare tickets allow you to change the date and time of travel at a moment's notice and offer a full refund should you decide not to travel. When buying apex and other discounted tickets, always make sure that you fully understand any ticket restrictions. Return fares from Australia to Europe are higher than when travelling in the opposite direction. The best deals are from Sydney, although bargains can be found from Melbourne and Perth (discount fares are advertised in the major daily newspapers). A 'passenger movement charge' (previously called a 'departure tax') of $27 is payable for passengers aged 12 or over (since July 1995) when you purchase your ticket, which is endorsed to show that it has been paid.

Stop-overs & Round-the-World (RTW) Tickets: When travelling to Australia you can travel one-stop or take advantage of a number of stop-overs, e.g. in Asia, the Pacific and North America. Most return tickets from Europe include 'free' stopover options on outward and return journeys, usually in Asia or the Pacific. Round-the-world tickets to Australia from London via Asia and North America start at around £700 for four stops, depending on the season. From Europe you can also fly via South Africa or South America, although these options are more expensive than the usual Asian or North American routes.

VISITORS' TICKETS

Visitors to Australia can buy a range of special tickets and passes for travel by air, rail and bus. Some passes can only be purchased outside Australia, although you should note that you can get better deals in Australia for some journeys. Beware of buying passes for longer or more travel than you need, which can provide a compulsion to keep going when you would rather stay put (passes are even more expensive when they aren't used!).

Fly-drive packages are also available from many airlines and travel companies overseas. Note that it's often important to book your seat well in advance, particularly in the peak season and when travelling on routes where there are infrequent services, e.g. one or a few trains or buses a week.

Air: Domestic air passes are good value if you wish to see a lot of Australia in a relatively short period. A range of passes are available including the Boomerang Pass from Qantas and the G'Day Pass from Ansett, both of which require a minimum purchase of two pre-paid flight coupons. Those travelling to Australia from the UK with Qantas can purchase a Boomerang Pass which costs around £90 for a single zone flight and around £115 for a multi-zone flight. Children pay two-thirds of the adult fare and infants under two years who aren't occupying a seat pay 10 per cent. The Boomerang Pass is valid on Qantas, Air Pacific and Ansett New Zealand flights. The Ansett G'Day Pass offers around 25 per cent discount on Ansett, Ansett Express and Ansett WA domestic flights. Passes can be purchased overseas or within 30 days of your arrival in Australia.

Note, however, that some flights are actually more expensive with air passes than buying a flight in Australia. International travellers can also purchase domestic air tickets in Australia at discounts of up to 50 per cent, although travel must be completed within 60 days of your arrival. Flights times can usually be changed and refunds are available without penalty. Some airlines offer a Backpackers' pass which can only be purchased in Australia and some air passes allow free access to local bus services, plus discounts on accommodation and rental cars.

Rail: Visitors to Australia can buy an Austrailpass for 14 ($485 economy class), 21 ($625) or 30 ($755) days (economy only), although seven-day extensions are available ($250). Passes allow unlimited first or economy class travel on most of the Australian rail network, including travel on suburban trains in Adelaide, Brisbane, Melbourne, Newcastle, Perth and Sydney. Passes can also be used on nominated coach services, where a rail link isn't available. Tickets can be purchased overseas and from Rail Australia and rail travel centres in Australia. Use of the pass must begin within six months of the date of issue. The Austrailpass allows visitors to make a return trip on the *Indian Pacific* across Australia for less than an Australian pays one way (the pass isn't available to residents).

An economy Austrail Flexipass allows travel for eight ($400 economy class), 15 ($575), 22 ($810) or 29 ($1,045) days within a six month period. The eight-day Flexirail pass excludes travel from Adelaide to Perth and Adelaide to Alice Springs. There's a surcharge on all passes for sleeping berths and a compulsory meal charge for first class sleeping berth passengers on the *Ghan, Indian Pacific* and *Queenslander* trains. Upgrading to first class is permitted only when economy seats or sleepers aren't available. A Kangaroo Road 'n' Rail Pass allows travel on all trains and Greyhound Pioneer Australia buses for 14, 21 or 28 days.

Individual states also offer rail passes including the Sunshine Railpass (Queensland, 14, 21 or 30 days), the Victoria Pass (seven or 14 days), the Westrail Premier Discovery Pass (21 days), the Westrail Southern Discovery Pass (28 days), the East Coast Discovery Pass (valid for six months for travel from Melbourne to Cairns or parts of this route) and the NSW Discovery Pass (valid one month). All passes must be presented with your passport at the departure station of the initial journey for validation and no refunds are possible once travel has commenced.

Rail passes are available from Rail Australia agents, Thomas Cook travel offices, offices of the Tour Pacific/Australian Travel Service, Qantas and Jetabout Tours' offices, and from other travel agents in many countries. Rail Australia publish a leaflet, *National and State Passes*, for visitors available from agents (e.g. Leisurail in Britain, tel.

01733-335599) and Australian tourist commission offices overseas. For more information contact Rail Australia, 1 Richmond Road, Keswick, SA 5035 (tel. (08) 8217 4321).

Bus: A number of bus passes are available in Australia from Greyhound Pioneer Australia and McCafferty's, which are of particular interest to backpackers. Greyhound offer the Aussie Pass which allows unlimited travel for seven to 21 days (see below) and Aussi Pass Value packages (valid six to 12 months), which include transfers, touring and unlimited stopovers. Value packages are available for a number of set routes, which you have six or 12 months to complete, including an 'All Australian' pass costing $1,420 and valid for one year. The Greyhound Travel Oz Adventure Pass allows you to travel on Greyhound buses along a pre-set route and stop as often as you wish. It includes an option to pre-pay for YHA accommodation from five to 50 nights (which can be used before, during or after the bus pass validity period), plus a discount voucher booklet with over 600 discounts at some 100 attractions throughout Australia.

The Greyhound Aussie Pass is valid for travel on seven to 21 days as shown below:

Days Travel	Validity Period	Cost
7	30 days	$475
10	30 days	$610
15	30 days	$710
21	60 days	$935

Greyhound also offer an 'Aussie Kilometre Pass' where you decide how many kilometres you wish to travel, from a minimum of 2,000km/1240mi ($176) after which passes can be extended in multiples of 1,000km/621mi (Australia is a BIG country). A 20,000km/12,427mi pass costs $1,344, although there's no maximum. It's valid for 12 months, although travel must commence within three months of purchase.

McCafferty's Express Coachline offers 15 set-route Travel Australia Passes (valid three to 12 months), at discounts of up to 50 per cent. Passes include travel on *Indian Pacific* trains from Adelaide to Perth where the route crosses the Nullabor Plain in Western Australia. Tasmanian Wilderness Transport and Hobart Coaches offer a scheduled service pass of from seven to 30 days, and unlimited travel passes can also be purchased on Tasmanian Redline Coaches for the same periods. Travellers who are YHA, VIP, ISIC and Euro 26 ticket members (or ID holders) receive a 15 per cent discount on bus passes purchased outside Australia, or a 10 per cent discount when they are purchased in Australia. Children under three years of age travel free and those aged three to 11 receive a 15 per cent discount.

11.
MOTORING

Australians are devoted to their cars and (like Americans) rarely go anywhere without them. It's essential to have your own transport in Australia if you live anywhere other than in one of the main cities. Travelling interstate involves vast distances (on the North American scale) and driving in the outback is reminiscent of driving in North Africa. Australians are used to driving long distances and think nothing of driving hundreds of miles to visit relatives or friends for a few days or even a day out. Almost 80 per cent of all goods in Australia are transported by road, and passenger travel is also dominated by road transport.

Australian cities are often sprawling (particularly Sydney) and therefore people are inclined to use their cars rather than public transport. However, Australians haven't learnt how to co-exist with the motor car in their cities, where traffic jams, parking problems and vehicle pollution are a way of life. Traffic congestion and pollution is chronic in Sydney (where traffic congestion has been estimated to get six times worse in the next 20 years) and Melbourne, where rush hours should be avoided if at all possible. Drivers could be urged to leave their cars at home on days of high pollution in some cities (e.g. Sydney), although it's unlikely that many Australians would voluntarily abandon their cars for public transport (assuming it's an alternative). There are 'park and ride' facilities in cities to encourage commuters to use public transport, although they aren't widely used (car pooling is also a hard slog).

Australia has a relatively high accident rate and around 2,000 people are killed and 20,000 injured on Australian roads each year, although the numbers are falling partly due to the introduction of widespread random breath testing, reduced alcohol/blood levels, and speed cameras. However, the prevalence of alcohol (and drugs) in fatal accidents remains a major problem. The risk of young males aged 17 to 25 dying on the roads is around three times that of other age groups, and they are five times more likely to die in a car accident than women of the same age. Public holiday periods are the most dangerous times to be on the roads.

The individual states and territories have jurisdiction over the registration of motor vehicles, drivers' licences and traffic rules, which vary depending on the state or territory. For specific information obtain a copy of your state or territory's 'highway code' (it has various names such as the *Road Users' Handbook* in New South Wales). If you're going to Australia for a limited period, don't forget to take your foreign licence, international driving permit (if applicable), car insurance policy, no-claims' discount entitlement, and records of membership of motoring organisations.

VEHICLE IMPORTATION

If you plan to import a motor vehicle or motorcycle into Australia, either temporarily or permanently, first ensure that you're aware of the latest regulations. Any vehicle imported into Australia must meet the registration requirements of the state or territory where it's going to be registered (or it must be modified). If you're in doubt, check with the relevant motor vehicle registration authorities (see **Appendix A**). The current conditions governing the importation of vehicles are provided in various publications produced by the Australian Customs Service including *Customs Information for Travellers* and *Importing a Motor Vehicle or Motorcycle*. They are available from Australian embassies and high commissions overseas or from the Comptroller-General, Australian Customs Service, Customs House, 5-11 Constitution Avenue, Canberra ACT 2601.

Exporting a car to Australia can save you a considerable amount of money, particularly if you own a luxury or sports car and have owned it for a number of years. European manufactured cars usually cost around double the price in Australia. However, you must take into account shipping costs, insurance, port/unpacking and quarantine charges in Australia, and Australian customs' duty and sales tax. It costs around £1,000 to ship a small family car (e.g. a Ford Escort or VW Golf) from the UK to Sydney plus around £500 in other fees. Before deciding to import a car, it's advisable to compare Australian prices of both new and secondhand cars, and the cost of shipping and importing a vehicle into Australia. You may also wish to check that spare parts and servicing are available and what they will cost. Note also that Australian insurance companies may refuse to provide cover on vehicles that aren't sold in Australia due to the high cost of accident repairs.

Permanent Importation: Personal imports are available to Australian citizens and migrants with Australian permanent residence, providing they haven't imported a vehicle under the concession in the previous 12 months. A vehicle must have been owned and used overseas for at least three months (unless it's over 15 years old) and must be right-hand drive. Although a left-hand drive vehicle can be converted to right-hand drive it's expensive and usually isn't worthwhile (and the conversion may not be accepted by the Australian authorities). Vehicles can be imported without proof that they meet Australian Design Rules, but are expected to provide a level of safety similar to Australian vehicles and must pass a roadworthiness inspection. Any vehicle imported into Australia must also meet the registration requirements of the state or territory where it's going to be registered. If in doubt, check with the relevant motor vehicle registration authorities (see **Appendix A**).

Vehicle Standards: All imported vehicles must meet Australia's safety, emissions and anti-theft standards, and must comply with safety requirements relating to lighting, seat belts, child restraint anchorages and glazing. The standards are contained in a booklet (*Importing Vehicles to Australia*) available from the Federal Office of Road Safety (see address below). It's illegal to import a new or secondhand vehicle unless it meets the emission standards applying to vehicles to be used on Australian roads, or arrangements have been made to modify the vehicle to meet these requirements after its arrival in Australia. Before importing any vehicle, it's essential to ensure that it will meet the necessary standards in Australia. This can be done by contacting the Administrator Motor Vehicle Standards, Department of Transport and Communications, Federal Office of Road Safety, GPO Box 1553, Canberra ACT 2601 (tel. (02) 6274 7506).

Temporary Importation: Vehicles can also be imported temporarily for up to one year by overseas visitors from certain countries, by submitting an application to import a vehicle or presenting a valid *Carnet de Passage en Duane* at your port of entry. The overseas organisation issuing the *carnet* must have a reciprocal arrangement with the Australian Automobile Association (AAA), otherwise you will need cash or a bank security equal to the amount of duty and sales tax otherwise payable. You're permitted to import a left-hand drive vehicle temporarily, but it must display a 'Caution Left-Hand Drive' sign on its rear.

In most states and territories it's necessary to present the vehicle for inspection at the nearest motor vehicle registration authority as soon as possible after importation. You will need the following papers:

- evidence that a security has been paid to the customs' authorities (*Carnet de Passage*);
- evidence that the vehicle has Australian third party insurance;
- your home driver's licence or an international driving permit;
- the vehicle's current registration certificate.

After the vehicle has passed the mechanical and safety inspection and the documentation has been checked, a temporary permit is issued allowing it to be driven in Australia until the expiry date.

Shipment: Most international shippers serving Australia can arrange for the shipment of vehicles and there are also specialist vehicle shipping companies in some countries. Shippers usually offer a range of services including shared containers, 'sole use' containers and roll on/roll off (where vehicles are driven onto and off a ship). Shop around and obtain a few quotations. Containerisation is best, but also the most expensive.

Import Application: An 'Application for Vehicle Import Approval' form must be completed at least four weeks prior to the planned arrival of a vehicle in Australia (the fee of $50 must accompany the application). An application form is contained in the booklet, *Importing Vehicles to Australia*, mentioned above. The importer requires the application form to obtain clearance at the port of entry and there will be a delay if he doesn't have the form when the vehicle arrives in Australia. To avoid delays you should also have available documents such as your passport, driver's licence, purchase and transportation documents, bill of sale, registration and insurance papers, service records and log book.

Quarantine Clearance: Quarantine clearance is required from the Australian Quarantine and Inspection Service after a vehicle arrives at the port of entry. A car should be steam cleaned before shipment, as it will need to undergo a quarantine inspection on arrival in Australia. When a vehicle arrives in Australia it's inspected internally and externally for soil, seeds, insect and disease bearing organisms. If any suspect traces are found (which is usually the case), the car must be thoroughly cleaned inside and out, and the engine and undercarriage steam cleaned (at your expense).

Duty & Tax: Customs' duty, sales tax and customs' clearance is performed at the port of entry. Details of combined duty rates, customs' values, depreciation allowances and personal import approvals are available from Australian Customs and Registration Departments and shipping agents. The duty and tax payable is revised annually and in 1997 was as follows:

Vehicle Type	Vehicle Age	Customs' Value	Duty & Tax*
passenger	up to 30 years	up to $25,167	54.84%
"	"	over $25,167	88.65%
passenger	over 30 years	up to $30,830	26.40%
"	"	over $30,830	54.00%
4-wheel drive	Any	up to $29,362	32.72%
"	Any	over $29,362	61.70%
Campervans	Any	Any	54.84%
Commercial	Any	Any	32.72%
Motorcycle	Any	Any	26.40%

* The higher duty and tax rate is levied only on the 'customs' value' amount in excess of the lower customs' value. For example if a car passenger vehicle (car) less than 30 years old is valued at $30,000, the higher rate of duty and tax (88.65%) is levied only on the amount above $25,167, i.e. $4,833. A sales tax only is levied on motorcycles.

The customs' value is the purchase price plus the cost of any modifications or improvements, less a depreciation allowance of 5 per cent for the first month of use and ownership, plus 1 per cent for each subsequent month of use and ownership up to a maximum of 76 per cent (equal to six years' ownership). If there's insufficient evidence of the purchase price paid or a vehicle's purchase price was unrealistic, the customs' value is determined as 40 per cent of the current Australian market value of the vehicle. To claim depreciation, you must present your passport and all purchase documents, bill of sale, registration papers, service records and the shipping Bill of Lading, together with any other documents that may assist customs in determining the 'customs' value'. Ownership and use is determined by documentation in the importer's name and extends from the date of purchase or delivery (whichever is the later) until the date the owner or the vehicle left the foreign country (whichever is the earlier). The value is calculated from local value to Australian dollars on the date the vehicle was exported to Australia.

Australian manufactured vehicles aren't subject to customs' duty and may be re-imported into Australia free of sales tax, providing tax was paid prior to exportation and no refund was obtained.

VEHICLE REGISTRATION

Vehicle registration (referred to as 'rego') in Australia includes road tax and compulsory third party insurance and must be renewed annually. Registration is the responsibility of the individual states and territories and fees vary, but are usually $400 to $600 for an average vehicle (Western Australia is cheapest and the ACT is the most expensive). Registration of a vehicle is done with the local state traffic authority, e.g. the Road and Traffic Authority (RTA) in New South Wales (see addresses in **Appendix A**). Payment of vehicle registration can be made at any post office. Motorists who don't pay their rego within a few weeks of it falling due face fines (tens of thousands of motorists drive without rego).

Compliance Plate: Before a vehicle can be registered in Australia it must be fitted with an Australian compliance plate which indicates that it complies with Australian Standards (ADRs). A compliance plate is fitted automatically to a car manufactured in Australia. Imported vehicles must be tested and a compliance plate fitted. This involves having the vehicle inspected at a state government motor vehicle registration authority to insure that it meets the local safety requirements. Before a vehicle can be tested, evidence must be shown that import duty and tax has been paid, as applicable.

Number Plates: Registration (number) plates are issued by individual states and must be displayed front and rear on cars and at the rear of motorcycles. The registration plates must be those that are recorded on the vehicle's registration papers. A vehicle cannot be parked or driven on a public road without registration and plates must be returned to the issuing authority when they expire. Each state or territory has different coloured plates as shown below:

State/Territory	Colour
ACT	blue on white
NSW	black on yellow
NT	red on white
VIC	dark blue of white (new)/white on black (old)
SA	green on yellow
TAS	blue on white
WA	black on yellow (new)/black on white (old)

There are also commercial, official, diplomatic and personalised registration plates with different colours.

Change of Ownership: When buying a secondhand car the previous owner must sign the back of the registration paper, which you then take with the test certificate (if applicable) to the motor registry. The change of ownership must be registered with the state authority and a registration transfer fee paid, e.g. around $75 in New South Wales. It's necessary to have proof of compulsory third party (CTP) insurance (shown by a 'green slip' issued by the insurance company) to register a vehicle. When a vehicle is bought or sold, the CTP insurance transfers to the new owner until the registration expires. The current registration label must be displayed behind the car windscreen (make sure that it doesn't fall off by taping it in position). If you lose it a replacement costs around $20.

BUYING A CAR

Cars are relatively expensive in Australia and generally cost slightly more than in most European countries and up to twice the cost of cars in the USA, particularly for imported cars (on which there's a hefty import tariff). The Commonwealth Bank Australia quotes new and used car prices in its free annual *Cost of Living and Housing Survey Book*. Information regarding the purchase of both new and used cars is published by Australian motoring organisations (see page 268), e.g. in NSW the NRMA publish a booklet entitled the *Worry-Free Guide to Buying a Car*. New and used car guides are also available including the *New Car Buyers Guide*, the *Used Car Buyers Guide* and Universal's *New & Used 4WD Guide*.

New Cars

A number of foreign manufacturers make or assemble cars in Australia including Ford, Holden (General Motors), Mitsubishi, Nissan and Toyota, which comprise over 75 per cent of the new car market. Ford and Holden models are the most popular, and consequently the cheapest for spares and to get repaired. The Holden Commodore (the 1997 car of the year) is rated as one of Australia's best family cars followed by the Ford Falcon, Mitsubishi Magna and Toyota Camry. Note that local models are often different from those available in other countries, as manufacturers style their cars on what the local market demands (Australians are proud of their 'unique' cars, particularly old Holden models). Four-wheel-drive (4WD) cars are popular in Australia, particularly in country areas, although the running costs (fuel and maintenance) are around 30 per cent higher than two-wheel-drive cars. They do, however, keep their value well. Station wagons or estate cars are also popular and are often chosen in preference to a 4WD in suburban areas.

Although comparisons between new car prices in different countries are often difficult (e.g. due to fluctuating exchange rates and the different levels of standard equipment), prices in Australia are generally high and almost doubled between 1985 and 1995. A small 5-door, 4-cylinder saloon costs from around $15,000 and a 6-cylinder model from around $30,000. There's a high tariff on imports to protect local manufacturers, although Australia is pledged to reduce or abolish import duty and tax. The tariff was to have fallen to 5 per cent by 2005 and to be abolished altogether by the year 2010. However, after much debate (and fierce opposition from local car manufacturers) it was decided to reduce the tariff by 2.5 per cent a year until the year 2000, when it will be frozen at 15 per cent until 2005.

Australians are fond of big gas-guzzling, six-cylinder cars, although their fuel consumption has fallen considerably in recent years, and their engines last longer and aren't as likely to overheat as four-cylinder engines on long runs. Air-conditioning is standard on most cars in Australia and is essential for anyone who spends much time behind the wheel. It certainly isn't a luxury when stuck in a traffic jam in summer or on long-distance trips in the outback. Note, however, that air-conditioning decreases power and increases fuel consumption slightly. A basic air-conditioning unit costs from around $1,000 (installed) for a small family car. Fuel consumption isn't so important in Australia, where petrol is a lot cheaper than in many other countries. Note that the cost of labour and parts for even the least expensive family cars can be very high, so it may pay to buy a car with a long or extended warranty. Popular local-manufactured cars are best if you don't want high repair bills (spares and servicing for some German and Japanese cars are astronomical).

Used Cars

Used cars can be excellent value for money in Australia, particularly low mileage cars less than one year old, where the savings on the new price can be as high as 25 per cent. (The minute a new car leaves the showroom it's usually worth 10 per cent less than the purchase price.) Some models (e.g. luxury models) depreciate much quicker than others and often represent excellent secondhand bargains. Australians tend to keep their cars longer than people in many other countries, with the average age over 10 years.

Dealers: Like most countries, Australia has its share of dodgy used car dealers, who employ every underhand trick in the book when selling to unsuspecting buyers. It isn't unknown for salesmen to include details after you have signed a form, so make sure that everything is completed before signing and obtain a copy. Never sign a form with some details left blank (such as the price, repayment period and payments), which is akin to signing a blank cheque! Avoid signing a purchase form that's subject to a 'satisfactory' mechanical inspection, as this may mean that unless a vehicle is found to have major faults you could still have legally bought it.

It's always best to buy a used car from a licensed dealer who's bound by the Auctioneers and Agents Act (and who may be a member of a Motor Traders Association), when, if there's any question about a car's history (e.g. it's stolen, still under finance or not as it appears), the dealer must rectify the problem. When you buy from a car dealer, he will usually help you with the paperwork and provide a roadworthy certificate and warranty, which is compulsory in most states. A dealer may also include free membership of the local motoring organisation. Always carefully check what's included or excluded from a used-car warranty, as many warranties contain a number of conditions, which, if you don't adhere to them, will void the warranty. Note, however, that if you're buying a car to travel round Australia, the warranty won't do you a lot of good if you buy it in Sydney and break down in Perth! You may just as well save money and buy privately.

Buying Privately: If you're buying a car privately from an individual, you should ask to see a current road worthiness certificate, which should be less than one month old. To sell a car legally in Australia the seller must have the car inspected within one month prior to the sale and present the inspection certificate to the buyer. You should only buy a car that carries a valid 'pink slip' insuring that it meets safety and roadworthiness criteria at the time it was inspected. It's best to buy a car with around 9-10 months' registration (rego), which means that you avoid the cost of registration and need only pay a rego transfer fee plus stamp duty on the declared value of the vehicle. Note that many people understate the price when buying privately, as stamp duty and transfer tax totalling around

8 per cent of the stated value must be paid when registering a car. It's estimated that some 60 per cent of declared values are low.

Visitors & Travellers: Short time residents such as long-stay tourists, backpackers and working holidaymakers may wish to consider the flexibility of having their own transport, which can also be economical when split between a number of people. If you want an old reliable car, it's best to buy a Ford Falcon or Holden Commodore, which are engineered to survive Australia's rough outback roads, have strong 6-cylinder engines and relatively inexpensive parts that are easy to obtain. Secondhand parts for most older Australian-made cars can be picked up cheaply from car breakers' yards throughout the country. Station wagons and panel vans are popular among travellers, as you can put a mattress in the back for sleeping. Note, however, that imported cars (e.g. German and Japanese) are generally considered more reliable than Australian-built cars, although they are also much more expensive. Expect to pay from $1,000 for an old 'banger' (which should, however, be mechanically reliable) and from around $5,000 for a decent secondhand car that will last a number of years.

Cheap Cars: Cheap cars can be purchased through car markets in most cities, where owners gather to sell their vehicles. For example, in Sydney you can buy or sell a vehicle at the Kings Cross Car Market, which is dedicated to travellers buying and selling cars and campervans. Note, however, that there are no guarantees, so you need to know what you're buying. One of the advantages of buying from a traveller is that they may include camping equipment, spares and other useful items in the price. You can also pick up interstate registered cars (i.e. cars registered in a state other than the one where it's being sold) which can be good buys, particularly if you plan to sell in the state where a vehicle's registered. It's also possible to buy at auction, although this isn't recommended unless you're an expert mechanic. The main disadvantage of buying a cheap car is that it will have high mileage and may be in poor mechanical condition.

A number of dealers (car yards) in the major cities specialise in selling cars to travellers and most are honest as their reputation depends upon it. Many offer to buy vehicles back at an agreed price (providing you don't wreck it), which is usually 50 per cent of the price paid. Note, however, that dealers may try to knock down the buy-back price by finding fault with the car, even when it has been agreed in writing. If this happens you may get a better deal selling it privately (you should get around two-thirds of the price paid after six to nine months, providing that you didn't pay too much). Obviously a buy-back deal is worthwhile only if you're returning to your starting point.

Mechanical & Other Checks: If you're a member of an Australian motoring organisation (see page 268), you can get them to check a car before you buy it for a fee of around $100, or alternatively a 'mobile' mechanic will do it for around $25. It's important to contact the state Registry of Encumbered Vehicles which will tell you if a car is under finance, whether it has been stolen or there are any outstanding fines (e.g. parking) against it (when you buy a car you assume responsibility for any outstanding fines). The small fee levied could save you thousands of dollars.

Publications: The best days for car advertisements in local newspapers are Wednesdays and Saturdays. There are also advertisements in publications such as the *Trading Post* (Sydney) and car magazines. You can also buy interstate newspapers, although it's rarely worth travelling far to inspect a car unless it's a rare model or exceptional value for money (you can travel a very long way to inspect a 'lemon' which wasn't worth walking around the block to see). Note that deciphering car ads. can be difficult unless you speak 'Australian', e.g. a panel van is a van with no rear windows and front seats only and a ute is a utility or pick-up truck (an open backed van).

TEST CERTIFICATE

In most states and territories, vehicles must pass a periodic technical inspection. For example in New South Wales a vehicle over three years old must pass an inspection every year (fee around $20) before its registration can be renewed. In order to sell a car in Australia you must have the car inspected within one month prior to the sale and give the inspection certificate to the buyer. The technical inspection is carried out by authorised garages and includes checking all lights (i.e. headlights, brake lights and indicator lights), brakes, steering, windscreen wipers and washers, horn, tyres (which must have 1.5mm of tread across the whole surface) and seat belts. If your car passes, you're given an inspection report ('pink slip') which must be displayed behind the windscreen. If your car fails the test, you will be given a defect notice ('black slip') listing the points on which it has failed. Note that you can get a defect notice if your car is too noisy, drips oil or blows too much smoke, and it can even be failed if the inspector thinks it's too dirty to test. If you get a defect notice you may be permitted to drive home or to a garage for repair, depending on why it failed.

The police can stop and test your vehicle at any time and if you get a defect notice it must be repaired and officially cleared before you can drive it. The police will affix a yellow sticker (called a 'canary') to your windscreen which allows you to drive your car home or to a garage for repair (they may also do this to a stationary car, which means that they wish to inspect it). If a red sticker is attached to a vehicle, it means that it's considered to be unroadworthy and cannot be driven until it's repaired on the spot (or it can be towed away).

SELLING A CAR

The main points to note when selling a car are:

* A potential buyer shouldn't test drive your car unless he's covered by your or his own insurance. You're responsible if someone drives your car with your permission without valid insurance.

* If you're planning on selling your car, you must usually (e.g in NSW) have it safety inspected one month before the sale and give the test certificate to the prospective buyer. It's illegal to sell a car in an unroadworthy condition, unless you're selling it as a non-runner without a test certificate (see page 243). Never describe a car as being in a better condition that it is, e.g. excellent condition. If it's subsequently found to have any faults, you could be liable to reimburse the buyer or pay for repairs.

* You must sign the back of the registration paper and give it to the buyer. When a vehicle is sold the compulsory third party insurance transfers to the new owner with the registration until it expires.

* Inform your insurance company. Either cancel your insurance or transfer it to a new car. Note that if you cancel your insurance, even for a short period, this may affect your no-claims' discount when you take out insurance on a new car. When you sell a car, you're required to notify the motor vehicle registration office by completing the appropriate part of the vehicle registration papers (see page 239). The new owner of the car must also register his ownership with them (this is intended as a cross check of ownership).

- If you're selling your car privately you should insist on cash. It's usually a formality for the buyer to accompany you to your bank and make a cash transfer on the spot. There are confidence tricksters (crooks) who will, given half a chance, happily give you a dud cheque and drive off with your car. If someone insists on paying by cheque, you should *never* allow them to take your car until the cheque has cleared. Don't allow a dealer or car auctioneer to take your car until a cheque has cleared as cheques sometimes bounce after companies have ceased trading.

- Include in the receipt that you're selling the car in its present condition (as seen) without a guarantee, the price paid and the car's kilometre reading. The new owner may ask for a declaration in writing that the car is accident free, which applies to major accidents that have caused structural damage and not slight bumps.

- The buyer must pay stamp duty which is based on the declared value of the vehicle, which is why many people understate the price when buying privately.

You can advertise a car for sale in local newspapers, on free local notice boards, in the local or national newspapers (Wednesdays and Saturdays are best), and in many motoring newspapers and magazines. The best place to advertise a car depends on the make and value of the car. Cheap cars are probably best sold in local newspapers, while expensive vehicles and collectors cars are often advertised in the motoring press or in national newspapers such as *The Australian*. Buyers will travel a long way to view a car that appears good value for money (if nobody phones, you'll know why). Note that it's usually difficult to sell a vehicle outside it's 'home' state (i.e. where it's registered), as it must undergo a new inspection, and receive new registration plates and papers. For this reason, if you sell a car in a state other than where it's registered, you will normally receive less than its market value.

DRIVER'S LICENCE

The minimum age for driving in Australia is 17 or 18 for a car or motorcycle, depending on the state or territory. A young driver may obtain a licence before he reaches the required age after passing a written road knowledge test, e.g. at age 16 in NSW. There are special licence classes for heavy goods' vehicles, buses, taxis, tow trucks and driving instructors. If you're a resident of Australia, you must have a licence issued by the state or territory where you're resident, and if you move states you must apply for a new licence and return your old licence. Foreign licence holders coming to Australia as permanent residents must obtain (not just apply for) a state licence within three months (this also applies to those moving between states and territories).

The following information is based on vehicle licences in NSW, which is similar to other states. In NSW, the basic licence class (category 1A) permits you to drive a motor car or vehicle with a maximum of 12 seats (including the driver) weighing less than 4.5 tonnes. A category 1B licence is required to drive heavy goods vehicles and vehicles with more than 12 seats. You must be aged 17 or over to hold a 1A licence and 18 to hold a 1B licence. A category R licence is required to ride a motorcycle. The various levels of licences in NSW are distinguished by their colour: learner's licence (green), provisional licence (red), unrestricted licence (silver or gold). A silver unrestricted licence is issued for one or three years after you first pass your test. After five years you qualify for a gold licence which is valid for five years. A NSW driver's licence costs $33 a year, $80 for three years and $108 for five years (prices are similar in other states).

To obtain a driver's licence in New South Wales you must:

- provide your foreign licence (with a translation if necessary) which is photocopied and returned;

- prove your identity, e.g. with a passport and another document such as a credit card, or an account card from a bank, building society or credit union;

- pass an eyesight test;

- pass a road knowledge test;

- pass a driving test*;

- pay the fee.

* Holders of American, British and New Zealand drivers' licences don't need to take a driving test.

If you fail the knowledge test you can take it again (e.g. on the next working day) and you will only be asked the questions which you got wrong. It's necessary in most states to undergo an eyesight test and in certain cases a medical examination, e.g. sufferers from diabetes and epilepsy.

If you (i.e. a person holding a foreign licence) fail the driving test, you can no longer drive until you pass the test. You must then obtain a learner's licence which allows you to drive while supervised by a licensed driver with a clean licence (no demerit points) who has held a licence for at least seven years. If you have held a foreign driver's licence for less than a year you will be eligible only for a provisional licence (a licence issued to NSW drivers for one year after they pass their driver's test). This means that you must display a 'P' plate (front and rear) on your vehicle at all times and are restricted to lower speeds (maximum 80kph/50mph), a reduced alcohol level (0.02) and are permitted to accumulate less than four demerit points (see below) during the term of your licence.

In some states, learner drivers must keep a logbook (teenagers are supervised by their parents) to prove that they have gained experience driving under a range of driving conditions and their L-plate training period has extended to a year. A three-month L-plate period is in place in many states. The RTA in NSW publish a booklet, *Licence to Drive*, and a *Guide to DART* (Driving Ability Road Test), both of which are available from local motor registries. If your last licence expired over five years ago or you're aged over 85 and fail a driving test, you may be required to return to a learner's licence. Learners must take a written road knowledge test before taking a practical driving test. A driving test costs $35 or around an extra $60 if you use a driving school vehicle (check in advance as fees can be excessive).

Demerit Points: Fines as well as demerit points are issued for traffic and driving infringements, which depend on the severity of an offence. Demerit points range from 1 (e.g. failing to dip your headlamps) to 6 points (exceeding the speed limit by over 45kph/28mph), although most offences carry three demerit points. A list of the infringements and consequent demerit points is provided in a state's *Road User's Handbook* and you should check with the Roads and Traffic Authority for the point limit for the type of licence you carry. If you accumulate a certain number of demerit points within a limited period (usually two years), it can lead to your licence being revoked. The number you need to accrue in order to be banned from driving depends on the type of licence you carry. If you accumulate 12 points your licence will usually be cancelled for a minimum of three months. Your licence can also be cancelled for up to five years (and you can be imprisoned) for serious offences such as failing or refusing to take a breath test (see page 261), failing to stop after an accident in which someone has been injured or killed, and exceeding the speed limit by over 45kph/28mph.

Visitors: Most foreign licences are valid for a year in Australia, although it's usually worthwhile obtaining an international driving permit, particularly if your national licence doesn't contain your photograph (e.g. a British driver's licence). If a foreign licence isn't written in English, an official translation must be obtained. This can be obtained in Australia from the local state Ethnic Affairs Commission or the Translating and Interpreting Service of the Commonwealth Department of Immigration and Ethnic Affairs. Your driver's licence, translation and passport must be carried when driving.

Note that there are heavy penalties in Australia for driving without a licence (or with an expired licence) including fines of up to $2,000, a prison term of up to six months and a ban from driving for a period.

CAR INSURANCE

General

The following categories of car insurance are available in Australia:

Third party: The minimum insurance cover required by law is third party, usually referred to as compulsory third party (CTP), which is required in all states and territories. CTP covers bodily injury only (plus injuries to third parties caused by passengers) and doesn't cover damage done to third party property, for which **third party property** insurance is required (see below). Under common law, compensation is paid for both economic loss (medical costs and loss of earnings) and non-economic loss (e.g. pain and suffering), if applicable. The insurance 'green slip' must be produced when registering a vehicle. When a vehicle is bought or sold, the CTP insurance transfers to the new owner until the registration expires. CTP is included in a car's annual registration fees, but in the case of imported vehicles which are exempt from the first year's rego insurance, it must be independently arranged. Note that it can be difficult to insure some imported vehicles that aren't sold in Australia. Foreign insurance policies aren't valid in Australia and all vehicles operated there must be insured with an Australian company. **This insurance isn't advisable as you could be faced with a huge bill if you damage someone else's property.**

Third party property (TPP) protects against liabilities for damage caused to other third party property in an accident, e.g. if you damage another car or knock down a fence. TPP cover usually includes a provision of $3,000 to $5,000 for your own car if it's damaged by an uninsured driver (but you must be able to identify the driver).

Third-party, fire and theft (TPF&F): Known in some countries as part comprehensive, TPF&F includes (in addition to third party cover) loss or damage caused to your car and anything fitted to it by fire, lightening, explosion, theft or attempted theft. It usually includes broken glass. Note that the amount you can claim may be limited, e.g. to $5,000, unless otherwise agreed when you take out the policy. Bear in mind that it isn't unusual for a car to overheat and catch on fire in Australia, so unless you're driving a worthless heap it will pay you to have TPF&T insurance (and carry a fire extinguisher!). It's also important to insure your belongings, particularly if you're travelling around Australia in a camper van and are carrying all your 'worldly possessions' with you. Check the small print of your insurance policy and note that travel insurance (see page 314) isn't intended for those who lose everything and won't usually cover all your belongings.

Comprehensive insurance covers you for all the risks listed under the CTP and TPP above, plus damage to your own car, theft of contents, broken glass (e.g. windscreen replacement), personal accident benefits and medical expenses. It also usually includes damage due to natural hazards, e.g. storm damage. Extra cover may be included free or for an additional fee and may include the cost of hiring a car if yours is involved in an accident or stolen, legal assistance, no-claims' discount protection, and extra cover for a car stereo or phone. Comprehensive insurance may also cover you against loss when your car is in a garage for service or repair. Check a policy for any restrictions, for example you may not be covered against theft if your car isn't garaged and locked overnight. Most lenders usually insist on comprehensive insurance for leasing, contract hire and hire purchase agreements.

Comprehensive insurance can be extended to include other vehicles not belonging to or hired to the policy holder, and any insurance policy can include other people to drive your car (either individually named or any driver). Note that comprehensive insurance generally covers you for third-party only when you're driving a car that doesn't belong to you. Separate passenger insurance is usually unnecessary as passengers are automatically covered by all Australian motor insurance policies. Personal accident, medical expenses, clothing and personal effects cover, are usually included in comprehensive policies.

Premiums

The most important factor influencing premiums is a car's insurance class (although not all insurers place cars in the same class), which is calculated according to the new cost; the cost of spare parts, bodyshell and labour; repair times; and its performance. In addition to the car's insurance class, other factors affecting the cost include:

- the type of insurance cover required;
- the make and type of car (and how expensive it is to repair);
- the age and value of the car;
- your driving experience and driving record (demerit points or loss of licence);
- your age, sex (women drivers usually pay lower premiums as they have fewer accidents) and occupation;
- what you use your car for, e.g. business or pleasure;
- your accident record and no-claims' discount;
- who will drive the car besides the owner;
- your health (you may be required to pay an excess if you suffer from epilepsy or diabetes);
- where you live and whether your car is garaged overnight;
- the number of miles you do a year (some policies offer reduced rates for those who do low mileage);
- any extras you require, such as a protected no-claims' discount.

Australian cities and states are divided into zones, and premiums are much higher for those living in inner cities than the outer suburbs and small country towns. Driving conditions are more hazardous in cities (due to the high volume of traffic) and there's usually a high risk of theft. Some insurers insist that a car (particularly a high-risk car) has an engine immobiliser.

Note that the cost of CTP insurance is fixed in most states and varies from around $165 in South Australia (over 40km/25mi from Adelaide) to around $275 in Melbourne (metropolitan). The exception is NSW, where the cost can vary considerably (so shop around). With comprehensive insurance, you must usually pay a standard excess of from $100 to $400 when you make a claim. You must ensure that you state any previous accidents or driving offences when applying for car insurance, otherwise your insurer can refuse to pay out in the event of a claim. Drivers under 25, inexperienced drivers (holders of a licence for less than two years) and drivers with a bad accident record, must usually pay a larger compulsory excess. You're usually also required to pay an excess, e.g. $50, if you make a claim on your windscreen cover (which normally covers all glass), but this doesn't affect your no-claims' discount. Drivers who have lost their licence due to drunken or dangerous driving must usually pay a much higher premium for a number of years.

For a small extra premium, most insurance companies will cover you for legal costs arising from road accidents (it's also available separately from Australian motoring organisations, but is more expensive). If you cannot live without a car, ensure that your policy will pay for car hire in the event of an accident or your car being stolen (or that you have separate 'uninsured loss' insurance to cover this). Special 'mobility' insurance is available to pay for the cost of alternative transport after losing your licence due to a motoring offence, medical revocation of your licence or being unable to drive due to injury.

Motor insurance policies are valid for one year from the date you're first insured. You must usually pay in advance, although some companies allow you to pay in instalments either monthly, quarterly or half-yearly by direct debit from a bank account, possibly without incurring an additional charge (if there's an extra charge, check the interest rate). Initially you'll receive a 'cover note' to prove that you're insured, until your insurance certificate is issued. Check that the details on the cover note are correct, particularly the type of cover required and the date and time it commences. Towards the end of your insurance period you'll receive a renewal notice from your insurance company.

You aren't required to renew your car insurance with the same company, but may shop around for a better deal. **Note, however, that if you don't renew your motor insurance by the date due, your cover will cease automatically.** You can change your insurance company and policy whenever you like in Australia, for example by giving seven days notice and returning the certificate, whereupon you'll receive a portion of your premium back, providing you've made no-claims. If you're staying in Australia for a short period, you can usually take out a fixed period policy, e.g. for three or six months, although this may be much more expensive than cancelling an annual policy and obtaining a refund.

It's important to shop around and obtain quotations from a number of insurance companies (including direct insurance companies who sell policies over the phone) when obtaining insurance, as quotes can differ by thousands of dollars!

No-Claims' Discount

A foreign no-claims' discount (or bonus) is usually valid in Australia, although some Australian insurance companies won't accept a no-claims' discount earned overseas with a foreign insurance company. You must provide written evidence from your present or previous insurance company, not simply an insurance renewal notice. The maximum no-claims' discount in Australia is usually 60 per cent. Some insurance companies offer an introductory discount. The no-claims' discount offered by insurance companies is typically: one year (25 per cent), two years (35 per cent), three years (45 per cent), four years (55 per cent) and five years (65 per cent).

Normally when you make a claim you lose two years' no-claims' discount (which also applies to a claim for fire or theft), so it's sometimes cheaper to pay for minor damage yourself. Damage to glass doesn't affect your no-claims' discount, but you're usually required to pay the first $50 or $100 of a claim. Most insurance policies offer a protected no-claims' discount policy or allow you to insure your no-claims' discount. This means that you can usually make one 'at-fault' claim within a certain period (e.g. three years) or two 'at-fault' claims (e.g. within five years), without losing any of your no-claims' discount.

Some companies provide an extra no-claims' discount or lower premiums for experienced motorists with a clean licence and an accident-free driving record. If you insure two or more vehicles, you can claim a no-claims' discount on one vehicle only, although you may be given a discount on the premium for the other vehicles. Note that if you're uninsured (e.g. don't drive) for longer than two years, you usually lose your entire no-claims' discount.

GENERAL ROAD RULES

Each state and territory has its own driving laws, but in general the variations are minor. However, it's essential to familiarise yourself with the local idiosyncracies in the law by obtaining a copy of a state or territory's 'highway code' (such as the *Road Users' Handbook* in New South Wales) from the local 'Motor Vehicle' authority (e.g. the Roads and Traffic Authority in NSW) and motoring organisations. Handbooks contain advice for all road users, including motorists, motorcyclists and pedestrians. The NSW handbook is available in English, Arabic, Chinese, Croatian, Greek, Korean, Japanese, Serbian, Spanish, Turkish and Vietnamese (they may also be available on audio cassette). A *Heavy Vehicle Drivers' Handbook* and a *Motorcycle Riders' Handbook* are also published in NSW. The Australian Automobile Association (AAA) publishes a free booklet, *Motoring in Australia*, which contains sections in English, French, German, Japanese and Spanish.

The following general road rules are mostly taken from the NSW *Road Users' Handbook* (unless otherwise noted) and may help you adjust to driving in Australia and avoid an accident:

- Among the many strange habits of the Australians is that of driving on the left-hand side of the road, which they inherited from the British. You may find this a bit strange if you come from a country which drives on the right, however, it saves a lot of confusion if you do likewise. It's helpful to have a reminder (e.g. 'think left!') on your car's dashboard. Take extra care when pulling out of junctions, one-way streets and at roundabouts. Remember to look first to the *right* when crossing the road on foot. If you're unused to driving on the left, you should be prepared for some disorientation or even terror, although most people have few problems adjusting to it.

- At crossroads and junctions in Australia where no right of way is assigned, traffic coming from the right has priority (as on the continent of Europe). At major junctions, right of way is always indicated by a triangular 'GIVE WAY' (yield) sign or an octagonal red 'STOP' sign. There are also usually road markings. When faced with a stop sign you must stop completely (all four wheels must come to rest) before pulling out onto a major road, even if you can see that no traffic is approaching. At a give way sign, you aren't required to stop, but must give priority to traffic already on the major road. You must also give way to traffic on your right when entering a freeway or dual carriageway from a slip road.

• The different types of traffic signs in Australia can usually be distinguished by their shape and colour as shown below. Apart from the international octagonal 'STOP' sign (white on red) and the triangular 'GIVE WAY' sign (black on white with a red border), most Australian road signs don't follow international standards.

 – **warning signs** tell you that there may be dangers ahead and are usually diamond shaped with black diagrams (sometimes accompanied by red) and symbols (such as a kangaroo) on a yellow background;

 – **regulatory signs** give instructions (in words) that must be obeyed and are usually rectangular with black letters on a white background (some also have red markings). Some parking signs are green on white.

 – **freeway signs** give information about the start, end and exits from freeways;

 – **stock signs** are used in rural areas to indicate areas where live stock can be expected on or near roads (you must slow or stop as required and can be fined for disobeying signs);

 – **temporary signs** are used at roadworks;

 Some of the most important signs are shown in a state or territory's 'road users' handbook'. Signs may be reinforced by painted warnings on the road.

• On roundabouts (traffic circles), vehicles on the roundabout (coming from your right) have priority and not those entering it. Traffic flows clockwise round roundabouts and not anti-clockwise, as in countries where traffic drives on the right. Some roundabouts have a filter lane which is reserved for traffic turning left. You should stay in the lane in which you entered the roundabout, follow the lane markings to leave and signal as you approach the exit you wish to take. There are many roundabouts in Australia, which although they are a bit of a free-for-all, speed up traffic considerably and are usually preferable to traffic lights, particularly outside rush hours (although some busy roundabouts also have traffic lights).

• Australia was one of the first countries to make of seatbelts compulsory. The use of seatbelts is compulsory for all front and rear seat passengers when they are fitted and children must be properly restrained by an approved child restraint or adult seatbelt if fitted to a vehicle. In the absence of an approved restraint or seatbelt, they must travel in the back seat of a car. In Victoria, a child under the age of one year isn't permitted to be carried without being properly restrained in any vehicle required to have child restraint anchorages. The exceptions are taxi cabs, vehicles registered in another state or territory, or when there's isn't an unoccupied seat. Children aged one to 13 must use an approved child seat that meets the Australian Standard or a firmly adjusted adult seatbelt when available. A child must *never* travel in the front seat without using a child restraint or seatbelt, even when the back seat is full. Seatbelts or restraints must be approved (to the requisite Australian standard) and be appropriate for the age and weight of a child, as follows:

 – **under six months (weighing less than 9kg):** a rear-facing baby seat with a built-in harness in either the front (but not when the front seat is fitted with an air bag) or rear of a car;

 – **from around six months to five years (from 8kg to 18kg):** a rear-facing seat or, if there's insufficient space, a front-facing restraint with a built-in harness;

- **from around three to 10 years (14 to 32kg):** a child safety harness which should be used where only a lap belt is available (do Australian police officers carry weighing machines?).

A booster seat or cushion can be used in the front or rear seats with an adult three-point (sash) seatbelt or in a rear seat with a child harness. Special harnesses and belts are also available for the handicapped. Note that all belts, seats, harnesses and restraints **must be correctly fitted and adjusted, without which they may be useless (many child seats are wrongly fitted).** Some child seats have fatal flaws and many cars have seatbelt straps that are too short for rear-facing baby seats. If all available restraints in a car are in use, children may travel unrestrained (although this is *extremely* unwise).

It's estimated that seatbelts would prevent around 75 per cent of deaths and 90 per cent of injuries suffered by those involved in accidents not wearing seat belts. In addition to the risk of death or injury, you can receive a $75 or $100 fine for ignoring the seatbelt laws (and will also lose three points on your licence) and for each unrestrained child under 14. Note that it's the driver's responsibility to ensure that children are properly fastened. If you're exempt from using a seatbelt for medical reasons, a safety belt exemption certificate is required from your doctor.

Drivers not using seatbelts are apparently more likely to drive under the influence of alcohol or drugs or speed, and police are more likely to breathalyse drivers not using belts. One in five drivers killed in accidents since 1994 wasn't using a seatbelt and almost half the drivers killed with illegal blood-alcohol levels were unbelted. Drivers not using seatbelts are three times more likely to be killed than those using them. The vast majority of Australians use seat belts, due in no small part to an effective advertising campaign in the '80s ('Click clack, front and back'). More information can be obtained from motoring organisations and 'Motor Vehicle' authorities.

- Railway level crossings can be dangerous places, especially where there are no gates, booms or flashing lights. Always approach a railway level crossing slowly, look and listen for trains, and be prepared to **STOP**. There are usually warning signs ahead of crossings. Where there are gates, booms or flashing lights, start to cross only when the signals have stopped flashing and the gates or booms are fully open. You must stop at a crossing when:
  - there's a stop sign;
  - there's a gate or boom across the road;
  - red lights are flashing;
  - a railway employee signals you to do so;
  - you're carrying flammable, explosive or dangerous goods.

Crossings without gates (e.g. in country areas) must be approached with extreme caution, including pedestrian railway crossings. Even a car that's built like a tank won't look so smart after a scrap with a 70-tonne locomotive.

- Be particularly wary of cyclists, moped riders and motorcyclists. It isn't always easy to see them, particularly when they are hidden by the blind spots of a car or when cyclists are riding at night without lights. **When overtaking, ALWAYS give them a wide . . . WIDE berth.** If you knock them off their bikes, you may have a difficult time convincing the police that it wasn't your fault; far better to avoid them (and the police).

- When loading and unloading children, school buses flash orange lights at the front and rear, and may also display a 'GIVE WAY' sign at the rear. You must drive slowly near school buses and give way to children crossing the road. Lights remain flashing for around 30 seconds after which the doors close and the bus moves off.

- If you needed spectacles or contact lenses to pass your sight test, you must always wear them when driving. It's advisable to carry a spare pair of glasses or contact lenses in your car.

- White or yellow lane and road markings are painted on the road surface in towns and cities, e.g arrows to indicate the direction traffic must go in a particular lane. You should always stay in the centre of the lane in which you're driving and, where there are no lane markings, keep to the left side of the road. In many cities there are transit lanes in operation during rush hours, e.g. 6am to 10am Monday to Friday, which may be used by buses, taxis, motorcycles, bicycles and emergency vehicles. A passenger vehicle may use these lanes *only* if it's carrying one or two passengers (real passengers, not dummies!), e.g. in NSW a passenger vehicle in a T2 lane must have at least one passenger and in a T3 lane at least two passengers. Otherwise these lanes may be used only if you intend to make a turn within 100 metres. There are also 'BUS ONLY' lanes in cities.

- In cities such as Melbourne, tram lines are delineated by solid yellow lines, which you should remain clear of unless you want a close encounter with a tram (continuous yellow lines cannot be crossed, but broken lines can be crossed if you don't obstruct a tram). When a tram has started to cross an intersection it has right of way over all other vehicles. There are special rules when overtaking trams and you must not pass a tram when it stops to pick up or drop off passengers (unless there's a central island). Note that tram tracks can be slippery when wet and cyclists and motorcyclists should take care.

- White lines mark the separation of traffic lanes. A solid single line or two solid lines means no overtaking in either direction. A solid line to the left of the centre line, i.e. on your side of the road, means that overtaking is prohibited in your direction. You may overtake only when there's a single broken line in the middle of the road or double lines with a broken line on your side of the road. Note that double lines may be crossed when making a right turn in some states, but not in others, and U-turns are usually prohibited across any unbroken centre line even if associated with a broken line.

  It's usually illegal to overtake on an inside lane unless traffic is being channelled in a different direction. However, overtaking on the inside (i.e. undertaking) is permitted on a highway with three or more lanes in each direction in some states. In Australia, the right-hand land isn't usually just for overtaking and although you should keep to the left, it isn't obligatory. Motorists must indicate before overtaking *and* when moving back into an inside lane after overtaking, e.g. on a dual carriageway or freeway.

- Headlights must be used when driving between sunset and sunrise or at any time when there's insufficient daylight to be able to see a person wearing dark clothing at a distance of 100 metres (so keep an eye out for people in dark clothing). It's illegal to drive on side (parking) lights in Australia and headlights must usually be dipped (low beam) when driving in built-up areas where there's street lighting. Headlamps must also be dipped within 200 metres of an approaching vehicle, immediately an oncoming vehicle has dipped its headlights and when travelling within 200 metres behind another vehicle. If you happen to be riding a camel on a road at night in Broome (WA), you must have a rear light.

- Headlight flashing has a different meaning in different countries. In some countries it means "after you", while in others it means "get out of my way". It can even mean "I'm driving a new car and haven't yet worked out what all the switches are for". **In Australia headlamp flashing has only one legal use — to warn another vehicle of your presence**, although most people use it to give priority to another vehicle, e.g. when someone is waiting to exit from a junction. Note that it's illegal in some states to warn other vehicles that they are approaching a speed trap or police road block by flashing your lights (although many drivers do it). Hazard warning lights (all indicators operating simultaneously) are used to warn other drivers of an obstruction, e.g. an accident or a traffic jam on a highway.

- The sequence of Australian traffic lights is red, yellow, green, yellow and back to red. Yellow is a warning to get ready to go, but you must not start moving until the light changes to green. Yellow (after green) means stop at the stop line and you may proceed only if the yellow light appears after you have crossed the stop line or when stopping might cause an accident. A green filter light may be shown in addition to the full lamp signals, which means you may go in the direction shown by the arrow, irrespective of other lights showing. Cameras are often installed at busy traffic lights to detect motorists driving through red lights (a favourite pastime of many Australian motorists).

  In some cities (e.g. Adelaide) there are flashing 'no right turn' signs at some junctions during business hours. In Melbourne, to accommodate the city's trams, a special rule applies at intersections where there's a 'Right Turn From Left Only' sign (known locally as the 'hook turn') accompanied by curved broken lines on the road surface. At these intersections you must keep to the left hand lane and wait until you get a green light to make a right turn. At traffic lights in some states there are 'TURN LEFT AT ANY TIME WITH CARE' or 'LEFT TURN ON RED PERMITTED AFTER STOPPING' signs, permitting vehicles to turn left even when faced with a red light (as in most of the USA). However, drivers must first stop if indicated and only proceed when they can do so safely. Flashing yellow lights and stop signs with three large black dots are used at some intersections, which mean that you must stop and give way to all traffic. A sign of a white 'B' on a black background indicates traffic lights for buses in a special bus lane marked 'BUSES ONLY' (you should never drive in bus lanes — unless you're driving a local bus). In Queensland, motorists must give way to buses pulling out into traffic in towns (i.e. a 60kph/37mi zone).

- Always approach pedestrian crossings with caution and don't park or overtake another vehicle on the approach to a crossing (usually shown by zigzag lines or a large white diamond). At some crossings a flashing amber light follows the red light, to warn you to give way to pedestrians before proceeding. **Note that pedestrians have the legal right of way once they have stepped onto a crossing without traffic lights and you must STOP. Motorists who don't stop are liable to heavy penalties.** Where a road crosses a public footpath, e.g. when entering or emerging from a property or car park bordering a road, motorists *must* give way to pedestrians.

- Tail-gating (driving too close to the vehicle in front) is commonplace in Australia and most other countries, where few drivers have any idea of safe stopping distances (including thinking distance, i.e. the time it takes a driver to react). In good conditions you should leave a gap equal to three seconds between your vehicle and the one in front in order to be able to stop in an emergency. Note that the three-second rule applies to cars with good brakes and tyres, on dry roads, in good visibility and with an *alert driver*. If you're half asleep and driving an old banger on a wet or icy road, you had better not exceed 20kph/12mph, otherwise you'll never stop in an emergency! As a safety precaution, always try to leave a large gap between you and the vehicle in front. This isn't just to allow you more time to stop, should the vehicles in front decide to get together, but also to give the 'tail-gater' behind you more time to stop. **The closer the car behind you, the further you should be from the vehicle in front.**

* Fines can be exacted for a wide range of motoring offences, some of which are imposed on-the-spot, e.g. for marginal speeding and other 'minor' offences. A conviction for most motoring offences results in a fine and demerit points on your licence, which, if you collect enough, will result in the suspension of your licence for a period (see page 244). Serious offences such as dangerous or drunken driving involving injury or death to third parties can result in a prison sentence.

AUSTRALIAN DRIVERS

Like motorists in all countries, the Australians have their own idiosyncracies and customs. Although they aren't recognised as the best in the world, most Australians are good and careful drivers, who take their driving seriously. Northern Territorians are reckoned to be Australia's worst drivers, particularly in traffic, and are scornfully referred to as bush motorists (who tend not to bother with the niceties of driving, such as indicating, stop signs, red lights, lanes, etc.). Running red lights is commonplace in Australian cities and the all-red period (when all vehicles are required to stop) has been increased to help combat this problem (maybe there's a higher than average incidence of colour-blindness in Australia?). Australia has its fair share of seriously crazy drivers, added to which (according to a specialist's report in 1997) there are also some 80,000 drivers with dementia on Australian roads (you may be forgiven for thinking that they are ALL driving on the same roads as you or that perhaps they made a mistake and there are *only* 80,000 drivers *without* dementia).

Australian drivers tend to be aggressive, particularly truck drivers, and it's usually every man (or women) for himself, particularly in Sydney. On the outback roads of central and northern Australia you're likely to come across road trains, which are multi-trailer, articulated lorries up to 50 metres in length and weighing over 100 tonnes, driven by maniacs who don't move over for anyone (except perhaps another road train). It's best to pull over and let them pass (allow at least a kilometre if you plan to overtake one). Most Australian men have a cavalier attitude to driving and believe they are wonderful drivers (it's a macho thing), although the accident statistics tell another story. Drinking and driving is still fairly commonplace, despite regular spot checks. The macho attitude among young male drivers is a killer and the risk of young people aged 17 to 25 dying on the roads is around three times that of other age groups. However, the once appalling accident rate has decreased in recent years through improved roads, random breath testing, stricter laws, safer vehicles, and better driver training and education. Women generally drive as well as men, have far fewer accidents (particularly the under 25s), and are much less likely to drink and drive. However, young women drivers are increasingly showing aggressive driving behaviour normally associated only with men.

Beware of kangaroos and assorted other animals which stray onto country roads, particularly at night (attempts to teach them the 'blue cross' code have failed miserably). An encounter with a big boomer can seriously damage your vehicle, which is why most car and truck owners who regularly use country roads fit their vehicles with 'roo bars' (the steel bars you commonly see on 4-wheel drive vehicles in many countries). Some cars are fitted with an alarm ('shu-roo') which emits a high-pitched noise that frightens kangaroos. Many Australians try to avoid travelling when it's dark because of the dangers posed by animals (most are nocturnal and feed at night). Note that you should swerve to avoid a kangaroo only when it's safe to do so, as many people kill themselves trying to avoid them. Water buffalo are a problem in some northern parts of the country and grazing cattle can also be a menace in country areas. Take it easy when driving in inclement weather. Ice and snow is rare in most areas except the mountainous regions of New South Wales, Victoria and Tasmania (which being farthest south, experiences the worst winter weather). Fog can also make driving extremely hazardous in winter in some regions.

Tempers are rising on Australia's overcrowded streets and road rage ('invented' in California — where else?), where drivers blow their tops and attack or drive into other motorists, is becoming more common. It's often provoked by tailgating, headlight flashing, obscene gestures, obstruction and verbal abuse, so be careful how you behave when driving in Australia. However, despite their idiosyncracies, Australian drivers are usually above average (average is bad) and not as belligerent as those in many other countries. Don't be discouraged by the tail-gaters and road hogs, as driving in Australia is less stressful than in many other countries and can even be enjoyable in country areas (providing you avoid dirt tracks). Most people who come from countries where traffic drives on the right quickly become used to driving on the 'wrong' side of the road. Just take it easy at first and bear in mind that there may be other motorists around just as confused (and frightened) as you are.

AUSTRALIAN ROADS

There are some 850,000km (over 500,000mi) of roads in Australia, varying in quality from eight-lane highways to rutted dirt tracks which are impossible to negotiate in anything less than a four-wheel drive vehicle. Only one-third of roads are sealed, including 16,000km (10,000mi) of national highways linking the capital cities, plus Brisbane and Cairns in Queensland, and Hobart and Burnie in Tasmania. Roads are usually classified as primary or secondary routes. Primary routes are the major roads that link the states and territories, together with those serving the principle centres of population and industry within them. Secondary routes include those which facilitate the carriage of produce from farms and mines, forest roads serving tourist resorts, and most streets in towns and cities. Lighting is good on major urban highways and usually adequate on other urban roads.

Generally the roads between major cities and state capitals are excellent with dual carriageways (divided highways) in metropolitan areas, particularly in the eastern coastal areas of Sydney, Newcastle and Brisbane. In rural areas, where the traffic density isn't high and there are vast distances between towns, roads may have only two lanes and in the out-back dirt roads are common. In general, the quality of Australian roads is excellent, although some main roads and freeways are in a poor condition due to being constantly chewed up by juggernauts and the heavy volume of traffic.

There are wide roads in most cities, particularly in the suburbs, where they are usually laid out on a grid system (except Canberra and Sydney). Victoria's roads are the most crowded, as are urban roads in New South Wales. Driving in Sydney is a pain and to be avoided if at all possible (finding parking can be a nightmare), while Melbourne isn't much better. Most major cities are choked during rush hours, e.g. 6am to 10pm, and Sydney is congested at almost any time. Sydney Harbour bridge is an infamous bottleneck (a toll is charged when travelling south), although the harbour tunnel (included in the bridge toll) has relieved some of the congestion. Sydney has a 'Metroad' system which helps make travel into, through and out of the city (a tiny bit) easier. Major roads are prefixed with an 'M' and numbered 1 to 7, and indicated by distinctive hexagonal route markers. Driving in Adelaide, Brisbane and Perth is relatively easy, although rush hours should be avoided. Tasmanian roads are fairly traffic free (a few cars tail-to-tail practically represent a traffic jam) and driving there is fairly relaxed (except in winter). Note that many cities have tortuous one-way systems. Signposting in cities can be confusing and street names are often difficult to find. Signposting is virtually non-existent in the outback and can be a bit of a joke (e.g. Darwin 2,000km). Note that distances are shown in kilometres (km) in Australia and not miles.

Major roads, variously referred to as expressways, freeways and highways (as in the USA) have three or four lanes in each direction. In some cities there are toll roads, called tollways, such as the M2 tollway in Sydney. However, toll roads are unpopular with Australians and the M2 has been shunned by many motorists and it carries only around half the number of vehicles forecast. However, despite this setback more toll roads are planned. All major highways are sealed, although the Stuart Highway ('the track') extending 3,000km/1,850mi from Adelaide to Darwin was completely sealed only in 1987.

Highway number 1 goes right around Australia, mostly hugging the coast, and is Australia's most dramatic road. Note that road numbers are rarely used in Australia and most people refer to roads by their names. Highway 1 is known by various names depending on the particular stretch, such as the Princes Highway between Sydney and Adelaide. Some stretches are extremely picturesque and it passes through many interesting towns. The most direct route between Sydney and Melbourne is via the more busy inland Hume Highway (number 31). The most direct route between Melbourne and Adelaide is the Western Highway (number 8), but again the Princes Highway (1) offers the best views. The main roads between Sydney and Brisbane are the coastal Pacific Highway (1) and the inland New England Highway (15). The quickest route from Sydney to Adelaide is via the Great Western (32), Mid Western (24) and Stuart Highways (20). (In truth, it's by air!)

On national highways there are route markers (small shields by the roadside) every 5km/3mi bearing the initial letter of the last or next major town above the distance in kilometres. There are emergency telephones every kilometre on Australian freeways for use in the event of accidents and breakdowns. Some highways have a 'crawler' lane or hard-shoulder (for slow-moving vehicles) and uphill speed ramps are common on steep downhill stretches to slow vehicles if their brakes fail. National highways are a federal government responsibility and have been funded from an excise levied on fuel since the early '80s.

Note that the vast distances and the hot sun induce drowsiness in drivers and you should make frequent stops for refreshment and rests on a long journey. There are frequent roadside rest areas on main highways and free coffee is provided at stops on some main highways to help reduce driver fatigue. Drivers falling asleep at the wheel are a major cause of accidents on freeways, particularly at night (as the sign says, *Drowsy Drivers Die*!). It's always advisable to have company on long journeys.

Outback Roads: In some sparsely populated country areas (back-of-Bourke) there are long stretches of road with only one lane paved and wide unsealed shoulders. Even main highways such as the Western Australia coastal road (highway 1) have stretches consisting of a single lane with dirt shoulders. Many outback roads are dirt and in varying stages of neglect. In country and outback areas off the main highways, minor roads can be terrible, consisting mainly of dirt tracks. In some outback areas in Western Australia there are sealed roads built privately by mining companies and visitors may be allowed to use them with a permit.

There has, however, been a vast improvement in the outback road network in recent years making it possible for the average motorist to explore the country by car (on main highways) without the need of a 4WD vehicle. However, high ground clearance is necessary on unsealed outback roads and 4WD is often mandatory if you don't want to get stuck (although it isn't foolproof). Outback driving can be hazardous for the inexperienced driver and thorough preparation is essential as conditions vary from area to area and season to season. The best time to travel is during the cooler winter months between April and October. Many outback roads are deeply rutted and can be washed away by flash floods and remain impassable for weeks on end during the wet season (some roads in northern Australia are impassable from December until May). Dust can also be a problem during the heat of summer in central Australia (when air-conditioning is practically essential). Note that you should keep a close eye on the temperature gauge in hot weather.

When travelling in the outback, road conditions and routes must be checked with the local authorities, in addition to weather forecasts and the availability of fuel. On some roads in the outback, motorists are required to complete a police destination card giving their expected time of arrival at the next town. It's advisable to carry a two-way UHF radio tuned to the local Royal Flying Doctor Service (see page 276). Make sure a vehicle is roadworthy and carry plenty of spares including two spare tyres, plastic windscreen, tools, a week's supply of food and water (20 litres per person in a number of containers), first-aid kit, spare fuel (keep the tank topped up at all times), a workshop manual and maps.

If you break down, it's imperative to stay with your vehicle. As a last resort burn a tyre, as property owners in the outback never ignore smoke. Note that a motorist must (by law) aid someone who has broken down in the outback. In bygone days it wasn't unusual to come across a vehicle in the outback containing the skeletons of its occupants, although (despite the horror stories) people rarely die in the outback nowadays. Many books are published for outback travellers including *Outback Australia* (Lonely Planet), *Safe Outback Travel* by Jack Absalom (Five Mile Press) and Gregory's *Four Wheel Drive Handbook*. The Australian Tourist Commission also publishes a booklet, *Hit the Road*, for visitors planning long-distance trips.

Information about road conditions is provided by motoring organisations and state government roads' departments, e.g. in Queensland the Main Roads Department publishes *Queensland Road Conditions*. Road conditions throughout Australia can be obtained from the NRMA on (02) 11571, 24 hours a day.

TRAFFIC POLICE

Police in Australia don't require a reason to stop motorists and can stop you for a spot check at any time. In recent years random breath testing has increased considerably as police have cracked down on drinking and driving. Australian state police aggressively enforce all traffic regulations and use a variety of equipment and tactics to catch offenders. Roadblocks with mobile breath-testing units are used to check for drink-driving infringements and automatic cameras are installed at intersections to identify drivers running red lights. Radar units and speed cameras are employed to identify speeders, and airplanes and helicopters are used to catch speeding vehicles on rural highways. Never antagonise a police officer or make any smart cracks, as this is the fast lane to prosecution; remain courteous and obsequious and you may be let off with a caution.

Although you may have read about corrupt Australian police, don't even think about trying to bribe an officer unless you wish to be charged with a much more serious offence! Note that when crossing a state border, your vehicle may be searched for firearms, drugs, pornography, and fresh fruit and vegetables (which cannot be transported from one state to another to prevent the spread of parasites).

You're required by law to carry your car or motorcycle registration papers and your driver's licence (including an international driving permit if required) when driving in Australia. You must give a policeman your name and address when requested, although you aren't required to answer questions before obtaining legal advice. Marginal speeding and other minor offences (such as not having your driver's licence) are usually dealt with by on-the-spot fines (officially called a 'Traffic Infringement Notice'), which have increased considerably in many states in recent years and can be up to $250. Residents can pay an 'on-the-spot' fine within 28 days and aren't required to go to court. If you think you haven't committed an offence, you can contest a fine or prosecution in a court of law, although it isn't usually worthwhile unless you have incontrovertible proof of your innocence.

All states are owed tens of $millions (over $200m in NSW alone) in unpaid motoring fines. In Western Australia (since 1995), the licence of a motorist is automatically suspended until a fine is paid, and goods can be seized (such as a car or furniture) in lieu of unpaid fines. This move is followed by a community service order, with jail as a last resort (the system has proved such as success that other states such as NSW plan to follow suit).

MOTORCYCLES

The minimum age for riding a motorcycle in Australia varies depending on the state or territory, but is usually 17. A young driver may obtain a licence before he reaches the required age after passing a written road knowledge test, e.g. at age 16 years and nine months in NSW. The following information is based on vehicle licences in NSW, which is similar to other states. A learner is permitted to ride a motorcycle with a maximum engine capacity of 260ml with a power to weight ratio of no more than 150kw per tonne (whatever that means?). An 'L' plate must be displayed on the back and you mustn't carry a passenger. In some areas of NSW, learners must complete a pre-provisional licence course before taking a road knowledge test. The course can be taken at age 16 and six months, and allows the learner's licence to be issued at age 16 years and nine months. To obtain a provisional motorcycle licence (class R), you must take a riding test between three and six months after you receive your learner's licence. After passing the test, a 'P' plate must be displayed on the back of the motorcycle for a period of one year. If you have held a foreign motorcycle licence for less than a year you will be eligible for a provisional licence only, and if you fail the riding test you may be required to undertake further rider training.

Although Australia has an excellent climate for biking, it has declined in popularity in the last decade and bikes are more a fashion statement nowadays than a transport option, with many over 40s buying them for leisure riding. Large capacity bikes are best for long-distance travel. It's essential to take spares and tools when on a long trip and travelling alone in the outback isn't advisable (see page 255). Contact motorcycle clubs and motoring organisations for information about outback road conditions and the availability of petrol.

There has been a massive slump in motorcycle sales in the '90s (due to the Australian dollar's collapse against the Japanese yen), with sales running at around 25,000 a year compared with 80,000 at their peak. The average price is around $12,000 with top models costing close to $30,000. If you need a bike for a limited period only (e.g. a trip around Australia), some dealers offer buy-back options on secondhand bikes. There's a good market in secondhand bikes and you may be able to pick up a bargain from a departing visitor (the best time to buy a bike is at the start of the Australian winter in May). Motorcycles can be rented in Australia, although rates are high and range from $85 to $150 per day ($400 to $800 a week) depending on the engine capacity (there are usually discounts for rentals longer than a week). A deposit of around $1,000 is payable by credit card. One-way rentals are possible with a drop-off fee. However, it's cheaper to buy a secondhand bike and sell it when you no longer need it.

Helmets must be worn at all times (but remove it when going into a bank or they may thing that you're planning to rob it!). In recent years motorcycle accidents have been greatly reduced due to helmets, better bikes and protective riding gear, better training, and defensive riding by bikers. In general, laws that apply to cars also apply to motorcycles. Note that motorcyclists aren't popular in Australia with motorists, particularly in the major cities where lunatic motorcycle couriers have given bikers a bad name. The NSW Roads and Traffic Authority publishes a *Motorcycle Riders' Handbook*.

ACCIDENTS

If you're involved in (or cause) an accident in Australia, which results in injury to a person or animal, or damage to any third party's vehicle or property, the procedure is as follows:

1. Stop immediately. If possible move your car off the road and keep your passengers and yourself off the road. If you have an accident (or a breakdown) on a major highway, don't stay in your vehicle whatever the weather (even if it's parked on the hard shoulder) as there's a danger that another vehicle will run into you (many accidents on freeways occur on the hard shoulder). Wait on the embankment or nearby land (this also applies to stopping on other fast roads). Note that failing to stop after an accident or failure to give particulars or report to the police is a serious offence.

2. Warn other drivers of any obstruction by switching on your hazard warning lights (particularly on freeways) or by placing a warning triangle at the edge of the road at least 50 metres behind your car on secondary roads and 150 metres on a freeway. If necessary, for example when the road is partly or totally blocked, turn on your car's dipped headlights and direct traffic around the hazard. In bad visibility, at night, or in a blind spot, try to warn oncoming traffic of the danger, e.g. with a torch, or by waving a warning triangle up and down.

3. If anyone is injured, immediately phone for an ambulance, the fire brigade (if someone is trapped or oil or chemicals are spilled) or the police (dial 000). Emergency telephones are provided on freeways. Give first-aid only if you're qualified to do so. Don't move an injured person unless absolutely necessary to save him from further injury and don't leave him alone except to phone for an ambulance. Cover him with a blanket or coat to keep him warm (cool?).

4. The police may attend and investigate an accident where someone is killed or injured; damage is caused to property, animals or vehicles in excess of $500; a person fails to stop and exchange information; or a driver is believed to be under the influence of alcohol or drugs. If you think someone else involved in an accident is drunk or has otherwise broken the law (e.g. his vehicle is unroadworthy), you should call the

police. The police normally breathalyse everyone involved in an accident as a matter of routine. Note that calling the police to the scene of an accident may result in someone being fined or charged for a driving offence. In all cases you mustn't say anything which could be interpreted as an admission of guilt, even if you're as guilty as hell. Admitting responsibility for an accident, either verbally or in writing may **release your insurance company from responsibility under your policy (and could also result in a criminal charge)**. In other words you must say nothing (not even 'sorry') or only that your insurance company will deal with any claims. Let the police and insurance companies decide who was at fault.

5. If either you or any other driver(s) involved decide to call the police, don't move your vehicle or allow other vehicles to be moved. However, if it's necessary to move vehicles to unblock the road, mark the positions of their wheels with chalk and measure the distance between vehicles. Take photographs of the accident scene if a camera is available (you can keep a disposable camera in your car which costs around $10), or make a drawing showing the positions of all vehicles involved before moving them.

6. Check immediately whether there are any witnesses to the accident and take their names and addresses, particularly noting those who support *your* version of what happened. Write down the registration numbers of all vehicles involved (or possible witnesses) and their drivers' and owners' names, addresses and insurance details. Note also the identification numbers of any police present. You must (by law) give anyone having reasonable grounds for requiring them (e.g. the owner of damaged property) your name and insurance details, and the vehicle owner's name and address (if different).

7. If you're involved in an accident where damage over $500 or $1,000 (depending on the state) is caused to property, animals or vehicles, the nearest police station must be notified within 24 hours (if the police don't attend the scene). If you have caused material damage, you must inform the owner of the damaged property as soon as possible. If you cannot reach him, report the accident to a police station within 24 hours (this also applies to damage caused to other vehicles when parking). It's often advisable to report any accident involving another vehicle within 24 hours to avoid any repercussions later. Make sure your visit is officially recorded by the police officer on duty and that you receive signed verification of your report.

If you have an accident involving a domestic animal and are unable to find the owner, it must also be reported to the police or the RSPCA. If a domestic animal is injured, it should be taken to the nearest vet or animal shelter. If you have an accident with a wild animal you should try to lessen any suffering it may experience and remove it from the road (care should be taken as many Australian mammals carry their young in pouches). If a wild animal is injured you should notify the local Wildlife and Information Rescue Service (WIRES).

8. You may be asked to make a statement by the police or be asked questions, although you have the right to silence and aren't required to say anything (apart from giving your name and address). If you do make a statement, it should be short and unambiguous. However, it may be preferable not to make a statement until you have spoken with a solicitor, particularly if you're involved in a serious accident. **When you do make a statement, don't sign it unless you're certain that you understand and agree with every word.**

9. Lastly, you should report all accidents to your insurance company in writing as soon as possible, even if you don't intend to make a claim (but reserve your right to make a claim later). If you're injured and plan to make an insurance claim, you must obtain a doctor's report as soon as possible after the accident to verify your injuries (this will obviously be done automatically if you're admitted to hospital). Your insurance company will ask you to complete an accident report form, which you should return as soon as possible (don't forget to sign it). It's possible to avoid delays in insurance claims by completing a collision report at the nearest police station to where the accident occurred.

DRINKING & DRIVING

As you're no doubt well aware, drinking and driving make a dangerous cocktail. In Australia you're no longer considered fit to drive when your blood contains between 0.02g and 0.08g of alcohol (depending on the state and other factors) per 100ml of blood. The limit for experienced drivers is O.05g in the ACT, New South Wales, Queensland, Tasmania and Victoria (some states are thinking about lowering it to 0.02g), while in the Northern Territory, South Australia and Western Australia it's 0.08g. In most states the limit is 0.02g for drivers with a learner's or provisional licence; drivers under 25 who have held a licence for less than three years; anyone driving a bus, taxi or car for hire or reward; and drivers of heavy goods vehicles or anyone carrying a dangerous load. In some states, drivers with a learner's or provisional licence must not drive with any alcohol in their blood.

For a male of average body weight, the recognised maximum he can drink and remain under the 0.05g limit is around two standard glasses of beer or wine (or 30ml nips of spirits) in one hour (it's usually just one glass for a woman). One standard drink can put anyone over the 0.02g limit. Some pubs have machines where you can test your own blood/alcohol level, although they aren't foolproof. Note that you can still be over the legal limit the morning after a heavy night's drinking. If you're planning a business or social engagement where you know you will be drinking, you should leave your car at home and use public transport, a taxi or go with another driver who won't be drinking.

Random breath testing (RBT) is permitted in Australia (it commenced in Victoria in 1976) and the police frequently set up road blocks and breathalyse all drivers, particularly late at night on Thursdays, Fridays and Saturdays. Often the police employ special mobile testing stations (called 'booze buses'), although in some states (e.g. Victoria) all traffic police carry breath testing equipment and every motorist stopped (regardless of the reason) is breathalysed. RBT usually involves simply blowing or speaking into a meter. If you fail the breathalyser test, you'll be taken to a police station and be given a further test on a breath analysis unit. If you're still over the limit you will be charged and your licence can be immediately suspended. If you refuse to take a breath test the penalty is the same as for a high range drink drive charge, so you have nothing to gain and everything to lose by refusing a test.

The blood alcohol level of drivers who fail tests has fallen considerably in recent years, although there are still many drivers over the limit in some states. The vast majority of drunken drivers are males, particularly those involved in serious accidents. Around a quarter of drivers killed on Australian roads are over the blood-alcohol level. You can also be disqualified for driving while under the influence of drugs. If after passing a breath test under the limit for alcohol, the police still feel that you're under the influence of another drug, you can be arrested and taken to a hospital for further testing of your blood or urine (instant drug tests have also been developed in other countries, but aren't in use in Australia yet). Samples may be tested for such drugs as marijuana, heroin, morphine, cocaine, barbiturates, tranquilizers and sleeping tablets.

In NSW, fines for driving over the legal alcohol limit are usually a maximum of between $500 and $1,500 and the disqualification period varies from less than three months to life. Those who are well above the limit and repeat offenders can be jailed for up to one year in NSW (longer in some other states). If you have a blood alcohol level of 0.15 and are involved in an accident that causes injury or death, the penalties can be severe, e.g. up to 10 years' imprisonment in NSW. Drunken drivers must pay much higher insurance premiums after disqualification. Visitors who are apprehended for drunken driving in Australia are reported to their home country's traffic authorities.

If you have an accident while under the influence of alcohol, it can be very expensive. Your car, accident and health insurance could all be nullified. This means you must pay your own (and any third party's) car repairs, medical expenses and other damages.

CAR THEFT

Car theft is rife and on the increase in Australia, where a car is stolen every five minutes, and costs over $1 billion a year. Many stolen cars are broken up and sold for spares, while the rest are given a false identity and sold. If you regularly park your car in a city street, you have a high chance of having it or its contents stolen, although the favourite spot for thieves (particularly on Fridays and Saturdays) is suburban shopping mall car parks. Having your car stolen means more than just taking a taxi home. It may mean weeks of delay sorting out insurance, extra time and expense travelling to work, possible loss of personal (maybe irreplaceable) possessions, and loss of your insurance no-claims' discount. It may also involve hiring a solicitor or going to court to re-claim your car after it has been sold by the thief (if a car is stolen and sold, it can be a nightmare getting it back). For complete peace of mind, particularly in Sydney or Melbourne, you're better off using public transport!

If you drive a new or valuable car it's wise to have it fitted with an alarm, an engine immobiliser (preferably of the rolling code variety with a transponder arming key) or other anti-theft device, and to also use a visible deterrent such as a steering or gear change lock. This is particularly important if you own a car that's particularly desirable to car thieves, which includes all imported sports and executive cars, which are often stolen by professional crooks to order. A reflection of the high number of stolen cars in Australia is that it's standard practice for new cars to be fitted with dead locks and sophisticated alarm systems as standard equipment. Don't take unnecessary risks and always lock your car, engage your steering lock and completely close all windows (but don't leave pets in an unventilated car). Never leave you keys in the ignition (which is illegal in a public place in Queensland), not even when filling up at a petrol station or in your driveway. Put any valuables (including clothes) in the boot or out of sight and don't leave your vehicle registration papers in the car or any form of identification. If possible, avoid parking in commuter (e.g. at railway stations) and long-term car parks (e.g. at airports or malls), which are favourite hunting grounds for car thieves. When parking overnight or when it's dark, always park in a well-lit area, which helps deter car thieves.

Car theft has spawned a huge car security business in the (losing) battle to prevent or deter car thieves. These include a multitude of car alarms, engine immobilisers, steering and gear stick locks, personal wheel clamps, window etching with the car registration number, locking wheel nuts and petrol caps, and removable/coded stereo systems (a favourite target of thieves). If you plan to buy an expensive stereo system, buy one with a removable unit or control panel/fascia (which you can pop in a pocket), but *never* forget to remove it, even when stopping for a few minutes (although thieves sometimes steal the 'back box', leaving you with a useless facia).

A good security system won't prevent someone breaking into your car (which usually takes a professional a matter of seconds) or prevent it being stolen. What it will do is make it more difficult and may prompt a thief to look for an easier target. However, thanks to new tracking systems, most owners of valuable cars can be virtually assured that a stolen car will be recovered (usually within around four hours of being reported stolen). Tracking systems such as Mobiletrack have an almost 100 per cent recovery rate in tracking down stolen vehicles (so far thieves have been unable to find a way around them).

If your car is stolen, report it to the police and your insurance company as soon as possible. Don't, however, expect the police to find it or even take much interest in your loss. The Australian Consumers Association (see page 434) publishes an excellent book entitled *Safe and Secure - A Guide to Household and Car Security* by Richard Upton.

PETROL

Three grades of petrol are available in Australia: regular unleaded (92 octane), premium unleaded (96 octane) and leaded (97 octane). Premium unleaded isn't sold at all petrol stations. Specially treated petrol is sold in Sydney during the summer months in order to reduce ozone pollution. Diesel is also available at most petrol stations (the price is similar to unleaded) and two-stroke petrol is available for mopeds, boats, lawn-mowers, etc. Prices vary from area to area, even within cities, and in outback areas (where petrol stations are few and far between) and Tasmania, prices are around 15 per cent higher than in cities. Prices are usually between 65¢ and 75¢ a litre (or around $2.70 to $3.20 an imperial gallon). Premium unleaded is usually only a few cents more than regular unleaded petrol, which is from 65¢ a litre in urban areas. Petrol is usually cheapest at supermarkets, which sometimes prompts a price war (discounting has become commonplace in recent years). Petrol prices in Australia are similar to the USA and around half those in Europe. In recent years there have been claims of price fixing by the major oil companies. The big four companies, Mobil, Shell, BP and Ampol can own and operate only 4 per cent of the stations carrying their name, where they can fix the prices. The remaining outlets are franchises, who buy petrol from the oil company at a wholesale price and fix their own prices.

Many cars in Australia have been converted to run on liquid petroleum gas (LPG) or low propane gas, including most taxis. Most petrol engines can be converted to use both petrol and LPG (they can be switched between them), although you will lose around one-third of your boot space to accommodate the gas tank. The advantage is that LPG costs from around 25¢ to 35¢ a litre, although there's a loss of power of around 15 per cent. All urban areas and most large country towns have LPG outlets. However, a word of warning: LPG tanks occasionally explode, often with fatal results!

All new cars registered in Australia are fitted with a catalytic converter and run on unleaded fuel. Most cars that aren't fitted with catalytic converters can also run quite safely on unleaded petrol without any engine adjustments and without affecting their performance. However, tests in recent years have shown that using unleaded petrol in non-catalysed cars causes more pollution than using leaded fuel. **A car fitted with a catalytic converter must never be filled with leaded petrol.** To do so will damage the catalytic converter which is expensive to replace. To prevent errors, unleaded petrol pump pipes are usually coloured green and the nozzles of leaded petrol pumps are larger than those of unleaded pumps, and won't usually fit the petrol filler hole of a car fitted with a catalytic converter. Nevertheless, pay attention, particularly when a garage attendant is filling your car.

The trading hours of petrol stations vary considerably. Most open from 7.30am to 6.30pm Mondays to Saturdays and on Sunday mornings. Many petrol stations are open 24 hours a day in cities and on major highways. However, they run a high risk of robbery and even murder at night in some cities, and the number of 24-hour stations is expected to be reduced drastically in future. Some stations also have automatic pumps accepting $5 and $10 bills, and possibly credit and debit cards (however, don't rely on finding any outside major towns). Most petrol stations accept major credit and charge cards and local debit (EFTPOS) cards.

Most petrol stations provide additional services such as checking oil, water and tyre pressure, and cleaning windscreens. Some also have a car wash and most have a shop selling a wide range of motoring accessories and other goods. In fact, the main business of many petrol stations isn't selling petrol, on which profit margins are minimal. Today's petrol stations are more like convenience stores and sell a wide range of souvenirs, ice cubes, ice cream, confectionery, snacks, soft drinks, newspapers and magazines. Many petrol stations also have workshops and can usually handle minor repairs on-the-spot.

SPEED LIMITS

Needless to say, excessive speed is one of the major causes of accidents in Australia, and on country roads (where limits are widely ignored) one in three serious casualties involves speeding. Despite prosecutions and large fines, speeding is widespread in Australia and many motorists have a complete disregard for speed limits. In general, roads are posted with signs showing the maximum legal speed (in kilometres per hour and not miles per hour), e.g. in NSW white rectangular signs indicate the speed limit in black numerals within a red circle. Note that in addition to mandatory speed limits, there are square yellow signs indicating advisory limits, e.g. when approaching a sharp bend, which aren't compulsory. The following speed limits are in force for cars and motorcycles throughout Australia, unless indicated otherwise by a sign:

Type of Road	Speed Limit
any road with street lighting	60kph/37mph
streets without lighting	100kph/62mph

In some urban areas (e.g. in Sydney) a 50kph/31mph limit has been introduced on a trial basis (and is likely to become permanent) in an attempt to reduce accidents, particularly those involving pedestrians. In Western Australia the speed limit is 110kph/68mph on country roads and highways, and in the Northern Territory there's no speed limit outside built-up areas (although speeds are severely limited by potholes and ruts on most roads).

In some urban areas there are zones with lower speed limits including local traffic zones (40kmh/25mph); shared traffic zones, where pedestrians, bicycle riders and other vehicles all use the road (10kph/6mph); and school zones which have reduced speed limits on school days during school hours (e.g. 40kmh/25mph or 25kmh/15mph). However, after a court case and intervention by the federal Transport Minister, state governments were declared not to have the power to impose fines for speeders in a (temporary) 25km/15mph speed limit (school) zone (after thousands had already been fined). Note that in some residential areas there are speed humps (known as 'sleeping policemen' or 'traffic calmers' — although they certainly don't calm drivers!), designed to slow traffic.

They are sometimes indicated by warning signs and if you fail to slow down it's possible to damage your suspension or even turn your car over. Learners and provisional licence holders are limited to a maximum speed of 80kmh/50mph, even when a higher limit is in force. If you're towing a caravan, trailer or another vehicle you're also limited to 80kmh/50mph.

Speed limits are rigorously enforced in Australia and police employ radar units and speed cameras to identify speeders. Light planes and helicopters are used to spot speeding vehicles on interstate highways, where white lines may be painted on the road surface to help aerial police calculate speeds (by timing a vehicle between lines). Radar detectors are illegal in all states except Western Australia and the Northern Territory, and you can be fined up to $700 for using one in other states (it will also be confiscated). However, they are in widespread use throughout Australia. If an oncoming vehicle flashes his headlights at you, it may be that he has spotted a radar trap and is trying to warn you. If this happens it's wise to slow down if you're exceeding the speed limit.

Marginal offences are usually dealt with by on-the-spot fines, which can run into hundreds of dollars. You can also 'earn' demerit points on your licence and be disqualified from driving for a period. In NSW you receive one demerit point for exceeding the speed limit by less than 15kph/9mph; three demerit points (over 25kph/15mph and below 30kph/18mph); four demerit points (over 30kph/18mph and below 45kph/28mph); and six demerit points and cancellation of your licence for at least three months if you exceed the speed limit by over 45kph/28mph. Over Christmas and New Year 1997-98, double demerit points were introduced in NSW to deter speeding drivers and anyone caught driving at 30kmh (18mph) above the limit automatically lost his licence for one month. Driving more than 45kmh/28mph above the speed limit is considered dangerous driving and if it results in an accident causing injury or death the penalties can be severe (e.g. up to 10 years' imprisonment in NSW).

GARAGES & SERVICING

When buying (or importing) a car into Australia, you should bear in mind the local service facilities, as not all cars can be easily serviced. All the major European and Japanese manufacturers are well represented, but garages servicing American and exotic European cars are few and far between. If you drive a 'rare' car, it's advisable to carry a basic selection of spare parts, as service stations in Australia may not stock them and you may need to wait several weeks for them to be sent from overseas. Most garages are open from around 7.30am to 6.30pm, Monday to Friday. Small garages and workshops are cheaper, although the quality of work is variable and it's best to choose one which has been personally recommended. Ask your friends and colleagues if they can recommend a garage close to your home or workplace. Note, however, that if anything goes wrong (and it often does), you'll have a better chance of redress with a main dealer, or a garage that's a member of a trade association or approved by a motoring organisation. When a car is under warranty it must usually be regularly serviced (at the recommended service intervals) by an approved dealer in order not to invalidate the warranty. Servicing and repairs at main dealers is expensive, particularly for imported cars.

Always obtain a number of quotations for major mechanical work or body repairs and tell the garage if an accident repair is to be paid for privately, as they may increase the price when an insurance company is paying. Quotations for accident repairs usually vary wildly and some garages include the replacement of unnecessary parts. Always get a second opinion if you're quoted a high price for a repair, e.g. by simply ringing an approved dealer. Poor workmanship and overcharging by garages are the biggest concerns for motorists in Australia and generate the most consumer complaints. Always instruct a garage what to do in writing and for anything other than a standard service, get a written estimate that includes labour and parts. Ask the garage to contact you (give them a phone number) to obtain approval before doing anything that isn't listed or if the cost is likely to exceed the original estimate.

Many garages, including most main dealers, will provide a replacement 'rental' car while yours is being serviced, although you must book in advance and arrange comprehensive insurance. Some garages will collect your car from your home or office and deliver it after the service, or alternatively will drop you off at a railway station or local town and pick you up there when your car is ready for collection.

ROAD MAPS

Among the best road maps available in Australia are those produced by the major oil companies, obtainable from petrol stations. Good maps are also published by local Roads and Traffic Authorities and automobile associations such as the NRMA in NSW (see page 268), which may be free or discounted for members. These are usually cheaper and sometimes better than those produced by oil companies. One of the best 'commercial' maps available is the *Australian Road Atlas* (George Ohip/O'Neil). Free maps of Australia are available from tourist information centres, libraries and car rental companies. A good road map distinguishes between national and state highways and shows the distances between towns and cities and approximate driving times. It should also indicate the state of roads, i.e. whether they are sealed or dirt. Because of the vast distances between towns, a map should also indicate rest points and the distances between them. Street directories (e.g. Gregory's) are published for major cities and are available from bookshops and newsagents. Local town maps are also available from libraries and tourist offices.

CAR RENTAL

The car rental business is extremely competitive in Australia, where there are five nationwide companies (Avis, Budget, Hertz, National and Thrifty) and a plethora of smaller companies. The major companies have offices in cities and towns throughout the country and at most major airports. Nationwide companies provide one-way rental, which means you can rent a car at one branch and leave it at another. Note, however, that there are a number of conditions, they don't usually include Western Australia and the Northern Territory, and it's expensive (around $200 extra). Airlines offer fly-drive deals on flights to or within Australia, which must be booked in advance. Cars can be rented from garages and local car rental companies in most towns, which often have much lower rates than the nationals. Look in local newspapers and under 'Car Rentals' in the yellow pages. Shop around for the best buy as the car rental business is extremely competitive.

There's a wealth of companies in Australia renting old cars such as 'Rent a Ruffy' and 'Rent a Wreck', typically from around $25 a day. However, with insurance and stamp duty you shouldn't count on renting a car for less than $40 a day. You should also beware of cowboy rental companies offering 'rental cars from hell'. Be particularly careful when hiring older cars (cars from major rental companies aren't more than three years old and are usually less than one year old), as they could be in a dangerous condition. If you rent a car in an unroadworthy condition, you're responsible if you're stopped by the police or cause an accident. You may be better off buying an inexpensive vehicle and selling it when you no longer need it (see page 240 and 243).

Rental cars from major companies can often be ordered with a portable telephone, child restraints or a roof rack, for which some charge a fee. All rental cars from national companies are covered for roadside breakdown assistance from a motoring organisation (see page 268). You can also rent a four-wheel drive vehicle, campervan, motorhome, station wagon, minibus, prestige luxury car or a sports car, and a choice of manual or automatic gearbox is often available. Minibuses are also available and are accessible to wheelchairs. Performance cars can be rented from a number of specialist rental companies, although if you want to test drive a car for a few days with a view to buying one, you may get a better deal from a garage. Some companies also rent cars with hand controls for registered disabled drivers.

The rates charged by the national rental companies in major cities are almost identical, with average daily rates of $50 to $60 for a small family car, $75 for a medium-sized car and $100 for a large car. Four-wheel drive vehicles cost from around $100 a day. Smaller local companies are usually cheaper, although you shouldn't automatically assume that this is so, as the major companies offer special deals including standby, weekend (e.g. three days for the price of two), weekly and monthly rates. You may also be able to negotiate a lower rate if business is slow. In some areas where competition is fierce (such as Tasmania), rates are usually lower, particularly in the off-season. Compulsory third party insurance and a collision damage waiver (CDW) are usually included in rates (but check the small print as even with CDW you may be liable in certain circumstances). If CDW isn't paid, you must pay an excess (e.g. $300 to $1,500) which is forfeited if you have an accident. Personal accident insurance is available for an extra charge of around $2.50 a day. Stamp duty of 1 or 1.5 per cent is payable on car rentals.

When comparing prices, take into account all the costs, taxes and surcharges, as what initially looks a bargain may not be when you include all the extras. Unlimited mileage in usually standard in cities, but not always. When travelling in the outback there's a flat daily charge plus a charge per kilometre. Note that rental car insurance doesn't usually cover travel on dirt roads, with the exception of 4WD vehicles. Note that even with a 4WD vehicle, insurance doesn't usually cover off-road travel, i.e. anything that isn't a maintained (sealed or dirt) road. Trips to the outback require special planning (see page 255) and you should consider a four-wheel drive vehicle, although most rental companies expect you to have experience of driving 4WD vehicles before they will rent one to you. If you're planning to travel in rural areas or interstate, you should make sure that the rental includes membership of a local motoring organisation.

You should always check the kilometre restrictions, which may be only 100km to 300km 'free' per day, after which you pay a charge (e.g. 25¢) per km. Most companies restrict travel to sealed roads within 100km to 200km of the rental outlet or within the state or territory where they are rented (although ACT rentals usually cover the whole of New South Wales). If you breach the rules regarding the operating area, your insurance is automatically cancelled! Major companies usually quote different rates for metro (city), country and remote driving.

Campervans can be rented for around $900 a week (2/3 berth), and motorhomes between $1,200 (4 berth) and $1,400 a week (6 berth). Rates vary depending on the season, the period, and the state or territory. Rentals are usually for a minimum of seven days (although four-day rentals are available). The above rates are for peak periods for rentals of less than three weeks and are reduced considerably for off-peak periods and for rentals of three weeks or longer. Rentals must be paid in advance and a bond of around $700 is also payable, but is reduced if comprehensive damage insurance is purchased (daily rate around $30). CDW is around $12 a day and there are also government taxes to pay. Some companies offer older vehicles (e,g, over three years old) at lower rates. There's a surcharge of $10 to $15 a day during December and January (school holidays) for campervans and motorhomes.

Vehicles are usually equipped with air-conditioning, refrigerator, sink, gas stove/grill, wardrobe, convertible beds and a water tank, and some deluxe vehicles also have a shower and toilet. Essential items such as blankets, linen, crockery and cooking utensils are also usually provided. Note that rented campervans and motorhomes may not be used north of Mossman in Queensland or north of Geraldton in Western Australia, and vehicles aren't permitted to travel on unsealed roads, which voids the insurance cover. One-way rentals are possible with some companies, usually between major interstate cities.

To rent a vehicle in Australia you require a full national or international driver's licence, which must have been held for a minimum of two or three years. You must usually be aged over 21 to rent a car, although some companies set the minimum age at 23 or 25 (which usually applies to certain vehicles only such as 4WDs). A major credit card is usually necessary for identification and the estimated costs (including petrol) must be paid in advance. The petrol bond is refunded when a vehicle is returned with a full tank. Without a credit card, the estimated rental charge and a bond of around $200 must be paid in advance, which is returned, less any legitimate deductions. Deposits and insurance excess may range from $500 to $4,000 (in the Northern Territory) depending on the type of car, rental period and company.

Vans and utility vehicles (pick-ups) are available from major rental companies by the hour, half-day or day, or from smaller local companies (which once again, are usually cheaper). You can also rent a caravan, trailer, or a mini-bus, from a number of companies (prices vary with the season). In addition to self-drive car rentals, in many cities you can rent a luxury car with a chauffeur.

MOTORING ORGANISATIONS

There are motoring organisation in all Australian states and territories. The Australian Automobile Association (AAA) is the only national motoring organisation in Australia, which operates as an umbrella organisation for motoring organisations in individual states and territories. It provides no services to individual motorists and any requests must be directed to local organisations. The AAA publishes a booklet entitled *Motoring in Australia*. Some 75 per cent of Australian motorists are members of a motoring organisation, one of the highest rates in the world. The largest is the National Roads and Motoring Association (NRMA) in New South Wales, with almost 2m members.

There are few essential differences between the basic services provided by Australian motoring organisations, although membership costs vary. The primary service of motoring organisations is to provide emergency assistance in the event of an accident or breakdown. Most organisations offer different membership levels providing different levels of service, which usually include towing and vehicle recovery, free public transport or a rental car, home start and legal advice. Motoring organisations provide a fast and efficient service, usually arriving within one hour of notification of a breakdown. Note that a vehicle is covered (irrespective of the driver) and not the individual. The larger organisations offer both national and international accident or breakdown cover for no extra charge.

All organisations charge a joining fee and an annual membership fee, for example the NRMA (NSW) has a $40 joining fee and standard membership fee of $46 a year or $92 a year fee for the expanded NRMA plus service. Fees are similar in other states and territories. NRMA plus provides additional services including emergency accommodation, passenger transport, replacement rental car, vehicle transport and extended towing service (up to a maximum cost of $2,000). In this case you must be over 100km from your home and the breakdown or accident damage must take at least 24 hours to repair.

All organisations offer additional services which may include free publications; international driving permits; international camping cards; travel services; private clubs; crash repair centres; driving schools; holiday centres; road maps and itineraries; weather and road conditions; accommodation guides; car and household insurance (motoring organisations are among Australia's largest insurers); vehicle inspection and technical advice; legal advice; and emergency accommodation. Some motoring organisations (e.g. the NRMA) are expanding into financial services, ranging from home loans to cheque books, superannuation to cash management accounts.

If you break down, call the local motoring organisation by phoning a 24-hour service telephone number for assistance. Keep your membership card in your car and quote your membership number when calling for help. There are emergency telephones every kilometre on Australian freeways for calling for assistance from local motoring organisations. Non-members can also get assistance, but it can be expensive. Members of foreign motoring organisations (affiliated to the AAA) who break down anywhere in Australia can obtain free breakdown assistance from Australian organisations, plus free maps and accommodation directories at members' rates (on production of your membership card). Most Australian organisations also have reciprocal arrangements with motoring organisations in other countries (for when you're driving overseas).

The addresses and telephone numbers of Australian motoring organisations are listed in **Appendix A**.

PARKING

Parking in most Australian cities and towns is often a problem and can be a nightmare. On-street parking is a particular problem and most streets without parking meters or bays have restricted or prohibited parking. There's a distinct lack of short-term parking in the central areas of major cities, particularly Sydney and Melbourne. Australian companies don't usually provide employees with free parking facilities in large cities and towns, so check in advance whether parking is available at your workplace (if it isn't, it could be *very* expensive). Outside cities and towns, parking is usually available at offices and factories. In many areas there are 'park and ride' parking areas, where parking and/or public transport into the local city may be free, and there's also free parking at some suburban railway stations in major cities. Parking in public car parks and at meters is usually free on Sundays and public holidays (check the notice *before* buying a ticket). Many cities and towns produce car park maps showing all parking areas, available free from council offices, libraries and tourist offices.

There are numerous restricted on-street stopping and parking areas in cities and towns, each with it's own particular regulations, including the following:

No Parking. This means you must not stop a vehicle except to pick up or unload goods or passengers.

No Standing. This sign means that you may not stop your vehicle except to pick up or set down passengers.

No Stopping. Here you may not stop for any reason except in an emergency.

Hourly or Two Hour Parking. In these areas you're permitted to park free of charge only for the period shown (one or two hours) during certain hours on certain days, shown on a sign. Outside of these limits there are no restrictions.

Resident Parking. If you have a Resident Parking Authority you may park free of charge without restrictions (even where there are meters), otherwise you're limited to the time shown on a sign and, if applicable, must pay a fee.

Clearway. These are used to limit parking on major arteries during rush hours (the restrictions are shown on signs). The only exceptions are buses and taxis, which are permitted to pick up and set down passengers.

Taxi Stand. Only taxis may occupy taxi stands during the period posted.

Bus Zone. Only buses are allowed to stop in a bus zone to pick up and set down passengers.

Loading Zone. Only commercial vehicles loading and unloading goods may stop in a loading zone, e.g. for a maximum of 30 minutes.

Construction Zone. These areas are restricted to trucks delivering materials at construction sites. Picking up and setting down passengers is permitted.

Truck Zone. Only goods vehicles that are being loaded and unloaded may stop in these zones during the time shown on the sign.

Disabled Parking. A disabled driver (or a vehicle carrying a disabled person) with a current Disabled Persons's Parking Authority (available from local council offices) can park in special parking spaces allocated to disabled drivers in towns and cities. Mobility maps showing parking areas for the disabled are available from local councils.

Road Markings: On-road parking restrictions in Australia are often indicated by yellow lines at the edge of roads, usually accompanied by a sign indicating when parking is prohibited, e.g. 'Mon-Sat 8 am-6.30 pm' or 'At any time'. If no days are indicated on the sign, restrictions are in force every day including public holidays and Sundays. Yellow lines give a guide to the restrictions in force, but the signs must always be consulted.

Off-Road Car Parks: In most towns there are public (council) and private off-road car parks, indicated by a sign showing a white 'P' on a blue background. Off-street car parks (parking stations) in city centres are expensive and charge around $3 or $3.50 for half an hour. The method of payment in off-road car parks varies. On entering most private car parks you collect a ticket from an automatic dispenser (you may need to press a button) and pay either *before* collecting your car (at a cash desk or in a machine, which may accept both coins and notes), or in an automatic machine at the exit (keep some coins handy). Some machines don't issue you with a ticket with which to exit the car park, and after paying you must exchange your ticket at a special kiosk for yet another ticket. If you've already paid, you insert your ticket in the slot of the exit machine (in the direction shown by the arrow on the ticket).

Some multi-storey car parks are pay-and-display (see below), where you must decide in advance how many hours parking you require and buy a ticket from a machine for this period. When parking in multi-storey car parks, make a note of the level and space number where you park your car, as it can take a long time to find your car if you have no idea where to start looking. When parking at shopping centres in some cities, your parking fee may be reduced depending on the amount you spend. Out of town supermarkets and shopping centres provide free parking, which is a major attraction to shoppers (and car thieves!). Take care in car parks as accidents often occur there and you may not be covered by your car insurance.

Parking meters: The maximum permitted parking period usually varies from 30 minutes to two hours. Meter-feeding is illegal. You must vacate the parking space when the meter time expires, even if it was under the maximum time allowed, and you may not move to another meter in the same group. Meters normally accept a variety of coins and are usually in operation from 8am until 6.30pm, Monday to Saturday (check meters to be certain). Meter fees vary considerably. Some cities have sharply increased fees in recent years, e.g. Melbourne raised the two-hour fee from $1.20 to $4 ($1 for half an hour). Note that where there are double meters, you feed the one on the side where you're parked. Don't park at meters which are suspended, as you can be towed away. As in most other countries, parking wardens are among the most abused people in Australia. They mark your tyres with the time in white chalk and if you exceed the permitted (or paid for) period they (gleefully) give you a ticket.

Pay-and-Display: parking areas where you must buy a parking ticket from a machine and display it behind your windscreen. It may have an adhesive backing which you can peel off and use to stick the ticket to your windscreen or car window. When you have inserted sufficient coins for the period required, press the button to receive your ticket. Pay-and-Display parking areas usually operate from around 8am until 6.30pm, excluding Sundays and public holidays. There's a voucher system in use in some cities, although this is being replaced by pay-and-display.

Parking Fines: The fine for illegal parking depends on where you park and is usually from $20 to $60. Parking in a dangerous position or near a pedestrian crossing usually results in a higher fine than simply parking illegally, although parking offences don't usually result in licence demerit points (see page 244). If fines are not paid within the specified period, they are usually increased and it may be necessary to go to court. In certain areas you shouldn't even *think* about parking illegally, as your car will be towed away in the blink of an eye. You must then pay a parking fine and towing fee, plus a daily storage fee after the first 24 hours (so don't leave your car there too long). A car pound won't release your car until you've paid and may only accept cash. You cannot be towed away from a pay-and-display area or a parking meter unless the parking bay is suspended. Clamping is illegal in Australia (hurrah!).

Whether parking restrictions exist or not, when parking on a road be careful where you park, as you can be prosecuted for parking in a dangerous position and could also cause an accident. If your parked car contributes to an accident, you may also have to pay damages. In a two-way street, it's usually illegal to park on the right hand side of the road facing oncoming traffic. When parking, you must usually (by law) leave around one metre (front and back) between your car and others, and in an official parking area always ensure that you're parked within a marked bay (otherwise you can receive a parking ticket). Parking on footpaths is illegal everywhere. Note that using your hazard warning lights when parking makes no difference if you're parked illegally. Wherever you drive in Australia, keep a plentiful supply of coins handy for parking and pay-and-display meters. When parking in the sun it's advisable to place a heat deflector behind your windscreen (otherwise the steering wheel and gear lever will be too hot to touch after a short time).

12.

HEALTH

Australia is among the most advanced countries in the field of medicine and is noted for its highly-trained medical staff and modern hospitals equipped with the latest high-tech apparatus. Health care services in Australia are provided by both government (including Commonwealth, state, territory and local governments) and private organisations. The country spends around 9 per cent of its GDP on health care (compared with some 15 per cent in the USA), which is about average for OECD countries. Despite the rising cost of modern medicine, with its astronomically expensive equipment to diagnose and treat illnesses such as cancer and heart disease, costs have largely been contained in the last 15 years (although in 1998, both Medicare and health funds were facing a funding cricis). In recent years there has been a growing emphasis on preventive medicine and community care, including education programs to promote a healthy lifestyle. Two yardsticks used to measure the quality of health care are the infant mortality rate (around six deaths for every one thousand live births) and life expectancy (81 for women and 75 for men), both of which rate Australia among the 'best' in the world.

Australia has a national health system (Medicare) which provides free or subsidised medical care and free hospital treatment in public hospitals for all permanent residents (plus certain visitors) irrespective of their age, income or health status. The public health system is supplemented by a wide variety of private practitioners, hospitals and clinics, plus a range of voluntary agencies and non-profit organisations. Alternative medicine and natural remedies are popular in Australia, where acupuncture, homeopathy, chiropractic, osteopathy, physiotherapy and naturopathy thrive. Health facilities and doctors are unevenly distributed in Australia, with the major cities and urban areas having a huge over-supply of GPs, while in most country areas there's a shortage, particularly in the Northern Territory and Western Australia. Trying to encourage doctors to relocate from the major cities to remote country and outback areas is a major problem, which the government is trying to address by importing migrant doctors specifically to work in country areas. The Royal Flying Doctor Service provides medical services in remote country areas and evacuates urgent cases to hospital.

The Nation's Health: Australians are generally healthier than they were 20 years ago, due to a decrease in smoking and drinking and an improved diet (although Australia's love affair with junk food and red meat is largely undiminished). The amount of exercise Australians take is generally low and over half the adult population is either obese or overweight and a quarter of children are overweight to the point of being classified as obese (many children also have eating disorders and anorexia). Stress-related problems (often due to over-work or lack of sleep) are an increasing problem in Australia's cities and the country has a relatively high suicide rate, particularly among the young and the over 65s. Voluntary euthanasia is a topical subject in Australia, particularly since the world's first voluntary euthanasia law was passed in 1995 in the Northern Territory. This was subsequently overturned in 1997 by the federal government after four people had been medically assisted to die. In most states, patients can refuse life-sustaining treatment, but doctors cannot assist them to die (although in reality many doctors do assist terminally-ill patients).

The biggest killers in Australia are cancer (the cause of some 30 per cent of deaths), heart disease (e.g. strokes) and smoking-related illnesses. Alcoholism is fairly widespread as is drug addiction, which is a serious and increasing problem. The country has an unusually high degree of diabetes and is expected to have around one million sufferers by the year 2000. There are special health programs in Australia for Aboriginals and Torres Strait Islanders, many of whom have acute health problems (often related to alcohol abuse and poor diet) and a much lower life expectancy than other Australians.

Virulent flu (influenza) strains are a widespread problem and directly or indirectly kill some 1,500 people a year and affect as many as 30 per cent of the population (flu vaccinations are recommended for those aged over 65). Miscellaneous health problems in recent years have included outbreaks of salmonella poisoning (from cooked meats), hepatitis C (a life-threatening infection transmitted mostly by intravenous drug users), legionnaire's disease, dengue fever and meningococcal disease. Air pollution caused by high smog levels is an increasing problem in Australia's cities, particularly Sydney (where pollution is higher than London, New York or Tokyo) and Melbourne, where asthmatics, bronchitis sufferers and the elderly are particularly at risk. Sydney is reportedly the allergy capital of the world due to its numerous plants that send out pollens on breezy spring days.

Skin Cancer: Skin cancer is a major problem in Australia, which has the highest rate of melanoma in the world (although cases are reducing as people take heed of warnings). If you aren't used to Australia's fierce sun you should limit your exposure and avoid it altogether during the hottest part of the day (between around 10am and 3pm), wear protective clothing (including a hat) and use a sunscreen. Those with fair skin should take extra care, as it can take only 15 minutes to get burnt on a hot summer's day. The governments slogan in the battle against skin cancer is 'Slip, Slop, Slap': Slip (on a shirt), Slop (on sunscreen), Slap (on a hat). This is backed by a 'SunSmart' campaign begun in 1987 which is particularly targeted at teenagers. It's important to use a sunscreen with a high protection factor, e.g. a pH 15+ broad-spectrum, water-resistant sunscreen (even stronger sunscreens with a protection factor of 30 plus are now available).

Too much sun and too little protection dries your skin and causes premature aging, so care should be taken to replace the skin's natural oils (many Australian women in their 20s and 30s have the skin of people 20 or 30 years older). Medical experts recommend the wearing of good quality sunglasses, e.g. with UV400 polycarbonate lenses, to protect against eye cancer and other eye problems caused by the sun. Hikers should wear legionnaire or Arab style hats with neck flaps. Children are particularly vulnerable and should wear wide-brimmed hats in the sun and a T-shirt when swimming. Those who live the outdoor life (such as sports men and women) are particularly at risk and should follow the example of Australian cricketers and wear total block-out zinc cream on exposed areas when spending a long time in the sun. Drink plenty of water when in the sun to prevent dehydration (in extreme heat you should drink a litre every hour), and avoid excess alcohol and over-exertion (particularly if you're elderly). Other problems associated with too much sun include sunburn, heat exhaustion, sunstroke, prickly heat and fungal infections.

Wildlife: Australia has some of the deadliest creatures in the world including a plethora of poisonous snakes (e.g. the brown, black, yellow whip, tiger, death adder and the western taipan), venomous spiders (e.g. red-back, trap-door and funnel-web), scorpions, crocodiles, sharks, jellyfish, sea snakes, stonefish, catfish and assorted other unpleasant marine life, many of which can deliver a fatal sting. Note that although you're unlikely to have a close encounter with most of Australia's wildlife (unless you venture into the bush or the sea on unprotected beaches), many poisonous snakes can be found in suburban parks and gardens and near water courses. You should avoid undergrowth and country areas unless you're wearing protective clothing (i.e. not thongs or shorts) and try to avoid disturbing wildlife. Insects (e.g. mosquitos, ticks and wasps) are also a problem in many areas, although they are unlikely to kill you. Children are taught at school to recognise and avoid dangerous wildlife.

Immunisation: Child immunisation is a problem in Australia, where around 45 per cent of children aren't fully immunised against diseases such as whooping cough, tetanus and diphtheria, resulting in many unnecessary deaths. Many parents are concerned about the side effects, although these are tiny compared to the risks posed by the diseases. A further drawback in the campaign to immunise children is that in future parents may need to pay for shots, whereas in the past they were free. The government has proposed preventing children from enrolling in school (as in the USA and other countries) and reducing parents' benefits such as the maternity allowance and childcare assistance payment, if children aren't immunised. Children should have six sets of injections between the age of two months and four years in order to be fully immunised against diphtheria, tetanus, whooping cough, poliomyelitis, Hib, measles, mumps and rubella. Children aged between 10 and 19 years also need booster shots for most of these diseases. Immunisations can be provided by your family doctor, an immunisation clinic, local authorities and some public hospitals. An immunisation register was established on 1st January 1996 to record details of all immunisations given to children up to six years of age. From 1st January 1998, parents who fail to immunise their children will lose $200 in maternity allowance.

The Disabled: Australia provides better than average facilities for the disabled. General information is available from the National Information Communication Awareness Network (NICAN), PO Box 407, Curtin, ACT 2605 (tel. (02) 6285 3713) and the Australian Council for the Rehabilitation of the Disabled (ACROD), PO Box 60, Curtin, ACT 2605 (tel. (02) 6282 4333). All capital cities and most regional centres produce mobility maps showing accessible paths, parking and toilets for those with mobility difficulties, and nationwide facilities are listed in *Easy Access Australia - A Travel Guide to Australia.* Note, however, that accommodation and support services for the disabled are relatively poor in Australia. Many councils provide a directory of services for people with disabilities and for older residents.

You can safely drink the water in Australia, although the (red) wine tastes much better and taken in moderation even does you good (if you believe the winegrowers it isn't alcohol but medicine!).

EMERGENCIES

The action to take in a medical 'emergency' depends on the degree of urgency. If you're unsure who to call, ask the telephone operator (dial 1234) or call your local police station (N.B. a mobile phone can be a lifesaver in a remote area or when you need help and are on your own). They will tell you who to contact or even call the appropriate service for you. Whoever you call, always give the age of the patient and, if possible, specify the type of emergency. **Keep a record of the telephone numbers of your doctor, local hospitals and clinics, ambulance service, dentist and other emergency services, next to your telephone.**

* Dial 000 for an ambulance without a doctor (but usually with a paramedic) in **an emergency only**. Many ambulances are equipped with cardiac, oxygen and other emergency equipment (called intensive care ambulances). Ambulance services aren't covered by Medicare, although you can become a member of the St. John's Ambulance Association for around $15 a year in most cities, which entitles you to free ambulance services. Private health insurance may include ambulance costs. There are air ambulances (helicopters) in some cities.

* Remote outback areas are served by the flying doctor service, established as a non-profit organisation in 1927 and funded by the federal government and voluntary

contributions. The service covers some 80 per cent of outback areas from 12 main bases which ensure that most patients are less than two hours from medical help. Services includes regular clinic visits to remote communities, visits by specialists and, in some areas, dentists. The service also offers advice on touring and emergency procedures (travellers in remote areas can rent a transceiver set with emergency call buttons). For more information contact the Royal Flying Doctor Service of Australia, Federal Office, Level 6, 43 Bridge Street, Hurstville, NSW 2200 (tel. (02) 9580 9711).

• In minor emergencies or for medical advice, you should phone your family doctor if you have one. Failing this you can ask the operator (1234) for the telephone number of a local doctor or hospital (or consult your phone book). Police stations keep a list of doctors' and chemists' private telephone numbers, in case of emergency. In some cities and regions there are private, 24-hour, doctor services that make house calls (but check the cost before using them).

• If you're physically able, you can go to the Accident, Casualty or Emergency department of a public hospital, many of which provide a 24-hour service. Check in advance which local hospitals are equipped to deal with emergencies and the quickest route from your home. This information may be of vital importance in the event of an emergency, when a delay could mean the difference between life and death. Emergency cases, irrespective of nationality and the ability to pay, are *never* turned away in Australia and treatment may be free if you're a national of a country with a reciprocal health agreement with Australia (see page 292).

• If you have an emergency dental problem outside normal surgery hours, call a dentist providing an emergency service (listed in yellow pages).

MEDICARE

Medicare is the name of the national health service in Australia, established in 1984. It provides free treatment for public patients in public hospitals and free or subsidised treatment by doctors (including specialists), optometrists and dentists for specific services. All permanent residents of Australia are eligible to join Medicare and restricted access is also granted to citizens of certain countries with which Australia has a reciprocal health care agreement (see page 292). If you're working in Australia you're automatically covered for injuries or illness as a result of an accident by compulsory workers' compensation insurance (see page 60).

Contributions: Medicare is partly funded (less than 20 per cent) by a 1.5 per cent levy on taxable income (above $13,127) and by general taxation. Medicare benefits cost some $6 billion in 1996/97. The levy was increased from 1.5 to 1.7 per cent in 1996 to compensate gun-owners forced to give up their weapons under new laws (a novel way to raise taxes, see **Crime** on page 442), but returned to 1.5 per cent from 1st July 1977. In an effort to encourage (coerce) high earners to take out private health insurance, the levy was increased in 1996 by 1 per cent for single people earning over $50,000 a year and couples earning over $100,000 a year. If you're self-employed, the levy is included in your annual assessment. Certain people are exempt from paying the levy including single people on incomes below $13,127 (if your income is between $13,128 and $14,347 your levy is 20¢ for every dollar above $13,127), couples and sole parents earning below $22,152 (increasing by $2,100 for each child), pensioners with a pensioner concession card or a Commonwealth seniors health card, war veterans and widows, and defence force personnel without dependants. Couples and sole parents on low incomes (below $24,309 plus $2,295 for each child) are entitled to a reduction in their Medicare levy. The unemployed and dependants have automatic deductions made from their unemployment benefits or other allowances.

Enrolment: It's advisable to enrol in Medicare as soon as possible after your arrival in Australia, although it isn't necessary until you use the system as you can join retrospectively, i.e. you can claim a refund of previous medical expenses after joining Medicare. You can apply in person at a Medicare office in Australia or you can ring 132011 (local call cost) and have an application form sent to you. You can also obtain an application form from a post office. You're required to show proof of eligibility, e.g. your passport with a residence stamp, if you're a permanent resident. Applicants must also provide details of their residence, income and assets.

You receive a plastic Medicare card (green and gold) by post around two to three weeks after applying, which contains your Medicare membership number, address, the names of all dependants (e.g. spouse and children) entitled to use the card, and its expiry date. The card has a signature strip on the back and must be signed immediately. If you receive treatment before you obtain your card you will have to pay in full and claim a refund, or delay payment until you get your card. There's a three month waiting period before claims are met for new members. Cards are valid for five years, although you must obtain a replacement card if you change your address or other details on the card change (e.g. your family increases in size). The card can be used to:

* receive a cash benefit at a Medicare customer service centre;
* quote your Medicare number when making enquiries or a claim;
* receive treatment (without payment) from a doctor or optometrist who bulk-bills Medicare;
* obtain free hospital treatment in a public hospital.

Medicare *provides* benefits for the following:

* doctor's consultation fees including treatment by specialists (when referred by a GP);
* X-rays, pathology tests, other medical tests, examinations and certain surgical procedures (listed in the Medicare Benefits Schedule);
* eye tests performed by an optometrist;
* some surgical procedures performed by dentists registered with Medicare;
* specified items under the Cleft Lip and Palate Scheme;
* all associated treatment costs when you're treated as a public (Medicare) patient in a public hospital.

Medicare *doesn't* cover the following:

* private patient costs, e.g. theatre fees or accommodation;
* dental examinations and treatment (although certain essential dental surgery is covered);
* ambulance services;
* home nursing;
* physiotherapy, occupational therapy, speech and eye therapy, chiropractic, podiatry, and psychology;

* acupuncture (unless treatment is provided by a doctor);
* spectacles and contact lenses;
* hearing aids and other appliances;
* the cost of prostheses;
* medicines;
* medical and hospital costs incurred overseas.

Medicare also doesn't include medical treatment that isn't immediately necessary; elective surgery or hospital treatment that isn't of an essential nature; treatment arranged before arriving in Australia; accommodation and medical treatment in a private hospital; accommodation and medical treatment as a private patient in a public hospital; and medical repatriation or funeral costs. Medicare also doesn't cover situations where someone else is responsible for medical costs (e.g. a compensation insurer, an employer or a government authority); medical services which aren't clinically necessary; surgery solely for cosmetic reasons; mass immunisations; and examinations for life insurance, superannuation or membership of a friendly society. If you receive treatment under Medicare for an injury or accident which is subject to compensation by a third party such as an insurance company or workers' compensation, the insurer must reimburse Medicare for any benefits related to the injury before making any payments to you. You're usually required to indicate whether this is the position when making a claim.

Schedule Fee: The benefits provided by Medicare are based on a schedule of fees, the Medicare Benefits Schedule (MBS), set by the Commonwealth government, which are increased annually at half the rate of inflation. When a doctor charges more than the scheduled fee, patients must meet the additional cost. Medicare pays 85 per cent of the schedule fee or the schedule fee less an amount of up to $50 (adjusted annually on 1st November), whichever is the larger amount. The remaining 15 per cent, the difference between what Medicare pays and the Schedule Fee, is called the 'gap' amount. The unfunded gap can be covered by private health insurance (see page 306).

Medicare Safety Net: Those who require frequent treatment are protected from high costs by a Medicare safety net. When you (or your family members) have paid 'gap' contributions amounting to a total of $276.80 (adjusted annually on 1st January) in a 'Medicare' financial year (from 1st July to 30th June), benefits are increased to 100 per cent. Note that if your GP charges more than the schedule fee, the extra amount doesn't count towards the safety net (the gap amount for in-hospital services also doesn't count towards the safety net). It isn't necessary for individuals to register for the safety net, as Medicare keeps a record of gap amounts and the higher (100 per cent) benefits apply automatically as soon as the limit is reached. However, families (even when listed on one Medicare card) need to complete a 'Medicare Safety Net Registration Form' available from Medicare and take or send the completed form to a Medicare customer service centre. A family includes a spouse (or *de facto* spouse), children under 16 in your care and dependant full-time students aged under 25. It's important to register your family as soon as possible, as you receive 100 per cent of the schedule fee for a service only after you have registered for the safety net, i.e. it isn't paid retrospectively.

Bulk-Billing: Bulk-billing (also called direct-billing) is where a doctor (or optometrist) doesn't charge the patient, but the patient assigns his right to benefits to the doctor who bills Medicare directly. When a doctor bulk-bills you will be asked to complete a form after the service, of which you receive a copy. You don't need to pay anything and aren't required to make a claim to Medicare. Most doctors and specialists bulk-bill at least some of their patients, such as pensioners and health card holders. Some 80 per cent of visits to GPs are bulk-billed, where the GP bills Medicare at $20.85 for each standard consultation. However, GPs are not happy with the rebate schedule and want increased rebates, which have fallen in real terms in recent years. A doctor's remuneration is exactly the same per patient whether he spends six or 66 minutes with a patient, which are both classed as standard consultations. The standard length of a consultation (based on the schedule fee) is around six minutes, which encourages doctors to rush through consultations, derisively referred to as 'six-minute' or 'stop-watch' medicine. In order to give patients' the time they require, GPs would (not surprisingly) prefer to be paid for the time spent with patients.

Around half of Australia's GPs charge some patients extra (the average is around $9) on top of the government rebate. The Australian Medical Association (AMA) recommends a fee of $36 for a consultation of as little as five minutes, and many doctors who don't bulk-bill patients charge all or some patients up to $15 for a standard consultation, i.e. $15 above the amount they receive from Medicare. This has led to a two-tier system, with in some cases, fee-free patients (such as pensioners) having to wait days to see their GP.

Claims: If your doctor or optometrist doesn't bulk-bill, he will give you a bill for his services. You can either pay the bill and claim a refund from Medicare or send the bill to your local Medicare office with a claim's form. If you send the bill to Medicare you will receive a Medicare cheque made out to the practitioner, which you give to him plus the balance ('gap') payable by you (if any). Claims can be made by mail (addressed to Medicare, GPO Box 9822 in your state's capital city) or in person with a completed claims form and the original bills or receipts for payments. If you make a claim in person and have paid for treatment, you will receive a cash refund (a cash limit applies). Always take your Medicare card with you when attending a Medicare office. Claims made by mail are paid by cheque (you can also drop your claim's form in the box provided at Medicare offices, when you will also be refunded by cheque). Electronic lodgment of Medicare claims was introduced in 1997 and enables members to use their Medicare cards in EFTPOS-style machines (like bank ATMs) aimed at reducing delays in payments and improving access to Medicare for people living in rural and remote areas.

Retiree's: Retirees who aren't in receipt of a social security or veterans' affairs pension and whose income is below the pension cut-off point, may qualify for a range of free and concessionary health services. Retirees can apply for a Commonwealth Seniors Health Card (contact the Social Security Teleservice on 132468) and receive the following concessions:

* prescriptions at $3.20 each for medicines and drugs listed on the Pharmaceuticals Benefits Scheme (PBS), although where a particular brand charges a premium you could pay much more;

* free hearing aids through the Australian Hearing Services (tel. frecall 1800-813 762) plus an annual maintenance fee of $25;

* free general and emergency dental treatment under the Commonwealth Dental Health Program.

Restrictions/Ineligibility: Note that foreign retirees with a temporary visa (see page 96) aren't covered by Medicare and must take out private health insurance. Foreign diplomats and their families also aren't covered by Medicare. Medical expenses incurred by men aged over 55 and women aged over 51 who have been sponsored in the family reunion migration category are the responsibility of their sponsor for 10 years or until they reach retirement age.

Uncertain Future: As in many other countries, the rising cost of health care and health insurance has created severe problems for Medicare, which is over-worked, under-resourced and facing a funding crisis. It's also burdened by the increasing life expectancy of Australians (around 12 per cent of the population is aged 65 or older, which is expected to double by the year 2050). In recent years the cost of private health insurance, which usually supplements rather than replaces Medicare, has increased sharply and has led to people abandoning private health insurance in droves (thus adding to the burdens of Medicare). Before Medicare was introduced in 1984, some two-thirds of Australians had private cover, which has since fallen to less than a third. Many people believe that Australia now has a two-tier health system, with a costly private health sector with all the 'bells and whistles' for those who can afford it, and a neglected second-rate public system for those who cannot. However, there's little evidence that you get better health care in a private rather than a public hospital.

Many public hospitals are cash-starved and cannot cope with the demand, and even emergency patients are being refused admittance at some public hospitals. An increasing strain on services (particularly from the elderly) is leading to a crisis in public hospitals, many of which have a shortage of nursing staff and doctors. Although most urgent cases are admitted within 30 days, there are long waiting lists for elective surgery under Medicare and non-urgent cases may need to wait up to a year for admission. The public perception is that the quality of public health care has fallen in recent years, although patients who use it generally rate it highly. Common complaints include high costs, poor hospital service, concern over gap payments, insufficient Medicare cover, and confusion over how the system works. Many families would like to have private health insurance but find that it's unaffordable.

General information about Medicare in English is available from the Medicare Information Service (tel. 13 2011) and information in other languages is available from the Medicare Multilingual Telephone Information Service (131202).

PRIVATE HEALTH SERVICES

Private health treatment functions both within Medicare and independently of it, and most public hospitals admit private patients. In addition to specialist appointments and hospital treatment, people most commonly use private health services to obtain second opinions, private health checks or screening, and for complementary medicine such as acupuncture, chiropractic, homeopathy, naturopathy, osteopathy and physiotherapy (which aren't usually covered by Medicare or private health insurance). Around one-third of Australians have private health insurance, which is usually complementary insurance, so named because it complements rather than replaces Medicare. It's commonly used to pay the difference ('gap') between the Medicare schedule fee and what Medicare actually pays. The principal reason most people have private health insurance in Australia is to circumvent the Medicare waiting lists for specialist appointments and non-emergency hospital treatment. Private patients are usually free to choose their own doctor and hospital, and may be accommodated in a single hotel-style room with a radio, telephone, colour TV, *en suite* bathroom and room service, depending on their policy.

With the deterioration of Medicare services and lengthening waiting lists, you're strongly advised to consider taking out private health insurance, which will ensure you always receive the medical treatment you need, when you need it. Note, however, that the quality of private treatment isn't better than that provided by Medicare and you shouldn't assume that because a doctor (or any other medical practitioner) is in private practice, he's more competent than his Medicare counterpart. In fact you will often see the same specialist or be treated by the same surgeon under Medicare as privately. For information about private health insurance see page 306.

DOCTORS

There are excellent family doctors throughout Australia, who are generally referred to as General Practitioners (GPs). The best way to find a doctor, whether as a Medicare or private patient, is to ask your colleagues, friends or neighbours if they can recommend someone. There's a glut of doctors in most cities and metropolitan areas, and an acute shortage (of around 1,000 GPs) in many rural areas, where the ratio of doctors to population is less than half the national average. Therefore in rural areas or the outback (where you're also served by the Royal Flying Doctor Service) you may need to travel some distance to visit a doctor. The shortage has led the government to introduce a scheme to attract foreign doctors (on temporary work visas) to practise in rural areas (around half are from Britain and Ireland). In general, doctors are discouraged from migrating to Australia and receive a points penalty when being assessed.

Medicare Doctors: It isn't necessary to be registered with a doctor in Australia and you can choose to visit any doctor, either as a Medicare patient (providing the doctor is registered with Medicare) or a private patient. If you wish to be treated as a Medicare patient, you must check whether a doctor charges the schedule fee ($20.85) for consultations and bulk bills Medicare or whether he levies an extra charge (which may be $15 or more for a consultation). Note that many doctors now levy a fee and in some areas you may have difficulty finding a doctor who doesn't (although pensioners and health care card holders are usually exempt). Some doctors levy a 'co-operative charge' (e.g. $2.50) to discourage frivolous visits. The low remuneration paid to doctors by Medicare encourages doctors to rush consultations (referred to as 'six-minute' or 'stop-watch' medicine). If you're concerned that your doctor doesn't allow sufficient time to do a thorough examination, you should change doctors, although you may need to choose one who charges an additional fee. If you wish to see a GP privately, you (or your insurance company) must pay the full fee, which is left to the doctor's discretion. You should expect to pay around $36 or more for a routine visit to a GP.

Choosing a Doctor: It's advisable to enquire in advance (e.g. by asking a receptionist) whether a doctor has the 'qualifications' you require, for example:

- Is he or she of the right sex?
- Is he easily reached by public transport, if necessary?
- Is it a group practice? This may be preferable to an individual practice, where you may be required to see a locum (replacement) doctor when your doctor is absent (in a group practice, doctors cover for each other outside surgery hours).
- What are the surgery hours (Saturday and evening surgeries may be held)?
- What is the procedure for home visits?
- Does the doctor practise preventive or complementary medicine (e.g. acupuncture)?
- Does the doctor prescribe contraception?
- Does the doctor bulk-bill or does he levy an extra charge?
- If you're a private patient, what does a consultation cost?

Many doctors work at public clinics and medical centres in the suburbs of major cities, where a number of doctors have a group practice, at least one of whom will usually be female (there's a relatively large percentage of women doctors in Australia). Clinics and medical centres usually have an in-house pharmacy and medical tests (such as X-rays, and blood and urine analysis) may also be conducted in-house.

Surgery Hours: Surgery hours vary, but are typically from 8.30am to 6 or 7pm, Monday to Friday, with early closing one day a week, e.g. 5 or 5.30pm on Fridays (evening surgeries may also be held on one or two evenings a week). Emergency surgeries may be held on Saturday mornings, e.g. from 8.30am to 11.30am or noon. If you're an urgent case, you will usually be seen immediately, but should still telephone in advance if possible. Most doctors' surgeries have answering machines outside surgery hours, when a recorded message informs you of the name of the doctor on call (or deputising service) and his telephone number.

Appointments: An appointment must be made to see a GP, usually one or two days in advance. If you're an urgent case (but not an emergency), your doctor will usually see you immediately, but you should still phone in advance. Note, however, that surgeries often overrun and you may need to wait well past your appointment time to see a doctor. Australian doctors make house calls, although it can be expensive for private patients.

Specialists: Medicare patients must always be referred by a GP to a specialist, e.g. an eye specialist, gynaecologist or orthopaedic surgeon. If you would like a second opinion on any health matter, you may ask to see a specialist, although unless it's a serious matter your doctor may refuse to refer you. You may, however, be able to convince another doctor to refer you or you can consult a specialist as a private patient. Patients with private health insurance may be free to make appointments directly with specialists, although most insurance companies prefer patients to be referred by GPs. Note that most specialists have long waiting lists for Medicare patients.

Your GP can provide advice and information on any aspect of health or medical after-care, including preventive medicine, blood donations, home medical equipment and special counselling. If you're a Medicare patient, he should also be able to advise you about the range of medical benefits provided under Medicare, including immunisation, maternity care, contraceptive help and psychiatric treatment.

Note that patients in Australia have no legal right to see their medical records, as in many other countries.

DRUGS & MEDICINES

Medicines and drugs are obtained from a chemist (pharmacy) in Australia, which also provide free advice concerning 'minor' ailments and recommend appropriate medicines. Many drugs and medicines in Australia can be prescribed only by a doctor via an official form called a prescription (which is written in a secret language decipherable only by doctors and pharmacists). Some drugs and medicines requiring a doctor's prescription in Australia are sold freely in other countries, while certain drugs available over the counter in Australia are controlled in other countries. Over 175m prescriptions are dispensed each year in Australia.

At least one chemist is open in most towns during the evenings and on Sundays for the emergency dispensing of medicines and drugs, and there are 24-hour pharmacies in some cities. A rota is posted on the doors of chemists and published in local newspapers and guides. If you require medicine urgently when chemists are closed, you should contact your GP or the local police station. To obtain medicines prescribed by a doctor, simply take your prescription form to any chemist. Your prescription may be filled immediately if it's available off the shelf or you may be asked to wait or come back later.

The Pharmaceutical Benefits Scheme (PBS) subsidises the cost of around 1,700 necessary and life-saving medicines. Most medicines available on prescription are subsidised under the PBS, so just by having a prescription filled you receive the benefit of the subsidy. PBS medicines are available to all Australian residents and to visitors from countries with which Australia has a reciprocal health care agreement (see page 292). Proof of residency or nationality may be necessary. If you're eligible but unable to provide proof you may be charged the full price for medicines, although you can obtain a refund at a Medicare customer service centre or by posting your claim (plus the receipt and your Medicare card or proof of eligibility) to Medicare, GPO Box 9822 in your capital city. General patients below the safety net and without a concession card (see below) should pay a maximum of $20 towards the cost of each PBS medicine. Note that the cost of non-prescription medicines can vary considerably and if you need a medication regularly, it's worth shopping around. It's possible to buy prescription (and other) medicines by post (post free) at savings of up to 50 per cent from Reply Paid 388, Pharmacy Direct, 388 Victoria Road, Rydalmere, NSW 2116 (tel. freecall 1800-624563) or (02) 9638 3000).

In recent years the government has restricted the prescription of expensive drugs in order to reduce the escalating cost of pharmaceuticals. GPs must now prescribe the cheapest of a particular group of drugs and patients wishing to use a more expensive drug must pay a 'therapeutic premium' (the difference between the government subsidy and the cost of the drug). Patients using commonly prescribed drugs for high blood pressure, cholesterol, depression and ulcers now receive the cheapest of a particular group of drugs. Unless your doctor has ticked a box on the prescription form saying that there's no substitute, you can ask for the lowest-priced brand available and don't need to buy the one prescribed by your doctor. If a medication isn't available under PBS (i.e. is non-prescription), you must pay the entire cost. If you have private health insurance you may be able to reclaim the cost of prescriptions from your insurance company.

PBS Safety Net: If you or your family (spouse or *de facto* spouse, children aged under 16 and dependant full-time students under 25) spend $612.60 (adjusted annually on 1st January) on prescription medicines in a calendar year, you're entitled to receive all additional prescription medicines at the concession rate of $3.20 per item for the remainder of the calendar year. All purchases must be recorded on a Prescription Record form by your pharmacist.

Concession Card: If you have an approved concession card (issued to pensioners, the unemployed, low-income families, war widows and their dependants), you pay $3.20 per prescription until you reach the safety net threshold of $166.40, after which there's no charge for the rest of the year. There's a pharmaceutical allowance for pensioners of $5.40 per fortnight (single or couple combined) or $2.70 per fortnight for a couple where only one partner is eligible.

Foreign Prescriptions: Note that brand names for the same drugs and medicines vary considerably from country to country, so if you regularly take medication overseas, you should ask your doctor for the generic name. If you wish to match medication prescribed overseas in Australia, you need a current prescription with the medication's trade name, the manufacturer's name, the chemical name and the dosage. Most foreign drugs have an equivalent in Australia, although particular brands may be difficult or impossible to obtain. If you're visiting Australia, you may bring a maximum of four weeks' prescription medicines with you. You should also have a doctor's prescription which, after it has been endorsed by an Australian-registered doctor, will allow you to obtain medication in Australia.

Most chemists also sell non-prescription medicines and drugs, toiletries, cosmetics, health foods and cleaning supplies. A health food shop sells health foods, diet foods, homeopathic medicines and eternal-life-virility-youth pills and elixirs, which are quite popular in Australia (even though their claims are often in the realms of fantasy). **Always use, store and dispose of unwanted medicines and poisons safely, e.g. by returning them to a pharmacist or dispensing doctor, and never leave them where children can get their hands on them.**

HOSPITALS & CLINICS

Most Australian towns have a hospital or clinic, signposted by the international hospital sign of a white 'H' on a blue background. Australia has a variety of public and private hospitals and clinics. There are various kinds of public hospitals in Australia including district hospitals, teaching hospitals, general hospitals, children's hospitals, veterans affairs' hospitals, dental hospitals, psychiatric hospitals and day hospitals. Major hospitals are called general hospitals and provide treatment and diagnosis for in-patients, day-patients and out-patients. Major hospitals may have a maternity department, infectious diseases unit, psychiatric and geriatric facilities, rehabilitation and convalescent units, and cater for most forms of specialised treatment. Australia's public hospitals are funded jointly by the federal government and state and territory governments, and administered by state and territory health departments. There are an increasing number of private hospital operators in Australia (such as Australian Hospital Care) and some public hospitals are also operated by private companies under a contract.

Public Hospitals: Medicare pays for the full cost of accommodation and medical treatment performed by hospital appointed doctors for Medicare patients in public hospitals. Hospital bills for treatment under Medicare are always paid directly by Medicare. Note, however, that you will have no choice of doctors or hospital, or when you will be admitted for treatment or surgery. Medicare patients also receive free X-rays and pathology tests in public hospitals, and free out-patient services in some public hospitals. Patients are usually accommodated in general wards or twin rooms. If you want a TV or a telephone, you must pay extra for them. When you go to a public hospital you should take your Medicare card with you (if applicable). The staff may ask whether you wish to be treated under Medicare as a public patient or as a private patient.

In recent years there has been a funding crisis in public hospitals in many states, some of which have a chronic shortages of basic medical supplies, including bed linen, bandages, swabs, sterile dressings, syringes and drugs. Some public hospitals also have a lack of diagnostic equipment, e.g. for brain scans. Note, however, that there's usually no shortage of equipment or drugs that would put patients' lives at risk. In some over-worked public hospitals, patients are left lying for hours in emergency departments and in corridors waiting for ward beds. Some public hospitals suffer from a shortage of doctors and nurses, and are forced to recruit casual staff from locum and nursing agencies.

Private Patients/Hospitals: If you're a private patient in a public or private hospital, Medicare will pay 75 per cent of the schedule fee for medical services and the remaining 25 per cent will be paid by hospital private health insurance if you're a member of a health fund. If your doctor bulk bills (which means that they charge only 75 per cent of the schedule fee) you won't need to pay anything. You will also be charged for hospital accommodation and items such as theatre fees and medicines (as applicable). These costs may be recovered from your private health insurance, although you should check with your fund or insurer prior to admission. If you don't have private health insurance, you will be asked to pay the estimated costs at the time of admission. The average charge for a private bed is around $200 a day in a public hospital and almost $500 a day in a (5-star?) private hospital. Private patients are usually provided with single rooms equipped with all the comforts of home, including radio, TV, telephone, *en suite* bathroom and room service. If you're a private patient, you can choose the hospital and your attending doctor and surgeon, although if you want your own doctor to treat you in a public hospital there's a daily 'accommodation' charge. Note that doctors treating patients in private hospitals bill them independently. When you leave hospital, you will generally be asked to pay the difference (if any) between your health insurer's refund and the hospital fees. From mid-1998 patients in private hospitals will be given a quotation for the cost of surgery and out-of-pocket expenses, and will receive a single bill for the total cost. At the moment patients can receive dozens of separate bills for a stay of a few days in hospital.

CHILDBIRTH

Childbirth in Australia usually takes place in a hospital labour ward or birth centre (a small unit usually located in the grounds of a larger hospital), where a stay of up to five days is usual (although many women leave hospital within three days of giving birth). Public hospitals are under pressure to discharge mothers earlier and even privately insured mothers are being encouraged to cut their hospital stay in exchange for lower maternity (e.g. obstetrician) bills. If you wish to have a child at home, you must find a doctor or midwife (see below) who's willing to attend you. Some doctors are opposed to home births, particularly in cases where there could be complications (many births in Australia are induced) and when specialists and special facilities (e.g. incubators) may be required. You can hire a private midwife to attend you at home throughout and after your pregnancy. Relatively few people in Australia choose to give birth at home.

Medicare patients are usually unable to choose the hospital where they wish to have their baby and also won't be free to choose their obstetrician. Note that if you're insured with a health fund, you will need to make a large contribution (e.g. $700) towards the obstetrician's fees, as funds may pay only some $650 (or half the fee charged). If you have a choice, find out as much as possible about local hospital methods and policies concerning childbirth, either directly or from friends or neighbours, before booking a bed. The policy regarding a father's attendance at a birth varies depending on the hospital. A husband doesn't have the right to be present with his wife during labour or childbirth, which is at the consultant's discretion. If the presence of your husband is important to you, you should check that it's permitted at the hospital where you plan to have your baby and any other rules that may be in force. Women who don't speak English often have problems and are generally dissatisfied with their hospital treatment during pregnancy. Interpreters are rarely provided and information isn't usually published in foreign languages.

Midwives (nurses with specialist training) are responsible for educating and supporting women and their families during the childbearing period. They can advise women before they become pregnant, in addition to providing moral, physical and emotional support throughout a pregnancy and after the birth. Your midwife may also advise on parent education and antenatal classes for mothers. Note that some hospitals now charge (e.g. up to $120) for antenatal classes, which used to be free. There are Maternal and Child Health Centres in some states (e.g. Victoria), funded by the state government or local councils. However, there's a dearth of services for new mothers in many areas and post-natal care may be patchy or even non-existent, with new mothers being abandoned to their own devices.

Information: Family planning associations provide free teaching, counselling and related services. There are many publications for mothers including *The Babybook* published for Melbourne and Sydney (Universal Magazines, Private Bag 154, North Ryde, NSW 2113) and *The New Good Birth Guide* by Sheila Kitzinger (Penguin).

DENTISTS

There are excellent dentists in cities and towns throughout Australia, although they are thin on the ground in country areas. The best way to find a good dentist is to ask your colleagues, friends or neighbours (particularly those with perfect teeth) if they can recommend someone. Dentists are listed under 'Dental Surgeons' in the yellow pages and are permitted to advertise any special services they provide such as emergency or 24-hour answering service, dental hygienist, and evening or weekend surgeries. There are mobile dentists in some country regions and in remote areas emergency dental services are provided via the flying doctor service. Many family dentists in Australia are qualified to perform treatment such as endodontics or periodontics, carried out by specialists in many other countries. Water supplies are fluoridated in most parts of Australia in order to prevent dental decay.

General dental services aren't funded by Medicare, although it pays for 75 per cent of in-hospital medical procedures performed by an oral surgeon. The cost of dental treatment has risen considerably in recent years and it pays to keep your mouth shut during dental check-ups, which are recommended annually. Dental charges vary depending on the area and the individual dentist and, as in most countries, can be very expensive. Most dentists accept payment by credit card (plus dollars, gold, diamonds, bearer bonds, etc.). Dental teaching hospitals in the major cities treat patients for less than private dentists, although you may be something of a guinea pig. Pensioners and the unemployed with a Medicare concession card are entitled to free general and emergency dental treatment under the Commonwealth Dental Health Program, although there are waiting times of up to two years for treatment. Children in some states receive free school dental care. Note that if you miss a dental appointment without giving 24 hours notice, your dentist may charge you a standard fee (amazing how people who never forget anything, often forget dental appointments!).

Information about dental fees can be obtained from the Australian Dental Association, 116 Pacific Highway, North Sydney, NSW 2000. For information about **Dental Insurance** see page 310.

OPTOMETRISTS

As with dentists, there's no need to register with an optometrist or optician. You simply make an appointment with anyone of your choice, although it's advisable to ask your colleagues, friends or neighbours if they can recommend someone. Opticians and optometrists are listed in the yellow pages, where they may advertise their services. Optometrists (like spectacles) come in many shapes and sizes.

There are three kinds of professionals providing eye care in Australia. The most highly qualified is an ophthalmologist, who's a specialist physician trained in diagnosing and treating disorders of the eye. In addition to performing eye surgery and prescribing drugs, he may also perform sight tests and prescribe spectacles and contact lenses. You may be referred to an ophthalmologist by an optometrist or your GP. An optometrist is licensed to examine eyes, prescribe corrective lenses, and dispense spectacles and contact lenses. They are also trained to detect eye diseases and may prescribe drugs and treatment. An optician is not the same as an optometrist (as in some other countries) and may not examine eyes or prescribe lenses. Opticians are licensed to fill prescriptions written by optometrists and ophthalmologists, and to fit and adjust spectacles.

The optometrist business is very competitive in Australia and unless someone is highly recommended, you should shop around for the best deal. Prices for both spectacles and contact lenses vary considerably, so it's wise to compare costs (although make sure you're comparing like with like) before committing yourself to a large bill, particularly for contact lenses. Soft contact lenses or spectacles (frames and lenses) can be purchased in Australia from around $150-200 (usually inclusive of an eye examination). Special offers are common such as 'buy a new pair of spectacles and receive a spare pair free'. Note, however, that the lowest prices and special deals aren't necessarily the best value. Always ask about extra charges for eye examinations, fittings, adjustments, lens-care kits, follow-up visits and the cost of replacement lenses (if they're expensive it may be worthwhile taking out insurance). Many opticians offer insurance against the accidental damage of spectacles for a nominal fee.

Many Australians wears contact lenses. Disposable (one-day) and extended-wear (e.g. one or three months) contact lenses are widely available, although most medical experts believe extended-wear lenses should be approached with extreme caution, as they greatly increase the risk of potentially blinding eye infections. **Obtain advice from a doctor or eye specialist before buying them.** Medicare pays for 85 per cent of the cost of eye tests by optometrists as listed in the optometrical schedule. Note that you aren't required to buy your spectacles or contact lenses from the optometrist who tests your sight, and he must give you your prescription at no extra charge. There are optical retail chain stores in Australia, where you can get spectacles made within an hour. It's advisable to have your eyes tested before your arrival in Australia and to bring a spare pair of spectacles or contact lenses with you (also bring a copy of your prescription in case you need to obtain replacements in a hurry).

COUNSELLING

Counselling and assistance for health and social problems is available under Medicare, and from many local community groups and volunteer organisations, ranging from national associations to small local groups (including self-help groups). Local authorities provide social workers to advise and support those requiring help within their community. If you need to find help locally, you can contact your local council, local voluntary services or a Citizens Advice Bureau for advice. A list of 24-hour emergency services (including many counselling services) is included at the front of both white and yellow page telephone directories, plus community help and welfare services, and help for young people.

Many colleges and educational establishments provide a counselling service for students, and general hospitals have a psychiatrist on call 24 hours a day. Problems for which help is available are numerous and include drug rehabilitation; alcoholism (e.g. Alcoholics Anonymous); gambling; dieting (e.g. Weight Watchers); smoking; attempted suicide and psychiatric problems; homosexual related problems; youth problems; battered children and women; marriage and relationship counselling; and rape.

Trained counsellors provide advice and help for sufferers of various diseases (e.g. multiple sclerosis and muscular dystrophy) and the disabled (e.g. the blind and deaf).

They also help very sick and terminally ill patients (e.g. cancer, leukemia and Aids sufferers) and their families come to terms with their situation. A number of voluntary organisations and local authorities run refuges for battered wives (and their children) or maltreated children, whose conditions have become intolerable (some provide 24-hour emergency phone numbers). If you or a member of your family are the victims of a violent crime, the police will put you in touch with a local victim support scheme.

In times of need there's nearly always someone to turn to and all services are strictly confidential. In major towns, counselling may be available in your own language if you don't speak English. If you need help desperately, someone speaking your language will usually be found. **Lifeline** (13 1114) provides a confidential, 24-hour counselling service in periods of personal crisis (e.g. for the lonely, desperate and suicidal) throughout Australia for the cost of a local call. Many councils publish a directory of children's and family services.

DRUG & ALCOHOL ABUSE

Drug abuse is a serious problem in Australia, where it's estimated that heroin users alone spend around $3 billion a year on the drug (it also costs the country around $2 billion a year). The average beginner is just 16 and the average time between take up and death is just 10 years (around 700 people die each year from overdoses). The drug problem is of increasing concern to those in the fight against Aids (see page 290), as the sharing of needles among drug addicts (many of whom are HIV positive or have Aids) is a major cause of the spread of Aids. Free hypodermic needles are provided is Sydney (distributed via pharmacies) and Melbourne plans to provide premises ('shooting galleries') where addicts can obtain needles, inject drugs and be checked for overdoses. There's also a new experimental treatment for heroin addicts called rapid opiate detoxification.

The National Campaign Against Drug Abuse (NCADA) was established in 1985 to reduce the use of both legal and illegal drugs through community education, drug education programs for parents and children, and professional training. However, despite the NCADA campaign and increased vigilance by police and customs officers to reduce the supply of drugs from overseas (particularly heroin), high levels of drugs are still being imported into Australia (mostly via Sydney). Marijuana is widely grown and smoked throughout Australia. Each state has its own laws regarding marijuana which vary considerably. In some states it has been decriminalised and its use and possession is legal, while in others its use is punishable by huge fines and even imprisonment (see **Crime** on page 442).

Many people believe that the authorities are fighting a losing battle against the drug barons and that universal prohibition has actually increased consumption. Some experts would like to relax Australia's tough prohibitionist drug policies, although it's impossible without the USA's approval (and it has the opposite opinion, even though its tough uncompromising measures have proved an abject failure). Some people in the judiciary and police believe that punishing drug-users in the criminal justice system is debasing the legal system, and that they should treated in hospitals. Plans to give free drugs to addicts in a controlled program (as pioneered in Switzerland) have been strongly opposed by the USA.

Many government and voluntary organisations provide drug advice and rehabilitation services, including residential facilities (there are government-run detoxification units in the major cities). In cities there are voluntary groups providing counselling, advice and support for drug users, and their relatives and friends (see your local white or yellow pages). If you can afford to pay for private treatment, a number of private clinics and hospitals specialise in treating people for drug, alcohol and chemical abuse, and other health problems.

Apart from the direct or indirect loss of life, alcohol abuse costs Australian industry $millions a year in lost production due to absenteeism, and it's also a serious problem among children. The government has instituted a national alcohol program to warn people of the dangers of excessive drinking. Alcoholics Anonymous has self-help groups throughout Australia (see your telephone book).

SEXUALLY-TRANSMITTED DISEASES

Like most western countries, Australia has its fair share of sexually-transmitted diseases, including the deadly Acquired Immune Deficiency Syndrome (AIDS). The furore over Aids has died down in the past few years, which many fear may cause those most at risk to be lulled into a false sense of security (many Australian teenagers still practise unsafe sex). The explosion of Aids predicted by many 'experts' hasn't materialised, particularly among the heterosexual population, although the number of heterosexual cases is increasing. **Aids is always fatal and to date there's no cure.** All blood used in transfusions in Australia is screened for HIV (human immunodeficiency virus, which usually leads to Aids).

A total of around 20,000 cases of HIV had been officially recorded in Australia up to 1995, mostly among homosexual men (Sydney, Melbourne and Adelaide have thriving gay communities), around a third of which were later diagnosed as having Aids. However, the real figures for HIV cases are thought to be much higher. There has been a major education campaign to warn people of the risks of Aids in recent years, during which the number of HIV cases has fallen. However, the number of Aids cases in Asia is expected to explode in the next few years, which health experts believe poses a serious threat to Australia.

The spread of Aids is accelerated by the sharing of syringes by drug addicts, among whom Aids is rampant (many of Australia's heroin addicts are infected with the HIV virus). In an effort to reduce syringe sharing among HIV positive drug addicts, free needles and condoms are distributed to drug addicts. The spread of Aids is also accelerated by prostitutes, many of whom are also drug addicts. The best protection against Aids is for men to wear a condom, although they're not foolproof (against Aids or pregnancy) and the only real protection is abstinence (or 'NO!'). Condoms are on sale at chemists, some supermarkets, men's hairdressers, and vending machines in public toilets in pubs and other places.

Public hospitals and clinics provide free tests, treatment and advice for venereal diseases and Aids. All cases of Aids and HIV-positive blood tests in Australia must be reported to the local health authorities (patients' names remain anonymous). If you wish to talk to someone in confidence about Aids, there are many organisations and self-help groups providing information, advice and support in all areas (see your local telephone book).

BIRTHS & DEATHS

Births in Australia must be registered with the Registrar of Births, Deaths and Marriages within 60 days (even when a child is stillborn). When birth takes place in a hospital the parents are given the relevant form to register the birth. In the case of home births, a form can be obtained from a hospital or from the Registrar of Births. A child born to an unmarried mother is usually registered in her name, but can be registered in the father's name if both parents agree. The birth of a child to foreign parents or the death of a foreigner in Australia may need to be reported to a consulate or embassy, for example, to obtain a national birth certificate and passport for a child, or to register a death in the deceased's home country.

Deaths: When someone dies in Australia, it must be reported to the Registrar of Births, Deaths and Marriages within a certain period, which is usually 21 days. The registrar is normally notified directly by the hospital authorities when a death occurs in a hospital. He decides whether to issue a death certificate after obtaining a medical certificate and other details concerning the deceased. If someone dies suddenly, accidentally, during an operation, in unusual circumstances, or the cause of death is unknown, the registrar will notify the police and/or the coroner, who will decide whether an autopsy is necessary to determine the cause of death.

The registrar will need to know personal details of the deceased, including the date and place of birth and death, details of marriage (if applicable), and whether the deceased was receiving a state pension or any welfare benefits. The registrar then issues a death certificate which authorises the funeral to take place. The death certificate must be given to a funeral director (or undertaker) to organise the burial or cremation (or alternatively you can arrange for the body to be shipped to another country for burial). You may wish to announce a death in a local or national newspaper, giving the date, time and place of the funeral, and your wishes about flowers or contributions to a charity or research.

Costs: Traditional funerals are expensive in Australia, where cremation costs an average of around $3,500 and burial around $4,000 (undertakers only get one bite of the cherry and have to make the most of it!). A grave plot (which are in short supply in some cities) can cost anything from $400 to $3,000 plus digging fees of from around $400 to $900. Note that the tenure on a plot may be indefinite or limited, e.g. from 25 to 99 years, after which you must make an additional payment if you wish to retain the plot. Crematorium fees are typically around $500. You can pay in advance for your funeral through a variety of 'pay-now-die-later' schemes, with price and service guaranteed, although there are no legal safeguards and the prepaid funeral trade is ripe for fraud, mismanagement and over-selling. If you want to have a body buried overseas or have someone who died overseas buried in Australia, the body will probably need to be transported by air, which can be *very* expensive.

In the event of the death of a resident of Australia, all interested parties must be notified (see **Chapter 20**). You'll need a number of copies of the death certificate, e.g. for the proving of the will (probate), pension claims, insurance companies and financial institutions. If you need to obtain a copy of a birth, marriage or death certificate, the cheapest way is to apply to the registrar in the state or territory where it was registered. A brochure, *What to do when someone dies*, is available from the Department of Social Security. See also **Wills** on page 356.

SMOKING

As in most countries, smoking contributes to a huge loss of life and number of working days in Australia, although the number of smokers has steadily decreased over the last few decades to around 27 per cent of men and 22 per cent of women. It's estimated that some 20 per cent of pregnant women continue to smoke throughout their pregnancies, despite the dangers to their unborn child. An anti-smoking campaign ('Smoking, Who Needs It'?) launched in 1990 aims to reduce smoking among young women. Some 20,000 people die annually in Australia from smoking-related illnesses costing the state around $13 billion a year in health care costs, which has prompted some two-thirds of Australians (presumably all non-smokers) to think that smokers should pay a higher Medicare levy. However, although smokers place a higher burden on Medicare they also die younger and it has been calculated that the life-long health costs of smokers is actually less than that for non-smokers in some countries.

Smokers are under siege on all fronts in Australia and the Australian Medical Association has called on federal and state governments to sue tobacco companies to recoup the health costs of smoking. As in many other countries, tobacco companies face huge bills as a result of court cases brought by smokers for smoking-induced illnesses such as cancer. Over three-quarters of Australia's top companies restrict smoking (and the consumption of alcohol) in the workplace, with around half having a total ban on smoking at work and a third with designated areas where employees are permitted to smoke. It's legal for employers to specify in job advertisements whether they will hire smokers (employers are fearful of law suits from non-smokers).

In recent years there has been increasing concern about 'passive smoking', where non-smokers involuntarily inhale the smoke generated by smokers, although it hasn't generated the paranoia seen in the USA (where anyone who smokes in a public place is liable to be summarily executed). The National Health and Medical Research Council has recommended a statutory ban in all enclosed public spaces outside the home. However, the anti-smoking lobby is gaining ground fast and some states and territories already have a ban on smoking in many public places, including public transport, public buildings and restaurants (although exemptions can usually be granted). There's a smoking ban on Australia's international airlines and on all domestic flights. The attitude towards smoking varies from state to state (the ACT is toughest and Queensland the most lax). The ACT has introduced laws against smoking in all enclosed public places including hotels, restaurants, cafes, bars, pubs, clubs and sports stadiums, and this is likely to be followed by other states (although to date, most have stopped short of the blanket ban imposed in the ACT). Many restaurants and pubs already have smoking and non-smoking sections.

Action on Smoking and Health (ASH) provides advice on giving up smoking and information on smoking and the rights of non-smokers, and the anti-smoking group QUIT produces leaflets in 13 languages. There are also non-smoking clinics and self-help groups throughout Australia to assist those wishing to stop smoking. Contact your local health authority for information.

MEDICAL TREATMENT OVERSEAS

Australian residents are entitled to immediate necessary medical and public hospital treatment similar to that provided by Medicare in countries with which the Australian government has reciprocal health care agreements. This includes Finland, Italy, Malta, the Netherlands, New Zealand, Sweden and the UK (it also covers students studying in these countries). In order to obtain treatment under a reciprocal agreement, you must provide a current Australian passport (or a foreign passport which shows that you're a permanent Australian resident) and your Medicare card. Note that in certain countries, e.g. Canada, Japan, Switzerland and the USA, medical treatment is *very* expensive and it's advisable to take out travel or holiday health insurance (see page 314) when visiting these countries. **This is wise wherever you're travelling as it provides considerably wider medical cover than reciprocal health care agreements (and includes many other things such as repatriation).** If you do a lot of travelling overseas, it's worthwhile having an international health insurance policy.

Visitors to Australia: Australia has reciprocal health care agreements with a number of countries (including those listed above), citizens of which are entitled to free emergency health treatment in Australia.   Visitors from Italy and Malta are covered for a period of six months from their date of arrival in Australia; all others (listed above) are covered for the duration of their visit. The agreement covers emergency and essential treatment only and doesn't cover treatment or medication for pre-existing medical conditions. Agreements don't include prescription costs and there's a fee (maximum $10) for consulting a doctor. Foreign students on sponsored studies are also covered, but those paying full fees must pay an advance premium. It isn't necessary for you to enrol in Medicare until you require treatment, when you must produce your passport and proof that you're enrolled in your country's national health care scheme, e.g. with a national health care card or certificate.

13.

INSURANCE

The Australian government and Australian law provide for various obligatory state and employer insurance schemes. These include health, sickness and maternity; work injuries; state and private (superannuation) pensions; disability; and unemployment insurance. Australia is a nation of gamblers, which is reflected in the relatively low level of insurance, not only for such basic requirements as loss of income or life insurance, but also comprehensive insurance for cars, buildings and home contents. Many people tend to (or have to) rely on state 'insurance' benefits, which come under the heading of 'Social Security', including additional family payments, sickness allowance, income support, benefits for the unemployed, maternity allowance and various pensions. Note, however, that social security provides for the most basic needs only and those who are reduced to 'living' on it usually exist below the poverty line.

Most Australians and foreign residents and their families receive health treatment under Medicare (see page 277), the public health system. If you don't qualify for health care under Medicare it's essential to have private health insurance, which is obligatory for some temporary residents. If you're coming to Australia from overseas, you would be wise to ensure that your family has comprehensive health insurance during the period between leaving your last country of residence and arriving in Australia. This is particularly important if you're covered by private health insurance in your home country that doesn't cover you overseas. One way is to take out a travel insurance policy. However, if possible it's usually better to extend your present health insurance policy, particularly if you have existing health problems which may not be covered by a new policy.

There are only a few cases in Australia when insurance for individuals is compulsory including building insurance if you have a mortgage (because your lender will insist on it) and basic third party motor insurance (CTP), which is required by law. If you're an employee you must also belong to a superannuation fund. You may also need compulsory third party and accident insurance for high-risk sports. Voluntary insurance includes accident, income protection, private health, home contents, personal liability, legal expenses, dental, travel, motor breakdown and life insurance.

It isn't necessary to spend half your income insuring yourself against every eventuality from the common cold to being sued for your last cent, but it's important to be covered against any event which could precipitate a major financial disaster (such as a serious accident or your house falling down). **As with everything to do with finance, it's imperative to shop around when buying insurance.** Just picking up a few brochures from insurance agents and making a few phone calls could save you a lot of money (enough to pay for this book many times over). Regrettably you cannot insure yourself against being uninsured or sue your insurance broker for giving you bad advice.

In all matters regarding insurance, you're responsible for ensuring that your family is legally insured in Australia. If you want to make a claim against a third party or a third party is claiming against you, you would be wise to seek legal advice for anything other than a minor claim. **Note that Australian law may be very different from that in your home country or your previous country of residence, and you should never assume that it's the same.** Bear in mind that if you wish to make a claim on an insurance policy, you may be required to report an incident to the police within 24 hours (which in some cases may be a legal requirement).

Note that information in this chapter is intended only as a guide as the rules and rates regarding insurance matters are constantly changing particularly social security, superannuation and health insurance. You should therefore obtain the latest information from the appropriate authorities or an insurance company in

Australia. See also **Car Insurance** on page 246 and **Motor Breakdown Insurance** on page 268.

INSURANCE COMPANIES

There are numerous insurance companies from which to choose in Australia, providing either a range of insurance services or specialising in certain fields only. In Australia you can buy insurance from many sources including traditional insurance companies selling through their own salesmen or independent brokers, direct insurance companies (selling direct to the public), banks and other financial institutions, and motoring organisations. The major insurance companies have offices or agents (brokers) throughout Australia, including most large towns, most of whom will provide a free analysis of your family or business insurance needs.

Brokers: If you choose a broker, you should use one who's independent and sells policies from a wide range of insurance companies. Some brokers or agents are tied to a particular insurance company and sell policies only from that company (which includes most banks). An independent broker should research the whole market and take into account your individual requirements, why you're investing (if applicable), the various companies' financial performance, what you can afford and the type of policy that's best for you. He mustn't offer you a policy because it pays him the highest commission, which incidentally you should ask him about (particularly regarding life insurance).

Direct Insurance: In recent years direct marketing and direct response insurance companies (bypassing brokers) have resulted in huge savings for consumers, particularly for car, building and home contents' insurance. Direct marketing companies give quotations over the phone and often you aren't even required to complete a proposal form. Compare premiums from a number of direct sales insurance companies with the best deals from brokers before choosing a policy.

Shop Around: When buying insurance, you should shop 'til you drop and then shop around some more! Premiums vary considerably (e.g. by 100 to 200 per cent), although you must ensure that you're comparing similar policies and that important benefits haven't been omitted. Bear in mind that the cheapest policy isn't necessarily the best, particularly regarding the prompt payment of claims. Many analysts believe that it's better to pay for independent insurance advice rather than accept 'free' advice, which may be more expensive in the long run. You should obtain a number of quotations for each insurance need and shouldn't assume that your existing insurance company is the best choice for a new insurance requirement. Buy only the insurance that you *want* and *need* and ensure that you can afford the payments (and that your cover is protected if you're sick or unemployed).

INSURANCE CONTRACTS

Read all insurance contracts carefully before signing them. If you don't understand everything, ask a friend or colleague to 'translate' it or obtain professional advice. Policies often contain traps and legal loopholes in the small print. If a policy has pages of legal jargon and gobbledegook in *very* small print, you have a right to be suspicious, particularly as it's common practice nowadays to be as brief as possible and write clearly and concisely in language which doesn't require a doctorate in law. Take care how you answer questions on an insurance proposal form, as even if you mistakenly provide false information an insurance company can refuse to pay out when you make a claim.

Most insurance policies run for a calendar year from the date on which you take out a policy. All insurance policy premiums should be paid punctually, as late payment can affect your benefits or a claim, although if this is so, it should be noted in your policy. Before signing an insurance policy, you should shop around and take a day or two to think it over (never sign on the spot as you may regret it later). With some insurance contracts, you may have a 'cooling off' period during which you can cancel a policy without penalty.

Claims: Although insurance companies are keen to take your money, many aren't nearly so happy to settle claims. Like insurance companies everywhere, some Australian insurance companies will do almost anything to avoid paying out in the event of a claim and will use any available loophole. Fraud is estimated to cost the insurance industry $millions a year (particularly motor insurance fraud) and staff may be trained to automatically assume that claims are fraudulent. If you wish to make a claim, you must usually inform your insurance company in writing by registered letter within a number of days of the incident (possibly within 24 hours in the case of theft). **Failure to do so will render your claim void!** Don't send original bills or documents regarding a claim to your insurance company unless it's absolutely necessary (if necessary you can send a certified copy). Keep a copy of all bills, documents and correspondence, and always send letters by recorded or registered mail so that your insurance company cannot deny receipt.

Don't bank a cheque received in settlement of a claim if you think it's insufficient, as you may be deemed to have accepted it as full and final settlement. Don't accept the first offer made, as many insurance companies try to get away with making a low settlement (if an insurer pays what you have claimed without a quibble, you probably claimed too little!). When dealing with insurance companies, perseverance often pays. Insurers are increasingly refusing to pay up on the flimsiest of pretexts, as they know that many people won't pursue their cases, even when they have a valid claim. Don't give up on a claim if you're sure you have a good case, but persist until you have exhausted every avenue. If you cannot reach agreement, you can contact the General Insurance Claims Review Panel (tel. freecall 1800-363683) for independent arbitration or take legal action.

SOCIAL SECURITY

Social Security (welfare) is the name given to state welfare benefits paid to residents in Australia. Social Security is non-contributory and is financed from general taxation (although there's a taxation levy for Medicare), and comprises around 25 per cent of GDP. Australia has one of the most comprehensive social security systems in the world, which has engendered widespread welfare dependency with around one-third of all Australians relying on welfare payments as their main source of income (half of whom are pensioners). On the other hand, many people fail to apply for allowances and pensions to which they're entitled. If you apply and your application is rejected, you can ask for the decision to be reviewed by an Authorised Review Officer (ARO) and if it's turned down again you can appeal to the Social Security Appeals Tribunal and finally to the Administrative Appeals Tribunal.

Fraud: Social security fraud is huge, although the government has cracked down in recent years during which many people have lost their benefits or had them reduced (many have also been prosecuted). Around 2,500 people were convicted of cheating the welfare system in 1996/97 at a cost to taxpayers of some $25m. A further 300,000 were found to be receiving too much in payments and over 60,000 people too little. The most common form of welfare fraud is people claiming unemployment benefits while working. Many cheats are discovered through tip-offs from the public under the government's confidential 'dob in a dole bludger' initiative. Another method used to detect fraudsters is data-matching between the Department of Social Security and the Australian Tax Office.

Income & Means Tests: Eligibility for most social security benefits is subject to an income and/or means test. The poorest 10 per cent of Australians receive some 600 per cent more in government payments than the richest 10 per cent over their lifetime. If you're found to have sufficient income or assets after a means test, your social security payments are reduced or terminated. Assets which are means tested include most investments but not personal belongings such as your principal home, cars, holiday homes, antiques and superannuation pensions. Financial investments are deemed to earn a certain income (adjusted annually).

New Migrants: Since 4th March 1997, migrants have had to wait two years before they can claim most social security payments, although refugees and humanitarian entrants are excluded from the waiting period. Migrants can, however, claim Special Benefit or Widow's Allowance in exceptional circumstances and are able to receive the minimum rate of Family Payment (see below) during the two-year waiting period. Migrants also have access to Medicare during their first two years in Australia. Note that some sponsors of migrants need to provide an Assurance of Support (see page 80), which makes them liable to repay the government if certain welfare benefits are paid to the migrant during his first two years (ten years for children sponsoring a parent who's within 10 years of retirement).

The two-year waiting period for welfare has caused some migrants to become destitute and homeless according to the Welfare Rights Centre and there have been calls to have it suspended or cancelled. However, there's a glimmer of hope — a ruling in February 1998 by the Administrative Appeal Tribunal allowed new migrants easier access to welfare payments if they are destitute (the government had conveniently 'forgotten' to tell most migrants about the two-year rule). A NSW Ethnic Communities Council survey discovered that over two-thirds of newly arrived migrants were unaware that they couldn't claim benefits for two years. Migrant service units monitor and review services to migrants and refugees, and liaise with ethnic and voluntary groups, and there are also migrant resource centres in the major towns and cities. Settlement support is provided for migrants with genuine financial problems.

Benefits: The main benefits include pensions for the aged, disabled and sole parents; payments for those who are unemployed, sick or in special need; allowances for children; sheltered employment and rehabilitation allowances; and allowances for families with children. Benefits include a disability support pension, double orphan pension, carer pension, child disability allowance, parenting or guardian allowance (if a sole parent), newstart allowance, youth training allowance, sickness allowance, mobility allowance, multiple birth payment (triplets or more), pharmaceutical allowance, rent assistance, parenting allowance, partner allowance, widow allowance, bereavement allowance, family tax payment, maternity allowance and a health care card. A discretionary payment (called a special benefit) may be paid to those who aren't eligible for other forms of assistance and are unable to support themselves.

The federal and state governments jointly fund a wide range of welfare services based on home care for elderly and disabled persons and their families. Some 1,500 nursing homes (around a fifth are state-operated) and around 1,000 hostels receive federal support to provide residential care for elderly people. A federal government disability services program funds organisations to provide services that help people with disabilities maintain their independence and achieve their full potential. The Commonwealth

Rehabilitation Service employs a wide range of specialist to work with disabled people in order to help them return to economic and social independence.

Information: A range of publications detailing Social Security allowances, benefits and pensions are available from Social Security offices and community organisations. The Department of Social Security provides a telephone enquiry service on 132468 or 131202 for languages other than English. Calls are charged at local call rates from anywhere in Australia. For more information contact the Department of Social Security, PO Box 7788, Canberra Mail Centre, ACT 2610.

Family Payment

A family payment is paid to parents or guardians with dependant children aged under 16 or full-time dependant students aged 16 to 18 who aren't in receipt of an Austudy or Abstudy allowance. The amount paid depends on the age and number of children in the family, and the family's total income and assets. Payments are usually made fortnightly into the mother's bank account, although if you have large expenses such as school uniforms it's possible to receive part of the payment in a lump sum in advance twice a year (January and July). Families with low incomes may also receive a supplement. The maximum family payment per fortnight in 1997 was $96.40 for each child under 13, $125.40 for each child aged 13 to 15, and $60.20 for each student aged 16 to 18. The minimum payment was $23.50 per child per fortnight.

If your assets are less than $407,250 you receive the maximum family payment, but if they exceed $604,250 (excluding the family home), no payment is made unless hardship provisions apply. The income levels required to qualify for family payments are shown below:

No. of Children	Max. Payment	No Payment
1	$23,400	$65,941
2	$24,024	$69,239
3	$24,648	$72,537
4	$25,272	$75,835
Each Extra Child	$624	$3,298

If your income doesn't exceed the amount shown in the first column ('Max. Payment') in the above table, you receive the maximum family payment. If your income is above the amount shown in the first column but below the amount shown in the second column, you receive a reduced family payment. If your income exceeds the amount shown in the second column ('No Payment'), you receive no family payment. Family payment and other payments for children aren't taxable.

Unemployment Benefits

Australia has no unemployment benefit or 'dole' as such, but payments are made under the Jobsearch or Newstart allowances. If you're unemployed, you must register with the Department of Social Security where, providing you qualify, you will be given a form to complete and lodge within 14 days. You will need to provide proof of identity and your tax file number. If you have been terminated (sacked, retrenched, etc.) from a previous position, you will need your Employment Separation Certificate which states the reason you left work and your wages. For new immigrants there's a two-year waiting period before payments start. If you remain unemployed for over one year, you will need to apply for the New Start Allowance. Rates of payment depend on individual circumstances including you age, marital status and your number of children. In 1997, payments ranged from $145 a fortnight for a single person living at home with no dependant children, to $580.20 for a couple over 18 with children. Payments are subject to assets and income tests.

Job Search Allowance. To qualify you must be aged under 18, or over 18 and registered with the DSS for one year or less, have permanent residence status, and be actively looking for work. You must also convince the DSS that you're looking for work or that you're improving your job prospects by attending training or educational classes. To receive payments you must report in writing to the DSS every two weeks on your job searching activities. This is called the 'activity test' and if you don't have good reason for not meeting the requirements your allowance will be stopped.

New Start Allowance. To qualify you must be over 18, a permanent resident, unemployed and registered with the DSS for over one year. You must also be actively searching for work. In your initial interview with the DSS you must sign an undertaking agreeing to a plan of action to improve your employment prospects. Refusal to sign the agreement will limit or nullify your chances of qualifying for the allowance. You must also report to the DSS every two weeks. The new start allowance is usually paid from the day the job search allowance (see above) stops (if applicable). The income and assets tests for job search and new start allowances are the same, as are the rates.

In the last few years, a wealth of changes have been made to social security payments for the unemployed including the termination of payments to teenagers (which forced many of them to go back to school); a work-for-dole scheme; tighter rules for youths living at home (depending on their parents' income); stricter rules regarding the liquid assets of claimants (who must exhaust any payout from a previous employer before claiming the dole); and loss of benefits for failure to attend a job interview, withdrawal from a job program or non-disclosure of income from employment. Job Search and the New Start allowance aren't paid during an absence from Australia.

State Pensions

State pensions are paid to men at age 65 and women at age 61, although the pensionable age for women is gradually being increased to 65. The qualifying age was raised from 60 to 60.5 years on 1st July 1995 and to 61 on 1st July 1997, and will be further increased by six months at two-year intervals until 1st July 2013, when it will be 65 years (it will be 65 for anyone born on 1st January 1949 or later). A full Australian pension is payable after 25 years' residence during a person's working life, i.e. between the ages of 16 and 65 for men and 16 and 60+ for women. You generally need to have lived continuously in Australia for 10 years to qualify for a state retirement pension. However, Australia has reciprocal social security agreements with some countries (including Austria, Canada, Cyprus, Ireland, Italy, Malta, the Netherlands, New Zealand, Portugal, Spain and the United Kingdom) which may enable newcomers to receive a pension as soon as they reach pensionable age, irrespective of their residence period. In addition to the basic retirement pension, various other pensions are paid in Australia including a pension for a wife, widow, sole parent, disability support/wage, bereavement, mature age, double orphan and a carer. All pensions are paid at the same rates (listed below) and most are subject to an income and assets test. Other social security payments may be paid in addition to the retirement pension.

Unlike state pensions in most countries, which are paid irrespective of a person's wealth or income, most Australian pensions are subject to income and assets tests (the test which produces the lower rate of pension applies). This applies to all pensioners except invalid pensions for permanently blind persons and pensions for war and defence widows. Around 30 per cent of Australians are considered too wealthy to receive a state pension. Under the **income test**, a full pension is paid if your gross income doesn't exceed $100 a fortnight for a single person or $176 a fortnight for a couple, plus an additional $24 for each child. For each dollar earned above these amounts your pension payment is reduced by 50¢ for singles and 25¢ for each of a couple. No payment is made if your fortnightly income exceeds $806.40 (single) or $1,347.20 (couple). A private pension counts as income and therefore if you receive a pension (in Australia or from overseas) this could reduce your state pension. Under the **assets test**, the pension you receive depends on the market value of your assessable assets (which are indexed annually) as shown below:

Status	Full Pension	No Pension
single homeowner	$125,750	$243,500
single non-homeowner	$215,750	$333,500
married homeowner couple	$178,500	$374.000
married non-homeowner couple	$268,500	$464,000

Your pension is reduced by $3 for every $1,000 of assets above the 'full pension' limits listed above. There's no assets test for those aged over 70. The assets test doesn't include your principal family home or the land on which it's built up to two hectares (providing it's used for domestic purposes). Prepaid funeral expenses and aids for the disabled such as wheelchairs are also excluded (what generosity!).

In 1997, the maximum retirement pension was $347.80 for a single person and $580.20 ($290.10 each) for a married couple. The retirement pension is taxable, but on its own is below the tax threshold. Pensioners who delay their retirement become eligible for a cash bonus equal to 9.4 per cent of their pension entitlement for each year they continue working. State pensions are indexed twice a year in line with changes in the Consumer Price Index (CPI). Pensions are pegged at 25 per cent of average male earnings to ensure that the rates keep pace with the rest of the community (the full effect in expected by the year 2000). You can choose the day on which you want your pension paid in order to eliminate peak times at DSS offices and banks. Pensions are usually paid into a bank, building society or credit union account.

In order to claim a pension, you require at least three original documents which prove your identity; details of all bank, building society and credit union accounts, and any other money you have invested; and your latest rent receipts, rent book or other proof of the amount paid, if you're paying private rent. The documentation should be brought with you when lodging a claim (although it can be provided later). If you're married (or have a *de facto* partner) you should bring your partner with you and he must also complete a form, prove his identity and provide details of his assets.

Australian pensions can be paid overseas although pensioners going overseas for longer than six months must obtain a pre-departure certificate from social security. If the period overseas is expected to be for one year or more, pension payments may be sent to an overseas address. Under reciprocal agreements with other countries, a full Australian pension is payable after 25 years' residence during a person's working life, i.e. between the ages of 16 and 65 for men and 16 and 60+ for women. If you have lived in Australia for less than 25 years and then go to live overseas, you will receive an Australian pension proportionate to the number of years spent there, e.g. if you spent 12.5 years in Australia you will receive half of the full retirement pension.

UK Pensioners: The pensions of British state pensioners are frozen at the prevailing rate with no annual adjustments for inflation when they move to some countries. These countries include Australia and other Commonwealth countries such as Canada, New Zealand and South Africa, which affects over 350,000 pensioners. There are some 150,000 British state pensioners in Australia with frozen British state pensions (which may be equal to just a few £sterling), and of these, around 100,000 receive social security 'top-up' payments totalling some $80m a year from the Australian government. This a constant source of friction between the Australian and British governments, and the Australian government has threatened to reduce them if the British government doesn't pick up the bill (which is has continually refused to do).

There's a worsening crisis in state pension funding in Australia (and most western countries), where fewer and fewer workers must support an increasing number of pensioners. To make matters worse, most countries expect to at least double their over 65 population in the next 50 years. In 1995 there were 2.2m Australians over the age of 65 out of a population of around 18m, which is expected to rise to between 5.2m and 6.4m by 2051 when it's estimated the population will be between 25m and 28m. This will mean that there's double the number of pensioners in relation to the proportion of the total population. As in many countries, there are plans to transfer the burden from the public to the private sector, which is why the mandatory Superannuation Guarantee Scheme was created in 1992 (see below). However, despite the introduction of superannuation, some 75 per cent of people are still expected to be eligible for a full or part state pension for at least the next 25 years. The Commonwealth government spends around $20 billion a year on retirement benefits.

Australian pensioners are entitled to concessional dental treatment, prescriptions and optometrist services; concessions on public transport fares in most states and territories; and various other concessions (that vary from state to state) which may include reduced council rates, reductions on utility costs (e.g. telephone rental, water rates, etc.), free mail redirection service and reduced registration fees for dogs.

For further information about retirement pensions in Australia, contact the Department of Social Security, International Operations Branch, GPO Box 273C, Hobart, Tasmania 7000.

SUPERANNUATION

Superannuation (usually referred to simply as 'super') is the term commonly used in Australia for a private pension fund. As the number of retired workers has increased and the number of young workers to take their place has declined (partly due to higher unemployment), the pressure on government funds to pay state pensions has also increased. In order to reduce the burden, the federal government introduced compulsory employer superannuation funds in 1992 under the Superannuation Guarantee Scheme. Superannuation doesn't, however, replace the state pension (which continues to be available to those who need it), but is intended to supplement it and provide a greater level of income in retirement.

Super rules have been extended to include part-time and casual workers, and those who leave the workforce for up to two years. Generally if you earn over $450 a month, your employer must pay a minimum level of super for you, although some awards require employers to pay super for employees earning less than $450 a month. However, employees earning between $450 and $900 a month can choose to receive their Superannuation Guarantee contributions as additional salary. The self-employed non-resident employees paid for work undertaken outside Australia aren't required to belong to a super fund, and resident employees employed by non-resident employers and paid for work undertaken outside Australia also needn't be covered.

Funds are non-contributory for employees, although voluntary contributions can be made. There are around 7m super fund members (some 90 per cent of the workforce) with over $300 billion in superannuation assets. There are various types of super funds including employer-sponsored funds, industry funds, financial institution funds and private do-it-yourself funds (which hold an increasing share of super assets). Banks, building societies, credit unions and life insurance companies can all provide superannuation funds in the form of Retirement Savings Accounts (RSAs). Repayment of all RSA deposits are guaranteed, but investment earnings are usually modest, e.g. 4 per cent a year, and many believe they are a waste of time (some employers have been trying to push workers into RSAs that leave them worse off than superannuation funds). If you're self-employed or aren't part of a recognised superannuation scheme, you can contribute to an independent private or public scheme (or a number of schemes) and tax relief may be claimed against superannuation payments. Many people begin their super earnings with small contributions, particularly part-time, casual and seasonal workers. To help amounts under $1,000 grow, super funds are required to protect them against fees and charges.

You aren't obliged to join your employer's fund and from 1st July 1998 (although it's likely to be delayed for a year) all new employees must be given a choice of four funds, including an RSA (this choice is expected to be extended to all employees from 1st July 2000). Employees will have 28 days to make their decision, after which employers will decide. There's a huge difference between the best and worst performing super funds, so it's wise to shop around and compare fund performance over a five or 10 year period and the level of fees (smaller industry funds don't do as well as the larger ones). Note, however, that in most cases, you would be foolish to turn down the opportunity to join an employer's fund if it's a good one, as this usually provides extra benefits. These may include higher employer contributions, free life and disability insurance, and loss of earnings insurance due to injury or illness. Some funds offer members discounted home and personal loans and private health insurance. It's possible that in future employees will be able to use part of their superannuation funds to buy a home. Your super payout may be related to your final salary, which is the best option. If it isn't, you should ensure that the fund is invested safely as you could lose out if the share market or property prices collapse in the years just before retirement.

If you're an eligible employee (whether full-time, part-time or a casual worker), your employer must contribute to a superannuation scheme on your behalf, the contributions to which must be at least the minimum level laid down by the government, termed the Superannuation Guarantee (SG). If you change employers or professions, your superannuation benefits can be transferred into another fund. The following table shows the fixed percentage of an employee's gross earnings that must be paid into a superannuation scheme (for each employee) under the Superannuation Guarantee:

Financial Year	Superannuation Guarantee
1997-98	6%
1998-99	7%
1999-2000	7%
2000-2001	8%
2001-2002	8%
2002-2003 and beyond	9%

The amount paid has been phased in gradually (starting with 3 per cent for companies with a payroll of $1m or less in 1992) and will reach 9 per cent in the financial year 2002/2003, as shown in the above table.   Note that compulsory employer super contributions are too low (they were originally going to be higher) to maintain income levels in retirement, e.g. the 9 per cent contribution will deliver only around 40 per cent of your pre-retirement income, while it's estimated that most people will need around 75 per cent to have a comfortable retirement.   Some employers pay additional superannuation contributions, e.g. up to 15 per cent of your salary.

Some employers operate flexible 'fast-tracking' super schemes, whereby you can pay higher superannuation contributions and reduce your salary (called 'salary sacrifice' arrangements).   This is particularly worthwhile when your personal tax rate is high, although there's now a tax penalty for doing this. Since 20th August 1996, contributions to superannuation for high income earners have attracted a surcharge of up to 15 per cent.

The surcharge applies on contributions made by those earning $70,000 a year or more (for both employees and the self-employed) and is levied on top of the 15 per cent tax on deductible superannuation contributions (in other words, the tax is now double the previous rate).   The surcharge is phased in at 1 per cent for every $1,000 earned above $70,000, e.g. if you earn $71,000 you must pay a 1 per cent surcharge (16 per cent overall), on $72,000 there's a 2 per cent surcharge (17 per cent overall), and so on up to a maximum surcharge of 15 per cent (total 30 per cent) for those earning $85,000 or over.   The surcharge also applies to anyone who fails to provide his tax file number to his super fund, so many people pay the tax even though their income is below the $70,000 threshold (but it can be reclaimed).   Since the tax was announced many wealthy people have quit super to avoid the tax (over 1.5m super accounts have been closed).   Super has widened the gap between the poor and wealthy, with high income earners enjoying a huge advantage in the race to build up their superannuation assets through large tax concessions on their contributions (the majority of super tax deductions goes to the top 20 per cent of income earners).

Withdrawals: Undeducted contributions (those made out of after-tax salary) can be withdrawn at the age of 55 up to the year 2025. From the year 2025, superannuation will be able to be accessed only at the age of 60 and all super contributions will be 'preserved' (made into jam?) with effect from 1st July 1999. This measure is designed to prevent 'double dipping', i.e. taking super benefits early, spending the money and then applying for a state pension at age 65.   Those aged over 55 will be forced to exhaust their superannuation funds before being allowed to claim unemployment benefits. If you leave Australia permanently, your super benefits won't be released until you reach the 'preservation' age, i.e. 55 for those born before 1st July 1960 and 60 for those born after 30th June 1964. The maximum age limit for contributing to a super fund is 70, providing you work a minimum of 10 hours a week (if you work beyond the age of 65, you should check whether you're still eligible for superannuation). Benefits can be taken in a lump sum, an annuity or a regular monthly income (e.g. an allocated or lifetime pension), or a combination of these.

Since compulsory employer superannuation was introduced in 1992, a number of problems have surfaced and it has become increasingly complicated and difficult for the layman (or anyone) to understand. Although successive governments have tinkered at the edges (some 2,000 changes have been made), many analysts believe that it needs a complete overhaul. For example under the present system super savings are taxed three times: when contributions are made, when there are earnings and when benefits are paid out! However, super reaps some $2.5 billion a year in taxes (and rising) and the government is loathe to kill the golden goose.

HEALTH INSURANCE

The Australian Medicare (see page 277) public health system provides free or subsidised medical treatment for all permanent residents in Australia. Anyone living or working in Australia (even temporarily) who isn't eligible for Medicare treatment (and who doesn't like living dangerously) should have private health insurance. Private health insurance in Australia is usually complementary insurance, so called because it complements (rather than replaces) Medicare. It's commonly used to pay the difference ('gap') between the Medicare schedule fee and what Medicare actually pays. The main reason most people have private health insurance in Australia is to circumvent Medicare waiting lists for specialist appointments and non-emergency hospital treatment (e.g. elective surgery). Patients are also usually free to choose their own doctor and hospital. **Private insurance ensures that you receive the medical treatment you need, when you need it.** Note, however, that (despite what insurance companies might say) the quality of private treatment isn't better than that provided by Medicare and you shouldn't assume that because a doctor (or any other medical practitioner) is in private practice, he's more competent than his Medicare counterpart. In fact you're likely to see the same specialist or be treated by the same surgeon under Medicare as privately (but a few 'years' earlier).

Most private health insurance in Australia is provided by health funds, which are regulated by the Commonwealth government and follow the principle of 'community rating' to determine premiums, i.e. premiums don't vary according to age, sex or your state of health. This ensures that high-risk members such as the elderly, women and the chronically sick, aren't required to pay astronomically high premiums as in some other countries. However, most health funds are eroding this principle and have introduced a variety of conditions in recent years which exclude expensive treatment (called exclusion policies) and surgery such as joint replacements, and there may also be financial ($) limits. Many analysts believe this could be the thin end of the wedge, where insurance companies abandon the 'community rating' by stealth. Changes have been proposed by the government to health insurance, although they are strongly opposed by the Australian Medical Association, which fears that health funds will dictate clinical practices in order to reduce costs, e.g. where the fund decides on treatment rather than the doctor.

Prior to October 1996, funds were required to charge a family no more than twice the premium of a single person, irrespective of how many members a family had. This is no longer the case. Since October 1996, private health insurance funds are allowed to offer four categories of membership as follows:

• single person's membership;

• couple's membership;

• family membership, consisting of at least two adults and one or more other, which may include children or grandparents;

• single-parent membership, consisting of at least one adult (who's the contributor) and one or more dependant children;

When taking out family or single-parent membership, always carefully check what constitutes a dependant child, as your children may not be covered.

Each state has its own private health funds, the largest of which include Medibank Private, the Medical Benefit Funds (MBF), National Mutual Health Insurance and the Hospital Contribution Fund (HCF). By far the largest fund is Medibank Private, a non-profit health benefits organisation (established in 1976) operated by the state-run Health Insurance Commission. It's Australia's largest private health insurer, covering some 1.8m people (two-thirds of all people with private health insurance), with some 275 customer service centres throughout the country. **Medibank Private also provides Overseas Visitors Cover for temporary residents of Australia who aren't eligible for Medicare benefits.** It's possible to obtain health insurance from some banks (e.g. NAB), although they may only target high earners. Compare the benefits and costs provided by a number of health funds. Most provide a choice of basic, intermediate and comprehensive levels of cover, with intermediate and high levels usually providing private rooms in private hospitals and ancillary cover.

Types of Insurance: Health funds offer two basic types of insurance: hospital and ancillary. Hospital cover contributes to the cost of in-hospital treatment and accommodation as a private patient in a private or public hospital. Ancillary cover contributes to the cost of out-patient medical services that aren't covered by Medicare, such as dental treatment, spectacles or contact lenses, physiotherapy, acupuncture, chiropractic and other alternative therapies. Ancillary insurance may also include ambulance cover, home nursing and other services, although there's usually no refund for X-rays or prescriptions. There are payment limits for ancillary cover, both per visit and overall annual limits. Some funds (e.g. HCF) have a 'fit and well' policy which pays for gym membership or sports equipment such as running shoes.

Premiums: In mid-1997, the average costs of 100 per cent hospital cover for a family was around $1,700 and the average cost of 100 per cent ancillary cover around $800. Premiums vary considerably depending on the state or territory and are highest in Victoria and South Australia, and lowest in the Northern Territory and Western Australia. The average cost of private health insurance per year for a single person is: basic (private hospital expenses including choice of doctor) $500, top (covers 100 per cent private hospital expenses) $800, and ancillary (non-hospital expenses such as dental, optical, physiotherapy and chiropractic treatment) $350. Premiums differ little between couples, families and single parent families, who all pay around double the single premium. Premiums (which are tax deductible) can usually be paid monthly, quarterly or annually, and a discount may be given for prompt or annual payment.

Medicare automatically pays 75 per cent of the Medicare Benefits Schedule (MBS) fee for a doctor's services, accommodation in a private hospital or for a private bed in a public hospital, and the health fund pays the rest. Health funds have contracts with hospitals and doctors in order to assert some control over costs and therefore reduce their premiums. You may need to choose a hospital and doctor contracted to your health fund, otherwise you must pay the 'gap' between what the fund pays and what your doctor or hospital charges. Note that some funds have agreements with relatively few private hospitals, outside of which you're limited to a private bed in a public hospital, and you may not be covered outside your home state. You should receive a written quotation for non-emergency hospital treatment, including all costs and out-of-pocket expenses.

Extra Costs & Excess Charges: Note that the benefits (rebates) provided by health funds aren't usually 100 per cent and you usually need to make a contribution (an excess or co-payment) towards fees, called 'out-of-pocket' costs. These can be very high and can run into hundreds or even thousands of dollars (and can change at short notice). If you want your own doctor to treat you in a public hospital, you must pay a daily accommodation charge and some funds levy a fee per night (e.g. $50) for private hospital patients. In addition to out-of-pocket costs, there's also usually an annual excess charge, which can be up to $2,000 a year for a family and may be applied per person for a couple. When you leave hospital, you're generally asked to pay the difference (if any) between your health insurer's refund and the hospital's fees. **High out-of-pocket expenses are the main reason people have abandoned private health insurance.**

In recent years people have been deserting private health insurance in their thousands as premiums and surcharges ('gap' fees) have soared (what did the fools expect?). Before Medicare was introduced in 1984, over 50 per cent of Australians had private cover, which has since fallen to below a third (some 6m people) — the system ceases to be viable at 30 per cent! After increasing premiums by between 10 and 20 per cent in the last year, funds were losing around 1,000 members a day in 1997. The government is desperate to encourage people to return to (or remain in) private health cover, as Medicare is facing a funding crisis and its survival in its present form relies heavily on a strong private health sector. **If things go on this way, there could be a collapse of health funds AND Medicare (maybe you had better insure with a foreign company).**

The cost of private health insurance premiums has increased by over 100 per cent in the last eight years, from 1990 to 1997 (14 per cent in 1996/97 alone), compared with a cost-of-living increase of less than 30 per cent (and just 1 per cent in 1996-97). However, despite the high premiums, health funds are making very little (or no) money due to the spiralling costs of hospital stays and operations, and some are even on the verge of bankruptcy. The number of people cancelling their policies simply adds to the vicious circle of increasing premiums and the pressure on Medicare. From 1st July 1997, the government introduced a carrot and stick approach to encourage people to join a health fund, whereby those on low and middle incomes receive an incentive to take out private health insurance, while high earners are penalised if they don't have private health insurance.

Incentives: From 1st July 1997, lower and middle income earners have been able to claim between $100 and $450 in reduced premiums or as a tax deduction at the end of the year. Note that if you don't pay sufficient tax to qualify for the rebate, you will lose out on the incentive and therefore should claim a reduced premium instead. It's estimated that some 80 per cent of people are eligible for the incentives, shown below:

Eligibility/ Maximum Income*	Incentive* Hospital Cover	Ancillary Cover
Single $35,000	$100 ($250 premium)	$25 ($125 premium)
Couple $70,000	$200 ($500 premium)	$50 ($250 premium)
Family $70,000	$350 ($500 premium)	$100 ($100 premium)
+ $3,000 per child*		

*   The incentives listed above are for those earning up to the taxable (maximum) income shown in column one, plus $3,000 per child *after* the first one (i.e. you must have two children to claim the $3,000). Anyone earning above these limits doesn't qualify for an incentive. The premium (shown in brackets) is the minimum premium that must be paid in order to qualify for the incentives.

Despite the incentives, for most people the few dollars saved makes little difference when they are paying well over $1,000 a year for insurance. The incentives may have influenced people with insurance to stick with it, but they have done little to encourage people to sign up to a health fund.

Medicare Levy Surcharge: In an effort to encourage high earners to take out private health insurance, those who don't have private health insurance to at least cover doctor's fees and accommodation in hospital must pay an increased Medicare levy (see page 277). From 1st July 1997 the Medicare levy was increased by 1 per cent for single people earning over $50,000 a year and families earning over $100,000 a year, who don't have private health insurance (it applies pro rata if you have insurance for less than a full year). The taxable threshold increases by $1,500 for each child, excluding the first. This means that a single person with a taxable income of $50,000 must pay a surcharge of $500 a year and a couple with three children earning $110,000 a surcharge of $1,100. It may be cheaper to buy insurance with a large excess (which reduces the premium), even if you never intend to use it, than pay the increased levy. The government may have created the worst of both worlds, where it subsidises the health funds without relieving the burden on Medicare.

Waiting Periods: Note that all funds have waiting periods before new members are eligible to make a claim, e.g. a general two-month wait for all treatment, nine-months for obstetrics (i.e. you cannot join when pregnant) and one year for pre-existing conditions. This is to prevent you from making a claim directly after joining and then dropping your membership. However, accidents are covered from the day you join. Before changing funds, always check the waiting times for treatment, particularly if you have existing health problems. If you already belong to a private health insurance scheme (such as BUPA in Britain), you may be able to transfer your membership to Australia, in which case you won't be subject to waiting lists. Some insurance companies offer a short-term scheme for people staying in Australia for a limited period.

Students: Overseas Student Health Cover (OSHC) is obligatory for overseas students and their families in Australia, which must cover them for the duration of their visa (or the first 12 months). It's provided by a number of insurance companies, including Medibank Private. Your premium must be paid before you arrive in Australia and will depend on the length of your student visa, up to a maximum 12 months cover. If your student visa is for more than 12 months, a further premium is payable after 12 months. If you're a **private student**, your premium will be paid on your behalf by the school, college or university at which you will be studying. If you're a **government-sponsored student** (e.g. by the Australian Agency for International Development/AusAID), the agency or department of the Australian government which is sponsoring you will pay your premium to Medibank Private.

OSHC cover includes cover for doctors (including specialists) either at a surgery, your home or in hospital; pathology services such as blood tests; and X-rays. Payments are the same as for Medicare members, i.e. 85 per cent of the government schedule fee for outpatient treatment and 100 per cent of the schedule fee for hospital in-patient services. If a doctor charges more than the schedule fee, you must pay the difference. OSHC provides full cover in a general (shared) ward in a public hospital, including all charges for out-patient treatment. If you choose to be treated in a private hospital, Medibank Private will pay towards the cost of treatment and accommodation, but you will be responsible for paying the difference between the schedule fee and the actual fee charged. The services that aren't covered by OSHC are much the same as for Medicare (see page 277). If you wish to be covered for excluded services, you will need additional private health insurance.

International Health Policies: It's also possible to take out an international health insurance policy, which may be of particular interest to people living in Australia temporarily, or those whose work involves a lot of travel or who work part of the time overseas. Some policies offer members a range of premiums from budget to comprehensive cover. All policies offer at least two fee scales, one covering the whole world including North America (and possible other high cost areas) and the other excluding North America. Most policies include a full refund of hospital, ambulance, home nursing (usually for a limited period), out patient, emergency dental treatment and repatriation charges. All policies include an annual overall claims' limit, usually from $200,000 to $2,000,000 (the higher the better, particularly for North America).

Some comprehensive policies provide a fixed amount for general medical costs (including routine doctors' visits) and optional dental, optical and maternity expenses. Premiums range from around $1,500 to over $5,000 a year, depending on your age, level of cover and the areas covered (if North America is covered, premiums are much higher). If you don't require permanent international health insurance, you should consider a policy which provides limited or optional cover when you're overseas. Note that all bills, particularly those received for treatment outside Australia, must include precise details of treatment received. Terms such as 'Dental Treatment' or 'Consultation' are usually insufficient. It's also helpful if bills are written in English (although this is impossible in many countries).

If you're living or working in Australia and aren't covered by Medicare, it's risky or even foolhardy not to have private health insurance for you and your family. Whether you're covered by an Australian or foreign health insurance policy makes little difference (except perhaps in cost), providing you have the required level of cover, including international cover if necessary. (N.B. If you can afford private insurance, it would generally be considered foolish not to have it.) If you aren't adequately insured, you could be faced with some extremely high medical bills. When deciding on the type of policy, make sure that the insurance scheme covers *all* your family's health requirements. If your stay in Australia is limited you may be covered by a reciprocal agreement between your home country and Australia (see page 292), or by a private health insurance scheme. **Make sure you're fully covered in Australia <u>before</u> you receive a large bill.**

When changing employers or leaving Australia, you should make sure that you have continuous medical insurance. For example, if you and your family are covered by a company health fund, your insurance will probably cease after your last official day of employment. If you're leaving Australia, you must cancel an Australian health insurance policy in writing if you aren't a member of a company health scheme. **If you're planning to change your health insurance company, ensure that no important benefits are lost. When changing health insurance companies, it's advisable to inform your old insurance company if you have any outstanding bills for which they are liable.**

Complaints: If you're unable to resolve a complaint with your health fund, you can contact the Private Health Insurance Complaints Commissioner, Suite 1201, Level 12, St. Martins Tower, 131 Market Street, Sydney 2000 (tel. 1300-640 695 or (02) 9261 5944). See also **Chapter 12**.

DENTAL INSURANCE

It's unusual to have full dental insurance in Australia as the cost is prohibitive. Routine dental services aren't funded by Medicare, although it pays for 75 per cent of in-hospital medical procedures performed by an oral surgeon, and pensioners qualify for free general and emergency dental treatment under the Commonwealth Dental Health Program. Basic dental treatment is usually provided under a health fund's ancillary policy and most international health insurance policies offer optional dental cover or extra dental cover for an additional premium, although there are many restrictions and cosmetic treatment is excluded. Where applicable, the amount payable by a health insurance policy for a particular item of dental treatment is fixed and depends on your level of dental insurance. A list of specific refunds is available from insurance companies.

Some dentists also offer a dental insurance scheme. Patients must be 'dentally fit' (so if you have 'bad' teeth, you won't be accepted) and are graded according to the condition of their teeth. Insurance doesn't usually cover expensive items such as crowns, bridges and dentures. **Note that if you have healthy teeth and rarely pay for more than an annual checkup and a visit to a hygienist, dental insurance provides poor value for money.** See also **Dentists** on page 287.

BUILDING INSURANCE

For most people, buying a home is the biggest financial investment they will ever make. When buying a home, you're usually responsible for insuring it before you even move in. If you take out a mortgage to buy a property, your lender will usually insist that your home (including most permanent structures on your property) has building insurance from the time you sign the contract and legally become the owner. Even when it isn't required by a lender, you would be extremely unwise not to have building insurance, as homes can be severely damaged by inclement weather, landslides and subsidence.

Building insurance usually includes loss or damage caused by fire; theft; riot or malicious damage; water leakage from pipes or tanks; oil leakage from central heating systems; flood, storm and lightening; explosion or aircraft impact; vehicles or animals; earthquake, subsidence, landslip or heave; falling trees or aerials; and may include cover for temporary homelessness. Some insurance companies also provide optional cover to include trees and shrubs damaged maliciously or by storms. Note that there may be an excess, e.g. from $50 or $100, for some claims, which is intended to deter policy holders from making small claims. Building insurance must be renewed each year and insurance companies are continually updating their policies, so you must take care that a policy still provides the cover you require when you receive a renewal notice.

Lenders fix the initial level of cover when you first apply for a mortgage and usually offer to arrange the insurance for you, but you're usually free to make your own arrangements. If you arrange your own building insurance, your lender will insist that the level of cover is sufficient. Most people take the easy option and arrange insurance through their mortgage lender, which is generally the most expensive option, e.g. some direct insurance companies guarantee to cut building insurance costs for the majority of homeowners insured through banks and building societies. **The amount for which your home must be insured isn't the current market value, but the cost of rebuilding it should it be totally destroyed.** This varies depending on the type of property and the area. There's usually no deduction for wear and tear and the cost of redecoration is usually met in full. Note that building insurance doesn't cover structural faults that existed when you took out the policy, which is why it's important to have a full structural survey done when you buy a property.

Most lenders provide index-linked building insurance, where premiums are linked to inflation and building costs (premiums are usually added to your monthly mortgage payments). It is, however, your responsibility to ensure that your level of cover is adequate, particularly if you carry out improvements or extensions which substantially increase the value of your home. All lenders provide information and free advice. If your level of cover is too low, an insurance company is within its rights to reduce the amount it pays out when a claim is made, in which case you may find you cannot afford to have your house rebuilt or repaired, should disaster strike.

The cost of building insurance varies depending on the type of building and the area, and is calculated per $1,000 of insurance, e.g. from around $3 to $4 per $1,000 of cover (per year) in an inexpensive area up to $10 per $1,000 in the most expensive high-risk areas. Therefore insurance on a property costing $150,000 to rebuild costs from around $450 to $600 up to $1,500 a year. In recent years increased competition (particularly from direct insurers) has reduced premiums. The National Roads and Motoring

Association (NRMA) in New South Wales is the nation's biggest insurer and insures around 1.4m homes. Insurance for 'non-standard' homes such as those with thatched roofs or timber construction is usually higher. The highest level of cover usually includes damage to glass (e.g. windows and patio doors) and porcelain (e.g. bath, washbasins and WCs), although you may have to pay extra for accidental damage, e.g. when your son blasts a cricket ball through the patio window. Always ask your insurer what *isn't* covered and what it will cost to include it (if required).

Premiums can usually be paid monthly (although there may be an extra charge) or annually. Some home insurance policies charge an excess (e.g. $100) for each claim, while others have an excess for certain claims only, e.g. subsidence or landslip (when your house disappears into a hole in the ground or over a cliff), which is usually $2,000 or $4,000. Owners of houses vulnerable to subsidence and those living in flood-prone areas are likely to pay higher premiums.

Many insurance companies provide emergency telephone numbers for policyholders requiring urgent advice. Should you need to make emergency repairs, e.g. to weather-proof a roof after a storm or other natural disaster, most insurance companies allow work up to a certain limit (e.g. $2,000) to be carried out without an estimate or approval from the insurance company, but check first. Building insurance is often combined with home contents insurance (see below), when it's called home or household insurance, which is usually cheaper than taking out separate policies.

HOME CONTENTS INSURANCE

Home contents insurance is advisable for anyone who doesn't live in an empty house. Burglary and house-breaking is a major problem in Australia, particularly in the major cities. Although there's a lot you can do to prevent someone breaking into your home (see **Home Security** on page 139), it's usually impossible or prohibitively expensive to make your home completely burglar proof without turning it into a fortress. However, you can ensure you have adequate contents insurance and that your most precious possessions are locked in a safe or safety deposit box.

Types of Policy: A basic home contents policy covers your belongings against the same sort of 'natural disasters' as building insurance (see above). You can optionally insure against accidental damage and all risks. A basic contents policy doesn't usually include such items as credit cards (and their fraudulent use), cash, musical instruments, jewellery, valuables, sports equipment and bicycles, for which you may need to take out extra cover. You can usually insure your property for its secondhand value (indemnity) or its full replacement value (new for old), which covers everything except clothes and linen (for which wear and tear is assessed) at the new cost price. Replacement value is the most popular form of contents insurance in Australia. In the case of replacement value, it's best to take out an index-linked policy, where the level of cover is automatically increased by a percentage or fixed amount each year. Most policies have a maximum amount they will pay per item and/or a maximum amount per claim, e.g. $1,500 for each item of jewellery or work of art or a total claim of $7,500.

A basic policy doesn't usually include accidental damage caused by you or members of your family to your own property (e.g. 'accidentally' putting your foot through the TV during a political party broadcast) or your home freezer contents (in the event of a breakdown or power failure). A basic policy may include replacement locks, garden contents, personal liability insurance (see below), loss of oil and metered water, and temporary accommodation. If they aren't included, these items can usually be covered optionally. Some policies include legal expenses cover (e.g. up to $100,000) for disputes with neighbours, shops, suppliers, employers and anyone who provides you with a service (e.g. a plumber or builder). Most contents policies include public liability cover, e.g. up to $2m. Items such as computers and mobile phones may need to be listed as named items on your policy, and computers and other equipment used for business aren't usually covered (or may only be covered for a prohibitive extra payment). If you have friends or lodgers living in your home, their personal property won't be covered by your policy.

Premiums: Your premium will depend largely on where you live (and your insurer). All insurance companies assess the risk by location based on your postcode. **Check before buying a home, as the difference between low and high-risk areas can be considerable.** Annual premiums are usually calculated per $1,000 of cover and range from around $4 per $1,000 in a low-risk area to sround double this in a high-risk area. Many homeowners in high-risk areas would be willing to forego theft insurance, although insurance companies are unwilling to offer this option as premiums would be substantially reduced if theft was omitted (theft is a convenient excuse to load premiums).

As with building insurance, it's important to shop around for the lowest premium, which vary considerably depending on the insurer. If you're already insured, you may find that you can save money by changing insurers. (However, watch out for penalties when switching insurers.) Combining your home contents insurance with your building insurance (see above) is a common practice and is usually cheaper than insuring each separately. Having your building and contents insurance with the same insurer also avoids disputes over which company should pay for which item, as could arise if you have a fire or flood affecting both your home and its contents. Those aged over 50 or 55 (and possibly first-time home owners) may be offered a discount and some companies provide special policies for students in college accommodation or lodgings (ask an insurance broker).

Security: Most insurers offer a no-claims' discount or a discount (e.g. 5 or 10 per cent) for homes with burglar alarms and other high security features. In high-risk areas, good security is usually a condition of insurance. Beware of the small print in policies, particularly those regarding security, which insurers often use to avoid paying claims. You will forfeit all rights under your policy if you leave doors or windows open (or the keys under a mat or flower pot), particularly if you've claimed a discount due to your impregnable security. If there are no signs of forced entry, e.g. a broken window, you may be unable to claim for a theft (so break a window!). If you plan to leave your house empty for a long period, e.g. a month or longer, you may need to inform your insurer.

Sum Insured: Take care that you don't under-insure your house contents (including anything rented such as a TV or video recorder) and that you periodically reassess their value and adjust your premium accordingly. Your contents should include everything which isn't part of the fixtures and fittings, and which you could take with you if you were moving house. If you under insure your contents, your claim may be reduced by the percentage by which you're under-insured. Some insurance companies offer policies called 'no-sum' or 'fixed-sum', where you aren't required to value all your possessions, but are covered for a fixed amount depending on the number of bedrooms in your home. With this type of policy the insurance company cannot scale down a claim because of under-insurance, however, you're usually better off calculating the value of the contents to be insured. You can take out a special policy if you have high-value contents, which may be cheaper than a standard contents policy. **Always list all previous burglaries on the proposal form, even if nothing was stolen.**

Claims: Some insurers provide a 24-hour emergency helpline for policyholders and emergency assistance for repairs for domestic emergencies such as a blocked drain or electrical failure, up to a maximum ($) limit for each claim. Take care when completing a claims form, as insurers have tightened up on claims and few people receive a full settlement. Many insurers have an excess of from $50 to $100 per claim. Bear in mind that if you make a claim, you usually need to wait months for it to be settled. Generally the larger the claim, the longer you have to wait for your money, although in an emergency a company may make an interim payment. If you aren't satisfied with the final amount offered, don't accept it and try to negotiate a higher figure. If you still cannot reach agreement on the amount, you can contact the General Insurance Claims Review Panel (tel. 1300-363683) for independent arbitration or take legal action.

PERSONAL LIABILITY INSURANCE

Although common in Europe and North America (where people sue each other for $millions at the drop of a hat), personal (or legal) liability insurance is unusual in Australia. However, home contents policies (see above) usually include personal liability insurance up to $2 million and it's also included in travel policies (see below). Personal liability insurance provides personal insurance for individuals and members of their families against compensation for accidental damage, injury or death caused to third parties or their property. It usually covers anything from spilling wine on your neighbour's Persian carpet (N.B. if you pour white wine on a red wine stain, it will disappear) to your dog or child biting someone.

HOLIDAY & TRAVEL INSURANCE

Holiday and travel insurance is recommended for all who don't wish to risk having their holiday or travel spoilt by financial problems or to arrive home broke. As you know, anything can and often does go wrong with a holiday, sometimes before you even get on the plane (particularly if you *don't* have insurance). Travel insurance is available from many sources including travel agents, insurance brokers, tour operators, banks, airlines and motoring organisations.

Level of Cover: Before taking out travel insurance, carefully consider the level of cover required and compare policies. Most policies include loss of deposit or holiday cancellation; missed flight; departure delay at both the start *and* end of a holiday (a common occurrence); delayed baggage; personal effects; lost baggage (e.g. $3,000); medical expenses (up to $4m) and accidents (including evacuation home if necessary); personal money (e.g. $500 to $1,000); personal liability ($2m or $4m); legal expenses; and a tour operator going bust. You should also insure against missing your flight due to an accident or transport breakdown, as almost half of travel insurance claims are for cancellation (you should also be covered for transport delays at the end of your holiday, e.g. the flight home). With some policies, the amount you can claim for personal belongings may be limited to around $400 an item, which will be insufficient to cover your Rolex watch or expensive camera. Some home contents policies include cover for personal belongings worldwide. Note, however, that your insurance company won't pay out if you're negligent, e.g. you leave your camera in a taxi or on a beach.

Medical Expenses: Medical expenses are an important aspect of travel insurance and you shouldn't rely on reciprocal health agreements; cover provided by charge and credit card companies: house contents policies; or private medical insurance; none of which usually provide the necessary cover. The minimum medical insurance recommended by experts is $500,000 for Europe and $2m for North America and the rest of the world. Personal liability should be at least $2m for Europe and $4m for the rest of the world.

Note that most travel and holiday insurance policies don't provide the minimum level of cover that most people need. Always check any exclusion clauses in contracts by obtaining a copy of the full policy document, as all relevant information won't be contained in insurance leaflets.

Exclusions: Health or accident insurance included in travel insurance policies usually contains exclusions, e.g. dangerous sports such as white-water rafting, mountaineering, skiing, hang-gliding, scuba-diving, crocodile wrestling and kangaroo boxing, or even riding a motorbike in some countries. Check the small print and find out exactly what terms such as 'hazardous pursuits' include or exclude. Skiing and other winter sports should be specifically covered and *listed* in a travel insurance policy. Special 'winter sports' policies are available, which are usually more expensive than normal holiday insurance.

Cost: The cost of travel insurance varies considerably, depending on your destination. Many companies have different rates for different areas, e.g. Australia, Europe, North America and worldwide (excluding North America). Premiums for travel within Australia are around $15 per person for two weeks, European destinations are usually $30 to $40 for two weeks, and North America (where medical treatment costs an arm and a leg) and a few other destinations costs $70 to $100 for three weeks. The cheapest policies offer reduced cover, but may not be adequate for most people. Premiums may be higher for those aged over 65 or 70. Generally the longer the period covered, the cheaper the daily cost, although the maximum period may be limited, e.g. six months. With some policies an excess (e.g. $50) must be paid for each claim.

Annual Policies: For people who travel overseas frequently, whether for business or pleasure, an annual travel policy is often an excellent idea, costing around $200 to $300 a year for worldwide cover for an unlimited number of trips. However, always carefully check exactly what it includes and read the small print (some insist that travel is by air). Most annual policies don't cover you for travel within Australia and there's a maximum limit on the length of a trip, e.g. from one to six months. Some companies offer 'tailor-made' insurance for independent travellers (e.g. backpackers) for any period from a few days to one year.

Claims: Although travel insurance companies will quickly and gladly take your money, they aren't so keen to pay claims and you may need to persevere before they pay up. Fraudulent claims against travel insurance are common, so unless you can produce evidence to support your claim, the insurers may think that you're trying to cheat them. Always be persistent and make a claim irrespective of any small print as this may be unreasonable and therefore invalid in law. **Insurance companies usually require you to report any loss (or any incident for which you intend to make a claim) to the local police or carriers within 24 hours and to obtain a report. Failure to do this will mean that a claim usually won't be considered.**

Flight insurance and comprehensive travel insurance is available from insurance desks at most airports, including travel accident, personal accident, world-wide medical expenses and in-transit baggage. When you pay for your travel costs with some credit cards, your family (possibly including children under the age of 25) are provided with free travel accident insurance up to a specified amount, e.g. $300,000. **Don't rely on this insurance, as it usually covers only death or serious injury.** Special motor insurance providing added protection is available from some travel agents for anyone driving in the USA, where standard motor policies for rental cars *don't* include adequate insurance.

MOTOR BREAKDOWN INSURANCE

Breakdown insurance for cars and motorcycles is available from Australian motoring organisations (see page 268). Travel insurance for motoring holidays is also available.

CAR INSURANCE

Comprehensive or third party property car insurance is available from numerous insurance companies in Australia (see page 246). Third party (bodily injury) insurance (CTP) is compulsory in Australia.

LIFE INSURANCE

Although there are worse things in life than death (like spending an evening with a life insurance salesman), your dependants may rate your death *without* life insurance high on their list. Although it's often referred to as life *insurance*, Australian life policies are almost always for life *assurance*. Assurance is a policy which covers an eventuality which is certain to occur (for example, like it or not, you must die one day). Thus a life assurance policy is valid until you die. An insurance policy covers a risk which *may* happen, but isn't a certainty, for example, accident insurance (unless you're exceptionally accident prone). You can take out a life insurance policy with dozens of insurance companies in Australia. Be extremely wary of all insurance sales people (whose credibility is on a par with used car salesmen, real estate agents and politicians), some of whom use dubious soft and hard-sell methods to hook customers. You have no guarantee of receiving good or independent advice or indeed any advice at all. Most companies offer a variety of life insurance policies, e.g. term, whole life and endowment.

Commissions and Charges: One disadvantage with all life insurance policies is the large commissions paid to salesmen, which may be equivalent to a year's premiums, so it always pays to shop around and ask salesmen or brokers about their rates of commission. Added to commissions are expenses including management and administration fees. When buying life insurance, you're usually better off dealing with an independent insurance adviser or broker, who does business with a number of insurance companies. Note that most banks and building societies are unable to give independent advice on life policies and many are tied to a particular insurance company. Always try to ensure that you have a cooling-off period, during which you can cancel a policy without incurring a penalty.

Health: Whether you need to undergo a medical examination depends on the insurance company, your age, state of health and the amount of insurance required. You must complete a medical questionnaire and depending on your age and health record, your GP may be required to provide a medical report. If you have no family doctor or previous medical history, you may be required to have a medical examination. Many policies don't pay out when death is the result of certain illnesses, e.g. an aids-related illness. If you're a clean living, non-smoking, teetotaler, you may be able to obtain cheaper life insurance than an alcoholic chain-smoker (although you will probably die younger of boredom!).

Some companies provide free life insurance an employment benefit (although it may be accident life insurance only) and many superannuation schemes provide a death-in-service benefit. A life insurance policy can be used as security for a bank loan and can be limited to cover the period of the loan. Performance tables are published regularly in financial magazines showing the best-performing unit trusts, pension funds and other long-term investments. You would be wise to consult them and other independent sources of information before taking out a policy from which you expect either a lump sum on maturity or a regular income, as choosing the wrong investment can be *very* costly.

Finally, it's advisable to leave a copy of all insurance policies with your will (see page 356) and with your lawyer. If you don't have a lawyer, keep a copy in a safe deposit box. A life insurance policy must usually be sent to the insurance company upon the death of the insured, with a copy of the death certificate.

14.

FINANCE

Competition for your money is fierce in Australia and in addition to many Australian and foreign banks, financial services are provided by building societies, credit unions, investment brokers, insurance companies, mortgage originators/providers, Australia Post, and even supermarkets and service organisations (such as motoring organisations). Banks are facing increasing competition from a shakeup of the country's financial services industry, which it's estimated will eventually save $billions a year (although it's happening very slowly). Sydney is Australia's most important financial market, although it's relatively small in international terms. The country has a sophisticated financial system and in recent years has had a strong growth rate and low inflation (around 2 per cent). However, the Australian dollar suffered badly from the turbulence in Asian markets in 1997, which also hit the economy. In 1997, Australia's gross domestic product (GDP) per head was around US$22,000 and the average Australian's wealth is over $100,000 (although it isn't exactly evenly distributed).

Australia is a credit-financed society, and banks and finance companies queue up to lend you money or provide credit (interest rates on credit cards are high). Levels of personal debt are over 40 per cent of output (similar to the UK and USA) and in 1997 household debt reached record levels (over 90 per cent of disposable income), with Australians owing record amounts on credit cards and personal overdrafts. There are fears that if interest rates (which hit a 30-year low in 1997) were to rise rapidly, many people would be unable to service their debts (even with low interest rates, bankruptcies have been running at record levels in the last few years). Credit and assorted other plastic cards have largely replaced 'real' money and now account for the vast majority of retail purchases. Your financial standing in Australia is usually decided by the number of cards you have, including credit cards, cash cards, EFTPOS (debit) cards, charge cards, store cards and assorted specialist cards. Australia, like many western countries, is fast becoming a cash-less society. Personal savings in Australia are among the lowest in the western world.

Taxes in Australia vary considerably depending on the state or territory and overall per capita taxation is lowest in Queensland and highest in Victoria and NSW. Taxes are levied at Commonwealth (federal), state and local government levels. There are no wealth, inheritance or gift taxes in Australia (it's the only country among the OECD countries not to have some form of inheritance tax — although some states are eying this tax opportunity). States and territories don't currently levy income tax, but receive their income from stamp duty on commercial and legal documents (cheques, receipts, transfers of land, insurance policies and mortgage transactions); payroll tax (a state tax imposed on an employer's payroll and the biggest source of income for state governments); taxes on motor vehicles land and liquor; and miscellaneous licence fees. In recent years there has been an ongoing battle between state and federal governments over tax, which was brought to the fore with the high court's decision to outlaw state imposts on alcohol, petrol and tobacco. The main form of local government tax is property tax, augmented by charges for services such as sewerage and water.

The total of direct and indirect taxation in Australia is relatively low by international standards, although the government is continually inventing new ways of taxing people including various taxes on superannuation (pension) funds; a special tax to pay for the public health service; a tax for not having private health insurance; and fringe benefits tax. Australian politicians have been grappling with the problem of how to reform the tax system (it's the most unfair, contradictory and inefficient in the western world) for many years and there are advanced plans to introduce a goods and services tax (a form of value added tax) in the next few years.

Personal finance in Australia is a jungle and there are plenty of predators about just waiting to get their hands on your loot. Always shop around for financial services and never sign a contract unless you know exactly what the costs and implications are. Although bankers, financiers and brokers don't like to make too fine a point of it, they aren't doing business with you because they like you, but simply to get their hands on your pile of chips. It's up to you to make sure that their share is kept to a minimum and that you receive the best possible value for your money. **When dealing with 'experts' always bear in mind that while making mistakes is easy, fouling up completely requires professional help!** A new Consumer Credit Code was introduced in 1997 and is detailed in the Department of Fair Trading booklet, *Walking the Credit Tightrope is Now a Lot Less Risky* (don't you believe it!).

When you arrive in Australia to take up residence, ensure that you have sufficient cash, travellers' cheques, credit cards, luncheon vouchers, coffee machine tokens, silver dollars, gold nuggets and precious stones, to last at least until your first pay day, which may be some time after your arrival. Don't, however, carry a lot of cash. During this period you will find that a credit card (or two) is useful. Note that among the various Australian eccentricities is the government financial tax 'year', which runs from 1st July to 30th June of the following year.

There are numerous books and magazines published to help you manage your finances. *MoneyChoice* (operated by the Australian Consumers' Association — see page 434) will tailor a list of home loans, personal loans, overdrafts, and credit card options and interest rates to suit your needs (tel. 1900-170088, $1.95 a minute with a typical call costing $8). Personal finance information is published in the financial pages of the Saturday and Sunday editions of major newspapers. For information regarding pensions (including superannuation) and life insurance, see **Chapter 13**.

TAX FILE NUMBER

Your tax file number (TFN), consisting of nine digits, is probably the most important number you will receive in Australia. Without it you cannot open a bank account and you will be taxed the maximum rate (49 per cent) on your wages if you don't provide your employer with a TFN. You also need a TFN to claim unemployment and sickness benefits; invest in shares or make any investment; and to enrol in a fee-free course of higher education. It's also required when completing your annual income tax return. You can obtain an application form to apply for a TFN from your local Australian Tax Office (ATO) or most post offices. Proof of identification is necessary such as your passport with a valid visa, a birth certificate or a driver's licence. You should receive your TFN around two weeks after making an application. The Australian Taxation Office (ATO) publishes a brochure, *Applying for Your Tax File Number*. There are both personal and business tax file numbers.

When you earn interest income of $120 or more a year, receive dividends from shares or distributions from unit trust investments, Australian banks are required to deduct withholding tax if you don't provide a TFN (although it isn't compulsory to give your bank your TFN). Your bank is also required to report annually to the ATO the details of interest/dividend income earned, any TFN withholding tax deducted and the TFN quoted. Where necessary, withholding tax is calculated at the highest marginal tax rate plus the Medicare levy (see page 277). As you may be entitled to a tax refund, you need to include details of withholding tax deductions on your tax form.

Those exempt from withholding tax include pensioners; children aged under 16 (although a TFN should be obtained if investment income is likely to be above $420 a year); religious and voluntary organisations; government bodies and local authorities; and customers with special accounts where the interest doesn't accrue to the person named as the account holder. The tax rate is 30 per cent on dividends and royalties. Withholding tax is usually limited to 15 per cent on dividends under double-taxation agreements and to 10 per cent on royalties.

AUSTRALIAN CURRENCY

The Australian unit of currency is the Australian dollar (A$). It has been fairly strong in recent years thanks to a relatively strong economy and low inflation (around 2 per cent in 1997) However, in early 1998 the A$ fell to an 11-year low against the US$ due to the turmoil in Asian money markets and collapsing Asian currencies (it has derisively been referred to by Australians as the 'Pacific Peso' due to its fall in value in recent years). The $A lost over 15 per cent of its value against the $US in 1997, the biggest annual fall on record.

There's no limit on the amount of Australian or foreign currency that can be brought into Australia, but amounts of $10,000 or more (or the equivalent in foreign currency) must be declared on arrival. Currency refers to notes and foreign currency, and doesn't include travellers' cheques or other monetary instruments. Forms for reporting currency transfers are available from customs officers at ports and airports, and reporting is required by law (failure to do so is an offence). For further information contact the Australian Transaction Reports and Analysis Centre, GPO Box 5516W, West Chatswood, NSW 2057 (tel. (02) 9950 0055).

The Australian dollar is divided into 100 cents and coins are minted in values of 5¢, 10¢, 20¢, 50¢ (all silver-coloured cupronickel coins), and $1 and $2, which are gold-coloured bronze coins with irregular milling on the edge. Note that $1 and $2 coins are smaller than the 20¢ coin, which can cause confusion. Keep a supply of 20¢ and 50¢ coins handy for parking meters and other machines. Although the smallest coin is 5¢, prices are still shown in single cents and rounded up or down to the nearest 5¢. Australian banknotes have lurid designs and are printed in values of $5 (orange/mauve), $10 (turquoise/yellow), $20 (red/khaki), $50 (gold/green) and $100 (blue/grey). The $50 and $100 bills are treated with suspicion by many people and may not be accepted by small businesses, tax drivers, etc. Gold 'Australian nuggets' with a face value of $15 to $100 (their actual value is many times the face value) are available from banks and are a popular investment (except when the gold price is plummeting as it did in 1997).

Forgery is a problem in most western countries and there are a 'significant number' of forged $20, $50 and $100 notes in circulation, so be on your guard if someone insists on paying a large bill in banknotes. You should also check that you don't receive New Zealand coins in your change, which are worth less than Australian coins. New plastic $5 and $10 notes (made of polymer) have been introduced in recent years, which it's claimed were impossible to counterfeit (ha! — counterfeiters have already cracked them — back to the drawing board!). They last longer than paper notes and can be recycled when they are withdrawn (which is just as well).

It's advisable to obtain some Australian coins and banknotes before arriving in Australia, and to familiarise yourself and your family with them. You should have some dollars in cash, e.g. $50 to $100 in small bills, when you arrive, but should avoid carrying a lot of cash. This will save you having to queue to change money on arrival at an Australian airport (where exchange rates are usually poor and there are often long queues). It's best to avoid $50 and $100 notes (unless you receive them as a gift!) which sometimes aren't accepted, particularly for small purchases or on public transport.

FOREIGN CURRENCY

Australia has no currency restrictions and you may import or export as much money as you wish, in practically any currency. However, amounts of $10,000 or more in Australian or foreign currency (not including travellers' cheques) must be declared to customs on arrival in Australia (they are reported to the Cash Transaction Reports Agency, c/o The Treasury, Parkes Place, Parkes, ACT 2600, tel. (02) 6263 3762). This is to combat tax evasion and organised crime. Major Australian banks will change most foreign bank notes (but not coins) and offer a better exchange rate for travellers' cheques than for bank notes.

Buying & Selling Currency: When buying or selling foreign currency in Australia, beware of excessive charges. Apart from the difference in exchange rates, which are posted by all banks and (*bureaux de change*), there may be a significant difference in charges. Most banks and building societies buy and sell foreign currency, although apart from the major branches in capital cities, most don't keep foreign currency and you usually need to order it a few days in advance. It pays to shop around for the best exchange rates, particularly when changing a lot of money (it's possible to barter over rates in some establishments). Most banks have a wide spread (e.g. 5 to 10 per cent) between their buying and selling rates for foreign currencies. The A$ exchange rate against major international currencies is listed in banks and the major daily newspapers.

Travellers' Cheques: Travellers' cheques are widely accepted in Australia in all major international currencies. The commission for cashing travellers' cheques varies depending on the bank, e.g. of the big four banks, ANZ and Westpac don't charge a fee, the National charges $5 and the Commonwealth $6 per transaction (irrespective of the number of cheques cashed or their value). No fee is charged when cashing American Express or Thomas Cook travellers' cheques at their own branches. Australia Post charges a 1 per cent fee and other banks and travel agents 1.5 to 2 per cent or a flat fee of $5 to $10 (plus a stamp duty of 20¢ a cheque). Banks in rural areas (if you can find one) usually levy the highest fees for cashing travellers' cheques. You can also cash travellers' cheques at luxury hotels and some businesses, although exchange rates are usually poor. Note that you need your passport to cash cheques.

Most banks charge commission of 1 per cent of the face value when you're buying travellers' cheques. If you're planning to take up residence or spend some months in Australia, it's worthwhile buying A$ travellers' cheques, as you will avoid exchange rate fluctuations and save on commission and fees. When travelling outside Australia, it's best to buy travellers' cheques in £sterling or US$, which are the most widely accepted (US$ cheques should always be used when visiting the USA). Lost or stolen travellers' cheques can be replaced in Australia and most countries overseas (the easiest to replace are American Express), although you must keep a record of your cheque numbers (separate from your cheques).

Cash Transfers: If you have money transferred to Australia by banker's draft or a letter of credit, bear in mind that it can take up to two weeks to be cleared. You can also have money sent to you by international money order (via a post office), a cashier's cheque or telegraphic transfer, e.g. via Western Union (the quickest, safest and *most expensive* method). You usually need your passport to collect money transferred from overseas or to cash a banker's draft or other credit note. If you're sending money overseas, it's best to send it in the local currency, so that the recipient won't need to pay conversion charges. Note that some countries have foreign exchange controls limiting the amount of money that can be sent overseas. Insured mail is the only safe way to send cash, as the insured value is refunded if it's lost or stolen.

Postal orders can be sent to Commonwealth countries and a giro post office transfer can be made to most countries. Finally you can send money direct from your bank to another bank via an interbank transfer. Most banks have a minimum charge for international transfers, which generally make it expensive, particularly for small sums. Overseas banks may also take a cut, usually a percentage (e.g. 1 or 2 per cent) of the amount transferred (everbody wants a cut!).

Footnote: There isn't a lot of difference in the cost between buying Australian currency using cash, buying travellers' cheques or using a credit card to obtain cash in Australia. However, many people simply take cash when travelling overseas, which is asking for trouble, particularly if you have no way of obtaining more cash in Australia, e.g. with travellers' cheques or a credit card. **One thing to bear in mind when travelling anywhere, is to never rely only on one source of funds!**

CREDIT RATING

Whether you're able to get credit (or how much) in Australia usually depends on your credit rating, which is becoming increasingly important in today's hazardous financial world. Most financial institutions use credit scoring and a credit reference agency report to find out whether you're credit worthy. You may need to give signed consent on an application form or sign a special authority. If you're refused credit because of a credit report, you will be told and can ask to see the report and challenge anything which is incorrect. If you're a new arrival in Australia, a lender may use an agency in your previous country of residence. Individuals can also check the credit rating of a company or person with whom they're planning to do business. If you require access to your CRAA file contact the Public Access Division, Credit Reference Association of Australia (CRAA), PO Box 964, North Sydney, NSW 2059.

Banks and other financial institutions usually have a credit scoring system, based on information received from credit reference agencies. If you have a bad credit rating, it's almost impossible to obtain credit in Australia. Your credit score will depend on many factors such as your age and occupation; marital status; how long you have held your current job; whether you're a home owner; where you live; whether you're on the electoral roll; whether you have a telephone; and your credit track record. However, if you're able to provide collateral (i.e. security such as a property), for example for a bank loan, people will fall over themselves to lend you money (particularly those who charge extortionate interest rates). A life insurance policy can also be used to provide collateral for a loan. Finally, if you're refused credit, try looking on the bright side: without credit you cannot run up any debts!

BANKS

The major Australian banks with branches in cities and large towns throughout Australia are the Commonwealth Bank of Australia, (majority owned by the Australian government), National Australia Bank, Australia & New Zealand (ANZ) Bank and Westpac, collectively referred to as the big four. These banks also have the widest representation overseas. After making huge losses in the '80s, Australian banks are now highly profitable, with the big four alone making profits of over $5.5 billion in 1996. In addition to the national banks, there are also many regional, city and state banks (including drive-in banks). The major banks offer over 200 products ranging from current and savings accounts to personal superannuation schemes and home insurance. If you do a lot of travelling overseas, you may find the comprehensive range of travel and other services provided by the major banks advantageous. Note that many services provided by Australian banks are also offered by Building Societies (see below).

Banks are keen to attract migrants as customers and offer a range of special services to newcomers. The major banks (e.g. the Commonwealth Bank of Australia) provide financial advice and assistance to migrants in a number of countries, and also operate a network of Migrant Service Centres in Australia's capital cities. Most Australian banks (plus building societies and credit unions) have websites on the internet where you can investigate their accounts and services (and the major banks plan to introduce internet banking in 1998).

Many regional (bush or country) banks have closed in recent years (over a 1,000 branches have closed since 1993) as banks have slimmed down their branch networks. Many communities have been left without any local bank branches, although some towns have successfully fought closures by threatening to withdraw $millions in assets from a bank. In some communities, building societies and credit unions have stepped in to fill the void. With the proliferation of high-tech electronic banking (banking by remote means rather than in person at a bank branch) and the branch closure program, banks require a much smaller workforce and have shed thousands of jobs a year in recent years (bank is a four-letter word with many people in Australia, where they are generally held in low public esteem). In a small rural town or village, there's likely to be a post office agency, but no banks. A post office account is handy for travellers in rural areas or an account with one of the banks that allow withdrawals to be made from post offices (see page 157).

Telephone banking (or telebanking) is offered by most Australian banks (usually 24 hours a day, seven days a week) and has been a major growth area in recent years. Calls can go to an automatic menu or to an operator. Services provided include obtaining account balances; transferring funds between accounts; paying bills; displaying a list of the last five (or more) cheques cleared or the last five transactions; ordering statements and cheque books; obtaining interest rates earned/charged; and obtaining mortgages and other loans.

Australian banks are in the forefront of electronic banking and over half of all bank transactions are made through electronic banking methods, with some banks recording three-quarters of their transactions electronically. Electronic banking includes automatic teller machines (ATMs of which there are some 170,000 in Australia); electronic funds transfer; telephone banking; smart cards; stored debt cards; automated bill payment (BPAY); touch-screen customer service terminals; automated computer banking through dial-up services; and internet banking (although it's still in its infancy). In future, banks will have even fewer branches and it's expected that almost all banking transactions will be done via computer or telephone. Video telephone banking will soon allow customers to do business through video contact with centralised bank staff.

Australian banks have increased fees on retail transactions by as much as 100 per cent in recent years (to the fury of customers), although customers with large deposits or loans usually receive free banking. Banks are trying to lure customers away from branch transactions by levying increasingly high fees for over-the-counter transactions (up to $4!) and into electronic banking (which costs them a fraction of branch transactions). The major banks have also established low-cost 'kiosk' branches in supermarkets and shopping centres operated by just one or two people and open seven days a week. After initial indifference, supermarket bank kiosks have proved popular and are set to treble in number to over 500 in the next few years.

Most Australian banks are members of the Australian Bankers' Association (ABA) which has its own Code of Banking Practice that seeks to foster good relations between banks and their customers (providing it doesn't cost the banks any money). A banking ombudsman was established in 1989 by the ABA to mediate in disputes between banks and their customers. Complaints were running at over 40,000 in 1996/97, up 30 per cent on the previous year. If you have a dispute with your bank which you're unable to resolve with them, you can take the matter to the Australian Banking Ombudsman or another agency such as Consumer Affairs or a Small Claims Tribunal (see page 434). ABA members agree to abide by the decision of the Australian Banking Ombudsman (PO Box 14240, Melbourne City Mail Centre, Melbourne, Victoria 3000, tel. freecall 1800-337 444 or (03) 9613 7333), although if customers disagree with a ruling they aren't obliged to accept it and are free to take it up with a consumer affairs department, office of fair trading or take legal action. Note that there's no government or industry funded deposit protection system for deposits in Australia, as exists in many other countries. Deposit protection in Australia varies between banks, building societies and credit unions, none of which provide an explicit guarantee of deposits. This matter is currently under review by the Commonwealth government and new regulations may be forthcoming.

BUILDING SOCIETIES

Building societies (or permanent building societies to give them their full name) were established in the 19th century to cater for people saving to buy a home. Customers saved a deposit of 5 or 10 per cent of the cost of a home with the building society, who then lent them the balance. A building society would rarely lend to anyone who wasn't a regular saver, although this policy changed some years ago. Building societies have some 3m members and over $10 billion in assets, although this represents just 5 per cent of the Australian financial services market. Added competition in the financial sector in recent years (particularly from mortgage originators) has made life difficult and many societies are struggling to survive in their present form. Like banks, building societies have also been raising their fees in recent years to offset smaller margins on home loans.

Building societies (and credit unions) can now compete with banks on a more even footing and, after a long battle, they recently won the right to issue cheques in their own name (previously all cheques were issued by banks and cleared through a particular bank). Nowadays building societies offer many of the services provided by banks including current and savings accounts, cash cards, personal loans, credit cards, insurance and travel services. However, building societies don't all offer the same services, types of accounts or rates of interest. If you're looking for a long-term investment, the number of branches may not be of importance as members of most building societies are linked with the major banks and customers can use their ATM networks. Building societies don't have an independent dispute scheme, but follow a recommended procedure in the event of complaints.

Business Hours

Normal bank and building society opening hours are from 9am or 9.30am until 4pm, Monday to Thursday, and from 9.30am until 5pm on Fridays, with no shutdown over the lunch period in cities and most towns. Some city branches open from 8am until 6pm, Monday to Thursday, and until 8pm on Fridays, while in rural areas banks may open on one or two days a week only. Some banks and building societies open on Saturday mornings, e.g. from 9am until noon. There are bank branches with extended opening hours at international airports and in an increasing number of supermarkets and shopping centres (possibly open seven days a week). All banks are closed on public holidays.

Most banks, building societies and main post offices in Australia have 24-hour Automatic Teller Machines (ATMs) at branches for cash withdrawals, deposits and checking account balances (see page 332). *Bureaux de change* have longer opening hours, including Saturdays and Sundays in tourist areas and large cities, but should be used sparingly as they don't offer the best exchange rates and often charge high commissions.

Cheque Accounts

If you're planning to work in Australia and will be paid fortnightly or monthly, one of your first acts should be to open an account with a bank, building society or credit union, like most of the Australian working population. Your salary will usually be paid directly into your account by your employer and your salary statement will either be sent to your home address or given to you at work. Employees who are paid weekly or fortnightly are often paid in cash, in which case it's up to you whether you open an account (although it's difficult to survive without one nowadays).

The most common account for day-to-day money management is a transaction (current or cheque) account, which provides a cheque book, a credit card facility, ATM access, EFTPOS availability, telephone banking and the facility to pay your regular bills by direct debit. Many people have at least two accounts: a transaction (current) account for their out-of-pocket expenses and regular transactions, and a savings account for long term savings (or 'rainy day' money). Many people have both bank and building society/credit union accounts. Before opening an account, compare banks' charges and fees, interest rates (e.g. on credit cards and deposits) and the services offered by a particular financial institution or account.

An account can be opened overseas, either in person or by post. When opening an account by post, attach a certified photocopy of the pages of your passport showing its number, expiry date, your specimen signature, photograph and visa (if available). You may also need your driver's licence. If a copy of your passport is sent by mail, it must be certified by a professional person (such as a doctor, lawyer or teacher) or a person of similar standing with a public position such as a member of parliament, councillor, civil servant or police officer. When opening a bank account in Australia, banks and other financial institutions are required by law (under the Financial Transaction Reports Act 1988) to verify the true identity of each signatory to an account. This can be done in two ways, either by providing a reference from an acceptable referee or by providing specific identification documents. Under the 100 point identification system, each acceptable document is given a points rating and a total of 100 points is required to establish your identity. **Note that new arrivals can open an account during their first six weeks in Australia with only a passport.**

Most people pay their bills from their transaction accounts, either by standing order or by cheque. Bills can also usually be paid by phone by simply quoting your account details. Bank statements are usually issued monthly (optionally quarterly), interest is normally calculated daily and paid quarterly, and an overdraft facility may be provided. Note that transaction accounts pay *very* little interest on account balances, e.g. from 0.1 to 0.5 per cent, and Australians lose $billions a year by leaving excess cash in these accounts when they could be earning 2 to 5 per cent in savings accounts. If you regularly have $1,000 or more on deposit, you should consider keeping it an account that pays a 'reasonable' interest rate. The minimum opening balance may be as low as $1, although you should bear in mind that you usually need to maintain a much higher minimum balance in order to avoid bank fees and charges.

Fees & Charges: There has been a huge increase in bank fees and charges in recent years as banks have sought to recoup their reduced margins on mortgages and other loans from account holders (it used to be called 'profiteering'). Simple transaction fees have been raised sharply and an account-keeping fee is introduced when the balance falls below a certain minimum, e.g. $300 or $500. Those with loans and deposits of $20,000 or more or an account balance of $350 (e.g. Westpac Classic Plus) or more usually incur no fees, which includes between 66 and 80 per cent of customers. Most banks also charge a monthly 'account keeping' fee, e.g. from $2 to $7. Some accounts offer a fixed number of free transactions (e.g. 5 to 35) each month, after which a fee is levied. In order to reduce transaction fees, you should make fewer cash withdrawals and pay cash instead of using an EFTPOS card. There are also one-off fees (e.g. $10 to $35) for a range of services such as overdrawing an account, buying a bank cheque, stopping a cheque, obtaining a replacement statement and writing a rubber (bounced) cheque.

Banks are trying to introduce a user-pays system, where fees are related to the actual work involved in processing transactions, which means that there are lower fees for electronic banking than over-the-counter branch transactions. Some accounts are exclusively for those who use the electronic banking network to make withdrawals, and levy no fees (although there's a penalty rate for over-the-counter withdrawals). Some banks have fee exemptions for customers under the age of 18 or 21, tertiary students and pensioners. Always shop around for the lowest fees. Note also that few building societies and credit unions impose account-keeping fees.

Government Taxes: These are levied on transaction accounts by state and territory governments and in many cases exceed the cost of bank charges. There are two kinds of government tax, Financial Institutions Duty (FID) and Debits Tax. FID and debits tax are listed on bank statements and in account passbooks, and it may be possible to claim them as deductions in your tax return. Stamp duty is payable on cheques in South Australia, Western Australia and Norfolk Island, and is deducted from your account when a cheque book is issued.

FID is paid on all deposits paid into accounts in all states and territories except Queensland. It's usually levied at a flat rate of 0.06 per cent, which means that on a deposit of $100 you pay FID of 6 cents. Although this may seem innocuous, it can add up to a considerable amount over a year if your salary is paid into an account. FID doesn't apply to social security payments (although some banks charge it in error).

Debits Tax (or bank account debit tax, known as BAD!) is paid on all withdrawals from accounts that have a cheque facility, in all states and territories. It's levied on a sliding scale which penalises those who make regular small withdrawals rather than a few large amounts each month. In most state, debits tax is 30¢ on withdrawals of $1 to $99, 70¢ on $100 to $499, $1.50 on $500 to $4,999, $3 on $5,000 to $9,999, and $4 on $10,000 or more.

Cheques: Personal cheques aren't usually accepted in payment in retail outlets in Australia as they cannot be guaranteed (Australian banks don't issue cheque guarantee cards). When a cheque is acceptable, normally a bank card or driving licence is sufficient ID to pay by cheque. Cheques aren't usually crossed, although you can cross your own cheques by drawing two parallel lines across the face. This theoretically provides additional security, because a crossed cheque can be paid only into a bank account and cannot be cashed. To obtain cash from a bank, write the cheque in your own name or write 'cash' alongside 'Pay to' and don't cross it (but never send a cheque made out to cash through the post). Take great care when sending cheques by post, particularly for large amounts, as it isn't unknown for cheques to be stolen and paid into another account.

There are a number of ways to safeguard your cheques, one of which is to write 'not negotiable' between the two lines on a crossed cheque, which means it cannot be cashed by a third party (if a cheque was stolen and a third party cashed it, he would have to refund the rightful owner). An additional safeguard is to add the words 'account payee only' to the crossing (in between the two parallel lines), which means that the cheque must be paid into the account of the named payee. For extra security, you can add both 'not negotiable' and 'account payee only' to a cheque. If you cross out the words 'or bearer' on a cheque, this stops anyone except the named person from cashing it. You can also arrange with your bank that no cash cheques can be drawn on your account and print on cheques the $limit that can be drawn on any one cheque. **Note that a post-dated cheque can be honoured by your bank before the date written on it (cheques are valid for 15 months after the date written on them).**

Around $23 billion (some 4m cheques) a day is cleared via the Australian Payments Clearing Association system, which takes around five days. Clearance is to be cut to three days by the year 2000, although even this is painfully slow in the age of electronic banking, when cheques could easily be cleared the same day they are paid into a bank (if you make a cash withdrawal or payment you can bet your life that it's debited immediately!). The reason is simple: Banks invest the money on the overnight short-term money market and would lose $millions a year if they paid money out as quickly they received it.

SAVINGS ACCOUNTS

All banks, building societies and credit unions provide a range of savings accounts, usually referred to as deposit or investment accounts in Australia, many of which are intended for short or medium term savings, rather than long-term growth. Other types of savings accounts include deeming accounts; cash management trusts; mortgage offset accounts and redraw facilities; and savings investment bonus accounts. Retirement Savings Accounts (RSAs) are aimed at capturing the superannuation payments of casual and itinerant workers.

When choosing an account, the most important considerations are how much money you wish to save (which may be a lump sum or a monthly amount); how quickly you need access to it in an emergency; and whether you require additional services such as those provided by transaction accounts (see above). For example, you may wish to have instant access to your cash via ATMs with no limit on withdrawals. You may find a high interest cheque account (called fancy names such as a 'cash management call account') useful, as it provides all the usual facilities of a transaction account, plus high interest depending on the account balance (which must usually be a minimum of around $5,000).

Before committing your money to a long-term savings account or investment, you should shop around for the best deal, as interest rates, conditions and fees can vary considerably. Note that banks, building societies and credit unions frequently introduce new accounts paying increased rates of interest, **but they don't usually notify existing customers of this (they are not in the habit of giving money away unnecessarily).** Some banks automatically deposit your cash in a standard-rate term deposit paying a lower rate of interest when a super-rate term deposit ends. One thing you should *never* do is keep a large amount, say more than $1,000, in a transaction account, which pays a derisory interest rate. Note that interest rates are forever changing in Australia (increasing or decreasing in line with the official bank lending rate) and it may not pay you to tie your up money for a long period.

Most banks and building societies have two basic types of savings accounts: instant access and term deposit accounts. Instant access accounts, as the name implies, allow you instant access to your money. There's usually a minimum balance, which may be as low as $50 or as high as $5,000. With some high balance deposit accounts, all deposits and withdrawals must be a minimum of $1,000 or more. Interest rates usually depend on the account balance, e.g. $500, $1,000, $5,000 or $10,000. With a term deposit account, you're required to give notice before you make a withdrawal, which can be anything from 30 days to five years.

Note that term deposits can usually only be repaid earlier in exceptional circumstances, when a sharply-reduced rate of interest applies. Not surprisingly, term deposit accounts pay higher rates of interest than instant access. However, if there's any possibility that you will need immediate access to your money, you should keep it in an instant access account (in any case, the extra interest on short-term deposit accounts varies little from that of the best instant access accounts). Interest is usually calculated daily and paid monthly, quarterly, six-monthly, annually and/or at maturity. Note that non-residents are subject to a withholding tax of 10 per cent on income earned on bank deposits in Australia, which is deducted at source when interest is paid.

CASH & DEBIT CARDS

One of the most important innovations in banking in the last decade or so has been the introduction of cash and EFTPOS (debit) cards, which are routinely issued to all transaction account holders in Australia.

Cash Cards: A cash card allows you to withdraw money from Automatic Teller Machines (ATMs), commonly known as cash machines, 24 hours a day, seven days a week (providing they or you don't run out of money). The freedom from bank queues, banking hours and bank tellers provided by cash cards is very convenient, and you should think twice before opening an account which doesn't provide ATMs locally (although most small financial institutions have arrangements with larger banks or building societies). Most people prefer to use cash machines rather than deal with a bank clerk, which apart from being time-consuming, can also be *very* expensive. Cash (and EFTPOS) cards can also be used to pay at service stations, supermarkets and other retail outlets throughout Australia through the Electronic Funds Transfer at Point Of Sale (EFTPOS) system. You can also pay for telephone calls in special public telephones.

All banks, building societies and credit unions issue cash cards for account holders, which can be used to withdraw a maximum of around $500 a day from any of the participating bank's or building society's ATMs or those belonging to the same network. The big four banks' ATM networks are: ANZ (Night & Day), Commonwealth (Autobank), National (Flexiteller) and Westpac (Handybank). Some networks are linked so that you can use your cash or EFTPOS (and credit) cards in ATMs belonging to different banks. There's an agreement between some of the major banks to share each others ATMs, e.g. Commonwealth Bank/Westpac and ANZ/National Bank, with customers having access to some 5,500 ATMs. Customers of regional banks, building societies and credit unions also have access through reciprocal arrangements. Most banks and building societies allow free withdrawals from machines belonging to their network (there's a fee of 70¢ to $1 when using an ATM belonging to another bank or network). Other services provided by banks and building societies via ATMs include mini-statements (usually the last five transactions); account balances; the paying of bills (via a bank giro) and credit card payments; deposits (cash and cheques); transfers between accounts; cheque book and statement ordering; and the facility to change your Personal Identification Number (PIN). Note that these services are usually available only via cash machines at branches of your own bank.

When your application for a card is approved, your card and PIN are sent under separate cover (for security reasons). If you don't have a secure mail box (i.e. a private address or personal mail box), you should collect your PIN from your bank. For extra security, some banks activate cards only after customers have reported their safe arrival. **If you receive an unsolicited card, cut it up and return it to your bank or building society with instructions to cancel it.** For security reasons, you should **destroy your PIN as soon as you've remembered it and should never write it down (not even coded).**

The procedure for withdrawing money from ATMs varies from bank to bank and even between ATMs at different branches of the same bank, but is roughly as follows:

1. Check that the ATM is in service, which may be shown by an 'OPEN' sign, a light or a display on the screen. If the machine is out of service a message to this effect is usually displayed. If an ATM is out of service it usually means that the machine has run out of cash (common at weekends) or that the bank's computer is out of order. Sometimes an ATM will be unable to dispense cash, but will allow you to do other things such as check your account balance.

2. Insert your card as shown in the illustration on the machine. Most ATMs have a (usually transparent) protective cover which opens automatically. A screen message asks you to enter your PIN on the keyboard. **As a security measure, if you enter the wrong PIN a number of times (e.g. three), your card will be retained by the machine and you must contact your bank for its return.** You may need to press a 'proceed key' (usually coloured green) to continue after entering your PIN.

3. After you've entered your PIN the display will ask you which service you require, e.g. cash withdrawal (with or without a receipt). Press the 'button' corresponding to the service required (usually indicated by arrows at the edge of the screen).

4. If you're withdrawing cash, you must now enter the amount required (up to your card's limit) in multiples of $10, e.g. $20, $50 or $100, usually dispensed in $10 or $20 notes. Sometimes you'll need to press the 'proceed key' to continue.

5. At this point your card will be returned and your cash and receipt dispensed. Don't forget to take them all with you.

A 'cancel' or 'error' button (usually coloured red) is provided to terminate a transaction at any point. Your card will be returned and you can start again, if required.

Note that although it's relatively rare, ATMs do go wrong and occasionally give the wrong amount of cash, make mistakes on receipts, and 'phantom withdrawals' can turn up on your bank statement which you haven't made. You should always obtain a receipt for withdrawals and check them against your statement. If you have a problem with a machine, make a note of its location, the date and time, and exactly what happened. Notify your bank as soon as possible. Note, however, that you have only a slim chance of convincing your bank that their 'infallible' machine has made a mistake. Don't keep a lot of money in an account for which you have a cash card and *never* have a cash card for a savings account with a large balance. Beware of using ATMs in 'high risk' areas at night, as muggings occasionally occur. If you lose your cash card, you must notify the issuing bank immediately by telephone and confirm it in writing.

EFTPOS (debit) Cards: Most cash cards are also EFTPOS cards, which are accepted by most retailers and mail-order businesses in Australia and have largely replaced cheques. Over half of all card transactions in Australia are made with EFTPOS cards. There's no limit to the amount you can pay with an EFTPOS card, but you must have the money in your account (or have a pre-arranged overdraft). Many retailers, e.g. supermarkets, allow customers to obtain cash (known as 'cash-back') when buying goods with an EFTPOS card. Many cards can also be used overseas, e.g. as Visa or Mastercard 'EFTPOS' cards, to obtain cash and buy goods and services. They aren't, however, credit cards and you can only draw on funds in your account. There's a charge for obtaining cash overseas.

New Innovations: Australian banks have invested $millions into creating their networks of ATMs which some believe will become white elephants (or a herd) when new 'smart card' technology is introduced in the next few years. New smart cards contain computer chips (rather than a magnetic strip) and can be used to store a wide range of financial and personal information. New chip technology in smart cards will also combat credit card fraud, which is relatively low in Australia (compared, for example, with Europe) at just 5¢ for every $100 spent. New generation ATMs accept smart cards, cheque imaging and even ticketing. Reloadable 'electronic cash' cards with a stored-value are also being introduced in Australia, plus PC-linked credit cards compatible with computers and the internet. These allow you to order and pay for goods and services via your home or business computer. Both Mastercard and Visa have created 'virtual' credit cards to allow secure payments to be made over the internet.

CREDIT & CHARGE CARDS

Australia is one of the most credit-oriented societies in the world and credit card debt alone exceeded a record over $8 billion in early 1998. Most Australians have a number of credit and charge cards (with a credit limit of up to $5,000 on each) which are accepted by most retail outlets, whatever their size. The main difference between charge and credit cards is that with a charge card you can defer paying the bill for a few weeks or months, but you *must* pay the total balance outstanding when it's due (otherwise a penalty payment is payable), whereas a credit card allows you to spread your repayments over a period. Credit cards are much more popular than charge cards, both with cardholders and businesses. New smart cards (with a microchip) are set to revolutionise the way we pay for goods and services and are eventually expected to replace cash for most transactions.

One of the major advantages of international charge cards (e.g. Amex and Diners Club) is that if they are lost or stolen they can usually be replaced at short notice when you're travelling, e.g. within 24 hours in some countries. Apart from on-the-spot replacement of lost cards, you may find that charge cards offer few advantages over credit cards (see below), some of which, e.g. Visa or Mastercard, are more widely accepted, both in Australia and worldwide. Credit cards are also cheaper and more convenient to use. Charge cards do, however, generally offer more benefits than credit cards, particularly for international travellers. Both credit and charge cards are issued as ordinary, gold and platinum cards, with different credit and benefit levels. Gold card holders must usually have an annual income of over $50,000 a year and net assets of over $100,000.

The most commonly accepted credit cards in Australia are Bankcard (Australia's own credit card organisation), Mastercard and Visa (and affiliates). Most outlets that accept Bankcard usually also accept Mastercard and Visa. American Express, Diners Club and Carte Blanche cards are also widely accepted. You may have a problem using a credit card in remote areas and small towns or in small shops and restaurants. All banks, building societies, and many credit unions and major retailers offer their own credit cards in Australia. It isn't always necessary to maintain an account with a financial institution to obtain a credit card.

Costs: Banks compete fiercely for credit card customers, both on interest rates and the supplementary services attached to cards. The annual fee varies from no fee up to $30 for a standard card and up to $85 for a gold card. The lowest rates are usually charged by credit unions with no annual fee, although they may not give you any interest-free credit days. If you spend over a certain sum on your card, e.g. $1,500, the annual fee may be waived. A number of cards can be issued for a single account (a second card is usually issued free). When choosing a card, bear in mind that a free card with no annual fee may have a high interest rate (which is fine if you plan to pay off the balance each month). The best cards are those with no annual or a low annual fee *and* a low interest rate, which are usually restricted to homeowners and/or those with an excellent credit rating.

Interest: The interest rates charged on credit card balances in 1998 was between around 15 and 18 per cent. Most cards offer 14 to 55 days' interest-free credit, although there are no free credit days on some cards. Note that banks rarely pass on interest rate cuts to credit card holders. Card issuers use various methods to calculate the interest on cash advances and outstanding balances. (Interest is always charged on cash advances immediately and the interest-free period doesn't apply.) Note also that if the amount owing isn't paid in full, then interest is charged from the date of purchase and the interest-free period is lost altogether.

Some cards allow an interest-free period on new purchases only if the balance at the start is zero. A higher interest rate is usually charged on cards offering an interest-free period and there's also usually an annual fee. If you intend to pay off the amount owed in full each month, choose a card with no fee (or a low fee) and the longest interest-free period. Otherwise choose a card with a low fee and a low interest rate. Credit cards are definitely not for long-term borrowers, although if you borrow less than £1,000 and pay it off within one year, it may be cheaper than a loan. Interest is usually paid when your credit card account has a positive balance, i.e. you pay more money to your bank than is owed on a card (you may wish to do this when you plan to overspend your usual credit limit, but want the security of using a credit card).

Benefits: You should also compare the benefits offered by card issuers, which may include cash discounts on travel bookings; holiday discounts; foreign currency ordering; helplines; discounts on new cars; air miles and other points' schemes (see below); reduced hotel and car rental rates; free accident travel insurance; commission-free travellers' cheques; and free insurance on goods purchased with cards. Some cards, called affinity cards, have ties with registered charities, where a charity (or a number of charities) benefits each time a card is used (although it's peanuts).

Loyalty & Frequent Flyer Points: Loyalty points are a big attraction for cardholders, where you receive reward points for each transaction (usually one point for each $1 spent). Benefits include free travel, discounted goods and other freebies. Cards are offered by banks in conjunction with companies such as Telstra, General Motors-Holden, Qantas and Ansett. Frequent flyer points can be earned when using American Express (Qantas), Diners Club (Ansett) and Visa (Ansett and Qantas) cards. Points earned through Amex can be held in the card account indefinitely, thus protecting them from airlines' expiry dates. Note that if you don't settle up an Amex or Diners Club account in full each month, you don't earn any points. Card issuers sometimes offer promotions such as 1,000 bonus points for new customers and free prize draws. However, whatever the benefits on offer, you should always check a card's fees and interest rates.

Credit Limit: The credit limit for most card holders starts at around $2,000, although some card issuers allow you to choose your spending limit up to $10,000. Gold and platinum cards have higher credit limits than ordinary cards (or no limit at all). Increasing your credit limit is usually a formality, providing your credit rating is good and you always pay your bills on time. When changing card companies, check that you'll be able to keep your previous credit limit and that you don't lose any important benefits. Many card companies allow existing card holders to transfer their card balance when switching cards and offer a lower rate of interest (for a limited period).

Cash Withdrawals: Credit cards can be used to obtain cash from ATMs in Australia and overseas. You need a PIN to withdraw cash. When you use your card to obtain cash there's a handling charge and/or commission and a daily limit, e.g. $500 or $1,000. Interest is levied on cash withdrawals from the date of the withdrawal.

Bills: Most credit cards require you to repay a minimum of $10 or 5 per cent of the balance each month, whichever is the greater. If you pay off the full amount outstanding, you won't be charged interest and will receive up to seven weeks' free credit. Some credit card issuers offer protection insurance which covers payments in case of sickness, accident or unemployment (check exactly what's covered), which is worth considering. Protection insurance premiums are calculated according to your account balance and are added to your card payments each month.

Lost or Stolen Cards: If you lose a credit card or it's stolen, report it immediately to the police and the issuing office, and confirm the loss in writing as soon as possible. Credit card fraud costs $millions a year, although much of it could be virtually eliminated by adopting cards containing the holder's photograph and using a PIN number (which must be entered via a special keypad each time a card is used), as is the case in some other countries. Most retailers don't bother to check signatures, many of which are usually illegible anyway. Most banks allow customers to choose their own personal identification number (PIN), although if you use your birth date or telephone number as your Personal Identification Number (PIN) you may not be compensated if a card is stolen and used. The PIN must be reasonably disguised and mustn't be written down or contained in documents carried with a card.

Cards can be used to purchase goods by mail or over the telephone, both in Australia and overseas, although goods should only be sent to the cardholder's address. It's sometimes advisable to ask for the carbon paper when you purchase goods in person, as it can be used to obtain your credit card number and a copy of your signature. Always check that a credit card slip is made out for the correct amount before signing it.

Store Cards: Many major department and chain stores in Australia issue their own account credit cards and some don't accept any cards other than their own. Interest rates are quoted monthly and are usually *very* high, e.g. up to double what you pay with a Visa or Mastercard.

Even if you don't like plastic money and shun any form of credit, credit cards do have their uses. For example, no deposits on rental cars, no pre-paying hotel bills, safety and security, and above all, convenience. However, in the wrong hands they are a disaster and should be shunned by spendthrifts and should never be given to politicians.

OVERDRAFTS

Generally if you wish to overdraw your current account, you must make a prior arrangement with your bank, although some accounts allow an automatic authorised overdraft of around $500. Note that some banks have a standard charge (e.g. $20) for using an authorised overdraft, even if you overdraw by only 10¢. Some accounts allow holders an overdraft of up to $5,000 at preferential interest rates or without incurring any charges. Over $5 billion was borrowed on overdrafts in 1997. If you overdraw your account without a prior arrangement, you will find that your cheques bounce (i.e. they aren't paid) or that you're charged a punitive rate of interest (as much as 10 per cent above that charged on authorised overdrafts). An administrative charge (fine?) of $10 to $35 is made by most banks for unauthorised overdrafts, ostensibly for letters, interviews or other administration work.

It's usually easier to obtain an overdraft than a loan, particularly if your need is only short-term (longer than six months and you should consider a loan). The advantage of an overdraft over a loan, is that you pay interest only when you're actually overdrawn, so although you may have a $5,000 overdraft at the end of the month, this may be cleared by your salary at the beginning of the next month. Migrants may find it easier to get an overdraft than a loan, particularly during their first year in Australia, although credit may be limited and you will need a stable, long-term job.

The interest rates for authorised overdrafts vary, so shop around (it was around 12.5 per cent in late 1997). Business overdrafts are the best value and are usually only a few percentage points above the base rate. Try to ensure that you're charged a low interest rate on your overdraft, as interest rates for short-term, small overdrafts can be high. Overdrafts are insured free of charge by some banks against customers being unable to pay. Note that for some people, short-term borrowing is cheaper with a credit card (see page 332), for which you don't need permission and which can be repaid more or less at any time.

LOANS

It pays to shop around when you want a loan as many borrowers pay too much interest on their loans. Interest rates for borrowers vary considerably depending on the bank, the amount, the period of the loan, and most importantly, whether the loan is secured or unsecured. In late 1997, interest on an unsecured loan was around 12.5 per cent. A secured loan is cheaper, for which you must offer collateral as a guarantee against defaulting on the repayments, e.g. a life insurance policy (75 to 90 per cent of the surrender value is usual) or your home. However, you should beware of loans where your home is used as security, as if you fail to pay back the loan you can lose your home (if you have spare equity in a home, remortgaging may be the best way to raise money). If you want a loan to buy a new car, the best deals are usually provided by car manufacturers.

The rate of interest charged on loans in Australia is quoted as a flat rate or the Annual Percentage Rate (APR), which is the true rate of interest and includes all charges (e.g. documentation fees and maintenance charges). APR is usually just under double the flat rate. All interest rates on goods must, by law, quote the APR figure, so you're able to instantly compare rates. Most personal loans offer a fixed rate of interest throughout the term of the loan. Always shop around and compare APRs for personal loans from a number of financial institutions, as they can vary considerably. (It isn't always necessary to have an account with a bank to obtain a loan from them.) If you're able to offer security for a loan or can get someone to stand as a guarantor, you'll usually be eligible for a lower interest rate. However, you should be wary of acting as a guarantor for someone else's debts without some sort of security (or at least being prepared for the worst).

In addition to a personal loan from a bank or building society, 'loans' are available from a variety of sources including credit cards (a gold credit card may offer an unsecured overdraft facility of up to $20,000, although credit cards should be used for short-term borrowing only), bank overdrafts and interest free credit. Some banks have savings accounts where you pay a set amount each month (e.g. $20 to $200) which allows you to borrow up to 20 or 30 times your monthly payment.

If you want a loan (e.g. to start a business) and don't have sufficient security, one of the places you're least likely to get it is from your friendly bank manager. Banks are awash with money but they have few people to lend to since they tightened up their lending criteria a few years ago (although they have recently been relaxed due to increased competition). Business loans are generally even harder to obtain than personal loans. If there's the slightest risk involved your bank manager will demand security in the form of property or a water-tight insurance policy (or your first born) before he commits himself. It's a sad fact of life that when you most need money it will be hardest to come by, but when you're flourishing (and don't need it) people will fall over themselves to lend it to you.

Borrowing from private loan companies (moneylenders), as advertised in newspapers and magazines, is expensive (very high interest rates, plus fees and commission). Use them only as an absolute last resort when all other avenues have been exhausted and the loan is a matter of life and death. In general, the more desperate your financial situation, the more suspicious you should be of anyone who's willing to lend you money (unless it's your mum).

If you take out a loan, you can usually take out a credit protection insurance policy at the same time (sometimes included 'free'). In this case, if you're unable to pay your loan due to sickness, accident or unemployment, the insurance policy pays your loan instalments. If you're in doubt about the terms of a loan, you should seek independent advice from a citizens advice bureau (CAB) or consumer advice centre, which provide free advice (see page 451) about loans.

MORTGAGES

Mortgages (home loans) in Australia are available from many sources including banks, building societies, credit unions, mortgage originators/providers, mortgage managers, finance and insurance companies, motoring organisations and state housing authorities. The Commonwealth Bank is the largest lender (around $10 billion annually) followed by the Westpac Banking Corporation. Competition to lend you money is fierce and homebuyers in Australia have a wider variety of home loan finance than is available in many other countries. However, despite the increased competition, banks still handle around 80 per cent of new home loans. The usual home loan period is 25 years, although it can be anything from five to 30 years (or before the age at which a state pension is paid), while the maximum term for land loans is usually 20 years. Many lenders offer additional benefits such as free home and life insurance.

Government Loans: The Commonwealth and state governments provide funds for housing loans through the Commonwealth/State Housing Agreement, with loan repayments linked to the borrower's income. Interest subsidies provided during the early years of the loan are generally recovered when the borrower's income permits. In most states, the loans are made through co-operative building societies, a list of which is maintained by the state Registrar of Co-operative Societies. Housing Commissions and state banks in some states also provide loans, although eligibility is restricted to low to moderate-income families and there are often long waiting lists.

Interest Rates: In the last few years, the cost of mortgages has fallen considerably to stand at around 6.5 per cent in mid-1997 for variable-rate mortgages, the lowest in 30 years. Under the new Liberal-National coalition government that came to power in March 1996, the mortgage interest rate had been cut from around 10.5 to 6.5 per cent.

Note, however, that most banks are slow to cut their rates after the Reserve Bank lowers interest rates, which was the cause of a heated dispute between banks and the Commonwealth government in 1997. Despite lower interest rates, many lenders continue to make the same repayments as previously in order to pay off their mortgages faster. Interest is calculated on the daily loan balance and charged monthly.

However, low rates also have their down side, as they encourage people to borrow more than they can afford, and according to surveys a high percentage of Australian families are burdened by their loan repayments. Household debt levels have soared to almost 80 per cent of household disposable income and there are fears of a mass of defaulters if rates increase again. In recent years home loan defaults have increased due to a decline in the quality of lending, particularly by mortgage providers, who tend to market loans more aggressively and lend to people that banks reject. It's advisable not to rush into taking out a mortgage, particularly if your income isn't secure. Many people are denied mortgages because of bad credit ratings or insecure employment, which may include the self-employed, who usually need to produce a number of years' tax returns (usually two). It's possible to take out a mortgage protection policy in case you fall ill, have an accident or are made redundant and are unable to pay your mortgage, although it can be expensive and there are many loopholes. Most lenders offer a 'home loan protection plan' which guarantees repayments in case of death or permanent disability.

In recent years, loans have also been cheaper thanks to increased competition between the banks and other lenders (isn't competition wonderful!). The major banks have been savaged by smaller, non-bank rivals offering better deals, which has resulted in some excellent offers for borrowers. Banks have been forced to cut their margins (the difference between what they paid on deposits and the home loan rate) from 4 or 5 per cent to around 3 per cent in order to compete with mortgage originators such as Aussie Home Loans, who charge borrowers only some 1.7 per cent above the cost of obtaining funds. In 1997, banks were offering lower interest rates to selected customers such as professionals and other 'high net-worth' individuals.

Repayments: Your monthly mortgage repayments mustn't usually be more than 30 per cent of your gross basic income (a couple's incomes are combined — some 60 per cent of families paying off a home loan in Australia have two or more wage earners). The average home loan repayments are around 25 per cent of average family earnings (down from around 35 per cent in the late '80s), with the average home loan at $110,000 and average repayments around $850 a month (ranging from around $700 in Tasmania to $1,150 in NSW). Sydney owner-occupiers are generally more highly geared than Melbourne families. Note that it's usually necessary to have a high income and a secure job to get into and stay in home ownership in Australia, and only some 40 per cent of buyers pay over 30 per cent of their wages towards a mortgage. Repayments can be paid fortnightly (which can save a considerable amount over the term of a loan) or monthly. Some lenders allow you to reduce your payments by up to 50 per cent for up to six months when taking maternity or paternity leave.

Using the table below it's easy to calculate your monthly and total repayments. For example if you borrow $100,000 at 7 per cent over 25 years, your monthly payments will be $707 (100 x $7.07) and your total repayments over 25 years will be $212,100.

Interest Rate	Term of Loan (Years)/Monthly Payments per $1,000 Borrowed					
	5	10	15	20	25	30
6%	19.33	11.10	8.44	7.16	6.44	6.00
7%	19.80	11.61	8.99	7.75	7.07	6.65
8%	20.28	12.13	9.56	8.36	7.72	7.34
9%	20.76	12.67	10.14	9.00	8.39	8.05
10%	21.25	13.22	10.75	9,65	9.09	8.78
11%	21.74	13.78	11.37	10.32	9.80	9.52
12%	22.24	14.35	12.00	11.01	10.53	10.29

Deposit: Although it's still possible to obtain a loan for the whole cost of a property (a 100 per cent mortgage) from some developers, particularly if you're a first-time buyer, most lenders expect borrowers to pay a deposit of from 5 to 20 per cent of the purchase price. Note that borrowers usually pay a higher interest rate with a 100 per cent mortgage. The average deposit paid is around one-third of the value of a property in Sydney and some 40 per cent in Melbourne. Housing loan insurance is payable when a loan is greater than 75 or 80 per cent of the value of a property. The insurance premium is usually between $250 and $500 or 1 per cent of the loan, and is usually added to the loan amount. Expensive 'captive' mortgage insurance is offered by some lenders, where borrowers have no other option, when you pay around 20 per cent above the market rate (shop around for independent mortgage insurance). Note that mortgage insurance contracts cover the lender and not the borrower.

Fixed/Variable-Rate: In Australia, you can usually choose between fixed and variable-rate mortgages, where the interest rate goes up and down depending on the bank base rate. Those who cannot afford an increase in their mortgage repayments are usually better off with a fixed-rate mortgage, where the interest rate is fixed for the term of the loan or a number of years (e.g. one to 10), irrespective of what happens to interest rates in the meantime. The longer the fixed-rate period, the lower the interest rate offered. If interest rates go down, you may find yourself paying more than the current mortgage rate, but at least you'll know exactly what you must pay each month. Most variable-rate loans offer borrowers the option to fix the rate at any time, e.g. when interest rates are rising.

To judge whether a fixed-rate mortgage is worthwhile, you must estimate in which direction interest rates are heading (a difficult feat). Some mortgages combine fixed and variable-rate loans (split fixed/variable rate), which some analysts recommend as the best compromise between a 100 per cent fixed or variable-rate loan. Note, however, that this means taking out two loans and incurring higher fees. Homebuyers have shunned fixed-rate loans in recent years as rates have tumbled and in 1997 less than one in 10 borrowers took out a fixed-rate loan (although the number is increasing sharply ahead of fears of interest rate rises). The average size of a fixed-rate loan in 1997 was around $105,000 and the average for a variable-rate loan around $115,000. The average size of a home loan has risen by 60 per cent since 1990 to twice disposable incomes.

Types of Loans: There are few different types of home loans in Australia, where most are repayment mortgages (endowment, pension and other types of mortgages are rare). Standard home loans often include extra flexibility including additional payments, offset accounts, redraw facilities, variations to payment frequency and fixed-variable splits. Many lenders offer basic variable-rate loans with fewer features than standard loans (such as no offset account or redraw facility). Most lenders also offer low-start (honeymoon-rate loans), which reduce your mortgage payments for a number of years (usually one or two), and fixed-rate mortgages where you fix the rate for a period, e.g.

one to 10 years. Note that around a third of all complaints against banks concern home loans, in particular honeymoon-rate loans (on which banks levy high fees).

A new type of loan introduced in recent years is an equity overdraft loan, where the mortgage is run like a bank account. It works like a standard overdraft account where the more money you pay into your account the lower the amount owed (and hence less interest is payable), and you can borrow money whenever you wish (usually up to your original mortgage limit) at the same rate of interest as your mortgage. An equity overdraft loan may operate like a normal transaction account, although because of the flexibility and ease of borrowing it isn't recommended for spendthrifts.

Reducing the Term: Variable-rate mortgages usually allow extra optional payments to be made. Note that paying an extra 10 per cent each month can knock five or six years off the repayment term of a 25-year mortgage. One of the advantages of standard bank loans is that they usually have greater flexibility than other loans and offer additional features, such as redraw facilities and offset accounts. If you make extra payments, a redraw facility allows you to 're-borrow' the money later if the need arises. An offset account enables you to deposit money in a special account and receive interest in the form of a reduction in the interest payable on your loan. This means that a larger part of your repayments goes towards reducing the principal, resulting in significant interest savings and the loan being paid off quicker. An example of an offset account is the Commonwealth Bank's 'mortgage interest saver account' (MISA). Money lodged in a MISA is available on call and you don't pay bank fees on deposits and withdrawals (each of which must be a minimum of $1,000), although no interest is paid. A minimum balance of $2,000 must be maintained. Making payments fortnightly instead of monthly will also help you pay off a loan quicker.

Fees & Charges: A range of fees are associated with mortgages including a mortgage application and establishment fee, a valuation fee and loan registration. A Mortgage establishment fee is usually between $300 and $800, although some banks (e.g. The Commonwealth Bank and Westpac) have cut or eliminated fees for setting up mortgages (although they may be clawed back by administrative or maintenance fees). Most lenders don't charge a valuation fee, although it can be up to $200. Legal fees are usually waived. Some mortgages have a maintenance fee, e.g. $60 to $100, which may apply only to certain types of loans. Stamp duty is payable on mortgages in all states, but not in the ACT or Northern Territory (the average is around $350 on a $100,000 mortgage and $750 on a $200,000 mortgage). Mortgage registration costs from $55 (NSW) to $90 (NT).

Some mortgages carry crippling discharge (redemption) or exit fees if they are repaid early, which may entail paying all the interest on the balance of your loan running into thousands of dollars. However, this has usually been replaced nowadays by a discharge fee of from $100 to $650. While most borrowers never change their lenders, some homeowners remortgage every two or three years after shopping around for the best deal available. However, you must do your sums carefully, as changing lenders can be expensive. Some banks offer lower 'loyalty rates' of interest for customers who have maintained a loan for five years or more. While mortgage interest rates have been going down in recent years, fees have risen. Always make sure that you receive a list of all costs associated with a loan, including discharge fees.

Foreign Currency Mortgages: It's possible to obtain a foreign currency mortgage, e.g. in Swiss francs, US dollars, Deutschmarks or Japanese yen, all currencies which, with their historically low interest rates, have provided huge savings for borrowers in recent years. However, you should be cautious about taking out a foreign currency mortgage as interest rate gains can be wiped out overnight by currency swings. In the '80s many Australians took out Swiss franc loans and were unable to maintain their payments when the value of the A$ plummeted against the Swiss franc in later years. Most mainstream lenders advise against taking out foreign currency home loans. The lending conditions for foreign currency home loans are much stricter than for A$ loans and are generally granted only to high-rollers (e.g. those earning a minimum of $100,000 a year) and are usually for a minimum of $200,000 and a maximum of 60 per cent of a property's value.

Advice & Information: Whatever type of home loan you choose, take time to investigate all the options available and bear in mind that mortgage advice offered by lenders is often deliberately misleading and isn't to be trusted. One way of finding the best deal is to contact an independent mortgage broker. One such company is Mortgage Choice in Sydney (tel. (02) 9922 2599), a one-stop shop for those seeking the best mortgage deal offering hundreds of home loan deals from which to choose. Note, however, that they earn their living from fees paid by lenders, and therefore may not always be impartial. Solicitors in some states (e.g. NSW) offer homebuyers a free home loan service. This is a one-stop mortgage service managing every part of the home buying process including conveyancing, mortgage searches and advising on the best lender. Note, however, that although solicitors are bound by fiduciary duty to give independent advice, they may receive fees from lenders. MoneyChoice (operated by the Australian Consumers' Association, see page 434) offer a 24-hour automated telephone service which gives you a list of the five lowest-cost lenders over the phone and you can have an optional more comprehensive printout faxed or mailed to you (tel. 1900-170088, $1.95 a minute with a typical call costing $8). Wherever you obtain advice, always ensure that it's impartial (**always ask whether an adviser is being paid a commission by a lender**). Invaluable independent advice and comparative tables of lenders are published in specialist magazines such as *Your Mortgage* (quarterly). For information about buying property, see **Chapter 5**.

PROPERTY & LAND TAXES

Property taxes are called council rates in Australia and are levied by local councils on residents to pay for local services. These include town planning and building control, health inspections, garbage collection and disposal (which may be charged separately), roads, footpaths, parks and recreational facilities, libraries, and community and welfare services. Rates are based on the 'rateable value' of a property, officially called the 'unimproved capital value', which is reassessed every few years by the Valuer General's Department. In some states there's a swimming pool levy to ensure compliance with safety standards. Rates are levied annually but are usually paid quarterly. Check the current rates before buying a property, as in some areas they can be very high (pensioners may receive a concession). Rates usually also increase when land valuations go up, although there's a limit on what councils can charge.

Land Tax is levied on the ownership of land in all states and territories except the Northern Territory. It's based on the unimproved value of land (excluding the value of any buildings or capital improvements) at a prescribed date, e.g. 31st December in NSW, which is determined by a state's Valuer General. There's usually a threshold, below which no land tax is payable. In NSW, land tax is payable on investment property holdings whose land content is valued at more than $160,000 at a standard tax of 1.85 per cent. In 1997, the NSW Labor government (not many Labor votes among rich landowners) extended land tax to include owner-occupied residential land with a threshold value of $1m or more. Land tax is payable at a standard tax rate of 1.85 per cent on the amount above $1m plus $100 (tax on a property valued at $1m is exactly $100). For example, tax on land valued at $1.5m is $9,350 ($9,250 plus $100). Not surprisingly, the new land tax caused outrage among homeowners, many of whom are pensioners on modest fixed incomes. To make matters worse, revaluations have doubled or trebled land values in many areas in recent years, which has pushed many owners over the $1m threshold (at least it has taken the heat out of the booming property market). In stark contrast, Victoria scrapped land tax on family homes from 1st January 1998 and it now applies only to business land holdings, investment properties and holiday homes.

WHOLESALE TAX

Australia has no system of sales tax or value added tax (VAT), but levies a wholesale tax (WST) which is applied (completely arbitrarily) at varying rates on the wholesale price of a limited range of 'new' goods, i.e. goods that haven't previously gone into use or consumption in Australia. Services aren't subject to wholesale tax. A manufacturer or wholesaler is required to register for wholesale tax, which must be paid to the Commissioner of Taxation monthly. Wholesale tax is levied at the following rates:

Tax Rate (%)	Application
12	household goods, some foodstuffs
22	all other goods not specifically covered by schedule rates
26	wine
32	jewellery, furs, radios, TVs, cosmetics and photographic equipment
45	luxury motor vehicles

For sales tax on motor vehicles and motorcycles, see **Vehicle Importation** on page 236.

Goods that are exempt from WST include plant and machinery used for goods' production, agricultural equipment, primary products, building materials, drugs and medicines, books, clothing and most foodstuffs. Exemptions also apply to goods used in research, development, engineering and technical design; production related activities involving the ordering of goods and the controlling or costing of production processes; the storage, handling and despatch of own-produced goods; and certain cargo handling activities. Exports are also exempt.

Tax Reform: There are plans to reform the tax system and introduce a Goods and Services Tax (GST) or consumption tax to replace WST, which would be similar to the system of value added tax (VAT) applied in European Union countries. GST would be much broader based than WST and would include services. A rate of around 10 per cent has been suggested, with lower rates or exemptions for food and certain services. It's expected that a GST would help combat the black economy, which is estimated to cost the government up to $15 billion in lost taxes. Under GST, the price of many goods would be reduced, while others would be increased, although whatever is decided overall taxes are likely to rise (regardless of what politicians may say). As in most countries, low-income families bear the heaviest burden of indirect taxes and pay a much higher percentage of their income in taxes.

Reforms would include a limited range of state taxes, although there has been widespread disagreement between the states and the Commonwealth government, with states wanting to impose their own rates of GST (which would face constitutional hurdles) and income tax. The introduction of a consumption tax has been around for years, but its chances of being introduced were greatly enhanced in 1997 when the states' ability to levy taxes was reduced when the high court revoked the state levy of up to $5 billion in taxes on tobacco, alcohol and petrol. A reduction in income tax has been offered by the government in return for the introduction of a GST, although it won't be introduced before the next general election expected to be in late 1988 (it must take place by March 1999).

INCOME TAX

Residents of Australia are taxed on their worldwide income and non-residents on Australian-sourced income only. There's no state income tax in Australia, although it may be introduced under wide-ranging tax reforms currently under consideration. The income tax year in Australia runs from 1st July to 30th June of the following year (for reasons known only to the tax office). Tax is calculated on taxable income derived during the income tax year, although in certain circumstances a substitute accounting year beginning on a different date may be used. Changes in federal taxation are usually announced in the annual budget in May. Australian income tax law recognises the following general types of taxpayer: individuals, companies, partnerships and trusts. Specific provisions apply to minors, superannuation funds, insurance companies, primary producers, mining operations and certain other businesses.

Domicile: An individual is resident in Australia for tax purposes if he generally resides in Australia or he's domiciled in Australia and doesn't have a permanent place of abode outside the country, or he spends at least 183 days a year in Australia in a financial year (unless he doesn't intend to take up Australian residence and has a usual place of abode outside Australia). A citizen of a treaty country who works in Australia for a foreign employer for less than 183 days in a year, isn't considered a resident of Australia. However, double-taxation agreements contain particular articles dealing with government services, professors, teachers, directors and entertainers, which may alter this position.

Double-Taxation Agreements: Australia has double-taxation agreements with over 35 countries including Austria, Belgium, Canada, China, the Czech Republic, Denmark, Fiji, Finland, France, Germany, Greece, Hungary. India, Indonesia, Ireland, Italy, Japan, Kiribati, the Republic of Korea, Malaysia, Malta, the Netherlands, New Zealand, Norway, Papua New Guinea, the Philippines, Poland, Singapore, Spain, Sri Lanka, Sweden, Switzerland, Thailand, the United Kingdom, the USA, and Vietnam. Despite the name, double-taxation agreements are to prevent you paying double taxes and not to ensure that you pay twice. Under double-taxation treaties, certain categories of people are exempt from paying Australian tax. If part of your income is taxed overseas in a country with a double-taxation treaty with Australia, you won't be required to pay Australian tax on that income.

Foreign employees working in Australia for Australian companies or organisations are subject to Australian tax on their earnings. However, short-term visitors of less than six months aren't considered Australian residents and are subject to Australian tax at the rates applicable to non-residents (see page 346). Non-residents who are in Australia for longer than six months may be considered Australian residents and will then pay tax at the same rates as residents. Salary and wage income earned by residents from services performed overseas is exempt if the taxpayer has been employed outside Australia for a continuous period of at least 91 days, providing the income has been taxed overseas.

In addition to Australian taxes, you may also be liable for taxes in your home country. Citizens of most countries are exempt from paying taxes in their home country when they spend a minimum period overseas, e.g. one year. One exception is citizens of the USA. It's usually your responsibility to familiarise yourself with the latest tax procedures in your home country or country of domicile. If you're in doubt about your tax liability in your home country, contact your embassy or consulate. American citizens can obtain a copy of a brochure entitled *Tax Guide for US Citizens and Resident Aliens Abroad* from American Embassies.

Tax Evasion: Tax evasion is illegal and is a criminal offence in Australia, for which you can be heavily fined or even imprisoned. Nevertheless, there's a flourishing black economy, which the ATO estimates costs around $15 billion a year in unpaid tax on undeclared income. Most Australians don't consider it a crime to cheat the tax office — an attitude that has spawned a nation of tax fiddlers (it's a national sport). As in many countries, the wealthiest Australians use elaborate schemes to avoid paying tax and take maximum advantage of low-tax investments (while the ATO targets Aussie battlers!). Many wealthy Australians avoid or minimise their income tax by establishing trusts, which cost the government $millions a year in 'lost' tax. However, the tax office is planning a crackdown on overseas tax shelters and trusts (new legislation is imminent and expected to be applied retrospectively from 1995). An estimated up to 2m Australians use trusts in some form. Note that Australian banks and other institutions paying interest and dividends must provide details of all payments made to the tax office (which is why some people invest their money overseas, although not declaring income earned overseas is illegal).

Tax Audits: The number of taxpayers audited has more than doubled since self-assessment was introduced in 1987, to almost 500,000 a year. Some 70 per cent of those audited are found to have made mistakes, usually (not surprisingly) in their own favour. Among the individuals who come under close scrutiny are academics with travel claims; those who have received eligible termination payments or rental property deductions; hobby farmers; hobby businesses (such as musicians, glass blowers, knitters, candle-makers, photographers, wood-turners, etc.); small businesses (especially), the self-employed and contractors; those selling Amway and other home products; and those making claims for motor vehicles, self-education and home offices. An estimated 75,000 people falsely claim they are self-employed, thus claiming extra deductions.

Under self-assessment, the ATO doesn't conduct a detailed check of tax returns before issuing an assessment. However, there are heavy penalties if you make mistakes, which can be as high as 90 per cent of the tax owed plus interest. The ATO receives information from a variety of sources including banks, building societies, credit unions, employers and companies paying dividends. The ATO also provides incentives to those who 'dob in' (report) tax cheats and has tightened up its ability to collect tax and catch tax dodgers in recent years. Note, however, that the ATO is bound by privacy legislation and can only give information about a taxpayer to government agencies authorised to receive it. The ATO has a 'Taxpayers' Charter' to protect the public from 'rogue' tax officers.

Tax Avoidance: Tax avoidance, i.e. legally paying as little tax as possible, if necessary by finding and exploiting loopholes in the tax laws, is a different matter altogether to tax evasion. It's practised by most companies, wealthy individuals and self-employed people, although the opportunities for tax avoidance for anyone paying direct or PAYE tax are virtually non-existent. As in many countries, there's a two-tier tax system in Australia, first class for the self-employed and a second class system, called pay-as-you-earn (PAYE), for employees. The self-employed pay their tax in arrears, whereas an employee's income tax is deducted at source from his salary by his employer. If you own a company or are self-employed, you can also delay paying your tax for a period by appealing against a tax demand. Unfortunately there are few (legal) ways an individual paying PAYE tax can reduce his income tax bill (dying is one of them), although it's possible to appeal against your tax bill or anything connected with your tax affairs which you believe is incorrect. Whether you're self-employed or an employee, you should always ensure that you don't pay any more tax than is necessary.

Company/Corporate Tax: For taxation purposes, companies include all bodies or associations (corporate or uncorporated), but not partnerships, where partners are taxed individually. Companies are liable to pay tax on profits at a flat rate of 39 per cent. Employers are also liable to a fringe benefits tax on non-cash benefits made available to employees (such as company cars and low-interest loans). A company has its own tax file number and may also need a sales tax registration number. The date for filing depends on the company's financial year and they usually pay tax in instalments in the year following the year of the tax liability, e.g. tax owed on 1998 income is paid in 1999.

Accountants: If your tax affairs are complicated or you're unable to understand your own finances (like many people), you should consider employing an accountant or tax consultant to deal with your tax affairs (many banks also provide a personal tax service). This applies to most self-employed people, but very few who are on PAYE (see page 346). However, don't just pick an accountant with a pin from the phone book, but ask your friends, colleagues or business associates if they can recommend someone. If you're self-employed, you should choose an accountant who deals with people in your line of business and who knows exactly what you can (and cannot) claim.

Substantial tax savings can be made with regard to pensions, trusts and other tax-avoidance schemes, although some schemes apply only to the very rich as the cost of using them is prohibitive to anyone else. As soon as the ATO closes one loophole, tax accountants find another one. Accountant's fees vary from $100 to $300 an hour, so ask in advance what the rates are (they're highest in the major cities). Avoid 'high-power' accountants who will cost you the earth. You can reduce your accountant's fees considerably by keeping itemised records of all your business expenses (preferably on a computer), rather than handing your accountant a pile of invoices and receipts. Note, however, that a good accountant will usually save you more than he charges in fees.

Australia has byzantine tax regulations (the Income Tax Act runs to around 3,300 pages!) and it's possible to receive conflicting information from different tax 'experts' and even from different branches of the tax office. Taxpayers constantly complain of inconsistency in the way the ATO makes its rulings and some businesses use this to their advantage by shopping around for a better tax ruling! Never trust the ATO to take only what they should or to allow you the correct allowances and deductions, as although they won't cheat you deliberately, it isn't uncommon for them to make mistakes. If you pay PAYE tax, make sure that the tax deducted is correct (see page 346) and never hesitate to dispute a tax bill with which you disagree. A tax appeals system was introduced in 1997 and the ATO also has a problem resolution service (tel. 13 2870).

Information: 'Tax Help' is a volunteer service to help certain people complete their tax returns including those on low incomes (includes senior citizens); people from non-English speaking backgrounds; Aboriginals and Torres Strait Islanders; and people with disabilities. The Translating and Interpreting Service (TIS) helps non-English speaking people with tax questions by setting up a three-way telephone conversation with an interpreter and the tax office. The languages covered include Arabic, Chinese, Croatian, Greek, Indonesian, Italian, Japanese, Korean, Macedonian, Polish, Serbian, Spanish, Turkish and Vietnamese.

From July until the end of October, the ATO provides a telephone service for ordering publications (freecall 1800-150150, 8am until at least 10pm on weekdays and from 10am until 5pm at weekends, eastern standard time). If you need help you can telephone 13 2861 for all your income tax enquiries. General enquiries can also be made to the Australian Taxation Office (ATO), 40 Cameron Avenue, Belconnen, ACT 2617 (tel. (02)

6216 1111) or the Commissioner of Taxation, GPO Box 9990, Canberra, ACT 2601. TAFE colleges (see page 209), in conjunction with the ATO, run a course explaining the tax system and how to complete tax returns.

There are many books published annually about how to reduce your income tax bill including the *Longmans Australian Tax Guide* and the Australian *Master Tax Guide*, plus various tax computer programs such as *QuickTax* (Reckon Intuit) and *SmartTax* (Mysterious Pursuit), although they are still mainly for 'experts'.

Tax Income & Rates

Taxable income includes income derived directly or indirectly from all sources except where it's specifically exempted. It includes salary or wages; pensions; lump sum payments; termination payments; allowances and benefits; interest; income from partnerships or trusts; capital gains; foreign income; rental income; dividends; and bonuses. The tax law makes a basic distinction between income and capital receipts, and generally only income is assessable. However, real capital gains (see page 355) made from the sale of assets acquired after 20th September 1985 are included in your assessable income. Profits from the sale of assets acquired before 20th September 1985 in order to make a profit are also included in your assessable income, regardless of the period that they have been owned.

Some income is tax exempt and may include certain pensions, social security allowances and payments, education payments, and defence and United Nations' payments. Other income that's exempt from income tax includes family payment; certain scholarships, bursaries and other educational allowances; and the income of certain non-profit organisations. Most government pensions are subject to tax, although a system of rebates ensures that no tax is paid by a pensioner who earns only pension income plus a small amount of other income. Special provisions deal with other types of income including lump-sum payments received on retirement, non-cash benefits, irregular income earned by artists, sportsmen and the like, and the income of farmers. There are concessionary tax rates for some residents, e.g. those who work north of the 26th parallel (Tropic of Capricorn) and those who work in the fruit and vegetable industries (who pay only 15 per cent income tax). Those with irregular income are permitted to average their earnings out over five years. The tax payable is calculated according to a complicated formula taking into account 'normal' income and adding this to one-fifth of the taxpayer's 'abnormal' income over a five-year period. Special tax rules apply to those under the age of 18, when income is generally taxed at a higher rate.

Tax Rates: Australia has four income tax rates, from 20 to 47 per cent, as shown in the table below, which have remained the same since 1993. However, although the tax bands and rates have remained the same, increasing salaries mean that people inevitably pay more tax. The top marginal rate of tax (47 per cent) cut in at 14 times average weekly earnings 40 years ago, although today it's payable at just one and a half times average earnings. Around half of all Australian taxpayers pay tax at 43 per cent or above (without reform, it's estimated that within four years the average wage earner will be paying tax at the top rate). Anyone who isn't resident in Australia for a whole financial year receives a pro rata portion of the tax-free allowance ($5,400 a year), e.g. if you're resident in Australia for half the tax year your tax-free allowance is $2,700. Your taxable income, is your income after all allowances and deductions have been made from your gross income from all sources. The tax bands are as follows:

Taxable Income Band	Rate (%)	Tax on Band	Aggregate Tax*
under $5,400	0	nil	nil
$5,401 to $20,700	20	$3,060	$3,060
$20,701 to $38,000	34	$5,882	$8,942
$38,001 to $50,000	43	$5,160	$14,102
$50,0001 and over	47	-	-

* In the above table the first column shows the taxable income band, the second column (Rate) shows the percentage of tax payable on the income band in column one, the third column (Tax on Band) shows the tax payable on the maximum income in the band, and the fourth column (Aggregate Tax) gives the aggregate tax payable on the upper amount in the income band. For example if your taxable income is $40,000, you would pay tax of $8,942 on the first $38,000 of income plus 43 per cent on the balance of $2,000 ($860), making a total income tax bill of $9,802. If you earn $60,000 a year, you would pay $14,102 on the first $50,000 plus 47 per cent ($4,700) on the balance of $10,000, making a total tax bill of $18,802. The above rates exclude the Medicare levy (see page 277).

There's no tax-free allowance for non-residents who are taxed as shown below on income earned in Australia:

Taxable Income Band	Rate (%)	Tax on Band	Aggregate Tax
up to $20,700	29	$3,060	$6,003
$20,701 to $38,000	34	$5,882	$11,885
$38,001 to $50,000	43	$5,160	$17,045
$50,0001 and over	47	-	-

Individual Taxation

The joint filing of returns by spouses isn't permitted in Australia, where the same tax rate applies to married or single individuals. There are three main systems of collecting tax from individuals in Australia:

- Pay-As-You-Earn (PAYE);
- Prescribed Payments System (PPS);
- Provisional tax system.

PAYE: PAYE or direct income tax applies to salary and wage earners, including superannuation and termination payments. Under the PAYE or direct income tax system, an employee's tax is deducted from his gross salary at source by his employer, who forwards it to the tax office. Providing that you have no income apart from your salary or wages, PAYE is designed to cover your tax liability. Any additional income, e.g. part-time employment or income from investments or savings, whether tax is deducted at source or not, must be declared to the ATO. PAYE tax applies to all income tax payable on earnings to which the scheme relates and includes tax at all rates. At the end of the financial year (30th June), you must submit a tax return (see page 353) declaring your annual income from all sources. You receive a credit for your PAYE payments, which are offset against any tax payable. You must ensure that you give your employer your Tax File Number (see page 321) or you could be taxed at the highest rate.

Some employers may not deduct PAYE tax from an employee's earnings, particularly in the case of casual, contract or part-time workers, and where the distinction between employee and self-employed is blurred. This is illegal and a risky practice for employers, who are responsible for deducting all their employees' income tax at source, unless a person is categorised as self-employed by the tax office. The PAYE scheme is disadvantageous to employees, who in many cases would be entitled to claim larger and more allowances if they were classified as self-employed, and would also have the benefit of paying their tax in arrears. For this reason, many employees disguise themselves as independent contractors in order to avoid PAYE and reduce their tax (estimated to cost the government up to $100m a year).

The **Prescribed Payments System (PPS)** is a system for deducting tax from payments for certain work or services in prescribed industries that aren't covered by the PAYE system. For example, payments to sub-contractors in the building and construction industry are covered by PPS. Under PPS, when payments are made to, for example a sub-contractor, tax is deducted at source and sent to the tax office. This is then credited when the sub-contractor submits his tax return at the end of the tax year. It also obliges householders to report to the tax office sums over $10,000 paid under private construction contracts.

Provisional tax is paid by taxpayers who (in a particular tax year) earn over $999 of non-salary or wage income, e.g. in interest or other investment/business income, or who don't pay sufficient tax on their salary and wage income through the PAYE system. You need to pay provisional tax if you received income from a wage or salary, and the tax payable on your assessment was $3,000 or more and the shortfall in tax instalments deducted was also $3,000 or more. Provisional tax due is calculated on your previous year's income plus an 'uplift factor' which assumes that your income will grow. If you think the rate of provisional tax payable is higher than the amount of tax you will pay for the next financial year, you can apply to vary your provisional tax by completing a Provisional Tax Variation (PTV) form available from tax offices. Note that provisional tax is something of a mine-field and it's often worthwhile employing a tax agent to sort it out. Provisional tax isn't payable if your income is below the relevant threshold, shown below:

Marital Status	Threshold
Single	$21,377
Married/*de facto*	$33,368
Married/*de facto* (separated due to illness)	$41,116

Provisional tax is a prepayment of tax for the coming tax year, based on an estimate of your income in that year, and is allowed as a credit against your actual tax liability. If provisional tax exceeds $8,000, it's paid in quarterly instalments. However, if the amount paid (based on your previous year's income) is less than the amount assessed by the tax office at the end of the financial year, the balance owed must be paid within 30 days or by 1st February of the following year. Any shortfall between the provisional tax levied and the amount owed must be paid within 30 days of receiving a notice of assessment from the tax office.

Individual Tax Calculation:

Base Salary	$50,000
Bonus	$10,000
Company Car	$ 6,000
Interest (Australian source)	$ 6,000
Capital Gain	$ 8,000
Gross Income	**$70,000**
Less exempt income:	
Fringe Benefits Tax (Car)	($7,500)
Taxable Income	**$62,500**

Tax Calculation:

Tax on $ 5,400 at 0%	0
$15,300 at 20%	$ 3,060
$17,300 at 34%	$ 5,882
$12,000 at 43%	$ 5,160
$12,500 at 47%	$ 5,873
$62,500	$19,977
Medicare levy on $62,500 at 1.5%	$ 937.50
Income Tax Liability	**$20,914.50**

Self-Employed

You're generally better off if you're self-employed, as you can claim more in the way of expenses than employees (paying PAYE tax). Another advantage for the self-employed is the delay between making profits (hopefully) and paying tax on them. An estimated 75,000 people falsely claim that they are self-employed, thus claiming extra deductions. Recent court cases have declared that under the current tax laws, taxi drivers, bicycle/motorcycle couriers and airline pilots are independent contractors, and are therefore entitled to be treated as self-employed. In the light of these decisions, the ATO sidelined proposals that would have re-classified thousands of self-employed contractors as employees subject to PAYE tax.

Many companies pay 'employees' as contractors, thus avoiding payroll tax, workers' compensation, fringe benefits tax and the superannuation guarantee charge. Many people receive their pay through a company, trust or partnership, thus moving out of the PAYE system. The self-employed are eligible to claim more deductions in legitimate business expenses such as travel to and from work, phone bills, and work clothes or uniforms.

Note, however, that small businesses are frequently targeted by tax inspectors investigating tax evasion.

To be classified as self-employed, you must convince the ATO that you're genuinely self-employed and in business for yourself. The three-point test (contract, risk and labour versus completion of the job) to decide whether you're an employee or a contractor is as follows:

* **the contract test:** whether the payer can control the activities of the worker while the work is being done, as in an employer-employee relationship;

* **the risk test:** a contractor often owns his own equipment and only gets paid if the work is done, unlike an employee, who's paid regardless;

* **labour versus completion of the job test:** whether the worker is paid for hours worked, like an employee, or for completing a job, like a contractor.

If the ATO agrees that you're self-employed, get them to confirm their decision in writing.

Deductions: Expenses are usually fully deductible to the extent incurred in producing assessable income or necessarily incurred in carrying on a business for that purpose. Expenses of a capital, private or domestic nature, and those incurred in the production of exempt income, aren't deductible. Separate records must be kept of business travel and motor vehicle expenses. Entertainment expenses aren't tax deductible unless they're incurred for the provision of fringe benefits to employees. Deductions are allowed for salaries and wages paid to employees, interest, rents, maintenance, repairs, commissions and similar business expenses, although expenditure for the acquisition or improvement of assets aren't deductible (but depreciation may be claimed as an allowable deduction). However, expenditure for acquisitions or improvements may be added to the cost base of an asset for capital gains tax purposes and will reduce any taxable gain arising from a later disposition. Australian-source losses may be deducted against the same or different sources of income, and excess losses incurred on or after 1st July 1989 may be carried forward indefinitely, as can excess capital losses after 19th September 1985. Capital losses can be offset against capital gains (see page 355).

You shouldn't hesitate to claim for anything which you believe is a legitimate business deduction. The ATO will disallow them if they don't agree, but what they won't do is allow you a deduction to which you're entitled and have forgotten to claim. The profit earned by a sole trader or partnership is added to any other income and you're taxed on the total. Each partner in a partnership is taxed individually on his own share of partnership income. The self-employed and small businesses usually pay their tax under the provisional tax system outlined above.

The business structure you choose when establishing a business is vital in ensuring that you pay no more tax than is necessary (most family businesses operate a family trust in order to reduce taxes). It's important to obtain expert legal advice before establishing a business or starting work as a self-employed person in Australia. Like everything to do with tax law, the regulations applying to the self-employed and small businesses is complicated and time-consuming, and is estimated to cost some $7 billion a year in lost time. Not surprisingly, some 90 per cent of the self-employed and small businesses use a tax agent to complete their tax returns. A company must assess its own tax liability in its tax return, known as 'full self-assessment', which is being extended to all taxpayers. Self-employed, as used in Australia, means a 'sole trader' or someone in a partnership, and not a limited company or trust. If you have a limited company, you must pay **Corporate or Company Tax** on your profits, and will need the services of an accountant to deal with this. Company or corporate tax is levied at a flat rate of 36 per cent.

Deductions & Rebates

All taxpayers may claim allowable deductions and rebates in addition to credit for tax paid during the relevant financial year. The gross tax payable on taxable income is calculated at set rates by the government and is then reduced by any relevant deductions, rebates and credits to obtain the net tax payable. There's a big difference between a deduction and a rebate. Deductions reduce taxable income, but rebates are subtracted from the tax payable on your taxable income. Rebates are essentially available only to Australian residents whose dependants also live in Australia. There's no system of fixed allowance, deductions or rebates which apply to all taxpayers.

Deductions: Deductions are subtracted from your gross income to calculate your taxable income. Most deductions are occupation specific and must be legitimate expenses incurred in earning your assessable income, providing they aren't capital, private or domestic. They are commonly claimed by employees and include work, car, travel and self-education expenses, which must usually be substantiated by documentation. Deductions are also allowed for certain non-business expenses such as gifts to approved charities. Special documentation requirements must be provided where employment-related expenses exceed $300 a year. Allowable deductions include:

- Car expenses relating to work;
- Travel expenses relating to work;
- Occupational clothing expenses (e.g. specific and protective clothing or uniforms);
- Work-related, self-education expenses;
- Other work-related expenses including Financial Institutions Duty (FID), union fees, overtime meals, education courses, books, journals, tools, insurance premiums, telephone, computer and office expenses;
- Tax losses carried forward from previous years;
- Investments in the Australian film industry;
- Personal (non-employer sponsored) superannuation contributions;
- Interest and dividend expenses such as taxes and fees;
- Gifts or donations to recognised charities, funds, organisations and political parties;
- Expenses for managing your tax affairs;
- The undeducted purchase price of a pension or annuity.

Rebates: Rebates provide you with tax relief and are subtracted from your taxable income. The ATO calculates the tax payable on your taxable income and any allowable rebates are then deducted from the tax due. If rebates are greater than the tax due, you don't pay any tax. Rebates don't, however, reduce your Medicare levy (see page 277). In the 1997-98 tax year, the following rebates were allowed for dependants:

Dependant	Rebate
spouse (including *de-facto*)	$1,298
spouse (with dependant child/student)	$1,452
child-housekeeper	$1,298
child-housekeeper (with dependant child/student)	$1,556
invalid relative	$584
parent or parent-in-law	$1,167
sole parent	$1,219

Whether you can claim a rebate usually depends on such things as maintaining a dependant or living in a remote area, and not on the amount of taxable income you earned. However, some rebates (such as beneficiary and pensioner rebates and the rebate for low-income taxpayers) do depend on your income. Rebates include dependants, zone or overseas forces; superannuation payments; and medical expenses. A 20 per cent rebate can be claimed for net medical expenses (including medical, dental and optical aids) over $1,250 that aren't reclaimable from Medicare or private health insurance. Zone rebates are for people living in some remote or isolated areas of Australia (there are also special areas within these zones). Most apply to areas in northern and central Australia. The following rebates are available:

- all taxpayers are eligible for a 15 per cent tax rebate on the first $3,000 of taxable income from savings with a maximum benefit of $450; in 1998/99 a transitional rebate will apply at the rate of 7.5 per cent (maximum rebate $225) and from 1st July 1999 there's a 15 per cent tax rebate on the first $3,000 of taxable income from savings (maximum rebate $450).

- HECS tax (see page 205) is deducted from your gross salary at source by your employer if you pay PAYE tax;

- Medicare levy (see page 277) — the amount payable is calculated by the tax office;

- Tax rebates for the cost of private health insurance of up to $450 a year for families earning less than $70,000 a year, $250 for couples earning less than $70,000 a year and $125 for singles earning less than $35,000 a year.

- Superannuation contributions are taxed through a levy for top taxpayers (see page 303) and income from superannuation funds is taxed at 15 per cent. This applies to both the income from funds and deductible contributions, although super remains an attractive tax shelter as high-earners can choose to pay 30 per cent on income directed into superannuation rather than paying 47 per cent income tax. PAYE taxpayers can also reduce their tax by paying more into their superannuation funds (e.g. salary sacrifice), up to a specified amount.

Family Tax Assistance: Since 1st January 1997 there has been family tax assistance for families with at least one child. It consists of the following two elements (called part A and part B):

Part A provides assistance by increasing the tax-free threshold for one member of a couple or for a sole parent by $1,000 for each dependant child up to the age of 16 or each dependant secondary student up to the age of 18, where family taxable income is less than $70,000. The $70,000 threshold is increased by $3,000 for each child after the first. Part A of family tax assistance increases your tax-free threshold by $1,000 for each dependant child, which means a saving of $200 for each dependant child at the minimum rate of tax. Part A family tax assistance can also be paid via wages when it's $7.60 per fortnight for each dependant child. The income threshold for PART A family tax assistance is shown below:

Number of Dependent Children	Annual Income Threshold
1	$70,000
2	$73,000
3	$76,000
4	$79,000
5 or more	$67,000 plus $3000 for each dependant

Part B provides further assistance to single income families (including sole parents) with at least one child under the age of five, by increasing the tax-free threshold of the main breadwinner by $2,500, which means a saving of $500 for each dependant child at the minimum rate of tax. Part B family tax assistance can also be paid via wages when it's $19 per fortnight (irrespective of how many dependant children you have). This assistance is available where the taxable income of the main breadwinner is less than $65,000 and the annual income (excluding government payments) of the 'non-working' spouse is less than the income cut-off for the basic Parenting Allowance. The $65,000 threshold is increased by $3,000 for each child after the first. PART B family tax assistance is paid when the taxable income of the main breadwinner is less than the threshold listed below and (for two-parent families) the income of the other partner is less than $4,571:

Number of Dependent Children	Income Threshold
1	$65,000
2	$68,000
3	$71,000
4	$74,000
5 or more	$62,000 plus $3000 for each dependant

PART B benefits are payable in addition to PART A benefits listed above. Family tax assistance allows low income families to receive their benefits through the social security system, rather than the tax system. Payments are exempt from income tax and are excluded from separate net income for dependant rebate purposes.

Full details of all deductions and rebates for individual taxpayers are contained in the free *TaxPack* (see page 353).

Fringe Benefits Tax

Fringe benefits tax (FBT) was introduced in 1986 in order to reduce the amount of non-cash, non-taxable benefits (or 'perks') offered to employees by employers as part of their salary package. It includes company cars for employees' private use; private health insurance; free children's private education; low interest or interest-free loans; free or subsidised accommodation; and free holiday travel. The level of taxation on company cars depends on the business 'mileage' and is from 6 to 24 per cent. However, novated leases of luxury cars as part of executive salary packages are exempt.

FBT also includes discounted goods or services provided by an employer in excess of a specified threshold; payment or reimbursement of private expenses on behalf of employees; entertainment expenses; airline transport provided free or at a discount to employees in the airline travel industry; and the waiver of employee loans or debts. A portion of a living-away-from-home allowance paid to employees may also be subject to FBT, although 'reasonable' costs for food and accommodation aren't subject to FBT. Staff canteens, employer superannuation schemes and employee share acquisition schemes are exempt from FBT. Frequent-flyer schemes aren't taxable, even when your employer pays the membership fees, and child care provided on 'business premises' or a building controlled by your employer is also exempt from FBT (including employer-sponsored/leased places at childcare centres).

FBT is paid at the rate of 48.5 per cent. The FBT tax year is different from the financial year and runs from 1st April to 31st March. Payments are made quarterly by the 28th of July, October, January and April; each payment being equal to 25 per cent of the previous year's liability, with the balance payable when your annual tax return is filed. An employer must generally file an annual fringe benefits tax return by 28th April each year.

Income Tax Returns

All residents of Australia *must* lodge a tax return if any of the following applied (with certain exceptions) during the previous financial year:

- You received a government benefit or allowance and had other income;
- You received a government pension or allowance which was reduced because you had other income;
- You received more than $5,400 in taxable income during the financial year;
- You received more than $643 in income other than salary and wages, and you were under the age of 18 on 30th June of the financial year in question;
- You're a non-resident and earned more than $1 which had not already had non-resident withholding tax deducted from it;
- If you stopped full-time education, became an Australian resident or stopped being an Australian resident, and your income exceeded the part-year threshold amount.
- You paid tax during the previous tax year (with certain exceptions);
- You were liable for child support under the *Child Support (Assessment) Act 1989*;
- You made a loss or can claim for a loss made in a previous year;
- You carried out business in Australia;
- You were entitled to a distribution from a trust or had an interest in a partnership which carried out a business of primary production;
- You were an Australian tax resident and any of your income came from overseas.

If you don't need to lodge a return for the financial year in question, but lodged one for the previous financial year, you must complete a 'Non-lodgement Advice' and send it to the ATO (one is provided in the *Tax Pack*, see below).

Some 6.3m people lodge a tax return each year in Australia, around one-third of whom complete their own returns. Returns must be lodged by 31st October for the previous tax year, e.g. the tax return for the 1997-98 tax year ending 30th June 1998 must be lodged by 31st October 1998. If you're expecting a refund, the earlier you lodge your return, the quicker you're likely to receive it. If you're unable to meet the deadline due to circumstances beyond your control, you should request an arrangement to lodge at a later date in writing to the office where you last lodged, **before the deadline**.

Tax Pack: The ATO provides a comprehensive free *Tax Pack* (almost 150 pages) for individual taxpayers which is available from tax offices, post offices and newsagents (it's also available overseas in some countries). A copy is also delivered to all households just before the end of the financial year (30th June). The pack contains two (long form) tax returns (consisting of six pages) at the back, one of which is to be completed and sent to the ATO (the other is in case you make a mistake or to make a copy for your records, or alternatively you can photocopy your tax return before sending it). A 'short form' tax return is available for those with simple tax affairs (it will be sent to you automatically if you answered a relatively small number of questions on your previous tax return). If applicable, attach statements (group certificates or tax stamp sheets) issued by your employer to your tax return. If you don't have them, you should obtain a statement from your employer showing salary and income tax payments, otherwise you must complete a Statutory Declaration for missing or lost group certificates or tax stamp sheets.

Don't forget to sign and date the return on the last page before mailing it. If you use the TaxPack to complete your return and make a mistake, you won't be subject to any penalties, although you may be required to pay interest on any tax owed (unless the mistake was due to misleading information contained in the TaxPack). Although the return is relatively easy to follow and understand, many people still use a tax agent to complete their tax returns.

Tax Agents & Accountants: Many people use a registered tax agent or accountant to complete their tax return, the cost of which is tax deductible. He then has the responsibility for completing the return correctly and will (should) ensure that you claim for all the allowances and rebates to which you're entitled. The fee charged by a tax agent is usually around $75 to complete a tax return for an average taxpayer, although additional fees are charged for extra services (accountants are more expensive). Shop around and obtain a few quotations (some offer a free initial consultation).

The tax office where you lodge your return is determined by your postcode, a list of which is given in the TaxPack. You can post your tax return or lodge it personally in the box provided at tax offices. You can also lodge your tax return electronically by using *TaxPack Express* at a post office or at the office of a participating registered tax agent. There's a fee of $20 for this service, although you can claim a deduction in your next return. The tax office also plans to allow taxpayers to lodge their returns over the internet for the tax year 1997-98. **Always keep a copy of your tax form and anything else you send to the ATO. This is useful if your tax form gets lost in the post or there are any queries.** Keep a copy of all documentation (receipts, invoices, statements, etc.) which substantiate claims made in your tax return. Records must be kept for three and a half years for salary and wage earners and five years for the self-employed (seven years for car and travel-related expenses). Selected tax returns are audited and you may be penalised if the information provided is found to be incorrect. As in most countries, the self-employed are *much* more likely to be audited than employees.

Tax Bill: After around eight weeks you will receive a 'notice of assessment' from the ATO, which is an itemised account of the tax you owe on your taxable income. At the bottom of the assessment will be your tax debt or, if you're due a refund, your refund cheque (lucky you!). Your notice of assessment will tell you when you must pay your tax bill in order to avoid incurring a penalty for late payment. If you don't agree with the ATO's assessment you can lodge an appeal. If the amount owed doesn't include provisional tax (see page 346), the payment date will be around 30 days after receipt of the notice of assessment. If the notice includes provisional tax, the payment date won't be earlier than 31st March and if over $8,000 is owed, you can make the payment in four quarterly instalments. Tax can be paid in person at a tax or post office, or by post by cheque or postal order (payable to the 'Deputy Commissioner of Taxation'), which must be sent with the bottom section of your notice of assessment. If you use a tax agent who lodges returns electronically, your tax bill or refund can be paid directly from or into a bank, building society or credit union account. If you're unable to pay your bill on time, contact your tax office and ask for an extension. You will need to provide a reason why you need the extension (penniless?) and, if granted, you will be charged interest at a daily rate (equal to 20 per cent per annum) on the amount outstanding after the due date.

CAPITAL GAINS TAX

Australia doesn't have a separate Capital Gains Tax (CGT) as such, but provides for the inclusion in assessable income of any profits made on certain assets during the financial year. The part of a gain that's subject to income tax (i.e. the proceeds of a sale less the purchase cost after being reduced by indexation and any losses) is treated as ordinary income and subject to the same income tax rates. However, the amount of tax you pay is calculated by adding 20 per cent of the total gain to your other income, working out the extra tax due on this portion, and then multiplying it by five (the ATO *never* makes anything simple).

Tax is payable on the sale of certain assets including real estate (other than your principal home), shares, personal use assets, trust distributions, equipment and plant, and goodwill on the sale of a business. What are termed 'listed personal use assets' such as works of art and antiques, fall within CGT, providing the purchase price was over $100. It includes money or property received other than as gifts or loans, but doesn't apply to an inheritance arising from the death of an asset-holder. Exemptions from CGT include your principal residence and up to two hectares of attached land; motor vehicles (whether acquired for personal or business use); superannuation and insurance policies; debentures, bonds and other loans without a deferred interest element; certain personal use goods with a disposal value of less than $10,000; and any assets acquired before 20th September 1985.

Under Australian income tax laws, any realised capital gain from the disposal of assets acquired after 19th September 1985 are taxable. The cost of an item is indexed for inflation, although this doesn't apply when an asset is disposed of within one year. The excess of the sale price over the indexed cost base is the taxable capital gain, which is added to your other income and taxed at your marginal tax rate. Capital losses can be used to offset gains, either in the current year or in future years without a time limit, but cannot be used to offset other income. New residents are deemed to have acquired non-Australian assets for their fair market value at the time of becoming a resident (except for assets acquired prior to 20th September 1985, which are exempt). Upon ceasing to be a resident, you can choose to treat all non-Australian assets as 'taxable Australian assets', thereby deferring payment of CGT until the assets are disposed of or you resume resident status. Overseas employees who become residents during their Australian assignments are subject to complex CGT rules that may affect their assets located outside Australia. If you're in this position you should obtain expert advice regarding capital gains.

Gains made on the sale of your principal residence in Australia are usually exempt from CGT. However, tax is payable on capital gains made on the sale of an investment property or a second home. There's a federal government taxation incentive for those who let a property for less than their mortgage repayments on a property, when the loss can be offset against other income. There's a qualifying period of two years for exemption from CGT on an inherited home and if you choose not to live in an inherited home and sell it after two years, no CGT is payable.

If you sell a business for less than $2.1m, you're subject to CGT on only half of the portion of the proceeds described as goodwill, although lease premiums are fully taxable. When a small business is sold for retirement, the first $500,000 of the proceeds are exempt from CGT. Note that CGT complications can occur when a business undergoes re-organisation or re-structuring, when you should seek prior advice from an accountant or tax consultant.

The ATO publish a number of booklets including, *Capital Gains Tax — What you need to know*; *Capital Gains Tax and your home*; *Capital Gains Tax and investments in shares and units*; *Capital Gains Tax after divorce or involuntary disposal of assets*; and *Capital Gains Tax and the assets of a deceased estate*.

WILLS

It's an unfortunate fact of life, but you're unable to take your worldly goods with you when you take your final bow (even if you have plans to return in a later life). Once you've accepted that you're mortal (the one statistic you can confidently rely on is that 100 per cent of all human beings eventually die), it's advisable to make a will leaving your estate to someone or something you love, rather than leaving it to the government or leaving a mess which everyone will fight over (unless that's your intention). The good thing about dying in Australia (at least for your beneficiaries) is that there's no inheritance tax or death duties, and no probate or estate duty is payable (although some states are considering this tax option). Many people in Australia die intestate, i.e. without making a will, in which case their property is subject to the provisions and statutory orders of the various statutes in the state(s) dealing with intestacy.

If you own a home as a joint tenant with your spouse (as most couples do), it automatically passes to your spouse as the survivor of the joint tenancy. For example, in NSW if you die leaving a spouse and no children, then your spouse would inherit the whole of your estate. If you leave a spouse and children, then the spouse may get the bulk of the estate and the children may get only a part of it, depending on its size and the nature of its assets. If a beneficiary who's a child of the testator dies before the testator, his share will be distributed among his children. Property left to a child under a specified age must be held in trust on his behalf until he reaches the specified age.

It isn't necessary to leave a fixed percentage of your estate to your children in Australia or even to your spouse. However, a married person must make proper provision for his family in his will and if an estate is likely to be small it should usually all be left to the surviving spouse. If proper provision isn't made for the family, any family member can apply to a court under the Testators Family Maintenance Act for 'adequate provision' from the estate. Note that *de facto* couples don't have the same inheritance rights as married couples and should therefore ensure that their wills reflect their wishes.

A will must be in writing and be signed by the testator, whose signature must be witnessed by at least two other people, who must attest to the fact that they were present with each other and saw the testator sign the will (they must also sign the will with the same pen as the testator). A beneficiary mustn't be a witness, otherwise any gift to the beneficiary will be void. It's possible to make a do-it-yourself will in Australia, but it must be drawn up according to the laws of the particular state or territory where you live. There are various do-it-yourself will packs including *How To Make Your Own Will in*

Australia (Legal Kits of Australia), *The National Will Kit* (Citizen's Legal Information) and the *Australian Legal Will Kit*.

Will forms can also be purchased from newsagents and law stationers in Australia for around $2, although these are only recommended for small, straightforward estates, for example when spouses are planning to leave their assets (consisting mainly of the family home and investments) to each other or their children. If you wish, you can list all your 'valuables' and who's to get what (the list can be kept separate from the will and can then be changed without altering the will itself). Some businesses such as Credit Unions offer a free or cut-price will-writing service to their customers. In most cases it's advisable to consult a solicitor when writing a will, as the cost is relatively small (usually around $100 for a basic will). If you have a large estate it's essential to obtain expert legal advice, as there may be important tax implications. Bear in mind that a will must be written in a tax-efficient manner — solicitors have a field day sorting out home-made wills.

If you're a foreign national and don't want your estate to be subject to Australian law, you may be eligible to state in your will that it's to be interpreted under the law of another country. To avoid being subject to Australian inheritance laws, you must establish your country of domicile in another country. If you don't specify in your will that the law of another country applies to your estate, then Australian law will apply. A legal foreign will made in an overseas country dealing with overseas assets is valid in Australia and will be accepted for probate there. However, you should have an Australian will to deal with your Australian assets.

If your circumstances change dramatically, for example you get married, you must make a new will, as under Australian law marriage automatically annuls an existing will. Both husband and wife should make separate 'mirror' wills. Similarly, if you separate or are divorced, you should consider making a new will, although divorce doesn't automatically annul a will (there are special rules which apply). A new bequest or a change can be made to an existing will through a document called a 'codicil', without writing another will. You should check your will every few years to make sure it still fulfills your wishes and circumstances (your assets may also increase dramatically in value). A will can be revoked simply by tearing it up.

You'll also need someone to act as the executor of your estate, which can be particularly costly for modest estates. Your bank, building society, solicitor, or other professional will usually act as the executor, although this should be avoided if at all possible, as fees can be very high. The Public Trustee's Office in each state will prepare a will free of charge, although they will insist on being appointed the executor and will also charge commission fees for administering the estate as executor. If you appoint a professional as executor of your estate, always check the fees in advance (and whether they could increase in future). **It's best to make your beneficiaries the executors, who can then instruct a solicitor after your death if they need legal assistance.** Probate usually takes no more than three months in Australia,

Keep a copy of your will in a safe place (e.g. a bank) and another copy with your solicitor or the executor of your estate. It's useful to leave an updated list of your assets with your will to assist your executor in distributing your estate. You should keep information regarding bank accounts and insurance policies with your will(s), but don't forget to tell someone where they are!

COST OF LIVING

No doubt you would like to know how far your dollars will stretch and how much money (if any) you'll have left after paying your bills. The standard of living in Australia has increased considerably for all income levels in the last 20 years, although incomes have increased much faster for the rich than for the poor. However, in recent years many people in 'middle Australia' reckon that life is getting more expensive. Australia's inflation rate is based on the Consumer Price Index (CPI), which gives an indication of how prices have risen (or fallen) over the past year. The CPI (which sceptics believe stands for 'Con People Incessantly') is calculated from a basket of basic goods and services. It received a revamp in 1997 when mortgage interest rates were removed and computer equipment, financial fees and higher education fees were included.

In stark contrast to Australia's international image of affluence and plenty, poverty is widespread and there's a widening gap between the rich and poor, with the richest 20 per cent earning some 13 times as much as the poorest 20 per cent. Over 50 per cent of Australian families struggle to pay their bills and many people receive assistance from their families. Some 40 per cent of children live in families with very low incomes, including many one-parent families, and some 2m adults and children are dependent on government allowances (some 2m Australians also live in households with income below the poverty line). Many elderly people also struggle on state pensions (or no pensions) — elderly women are among the poorest sections of society. Many immigrants with families strive to live on $300 to $400 a week, with low-income families in major cities paying half or more of their weekly wage in rent payments. In recent years low-income families have been deserting inner-city suburbs in droves for cheaper outer suburbs and rural areas.

In a survey conducted by the *Economist* magazine in 1997, Sydney was rated the most expensive city in the southern hemisphere and ranked 22nd in the world. Perth is the second most expensive Australian city (33rd on the *Economist* list) and Melbourne the third (38th on the list). Sydney shares its position with New York and Helsinki, but is more expensive than Brussels, Houston, Los Angeles, Miami, Milan, Rio de Janeiro and San Francisco. Note that although most surveys agree that Sydney is Australia's most expensive city, most don't agree on the position of other Australian cities. There's little difference in the cost of living between Adelaide, Brisbane and Perth. The cost of living in rural areas is, not surprisingly, lower than in major cities (particularly housing).

It's difficult to calculate an average cost of living, as it depends on an individual's particular circumstances and life-style. What is important to most people is how much money they can save (or spend) each month. Manufactured goods tend to be expensive in Australia, particularly imported goods including automobiles, clothes and other manufactured items which are generally more expensive than in Europe or North America. If you do a lot of travelling, transportation costs will be high due to the large distances involved.

Your food bill will naturally depend on what you eat and is similar to the USA and around 25 per cent less than most European countries. Approximately $350 should be sufficient to feed two adults for a month in most areas (excluding alcohol, fillet steak and caviar). The price of staple foods in Australia's capital cities are listed in the monthly British newspaper *Australian Outlook* (see **Appendix A**) and a free *Cost of Living and Housing Survey* is published annually by the Commonwealth Bank of Australia. Even in the most expensive cities (i.e. Sydney), the cost of living needn't be astronomical. If you shop wisely, compare prices and services before buying and don't live too extravagantly, you may be pleasantly surprised at how little you can live on.

A list of the approximate **MINIMUM** monthly major expenses for an average person or family in a typical town or suburb are shown in the table below. **Note that these are necessarily 'ball park' figures only and depend on your lifestyle, extravagance or frugality, and where you live in Australia (almost everyone will agree that they are either too low or too high!).** When calculating your cost of living, deduct the appropriate percentage for income tax (see page 342) and other deductions from your gross salary.

	MONTHLY COSTS ($)		
ITEM	**Single**	**Couple**	**Couple with 2 children**
Housing (1)	400	600	800
Food	300	350	600
Utilities (2)	100	150	200
Leisure (3)	75	150	300
Car/travel (4)	200	250	350
Insurance (5)	50	100	100
Clothing	150	200	300
Rates	50	75	100
TOTAL	**$1,325**	**$1,875**	**$2,750**

(1) Rental or mortgage on a modern apartment or semi-detached house in an 'average' small town or city outer suburb. The cost for a single person is for a bedsitter or sharing accommodation. Other costs are for a two (couple) or three-bedroom property (couple with two children). They don't include council or other subsidised housing.

(2) Includes electricity, gas, water and telephone, plus heating bills.

(3) Includes all entertainment, sports and holiday expenses, plus newspapers and magazines (which could of course be much higher than the figure given).

(4) Includes running costs for an average family car, plus third-party insurance, road tax, petrol and servicing, but not depreciation or credit costs.

(5) Includes all 'voluntary' insurance, excluding comprehensive car insurance.

15.

LEISURE

The leisure and tourist industry is one of Australia's largest, earning some 7 per cent of GDP and providing direct or indirect employment for over 500,000 people. Australia is one of the world's top tourist destinations and overseas visitors (mostly from Japan, New Zealand, Britain, the USA and South Korea) numbered over 4m in 1996/97, accounting for over $15 billion (some 15 per cent) of the country's export earnings (one of Australia's biggest sources of income is from 'frugal' backpackers who spend an average of around $5,000 each). The 2000 Olympics in Sydney will give a further boost to Australia's position as one of the world's leading tourist destinations. However, the fallout from Asia's currency crisis in 1997 meant that tourist arrivals from Asia fell dramatically and was expected to hit revenue hard in 1998 (although offset to an extent by the weaker A$).

Australia is one of the world's most beautiful countries with a wide range of unusual landscapes. It's a country of infinite variety, offering something for everyone: magnificent beaches for sun-worshippers; beautiful and spectacular countryside and parks for greens; a wealth of mountains and seas for sports lovers; historic towns and bustling cosmopolitan cities for townies; a vibrant night-life and music scene for the jet set; superb wines and cuisine for oenophiles and gourmets; a wealth of culture, art and serious music for art lovers; and tranquillity for the stressed.

Until the '70s, Australia was (with some justification) considered to be a cultural desert (cultural cringe was a national trait) and a nation of philistines (with the notable exception of the country's 40,000-year Aboriginal cultural heritage). However, the arts have flourished in the last few decades and now match or exceed those found in many 'old world' countries. Australia has a rich history of achievement in the high arts such as drama, ballet, opera, music, literature, painting, sculpture, architecture and film. However, while not the cultural wasteland depicted by its critics, an appreciation of the arts still lags far behind that of sport, which is the country's most popular leisure activity (whether taking part or spectating).

The most popular leisure activities in Australia include cinema, botanical gardens, libraries, animal and marine parks, museums, popular music, art galleries, zoos, operas and musicals, theatre and dance. There are modern performing arts centres in the main cities, many of which vie for the title 'arts capital of Australia', while galleries, theatres, concert halls and cinemas abound in the major towns and cities. The main funding (over $50m a year) for the arts comes from the Australia Council, plus further contributions from state and local governments and corporate sponsorship. In addition to the more formal events, a profusion of free concerts and entertainment is staged in public parks, shopping and entertainment centres, including jazz, folk, rock, opera and classical concerts, plus impromptu shows by an assortment of jugglers, fire-eaters, buskers, acrobats, dancers and mime artists.

A wealth of festivals and carnivals are held in Australia throughout the year and include music, art, folk, food, wine, beer and harvest festivals; surf life-saving carnivals; and agricultural shows. Most states stage a Royal Agricultural Show, usually in September or October (although Sydney's Royal Easter Show is held at, you guessed it, Easter). They are much more than 'simply' agricultural shows and include a wide range of displays and entertainments. One of the wackiest events is the Todd River Regatta held in Alice Springs in September, notable because the Todd River is dry!

Australia offers an abundance of leisure and entertainment facilities, and many beautiful and manageable cities, some of which resemble large country towns. Sydney and Melbourne, two of the world's great cities, enjoy an intense rivalry for Australia's premier city. Sydney (Australia's most sophisticated and exciting city) usually wins hands down, thanks largely to its peerless setting ('Venice of the 21st century'), although

Melbourne is Australia's cultural and gastronomic capital, and its subtle charms tend to grow on you. The capital Canberra is home to the foremost art collections in the country, although many people consider it a boring, modern town with little charm. Other major cities include Adelaide, Perth, Hobart and Darwin, all of which have their own unique attractions.

However, despite the multifarious attraction of its lively cities, Australia's foremost and most enduring appeal is its immense natural beauty, which owes little to man's intervention (except perhaps on the debit side). Getting away from it all isn't difficult in Australia, with it's many lakes and rivers, miles of excellent beaches, and areas of wilderness bigger than many countries (the Northern Territory is one of the world's last frontier lands, where you can still imagine that you're an explorer). Australia is a time-honoured land of unbounded beauty and one of the world's most fascinating countries. It's a vast country of endless contrasts and colour with an amazing variety of environments ranging from bleak, unearthly deserts to lush tropical rain-forests; palm-fringed sandy beaches and stunning reefs to majestic snowfields; sparkling blue seas and remote tropical islands to rugged mountains and spectacular rock formations; and rolling farmlands and vineyards to wild rivers and vast lakes.

Australia boasts a wealth of natural wonders, many of which are World Heritage sites, including the Great Barrier Reef (the world's most magnificent coral reef), Ayers Rock, Kakadu National Park, the Flinders Ranges, the Murray River, the Grampians, the Yarra Valley, the Dandenongs and the Ranges, the Naracoorte Caves, Bool Lagoon, Katherine Gorge, the Snowy Mountains, and the Tasmanian Wilderness, to name but a few. It home to a plethora of unique and fascinating flora, fauna and wildlife, including astonishing mammals such as kangaroos, possums, wallabies, duck-billed platypus, wombats, koala bears, and the Tasmanian devil.

If you're spending a limited time in Australia, bear in mind that it's a vast country, so don't try to see it all in a few weeks or even months, which is impossible. If you rush through the outback by train or car, you will see little and the country will appear to consist of a vast nothingness. However, if you take your time and do a bit of walking, you will experience unexpected, untold wonders. Many visitors seek soft-adventure holidays (e.g. crocodile or shark watching, rather than a close encounter with the sharp end) and eco-tourism such as a camel safaris in the outback (the most uncomfortable means of transport invented).

Tickets for most large entertainment and sporting events can be purchased from BASS, Ticketek and Ticketmaster ticket agencies (they can also be purchased via the internet), which have outlets in all the main towns and cities (there's a surcharge of around $5 per ticket). Free entertainment guides are published in the major cities (e.g. the *Sydney Review*) and major newspapers also publish weekly guides, in addition to which there's a variety of commercial entertainment magazines (such as *What's On* magazine in Melbourne). A plethora of travel guides are dedicated to Australia including the excellent Lonely Planet *Australia* travel survival kit, which is a *tour de force* containing 1,000 pages and the most comprehensive guidebook to Australia. Other leading guide books include *The Rough Guide Australia, The Michelin Green Guide to Australia, Frommers Australia On $45 A Day* and the *Insight Guide to Australia*. Leisure information is also available via the internet, e.g. Sydney City Search (linked to www.smh.com.au). Many local councils publish a 'Leisure Directory'.

For information about sports facilities in Australia, see **Chapter 16**.

TOURIST INFORMATION

There are tourist offices, travel centres, visitors centres and visitors information bureaux in all cities, large towns and resorts, although few organisations maintain information desks at airports or major railway stations. All states have Tourist Commissions that publish a wealth of information and also act as booking agencies for transport companies, hotels and other accommodation. There are official state tourist offices in all state capitals, on major highways at state boarders and some regional centres. Many smaller towns also have tourist offices run by local councils and regional tourist associations. There are no state-run tourist information offices in Queensland, where tourist offices are often privately operated and act as booking agents for hotels, and travel and tour companies. State motoring associations (see page 268) also provide tourist and touring information.

The opening hours of city offices are relatively restricted by international standards, e.g. from 9am until 5pm Monday to Friday and Saturdays from 9am to between 1 and 4pm. Offices in the main cities and resort towns are also open for a reduced period on Sundays, e.g. 10 or 11am until 4pm. Tourist offices will provide you with a wealth of information about local attractions, restaurants, accommodation, sporting events, sports facilities, package holidays, tours, public transport, car rental and much more. Offices can provide information on a wide range of leisure activities and sports, so you should mention any special interests when making enquiries. Most cities and regions publish free entertainment magazines and newspapers containing maps and a wealth of useful information about local attractions and events (distributed by tourist offices, hotels, transport companies and information bureaux).

Australia is promoted overseas by the Australian Tourist Commission (ATC) and most Australian states also maintain tourist offices in a number of countries including the UK and USA. The ATC has offices in Auckland, Chicago, Frankfurt, Hong Kong, London, Los Angeles, New York, Osaka, Singapore, Tokyo and Toronto. Note that the ATC is strictly an external organisation which promotes Australia overseas and it doesn't maintain any offices in Australia. The ATC publishes a wealth of information including an excellent annual *Travellers Guide*, *Australia Unplugged* (a guide for young people) and *On the Loose* (for backpackers). They also publish fact sheets on many topics including disabled travel, camping, skiing, fishing and national parks, plus a good map of Australia (for which there's a small fee).

A lot of information is published specifically for backpackers and budget travellers such as the free magazine *TNT for Backpackers*, available from TNT, 5th Floor, 55 Clarence Street, Sydney, NSW 2000 (tel. (02) 9299 4811). TNT publishes editions for Sydney, NSW and the ACT; Melbourne, Victoria and Tasmania; Queensland and Byron Bay; and the Outback (which includes South Australia, Western Australia and the Northern Territory). The Sydney/NSW/ACT edition is published monthly, the other editions quarterly.

HOTELS

The quality and standard of Australian hotels and other accommodation varies considerably and includes superb international five-star luxury hotels, resort hotels, boutique hotels, budget hotels, motels, farms, apartments, guesthouses, hostels, and bed and breakfast accommodation. Sydney has a huge range of accommodation including 13 five-star hotels (the Regent Hotel in Sydney is rated one of the best in the world). However, the widest choice of accommodation is to be found in Queensland (where tourism is the main industry), which has a wealth of luxury hotels, motels, apartments and backpacker hostels in all resort areas. On the other hand, when travelling in country and remote areas the choice of accommodation is severely restricted, and it's advisable to obtain recommendations unless you're prepared to put up with the most basic of accommodation.

Rates usually vary depending on the season. The low season is generally from May to November (winter). However, in the centre and tropical north (the 'top end') winter is normally the best time of year to visit and is therefore the high season. In the summer, hotel rates in the top end drop by up to 30 per cent. There's a lack of accommodation in some cities (such as Sydney, where many hotels average over 90 per cent occupancy), particularly budget accommodation, although prices remain reasonable. The busiest period is between November and mid-May, with beds being almost impossible to find from mid-December to late January in cities and resorts unless you have booked. You can obtain discounts of up to 50 per cent for weekly bookings, stand-by prices, weekend specials and during the low season. Travel agents who buy rooms in bulk may be able to offer you a better rate than you can get yourself and motoring organisations also offer members' discounts. Many airlines sell vouchers offering reduced rates at motel chains.

Major hotel groups operating four and five-star hotels in major cities include Hilton, Sheraton, Regent, Hyatt, InterContinental, Ramada, Ritz Carlton, Radisson, Matson, Mirvac, Nikko, Parkroyal, Holiday Inn, Jewel Hotels and Resorts, Accor, ANA, Beaufort, Peppers, Select, Southern Pacific Hotels, Rydges, Waratah Inns, Tradewinds and Vista. Most top hotel chains have freecall 1800 booking numbers. Three to four star chains include Flag, Centra, Travelodge, Best Western, Metro Inn, All Seasons Resorts, Quality Pacific and Country Comfort. The following table can be used as a *rough* guide to accommodation prices in Australia:

Star Rating	Price Range
hostels	$7-20 (dormitory)
1/budget	$20-50
2	$55-85
3	$80-150
4	$125-250
5	$220-350 +++

Prices are usually quoted per room and not per person and generally include all taxes. A 10 per cent bed tax was introduced in New South Wales in 1997 (which caused an uproar in Sydney) and there's a 2.5 per cent tax at hotels in Ayers Rock and Alice Springs. Note that some hotels close on Sundays and public holidays as they cannot afford to pay staff the high penalty rates demanded.

Facilities: Note that a double room usually has twin single beds and if you want a double bed you should ask for one when booking. Top class hotels provide air-conditioned rooms with tea and coffee making facilities; room service; radio and colour TV (maybe with an in-house video film service); *en suite* bathroom or shower; telephone (often direct dial); mini-bar; hair drier; and trouser press. Some hotels provide no smoking rooms and special rooms for the disabled. Many top class hotels have a choice of restaurants and bars; provide secretarial, business and conference facilities; and have health and leisure centres with swimming pools, a gymnasium, solarium, sauna, jacuzzi, and a range of other sports facilities. Top class hotels in major cities also provide theatre booking agencies, hairdressing salons and a range of shops. Note that some luxury hotels discourage room service and impose surcharges at weekends.

Breakfast in top class hotels is expensive at around $12 to $15 for a continental buffet breakfast and $15 to $20 for a cooked breakfast. In some hotels a toaster is provided, in which case you will be given sliced untoasted bread for breakfast. Many hotels have a refrigerator stocked with cold drinks (where you can also keep your own drinks cold) and operate an honour system whereby guests are trusted to pay for what they consume. Note that telephone calls are expensive from hotel rooms and it's best to stock up on 20¢ coins and call from the lobby. When calling from your room, you must usually dial '9' for the hotel operator and '0' to get an outside line.

Budget Hotels: Budget hotels are in short supply in Australia and if you're looking for budget accommodation, your best bet is a hostel (see page 368), bed and breakfast (see page 367) or a pub. If you don't need to be in the middle of town, suburban hotels offer better value for money. Rooms in budget hotels and guest houses are usually from $30 to $50 for a single and $45 to $60 for a double (some also have suites/triples). Rooms are usually significantly cheaper by the week, e.g $110 for shared rooms and $160 for doubles. Pub hotels generally charge from around $25 to $35 for a single room in country areas, usually with a shared bathroom. Check whether breakfast is included. Breakfast at old hotels and private hotels are usually huge and excellent. Air-conditioning (or at least ceiling fans) is an important consideration in summer, particularly in Western Australia, Queensland and the Northern Territory.

Hotels must provide a public bar to serve alcohol, although this isn't required by motels and private hotels, and guest houses also don't have permits to serve alcohol. The term 'private hotel' is used to denote an hotel which doesn't serve alcohol. Other terms used for an unlicensed hotel are guest house, lodge and inn. You may also come across 'boutique hotels', which are small hotels more like guesthouses. There are old colonial-style hotels in country and outback areas, many of which have been refurbished in recent years. These include National Trust accommodation in pre-1901 buildings, full of character (the bar may also be full of characters) with eccentric owners and bizarre regulations.

Pub Hotels: Pubs are called hotels because they originally had to provide accommodation by law, although nowadays many 'pub hotels' don't have any accommodation. Some pubs provide tourist accommodation and may call themselves hotels/motels. Pubs in country areas, which may be called 'commercials' as the guests were traditionally commercial travellers (salesmen), are more likely to offer accommodation than those in cities. Pubs are usually basic (so don't expect a trouser press and bidet — or a bedtime mint on your pillow) with a bar downstairs and rooms upstairs which can be noisy (it's best to get a room at the top of the building).

Motels: There's a wide choice of modern comfortable motel (also called motor hotels and motor inns) chains throughout Australia including A1, Budget, Country Comfort, Flag International, Metro Inns, Quality Inns and Best Western. In remote areas there are road stations (similar to freeway rest stops) with motel-type portable units called 'demountables'. All motel chains will book you a room at another motel in the same chain free of charge, although you should note that not all motels are the same standard within a particular chain.

Motel rooms have a private bath or shower, telephone, TV, tea and coffee-making facilities and a refrigerator. Some luxury motels have a swimming pool or spa. At smaller motels you can park outside your door. At most motels you can order room-service breakfast, although most don't have bars, restaurants or dining rooms. Some motels have self-catering facilities (particularly in resort areas), although motel units (apartments) don't usually include cooking facilities but may have small ovens or microwave ovens. Singles usually start from $30 or $35 a night and doubles from $40 to $70 (rising to $140 for a luxury motel). Lower rates are usually available if you're planning to stay for more than a few days. Prices in resort areas are around double those in small towns or country locations. Breakfast isn't usually included in the price. Shared rooms in motels can be economical for a family or a group of three or four, and are popular with Australian families.

Hotel Guides: Motoring organisations (see page 268) publish guides to hotels, motels and other accommodation. These include the *A-Z Australian Accommodation Guide*, the NRMA *Accommodation Directory* and *Weekends for Two*, an accommodation guide published bi-anually. The NRMA *Accommodation Directory* lists hotels, motels, serviced apartments, guesthouses, and bed and breakfast accommodation throughout Australia. For general information, contact the Australian Hotels Association (tel. (02) 9281 6922).

Bookings: In cities there are hotel booking agencies such as the Countrylink New South Wales Travel Centre in Sydney (tel. (02) 9224 2742). Ausres is a one-stop central booking service for accommodation, tours and travel services (tel. 13 1066 or (03) 9696 0422). There are accommodation information boards with direct-dial free phones to book rooms at major airports, and rail and bus stations, although these generally apply to up-market hotels only.

BED & BREAKFAST

Bed and breakfast (B&B) accommodation consists of a room in a private house, pub, farmhouse or even a university campus, and is found throughout Australia from cities and large towns to small villages and outback stations. B&B accommodation is more informal than an hotel and provides a friendly place to meet Australians in their own homes. It usually includes farmstays, pubstays and homestays, and encompasses a huge variety of abodes including historic houses, country homesteads, inner city townhouses and conventional family homes. Farmstays are becoming big business (as outback tourism increases in popularity) and range from fairly basic to luxurious. They include ranch-style homesteads; small holdings in farming regions; outback cattle and sheep stations; and special interest farm holidays. Most are working properties where guests become one of the family and are accommodated in the homestead or in an adjoining cabin or cottage.

B&B is a relatively new concept in Australia, but has become popular in the last decade or so during which an increasing number of Australians have opened their homes to guests (a trend encouraged by the tourist authorities). However, it isn't an inexpensive option (as it is in Europe) with single rooms costing from $40 to $100 and doubles from $70 to $120. Homestays, which are similar to a B&B except that meals are provided, cost from $40 to well over $100 a night, depending on the meals and activities provided. Prices for full board at an outback farm (station) are from around $70 a day, although some farms offer inexpensive 'backpacker' accommodation in barns from around $7 a night (sleeping with the cows and pigs). Guesthouses are generally cheaper than B&Bs, with guests usually staying for a minimum of a week (like homestays, meals are usually provided). Most B&Bs don't accept credit cards.

Although it's advisable to book in advance, particularly during busy holiday periods or in major cities, it's usually unnecessary, particularly if you're touring and need a room for one or two nights only. If you're a smoker, you should ask whether smoking is permitted when booking. If you don't book in advance you'll have more freedom to go where you please, but you should bear in mind that some B&Bs have a minimum stay of two or three nights. When booking in advance, confirm your arrival time to ensure that your hosts will be at home. If you're staying for more than one night, you may be expected to vacate your room for most of the day and to leave by noon (or earlier) on your last day.

Guide Books: There are a number of guide books to B&B accommodation in Australia including *Robinson's Guide to B&B's & Rural Retreats* by Wendy Robinson (Periplus Editions), *Guide to Bed & Breakfast in Australia & New Zealand* by Jeannie Fairlie (Periplus Editions), *The Australian Bed & Breakfast Book* by J & J Thomas (Pelican) and the *Australian Bed & Breakfast Book* (Moonshine Press).

SELF-CATERING

There's a wide choice of self-catering accommodation in Australia which usually consists of apartments (units), although cottages, houses, chalets and mobile homes are also available for rent in country and resort areas. An apartment is often a good choice for a family, as it's much cheaper than an hotel room, provides more privacy and freedom, and allows you to prepare your own meals when you please. Standards, while generally high are variable, and paying a high price doesn't always guarantee a well furnished or well appointed apartment (most look wonderful in a brochure). Holiday apartments are generally found in tourist areas and serviced apartments (units) in cities and large towns. Serviced apartments with one to three bedrooms with living area, kitchen, laundry and bathroom cost from around $120 to $200 a night (there may be discounts for stays of a week or more). There's usually no low season in major cities such as Sydney, where rates are constant throughout the year.

Holiday apartments are usually rented on a weekly basis and are generally well equipped with cooking utensils, cutlery and crockery. However, small studios may have only an electric frying pan and a microwave for cooking, while larger apartments also have a stove. Check when booking if you plan to do a lot of cooking. You may need to provide your own linen and towels, although they can usually be hired for an additional fee. Prices vary considerably depending on the location and season, and are higher during school and public holiday periods. Before booking self-catering holiday accommodation check the holiday changeover dates and times; what's included in the rent (e.g. cleaning, linen); whether cots or high chairs are provided or pets are allowed; if a garden or parking is provided; access to public transport (if required); and anything you consider essential (such as a TV, heating, air-conditioning, etc.).

Self-catering accommodation is listed in guides such as the NRMA *Holiday Units and Cottages Directory* and lists are also maintained by tourist offices. If you're seeking longer term self-catering accommodation, see **Rented Accommodation** on page 132.

HOSTELS

For those travelling on a tight budget, one way to stretch limited financial resources is to stay in hostels. Hostels include everything from beach huts and tree houses in Queensland to mountain cabins in Tasmania, from historic renovated buildings and disused railway stations to huge purpose-built buildings. Some hostels call themselves resorts, although rates remain firmly in the budget bracket. Modern hostels generally provide the best facilities, although they lack character and warmth, and many people prefer the more intimate, smaller, owner-operated hostels. Standards vary enormously, even among hostels operated by the same organisation. One of the ways to discover the best hostels is to ask your fellow travellers.

There's fierce competition between hostel groups in resort areas, particularly on the Queensland coast, where many hostels have touts at the main public transport termini. The competition often leads to a range of extra services and perks, although it's advisable to book during the peak season and on public holidays. If you don't book, you may find it difficult to get a bed in cities and at popular tourist spots at any time. Many hostels have a toll-free (1800) number so you can book from anywhere in Australia free of charge. Note that some city hostels may admit overseas backpackers only, due to locals treating them as cheap dosshouses.

Facilities: The larger hostels have high standards and good facilities which may include personal lockers, security lockers or safety deposit boxes; free tea and coffee-making facilities; a self-catering kitchen (with allotted cupboard space and a shared refrigerator); laundry room and ironing facilities; telephones; travel booking service; luggage storage; fans or air-conditioning; and heating in winter. In larger cities, hostels usually have an inexpensive cafeteria. Resort hostels may offer a swimming pool, spa pool, sauna, gymnasium, billiard tables, tennis court, BBQs, TV lounge, launderette, shop, bar, cafe, restaurant and a travel shop. Many hostels offer a range of sports equipment on free loan or for rent (e.g. bicycles) and may also organise free tuition (e.g. sailing), day trips and tours. Most hostels provide free transport to and from local towns, airports, railway stations and bus termini.

There are few restrictions at hostels in Australia, which generally have no curfews (24-hour access), although private hostels may have fewer restrictions than YHA hostels and the standard of accommodation and facilities may also be higher. All hostels provide sheets, pillow slips and blankets, although they may need to be rented (which saves you carrying a sleeping bag and sheet). Note that some hostels are what's called 'party hostels', which stage backpacker party nights, barbecues and other entertainment. If you're looking for a quiet place to stay, these should be avoided!

Accommodation: Accommodation may include single and double rooms, family rooms and dormitories (sleeping up to 24). Most hostels have dormitories for from four to 12 people, which may be single sex or mixed (some hostels advertise separate dormitories but put men and women together). Note that dormitories can be noisy and lack privacy. The cost of a hostel is usually from around $10 a night for a bed in a dormitory to $25 per person, per night for a double. Some hostels have two-bedroom, self-contained units where around six people share a lounge, bathroom and kitchen. Many hostels offer discounts of $10 to $25 for stays of a minimum of four or five days, or weekly rates which usually save you a few dollars a night. Note, however, that some hostels have limits on the length of stays during peak periods. Security can be a problem and if you haven't got a safe place for your valuables never let them out of your sight, even when taking a shower (some travellers live off others and will steal *anything*).

There are a number of hostel chains in Australia which include the Youth Hostel Association (YHA), Backpacker Resorts of Australia (BRA) and Nomads Backpackers International, in addition to many privately-owned independent hostels. In outback areas there are Aboriginal hostels (operated by the Aboriginal Hostels Association) that may also take in non-Aboriginals.

YHA: The Youth Hostel Association (YHA) has around 140 hostels in Australia (around a third of the total number) classified as simple, standard and superior, with a grading of one to five backpacks. All guests must be YHA members. The annual membership fee (1997) was $44 (renewals $27) for over 18s and $13 for under 18s. There are discounts for two or three-year or life membership (certain conditions apply). Children under 17 receive free membership when their parents are members (called family membership) and group membership is also available. Senior Australian members receive two vouchers (worth $8.50 each) towards hostel accommodation in the state of issue. It may be cheaper to join the YHA overseas before arriving in Australia. Visitors can purchase a one-year Hostelling International Card (HIC) for $27 in Australia (overseas residents don't pay the joining fee) at YHA membership and travel centres in capital cities or at hostels. Introductory membership is also available, where you pay an extra $3 per night and after nine nights receive full membership (stamps are issued and an 'Aussie Starter Card').

There are few restrictions at YHA hostels, although the length of stays may be limited to a maximum of five to seven days. There are no age restrictions and no rules requiring early check-out. Guests must have sleeping sheets or bed linen (these can be purchased at hostels or hired for around $3 a night). Sleeping bags alone aren't permitted and blankets and pillows are provided. The YHA has an International Booking Network (IBN) and bookings can be made up to six months in advance (a fee of $2 may apply when booking in Australia). The YHA provides accommodation packs of 20 ($250 valid for six months) or 10 nights ($130 valid for two months). A range of discounts are offered to YHA members including 10 per cent off Greyhound Pioneer Australia's coach passes, up to 30 per cent discount on car rental, and over 800 other discounts across the country. The YHA publishes a free annual *Accommodation and Discounts Guide* plus a free *Australia Visitors Map* showing the location of its hostels. For further information, contact the Australian Youth Hostel Association, Level 3, 10 Mallett Street, Camperdown, NSW 2050 (tel. (02) 9565 1699).

BRA & Others: Backpacker Resorts of Australia (BRA) is an association of around 110 hostels throughout Australia. It offers VIP membership (not compulsory) which provides accommodation, travel, entertainment and equipment discounts. BRA allow guests to use their own sleeping bags, although sheets and blankets are available for hire. Rates are from around $12 to $16 a night and bookings cost $1.50. For information contact Backpacker Resorts of Australia, PO Box 600, Cannon Hill, Brisbane, QLD 4170 (tel. (07) 3890 2767). Nomads Backpackers International (tel. freecall 1800-819 883 or (08) 8224 0919) offer a 'dreamtime card' providing a range of accommodation (e.g. the seventh night free at all hostels) and other discounts throughout Australia.

Other Options: YMCAs and YHCAs offer casual accommodation, although their prices are around double those charged by hostels. They have single rooms and some dormitories, and are mainly located in the major cities. Out of term-time and during summer holidays (i.e. from November to February), many university colleges let rooms in their halls of residence to student travellers for around $12 to $15 a night for a single room or $20 for bed and breakfast. Rooms must be booked in advance and priority is given to students (others pay a surcharge of 50 to 100 per cent). Note that many universities are located outside cities and towns.

Publications: There are many publications for independent travellers including *Go Australia* (available from Go Publishing, 70 Brunswick Street, Stockton-on-Tees, Cleveland TS18 1DW, UK) and the *Australia and New Zealand Travel Planner* (published by TNT Magazine, 14-15 Child's Place, Earls Court, London SW5 9RX, UK), which provides invaluable advice for backpackers and travellers plus a complete hostel directory. TNT also publish *TNT for Backpackers* magazines. A free monthly magazine, *For Backpackers, By Backpackers*, is available in Sydney and the YHA also publishes a free magazine, *The Hosteller*, available from YHA hostels. The Australian government produces a backpacker hostel guide listing over 300 hostels which have been assessed by the Australian Automobile Association (AAA) since 1995 and given a one to five rucksack rating. The guide is available from hostels, transit points, hostel booking offices, travel agents and automobile associations in Australia. Books for hostellers include the

Aussie Backpacker Accommodation Guide (North Australian Publishing, PO Box 1264, Townsville, Queensland 4810) and the *Independent Travellers Guide to Australia* (STA Travel).

CARAVANS & CAMPING

Australia is a great country for camping due to its mild climate and the general lack of camping restrictions. Most towns have at least one campsite or caravan park. In the outback you can pitch a tent virtually anywhere you please, although permission is required to camp on private property and there are local regulations restricting camping in some areas. For example in Western Australia you aren't permitted to camp wild within 16km/10mi of a caravan or campsite, although you can try camping on green areas outside the city centre (but should be on your way early to avoid the attention of the local police). In Brisbane it's illegal to camp within a 22km/14mi radius of the city centre, although short-term camping is permitted in roadside rest areas in most of Queensland.

In national parks, camping is permitted in designated areas only, although some also allow bush camping (there's usually a small fee). Special environmental and safety regulations apply and most don't permit open fires (so you will need a portable stove). A supply of chopped wood is often provided. Fees vary from park to park but are usually from around $5 per person, per night (you may need to book at popular camp sites in national parks). When spending an extended period in a national park, you should let the park ranger know your route and when you expect to return. You must observe all fire ban warnings; take your rubbish with you; wash away from streams, rivers and lakes; stick to existing campsites where available, rather than creating new ones; use only fallen dead wood for fires; take no pets with you; take care not to desecrate Aboriginal sites; and must not interfere with the flora and fauna or disturb the wildlife (apart from these rules you can do what you like!). All state's publish information about camping in national parks.

Camp sites and caravan parks are common and are available in all major towns and tourist centres (many are located on the edge of beaches). Facilities vary but basic amenities usually include electricity hook-ups, hot and cold water, showers, toilets and laundry facilities. At large sites there's usually a range of indoor recreation areas, shops, restaurants, lock-up storage for valuables, and a wide variety of sports facilities which may include a swimming pool, tennis courts, volleyball, cycling, table-tennis, trampolining, canoeing, fishing and boating. Camp or caravan sites cost from around $10 a night for two people. A 'night' is usually from noon to noon and some sites charge extra to use showers, sports facilities (such as tennis courts) and other amenities such as ironing facilities or a freezer. Many caravan parks (such as BIG 4) have on-site caravans, cabins, villas and holiday units, which can be rented from around $20 to $30 a night for a caravan and $30 to $60 for a cabin. Linen and blankets can usually be hired, although a portable heater is useful in winter as many caravans and cabins are unheated.

Many campsites in Australia are primarily caravan parks, intended more for caravanners (trailers) and motor homes than for campers. Many have gravel surfaces (or hard ground) rather than turf, so pitching a tent can be hard work. Most campsites near to major cities are well away from the centre, which means that you need your own transport to get the most out of camping. It's important to book if you have a caravan and require an electricity hook-up. Outside peak periods you can usually find a campsite without difficulty on the spot, but don't leave it too late in the day when you're in a popular area (after noon is too late at some sites).

A swag (sleeping bag) is all you need when camping under the stars in the outback. Many different types are manufactured (e,g, by the Jolly Swag Company of Australia), the best of which include a mattress, sheet, down filled sleeping bag, blanket and pillow inside a sturdy canvas envelope. You can buy an optional tarpaulin cover in case of rain. When camping wild, avoid dried-up river beds in the wet season due to the danger of flash floods (when you will also need a life jacket!).

Camping tours are popular and many companies offer organised tours in air-conditioned coaches or 4WD vehicles. You can buy or rent (see page 266) a campervan or mobile home throughout Australia (many people purchase a secondhand one from a departing visitor).

Interesting magazines for campers and caravanners include *Outdoor Australia* and *Wild*. Excellent guide books are available from automobile associations such as the NRMA's (see page 268) *Camping and Caravan Directory*. See also **Australian Roads** on page 255for information about driving in the outback.

PARKS, GARDENS & ZOOS

There are some 2,000 national parks and reserves in Australia covering an area of over 40m hectares (100m acres), or over 5 per cent of Australia's land area, plus a further 38m hectares (95m acres) of marine and estuarine protected areas. Australia has 11 World Heritage areas including the Great Barrier Reef, Eluru-Kata Tjuta (Ayers Rock/Mount Olga), Kakadu National Park (Northern Territory, where *Crocodile Dundee* was filmed), the Queensland (wet tropics) rainforests, Fraser Island and the Tasmanian Wilderness. National parks include every possible habitat and many are of great scientific interest. Australia was the second country (the first was the USA with Yellowstone Park) to proclaim a national park (the Royal National Park in Sydney in 1879).

Each state has its own independent national parks authority, most of which publish guides detailing park facilities. Some parks charge an entrance fee, e.g. $7.50 for a car in NSW (less for motorbikes and pedestrians), although entry to smaller parks is often free and larger parks also provide free entry at weekends. A two-month holiday pass is available in Tasmania for $25 for a vehicle and $10 for motorcyclists, cyclists and bushwalkers, and an annual pass ($40) for vehicles is also available. All national parks and World Heritage sites have information or visitors' centres with maps, leaflets, slide shows and films, and guided tours are organised during peak times. Some parks provide numbered pegs indicating points of interest, natural features and unique habitats that can be cross-referenced with information sheets. For information about national parks, contact the Australian National Parks and Wildlife Service, 217 Northbourne Avenue, Turner, ACT 2601 (tel. (02) 6250 0250).

Australia has many excellent zoos, wildlife parks and aquariums throughout the country. The most famous is the Royal Melbourne Zoological Gardens (Australia's oldest dating back to 1857 and the third oldest in the world) housing around 4,000 species of animals and birds in their natural habitats. Taronga Zoo in Sydney is home to Australia's largest collection of native and exotic animals and has a peerless setting beside Sydney Harbour (best visited by ferry from Circular Quay) and extensive breeding facilities, some of which are located at its 'sister' zoo (Western Plains Zoo in Dubbo). Other top zoos and wildlife parks include the Alma Park Zoo north of Brisbane (which houses a large collection of Australian wildlife), Perth Zoo (40 acres of exotic and native Australian fauna), Adelaide Zoo, the Tidbinbilla Nature Reserve (west of Canberra) and the Lone Pine Koala Sanctuary (near Brisbane). There are aquariums in many of Australia's major cities (e.g. the Sydney Aquarium and Manly Oceanarium) and tourist resorts (e.g. Sea World on the Gold Coast).

Australia's cities were designed with people in mind and they generally have an abundance of green spaces and wide boulevards, with both formal and informal ('native') parks in or close to cities. All major cities have impressive botanical gardens such as the Royal Botanic Gardens in Melbourne, home to some 12,000 plant species and the finest in Australia, and the City Botanic Gardens in Brisbane (the Mount Coot-tha Botanic Gardens 12km/7mi west of the city are also impressive). Sydney has its own Royal Botanic Gardens, located adjacent to the harbour and the Sydney Opera House, and an exquisite Chinese Garden (Darling Harbour), while Canberra is home to the National Botanic Gardens on Black Mountain containing over 6,000 native plants. Some cities such as Melbourne publish a *Parks and Gardens* brochure. The National Trust (PO Box 3173, Manuka, ACT 2603, tel. (02) 6239 5222) is dedicated to preserving historic buildings and parks throughout Australia and owns a number of properties which are open to the public. You can join for $44 a year for individuals ($31 concession) and $62 for families ($44 concession). There are local National Trust offices in each state.

Information about national parks, botanical gardens, aquariums and zoos is available from the Australian Tourist Commission or any good guide book. All tourist offices and visitors' centres provide information about local attractions.

MUSEUMS & ART GALLERIES

There are over 1,000 museums in Australia visited by over 7m people annually, including federal and state museums, regional exhibitions and privately owned collections, plus a wealth of private art galleries in major cities. The most important national collections are housed in Canberra and include the National Museum of Australia, the National Gallery of Australia, the National Portrait Gallery, the National Library, the Australian War Memorial (which houses one of the best military museums in the world), the National Film and Sound Archive (free admission), the National Science and Technology Centre and the National Aquarium and Wildlife Sanctuary (admission $10). Admission to most state museums and galleries is $2 to $5, although this may be increased for special overseas exhibitions. Most museums are open daily from around 9 or 10am until 5pm, seven days a week.

The state capitals also have interesting collections, the most important of which include the Art Gallery of NSW, the Australian Museum, the Powerhouse Museum (science, decorative arts and social history), the National Maritime Museum and the Museum of Contemporary Art (all housed in Sydney); the National Museum of Victoria, the Victorian Arts Centre (housing the National Gallery of Victoria) and the Australian Gallery of Sport and Olympic Museum in Melbourne; the Art Gallery of South Australia and the South Australian Museum (both in Adelaide), and the National Motor Museum (Birdwood) in South Australia; the Western Australian Museum and the Art Gallery of Western Australia (Perth); the Queensland Museum and Queensland Art Gallery (Brisbane); the Tasmanian Museum and Art Gallery (Hobart); and the Northern Territory Museum of Arts and Sciences (Darwin), which houses one of the best collections of Aboriginal art in Australia. New museums due to open in the next few years include the Melbourne Museum (2000), the National Museum in Canberra (2001) and the Museum of Australian Art in Melbourne (2001). Admission is usually between $3 and $6 and students normally pay half price. Most museums and galleries are open daily, although many have reduced opening hours on Sundays.

There's a strong market for contemporary Australian art, particularly Aboriginal art, which has become fashionable in recent years and can be seen in many galleries. It is, however, usually expensive (apart from mass-produced tourist artifacts which aren't the genuine article). Famous Australian painters include Sidney Nolan, Arthur Streeton and Tom Roberts, although they aren't known internationally outside the art world (most Australian artists tend to become famous only after they have died).

All states have National Trusts that work hand in hand with the federal Heritage Commission to preserve historic buildings and sites. There are many reminders of Australia' past as a penal colony and many former prisons have been preserved as museums, notably the Old Melbourne Gaol and the Port Arthur penal colony in Tasmania.

CINEMAS

Cinema is the most popular leisure activity among Australians, over 60 per cent of whom visit a cinema each year (ticket sales are expected to hit 100m a year by the year 2000). Australian cinemas are split between first run and arthouse (which show old classics, foreign, cult and experimental films), plus films shown by cultural organisations, the State Film Centre (Melbourne) and film festivals. Australia is dominated by three large cinema chains: Greater Union, Village and Hoyts, which together account for around 50 per cent of screens in Australia and some 60 per cent of tickets sold. Independent (indies) operators control around 30 per cent of Australia's cinemas, although they are being hard hit by the multiplexes which have as many as 30 screens (but usually two to 10) and are often owned by the film distributors (film distribution rights are a constant battle for indies). At the other extreme, small towns usually have just one single-screen cinema, many of which are ancient. There are private film clubs in the major cities and local film societies in all areas.

Some cinemas (such as Cinema Plus) have giant screens employing IMAX 3-D technology. New centres have extra-wide comfortable seats with ample leg-room, dolby stereo or THX surround sound, air-conditioned (non-smoking) auditoriums and free parking. Many also have cafés, restaurants, bars and games rooms. There are also open-air, drive-in cinemas throughout Australia, particularly on Saturday evenings (you usually pay for the vehicle rather than the number of passengers). Most operate in summer, although in winter you may be able to rent an in-car heater. There's even a Deckchair Cinema in Darwin where you can watch a film while reclining in a deckchair.

All films on general release in Australia are given a film certificate classification (shown below), which denotes any age restrictions:

Classification	Age Restrictions
G	General release, no age restrictions
PG	parental guidance for children under 15; not recommended for children under 12
M	Mature - those aged over 15
R	Restricted - those aged over 18

Children (or adults) who look younger than their years may be asked for proof of their age (e.g. a school identity card, student card or driving licence) for admittance to age-restricted performances.

Tickets cost up to $12.50 ($7.50 for children aged under 15) in cities and a bit less in country areas. There are reduced prices for matinees, Tuesday evenings and sometimes also on Mondays. There was something of a price war in Sydney in 1997, where heavy discounting resulted in prices dropping to as little as $5 on Tuesdays (usually around $8.50). Most cinemas offer reductions for children, pensioners and students, although you should check in advance as some reductions apply to certain performances only. Many cinemas (including all new cinemas) have special facilities for the disabled in wheelchairs. Most chains provide passes which offer large discounts. Most cinemas accept telephone bookings (major credit cards accepted, although some cinemas charge a booking fee for each seat, e.g. $1.50) and tickets can usually be purchased in advance. Cinemas usually have a number of shows a day including late-night and all-night shows on Friday and Saturday evenings. Smoking is prohibited in all cinemas. Cinema programs are published in major daily and local newspapers.

Australia has a thriving film industry which has produced many international hits in the last few decades. (The world's first feature film, *Soldiers of the Cross*, was made in Australia in 1900 by the Salvation Army — not many people know that!). The Australian film industry is aided by the Australian Film Commission (AFC) established in 1975 to assist in the development of low budget, innovative film productions. In its heyday around 40 films a year were produced in Australia including such classics as *Picnic at Hanging Rock, Sunday Too Far Way, Gallipoli, My Brilliant Career, Breaker Morant, Newsfront, Mad Max, The Man From Snowy River, Crocodile Dundee, The Chant of Jimmy Blacksmith, Evil Angels, Strictly Ballroom, Death in Brunswick, Shine, Babe, The Piano, The Year of Living Dangerously, The Adventures of Priscilla, Queen of the Desert,* and *Muriel's Wedding.*

However, in recent years state funding has been reduced and the Australian film industry faces an uncertain future. Australian film stars include Mel Gibson, Nicole Kidman, Paul Hogan, Judy Davis, Greta Saachi, Jack Thompson and Toni Collette (Errol Flynn and Chips Rafferty were also born in Australia), plus a number of celebrated directors and producers. However, like most countries, Australia loses most of its talent to Hollywood which is quick to snap up foreign artists in order to cement their dominance of the silver screen. Major film festivals in Australia include the Melbourne International Film Festival and the Sydney Film Festival, both held in June.

THEATRE, OPERA & BALLET

Australian theatre is of a surprisingly high standard (particularly to those who think Australians are philistines) and extremely varied, thanks to the country's cosmopolitan and multicultural cities (particularly Sydney and Melbourne). In addition to mainstream traditional theatre (where classic plays and international musicals are performed to a very high standard), Australia has a thriving contemporary theatre scene where anything goes. It's far-ranging performances include outrageous Australian comedy, image-based theatre, experimental plays, pub and coffee shop theatre, and outdoor performances.

Melbourne has the most dynamic theatre life in Australia and boasts over 70 theatres including the State Theatre, Playhouse and the George Fairfax Studio (all of which are housed in the majestic Victorian Arts Centre), plus Her Majesty's, the Comedy Theatre, the Russell Theatre (home of the Melbourne Theatre Company), the Princess Theatre and the Athenaeum Theatre, and various fringe theatres. Sydney's main theatres include the Opera House, the Belvoir Street Theatre, the Griffin Theatre, the York Theatre, the Pilgrim Theatre, the Symour Theatre (in Sydney University) and the Wharf Theatre, home of the Sydney Theatre Company. The oldest surviving theatre company in Australia is the New Theatre in Sydney (over 65 years old). Other major Australian theatres include the Canberra Theatre Centre; the Queensland Cultural Centre and Performing Arts Complex in Brisbane (housing the Lyric Theatre, the Concert Hall and the Cremorne Theatre); and

His Majesty's Theatre and the Subiaco Theatre Centre in Perth (home of the State Theatre Company of Western Australia).

Major international productions such as *Les Miserables, Phantom of The Opera* and *Miss Saigon* are regularly staged in Australia's major cities. Most plays performed in Australia have traditionally been written by American and British playwrights. However, Australian theatre has blossomed in the last few decades and plays such as *Stretch of the Imagination* (Jack Hibbert) and *The Removalist* (David Williams) have become Australian classics. The Australians excel in comedy and love to send themselves and everyone else up. The most famous Australian comedy actor is Barry Humphries, whose larger-than-life characters include Dame Edna Everage, Barry McKenzie, Sir Les Patterson and Sandy Stone. Melbourne is the comedy capital of Australia and stages the annual International Comedy Festival in April, while Sydney has the Comedy Store with a different show each night. Tickets for most major productions vary considerably in price, but usually cost between $20 and $40, while performances at fringe theatres cost around $10. Half-price theatre tickets can be purchased on the day of performances in Sydney from the Halifax kiosk in Martin Place (tickets must be purchased in person and paid for in cash).

Opera: The Australian Opera was established in 1970 and is largely dependent on government subsidies and sponsorship (although it and other performing arts companies still run up huge losses). The Victoria State Opera and the Australian Opera (Sydney) were merged in 1996 to form a new integrated company, Opera Australia, which performs at the State Theatre in Melbourne and the Sydney Opera House. The standard of opera, ballet and classical concerts produced at Australia's main venues is among the best in the world and international stars regularly perform there. Home-grown stars include Joan Sutherland, Dame Nellie Melba, Joan Hammond, John Brownless, Yvonne Kenny and Peter Dawson. There are small professional opera companies in some states.

The Sydney Opera House is one of the architectural landmarks of the 20th century and has become the symbol of the city since its completion in 1973 after 14 years at a cost of $102m (it was begun in 1959 and was scheduled to be completed in five years at a cost of $7m!). In addition to an opera house, it also houses two main auditoriums (the larger for symphonies seating 2,690, the smaller for opera and ballet), a drama theatre and a small playhouse, three restaurants and a café. Despite its imperfect acoustics, it's often compared with Covent Garden in London, La Scala in Milan and the Carnegie Hall in New York as a serious music venue (it's to be modernised which hopefully will improve the acoustics). Opera Australia also performs outdoor concerts such as the Opera in the Park in Sydney in January. The opera season usually runs from July to August and November to December. Most events at the Sydney Opera House are expensive although tickets start at $15 for some concerts (rising to over $100). Information can be obtained from the Opera Centre, 480 Elizabeth Street, Surrey Hills, Sydney, NSW 2000 ((tel. (02) 9319 6333 for information and (02) 9319 1088 for 24-hour bookings — there's a $4 surcharge for telephone bookings).

Dance: Ballet is popular in Australia (where there are hundreds of ballet schools) where it's the most healthy art form and survives largely on box-office receipts. The world-famous Australian Ballet was founded in 1962 and has it's headquarters in Melbourne, although it performs a summer and winter season at the Sydney Opera House and also tours Australia. Tickets cost from around $30. Australia also has a number of contemporary dance companies, the most famous of which is the Sydney Dance Company (which performs at the Sydney Opera House). `

Festivals: In addition to the extensive concert program, Australian cities stage a number of prestigious arts' festivals including the biennial Adelaide Festival (1998, 2000, etc). It's one of the most prestigious in Australia (modelled on the Edinburgh Festival) and includes theatre, dance and musical performances from around the world. There's also a fringe festival. Other major arts' festivals include the National Festival of Australian Theatre (Canberra, October), the Festival of Perth (February), the Melbourne International Festival (October) and the Melbourne International Comedy Festival (April).

Theatre and concert listings are provided in weekly and monthly entertainment guides, available from tourist offices in major cities and many daily newspapers publish free guides such as the 'Metro Guide' on Fridays in the *Sydney Morning Herald* (which includes a theatre directory).

MUSIC

Classical concerts, music festivals and solo concerts are regularly staged throughout Australia by Australian and international musicians and performers. Australia has eight professional orchestras: six symphony orchestras (one in each state capital) run by the Australian Broadcasting Corporation (ABC), the Australian Opera and Ballet Orchestra in Sydney, and the State Orchestra in Victoria (both of which work with the Australian Opera and the Australian Ballet). Many Australians are enthusiastic about classical music and a number of festivals are staged including the Sydney International Music Festival (July), the Sydney Festival (January) and the Melbourne Music Festival (February). The Sydney Symphony Orchestra performs outdoor concerts such as the Symphony in the Park in Sydney in January. Musica Viva (Sydney) is the best known chamber music society (and the world's largest) and stage a concert series of international groups and artists. Regional companies (supported by state governments) perform in state capitals and provincial centres.

Rock Music: Rock music is an important part of the national popular culture and over the last 25 years Australia has produced some of the world's best rock music. Australia also has a thriving home-grown band scene, mostly performing in pubs, where the best of real Australian music is found, and clubs (e.g. RSL and working mens' clubs). Many amateur bands are surprisingly good (often performing their own songs), although due to their abundance and variety they can also be excruciatingly bad. Australia is said to be among the hardest training ground in the world for rock bands, where internationally famous bands such as AC/DC, Air Supply, Cold Chisel, InXs, Men at Work, the Little River Band, The Angels, Midnight Oil and Mental as Anything did their apprenticeship. There's usually an admission fee of $5 to $10 to clubs and pubs with live music, although many concerts are free (depending on who's performing).

Major Australian cities, particularly Sydney, Melbourne and Brisbane, are on the international itinerary of most international rock stars, many of whom perform in Australia around the Christmas (summer) season. In Sydney, the main venue for rock concerts is the Sydney Entertainment Centre and the Sydney Town Hall is also an important venue, while in Melbourne it's the Sport and Entertainment Centre on the banks of the Yarra River. Concerts are also held at the Myer Music Bowl in Alexandra Gardens, Olympic Park and Kooyong Stadium. In Brisbane, the big stars play at the Brisbane Entertainment Centre and in Perth the main venue for rock concerts is the Perth Entertainment Centre. Free rock concerts are held on summer Sundays in some cities (if it's very hot and the band sounds a bit off key, it may be the result of high humidity, which cause instruments to go out of tune — it's certainly an original excuse!). Big Day Out is an all-day Australia-wide popular music festival featuring top bands staged in January and February.

Jazz, Folk, Country and Bush Music: Jazz has a lively following on the pub circuit, particularly in Sydney, where there are many regular venues (bands also perform in a variety of outdoor venues). A number of jazz festivals are staged in Australia including the Montsalvat Jazz Festival (Eltham, VIC), held on the Australia Day weekend (January), and the York Jazz Festival in Western Australia in September. Australian folk and country music has strong local themes and there are clubs in all major cities, and many pubs also feature folk and country groups. Folk and bush music is also popular (it has its roots in English, Irish and Scottish folk music), where fiddles, tin whistles and banjos predominate along with a home-grown instrument called the 'lagerphone' (or zob stick), consisting of a wooden frame covered in metal bottle tops which is bashed on the ground, shaken or hit with a stick. The main festivals are the Australasian Country Music Festival in Tamworth (NSW) in January (featuring over 700 events) and the Australian Bush Music Festival (Glenn Innes, NSW) in November.

Aboriginal Music: Few people will forget the haunting sound of a didgeridoo (made famous by Rolf Harris in his song *Tie Me Kangaroo Down, Sport*) which is used in the bush to accompany tribal dances (called corroborees). Busking (often non-Aboriginals) didgeridoo players are common in the main cities and performances are staged for tourists in northern regions (although they are a pale imitation of a real corroboree). It's possible to hear the real thing at an Aboriginal cultural festival and there are some contemporary Aboriginal bands such as Yothu Yindi, although few have had any commercial success. Other forms of native music are Koori, a cross between traditional Aboriginal music and country music, and 'gum-leaf' bands, where Aboriginal performers make 'music' by blowing on gum leaves.

There are also a wide variety of amateur musical groups in Australia including orchestras, military bands, choral societies and even barbershop singers, most of which are constantly on the lookout for new talent. Free music is provided by an army of buskers, many of whom are excellent.

Concert and gig guides are available free in local daily newspapers, many of which also publish a weekly entertainment guide (usually on Fridays). There are free music weeklies in most cities distributed through pubs, record stores and bottle shops. These include *Beat*, *In Press* and *Storm* in Melbourne, *OTS* (On The Street) and *Drum Media* in Sydney, *Time Off* in Brisbane, the *Adelaide Review* and *X-press* in Perth. Gig guides are also broadcast on local music radio stations.

SOCIAL CLUBS

There are numerous social clubs and organisations in Australia catering for both foreigners and Australians including Ambassador clubs, Apex clubs, Business clubs, Church clubs and groups, the Freemasons, International Men's and Women's clubs, Kiwani Clubs, Lion and Lioness clubs, Rotary clubs, Round Table clubs, ex-Servicemen's clubs, Sports clubs, Women's clubs, Working Men's clubs and Returned Services League (RSL) clubs. RSL (or leagues) clubs are an institution in Australia and constitute the main social centre in country towns. They are run by the Returned Soldiers League/Returned and Services League (RSL) or local football clubs and associations, and are among the most popular social venues in Australia. Many have huge halls where a variety of shows are regularly staged, plus restaurants, bars, pay/satellite TV, gambling (poker machines), discos, live rock music and ballrooms. Although ostensibly for members (and their guests) only, many admit overseas visitors.

Expatriates from many countries run a wealth of clubs, associations and organisations in major cities (ask at local consulates for information). Many local clubs organise activities and pastimes such as chess, bridge, whist, art, music, sports activities and outings, theatre, cinema and local history. If you want to integrate into your local community or Australian society in general, one of the best ways is to join a local social club (even better join a number). In major cities there are singles clubs which organise a comprehensive range of activities on every day of the week. At the other end of the scale, if you're retired, you may find that your local council publishes a program of recreational activities for the retired in your area. Most local councils publish a calendar of local sports and social events, and most libraries provide information about local clubs, groups, associations and organisations.

NIGHTLIFE

There are discotheques and nightclubs in all major Australian towns and cities. Nightlife includes nightclubs, discotheques (discos), dance clubs, karaoke clubs, comedy clubs, cabaret bars, gay clubs, pool halls, RSL clubs and casinos (described under **Gambling** below). Note that the difference between a bar, pub, restaurant and nightclub is often marginal in Australian cities, and some establishments are a combination of all four. Sydney and Melbourne have the most cosmopolitan nightlife in Australia, with venues to suit every taste in music, fashion and atmosphere. There's also a huge variety of gay clubs in some cities such as Sydney (information is published in the gay press such as the *Sydney Star Observer* and *Capital Q*).

Admission to discos varies but there's usually a $6 to $15 cover charge, which may include a free drink, and venues with live music may charge as much as $20 for entry and $4 or $5 a drink. Some offer free entry for women on certain days (e.g. Wednesdays) and half-price drinks before 9pm (before the real 'action' starts) on some days. Some up-market discos and dance clubs allow admission to couples only. Note that drinks are usually expensive and even water usually costs from $2.50 to $3.50 a glass. The dress code is usually smart casual, which usually excludes jeans, leather, T-shirts and trainers, although in some establishments this may represent the perfect outfit (fashion usually dictates, depending on the venue). Dress may also be at the whim of the doorman (bouncer) and if he doesn't like the look of you, you're out (or at least not in). Many discos are open until 3am or later, although some have variable closing times.

There are some huge clubs in the major cities such as the *Metro* in Melbourne, which is the largest nightclub in the southern hemisphere. Many clubs and discos play a combination of live and recorded music. The main nightlife area in Sydney is Oxford Street and the sleazy Kings Cross area (British conservative politicians would feel at home here!), where drugs are freely available and violence is never too far away at some venues. Melbourne has some of the liveliest nightlife in Australia and a plethora of clubs. Some nightclubs are exclusive 'members-only' clubs with strict dress codes and high prices, which attract an older, more up-market clientele. Like discos, some nightclubs remain open until dawn.

Daily newspapers and free entertainment newspapers and information sheets (e.g. *3D World* and *Beat* in Sydney) in major cities provide a comprehensive lists of entertainment venues and events.

GAMBLING

Gambling is one of Australia's favourite pastimes (sometimes it's an occupation) and includes horse and greyhound racing; camel races; football pools; lotteries; bingo ('housie'); casinos; poker machines (pokies); card games; two-up; raffles; and the results of general elections, public appointments, football matches and other sports events. Aussies are compulsive (and impulsive) gamblers and will bet on almost anything, even the proverbial two flies climbing a wall, and in the outback (where you need to make your own amusement) there are even cane toad, cockroach, lizard and snail races!

Gambling is a $10 billion industry in Australia, where the residents of NSW are among the heaviest gamblers spending over $12m a day on lotteries alone (the record jackpot is $7.1m in January 1998). Gambling revenue is a favourite target of the tax man (around 30 to 40 per cent of the profit on poker machines alone) and taxation raised from gambling is a huge source of income for state and federal governments. Thanks to the revenue received from gambling, New South Wales residents paid the highest per capita taxes in Australia in 1996/97.

Casinos: Most states have one or more casinos and there are now around 15 in Australia including four in Queensland, two in Sydney, two in Melbourne, two in Tasmania (Hobart and Launceston) and one each in Adelaide, Alice Springs, Canberra, Darwin and Perth. New casinos in recent years have included the Sydney Star City and Sydney Harbour Casinos and the massive Crown Casino in Melbourne (open 24 hours a day). Games on offer include baccarat, roulette, blackjack, craps, poker, two-up, Sic Bo and Pai Gow (Chinese card games) and keno. Keno is similar to bingo except that you mark from one to 15 numbers out of 80 on your card and if your numbers are among the 20 drawn you win. Many casinos have a separate TAB area (see below) where you can place bets on horse and greyhound racing. Dress rules require 'smart casual dress' which usually means a shirt with a collar and no T-shirts, shorts, sports shoes (trainers) or thongs (flip-flops), although jeans are usually okay. However, some ban jeans and insist on a tie for men, so check in advance. Many casinos are open 24 hours a day. Games usually have a $2 minimum bet, although bets may start at $10 and up. Usually you must pay for drinks. Most casinos publish a free *Casino Gaming Guide*, but don't expect any insider tips on how to break the bank!

Pokies: Poker machines (pokies) have spread like wildfire in recent years and are now seen almost everywhere (except Western Australia, where they are banned), as state governments have rushed to cash in on Australia's gambling fever. There are over 85,000 pokies in NSW (10 per cent of the world's poker machines and more than in Nevada, USA) and some 27,500 in Victoria; the total in Australia is expected to reach around 200,000 by the year 2000. Pokies aren't just restricted to casinos and are common at leagues and other social clubs, where they are blamed for fueling gambling among the elderly. Many can be played from as little as 20¢ and some boast jackpots of up to $25,000. In some states (e.g. Tasmania) there are limits on the amount that can be gambled on video gaming machines, and in others (e.g. Victoria) there has been a backlash against pokies which have fuelled gambling among the poor in disadvantaged areas.

Racing: Horse and dog racing is a popular form of gambling in Australia and includes horse racing, harness-racing (trotting) and greyhound racing. Gambling on horse and greyhound racing operates on the tote system (an Australian invention) by state Totaliser Agency Boards (TABs). TABs have outlets in all towns and cities (around 1,000 in Sydney alone) where offices (which also accept bets on the football pools) are open from around 11am until 6pm Mondays to Fridays, and from 10am until 8pm on Saturdays. The TABs' annual turnover exceeds $4,000m, including around $100m waged on the

Melbourne Cup alone (Australia's premier horse race). To place a bet (win, place, quinellas, trifectas, etc.) you simply write the name of your horse(s) and the race number on a betting slip and give it to the clerk with your stake. If you win you can collect your winnings immediately after the race (providing you don't lose your receipt). There are no off-course starting price (SP) bookmakers in Australia, although there's on-course SP betting where odds are given by bookmakers for each horse and you're given a fixed price. However, illegal telephone bookies flourish and betting syndicates are active throughout Australia, which also accepts bets on events not covered by the TAB.

Lotteries: Lotto (or lottery) is also a popular form of gambling in Australia, where you choose six numbers from one to 40. Numbers are drawn once or twice a week and those who select three or more correct numbers win a prize. The minimum stake is $1 and the first prize is usually in the hundreds of $thousands or $millions (the average payout is some 60 per cent of the amount staked). Results are published in the press and are also available on special telephone information numbers.

Football Pools: Football pools were traditionally the most common form of gambling in Australia, although they have been overtaken by lotteries and other forms of gambling in recent years. Operated by Australian Soccerpools, punters forecast the results of football matches (Australian in the winter and British matches in the Australian summer) and can win huge cash prizes. The treble chance is the most popular bet, where punters guess which matches will be score draws (matches which end in a draw where each team scores at least one goal). If you don't want to fill out a coupon each week, you can have a standing order using the same numbers.

Two-Up: The national game of chance is called 'two-up', invented by soldiers in the first world war. It's illegal outside casinos (except on ANZAC Day) and a few licensed two-up schools (not that this means anything to Aussies). Not exactly the most sophisticated of games, bets are placed on two coins that are tossed into the air together using a stick called a 'kip'. If one lands heads and the other tails, there's no result and all bets are held for the next throw. If both coins show the same, then you win or lose depending on whether you chose heads or tails. Coins must spin when tossed otherwise the arbitrator (called the 'spinner') calls the game void. Bets are placed with the 'boxer'. Casinos keep the stakes when there's a sequence of five identical results (unless you bet on this), which amounts to around 3 per cent of the total stakes.

Compulsive gambling is a huge problem in Australia where an estimated 3 per cent of the population has a gambling problem. Like alcoholism, gambling is a disease which can be controlled but never cured. There are a huge number of Gamblers Anonymous groups and meetings in Australia, and also meetings for the relatives of compulsive Gamblers to help them cope with their loved ones addiction. Compulsive gamblers can ban themselves from casinos under the Casino Control Act. However, you can now gamble at cyber space casinos on the internet without leaving home, a form of gambling which is set to spiral in coming years. Note, however, that it's totally unregulated and that there's no guarantee of getting paid from 'casinos' located overseas (often they are 'based' in off-shore jurisdictions)

BARS & PUBS

Australia is famous for it pubs (an abbreviation of public house) which are a tradition inherited from the British, often referred to as hotels (although nowadays most don't provide accommodation). Australia has a huge variety of drinking establishments including bustling music pubs, hotel bars, pubs with restaurants and barbies; gay and lesbian pubs, trendy downtown lounge bars; luxury hotel cocktail bars; restaurant bars;

wine bars (although rare); earthy country and outback hotels with sawdust floors (where women aren't made welcome); elegant restored Victorian and Edwardian pubs (many with verandas and balconies); boisterous barn-like drinking dens; and tropical, niche and cabaret bars. Returned Soldiers League (RSL) clubs and other private (often ethnic) clubs are popular drinking places, and usually have low prices and an inexpensive restaurant. Many RSL clubs are open to allcomers and not just ex-servicemen (of which there are fewer and fewer in Australia). There are guides to local pubs published in some cities, e.g. the *Guide to Melbourne's Pubs* (Melbourne is reckoned to have the best variety and most interesting pubs in Australia).

Australia is traditionally a beer-drinking country (Darwin is reputedly the world's premier beer-drinking city per head), ranking around third worldwide. The annual average per capita consumption is around 110 litres (almost 200 pints), although it has fallen by some 20 per cent in the last decade or so as wine has become more popular. Despite their awesome reputation and the plethora of watering holes, most Australian's aren't great drinkers, although there's a hardened minority who do their utmost to compensate for this slur on the Australian character. Australians drink less alcohol per head than the inhabitants of most European countries, although they do, however, drink more than the average American, Briton or Canadian. It's hard to imagine it, but some states such as South Australia actually started life as temperance states!

Drinking is an art form and a way of life in Australia ('land of the liquid lunch') and most social activities revolve around a bottle of wine (or three) and a few dozen tinnies. It has even spawned its own language, for example beer is variously known as a frosty, tinny, tube, stubby, amber fluid, amber nectar, neck oil, throat charmer, singing syrup or brewery broth, and being drunk may be referred to as stinko, inked, off your face, full as a tick (or a goog), drunk as a fowl (or Chloe?), on the slops or schicked (a teetotaler is a 'waterbag'). Buying a round of drinks is called a 'shout' and you won't be popular is you miss your shout when your turn comes around. In Australia you usually buy your drinks at the bar and pay when you're served (you cannot run up a tab as in continental Europe and the USA). However, some trendy lounge bars insist on serving you at your table (and charging you extra for the privilege), although you still pay as you go. Beer gardens and courtyards are common throughout Australia and many pubs have live music (jukeboxes are also common).

Beer: Brewing and drinking beer is an art form in Australia, which boasts probably the best selection of beers to be found anywhere. Some bars and clubs boast over 100 different types of beer from around the world. The most popular foreign beers include Guinness (brewed in Australia); Sol and Dos Equis from Mexico; Budweiser and Slitz from the USA; and Heineken, Stella Artois and Löwenbräu from Europe. The most famous Australian beers include Fosters, Carlton Draught and Victoria Bitter (VB), all from Victoria; Castlemaine XXXX (pronounced four-ex, said to be so-named because Queenslanders cannot spell beer) and Powers from Queensland; Toohey's, Tooth's and Reschs from New South Wales; Emu, Swan Lager (derisively called 'black duck' outside WA) and Redback from Western Australia; Cooper's (one of Australia's best beers) and West End Bitter from South Australia (SA); and Boag's and Cascade from Tasmania.

Most Australian beers have a fairly high alcohol content (around 5 per cent), which is higher than most American and British beers, but lower than German and Czech beers. There's also a range of low-alcohol (LA) beers (from around 2 to 3.5 per cent alcohol) which include Carlton Cold, Diamond Draught, Fosters LA, Swan Light and Toohey's Blue. The best and strongest beers (as high as 9 per cent alcohol) are often those brewed by pubs with in-house breweries (called 'boutique' or brew pubs) which are extremely popular. These include the Matilda Bay Brewing Co. in Perth and the Redback Brewery in Melbourne (which makes a German-style *weiss* beer that the locals drink with lemon). Note that boutique and imported beers are more expensive than the local commercial brands.

Most beer drunk in Australia is of the lager (export) variety, which is generally sweet-tasting as it's made with sugar. The taste will be fairly familiar to Americans (whose drink tasteless coloured water) but will taste like 'dishwater' to real ale drinkers. Fortunately for real beer drinkers, real ales have become more popular in Australia in the last decade and there are now a variety of natural conditioned (cask or bottle) real ale beers available from brewers such as Coopers of South Australia. This is the sort of beer generally made by 'boutique' breweries and sold in their in-house pubs for around $4 to $5 a pint. Real ale is served warmer than lager beers, but is still served much colder than the same beers in other countries (e.g. Britain). Australians drink their beer almost ice cold (around 2°C), often in chilled glasses, so that when it hits your stomach on a hot day it freezes your insides. Not surprisingly, cold-filtered ice beers are gaining in popularity.

Beer is usually served in small measures ranging from 115ml (small beer) up to 575ml (an imperial pint/20fl oz). Both the names and standard sizes of beer glasses vary considerably from state to state. In Sydney the most common size is a middy (285ml) while in Melbourne it's a glass (225ml). Other measures include a beer six (6oz/170ml); a seven (7oz/200ml); a middy, handle or pot (285ml); and a schooner (usually 425ml, but 285ml in South Australia). Some pubs serve beer in imperial measures of a half-pint (285ml) or a pint (575ml). The easiest way to order is to simply ask for a small or large beer, but take care, as what passes for a small beer in one state may be twice as large in another (a large beer in Darwin is a 'stubby' weighing in at 2.35 litres or almost five pints!). Beer is usually drunk direct from bottles and cans in country areas. In really hot weather, bottles and cans are kept cool in a foam or polystyrene 'stubby holder' or cooler and Australians transport their cold beer in an insulated cold box called an 'esky' (after a well known brand name).

Beer is around the same price in Australia as in Europe and North America, with a 285ml (half-pint) costing around $1.50 in most pubs, although it can easily be double this in a fancy place. Low-alcohol beers are generally slightly cheaper than full strength beers. Bottled beer is sold in 375ml or 750ml bottles (many up-market bars don't sell beer on draught) and draught beer is also sold by the jug, which is slightly cheaper than by the glass. Not surprisingly, beer is much cheaper to buy from bottle shops (around half the price). Some bars and pubs have a 'happy hour' (e.g. from 5pm to 7pm) when drinks are sold at half price or even less, and some watering holes even offer half price drinking from 5pm to 9pm. Many pubs also offer special prices or free drinks to women (the idea being that where women congregate hard-drinking men will follow in large numbers).

Wine: Australian wines have become famous worldwide in the last few decades. Wine consumption in Australia is steadily rising at the expense of beer and is around 25 litres per head, per year — higher than any other English-speaking country but still well below the major European wine-producing countries. There are few wine bars in Australia which haven't caught on with the public (although the Casino Wine Bar in Adelaide boasts over 300 wines). Wine is usually reserved for drinking with food (pubs that serve good food generally have a good wine list), although some bars and pubs sell wine by the glass (e.g. $2.50) or the bottle (from around $10). Cheap wine, which may be referred to as bombo, lunatic soup or steam, is best avoided. For information about Australian wine, see **Alcohol** on page 423.

Other Drinks: Designer drinks include (wine) coolers, which are blends of inexpensive wine with sugar and fruit juice or fruit flavouring (they taste like punch). Other popular drinks include alcopops such as Two Dogs Lemonade (an alcoholic lemonade), Sub Zero (alcoholic soda, 5.5. per cent alcohol), Strongbow White (cider), Razorback Draught (a shandy), XLR8 (alcoholic cola) and alcoholic spring water such as DNA (containing 5 per cent alcohol). Alcoholic soda is mixed with lime, grenadine, midori or cranberry juice to make a long cool drink. Coke and other colas are drunk in copious quantities in Australia and costs around $1 a glass in a pub. Spirits are rarely drunk in pubs, where a shot of whisky (30ml) or other spirits costs around $2.

Licensing Laws: Licensing laws vary from state to state and even from pub to pub, and aren't as liberal as in most European countries (a hangover from the British, who cannot be trusted with alcohol). Pubs are usually open from 10am until 10pm or 11am until 11pm, Monday to Saturday and from 12pm until between 8pm and 10pm on Sundays. Sunday pub opening is restricted in most states, e.g. to between six or eight hours only (the churches still have some clout). In market areas, pubs may open as early as 6 or 6.30am and close at 6 or 6.30pm. Pubs aren't obliged to open for any set hours and landlords decide their own opening hours (usually) within state licensing laws.

There are no licensing restrictions in Canberra where pubs can stay open as long as they wish, and in Tasmania pubs can virtually open when they like, although most close by midnight. Some pubs stay open until midnight or 1am on Fridays and Saturdays, particularly in tourist areas, and in cities some establishments with a number of bars and a disco manage to serve alcohol for 24 hours. In some cities there are longer opening hours in summer than in winter. Nevertheless, a lot of drinking still takes place after licensing hours, particularly in country areas where the local policeman is likely to be one of the customers, and when the pubs close there are usually other places to get a drink (restaurants, nighclubs, casinos, discos, etc).

There are some odd local laws in Australia designed to reduce drunkenness, for example it's illegal to sell alcohol before 10am each day in Darwin (although even here most people don't start drinking so early in the day!) and in Melbourne it's prohibited to drink at the bar after 10pm, when you must occupy a table (the table helps stop you from falling down). Alcohol can be purchased from licensed 'bottle' shops (it isn't sold in food shops or supermarkets) and from pubs and restaurants. The minimum age for drinking in public places is 18 and if you look under age you may be asked for some ID (which you should always carry if you're under 20 or look under 18). In some outback towns, pubs have doormen (bouncers) to deter undesirables (waterbags and others who don't drink enough?).

Drunkenness and alcoholism is a huge problem in Australia, where the Aboriginals have been ravaged by it for decades (which has led to the consumption of alcohol being restricted or banned in and around some Aboriginal settlements and towns). The possession or consumption of alcohol in these areas can result in a huge fine (e.g. $1,000), six month's jail or even the confiscation of a vehicle used to transport alcohol. Drunken driving is also a widespread problem in Australia, although there has been a crackdown in recent years and a lowering of blood-alcohol limits for motorists. It's estimated that over 6,000 Australians die each year from alcohol-related causes (including some 30 per cent of road deaths). Many pubs have a DIY breathalyser which will tell you when you're over the limit, although it's wise to go to the pub with a teetotal friend or abstain from driving altogether when you're drinking alcohol. In future pubs may be forced to provide over-the-bar breath tests before serving customers, in order to protect themselves from negligence claims concerning drunks and drunken drivers.

RESTAURANTS & CAFES

Australians love their food (tucker) and dining out, accompanied by some of the best wines and beers in the world, is one of the greatest pleasures of life in Australia (which is why so many Australians are overweight). The greatest changes in Australia in the last few decades have been in its cuisine, which in the major cities is among the best and most varied in the world. However, it wasn't always so. Conservative British-influences and tastes persisted until the '70s when they were swept away by the culinary revolution led by migrants (Australia's most important gastronomic resource) and a new breed of young Australians who had travelled (and ate) the world. BYO (see below) and the rapid rise of Australian wines also had a huge impact on the proliferation of good cheap restaurants, and today Australia boasts the most cosmopolitan and diverse menus in the world.

Prior to the '70s, the staple diet of most Australians consisted of meat pies and gravy, fish and chips, and steak, egg and chips (or over-boiled vegetables) supplemented by vegemite (made from yeast slops) sandwiches, chico rolls (a distant cousin of the Chinese spring roll) and burgers. Australians are ardent carnivores, although not as much as previously when many people would eat steak and chops for breakfast (a habit still common in the outback). Nowadays there's an increasing number of vegetarians and vegetarian restaurants are fairly common in the main cities (most restaurants also serve some vegetarian dishes). However, there still isn't a lot of choice in small country and outback towns where you shouldn't expect to find any decent restaurants or anything other than basic 'Australian' cooking or an Australianised chinese restaurant.

Melbourne is generally recognised as the gastronomic capital of Australia, followed closely by Sydney, both of which can hold there own with most world capital cities and rate up there with Hong Kong, London, New York and Paris for choice, quality and value for money. Both Melbourne and Sydney boast over 2,000 restaurants (so many in fact, that there's a shortage of good chefs). Perth and Adelaide aren't far behind and have more than enough eateries to satisfy a starving gourmet. Brisbane isn't distinguished by it restaurants, although it also has many good places to eat, and even Darwin isn't bereft of decent restaurants, although it's relatively expensive compared to other capital cities. However, outside the cities, the towns and villages of Australia are generally a culinary wasteland, so stick to the cities for gourmet food.

Australian restaurants have to be good because there's so much competition, with new restaurants opening (and closing) with surprising speed in the major cities. Many people eat out around three times a week and Australian households spend over a quarter of their weekly food budget on eating outside the home. The appreciation of good food and wine is universal in Australia and isn't an elitist or class thing as in some other countries. Australian food is noted for the freshness and variety of its produce, meat and fish — most ingredients are grown or caught locally, which means that they're fresh and generally inexpensive.

Ethnic Restaurants: Australia doesn't have its own national cuisine and modern Australian cuisine borrows heavily from various foreign cuisines, with the dishes often having a distinctly Australian flavour. Most cities have a proliferation of ethnic restaurants, reflecting the countries from which most immigrants came. For example, Melbourne is known for its Greek and Italian restaurants, Sydney for its Lebanese and Thai restaurants, Adelaide its German restaurants, while Perth and Darwin have a wealth of Asian restaurants. Ethnic restaurants in the major cities are often clustered in groups in areas or suburbs where large ethnic communities have been established. Today, Australia leads the world in ethnic dining and take-away meals.

Australia has a huge variety of European, Middle Eastern, South American and Asian restaurants, which include Chinese (many regions are represented), French, Greek, Indian, Indonesian, Italian, Japanese, Korean, Lebanese, Malaysian, Mexican, Mongolian, Polish, Portuguese, Spanish, Russian, Sri Lankan, Thai, Vietnamese and Yugoslavian, to name but a selection. There are bustling 'China Towns' in Sydney and Melbourne rivalling those in most European and North American cities. In many shopping and entertainment centres there are Southeast Asian 'food halls' (also called food markets or food courts), where you can buy food from the surrounding kiosks and eat it at a central eating area, thus allowing you to mix dishes from various countries. Note, however, that Chinese and other Asian food, may be Australianised to such a degree that it's unrecognisable and some other foreign cuisine is often 'tailored' to suit Australian tastes and may bear little resemblance to authentic dishes.

Seafood: Australia is renowned for its seafood (many people reckon it's the best in the world) and each state or city has its own specialities. Australia's seas have yet to suffer from widespread over-fishing (although some stocks are threatened) or pollution, so an abundance of fresh fish and seafood is available, although there isn't the choice found in many traditional fishing countries. The best and widest choice of fish comes from the waters surrounding Tasmania which include brown and rainbow trout, sea-run trout, farmed Atlantic salmon, trevally, trevella, orange roughy and stripey trumpeter. Australia is also famous for it crustaceans and molluscs which include crayfish, abalone, oysters, mussels and scallops. Other Australian specialities include Sydney Rock oysters, Coffin Bay oysters (from South Australia), yabbies (hard-shelled freshwater shrimp), crabs (e.g. sand and mud crabs), Balmain Bugs (slipper lobsters from Sydney) and Moreton Bay Bugs (a type of lobster caught in the mouth of the Brisbane River). Australia's best fish include barramundi (a breed of perch which grows to over a metre in length and is one of the tastiest fishes in Australian waters), snapper (schnapper), shark (called 'flake' when served in fish and chip shops), King George whiting (South Australia), coral cod/coral trout (Great Barrier Reef), John Dory, ocean perch, reef fish (Queensland) and tuna.

Bush Tucker: Some restaurants specialise in bush (tucker) or aboriginal cooking, where you may be offered witchetty grubs (usually eaten alive!), emu egg omelettes and pies made from native fruits such as quandongs, boabs and billygoat plums. Other common dishes are emu steaks (from farmed birds), kangaroo (a delicious, almost fat-free meat), water buffalo steaks, camel and crocodile (which tastes like a cross between chicken and pork). Damper is Australian bush bread (made with flour, salt and water) baked in hot coals (usually on a camp fire). Note, however, that bush tucker is generally trendy and expensive, e.g. $40 a head plus wine.

Bring Your Own (BYO): Somewhat surprisingly the majority of Australian restaurants don't have liquor licenses (which are expensive), except in Canberra where most are licensed. Restaurants without a liquor licence are know as BYO ('bring your own') or BYOG ('bring your own grog'), where customers bring their own wine and other drinks. This is an excellent idea which unfortunately hasn't caught on widely in most other countries, mainly due to the huge profit that restaurants make on wine. There may be a charge of $1 to $2 for corkage (opening bottles and providing glasses), although many restaurants make no charge. Some up-market restaurants with liquor licenses also allow BYO, but charge around $5 corkage (which still saves you money providing you don't buy some cheap plonk). Regular diners (and drinkers) always carry a few (dozen) bottles of wine in their cars (which isn't illegal in Australia) so that they are never caught short when visiting a BYO restaurant (but get a ride or taxi home if you drink more than one or two glasses). Eating at BYO restaurants is excellent value compared with most of Europe and North America, where you can eat an excellent meal for around $20 or less a head (plus the cost of your wine). House wine in Australia usually starts at around $10 for a mediocre bottle and can be expensive, although some restaurants sell wine at bottle shop (retail) prices, but are likely to be more expensive than the cheapest bottle shops (e.g. Liquorland). In wine-growing areas, the wine list may be substituted by a wine tasting room, where you can choose from wines made on the property to accompany your meal. Note that Australians don't usually drink water with their meals and if you want water you may need to ask a few times before you get it.

Prices: Eating out is inexpensive in Australia where a good meal can be had from around $10 a head without wine. Expect to pay between $15 and $25 a head (plus wine) in a mid-range restaurant for three courses and coffee, while for top class restaurants the sky's the limit. If you're on a tight budget, some restaurants offer discounts to 'backpackers' and many employer's operate canteens which are open to the public where food is served buffet style and you can help yourself (not great food, but cheap and filling). Many restaurants do special priced lunches which are less expensive than the same meals served in the evening. However, you should avoid tourist-trap restaurants in cities and resorts. There are usually no additions for tax or service, although a surcharge may be levied at weekends and on public holidays to pay extra staff costs. Few people tip (see page 461) in inexpensive places, although many people leave 5 to 10 per cent in mid-range and top class restaurants. In a busy establishment, it's customary to leave the correct money on the table and leave, rather than pay the waiter/waitress personally. It's common to split the bill when eating with friends, rather than one person paying for a whole group (unless he's celebrating winning the lottery).

Pub Grub: The quality of pub food in Australia varies enormously from basic to excellent (it's at its most refined and varied in Sydney). At its worst it's boring and disappointing, but at its best it's delicious and excellent value for money. However, pub grub is rarely exotic and usually consists of grilled or barbecued steaks and chops, fish and seafood plus roasts, curries and salads. Many pubs also serve ethnic food or a combination of traditional Australia food and ethnic specialities. Outdoor eating is popular (although there's a surprising lack of pavement and garden tables in some Australian cities) and often consists of anything and everything barbecued including steak, burgers, chops, sausages (snags), chicken, fish and seafood. Many pubs have large courtyards or gardens where they operate non-stop, self-service barbies, where you buy a piece of meat and cook it yourself on the BBQ provided (condiments are supplied). You can also buy salad, bread and side dishes. A typical meal costs around $10, although some pubs have special offers and promotions when meals can be had for a little as $3 or $4. Many also have a self-serve salad bar and basic bar meals from $5 to $10. Meals are usually served in a dining room or lounge bar from noon to 2pm and from 6 to 8pm, although some pubs serve meals until late evening.

Fast Food: Fast food outlets proliferate in Australia and at the bottom end of the market can be as bad or worse than that found in any country. However, 'fast' or 'snack' food isn't (always) synonymous with junk food, as evidenced by the increasing quality and amazing variety of fast food establishments in Australia. Australians are hooked on fast food and over 80 per cent of the population eats fast food take-away meals at least once every two weeks, spending around $2 billion a year on it (or some 10 per cent of their food budget). Common snack outlets include sandwich shops, delicatessens and milk bars (shops selling snacks, sandwiches, rolls, meat pies, pasties, milkshakes, soft drinks, etc.). Fast food 'snacks' include sandwiches, hamburgers, sausages, hot dogs, pies, fish and chips, stuffed potatoes, vegetarian snacks, fried or grilled chicken, seafood, crepes and pancakes, and a huge variety of ethnic snacks such as pizza, kosher food, tacos, samosa, calamari, dim sum, focaccia, sushi, gyros, falafel, couscous, tabouleh, doner or shish kebab, pitta bread, tortilla, filled croissants and bagels.

As in all western countries, American fast food joints abound and McDonalds, Hungry Jack's (HJ's, trading as Burger King in other countries), Kentucky Fried Chicken and Pizza Hut can be found throughout the country. A popular budget restaurant chain is Sizzlers, an American-style restaurant chain serving steak, chicken and fish, and a selection of self-serve salads, pasta dishes and desserts. Barbecued take-away chicken chains include Chicken Treat and Red Rooster. Some fast food joints such as the American-style Fast Eddy's in Melbourne and Perth are open 24 hours a day. Note that authentic Australian hamburgers are often much better than the mass-produced variety served in chain restaurants. Many places also offer more healthy food for vegetarians and anyone who isn't planning to put on weight, such as salads, skinless chicken, etc. At most fast food joints you should expect to pay around $5 for a filling meal.

The most popular Australian take-away remains the humble meat pie (which could contain anything from beef or pork to camel, buffalo, kangaroo, crocodile or barramundi). It's Australia's national 'dish' (Aussies, mostly male, eat some 2m a day!) and is eaten swamped in gravy or tomato ketchup. A 'pie floater' is a meat pie floating in a bowl of pea soup. Meat pies are typically served in milk bars, cafés and from mobile food vans (a common sight in major cities and at tourist spots) and are the reason foreign food is so popular in Australia. However, at their best they can be delicious (at their worst dog food is tastier). **Beware of self-serve and other places where food is kept warm for hours on end, which can lead to food poisoning.**

Cafés: The Australians take after the British and drink a lot of tea and an increasing amount of coffee. Café society (and caffeine culture) is all the rage in Australian cities, where there's a huge variety of trendy and elegant cafés, the best of which are invariably Italian. All cafés serve food, although it's usually of the snack and fast food variety ('all-day breakfast' is common) rather than 'a la carte' meals. Few cafés have table service or printed menus and you must usually check the blackboard and order from the counter, where you also pay. Many people finish their meal in a café where they may have coffee and a sweet (e.g. ice cream or pastries). Cafés in capital cities are often open until midnight or early morning. Note that cafés don't usually serve alcohol in Australia unless they are also licensed restaurants.

Sweets: Among the few real Australian dishes are pavlova, a delicious meringue concoction created for the ballerina Anna Pavlova on her Australian tour in 1935. Others include Peach Melba (created for the Australian soprano Dame Nellie Melba), puftaloons (a fried dough scone) and lamingtons, an Australian institution consisting of a sponge cake dipped in raspberry jam, covered in chocolate sauce and then rolled in coconut. Australian ice cream is popular and one of the best is Norgen Vaaz (a take off of the American Haagen Daz).

Meal Times: Australians are fairly inflexible about their meal times and many restaurants have limited hours. For example dinner (often called tea after the British working class habit) is often served as early as 6 or 7pm and the last orders in proper restaurants may be as early as 9pm and the staff will be packing up to go home around 10pm. In small towns it's usually difficult to find anywhere serving food after 7.30 or 8pm other than a fast food joint or a fish and chip shop (lunch may also be served for one hour only, e.g. from 12.30 to 1.30 pm). However, in the major cities many restaurants stay open late and usually allow diners to circumvent the local licensing laws. In order to drink legally at a restaurant outside official licensing hours you must plan to dine, although you can order anything and aren't obliged to eat it (some places may provide a plate of free food to encourage drinkers). Note that the most common closing day for restaurants is Monday.

Bookings: Most restaurants accept bookings and payment by credit card, although you should check in advance at budget restaurants, otherwise you may discover to your embarrassment that: 'that *won't* do nicely sir'! Note that some top restaurants have a 'no-show' penalty of around $10 a head for those who don't bother to turn up or cancel at short notice after booking a table, although many restaurants over-book to compensate for 'no-shows'. Some restaurants have dress rules (smart casual is usual, even for the most exclusive establishments) and ban thongs (flip-flops) and shorts (unless perhaps when worn with shoes and socks — not a common habit in Australia). Smoking is banned in many restaurants and if you're a smoker you should check that it's permitted before booking.

Guides: There are many restaurant guides in Australia including annual *Cheap Eats* guides to budget restaurants in Melbourne, Perth and Sydney (each listing over 500 restaurants). There are free magazines in many cities such as *Dining Adelaide* and *Dining Out: Brisbane*, although these tend to feature mainly expensive, up-market restaurants. The *Courier Mail Good Food Guide* is a comprehensive guide to Brisbane's best restaurants. There's a free telephone Restaurant Advisory Service in Melbourne (tel. (03) 9328 4442), although it's sponsored by restaurants, so you shouldn't expect to receive impartial advice.

16.

SPORTS

Australia is a sporting paradise thanks largely to its generally mild (year-round) climate. Sport is an integral part of the nation's culture, the favourite topic of conversation (people even call each other 'sport') and has the status of a religion to many Aussies. It's both a unifying and divisive pastime (competition is fierce between rival teams), although Australians are generally good sports and appreciate plucky opponents (unless they are poms). Melbourne is the most sports-mad city (Sydney isn't far behind) and is home to Australia's unique football code, Australian Rules. Sports centres abound in all towns and cities, and offer facilities for a wide range of sports.

Aerobics is Australia's favourite form of exercise among young people followed by netball, basketball, swimming, cricket, soccer and Australian Rules football (the top spectator sport in the country). Other popular sports are golf, hiking, jogging/running, cycling, tennis, squash, lawn bowls, martial arts, tenpin bowling, horse racing and motor sports (in no particular order). Australia is famous for its beach culture and water sports are also very popular (80 per cent of Australians live within around 30km/18mi of the coast). Australians like their sports tough (like their he-man image) and love endurance tests such as ironman/ironwoman competitions and triathlons (a 1,500m swim, 40km/25mi bike ride and 10km/6mi run). However, even these aren't tough enough for 'real' men and they have recently come up with the 'eco-challenge race' which consists of 500km/310mi of bushwalking, canoeing, climbing, cycling, rafting, trekking, horse-riding and kayaking in the outback, rainforests and reef in northern Queensland. All in a day's work sport!

In Australian schools, sports are incorporated into the normal school day and aren't extra-curricular activities as in many other countries. Schools have a wide variety of teams for all sports and participate in inter-school and interstate competitions (Saturdays are the most busy school sports days and parents are called upon to ferry their children around the country to compete). Children come under pressure from parents, teachers and coaches to perform at their highest level and club scouts scour school sports meetings for talent. Two-thirds of Australian children join a sports club by the age of 11 and almost half the population is registered to participate in sports (Some 6m Australians take part in organised sport each year). Children who fail at sport can be made outcasts by their fellow pupils.

There's no such thing as just taking part and playing sport just for fun in Australia, where (as in America) winning is everything. Only the Americans devote more time, effort and money to sports' perfection than Australians, who are consumed by sport (although more often than not it's only as spectators or gamblers). The country has some 15 national leagues involving team sports (remarkable when you consider the vast distances involved). However, despite the popular image of Australians as bronzed beach muscular lifesavers and bathing beauties, most Australians are overweight and unfit, and the nearest they ever get to working up a sweat is jumping up and down in joy/anger while hurling abuse at the TV (soap opera for blokes). Less than a third of Australians participate in any form of physical activity (Sydneysiders are the biggest slobs).

Due to the seriousness (life and death) with which they approach international sport, Australians have an unfair advantage over most 'amateur' sporting countries. As a nation they excel at numerous sports including cricket, rugby, swimming, cycling, hockey, tennis, squash, surfing, rowing, lawn bowls, netball, golf, athletics, motor sports, sailing, horse riding, triathlon and many others. Australians also compete successfully at the world and Olympic Games for the disabled. The government provides financial assistance and coaching for the disabled through the Aussie Able Program. The country will receive a huge sporting (and economic) boost from hosting the Olympics in the year 2000 in Sydney (the first time since the Melbourne games in 1956).

The government and sports' bodies promote sport with slogans such as 'sport for all' and 'life be in it'. Sporting talent is nurtured in Australia and given the best possible encouragement through the Australian Institute of Sport (AIS), founded in 1981 in Canberra, and centres of excellence such as the Australian Cricket Academy. There are over 130 national sporting organisations in Australia and thousands of state, regional, city and local club bodies. Keen sports fans may be interested in visiting the Australian Gallery of Sport and Olympic Museum in Melbourne (open daily from 10am until 4pm). The Australian Tourist Commission (see page 364) publishes a wealth of fact sheets on every conceivable sport. Sports results can be obtained in Australia by telephone. Local municipal councils may publish a 'leisure directory' listing local sports centres and clubs. An annual *Sport Yearbook* (Gemkit Publishing) is available for those seeking an introduction to Australian sport.

AUSTRALIAN RULES FOOTBALL

Australian rules football (called 'Aussie rules' although it's also referred to simply as 'football') is Australia's leading ball game and considered by most people to be Australia's national sport (although fans and players of other football codes and cricket may disagree — they disparagingly refer to Aussie rules as aerial ballet or aerial ping-pong). Its rules were invented in 1858 and are unique, although it was based on Gaelic football and Hurley played in Ireland. Aussie rules is a fast, skilful, athletic and exciting game, in which the score can change quickly and the outcome may hinge on the last kick. It's a gruelling macho game and players are very fit and tough, most spurning any sort of protection (although some players do wear mouthguards, protective head gear and gloves to give them a better grip). They also wear sexy tight shorts and sleeveless shirts to show off their 'muscles' (not surprisingly it's popular with women who make up around half the spectators).

Aussie rules is played by teams of 18 players on an oval field (around three times the size of a soccer pitch) with an oval-shaped 'rugby' ball. The ball can be kicked, caught, hit with the hand, or carried and bounced (every 15 paces). If players don't bounce the ball regularly they are deemed to have 'run too far'. When a player catches a ball on the volley (before it touches the ground) he is said to have made a 'mark', for which he's allowed to stop and take a free kick. Players cannot be sent off during a game and consequently there are often scraps on the field (the game is often called 'an excuse for a punch-up' or an 'organised brawl'). However, disciplinary tribunals are held the following week if a player is deemed to have committed a breach of the rules (e.g. tripping, kicking, fighting or eye-gouging). Three players can be changed at any time (from the 'interchange bench') and players can come back into the game after being exchanged (as in ice hockey). A match lasts for four quarters of 25 minutes each, but can extend to around three hours when breaks between quarters and stoppages for injuries, disputes and punch-ups are included (plus 'time-on' added by the umpire).

The 'goal' consists of four evenly-spaced tall goal posts, the outer pair of which are slightly shorter than the inner pair. Six points are awarded for kicking the ball between the two central posts (a 'goal') and one point for kicking it through the outer posts (a 'behind'). The goal umpire (dressed in a white coat) waves two white flags to signify a goal and one finger and flag when one point is scored. A typical point score for each team is between 70 and 120 points. The score (goals and behinds) is shown in newspapers for each quarter with the final points total shown in brackets as follows:

Collingwood	4.5	6.7	7.9	10.12	(72)
Essendon	3.6	5.9	8.11	11.14	(80)

In the above table, Collingwood scored 4 goals and 5 behinds in the first quarter and by the end of the match had scored 10 goals and 12 behinds. Drawn games are extremely rare.

The national professional league is the Australian Football League (AFL) comprising 16 teams. Melbourne is the centre of Aussie rules and provides 10 of the 16 teams in the AFL, the others coming from Adelaide, Brisbane, Fremantle, Perth, Port Adelaide and Sydney. Aussie rules is the number one sport in five states; the Northern Territory, South Australia, Tasmania, Victoria (where it's a religion) and Western Australia. The Sydney Swans were transplanted to Sydney from Melbourne (they were originally named South Melbourne) in the early '80s in a first move to create a national competition.

Matches are played on Friday evenings, and Saturday and Sunday afternoons throughout the winter and attracted a total of over 6m spectators during the 1997 season. Crowds in Melbourne regularly top 30,000 at major games and 80,000 attend finals. Crowds are noisy but peaceful and there's rarely any crowd trouble. Matches are also televised and shown on national TV in Australia and a number of other countries. The grand final is played in September or October at the Melbourne Cricket Ground before 90,000 fans. It rivals the FA Cup Final in England or the American Super Bowl for atmosphere and passion.

An excellent book which describes the history of Australian Rules is *Up There, Cazaly? The Story of Australian Rules Football* by Leonie Sandercock and Ian Turner (Granada Books).

RUGBY FOOTBALL

There are two separate codes (excluding Aussie Rules) of rugby football in Australia: rugby union and rugby league. The main difference between the codes is that rugby union (which has always been strictly amateur) has teams of 15 players and rugby league 13 players to a team (two less to pay). Both codes are played internationally, although union is played by more countries.

Rugby League: Rugby is the main football game in New South Wales, Queensland and Canberra, where rugby league is the most popular code. Like Aussie rules, rugby league players are super fit, fast and tactically intelligent. The Winfield Cup is the world's premier rugby league competition and Australia is the world's premier rugby league nation, usually easily beating the main opposition in England, although it has few other international competitors. The national rugby league team is known as the Kangaroos.

There has been a battle over control of Australian rugby league in recent years between the Australian Rugby League (ARL) and the upstart Super League (established by Rupert Murdoch in 1995 to boost the audience for his Foxtel cable TV network). This was resolved in late 1997 when both sides agreed to establish a new united premiership competition from 1998 with 20 teams (which is expected to reduce in number in the next few years). ARL matches are played on most Friday and Saturday evenings and Sunday afternoons between April and September. The Newcastle Knights were the surprise (snow in summer in Sydney would have been less of a shock) first-time winners of the ARL grand final in 1997 beating Manly Sea Eagles.

Most rugby league teams are based in Sydney (11 of the top 20) with others in Newcastle, Wollongong, Brisbane and the Gold Coast of Queensland. Sydney is the only major city in the world where rugby is more popular than soccer (it's estimated that some

80 per cent of the world's best league players live within 30km/18mi of downtown Sydney). League is popular among the masses, although attendances are much lower than for AFL (Aussie Rules) games. The State-of-Origin series between the Australian states in May/June is the premier interstate competition, although it's poorly supported by the public. In 1997, in the inaugural world club challenge (so called because of the presence of Paris) the Australian clubs thrashed the English (and French) teams out of sight, demonstrating a huge gulf in quality between the two countries.

Rugby Union: The national team (called the Wallabies) were world champions in 1991 and 1995, and play around six internationals a year. Union is played at the highest level by (in addition to Australia), New Zealand (the All Blacks), South Africa (the Springboks), France, England, Ireland, Scotland and Wales (and at a lower grade by a number of other nations including Argentina, Italy and Papua New Guinea). Rugby union was previously a strictly amateur code in Australia, but is now fully professional at the top level. A few times a year, NSW and Queensland representative state teams play each other in a 'state of the union' series.

CRICKET

Cricket is a strange sport (baseball on valium to outsiders) which usually takes uninitiated foreigners some time to understand (even many Australians don't understand the finer points). If you don't know the difference between a stump and a bail or an over and a wicket you may as well skip this bit, as any attempt to explain would take around 100 pages and almost certainly end in failure.

There are some 500,000 registered cricket players in Australia, where there are leagues at all levels from tots to oldies, men and women, indoors and outdoors. Cricket, like footy, dominates its season (from October until March) and attracts big TV audiences. Half of all Australians watch cricket on TV and around 20 per cent go to matches, where tickets for top class games cost $20 for a one-day match up to $100 for a five-day test match. State cricket is played to a high standard (higher than the English county game), although it isn't a fully professional sport. The main national competition is the interstate Sheffield Shield, in which matches are played over three or four days, and there's also high-quality district cricket. Cricket players aren't usually the fittest of sportsmen, which was highlighted in 1997 when concern was raised over the weight and fitness of some of Australia's elite cricketers (spin bowler Shane 'tubby' Warne walked out of a press conference when questions were asked about his paunch).

Cricket is also played at international level (called test matches) by a number of countries including England, India, New Zealand, Pakistan, South Africa, Sri Lanka, the West Indies and Zimbabwe. During each year the Australian cricket team is usually engaged in one or two minor series of international matches (three tests) or a major series (five or six tests). If you thought four days (Sheffield Shield matches) was a long time for a single match to last, a test match lasts five days, usually with a rest day after two or three days play. One-day internationals (usually day-night, played under floodlights with players wearing brightly-coloured pyjamas) are also played. Test matches in Australia are played in Adelaide (the Adelaide oval), Brisbane (the 'Gabba'), Melbourne (the Melbourne Cricket Ground/MCG), Perth (the Western Australian Cricket Association or 'WACA' cricket ground, pronounced 'whacker') and Sydney (the Sydney Cricket Ground). The Melbourne Cricket Club was established in 1838 and play at the MCG (the world's largest).

The Australian cricket team also takes part in overseas tours during the Australian winter, when they play a series of test matches. The old enemy in cricketing terms are the poms (English), with whom Australia competes every few years for the ashes (not human, but from the stumps which were ritually incinerated when the Australian upstarts first beat England in 1882). A world cup, one-day, knockout competition also takes place every few years. Australian cricketing legends include Don Bradman (the greatest batsman ever), Ray Lindwall, Keith Miller, Richie Benaud, Dennis Lillee, Jeff Thompson, the Chappell brothers (Trevor, Greg and Ian), and Allan Border, to the present day crop of Shane Warne, Mark Taylor (the Aussie captain) and the Waugh twins (Mark and Steve). Even today people still talk about the bodyline series in 1932-33, in which the England bowlers broke the unwritten rules of cricket by bowling at the batsmen rather than at the wicket (a bit like the West Indies' fast bowlers in recent decades). It caused a major diplomatic incident and almost caused Australia to cede from the British Empire (the Aussies were upset because they hadn't thought of it first!).

Thrashing the Poms and winning, or more likely keeping, the Ashes (which Australians think are the remains of the English game!) is sporting heaven to most Australians. However, some Australians have questioned whether it's worthwhile playing England in recent years, during which England have hardly been able to muster any sort of opposition (Q. What's a Pommy batsman wearing zinc cream called? A. An optimist.). Even the apprentices in the Australian Cricket Academy can beat England these days and test matches are often no contests. Australian cricketers, like all Australian sporting heroes, have a ruthless streak, and have consistently hammered England since 1989. In the 1997 test series between the Aussies and Poms, the Aussies won 3-2 (the final score flattered the Poms) to retain the Ashes. The Aussies wanted to take the Ashes home with them (they are traditionally displayed at Lords Cricket Ground in London), although there's no way the Poms were going to let the Aussies have them (they may never have seen them again). Australia is the most successful country at international test cricket, although they haven't been so successful at limited-over, one-day matches in the World Cup (which prompted them to pick two national teams in 1997, one for one-day matches and another for test matches). Australia is also a top nation in women's cricket and they won the women's World Cup in India in 1997.

SOCCER

Soccer is a minor sport in Australia, where's it's played mostly by immigrants (it's referred to insultingly as 'wogball' by footy fans) and is a poor cousin to the various rugby codes and Aussie Rules. The professional National Soccer League (NSL) or A-League is played in the summer and attracts a relatively small following (most fans prefer overseas soccer), although it's gaining in popularity thanks to the success of the national team. Many top Australian players now play professional soccer overseas, notably in the English Premiership. The majority of clubs in the NSL are dominated by Italians, Greeks, Croatians, Slavics, Maltese, Dutch, Macedonians and assorted other 'foreigners' (who represent the ethnic origins of the local populace). The standard is on a par with top amateur teams in England and other European countries. Some Australian clubs have links with foreign clubs to develop young players (European professional clubs are looking to Australia to pick up cheap players, now that they have become so expensive in Europe).

The national team (called the 'Socceroos') has improved beyond all recognition in recent years and in 1996 engaged a top English coach (Terry Venables). However, the future of football in Australia suffered a major setback when the national team failed to qualify for the 1998 World Cup finals. In their final match they drew 2-2 (after leading 2-0) with Iran at home and went out on away goals after the two-leg qualifier. A month later they showed their true potential by reaching the final of the Confederations Cup in Saudi Arabia in late 1997. On the way to the final they drew 0-0 with Brazil, although they lost to them 6-0 in the final (which was a more realistic indication of the gulf between Australia and the world champions).

SKIING

Skiing in Australia dates back to the 1860s and is a popular sport, despite the fact that there's only one real skiing area (the Australian Alps, straddling the New South Wales-Victoria border). A lot of money has been spent on improving the infrastructure in recent years and the facilities and lifts at the larger resorts now compare favourably with the best that Europe and North America have to offer. Australia has an unreliable snow record (1997 was a particularly bad year) and in some years there's barely enough natural snow to cover even the highest resorts, and conditions can be hazardous for all but expert skiers. However, in the last decade snow cannons have been installed in most resorts, which can now guarantee at least some snow for part of the season (a lack of snow is no handicap to most Aussie skiers, as their main activity is getting drunk). Many Australians ski in New Zealand which has a more reliable snow record and many more resorts (professional skiers and ski bums from the northern hemisphere also ski and train in New Zealand during the northern hemisphere's summer). There are artificial snow slopes at Corin Forest Alpine Recreation Area 30 minutes from Canberra, where wheeled bobsleds achieve speeds of up to 80kph (50mph) on a stainless steel slide. Australian resorts have a good safety record, although 18 people were killed in 1997 when a landslide swept away two ski lodges in Thredbo.

The ski season traditionally begins in early June (sometimes in May if there's good early snow) on the Queen's Birthday weekend holiday and continues until around October. However, even in a good year there's usually adequate snow cover only in July, August and early September. Ski runs cater for all standards, from beginners to experts, although most long runs are relatively easy, while the more difficult runs are short. Snowboarding is increasingly popular in Australia (the major resorts have purpose-built runs and bowls) and equipment can be hired and lessons are available. The conditions are usually excellent for cross-country and telemark skiing. The major resorts have ski schools and child-care centres. Ski lessons including lift tickets cost around $60 a day (less for five or seven days) and the hire of boots and skis around $30 a day. (Costs are relatively high due to the short season). Major resorts have a reasonable choice of *après ski* entertainment and a selection of mountain restaurants, and there's a lot of partying among the lodges, although there's little nightlife compared with most European and North American resorts.

It's possible to travel to the Snowy Mountains from Sydney or Melbourne for a day's skiing, although it's more practical to ski for at least a weekend or a few days. You can fly to Cooma from where it's just a short trip by road to most resorts. The NSW snowfields are around four hours by road from Canberra. Note that if you drive, snow chains are compulsory (they can be hired) and there are heavy fines for motorists without them, even if there's no snow! Most resorts have a wide choice of accommodation including hostel dormitories, luxury hotels and self-catering chalets and lodges, a lot of which is close to ski lifts and runs. The cheapest way to enjoy skiing is to rent a resort lodge or apartment with friends and bring most of your food and drink with you, as prices are high in resorts. Accommodation is cheaper in Cooma and Jindabyne, from where there's a bus service to the ski slopes. Accommodation at a lodge in Thredbo or Perisher costs from around

$500 to $1,000 per person, per week sharing a double room depending on the season or $400 to $800 with four to a room.

NSW Resorts: Thredbo is Australia's leading ski resort (popular with overseas skiers) and has 65 marked runs (including the longest in the country of 5km/3mi with a vertical drop of 672m/2,200ft) and a specially designed snowboarding park. A day ticket costs around $60 and a five-day pass around $250. Perisher Blue (1,680m/5,500ft) includes Perisher Valley, Smiggin Holes, Mount Blue Cow and Guthega, and has 30 lifts, some floodlit runs for night skiing and special snowboarding runs. Most accommodation is in nearby Jindabyne, which is cheaper as it's a 40-minute drive to the major resorts or a few minutes on the Skitube which links it to Perisher and Perisher Blue (previously named Blue Cow), the largest ski resort in the southern hemisphere with 506 acres of snow terrain. One of the advantages of staying in Jindabyne is that you can travel to whichever resort has the best snow conditions each day. Other resorts include Lake Crackenback and Charlotte Pass (1,780m/5,850ft), which is the highest and oldest ski resort in Australia and only reachable by snowcat from Perisher Valley (8km/5mi). Mount Selwyn (1,492m/4,900ft) is a day resort (no accommodation) with 12 lifts and ideal for beginners. A one day lift pass costs $25 and five days plus lessons $200.

Victoria: Victoria is home to the vast High Country and the southern end of the Great Dividing Range and the Victorian Alps, which have three major and six minor ski areas. The best resorts include Mt. Buller, Mt. Hotham, Falls Creek, Mt. Buffalo, Mt. Baw Baw and Lake Mountain. There's a resort entry fee of $15 a day in winter. Mt. Buller is Australia's largest and most popular resort with 80km/50mi of runs and an extensive lift system, within easy access of Melbourne's airport, rail and coach stations (from where buses take you direct to the resorts). Falls Creek has 30km/18mi of runs, 23 lifts and a vertical drop of 267m/875ft (you can also ski directly from the village to the lifts and back) and a recent merger with Mount Hotham has created a larger resort with improved facilities. There are also a number of cross-country (nordic) ski centres in Victoria, e.g. Lake Mountain, which is the closest ski resort to Melbourne (just 100km/62mi away) with around 40km/25mi of trails. There's a $5 trail fee ($2 for children).

Tasmania: There are also some small snowfields in Tasmania which has two minor resorts: Ben Lomond (60km/37mi from Launceston) and Mount Mawson (Mount Field National Park). They are less developed and even less challenging than the major resorts in NSW and Victoria. However, they are also much cheaper, e.g. a day pass at Mount Field costs just $10 and at Ben Lomond around $20.

A free monthly newspaper, *Alpine News*, is available from tourist offices in winter. Snow and road reports are available by telephone on 0055-12370 (recorded service) or 0055-34320 for Thredbo. Cross country (also called *langlauf* in Australia) snow reports are available on 0055-26028.

Footnote: Although most Aussies cannot ski for toffee, Zali Steggall (who can ski) won a bronze medal (in the slalom) at the 1998 winter Olympics in Nagano (Japan).

CYCLING

Most people in Australia buy bikes for getting around town, rather than cycling purely for pleasure, exercise or sport (e.g. touring or racing). However, competitive cycling is also popular in Australia and includes road and track racing, cycle speedway, time-trialling, cross-country racing, touring, bicycle polo and bicycle moto-cross. Australia has had considerable success in international cycle racing in recent years, particularly track racing at the Olympics and world championships, and is fast becoming a major force in road racing (such as the Tour de France).

Apart from cycling to work or into town, cycling is an excellent way to explore the countryside at your leisure and get some fresh air and exercise at the same time. Note, however, that fresh air is in short supply in Australia's polluted cities, where you would be wise to wear a face mask to insulate yourself from traffic pollution (although, according to medical experts, they offer little or no protection against carbon monoxide). Cycling is an excellent way to get around most Australian cities (notwithstanding pollution), due to their relatively small size. Most Australian cities have an extensive network of cycle paths and tracks (Melbourne's cover 500km/310mi), with the exception of Sydney. Cyclists in some cities such as Canberra and Perth can legally ride on footpaths and pedestrians can also use cycleways. There are children's off-road bike circuits in cities and towns. In most cities, bikes can be transported on suburban trains free of charge or for a small fee during off-peak times, although a special permit may be required during peak periods (e.g. 6 to 9am and 3 to 6pm on weekdays) or it may be impossible). It's usually mandatory when transporting a bike on a plane or bus to dismantle and box it.

The climate and topography (in most regions) of Australia lends itself to cycling and is a good way to explore coastal areas. You can ride a long way in some regions without encountering any hills, although if you're actually looking for hills you're also well catered for. Long-distance bike riding or touring in Australia is a serious pursuit, although you must *never* go on a long trip in remote areas without being fully equipped and with sufficient water (always check local water sources when travelling in remote areas). When touring you also need to be wary of poor roads, broken bridges, rabid dogs, crazy drivers and inclement weather. You will need a mountain bike if you want to get off the beaten track, where the terrain can be very demanding (on both riders and bikes). Note that cycling isn't permitted off sealed roads in national parks. A hat and a plentiful supply of sunscreen are necessary in hot weather. Many companies arrange organised tours throughout Australia inclusive of bikes (although you can use your own), a support vehicle, accommodation and cooking.

A wide range of bikes are available in Australia to suit all pockets and needs, ranging from a basic 'town' bike costing a few hundred dollars to a professional racing cycle costing many $thousands. In between these extremes are shopping bikes, touring bikes, mountain bikes, BMX bikes, tricycles, tandems and bicycles with folding frames. Before buying a bike, carefully consider your needs, both current and future, obtain expert advice (e.g. from a specialist cycle store) and shop around for the best deal. Make sure you purchase a bike with the correct frame size. If you're a visitor and need a bike for touring, it's cheaper to buy a secondhand bike and sell it when you no longer need it (some cycle shops will buy back secondhand bikes at a guaranteed price).

A new ten-speed touring or mountainbike costs from around $400 or alternatively you can buy a good secondhand mountainbike from around $150 (try the weekly *Trading Post* in Sydney). Mountain bikes have become increasingly popular in recent years and cost from around $400 up to $10,000. Bicycle theft is common in Australia, so it's advisable to insure your bike if possible and buy a good lock. Australian Bikefile (PO Box 137, Caloundra, QLD 4551, tel. (07) 5491 9011) is a nationwide registration and insurance scheme where you pay an annual fee of $10 plus $20 if your bike is worth less than $300 and up to $45 if it's worth over $300 and less than $1,000.

Bikes can be rented in all cities and large towns and may include tandems, tricycles and folding bikes. Ask at the local tourist office for information. Touring and mountain bikes can be rented from around $10 a day, $20 a weekend and around $60 a week (or from $30 a day, $60 a weekend or $120 a week in Sydney). They can sometimes also be rented by the hour from around $3. There may be lower rates for children. Usually a deposit is required or you must leave your passport or a credit card as security. Note that many backpacker hostels provide free bikes for guests, although you should ensure that a rented or loan bicycle is insured against theft or damage and that you have a good lock.

It's important not to underestimate the dangers of cycling (particularly for children) in Australia, as many cyclists are killed or injured each year. Australian motorists don't respect cyclists as much as they do in some other countries, particularly in country areas (although many roads carry little traffic). Main roads can be particularly dangerous and many roads can deteriorate into gravel or rutted mud in country areas. Cycling in most cities is fairly safe, particularly where there are off-road cycle tracks and paths (Sydney is the main exception, where cyclists take their life in their hands). Cycling helmets are compulsory in all states and territories, and you can be fined on-the-spot (e.g. $25 to $50) for not wearing one. They can be uncomfortable in hot weather, but aren't as uncomfortable as brain surgery. Reflective clothing and bright (preferably flashing) lights at night may help to prevent an accident. If you have a child with a bicycle, it's important to impress upon him the need to take care and not take unnecessary risks, e.g. always observe traffic signals and signal clearly before making any manoeuvres. **Young children shouldn't be allowed to cycle on roads in towns and cities, as it's simply too dangerous.** Car drivers often cannot see or avoid cycle riders, particularly if they are stupid enough to ride at night without lights or dart out of side streets without looking.

Many books are published for cyclists in Australia including *Bicycle Touring in Australia* by Leigh Hemmings (Mountaineer Books); *Cycling Around Sydney*, *Seeing Sydney by Bicycle*, *Discovering Melbourne's Bike Paths* and a series of *Cycling The Bush* (Hill of Content) books by Sven Klinge which cover a number of states; plus *Cycling The Bush - The Best Rides in Australia*. Free brochures such as *Canberra Cycleways* are also available from tourist offices. Local cycling guides and maps are published by councils, conservation and cycling groups in many areas, many of which also publish safety booklets and brochures for children. 'Cycling' maps are available in the major cities from bookshops and local cycling clubs and organisations (the best are the government series of 1:250,000 scale).

If you're interested in joining a cycling club, your local library should have information about local clubs or you can contact the Australian Cycling Federation (tel. (02) 9281 8688) or Freewheeling (PO Box K26, Haymarket, Sydney, NSW 2000), a national organisation which publishes its own magazine. There are also bicycling organisations in all states such as the Bicycle Institute of New South Wales, GPO Box 272, Level 2, 209 Castlereagh Street, Sydney, NSW 2000 (tel. (02) 9283 5200) and Bicycle Victoria, 19 O'Connell Street, North Melbourne, VIC 3051 (tel. (03) 9328 3000).

BUSHWALKING

Whether you call it, walking, rambling, hiking, orienteering or bushwalking, getting from A to B for fun and pleasure (as opposed to not being able to afford a bus or train ticket) is popular in Australia and is the most common form of exercise (what's more it's free). Australians tend to call hiking, bushwalking, even when it's done far away from the nearest bush. However, real bushwalking generally refers to long-distance, serious walking in the outback, from a day trip to a number of weeks. There are marked trails in most national parks and state forests, although some offer tough walking and are for the seriously fit only, and there's generally a lack of marked long-distance trails. If you're lucky you may catch sight of some of Australia's rarer wildlife. You require a national park permit to enter certain parks and reserves costing around $10 a day for a vehicle or $50 or $60 a year. Day/night permits are also available in some areas for campers. Tracks are usually marked by coloured (e.g. red or blue) triangles on trees, posts, etc. Before setting out on a walk in a national park, you should sign on in the ranger's log book and sign off when you return, otherwise searches won't be initiated by rangers if you get lost. When on a long walk it's always wise to let someone know your plans and when you expect to return. Some trails are closed in the summer due to fire risks.

It's important to be properly prepared and equipped when going on a long walk and staying out overnight. Self-sufficiency is important as you cannot expect to find an hotel, restaurant or corner shop over every hill or around every bend. The outback doesn't suffer fools gladly and must be treated with respect (along with its animal life, flora and fauna). This means making adequate preparation (including fitness) and taking ample supplies of water, food, clothing, sun protection, maps and other essentials (such as an expert guide if you're inexperienced). Many excellent shops sell or hire bush clothing and equipment, and some youth hostels hire equipment.

Australia has a wealth of beautiful unspoiled hiking country in every state and territory. One of the major trails is the 5,000km/3,106mi National Trail from Cooktown (north of Cairns) to Melbourne, following the old stock routes, fire trails and bush tracks. Around Sydney there's the Royal National Park, Ku-ring-gai Chase National Park, the Blue Mountains and Kosciusko National Park in the Snowy Mountains. A 250km/155mi walk links Sydney with the Hunter Valley and in the west of the state the Hume and Hovell Track runs through high country between Albury and Yass. The Snowy Mountains (part of the celebrated Kosciusko National Park in NSW and Victoria) are a mecca for bushwalkers, where Thredbo is a popular summer hiking resort with a chairlift that takes you to the top of Mount Crackenback. One of NSW's most famous parks is the Warrumbungle National Park in the north of the state.

Victoria has some of the country's most spectacular and diverse countryside including the Australian Alps Walking Track stretching for 655km/407mi from Walhalla (144km/90mi east of Melbourne near Mount Baw Baw) to the Brindabella Ranges on the outskirts of Canberra. Other top walking areas in Victoria include the Little Desert National Park, Wilsons Promontory National Park, the Grampians National Park, Lederderg Gorg, the Great Dividing Range, Mt. Bogong, the Coastal Walking Track and the Snowy River National Park (where the film *The Man From Snowy River* was shot). Tasmania has some of the best bushwalking in Australia including the famous Overland Track from Cradle Mountain to Lake St. Clair (85km/53mi). One seventh of Tasmania is occupied by national parks, although they are under constant threat from mining and logging interests.

In South Australia there's the Mt. Lofty and Flinders Ranges, taking in the 1,500km/932mi Heysen Trail which crosses the state from Cape Jervis to Parachilna Gorge (in the Flinders Ranges). In Western Australia there's the Stirling Range and Porongurup National Park (both north of Albany), and Kalbarri, Karijini and Purnululu national parks. The 640km/400mi Bibbulman Track runs between Perth and Walpole on the southeastern coast. There are many excellent bushwalking possibilities in Queensland including Lamington in the southern Border Ranges, Main Range in the Great Divide, Cooloola north of the Sunshine Coast and Bellenden Ker south of Cairns, plus coastal islands such as Fraser and Hinchinbrook. The Northern Territory provides a wealth of walking areas including the Larapinta Trail in the Western MacDonnell Ranges (near Alice Springs), Trephina Gorge Nature Park in the Eastern MacDonnells, Gregory National Park, Kakadu National Park and Watarrka (Kings Canyon).

Orienteering is popular in Australia and is a combination of hiking and a treasure hunt, or competitive navigation on foot. It isn't necessary to be super fit and the only equipment that's required (in addition to suitable walking attire) is a special detailed map and a compass. There are orienteering clubs in many areas and bushwalking clubs in most towns and areas. In many towns and country areas, guided local walks are conducted throughout the year, ranging from sightseeing tours of towns to walks around local beauty spots, for which there may be a small fee. Walks are usually graded, e.g. easy, moderate or strenuous, and dogs can usually be taken unless otherwise stated. Ask for information at tourist information centres or local libraries.

A wealth of bushwalking books are published in Australia including *Bushwalking in Australia* by John Chapman (Lonely Planet), *Bushwalks in the Sydney Region* edited by Lord and Daniel, and a series of bushwalking books by Tyrone T. Thomas detailing walks in most states and popular walking areas including the *20 Best Walks in Australia* (Hill of Content). Bushwalkers may also be interested in the Australian magazines, *Outdoor Australia* and *Wild*. There are bushwalking associations in all states and territories such as the NSW Confederation of Bushwalking, GPO Box 2090, Sydney 2001 (tel. (02) 9548 1228).

On a less strenuous note for mere mortals, many municipal councils public local walking guides and there are short guided walks in the major cities.

See also **Camping & Caravanning** on page 371 and **Parks, Gardens & Zoos** on page 372.

MOUNTAINEERING, ROCK-CLIMBING & CAVING

Those who find walking a bit tame might like to try abseiling, rock-climbing, mountaineering, caving or pot-holing (subterranean mountaineering). They are also an ideal training ground for social climbers and yuppies who are willing to risk life and limb to get to the top (or bottom). If you're an inexperienced climber you would be well advised to join a climbing club before heading for the hills (an eight-hour beginner's course costs around $200). Contact the Australian School of Mountaineering, 182 Katoomba Street, Katoomba, NSW (tel. (02) 4782 5787) for information. There are abseiling and climbing schools in all the major cities, many with special indoor training apparatus (e.g. a climbing wall) for aspiring mountaineers. Ask about local clubs at climbing equipment stores.

Australia doesn't offer much in the way of mountaineering (Mt. Kosciusko in the Snowy Mountains, NSW is the highest point at 2,228m/7,307ft), although it has some of the best and most varied rock climbing in the world. Caving is particularly popular in Tasmania which has some of the most spectacular caves in Australia. Note, however, that some caves are open to experienced cavers only including the Kubla Khan and Croesus caves and the Exit Cave (permits are necessary to enter most caves, many of which are kept locked). There are caving (speleological) clubs and societies in all major cities.

Note that a number of climbers, cavers and pot-holers are killed each year in Australia, many of whom are inexperienced and reckless. Many more owe their survival to rescuers who risk their own lives to rescue them. **It's extremely foolish, not to mention highly dangerous, to venture into the hills (or holes) without an experienced guide, proper preparation, excellent physical condition, sufficient training, and the appropriate equipment and supplies.**

RACQUET SPORTS

There are excellent facilities in Australia for most racquet sports, including badminton, squash, racquetball and tennis. Some racquet clubs cater for both squash and tennis and possibly also badminton. Most private clubs have a resident or visiting coach, providing both individual and group lessons, and many sports clubs and resort hotels hold residential coaching courses and holidays throughout the year.

Tennis: Tennis is the most popular racquet sport and is played outdoors year round in most states. Local public (council-owned) courts and those owned by local associations can be hired for around $10 to $15 an hour, although it can be difficult to book a court during popular times. Many top hotels and resort hotels have tennis courts, and university courts can be hired during vacations for a token fee, e.g. from $2 an hour. Many companies and schools also have their own courts. There are also many private tennis clubs, although membership fees can be high and some have long waiting lists for new members. Indoor courts are rare in Australia, where outdoor courts can be used year round in most regions. Most courts in Australia are hard courts and there are few grass courts left (the Australia Open used to be played on grass before moving to it's current home).

Australia has a proud record in major competitions, particularly the Davis Cup (the world's premier team tennis competition), which Australia won 15 times between 1950 and 1969 and again in 1973, 1977, 1983 and 1986. Australians have also won the Wimbledon men's single title 15 times between 1952 and 1987 and the women's singles title five times between 1963 and 1980. Famous past players includes Frank Sedgeman, Rod Laver, Lew Hoad, Ken Rosewall, John Newcombe, Tony Roache, Pat Cash, Margaret Court and Evonne Goolagong. Although they are no longer the world-beaters they once were, Australia remains a leading tennis nation. Today's top Australian male players include Pat Rafter (US Open champion in 1997), Mark Philippoussis, Todd Woodbridge, Jason Stoltenberg, Mark Woodforde, Sandon Stolle, Scott Draper and Lleyton Hewitt.

The Australian Open Tennis Championships are held in Melbourne at the National Tennis Centre at Flinders Park, where the main court is unique in that it has a roof which can be closed when it rains or during extreme heat (above 40°C). It's staged over two weeks in January and is the first of the world's four most prestigious Grand Slam tournaments (with Wimbledon and the US and French Opens), although it's ranked below the others in importance and many of the world's top players don't compete. Anyone can play at the National Tennis Centre (except when the Australian Open is being held) for around $10 an hour and you can also take a tour for $5.

Squash: Squash (or more correctly squash rackets) is also a popular racquet sport in Australia and there's an abundance of courts in the major cities and towns. The cost of hiring a court is around $15 an hour and most clubs also have club evenings when members can play for a few dollars. Racquets and balls can be hired. The club standard is among the highest in the world and competitions are staged at all levels from club and state competitions to the Australian Open. Racquetball, the American version of squash, is played in Australia on a squash court and racquets and balls can be hired at some squash clubs. Australia is one of the top men's squash nations in the world (second only to Pakistan) and its women dominate world squash. It has five men in the world's top 20 and the world's top two women players (women's world champion Sarah Fitz-Gerald and Michelle Martin). Past champions include the legendary Geoff Hunt and Sue McKay, two of the best and most dominant players the world has ever seen. However, in the last five years squash has declined in popularity and the number of players has dropped by around 10 per cent. In some cities (e.g. Sydney) clubs have been closing in increasing numbers in recent years as the cost of maintaining or opening a club increases and real estate values rise (many former clubs have been redeveloped as office blocks, apartments and shops).

Badminton & Table Tennis: Badminton is also a popular sport in Australia, particularly among migrants from countries such as Indonesia, Malaysia and Singapore, although it lags behind tennis and squash. Most badminton facilities are provided by public sports centres and private clubs are rare. Table tennis is also quite popular in Australia where it's played both as a serious competitive sport and as a pastime in social and youth clubs. If you want to play seriously there are clubs in most areas. Costs vary although it's an inexpensive sport with little equipment necessary.

To find the racquet clubs in your local area look in the yellow pages, enquire at your local library or contact the appropriate national association.

SWIMMING

There's a wealth of public heated indoor and outdoor swimming pools in all towns in Australia, where the entrance fee is usually around $2 to $3. There are also salt-water, tidal pools on many beaches and Olympic-sized, 50-metre pools in all major cities. Many hotels, motels, apartment complexes and hostels also have their own swimming pools. In the major cities and resorts there are swimming centres with a number of heated pools, diving, solarium, sauna, spa and possibly a gymnasium. Outdoor pools may open only from around October until April in Melbourne and other southern cities. Australia has over 7,000 beaches (long, white sandy beaches are common) and all Australian coastal cities have a number of beaches, all of which are open to the public in Australia.

Sydney has miles of ocean beaches (30 in the Sydney metropolitan area alone) and also many along its harbour (e.g. Balmoral). Sydney's Bondi Beach is one of Australia's (and the world's) most famous beaches, although it's mainly for surfing. Manly (11km/7mi from the city centre) is another famous Sydney beach resort and the TV program 'Home and Away' is filmed at Sydney's Palm Beach. Topless bathing is common throughout Australia, although it isn't accepted on all beaches. South Australia was (surprisingly, considering they're supposed to be prudes) the first Australian state to have a legal nudist beach and the law was recently changed in NSW to permit nude bathing on selected beaches. Local councils can, however, designate any beach a nudist beach. Nude sunbathing is illegal in WA. There are sunscreen patrols on many beaches in Australia to warn people of the need to protect their skin from the sun.

Beach culture is an important aspect of life in Australia, where kids usually learn to swim 'before they can walk'. Beach life led to the surf lifesaving movement (which is both a sport and a community service), the surf ski and the surfboat. Australian beaches are among the best guarded and patrolled in the world and all public beaches are patrolled by lifesavers, who may be volunteers (over 50,000) or paid by the local council. They work each day during the summer season and year round in some resorts. When swimming off a protected beach, it's important to stick to the 'flagged' areas patrolled by lifesavers. Protected beaches also have shark and jellyfish nets (Sydney has an 80km/50mi underwater shark net along its coast — however, don't tell anyone but they aren't always there!), although they aren't foolproof. Note that there are dangerous rips (riptides), undertows and shallow sandbanks off some beaches which claim a number of lives each year (particularly on beaches which aren't patrolled by lifesavers). If you get caught in a rip, you should swim with it rather than against it.

Efforts are made to keep surfers apart from swimmers on protected beaches. On surfing beaches, swimmers must stay within the swimming area defined by red and yellow flags, which may be hoisted from around 6am until 6 or 7pm in summer (year round on some beaches). They are placed to indicate the safest swimming area in the prevailing conditions and also indicate the area under closest scrutiny by lifesavers. **Due to the**

dangers, swimmers are urged by lifesaving associations never to swim outside patrolled areas (almost all beach drownings are on unpatrolled beaches). If you get into trouble while swimming off a beach manned with lifesavers, you should raise one arm in the air which will alert the lifesavers. Take care not to venture too far out as it isn't uncommon for swimmers to be swept out to sea.

You should clear the water if a siren sounds, which may signal a shark sighting or a swarm of jellyfish. Shark attacks are rare (although widely reported) and on average only one Australian a year is killed by a shark. There's very little risk of being eaten alive by a shark, e.g. Sydney beaches have had only one fatal shark attack since 1937. The most common problem is jellyfish, particularly box jellyfish (known as sea wasps) whose sting can be fatal (another tiny jellyfish, irukandji, is found farther afield and is almost as deadly). During the jellyfish season, warning signs are posted along the Queensland coast from Mackay northwards and there's also a Marine Stingers Line (tel. freecall 1800-015 160). However, it's advisable to stay out of the sea during the wet season in the Northern Territory and northern Queensland (from October until May) as you usually only get stung once! Great Keppel island is generally the most northerly (or southerly) place where you can swim safely during the box jellyfish season.

Saltwater crocodiles can be a danger in the open sea near rivers and creeks, particularly tidal ones, and you should also keep a lookout for crocodiles if you're planning to swim in rivers in northern Queensland or the Northern Territory, or in swimming holes in the outback. You're apparently supposed to run away from a crocodile in a zig-zag pattern as they cannot run that way (unless the croc's had a few beers, in which case you may be in trouble!). Other dangers include poisonous coral, cone shells, stonefish, blue-ringed octopus, sea-snakes and catfish, all of which can kill you. In some places swimming is solely for sharks, crocodiles, jellyfish and *idiots*!

Note that the waters off many Australian beaches are polluted and many Australian rivers and lakes are also too polluted to swim in. Australians don't respect their beaches and litter can be found everywhere (wilderness beaches are the cleanest). A recent survey by the Surfrider Foundation found that around 20 per cent of Australian beaches are within 5km/3mi of a sewage outlet (3 billion litres of raw sewage is pumped into the sea every day), a quarter have stormwater pipes draining onto beaches, almost three-quarters have developments within just 250 metres of the high-tide mark (25 per cent are also affected by further developments), and around 80 per cent are strewn with litter (including used syringes).

Many beaches have completely lost their sand dunes due to beachfront development, and environmental groups believe that urgent action is needed to save what's left of Australia's beaches. Some resorts have a hotline where a recorded message updates callers on pollution from stormwater or sewer outfalls (e.g. (02) 9901-7996 in Sydney) and warns of other hazards such as stinging jellyfish and dangerous currents. Daily beachwatch reports are published in newspapers (e.g. the *Sydney Morning Herald*) reporting the location of sewage and stormwater. Pollution warnings are posted on some beaches.

Children learn to swim at school in Australia and regularly swim in the school or local public pool (adult lessons are also given at most pools). Students are divided into classes according to age and swimming ability, and are taught the finer points of swimming by qualified coaches. Students can obtain swimming certificates from junior through intermediate and senior certificates, up to lifesaver qualifications (to gold medal standard). Under a new law that came into effect in 1997, all private pools in Australia must have fences higher than 1.5m and be inspected by local councils. Legislation is designed to reduce the incidence of drowning among children aged under five, which is the most common cause of death for children of this age (almost 350 people in total died from drowning in 1996).

Private swimming clubs abound in Australia and help produce tomorrow's national Olympic team. Australians have an excellent record in the Olympics and World Swimming Championships, although there's increasing competition nowadays and they're unable to dominate as they once did. However, they still wipe the floor with other countries in the Commonwealth games held every two years. Australians also excel at water polo and diving.

WATER SPORTS

All water sports including sailing, windsurfing, waterskiing, rowing, powerboating, canoeing, surfing, parasailing and subaquatic sports are popular in Australia, which is hardly surprising considering it has a coastline of 36,738km/22,826mi (some 80 per cent of Australians live within around 30km/20mi of the coast) and numerous rivers and lakes. Boats and equipment can be rented from coastal resorts, lakes and rivers, and instruction is available for most water sports in holiday areas. Jet skis and surf skis can also be rented in an increasing number of resorts. Every beach resort worthy of the name stages a surf carnival in summer, in which individuals and teams compete for honours in swimming and surfboat races, board-paddling events, team lifesaving competitions and the highlight, iron-man/iron-woman competitions (a combination of swimming and surfski riding), There's even a professional ironman circuit which tours Australia in the summer.

Scuba Diving & Snorkeling: Australia is a mecca for scuba divers and snorkelers, particularly the Great Barrier Reef (2,000km/1,240mi in length), which offers some of the world's best diving and is one of the natural wonders of the world with some 400 types of coral and around 1,500 species of fish. Experts enthuse about the diving on the outer reef wall and you can rent underwater photographic gear (some boats also have on-board film-processing equipment). You can also wreck dive on the reef (e.g. the Yongala), which is the graveyard of over 500 ships. Many diving boats operate out of Cairns and other towns on the northern Queensland coast (boats are licensed to operate from around 20 sites). A day trip from Cairns costs around $80 for snorkelers and $110 for scuba divers, which includes two tank dives. Full snorkeling gear can be hired for around $15 a day, although some day trip organisers provide free snorkeling gear. Note, however, that during the wet season (January to March), floods can wash mud out into the ocean which can seriously affect viability. There are rules regarding where you can dive on the reef and what you can do (e.g. spearfishing is generally prohibited). Diving shops abound in resort areas and the major cities.

Divers in Australia need a PADI (Professional Association of Diving Instructors) certificate. To obtain a certificate in Australia you usually require a doctor's medical certificate certifying that you're fit to dive and must usually show that you can tread water for 10 minutes and swim 200m to be accepted on a course. Tuition in Australia is among the cheapest available in tropical waters and a PADI certificate course lasts five full days for beginners and costs between $300 and $500. There are diving schools in many coastal towns in Queensland, among the most popular of which are Airlie Beach, Cairns and Townsville. Shop around and ask about courses and avoid cheap 'cowboy' operators, as beginners have died after receiving poor tuition from these. Always learn with a qualified and reputable outfit. Some diving clubs offer free introductory lessons in a local pool. Note that not all courses offer good value for money and with the cheaper courses, you're likely to spend most of the time in a classroom or pool. A good mix is two days in the classroom and pool, a day trip to the reef, and perhaps two days on the reef spending the night on board. It isn't necessary to be a scuba diver or snorkeler to enjoy the Great Barrier Reef, which you can view from a glass-bottomed boat.

Although the Great Barrier Reef is the main destination for divers in Australia, there are other interesting alternatives including Fly Point at Port Stephens (north of Newcastle, NSW) and Ningaloo Marine Park (extending for 260km/161mi along the western side of the Northwest Cape in Western Australia), which is a smaller, more accessible version of the Great Barrier Reef (in places it's only a few hundred metres offshore). In some areas there are 18th century (e.g. off Rottnest Island near Perth, WA) and WWII wrecks, which make interesting dives.

Surfing: Surfing is a way of life rather than just a sport in Australia, where surfies (variously known as waxheads, seaweed munchers and shark-suckers) are mocked for their fanaticism. A number of international surfing competitions are staged in Australia, which has many top male and female professionals (Australian Mark Richards, who won the world title four times from 1979-1982, is considered the greatest competitive surfer of all time). There are surfing schools in all major (and many minor) surfing areas, which run beginners' courses usually lasting three to seven days. It's best to have a few lessons before buying your own board to see whether you take to it (surfboards can be hired for around $10 an hour and some resort hotels lend them to guests free of charge). A wet suit is usually necessary in winter. Some schools operate surfing safari trips, where you camp in remote locations and learn how to surf, fish and look after yourself in the wild. Surfing variations include surf mats, surfoplanes and boogie boards (small boards that you lie on which are used as an intermediary before progressing to a full-size surfboard). **Note, however, that boogie boards can be dangerous and users comprise a large number of those rescued by lifesavers.** Surfers can be a hazard for swimmers and if you impinge on the bathing areas of beaches you will be warned off by a lifesaver with a megaphone (if you fail to comply your board can be confiscated).

The best surfing in Australia is usually in New South Wales and Western Australia. In Sydney the best beaches are on the south shore including Bondi, Tamarama, Coogee, Maroubra and North Narrabeen. Cronulla, south of Botany Bay, is also popular and there are also many beaches between Manly and Palm Beach on the North Shore. Byron Bay in northern NSW is considered to be one of Australia's best surfing areas. If you live in Canberra, the nearest decent surfing is around 160km/100mi away at Batemans Bay. The best surf close to Melbourne is found at Mornington peninsula on the Great Ocean Road, and Bells Beach, Jan Juc, Torquay, Anglesea and Lorne are also popular surfing venues in Victoria. In South Australia you need to travel to Pondalowie for the state's most reliable and strongest wave's. Tasmania has some good surf beaches, the best of which is Marrawah on the west coast. Surfing condition are poor north of Brisbane and Surfers Paradise doesn't live up to its name. Cottesloe and Leighton are popular surfing venues in Perth, although the best surf is found at Yallingup further south. Note that on some beaches the local surfies are protective of their patch and may discourage newcomers. There are local surf reports in some areas where you can call a number (e.g. 0055-22995 in Sydney) to find out where the best waves are. Enthusiasts may wish to buy a copy of the *Atlas of Australian Surfing* by Mark Warren (Angus & Robertson).

Sailing: Boats of all shapes and sizes (from lasers and catamarans to motor cruisers and ocean-going yachts) can be rented from numerous coastal locations throughout Australia. A luxury yacht with up to eight berths costs around $300 a day or around $50 per person, per day (novices can charter a boat with a skipper). Some companies offer flotilla trips where you travel in a group with an experienced skipper. Sailing schools abound in resort areas and offer introductory lessons and courses for beginners up to racing standard. Many Australians fulfill their dream of owning their own boat and boat ownership is among the highest in the world. Airlie Beach and the Whitsunday Islands are the most popular sailing areas in Queensland, which is the centre of Australia's yacht charter business. In many resorts it's possible to get a job or a free ride as a crew member on a yacht.

Yacht racing is popular in all areas, including racing for 18-footers (an Australian invention) which are staged in Sydney Harbour on most Saturdays during the summer. Australia has an excellent record in international sailing events (including the Olympics and World Championships) and won the America's Cup in 1983 — the first nation to beat the Americans in over 100 years. One of Australia's major sporting events is the Sydney to Hobart yacht race (run annually since 1945) which starts on 26th December. It's a handicap race over 630 nautical miles and attracts entries from throughout the world.

Note that vessels arriving in Australia must call at a 'proclaimed' port (all major ports) where customs, quarantine and immigration facilities can be completed (usually three hours notice must be given via an OTC coastal radio station). Customs duty and sales tax is payable on any craft imported for private or commercial use in Australia and is payable on arrival, although those staying in Australia for less than 12 months can import a vessel duty and tax free (although a security bond may be required). A book entitled *Go Boating Safely* is published by the Australian Government Publishing Service.

MIscellaneous: Windsurfing is popular throughout Australia and windsurfing schools abound in beach resorts and on inland lakes. Note that you will probably learn faster on an inland lake than on coastal waters. Tuition costs around $150 for two half-days with a wetsuit included and a fully-rigged windsurfer costs around $50 a day to hire. Waterskiing has a large following in Australia and boats, skis and wetsuits can be hired in coastal resorts and on large inland lakes. Jet skis can be hired (around $15 an hour) in many beach resorts and on some inland lakes. However, unless you're an experienced rider it's advisable to steer well clear of jet (power) skis which are deadly in the wrong hands (both to riders and anyone who comes into contact with them). There are restrictions on the use of jet skis in most resorts. Parasailing is possible in many beach resorts, where you're attached to a parachute pulled along by a motor boat and float off into the wide blue yonder (it's less frightening than jumping out of a plane and you have a softer landing).

Rowing is a serious sport in Australia (Australia topped the Olympic medal table in Atlanta in 1996 and won five medals in the world rowing championships in 1997) and there are rowing clubs in all major cities and towns. Canoeing is popular on rivers and lakes, where there are numerous clubs offering courses, equipment hire and tours (the *Canoeing Guide to NSW* is published by the NSW Canoe Association). White-water rafting is popular in Australia with its many excellent rapid rivers graded from 1 (easy) to 6 (heeelp!!!!!). Among Australia's wildest rivers are the Franklin and Gordon in Tasmania. The Caltex Avon Descent is Australia's greatest whitewater classic covering 133km/83mi on the Avon River in Western Australia from Northam to Perth. Australia has a number of world champion canoeists.

AERIAL SPORTS

Most aerial sports have a wide following in Australia (which has an awful lot of airspace), particularly gliding, hang-gliding, paragliding, hot-air ballooning and microlighting. The main thing most aerial sports enthusiasts have in common is madness and money, both of which are essential in liberal doses in order to fulfil man's ultimate ambition.

Hang-gliding has become increasingly popular in Australia in the last decade and there are hang-gliding schools in many areas. Tuition costs round $10 for half an hour to fly in tandem with an instructor and a full course to obtain a pilot's licence costs around $1,000 and can be undertaken in around 10 days. Paragliding or parascending is the cheapest and easiest way to fly, and entails 'simply' jumping off a steep mountain slope with a parachute or being tow-launched by a vehicle or a boat. When you've gained enough height, you release the tow and float off on your own (or come crashing back to earth). Although generally safer than hang-gliding, paragliding can be dangerous or even lethal in the wrong hands. Paragliders must complete an approved course of instruction after which (if you survive) you receive a licence which allows you to purchase a paraglider and fly when supervised by an experienced pilot. Parasailing or paraflying is possible in many beach resorts and is like aerial water-skiing (a 10-minute 'flight' costs around $40).

Hot-air ballooning has a small but dedicated band of followers in Australia, although participation is generally limited to the wealthy due to the high cost of balloons (lawyers and politicians usually get a reduction for supplying their own hot air). Alice Springs is the country's ballooning centre. A flight in a balloon costs from around $100 ($50 for children) and is an unforgettable experience and a spectacular way to see some of Australia's most stunning landscapes (e.g. Ayers Rock). Balloon operators offer 30 or 60-minute dawn breakfast (including 'champagne') sunrise flights.

Aircraft and gliders (sailplanes) can be hired with or without an instructor (providing you have a pilot's licence) from many small airfields in Australia. There are many gliding clubs in Australia and parachuting and free-fall parachuting (sky-diving) flights can be made from most private airfields. Schools offer tandem jumps for beginners (where you're strapped to an instructor) and freefall courses cost around $350 for a full day's course. The latest craze to have taken off (literally) in Australia is the microlight (or ultralight), a low-flying go-cart with a hang glider on top and a motorised tricycle below. Microlights are designed to carry a maximum of two people and can be stored in a garage. It's one of the cheapest and most enjoyable ways of experiencing real flying without wings (you require a private pilot's licence). Flying lessons are cheaper in Australia than in most European countries and similar to North America. You can take a 'tourist' flight in a small plane from most airfields (seaplane flights are also offered in some areas, e.g. Sydney harbour).

Note that most aerial sports or private aviation are specifically excluded from many insurance policies, including, for example, health insurance and mortgage life insurance policies. Before taking up any aerial sport you should ensure that you have adequate health and accident insurance, sufficient life insurance and your affairs are in order. Why not take up fishing instead? A nice, sensible, <u>SAFE</u> sport (not that fish would agree).

FISHING

Fishing (or angling) facilities in Australia are excellent and it's one of the biggest participant sports in the country. There's good fishing in Australian waters, both inland and deep-sea fishing, with the main attraction being big game fishing. There's good trout fishing on inland lakes and rivers in many states, particularly in Tasmania. However, you should be wary of eating fish caught in inland waters as many are polluted, despite $millions spent on cleaning them up (many rivers are used as garbage disposal 'pipes' by industry). Overfishing of certain species is also an increasing problem for Australia's fishing industry. Note that there are bag and size limits in most areas for certain species of fish, e.g. Victoria limits trout catches to 10 a day and a licence may be required when fishing in inland waters. In WA, fishing licences ($10) are required only if you plan to catch marron and rock lobsters or will be using a net. Licences are available from the Fisheries Department. Some species such as turtles, clams, dugongs (sea cows) and triton shells are protected and are illegal to hunt in Australian waters.

The main Australian game fishing industry is based in Townsville, where prey includes black marlin (the prize catch), sailfish, saltfish, wahoo, tuna and Spanish mackerel. The main season is from June to November. Australia's most prized game fish, black and blue marlin, are protected by law and *must* be returned to the sea whether dead or alive (often after being tagged) on penalty of fines of up to $12,500! The Coral Sea off Cairns is one of the few places in the world where large black marlin are found. Game fishing competitions are regularly staged; one of the major events is the Gove Game Classic (NT) which attracts fishermen from throughout Australia. A game fishing boat for eight can be rented for around $1,000 a day, although marlin fishing can cost $1,500 a day for four to six passengers. 'Bottom' fishing boats are also available for hire and carry up to 30 passengers. Reef fishing on the Great Barrier Reef is also popular and fishing boats depart regularly from Cairns and Townsville for trips of from eight to 15 hours.

Good game fishing is also to be had in the waters off Broome (WA), where game includes mackerel, yellowfin tuna, wahoo, yellowtail, kingfish, hammerhead and bronze whale sharks. There's also good game fishing off New South Wales (tailor fish, marlin, mulloway, black marlin), Victoria and Tasmania (mulloway, bluefin tuna and Australian salmon), South Australia (tuna), Perth (blue marlin) and Darwin (queenfish, Spanish mackerel, barramundi and barracuda). Other popular prey include brown trout, English redfin, perch, eel and native blackfish (off the west coast of Tasmania), Australian Salmon, mulloway, shark, giant crabs, trevally, whiting and crayfish (off South Australia) and salmon, herring, tailor, trevally, sea pike, samson fish, spanish mackerel, bream, mulloway and crayfish (off the southern coast of Western Australia). Northern Australia is famed for its barramundi ('barra') fishing, found both offshore and inland. Fishing trips are organised for around $150 to $250 per day, usually between March and October, including accommodation, all meals, fishing guides, boat rental, equipment, tackle and bait. Note that in the NT there are limits on catches of barramundi and mud crabs (contact the local fisheries management service for information).

Tasmania has Australia's best fresh-water fishing including superb trout fishing (introduced in 1864 from England). A licence is required to fish in inland waters and there are bag, season and size limits for many species of fish. Licences cost $38 for the season, $20 for 14 days, $12 for three days and $7 for one day, and are available from sports stores, post offices, and state travel and information centres. The fishing season in most inland waters is from the Saturday nearest to 1st August until the Sunday closest to 30th April. However, there's a shorter season in many areas and in certain waters — a *Fishing Code* brochure is available detailing the seasons. Tasmania's coastal waters are also rich fishing grounds (fishing is permitted all year), where salmon, whiting and bream can all be caught from the shore.

GOLF

Golf was introduced in Australia in the 1820s and today there are around 1,400 clubs and some 1m golfers, making it the most popular participant sport in the country. Melbourne has over 100 golf courses (it claims to have more than any other city in the world) and Sydney has almost 100. There are many beautiful and spectacularly sited courses throughout the country, including many public courses. However, the best courses are usually private, although most allow non-members to play (but you may need to be invited by a member). Many private golf clubs are part of a larger country club or hotel sports complex where facilities may include a luxury hotel, restaurant, bar, tennis, squash, swimming pool and other facilities. Golf isn't an expensive sport in Australia, where a round usually costs from $10 to $25. Golf clubs can be hired for around $20.

Many golf clubs have golf nets and covered driving ranges, and most also have professionals to help you reduce your number of lost balls (beware of courses with lots of water, which have a voracious appetite for golf balls). Driving ranges are also provided in most areas and have all-weather, floodlit bays, practice bunkers and putting greens. The big advantage of a driving range (apart from the reasonable cost of a few dollars for a basket of 50 balls) is that you don't need to go and find your balls in the undergrowth or buy new ones when they land in the water (there isn't any).

Australia has produced many great golfers including the current world number one, Greg Norman. Other current top Australian male players include Peter Senior, David Graham, Craig Parry, Darren Cole, Peter O'Malley, Stuart Appleby, Robert Allenby, Brad King, Greg Chalmers and Robert Stephens. When not playing on the European or American circuits, Australia's top professionals play the ANZ PGA Tour of Australasia Order of Merit. The premier event is the Australian Open, staged in November at the Metropolitan Golf Club in Melbourne. Top Australian female golfers include Karrie Webb (who was world number one in 1997) and Karen Lunn. Crazy golf, miniature golf, pitch and putt, and putting greens (e.g. in public parks) are available in most areas for those who set their sights a little lower than winning the Australian Open.

GYMNASIUMS & HEALTH CLUBS

There are gymnasiums and health and fitness clubs (where sadists are employed and masochists go to torture themselves) in all cities and large towns in Australia, which include multipurpose fitness centres with swimming pools, aerobics and fitness machines. Many private health and fitness clubs organise aerobics and keep-fit classes, and may have a sauna, solarium, jacuzzi, steam bath and massage. Many top class hotels also have health clubs and swimming pools, which are usually open to the general public, although access to facilities may be restricted to guests only at certain times.

All clubs and centres have tonnes of expensive bone-jarring, muscle-wrenching apparatus, designed either to get you into shape or kill you in the attempt. Middle-aged 'fatties' shouldn't attempt to get fit in 'five minutes' (after all it took years of dedicated sloth and over-eating to put on all that weight), as overexertion can result in serious injuries. A good gymnasium or health club will ensure this doesn't happen and will carry out a physical assessment including a blood pressure test, fat distribution measurements and heart rate checks. All clubs should provide a free trial and assessment and produce a personal training program. In your rush to become one of the body beautiful it pays to take the long route and give the intensive care unit (or mortuary) a wide berth.

Private health and fitness clubs have been popping up overnight in all areas in what is a huge growth market. The cost of membership of a private club varies considerably, depending on the city, area, the facilities provided and the local competition. Note, however, that there has been a spate of closures in recent years which have left annual members out of pocket. This has led to a new law prohibiting gyms from offering annual membership specials that are much cheaper than a monthly payment scheme. Beware of fly-by-night outfits and choose a reputable, long-established club. Membership fees and value-for-money varies considerably, so you should shop around. Many gymnasiums can be used by non-members on payment of an admission fee, where a day ticket usually costs around $8 to $10 (monthly membership is also usually available). Some gyms in major cities (e.g. Sydney) are open 24 hours a day from Monday to Friday. Some clubs offer reduced rates for husband and wife or family membership.

MISCELLANEOUS SPORTS

The following are a selection of other popular sports in Australia, most of which are practised throughout Australia.

Athletics: Most towns have local athletics clubs, and organise competitions and sports days. Competitive running has a strong following in Australia and jogging is also popular in the main cities, where there are jogging tracks in many public parks and gardens. Races are organised throughout the year in all areas, from fun runs of a few miles up to half and full marathons. The ultimate 'jog' is the 1,060km/658mi ultrathon, the world's longest point-to-point race, run from Melbourne to Sydney in spring, taking over 50 days to complete. Australia isn't renowned for its prowess in athletics, but has a number of world-class athletes, notably Cathy Freeman, who won the 400m at the 1997 world championships. However, athletics isn't a popular spectator sport in Australia (unless it's the Commonwealth, World or Olympic Games) and Australia has few world champions in track and field sports (compared with their huge success in other sports). Australia is one of only three countries (Britain and Greece are the others) to have competed at every modern Olympics and Sydney will host the 2000 Olympics.

Baseball: To the uninitiated, baseball is the only game in the world that provides test cricket with any sort of challenge for the title of the most boring sport in the world (although it doesn't offer much competition, as games are far too short). Baseball is popular in Australia (particularly among insomniacs, who find that watching people run around in circles in pyjamas provides instant relief) where there's a national league and a national team, although it isn't a professional sport.

Basketball: A sport specially created for giants (and black American giants in particular), which is popular in Australia and one of the country's fastest-growing sports. There's a professional National Basketball League (NBL) and top matches are televised and attract crowds of over 15,000. The NBL has bolstered club standards and the national team (the Australian Crocodiles) is now rated in the world's top 10 (the import of foreign players is restricted in order to nurture home-grown talent).

Bowls: Once regarded mainly as a pastime for the elderly and retired, (lawn) bowls is increasingly popular with people of all ages, particularly the young (who are ruining the game's image). Top matches are well-attended and televised. There are hundreds of bowling clubs throughout Australia (almost every city suburb has one), which is one of the world's top bowls' nations and has produced many world champions.

Boxing: Legalised punchups for violent types. Popular throughout the country, particularly as a spectator 'sport' (many people enjoy watching a good fight, as long as they're out of (h)arms reach). Most towns have a boxing club and gymnasiums for budding professionals are common in the main cities. Australia has produced a number of world champions over the years.

Bungee Jumping: This 'sport' was invented in Australia (which says a lot about Australians) and is popular among macho Aussies. If your idea of fun is jumping 60m/200ft or more from a great height with an elastic rope attached to your body to prevent you merging with the landscape, then bungee jumping may be just what you're looking for. Jumps are usually made from specially constructed steel towers, but may also be made from bridges, cranes, hot-air balloons, etc. It's a strictly regulated sport which is actually very safe. You can also try rap-jumping in Australia which consists of rapelling (hence the name) or abseiling head first down a cliff at high speed.

Darts: Not actually a sport, but an excuse to get drunk (have you ever seen anyone playing darts in a milk bar?). A popular game in pubs, many of which have teams that play in local leagues.

Fencing: A sport which has lost a lot of its popularity since the invention of the gun, although a hard core of enthusiastic swordsmen are holding out in a small number of clubs.

Frisbee: Believe it or not, throwing plastic discs around has actually developed into a competitive 'sport', with league and cup competitions.

Gymnastics: Another popular sport in Australia and most schools and sports centres have 'gym' clubs.

Hockey: Hockey (grass) is a leading sport in Australia and both the Australian men and women's hockey teams are among the best in the world (the sport is equally popular among both sexes). The national men's team is called the Kookaburras. (For the record, Australia won the men's underwater hockey world title in 1996 — a sport reserved for those who can hold their breath for a long, LONG time.)

Horse & Greyhound Racing: Very popular in Australia, although not because Australians are a nation of equestrians or horse lovers, rather inveterate gamblers. Australia has a long tradition of horse racing and the Sydney Turf Club was established in 1825. Australia's premier horse race (and its greatest sporting event) is the Melbourne Cup run at the Flemington Racecourse in Melbourne on the first Tuesday in November. It's a blend of spectacle, carnival, fashion show, banquet and, yes, a horse race, and brings the country to a total standstill. In addition to flat horse racing, trotting (pacers or harness racing) is also popular in Australia (race meetings are always held at night). Greyhound racing is the poor relation of Australian racing and has a relatively small (but dedicated) following.

Horse Riding: Equestrianism (or horse riding to those who cannot spell 'ekwestranisem') is popular in Australia, where there's an abundance of space to ride and it's relatively inexpensive to own and keep your own horse. On cattle and sheep ranches in the outback, horses remain the primary means of getting around. There are many riding schools in rural areas throughout the country where horses can be hired. Trail rides abound in most areas, where most schools offer half and full-day trail rides and many also organise longer trips through the mountains, outback, rain forests and sand dunes. Australia has a proud tradition of horse breeding and horsemanship, and is one of the world's leading equestrian nations. You can also try camel riding in many areas, particularly in the Northern Territory and around Alice Springs. Camel treks are organised for periods of up to 14-days (take plenty of salve for your bottom!).

Martial Arts: For those brought up on a diet of Bruce Lee, unarmed (?) combat such as Aikido, Judo, Karate, Kung Fu, Kushido, Taekwon-Do and T'ai Chi Ch'uan, are taught and practised at clubs throughout Australia.

Motor Sports: Australians love all motor sports including formula one, Indycar, touring car, rallying, motor cycling, speedway and moto-cross. The Australian grand prix (staged at Albert Park in Melbourne) is one of the best organised formula one races in the race calendar and won the best race award in 1997 for the third successive year. Australia has produced a number of formula one champions including Jack Brabham and Alan Jones. An Indycar (USA) race is staged in Surfers Paradise (QLD) in March and is the only Indycar race held outside North America. Touring car racing has a huge following in Australia and attracts heavy sponsorship and wide TV coverage. The highlight of the season is the Bathurst (150km/93mi west of Sydney) 1,000k (629mi) held in October. The Australian Safari road rally is run over 6,000km (3,700mi) of rugged terrain in August, the route of which remains secret until the night before each race. Australia has a peerless record in 500cc motorcycling in recent years and has produced many world champions, including the current champion, Michael Doohan, who won the world 500cc motocycle title for the fourth successive year in 1997.

Netball: A popular sport in Australia where it's the most popular women's team game. There are clubs in all towns and competitions are staged at all levels including a televised national competition. Australia won the netball world cup in both 1991 and 1995.

Polo: Minority sport for princes and Australian millionaires (e.g. Kerry Packer), where players attempt to hit a ball into a goal while riding a horse at speeds of up to 40mph without falling off.

Rollerskating, Rollerblading, Skateboarding and BMX: Rinks and specially designed circuits are provided in many towns for skateboarding and BMX cycles (acrobatics on a bicycle). Participants should be protected against falls with crash helmets and elbow and knee pads (although not mandatory). It's difficult to hire equipment as it's too easily stolen, although BMX bikes can usually be hired. Rollerskating rinks are provided in major cities and towns, where skates can be hired and coaching is usually available. Many centres organise roller-discos for teenagers. A new craze sweeping the world is rollerblading, using skates where the wheels are set in a line. The promenades of beach resorts are popular roller-skating venues. Keen rollerskaters and rollerbladers also play roller hockey.

Shooting & Hunting: Shooting and hunting are both extremely popular in Australia, which has a long tradition of firearms' sports. However, shooters were dealt a blow in 1997 when many guns were outlawed after the Port Arthur massacre in Tasmania in 1996 (see page 442). Range shooting is popular in towns, and hunting has a large following in the outback, where locals will shoot anything that moves.

Snooker & Billiards: Many hotels, bars and sports clubs have billiard or snooker tables and there are snooker and billiards' clubs in the larger towns. American pool is also played in Australia and many clubs provide pool balls.

Softball: Similar to baseball, softball is played with a larger, slightly softer ball and teams have 10 players a side instead of nine. It's a popular sport in Australia, where it's also played on the beach.

Tenpin bowling: There are tenpin bowling centres in all the major cities in Australia, many with a restaurant and licensed bar. All centres stage competitions and there are tenpin bowling leagues and clubs in all areas (many companies have teams).

Trampolining: A popular sport among high fliers and gymnasts, with a large number of clubs (both junior and senior) around Australia, where courses are organised for all ages.

Volleyball: A really fun game for all the family which is widely played both indoors and outdoors (particularly beach volleyball) in Australia.

Wrestling: This refers to the real sport of wrestling (as practised in the Olympics) rather than the cabaret stuff shown on TV or what you do in bed with your partner. However, when it comes to mass popularity, showbiz wrestling is streets ahead.

Other Sports: Many foreign sports and pastimes have a group of expatriate fanatics in Australia including American football, archery, boccia, croquet, fencing, Gaelic sports (hurling, Gaelic football), handball, lacrosse and pétanque (or boules). For information enquire at council offices, libraries, tourist offices, expatriate social clubs, embassies and consulates.

17.

SHOPPING

A ustralia isn't one of the world's greatest shopping countries, either for variety or bargains, although the choice and quality of goods on offer has improved considerably in the last decade (although still limited compared with Europe and North America — many new products aren't available in Australia or cost a fortune). However, there's a wide choice of department, chain and international stores in the major cities, and exclusive boutiques and chic stores abound in arcades and shopping centres. In stark contrast to the cities, in small country towns there's likely to be a general store and a few other shops only. Prices are also necessarily higher in rural areas due to freight costs and most people who live in the country stock up on goods (and buy expensive items) when visiting a city or large town (or shop by mail-order).

There are many small, family-run stores in Australia, particularly in rural areas, small towns and the suburbs of major cities, although Australia's shopping scene has been transformed in the last few decades with the opening of numerous large shopping centres (malls) and vast supermarkets. Following the trend in most western countries, there has been a drift away from town centres by retailers to out-of-town shopping malls (introduced in the late '70s), which has left some town centres run down and abandoned. The biggest drawback to shopping in cities is parking, which can be a nightmare. However, in some areas too many shopping malls were built for too few customers and many are now being redesigned, redeveloped, reinvented or even demolished. Towns are now turning to 'street-scaping', i.e. reviving town streets by landscaping, installing traffic 'calmers' (speed bumps) or making them pedestrian-only, which many people prefer to bland malls. Australian cities invariably have excellent shopping centres, many housed in fine period buildings and pedestrian-only streets.

Australia doesn't exactly have a free and open marketplace and there are many protected industries, tariffs, monopolies and cartels, although new competition reforms have been introduced in recent years (e.g. the government plans to abolish import restrictions on recorded music). Consequently consumers don't always get the best deal and often pay much higher prices than in other countries. When buying expensive and luxury items you may be better off buying them overseas by mail or via the internet (see page 174). However, the price of many consumer goods such as TV and stereo systems, computers, cameras, electrical apparatus and household appliances has fallen dramatically in recent years. Furthermore, if your funds are in a currency that has increased in value against the Australian dollar in recent years (such as the £sterling or $US), you will be pleasantly surprised how far your money will stretch.

There's generally no bargaining or bartering in Australia, although if you intend to spend a lot of money or buy something expensive you should shop around and shouldn't be reticent about asking for a discount (except in department and chain stores and supermarkets, where prices are usually fixed). Many shops will also meet any genuine advertised price (although often reluctantly). Taxes are included in advertised prices and there's nothing more to pay (at least until Australia introduces a goods and services tax). Always shop around before buying, but make sure that you're comparing similar goods or services as it's easy to 'save' money by purchasing inferior products. In recent years consumer confidence has been low and the retailing sector has been relatively flat since the recession in the early '90s. Australians have become a nation of bargain hunters and have deserted department stores for no-frills retailers and discount stores such as Harris Scarfe, Kmart and Big W.

To encourage Australians to buy Australian-made goods, the government introduced the *Advantage Australia* loyalty program in 1997. Under this scheme, shoppers collect special stamps from companies selling Australian-made goods such as Ampol, Cadbury, Caltex, CSR and Edgell, which can then be used to redeem special offers, discounts and rewards (although the Australian Consumer Association suspects the real aim of the scheme is to obtain customers' personal details and purchasing information). Goods made in Australia often have a green and gold symbol to distinguish them from less expensive (and supposedly inferior) goods made in Asia. In general, Australian-made products are of high quality, although they are often more expensive than similar imported goods (however, top-branded, imported goods are much more expensive in Australia than in many other countries).

A wealth of quality arts and crafts are sold in Australia including hand-woven or knitted woolen garments, leather goods, hides and skins (particularly sheep and lambskin products), rugs, jewellery (e.g. gold, opals, pearls and diamonds), handbags, embroidery, paintings, ceramics, glassware, woodwork and traditional Australian 'outback' clothing. Aboriginal art (of which there are many styles made by different tribes) is popular and is best purchased directly from artists' co-operatives or Aboriginal-owned stores, rather than from tourist shops. It's cheapest in Alice Springs, Darwin and outback towns, although genuine Aboriginal art can be expensive. Aboriginal Arts Australia (AAA) was established by the government to market Aboriginal and Torres Strait Islander arts and crafts, through its stores in Alice Springs, Darwin and Perth. Note that much 'Aboriginal' artwork is mass-produced junk and cheap 'fake' Aboriginal souvenirs are also made in Asia (so before buying anything always check where it's made).

Most shops hold sales at various times of the year, the largest of which are held in December/January and July. The most popular sales are the post-Christmas (or end-of-year) sales, which traditionally start on 26th December, where savings of up to 60 per cent are possible. Some stores don't start their sales until the second week of January (e.g. David Jones and Myer) and in 1998 more stores plan to delay their post-Christmas sales until this time. Some stores seem to have a permanent sale, although retailers aren't permitted to advertise goods as reduced when they have never been advertised or sold at the advertised price.

Most shops accept major credit and debit (EFTPOS) cards, although you may be asked for proof of identification. Personal cheques aren't usually accepted and some stores don't even accept cash in order to deter robbers. Note that with the demise of one and two cent coins, prices are rounded up or down to the nearest five cents (this may also apply to electronic transactions, although there's no reason why it should). It's also possible to use stored value cards (SVCs), including disposable (in values of $20, $50 and $100) and reloadable cards, which are like a phone card and accepted as cash. In major cities and tourist areas you *must* be wary of pickpockets and bag-snatchers, particularly in markets and other crowded places. Don't tempt fate with an exposed wallet or purse or by flashing your money around.

The quality of service and assistance in shops ranges from excellent to poor, depending on the type of store, although generally Australian stores aren't known for their service. Many retail outlets require customers to allow staff to search their bags (excluding very small bags such as handbags) when paying or leaving a store to prevent shoplifting. This is usually shown by a sign and by entering a store you consent to having your bags searched (no sign, no checks). Many stores, particularly department and chain stores, provide free catalogues at Christmas and other times of the year. If you're looking for a particular item or anything unusual, you'll find that the yellow pages (see page 172) will save you a lot of time and trouble (and shoe leather). If you have any questions about your rights as a consumer, contact your local consumer affairs office, fair trading bureau or citizens advice bureau. Most retailers, particularly department and chain stores, will exchange goods or give a refund without question, but smaller stores aren't so enthusiastic.

Shopping guides are available in many areas including the essential *Bargain Shoppers* guides to Melbourne and Sydney (published by Universal Magazines, Private Bag 154, North Ryde, NSW 2113), *Shopping in Exciting Australia* by Ronald and Caryl Krannich, and the *Studentsaver Guide* which lists over 2,000 outlets offering ISIC students a discount (information is available from Student Services Australia, PO Box 399, Carlton South, Melbourne, VIC 3053). See also **Consumers' Rights** on page 434. For those who aren't used to buying goods using the metric system, a list of comparative weights and measures is included in **Appendix C**.

SHOPPING HOURS

Shopping hours in Australia vary depending on the city or town, the state or territory and the day of the week, and are among the most liberal in the world. Shopping hours have been extended in recent years and in some states stores can now open 24 hours a day, seven days a week, apart from a few public holidays. For example, trading is legal 24 hours a day, seven days a week in Victoria, except for Good Friday, Christmas Day and before 1pm on ANZAC day. However, shops cannot be required to open (e.g. in shopping centres) on New Year's Day, Australia Day, Labor Day, Easter Monday, the Queen's Birthday or Melbourne Cup Day, and trading is optional on Sundays. Sunday trading is a contentious issue in some states (e.g. Queensland), although shops in resorts (such as the Gold and Sunshine Coasts) open late at night, on public holidays and at weekends.

Normal shopping hours in country areas are usually from around 8.30 or 9am to between 5 and 6pm Mondays to Fridays, and from 9am until noon on Saturdays. In the major cities many stores open from 9am until between 2 and 5pm on Saturdays. Most stores have late night shopping until 9 or 9.30pm one evening a week in major cities, usually Thursday or Friday. In some areas, stores open an hour later in summer than in winter and department stores may open earlier on sales' days at 7.30 or 8am. Many stores are open for up to 12 hours a day (some are even open 24 hours) and on Sundays, and in the major cities stores may remain open all day Saturday and department stores in the main cities may open on Sundays (e.g. from 10am to 4pm). Harbourside shopping centres in Sydney (such as Darling Harbour) are open from 10am to 9pm Monday to Saturday and from 10am to 6pm on Sundays. Newsagents, chemists and delis. usually open on Sundays, e.g. delis. usually open from 8am until 8pm and chemists may open up to 24 hours a day in major cities. There are 7-11 (modelled on the American 7-11 stores) and Food Plus stores in the major cities which open 24-hours a day and may have a petrol station 'attached'. Many bookshops are open during the evenings and at weekends in major cities.

MALLS & MARKETS

In the last few decades, numerous vast indoor shopping centres (called malls after their American counterparts) have sprung up in out-of-town areas throughout Australia. Malls usually contain a huge selection of shops, including a large department store and many of the most famous chain stores, and are open seven days a week. The main attractions are one-stop shopping and free parking, which usually means you can simply wheel your trolley full of purchases to your car. The largest shopping centres incorporate a wide range of leisure attractions, including cinemas, games' arcades, food halls, fun parks, children's play areas, and a variety of restaurants, cafés and pubs. Most towns and cities also have covered shopping centres, although parking is often expensive and difficult in city and town centres, particularly on Saturdays, and parking areas may be located some distance from stores. Among the most famous city shopping centres are the vast Melbourne Central shopping centre (home to 300 stores) and the Queen Victoria Building (200 stores), Strand Arcade, Centrepoint Shopping Complex and the MLC Centre in Sydney. Many city malls are housed in restored period buildings, which are often connected by tunnels and walkways to other stores and centres.

Markets: Most small towns have markets on one or two days a week and in major cities and towns there may be a market (or a number) on most days of the week. Markets are cheap, colourful and interesting, and are often a good place for shrewd shoppers to pick up bargains, although you need to be careful what you buy (beware of fakes). Items commonly for sale in markets include fruit and vegetables, meat, fish, general food, clothes, arts and crafts, household goods, jewellery and books. Markets are the best place to buy fresh food, where the quality and variety rivals that of any country. Arts and craft markets are common in major cities and resort towns, where artisans can often be seen at work. Flea markets are popular in the major cities and sell secondhand goods including clothes, books, records, antiques and miscellaneous bric-a-brac. Some towns have permanent covered or indoor market places where markets are held from Monday to Saturday, and in some cities there are also popular outdoor Sunday markets. Check with your local library, council or tourist office for information (guides are available to markets in some states, e.g. Victoria).

FOOD & SUPERMARKETS

The quality and variety of food in Australia is superb and the equal of any country in the world. Food outlets include markets (where the freshest produce, meat and fish is usually available), delicatessens (delis.), ethnic food shops, general and corner stores, and, of course, supermarkets. There's a wealth of gourmet food shops in the major cities offering everything from bread and cheese to fruit and vegetables, cakes and pastries to coffee and tea. You can buy almost any ethnic food and ingredients somewhere in Australia, and in the major cities there are stores specialising in imported American and British foods (note, however, that with the plunge in the $A in 1997, prices are likely to rise sharply in 1998). Australia still maintains the quaint British tradition of delivering milk to homes in many towns and cities (home bread deliveries are also made) and many stores deliver groceries (either free or for a small fee).

Australia's biggest food retailers are Woolworth (around 35 per cent of the market), Coles Myer (25 per cent) and Franklins (15 per cent), with the remaining 25 per cent split between a few other large players and independents. Australian's spend over $40 billion a year in supermarkets which are (not surprisingly) among Australia's most profitable retailers (Woolworth and Coles Myer alone are expected to account for some 70 per cent of the food market by the year 2001). However, despite increasing pressure from the major supermarket chains, independent grocers are expected to survive by providing locally-oriented products and personal service. Supermarkets carry some 45,000 products in their major stores, although they have reduced the less popular brands in recent years. Coles also have Coles Express stores in city centres stocking around 13,000 products and offering up-market deli. products, gourmet take-home meals, a home catering service and personalised cakes (e.g. for office celebrations). Woolworth is planning a chain of Metro supermarkets to compete with Coles Express and also plans to introduce food shopping on the internet within the next few years (trials are already under way).

Supermarkets aren't usually permitted to sell alcohol, which must be purchased from bottle shops (liquor stores), grocers and hotels (pubs). However, in country areas, supermarkets and bottle shops may be combined. Supermarkets may have in-store bank kiosks and petrol stations, and they also have plans to introduce news agencies and pharmacies. Major supermarkets open seven days a week and in some cities they remain open until midnight. They provide trolleys which usually require a deposit of 20 cents and some insist that customers use a trolley or basket even when they're buying only a few items. Many supermarkets provide free 'exploding' plastic carrier bags and free boxes, and some provide staff to help you pack your purchases (although you may need to ask).

Australians have been eating more healthily in recent years, consuming less red meat (although they are still great meat eaters) and alcohol, and eating more fruit and vegetables. Meat is reasonable priced and of excellent quality, as is the superb fresh fish and seafood (although it can be expensive). Most supermarkets have a separate delicatessen and are usually good for fresh fruit and vegetables, due to the high turnover of stock (although you should avoid packaged produce, which may be stale or over-ripe). Many supermarkets bake their own bread on the premises and most have fresh fish, meat and cheese counters. Home cooking is one of the casualties of modern living and most Australians don't have enough time to shop and cook elaborate meals. Consequently, prepared, oven-ready meals, microwave food and take-away meals are increasingly popular, and all supermarkets cater for this lucrative growth market. Note, however, that some prepared and fast foods provide little or no nutritional value, and in some cases you would be better off eating the packaging!

Food prices vary depending on the city, shop and the season. Adelaide and Melbourne are generally regarded as the cheapest cities for food, while Darwin is the most expensive as most food must be shipped from outside the territory. In real terms (taking into account inflation and the increase in wages) food is cheaper now than it was 25 years ago, with the weekly food basket equal to around 7 per cent of average earnings compared with almost 9.5 per cent in 1972. Australians spend an average of around $120 a week on food (excluding alcohol), $30 of which is spent on take-away meals and eating out. The current food prices in Australia's capital cities are listed in the monthly *Australian Outlook* newspaper (see **Appendix A**). Note that all foods are sold by the metric measure in Australia (see **Appendix C** for imperial comparisons).

Labelling: Stricter guidelines on food labelling have been introduced in recent years and claims such as 'low fat', 'high fibre', 'sugar-free', 'light' and 'low cholesterol' must meet specific standards. However, don't always believe endorsements or labels, as many are paid for by manufacturers and aren't independent. Note that you usually pay a premium for anything labelled 'low fat', 'free-range' or 'low calory', many of which are bogus. Many manufacturers make unsubstantiated and wild claims for their products, particularly 'health' foods and environmentally-friendly 'green' products, which are deliberately misleading and often illegal. Until the standards and control of labelling is improved, you would be wise to treat health, diet and eco-friendly labels with scepticism.

There are also regulations concerning the vitamins and minerals that can be added to food and new rules about where food is produced. All highly perishable goods (e.g. fresh foods, dairy produce and prepared foods) must have a 'use by' date, after which their sale is illegal (perishable goods are usually discounted a day or two before the 'use by' date is due to expire). Note, however, that use by dates are widely ignored in country areas. Regulations regarding the handling and storage of food have also be tightened in recent years to restrict outbreaks of food poisoning, which is estimated to make thousands of Australians sick each year.

Scanning: All supermarkets in Australia use computerised (electronic point-of-sale) pricing systems where a bar code is included on the labels of goods and is read by a laser reader at the checkout. Always check your receipt carefully as customers are frequently overcharged, particularly on special offer items. Note, however, that unless you make a note of the price of everything you buy, any errors made when prices are entered into the computer may go unnoticed. In most supermarkets, if an item is scanned at a higher price than advertised (or displayed), you're usually entitled to get it free under the voluntary code of practice of the Australian Supermarket Institute. Self-scanning (where customers scan their own goods) has been introduced in some supermarkets in recent years and in future all supermarkets are expected to offer this option (spot checks are made to deter cheating). This reduces the time waiting at checkouts, although supermarkets won't do away with checkout staff (derogatorily called 'checkout chicks') altogether and will still offer the regular checkout service for those who don't wish to do their own scanning.

ALCOHOL

Alcohol (liquor) can be purchased from licensed 'bottle' shops (also called grog shops), pubs and restaurants (it isn't sold in food shops or supermarkets). There are drive-in bottle shops (possibly with 'express' and 'browse' lanes) in major cities, where the biggest and cheapest chains include Liquorland and Liquor Mart. The largest single liquor store in Australia is Dan Murphy's Cellar in Melbourne with some 8m bottles of wine (enough to throw a *really good* party and invite ever adult in Australia). Opening hours vary depending on the state or territory, e.g. from 8.30am until 8.30pm or 10am until 10pm, Monday to Saturday. There are reduced opening hours on Sundays. You must be aged over 18 to buy alcohol in Australia or consume it in a public place. Wine can also be purchased in Australia by mail-order (e.g. from Cellarmaster Wines) and Australians buy some 15 per cent of all bottled wines by mail-order (compared with less than 2 per cent in most other countries). The average Australian family spends around $20 a week on alcohol (mostly beer).

Wine: Although part of the new world, Australia isn't exactly a newcomer when it comes to wine production and vines were imported in 1788 by the first fleet. Commercial production started in the 1820s in NSW and Tasmania, which were followed by South Australia, Western Australia and Victoria in the 1840s. However, up to around 1960 some 80 per cent of all Australian wine was fortified (e.g. port and sherry), for which the country is still noted. Today over 90 per cent of Australian wine is table wine and the country has over 600 wineries.

Australia is ranked only around 15th among the world's grape growers. Nevertheless, wine is one of the country's fastest growing exports which were running at around 3m bottles a week in 1997 (three-quarters from South Australia) to some 80 countries. Exports were worth almost $700m in 1997, with the biggest markets being Britain (45 per cent), worth around $300m a year, the USA (15 per cent) and New Zealand. Australia hopes to increase exports to $1billion by the year 2000, although this seems unlikely due to growers being unable to plant sufficient vines fast enough. The grape harvest was 800,000 tonnes in 1997 (including 500,000 tonnes of premium grapes) and there are plans to double production by the year 2025. Only 10 years ago Australia imported more wine than it exported. However, while exports have soared, home sales have fallen in recent years, with the average annual consumption per head around 20 litres (Australians are increasingly choosing quality over quantity and drinking more premium wines). Many of the best Australian wines are rarely seen overseas.

South Australia produces around 55 per cent of Australia's wine, New South Wales (including the ACT) 35 per cent, with the remaining 10 per cent shared between Tasmania, Western Australia and Victoria (there's also a small production in Queensland and in Alice Springs in the Northern Territory). The most famous wine regions are the Barossa Valley, Coonawarra and the Clare Valley in South Australia; the Hunter Valley in New South Wales (famous for its white wines, particularly chardonnay); Rutherglen/Milawa (port and muscat), the Yarra Valley where sparking wines are produced, the Geelong area and the Mornington Peninsula in Victoria; and the Margaret River and Swan River Valley in Western Australia. Although each region is noted for a particular style of wine and specific grape varieties, there's also a lot of experimentation and blending of grapes between regions. The main producers include Penfolds, Lindemans, Seppelt, Seaview, Orlando (producers of Jacob's Creek, Australia's best known international brand), Wyndham Estate, Hardys and Wolf Blass. There are also many small independent producers (often called boutique vineyards) making high-quality wines.

Most producers welcome visitors and provide tastings, although you may need to make an appointment at the smaller wineries (which are often more attractive than the larger, more commercial places). Some wineries charge a small fee of a few dollars (to deter free-loaders), which is refunded if you buy. Note, however, that buying wine at wineries isn't necessarily cheap and can be more expensive than bottle shops. Some wineries have restaurants where you can sample the local food and the house wines at the same time. Most regions have a visitors centre, e.g. the Barossa Valley Visitors' Centre, which is open from 9am to 5pm Monday to Friday and from 10am to 4pm on weekends and public holidays.

Australian wines have earned an increasing international reputation and respect in recent years, with their distinctive deep fruity flavour, full-bodied character and consistency. Although many jokes have been cracked at the expense of Australian wine in the past, today's wines are useful for much more than hand-to-hand combat or sprinkling on your fish and chips. In fact Australian wines have been astounding the judges and competitors at international wine exhibitions for over a century (one apocryphal story tells of an Australian wine winning a competition in France in the 19th century and then promptly losing it when it was discovered where the wine was produced!). Today Australia is the most dynamic wine-producing country in the world (and easily the best of the new world producers) and the sophistication and quality of its wines have improved in leaps and bounds in recent years. Growers aren't afraid to experiment; indeed many go out of their way to introduce new grapes varieties and create exciting new blends (they threw out the rule book decades ago). Australian winemakers have a pragmatic approach and are quick to introduce the latest technology (coupled with more traditional methods) and are noted for their high yields and low production costs. The climate, soil, modern equipment and techniques, allied to the Australians' freedom from tradition and love of experimentation, combine to produce some of the best and most original wines in the world.

Australian wines are usually named after the grapes used rather than given fancy names or named after the region in which they are grown. The best Australian wines are varietal (wines made from one grape variety), although they also produce many excellent wines made from a blend of grapes. Australia is best known for its superb cabernet sauvignon, pinot noir and shiraz (called syrah in other parts of the world) red wines. Blended wines are also common including grenache/shiraz, grenache/cabernet sauvignon, merlot/cabernet sauvignon and cabernet sauvignon/malbec, some of which are unique to Australia. Australian wines are noted for their high alcohol content, which for reds can be as high as 14.5 per cent. The US magazine *Wine Spectator* voted Penfold's 1990

Grange Hermitage their 'Wine of the Year' in 1996 (it ought to be good at around $130 a bottle!). Like some French wines, it's becoming too expensive to drink and is hoarded and traded like gold.

The most common white wine grapes are riesling, sauvignon blanc and chardonnay, although sémillon, gewürztraminer, muscadelle, colombard, moselle, sauterne, chenin blanc, viognier, verdelho and marsanne are also grown. Blended white wines include semillon/sauvignon, semillon/chardonnay and Mitchelton's Marsanne/Viognier/ Roussanne (which must take first prize for originality and is also an excellent wine). The Miranda Rovalley Grey Series 1994 won the *Best Chardonnay Worldwide* at the 1997 International Wine and Spirit Competition in London. Often grapes are blended from different regions, which is why Australia has no national wine appellation or quality control scheme. Buyers need to rely on the reputation of individual producers, which is generally an excellent guide as there's little year-on-year variation in quality and reliability (you will also rarely come across a bad, i.e. corked, bottle of Australian wine). Note that Australia has some 10,000 labels and interpreting them can be difficult for the uninitiated (although label information has improved considerably in recent years).

Wine is no longer the bargain it was some years ago and it's generally more expensive than in many European wine-producing countries due to higher taxes. A good 750ml bottle costs around $8 to $10, while $15 to $20 buys an excellent bottle. However, for everyday drinking, the best cask (box) wines are good quality and excellent value, and much cheaper than bottled wines. The price of Australian wine has been increasing steadily over the years and the best wines are now among the most expensive in the world. Prices have also increased in recent years due to a shortage of quality grapes. Imported wines are available in Australia but are expensive compared with similar quality local wines.

Wine Casks/Boxes: Australia invented the wine box or cask ('chateau cardboard') in 1974, which consists of a plastic bag in a box with a built-in tap. Some two-thirds of all wine sold in Australia is sold in casks, over 60 per cent of which is dry white or near dry white wine, 20 per cent dry red or sparkling wine, 10 per cent fortified and 10 per cent other types. Wine casks are good value (but are no longer the bargain they once were) and cost from $5 to $10 for three or four litres, with up-market wines costing around $7 for a two-litre cask. Most wine sold in casks is every bit as good as the table wines sold in Europe and North America and some is outstanding. Casks are particularly popular for parties and barbecues, and are also good for having the odd glass (the wine won't go off as no air can get to it).

More Information: There are many books about Australian wine including *Australian Wine - A Pictorial Guide*, *The Wines of Australia* by Oliver Mayo (faber and faber) and *The Penguin Good Australian Wine Guide* by Huon Hooke & Mark Shield (Penguin), which contains ratings for all of Australia's premium wines.

Sparkling & Fortified Wines: Australia also makes excellent sparkling wines (both red and white), which are produced by the *méthode champenoise* (fermented in the bottle), although they are no longer permitted to call it champagne. An excellent bottle can be purchased for $10 to $15 (Yellowglen make some of the best). Australia is also noted for its fortified wines, although they aren't well known overseas. These include port (red and white), sherry, muscat, madeira, tokay and brandy. Port is a popular drink in Australia (it's made in Victoria) with the best vintages selling for $80 to $100 a bottle (and a match for the very best that Portugal has to offer), while a good non-vintage (such as Hardys Tall Ships Tawny Port) can be purchased for around $10. Australia is also noted for its excellent sherries, muscats and tokays (although it has little in common with the Hungarian wine after which it's named), the best of which are world-beaters.

Beer & Other Drinks: Prior to WWII Australia was largely a beer-drinking country and Australians still consume far more beer than wine (over 100 litres per head annually). Bottled beer is sold in 375ml (stubbys) and 750ml bottles and in 375ml cans. The cost of a dozen 750ml bottles is around $20 to $30 or around $1.60 to $2 a bottle (a single 750ml bottle usually costs around $2.25). Most beer bottles have twist off caps, so no bottle-opener is required. Canned beer costs around $1.35 for single cans (375ml) reducing to around a $1 a can when you buy a case of 24. Cheaper 'no name' beers cost around 20 per cent less than the market leaders and don't taste significantly different from the more expensive brands (although most people have their favourites). Note that aluminium cans are recycled and there's a refund of a few cents a can to encourage recycling. For more information about Australian beer see **Bars & Pubs** on page 381. Australians don't drink a lot of spirits such as whisky and gin (around one litre per head, per year). A bottle of scotch whisky or London gin costs around $20 to $25 for the cheaper brands or around the same as in Europe. Australia's most famous spirit is rum of which the Bundaberg ('Bundy') brand is the national spirit (there are also 'over-proof' varieties which are lethal).

DEPARTMENT & CHAIN STORES

Australia has a number of excellent department and chain stores. For the uninitiated, a department store is a large store, usually on several floors, which sells almost everything and may also include a food hall. Some stores have a department where shoe repairs, key cutting and engraving is done while you wait. Each floor is usually dedicated to a particular type of goods, such as ladies' or men's fashions or furniture and furnishings. Some stores are housed in beautiful art-deco or Victorian buildings and many are air-conditioned with a restaurant or cafeteria, telephones and toilets. Note that the floor at street level is designated the ground floor (not the 1st floor) in Australia, the floor above the ground floor is the 1st floor and the floor below the ground floor is usually called the basement.

The major department store chains in Australia include Grace Bros., Myer and David Jones. Sydney has David Jones (with an excellent international food hall), Coles and Grace Bros., while Melbourne has Buckley & Nunn, Myer, Waltons, David Jones, George's (considered the Harrods of Australia) and the Japanese store, Daimaru. Myer's store on Bourke Street Mall in Melbourne is the largest department store in the southern hemisphere and one of the 10 largest in the world. Others include David Jones, Myer and Fosseys in Canberra; Fitzgerald's and Myer in Hobart; Myer, David Jones and John Martin's (known locally as Johnny's) in Adelaide; and Ahern's, Boans, Cole's and Myer in Perth. Department stores have struggled in recent years, under pressure from no-frills retailers and discount stores, although some have been revitalised and are making a strong comeback.

A chain store is a store with a number of branches, usually in different towns, e.g. Woolworth, Target, Kmart and Harris Scarfe. There are dozens of chain stores in Australia, selling everything from electrical and household goods to books and clothes. Many department and chain stores provide customer accounts and allow the account balance to be repaid over a period of time, although this isn't usually wise as the interest rate can be high. Many department and chain stores offer gift vouchers which can be redeemed at any branch. Department stores (and many smaller shops) provide a gift wrapping service, particularly at Christmas time, and will deliver goods locally or send them by post/courier, both within Australia and worldwide.

CLOTHES

It used to be said (with some truth) that fashions arrived in Australia a decade after they had swept Europe and North America, although this is certainly no longer true. Today Australian clothes shops offer a wide range of attire, from traditional made-to-measure clothing to the latest ready-to-wear fashions, with prices ranging from a few dollars to a few thousand. Top quality and exclusive (i.e. expensive) international ladies' and men's fashion shops abound and all the leading international labels are available in the major cities. In addition to department and chain stores, all towns and cities have a wealth of independent stores covering the whole fashion spectrum and all price brackets. Bush clothes (or 'bush chic') can be purchased at specialist shops including R.M. Williams (whose clothing has achieved cult status worldwide) and the Thomas Cook Boot and Clothing Company in Sydney. These include oilskin raincoats (e.g. Drizabone), riding boots, wide-brimmed Akubra hats, work shirts, moleskins (trousers made of closely woven cotton), sheepskin coats and leather belts.

Good clothes are relatively expensive in Australia, as there are high tariffs on imported clothing and footwear. The good news is that due to the mild climate most of the year, most people don't need an extensive wardrobe. In the early '70s, Australia had a thriving clothing manufacturing industry, but this has been decimated in the last 20 years. Australia also has a number of celebrated designers, some of whom have received international acclaim. Nowadays, most clothes are imported from Asia and many aren't up to the quality common in Europe and North America. However, although the quality of foreign-made clothes may occasionally be suspect, you usually get what you pay for. Most shops provide a tailoring or alteration service (for a small fee) and many stores also provide a made-to-measure tailoring service. Note that women's clothes' manufacturers usually base their sizes on the average size 12 and many women find it difficult to find fashionable clothes that fit. Sizes are often based on the average American woman's size which is larger than the average in Australia (see **Appendix C** for a comparison of sizes).

Shopping malls are the best place to shop for reasonably priced clothes, although if you're after designer clothes, the best time to buy is during the sales. Markets are often a good place to shop for cheap clothes and mail order fashion offers (in newspapers and magazines) usually provide good value for money. Good clothes can also be purchased at huge savings from factory outlets, which also sell designer clothes (although you should always try them for size and check for faults). There are vintage and secondhand clothing stores and markets in most Australian cities, plus clothes hire shops where you can hire anything from a ball-gown to a wedding dress, a morning suit to evening dress (perfect for the office party).

Many clothes' stores sell shoes and there's also a wide range of specialist shoe stores in Australia. Note, however, that Australia has few good shoemakers and quality imported shoes can be very expensive. Many people stock up on shoes before arriving in Australia and replenish their wardrobe on trips overseas. There are also sportswear shoe stores in most towns specialising in sports and leisure shoes (e.g. trainers), which are particularly fashionable among the young. Shoe repair shops can be found in all towns and many department stores and high streets have a shop (or department) where repairs are carried out while you wait. Note, however, that the quality of repairs from a family cobbler may be superior to that of an 'instant' repair shop.

NEWSPAPERS & BOOKS

Australians read more newspapers per head than most other nationalities and some 600 are published including national, state, city, regional and suburban newspapers. In addition to the major daily newspapers, most large regional cities have daily newspapers and smaller towns publish weekly newspapers (there are also suburban weeklies in capital cities). There's an active foreign-language press in Australia catering to immigrants of many different nationalities and producing around 150 publications in 40 languages. In general, the Australian press is fairly parochial and provides scant coverage of foreign news (unless it's a major news item) and you shouldn't expect unbiased political reporting in Australian newspapers, which often reflect the political bias of a newspaper's owners. The law regarding cross-media ownership is restrictive and has led to clashes between the government and media interests (foreign ownership is limited to 15 per cent).

Most major newspapers are owned by a few press barons including Rupert Murdoch (whose News Corporation owns some 60 per cent of the Australian print media) and Kerry Packer (Consolidated Press). Daily and Sunday newspapers range from the broadsheet 'quality' newspapers (those that are difficult to read in confined spaces) for serious readers and the popular tabloids for those who just like to look at pictures. There are just two national dailies, *The Australian* (including *The Weekend Australian* on Saturdays) and *The Australian Financial Review* (Monday to Friday only). *The Australian* is Australia's foremost newspaper and is printed simultaneously at six sites around the country from Monday to Friday. Most Australian newspapers are published state-wide only and all capital cities have their own local newspapers. The newspapers with the largest circulation are *The Herald-Sun* (Melbourne), *The Daily Telegraph* (Sydney), *The Sydney Morning Herald*, *The West Australian* (Perth), *The Courier Mail* (Brisbane), *The Age* (Melbourne) and the *The Advertiser* (Adelaide).

Most dailies publish larger Saturday editions which usually sell around 50 per cent more copies than the weekly editions and may include weekend supplements, e.g. *The Weekend Australian* and the *The Sydney Morning Herald*. The major Sunday newspapers include *The Sunday Telegraph* (Sydney), *The Sunday Mail* (Brisbane), *The Sun-Herald* (Sydney), *The Sunday Herald-Sun* (Melbourne), *The Sunday Times* (Perth), *The Sunday Mail* (Adelaide) and *The Sunday Age* (Melbourne). Most Sunday newspapers are tabloids and aren't as good quality as some of the weekly newspapers. Most cities also have evening newspapers. The circulation figures of Australian newspapers are relatively small by international standards, ranging from around 300,000 for *The Australian* to 700,000 for *The Sunday Telegraph*.

Foreign newspapers are available from international news agencies in major cities and cost around $5, or $9 for the larger Sunday editions, although they are a few days old when they arrive in Australia. They are also available in some (e.g. state) libraries. Newspapers of particular interest to British expatriates include the *Guardian Weekly*, *Weekly Telegraph*, *International Express* and *UK Mail*, all of which are published weekly and contain a run-down of the week's most important news (they are also available on subscription).

Australians are avid magazine readers, around 1,000 of which are published every month plus a further 700 trade publications. Foreign magazines are also popular and widely available in the major cities (particularly British and American magazines). Popular Australian political and business magazines include the *Business Review Weekly*, *The Bulletin* (Australia's oldest magazine, but now effectively controlled by the American *Time* magazine), *Australian Business* and an Australian edition of the American *Newsweek* magazine. Women's magazines abound and include *The Australian Women's*

Weekly (which is actually published monthly and sells around 1m copies), *Women's Day* (which is a weekly), *Family Circle, New Idea* and *Australian Good Housekeeping*. There are also Australian editions of many international women's magazines including *Cleo, Cosmopolitan, Belle, Elle, HQ, Marie Claire* and *Vogue*.

Newsagents in the ACT, New South Wales, Queensland and Victoria have a monopoly on newspaper distribution to homes, milk-bars and convenience stores. Newsagents are open long hours in major cities and also on Sundays. Prices are generally higher in remote areas and states other than where a newspaper is published, due to the high cost of distribution. Some cafés and tea rooms provide free newspapers for customers to read (not take home) and newspapers can also be read in public libraries and at newspaper offices. The good news for foreigners and computer users is that most Australian and foreign newspapers and magazines can be accessed via the internet. You can also take out a subscription to your favourite foreign newspapers and magazines at a large saving over local newsagent prices (if you're willing to wait a few weeks or months for delivery).

Books: Australians are avid book readers and all Australian cities have a wealth of bookshops (hopefully all selling this book) and Australia also has a flourishing publishing industry. Angus & Robertson's Bookworld and Dymocks are the largest chains of bookshops in Australia and are represented in most major cities (Dymocks in Sydney claims to be the largest bookshop in the southern hemisphere). Many department stores also have book departments. Melbourne is reckoned to be the best city for bookshops in Australia, with Sydney not far behind. Many bookshops are open during the evening (some until midnight) and at weekends in major cities.

There are also specialist bookshops in major cities such as travel, art, children's, feminist, gay and lesbian, new age, backpackers, Australiana and antiquarian. In many towns there are 'remainder' or cut-price bookshops, where remaindered books that have been sold off by publishers can be bought at discount prices. In the major cities there are secondhand bookshops for collectors and bargain hunters. Many large bookshops in cities also have a selection of foreign-language books and there are ethnic bookshops in some areas serving the local ethnic communities. Government publications can be purchased at Commonwealth Government Bookshops in the major cities or by mail from the Australian Government Publishing Service, GPO Box 84, Canberra, ACT 2601.

Note that books aren't sold at fixed prices in Australia and locally published books are typically sold at a 10 per cent discount. However, imported books can be expensive and are usually marked up by 25 to 50 per cent. Book tokens are a popular present for people of all ages and are sold and accepted by most bookshops. Many organisations and clubs run their own libraries or book exchanges and public libraries usually have an excellent selection of books.

FURNITURE

Furniture is usually good value for money in Australia, where there's a wide choice of modern and contemporary designs in every price range, although (as with most things) you generally get what you pay for. Exclusive imported furniture is available (with matching exclusive prices), although imports also include reasonably priced quality leather suites and a wide range of cane furniture from Asia. Among the largest furniture chain stores in Australia are Harvey Norman, Freedom Furniture and KC Country Furniture, plus the major department stores, all of which offer a wide range of top quality Australian-made and imported furniture. It costs around $10,000 to furnish an average three-bedroom home, although secondhand furniture is widely available. Furniture can also be rented for around $200 to $300 a month for an average size home.

Note that when ordering furniture, you may have to wait weeks or months for delivery. Try to find a store which has what you want in stock or which will give you a guaranteed delivery date (after which you can cancel and receive a full refund if you wish). A number of manufacturers sell direct to the public, although you shouldn't assume that this will result in huge savings, and should compare prices and quality before buying. There are also stores specialising in beds, leather, reproduction and antique furniture, and a number of companies manufacture and install fitted bedrooms and kitchens. Note that fitted kitchens are an extremely competitive business in Australia and you should be wary of cowboy companies who are specialists in shoddy workmanship.

If you want reasonably priced, quality, modern furniture there are a number of companies selling furniture for home assembly (which helps keep down prices). Assembly instructions are generally easy to follow (although some people think Rubik's cube is easier) and some companies print instructions in a number of languages. Retailers will often assemble furniture for you, although this increases the price. All large furniture retailers publish catalogues, which are generally distributed free of charge. Some stores offer you $100 or $200 for your old suite, when you buy a new one from them. However, this may not be much of a bargain (particularly if your suite is worth more than the amount offered) and you should always shop around for the best price and quality available. Furniture and home furnishings is a competitive business in Australia and you can often reduce the price by some judicious haggling, particularly if you're spending a large amount. Some stores will match a competitor's price rather than lose a sale. Another way to save money is to wait for the sales. If you cannot wait and don't want to (or cannot afford to) pay cash, look for an interest-free credit deal. Check the advertisements in local newspapers and national home and design magazines such as *Australian Home Beautiful, Australian House & Garden* and *Better Homes and Gardens*. See also *The Bargain Shoppers* guides to Melbourne and Sydney (see page 420).

HOUSEHOLD APPLIANCES

Large household appliances such as cookers and refrigerators are usually provided in rented accommodation and may also be fitted in new homes. Many homeowners include fitted kitchen appliances such as a cooker, refrigerator, dishwasher and washing machine, when selling their house or apartment, although you may need to pay for them separately. Dishwashers (mechanical type, not the wife/husband) are still something of a luxury item in Australia and aren't usually found in rented accommodation. If you wish to bring large appliances with you, such as a refrigerator, washing machine or dishwasher, note that the standard Australian unit width isn't the same as in other countries. Check the size and the latest Australian safety regulations before shipping these items to Australia as they may need expensive modifications (they usually aren't worthwhile bringing to Australia). There's a wide range of household appliances in Australia, from both Australian and foreign manufacturers. Note that some appliances such as refrigerators cost twice as much to run as others (choose those with a high energy efficiency rating, which are cheaper to run). Note that refrigerators/freezers in Australia are normally 'tropicised' or fan-assisted to cope with the high average temperatures.

If you already own small household appliances, it's worthwhile bringing them to Australia as usually all that's required is a change of plug (but check first). If you're coming from a country with a 110/115V electricity supply (e.g. the USA) then you'll need a lot of expensive transformers (see page 141). Don't bring a TV to Australia as it won't work (see page 178). A huge choice of home appliances are available in Australia these days and smaller appliances such as vacuum cleaners, grills, toasters and electric irons aren't expensive and are usually of good quality. It pays to shop around, as quality, reliability and prices vary considerably (the more expensive imported brands are usually the most reliable). Before buying household appliances, whether large or small, it may pay you to check the test reports in *Choice* magazine (see page 434) at your local library. The cost of major household items is listed in the free *Cost of Living and Housing Survey* published annually by the Commonwealth Bank of Australia.

If you need kitchen measuring equipment and cannot cope with decimal measures, you'll have to bring your own measuring scales, jugs, cups (US and Australian recipe cups aren't the same size) and thermometers (see also **Appendix C**). Note also that Australian pillows and duvets aren't the same size or shape as in many other countries.

SECONDHAND BARGAINS

There's a lively secondhand market in Australia for almost everything, from antiques to motor cars, computers to photographic equipment. You name it and somebody will be selling it secondhand. With such a large secondhand market there are often bargains to be found, particularly if you're quick off the mark. Many towns have a local secondhand or junk store and charity shops (e.g. Salvation Army or Vincent de Paul), selling new and secondhand articles for charity (where most of your money goes to help those in need). There are a number of national and regional weekly newspapers devoted to bargain hunters such as the *Trading Post* in Sydney.

If you're looking for a particular item, such as a camera, boat or motorcycle, you may be better off looking through the small ads. in specialist magazines for these items, rather than in more general newspapers or magazines. The classified ads. in local newspapers are also a good source of bargains, particularly for items such as furniture and household appliances. Shopping centre (mall) and newsagent bulletin boards and company notice boards may also prove fruitful. Expatriate club newsletters are a good source of household items, which are often sold cheaply by those returning home. Another place to pick up a bargain is at an auction, although it helps to have specialist knowledge about what you're buying (you'll probably be competing with experts). Auctions are held in Australia throughout the year for everything from antiques and paintings, to motorcars and property. Local auctions are widely advertised in newspapers and via leaflets.

There are antique shops and centres in most towns, and antique street markets and fairs are common in the major cities (where you can pick up interesting Australiana — but you must get there early to beat the dealers to the best buys). For information about local markets, inquire at your local tourist office or library. Car boot (trunk) sales are gaining popularity in Australia and yard sales, where people sell off their surplus belongings at bargain prices, are also popular. Sales may be advertised in local newspapers and signposted on local roads (they are usually held on weekends).

HOME SHOPPING

Home shopping by mail, phone, fax or computer (using on-line computer services or the internet) has become increasingly popular in recent years. Direct marketing is worth some $5 billion a year in Australia, 75 per cent through direct mail and catalogues, with the remainder through tele-marketing. Mail-order catalogue shopping has long been commonplace in Australia, particularly among people living in remote areas. In addition to dedicated mail-order companies, most major department stores also provide mail-order catalogues. Direct retailing is fairly common in Australia, particularly for computers, office equipment and supplies, and financial and insurance services. TV shopping is also becoming increasingly popular and products sold through infomercials have already had a huge success. There are two, 24-hour pay TV shopping channels in Australia, the TV Shopping Network (TVSN) and The Value Channel (TVC). TVSN offers some 4,000 individual product lines, an unconditional money-back guarantee and delivery in five to 10 working days (at a fixed rate anywhere in the world).

Internet: Shopping via the internet is a fairly recent innovation, but is growing at a huge pace (Australia is second only to the USA in the number of internet users per head of population) and is expected to dominate retailing in the next century. Food retailers such as Woolworth and Coles Myer are likely to introduce internet food shopping in the next few years. Under present rules, consumers are exempted from sales tax and customs' duty when imported mail-order goods attract a total tax bill of less then $50. You can buy virtually anything over the internet and large savings can be made on goods that don't incur a high mail or shipping cost. Australians are increasingly using the internet to buy products such as CDs, books and sporting goods (e.g. fishing equipment) from the USA, on which savings can be substantial. Note that when buying expensive goods overseas, you should always insure them for their full value.

It's estimated that some $2 billion is lost in sales and taxes on overseas internet sales, which prompted the Australian government to launch an investigation. Australia is more concerned than many other nations, as overseas traders can easily undercut Australian prices and circumvent Australia's high import tariffs and taxes, which could become a real threat to Australia's economy in future. Note that Australian banks don't officially allow businesses to accept credit card orders over the internet, although many businesses ignore this edict as banks have no way of knowing whether an order was received over the internet or by some other method. However, new security standards have been introduced in recent years such as the Secure Electronic Transaction (SET) standard, which makes internet shopping much safer.

Note that home shopping can be a mine-field, although you have the same rights as when shopping in-store (however, they are more difficult to enforce). Before committing yourself to buying anything from home, always make sure you know your rights and don't send cash through the post or pay for goods in advance unless absolutely necessary (and you have a cast-iron, money-back guarantee). It's always advisable to investigate mail-order and internet companies and to pay by credit card, as you may then have redress against the credit card company if goods don't materialise or aren't as advertised. If a company is a specialist mail-order trading company, make sure they are a member of the Australian Direct Marketing Association (ADMA), which has a code of conduct and offers assistance to consumers (tel. freecall 1800-252 389). You should be wary of doing business with companies located in offshore locations, as there are a number of offshore scams (including fake credit cards, phoney lottery tickets, worthless phone cards, internet gambling and pyramid schemes). **If anything sounds too good to be true it almost certainly is!**

DUTY-FREE ALLOWANCES

Visitors or migrants coming to Australia are permitted to import the following goods purchased duty-free:

- 1,125ml (1.125 litres) of alcoholic liquor, including wine, beer or spirits, per person over 18 years of age;

- 250 grammes of tobacco products (for customs' purposes, 250 cigarettes are equal to 250 grammes) per person over 18 years of age;
- all personal clothing and footwear (excluding furs);
- articles for personal hygiene/grooming such as toiletries, but excluding perfume concentrate;
- articles taken out of Australia on departure, but excluding articles purchased duty and/or sale tax free in Australia (any duty/tax free goods are counted against your duty-free allowance);
- any other articles (except alcohol and tobacco) obtained overseas or duty and sales tax free in Australia, up to a total purchase price of $400 per person aged 18 or over ($200 for under 18s) — this includes goods intended as gifts or received as gifts, whether personal or carried on behalf of others;
- all visitors' goods (providing you intend to take them with you on your departure).

Members of the same family travelling together may combine their individual duty-free allowances. Duty and/or sales tax must be paid on any goods above the duty-free allowance, with excess articles being valued for duty/tax on the actual price paid for them, converted to Australian dollars. However, duty and/or sales tax up to $50 is waived on goods in excess of duty-free concessions, providing the goods are declared as excess to concessions and aren't for commercial purposes. If purchase receipts aren't available, alternative methods of valuation may be used. Note that some items (such as jewellery) are subject to high rates of duty and/or sales tax. Payment of duty and tax can be made in cash, by travellers' cheque (in $A) and by international credit card. Information can be obtained from state customs' offices (see **Appendix A**) or the Australian Customs Service, GPO Box 148, Fyshwick, ACT 2609.

One unusual feature at Australian airports is in-bound duty-free shops where you can buy alcohol and tobacco products, and a limited range of perfumes and cosmetics before you reach immigration and customs. There are also city duty-free shops where you can buy duty-free goods (upon presentation of a valid international air ticket) before going to the airport to catch your plane. Check the prices here first as they are usually lower than at airports. Purchases must usually be taken from the shop in a sealed bag (marked 'Important - Duty-Free Goods in Possession') that must be keep intact until you have boarded your flight. Alcohol, cigarettes, perfume and jewellery must be purchased within 10 days of your departure and kept sealed until you have left Australia. However, some goods such as cameras, film, watches and most electronic goods can be used as soon as they are purchased. The maximum permitted value of purchases is $400, which are listed on your ticket and must be shown to customs' officers at airports, so you must take them with you as hand baggage when leaving the country (so don't buy a life-size stuffed kangaroo!).

RECEIPTS & GUARANTEES

When shopping you should always insist on a receipt and keep it until you have left the store or have reached home. This isn't just in case you need to return or exchange goods, which may be impossible without the receipt, but also to verify that you have paid if an automatic alarm goes off as you're leaving the shop or any other questions arise. You should always check receipts immediately on paying (particularly in supermarkets), as if you're overcharged it's often impossible to obtain redress later. When you buy a large object which cannot be wrapped (such as a life-size stuffed kangaroo), a sticker should be attached as visible evidence of purchase (in addition to your receipt). You need your receipt to return an item for repair or replacement (usually to the place of purchase) during the warranty period.

It's advisable to keep receipts and records of all major purchases made while you're resident in Australia, particularly if your stay is for a limited period only. This may save you both time and money when you finally leave Australia and are required to declare your belongings in your new country of residence.

CONSUMERS' RIGHTS

If you buy something which is faulty, damaged or doesn't work or measure up to the manufacturer's or vendor's claims, you can return it and obtain a replacement or your money back. Note that extended warranties or money-back guarantees don't affect your statutory rights as a purchaser, although the legal status of a warranty may be unclear. Some stores offer an exchange of goods or a money-back guarantee for any reason, which isn't required by law, although this guarantee is usually for a limited period only and goods must be returned unused and as new. Some stores attempt to restrict your rights to a cash refund or to exchange goods when an item is faulty or unfit for use, which is illegal.

In Australia you have the right to a refund if you buy a faulty product (with the exception of goods purchased at auction). Signs such as 'no refunds given', 'no responsibility for loss or damage', 'goods left for repair at your own risk' and 'all care but no responsibility taken' are meaningless and unlawful (under state and federal laws). All goods must be of 'merchantable' (reasonable) quality and fit for the purpose for which they were sold, and it's illegal for sellers to include a clause in the conditions of sale that exempts them from liability for defects, product faults and lack of care. Most traders will back down once you show that you know the law and are determined to obtain your legal rights.

There are a number of 'consumer organisations' in Australia including consumer affairs bureaux, fair trading bureaux, citizens' advice bureaux, ombudsmen and small claims' tribunals (see also **Legal & General Advice** on page 451). A consumer affairs bureau will give general advice over the phone, but won't usually take any action on a complaint unless it's made in writing or in person. Note, however, that callers are often given poor or incorrect advice. If you make a complaint, the bureau will give you advice, write to the trader concerned on your behalf or may refer your complaint to another government or consumer body to investigate. If you're unable to resolve a dispute with a trader or tradesman, you can take a dispute to a small claims or consumer claims court or tribunal for a small application fee. Note that claims are limited to $2,000 in Tasmania, $3,000 in New South Wales (up to $25,000 for building disputes) and $5,000 in all other states and territories. Traders who fall foul of the Trade Practices Act can be fined up to $20,000.

The consumers' champion in Australia is the Australian Consumers Association (57 Carrington Road, Marrickville, NSW 2204, tel. (02) 9577 3333, internet: choice.com.au), which publishes a number of magazines for consumers including *Choice*, their general consumer magazine, *Choice Health Reader*, *Computer Choice*, *Choice Travel* and *Consuming Interest* (a quarterly magazine about consumer issues). The ACA also publishes and distributes a wide range of consumer-oriented books. *Choice* contains independent tests of products and services and is essential reading when buying major household goods. Magazines are available only on subscription (not from newsagents). The ACA also provides a Consumer Information Service (tel. (02) 9577 3399).

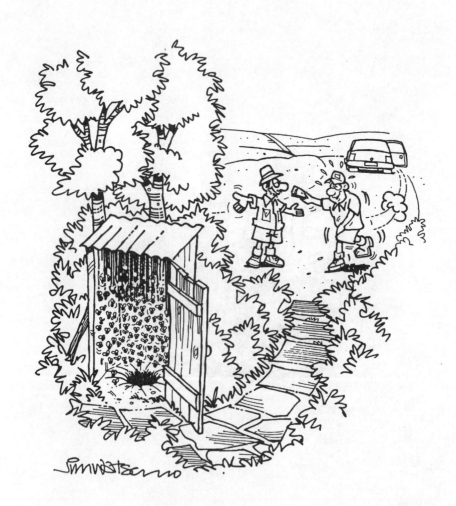

18.

ODDS & ENDS

This chapter contains miscellaneous information. Although all topics aren't of vital importance, most are of general interest to anyone planning to live or work in Australia, including everything you ever wanted to know (but were afraid to ask) about tipping and toilets.

AUSTRALIAN CITIZENSHIP

Immigrants are eligible for Australian citizenship after just two years' residence in the previous five years, including the 12 months immediately prior to their application. Applicants must be permanent residents; be at least 18 years of age; have a basic knowledge of the English language; be capable of understanding the nature of their citizenship application and understand the responsibilities and privileges of Australian citizenship; be of good character; and be likely to live in Australia or maintain a close and continuing association with Australia. The ability to speak English doesn't apply to people over 50 and those aged over 60 aren't required to understand the responsibilities and privileges of Australian citizenship.

Exceptions to the above rules apply to armed forces personnel (who need only to have served for three months), former Australian citizens (who need only to have been resident for 12 months in the last two years), spouses/widows/widowers of Australian citizens (who normally need to have been resident only for the 12 months prior to their application), permanent residents not present in Australia but engaged in activities beneficial to Australia, and various others. In certain cases such as spouses/widows/widowers of Australian citizens, applicants must show that they would suffer significant hardship or disadvantage if they weren't granted citizenship. Note that new citizenship requirements concerning language, residency and cultural knowledge may be introduced in 1999, and the residency requirement could be raised to four years.

Most people born in Australia before 26th January 1949 automatically became Australian citizens on that day and those born between 26th January 1949 and 20th August 1986 automatically became Australian citizens unless one of their parents was a foreign diplomatic or consular official. Since 20th August 1986, citizenship has been acquired if, at the time of a person's birth in Australia, at least one parent was either an Australian citizen or an Australian permanent resident. Those born overseas to a parent who's an Australian citizen can apply for registration as an Australian citizen by descent if they meet certain criteria. A child who's a permanent resident and legally adopted in Australia (after 22nd November 1994) automatically acquires Australian citizenship if at least one parent is an Australian citizen at the time of adoption.

New citizens must make a 'pledge of commitment': *From this time forward, under God*, I pledge my loyalty to Australia and its people, whose democratic beliefs I share, whose rights and liberties I respect, and whose laws I will uphold and obey.* (* the words *under God* may be omitted). The benefits of citizenship include the right to run for public office and to enlist in the defence and police forces and other public service jobs requiring citizenship; the right to be protected under Australian diplomatic arrangements overseas; the right to claim full welfare benefits; the right to register children born overseas as Australian citizens; and the right to vote. If you're granted Australian citizenship, you can retain your foreign passport (providing the country of issue permits dual nationality) and obtain an Australian passport. Once you're an Australian citizen, you must use your Australian passport to enter and leave Australia.

Around 16m people have Australian citizenship and a further 1.1m are eligible for citizenship. Some 120,000 people are granted citizenship each year, although only around one in 10 immigrants becomes an Australian citizen (despite the fact that some

80 per cent of immigrants interviewed within six months of their arrival claim they will take out citizenship). British immigrants are the least likely to become Australian citizens.

CLIMATE

The biggest attraction of Australia for many immigrants, particularly those from the northern hemisphere, is it's temperate climate and the lifestyle it affords. Australia is an 'upside down' country (weather-wise) with the warmest part (nearest the equator) at the top and the coldest at the bottom. It's less prone to climate extremes than other continents of comparable size, because it's surrounded by seas and has few high mountain masses. Australia's seasons are the opposite of the Northern Hemisphere, e.g. when it's summer in Europe it's winter in Australia and vice versa. The most pleasant seasons in most of Australia are spring and autumn, with the exception of Tasmania where is the most enjoyable season. Australia has climates to suit everyone (bar Eskimos), although it broadly has just two climatic zones. Some 40 per cent of Australia in the north lies in the tropical zone, while the remaining regions (south of the Tropic of Capricorn) are in the temperate zone and have four distinct seasons. The tropical zone has just two seasons: wet (November to April) and dry (May to October), while the temperate zones have four seasons: Spring (September to November), Summer (December to February), Autumn (March to May) and Winter (June to August).

The average hours of sunshine a day in Australia's capital cities ranges from five in Hobart to eight in Perth. January is the hottest month in most southern regions while February is hottest in Tasmania and southern Victoria. Average summer temperatures in January range from around 17°C (63°F) in Hobart to 29°C (84°F) in Alice Springs and Darwin. Temperatures reach over 30°C (86°F) in most areas during summer and the heat can occasionally be unbearable when temperatures soar to 45°C (113°F). The hottest place in Australia is Marble Bar (WA) where the temperature from October to March usually averages 40°C (104°F) or more. The highest recorded temperature in Australia is 53.1°C (127°F), measured at Cloncurry (QLD) in 1889. If you cannot stand extreme heat choose Hobart, Adelaide, Melbourne or Sydney rather than Perth, Brisbane or Darwin.

In winter, sleet and occasionally snow can fall on the urban areas of Hobart and even in Canberra or Adelaide. Australia has the lowest rainfall of any continent after Antarctica, with average annual rainfall for the capital cities varying from 1,536mm (60.4in) for Darwin in the monsoon region to 530mm (21in) in Adelaide. During the wet season in the north (January to March), roads can quickly become impassable as tracks become raging rivers after a downpour. In contrast, large arid inland areas get less than 250mm (10in) a year. Snow is rare except in the Australia Alps, straddling the New South Wales-Victoria border, where it's possible to ski between June and October, although temperatures can fall below 10°C (50°F) on winter nights in most regions.

NSW/Sydney: NSW has a huge variety of weather throughout the state, although it generally has an equable temperate climate. Sydney has the highest rainfall of any Australian capital city at 1,140mm (45in), which is spread fairly evenly throughout the year, although summer gets its fair share. In Sydney it rains on some 150 days a year with the wettest months being April to June. It has mild winters with daytime temperatures rarely falling below 10°C (50°F) and highs of around 17°C (63°F). Summer temperatures average around 25°C (77°F), although they can be quite humid (particularly from January to March). Occasionally the temperature in Sydney reaches over 40°C and can still be 30°C at midnight, although this is rare as cool sea breezes help lower temperatures during heat waves. Sydney frequently has high pollution levels in summer.

Canberra (ACT): Canberra has four distinct seasons, with hot dry summers and cold winters. It's situated inland and therefore the climate isn't moderated by the ocean as in Australia's coastal cities. Canberra is the coldest capital city in winter with temperatures plunging to around freezing at night, although it rarely snows. Winter mornings are frosty but most days are bright and sunny, with temperatures averaging around 12°C (54°F). Annual rainfall is low at around 660mm (26in). The ACT has an average of seven hours sunshine a day with summer temperatures averaging around 27°C (81°F). Canberra is noted for its clean air and isn't prone to pollution in summer.

Queensland/Brisbane: Queensland has a sub-tropical climate in the south and tropical in the north, with wet and dry seasons. Summer is the wet season, when rainfall averages around 1000mm (40in), particularly in the north, when violent thunderstorms and floods are common. The state has the wettest town in Australia, Tully, with over 4,000mm (160in) of rain a year (four times that of Brisbane). Extremes of flood and drought are common in country areas. Brisbane is one of the sunniest cities in Australia with an average of over 7.5 hours a day and mild sunny winters. Average temperatures are between 10°C (50°F) and 21°C (70°F) in winter and between 21°C (70°F) and 29°C (84°F) in summer. Summer temperatures can, however, reach over 38°C (100°F) and humidity can be very high, although it's usually tempered by cool sea breezes in coastal areas.

Victoria/Melbourne: The Victorian climate is somewhere between maritime and continental. The weather in Melbourne can be extremely changeable and it's said that you can experience all four seasons in one day (it's supposed to have almost English weather). Victoria has a generally mild climate, although it can experience very hot and cold periods. Melbourne experiences cold, wet and windy weather in autumn and winter, although temperatures rarely fall below around 5°C (41°F) with highs of around 14°C (57°F). Mountainous regions have snow in winter, when temperatures remain below freezing for long periods. It has low rainfall of around 660mm (26in), around half that of Sydney and Brisbane, which is fairly evenly spread throughout the year (June and July are the wettest months). Melbourne has mild autumns (the most pleasant season) and hot summers, when temperatures average 25°C (77°F) and occasionally soar to 40°C (104°F).

South Australia/Adelaide: South Australia has an almost Mediterranean climate, characterised by long, dry summers and short mild winters, and is said to have the best year-round climate in Australia. Adelaide is noted for its low rainfall (the lowest of any state capital) at just 530mm (21in), which falls mainly between April and October. South Australia is the driest state and its northern regions are mostly desert. It's sunny and not too cold in winter, when average temperatures are between 8°C (46°F) and 16°C (61°F). There's an average of four hours sunshine a day in winter and seven hours in summer. Summers are hot with maximum temperatures averaging over 27°C (80°F), although nights aren't usually too hot and there's low humidity. It's very hot in the northern desert regions where temperatures are frequently over 40°C (104°F).

Western Australia/Perth: The southern areas of Western Australia enjoy a Mediterranean climate, while northern areas have a tropical climate with dry and wet seasons. Perth is the sunniest capital city in Australia with an average annual temperature of 18°C (64°F) and over eight hours sunshine a day. Spring and autumn are the most pleasant seasons. The average rainfall is low at 914mm (36in) a year (although it's over 1,500mm/60in on the southwest coast), which falls mainly between April and October. The northern and eastern regions have very low rainfall and consist mostly of desert. Winters in Perth are mild (but wet) and sunny with average temperatures of between 9°C

(48°F) and 18°C (64°F), although frost is common away from the coastal areas. Summers are very hot with daytime temperatures frequently between 30°C (86°F) and 40°C (104°F) and hot nights, although it's a dry rather than humid heat. The summer heat is mitigated by cool breezes that blow in off the sea from Fremantle west of Perth, called the 'Fremantle Doctor' for its balming effect (some enterprising locals bottle it and sell it to tourists for $4.95 a go!).

Northern Territory/Darwin/Alice Springs: The Northern Territory has a tropical climate with just two seasons: wet from November to April (also known as the 'green' season), and dry for the remainder of the year. Basically the weather is as hot as hell all year round, with average daily temperatures in Darwin between 20 and 33°C (68 and 91°F) and reaching over 40°C (104°F) for weeks on end in the central desert regions (and Alice Springs). Rainfall is almost non existent in Darwin from May to September, which is more than compensated for between December and March when it's between 250 and 380mm (10 and 15in). The heat and humidity is often oppressive, with humidity as high as 95 per cent just before the start of the wet season. The Northern Territory is prone to cyclones and violent thunderstorms. Alice Springs has an average of 9.5 hours sunshine a day, with warm winters and hot and dry summers. Summer evenings can be cool and in winter the temperature often falls below freezing at night. Alice has low annual rainfall, with an average of around 40mm (1.5in) falling between December and February.

Tasmania/Hobart: Tasmania has a temperate climate with four distinct seasons without the extremes of the mainland cities. It's the coldest part of Australia and is occasionally hit by icy southerly winds from Antarctica, although it's still relatively mild by northern hemisphere standards. Nights can be cool throughout the year, although winters aren't as cold as in Canberra and Alice Springs. The average winter temperature in Hobart is between 5°C (41°F) and 12°C (54°F). It has around 620cm (25in) of rain a year (half that of Sydney and Brisbane), with rain falling on around half the days of the year, mostly between July and October. In the west, rainfall is around four times that of Hobart. Hobart receives an average of around five hours of sunshine a day with maximum summer temperatures averaging around 21°C (70°F). Water temperatures are much lower than the rest of Australia and it's generally too cold for sea bathing.

Australia is hit by frequent natural disasters including droughts, floods, cyclones, bushfires, earthquakes and tropical storms. Periodic droughts are a way of life and a constant worry for farmers. In late 1997, around three-quarters of NSW was in the grip of a drought (in 1995, 90 per cent of the state was hit by drought), which was lifted by rains in September and October. In many rural areas, rivers are sucked almost dry by the demand for water for irrigation, causing many to slow to a trickle and the water to become polluted by toxic algae (rivers are also polluted by salt and are dying). There are frequent (sometimes permanent) water restrictions in most regions of Australia, even in the major cities. The Australian weather is periodically (e.g. in 1997) affected by *El Niño*, an ocean warming phenomenon where prevailing cold water currents along the west coast of South America become warmer, thus upsetting weather patterns and leading to floods in North and South America and droughts in Australia.

Bushfires are a constant threat in country areas (mainly in summer) which are often caused by lightning strikes (many are also deliberately lit). They often threaten country towns and occasionally major cities, and deaths among firefighters and homeowners are frequent (some people needlessly lose their lives because they refuse to abandon their homes). Note that lighting fires in a bushfire zone is strictly forbidden (even where it's permitted you must ensure that every spark is extinguished before leaving and must *never* throw cigarette butts out of car windows). Although earthquakes are rare in Australia, in

1989 one struck Newcastle (NSW), killing 13 people and injuring 160, and causing damage costing $1.7 billion.

Cyclones (known as 'blows') are fairly common in the summer months (between November and April) in the northern regions of Australia (from Western Australia to Queensland). In 1974, cyclone Tracey flattened Darwin with gusts of up to 280kmh (174mph). It killed 66 people and destroyed over 5,000 homes leaving less than 500 intact, in what was the greatest natural disaster in Australia's modern history. The city has since been completely rebuilt to 'withstand' cyclones. Violent tropical and electrical storms are common in the north of Australia, particularly northern Queensland. In January 1998 torrential rains in Townsville caused widespread flooding when 500mm (20in) of rain fell in just 12 hours.

Approximate average daily maximum/minimum temperatures for the major cities are shown below in Centigrade and Fahrenheit (in brackets):

City	Spring	Summer	Autumn	Winter
Adelaide	22/11 (72/52)	28/17 (82/63)	22/12 (72/54)	16/8 (61/46)
Alice Springs	30/14 (86/57)	35/21 (95/70)	18/13 (82/55)	20/7 (68/45)
Brisbane	26/16 (79/61)	29/21 (84/70)	26/16 (79/61)	21/10 (70/50)
Cairns	29/21 (84/70)	31/24 (88/75)	29/22 (84/72)	26/18 (79/64)
Canberra	19/6 (66/43)	27/12 (81/54)	20/7 (68/45)	12/1 (54/34)
Darwin	33/24 (91/75)	32/25 (90/77)	32/23 (90/73)	30/20 (86/68)
Hobart	17/8 (63/46)	21/12 (70/54)	17/9 (63/48)	12/5 (54/41)
Melbourne	20/9 (68/48)	25/14 (77/57)	20/11 (68/52)	14/7 (57/45)
Perth	22/12 (72/54)	29/17 (84/63)	24/14 (75/57)	18/9 (64/48)
Sydney	22/13 (72/55)	26/18 (79/64)	22/14 (72/57)	17/9 (63/48)

A quick way to make a *rough* conversion from Centigrade to Fahrenheit is to multiply by two and add 30 (see also **Appendix C**). The weather forecast is available via the TV teletext services, in daily newspapers, and on TV and radio broadcasts. Warnings of dangerous weather conditions affecting motoring are broadcast regularly on ABC national and local radio stations. Many newspapers devote a full page (often in colour) to the weather and news programs on radio and TV are usually followed by detailed weather forecasts and analysis. Forecasts are usually extremely accurate, not least due to Australia's generally stable weather patterns.

CRIME

Australia is a safe country by international standards and you can usually walk almost anywhere at any time of the day or night in Australian cities without being mugged or murdered. However, it's important to take the usual safety precautions that you would in any country and to bear in mind that Australia has become a more violent society in the last decade. Crime rates vary from state to state and the Northern Territory is the most dangerous place to live, while Victoria is the safest. House-breaking and burglary is rampant in Australian cities, particularly Sydney, which has some reported 130,000 cases a year. Car theft is also widespread in Australian cities. Beware of pickpockets and opportunist thieves such as bag snatchers in major cities and crowded places, and keep a close eye on your belongings when travelling on public transport and when staying in hotels or hostels. Ramraiding used to be widespread in Australian cities, but has fallen off since retailers stopped displaying valuable goods in their windows.

Although basically honest, many Australians delight in 'beating the system' including cheating their employer (false sickies, bludging, etc.), fiddling their income tax (e.g. by not declaring income) and not paying motoring fines. In 1997 there were some 400,000 unpaid motoring fines (mostly for parking) in NSW alone, totalling around $235m. NSW plans to institute measures to recover unpaid fines (as other states have done) including the suspension of driving licences, cancellation of vehicle rego, seizure of assets and garnisheeing of wages. Many people take their lead from politicians, officials and the police, among whom corruption is widespread. Organised crime is rife in Australia's major cities, where much crime is linked to Asian gangs including Chinese, Thais and Vietnamese. It's estimated that crime costs Australia some $13 billion annually, including white-collar crime (e.g. fraud, forgery and false pretenses) which is thought to cost over $3 billion a year alone and is the country's largest crime cost (it's also the biggest crime growth area and the hardest to prosecute). Around $8 billion a year is spent on public and private crime prevention.

Violent crime is still relatively rare in Australia, although it has increased considerably in the last decades (along with most other western countries). There has been a huge increase in armed robbery in the last decade, and rapes, murders and assaults have all increased dramatically, although muggings are still relatively rare. Violent crimes by the young have soared (many children and youths are totally out of control) and gun (see below) and knife culture is widespread. Armed robbery is becoming fairly common in Australia, where banks, retail outlets and petrol stations are the most common targets (particularly all-night stores and petrol supermarkets). As a result some outlets have stopped accepting cash and many are considering closing at night. Women should avoid travelling alone at night and hitchhiking can be dangerous for both sexes (there have been a number of murders of backpackers in recent years, many involving a serial killer, thankfully now behind bars).

Drugs: Illegal drug use and trafficking is a vast and growing problem in Australia, although the authorities in some states have taken a more enlightened view of the use of soft drugs such as cannabis and marijuana in recent years, and there are nationwide moves to liberalise laws prohibiting their use. Smoking pot is widespread in Australia, where around a third of the adult population uses or has used cannabis and growing cannabis plants is a vast cottage industry (although the highest-grade cannabis comes from Papua New Guinea). The law regarding its use varies considerably. It has been decriminalised in the ACT and the Northern territory, where there's a fine of from $50 to $200 for its possession or production. However, its possession is still a criminal offence in New South Wales, Victoria, Queensland, Western Australia and Tasmania, where possession and/or production can result in a fine of from $2,000 to $300,000 (Queensland) and/or up to 15 years in jail. South Australia has abolished jail for small-time marijuana users and you're permitted to grow five marijuana plants, 30g of cannabis leaf, 2g of cannabis oil or 5g of cannabis resin. However, this may be reviewed since it was revealed that this is sufficient to yield enough marijuana for 4,000 joints! Unlike hard drugs there's little crime associated with cannabis use.

In stark contrast, the use of hard drugs is also responsible for a large proportion of crime in Australia, including over half of all thefts in the major cities (which are committed by drug addicts to finance their habit). It's also estimated that heroin trafficking is involved in some 40 per cent of serious crime. Despite the harsh penalties, Queensland is reckoned to be the worst state for drug use, particularly amphetamines such as ice, ecstasy and LSD. Some officials would like to decriminalise all drug use and treat users as victims rather than criminals, although this enlightened view cuts no ice with the USA, which has campaigned long and hard against any relaxation of international drug laws.

Guns: Like Americans, Australians have a fascination for guns and there are millions of legal and illegal guns in private hands. However, unlike America, the incidence of gun crime is remarkably low in Australia considering the number of weapons in circulation (only some 25 per cent of homicides involve the use of guns). Following the Port Arthur massacre in 1996 (when 35 people were shot dead when a gunman went on the rampage), the government instituted a buy-back of automatic and semi-automatic guns (including self-loading rifles and pump-action shotguns) financed by a Medicare levy. Owners were given 12 months to voluntarily hand in guns, although when the amnesty ended in 1997, it was conservatively estimated that a million people still held illegal guns. There has been compulsory registration of firearms since 1st July 1997 and owners must be aged over 18, undergo a training and safety course, and have a genuine reason to own a gun such as belonging to a shooting club. New penalties for possessing illegal firearms range from a $6,000 to $24,000 fine and up to four years imprisonment, depending on the type of firearm. However, Australia still has among the most liberal gun laws in the world.

Prisons: Australia has a tough sentencing and prison regime (including controversial private prisons), and the prison population has doubled since 1990 (prison violence is widespread). Tougher sentences have been introduced in recent years in many states, although it has had little or no effect on crime rates (the main reasons for crime are drug use, family breakdown, poverty and unemployment — particularly among youths). Western Australia has introduced controversial 'three strikes and you're out' legislation, whereby anyone convicted of a third burglary offence receives a mandatory, minimum one year's jail sentence. Many people are held in prison for up to 12 months on remand waiting for their case to go to trial, around half of whom are acquitted when they are brought to trial. Prisoners are also kept in police cells on remand where conditions are often appalling. A disproportionate number of Aboriginals and Torres Strait Islander people are convicted of crimes (mostly due to drunkenness and related crimes), who comprise just 2 per cent of the population but make up 15 per cent of prisoners in some states. Deaths in custody (including suicides) are high and include a disproportionately high number of Aboriginals.

Summary: Although the foregoing catalogue of crime may paint a less than rosy picture of Australia in the '90s, it's still a relatively safe place to live. In comparison with many other countries, Australia's crime rate isn't high and the incidence of violent crime is relatively low. If you take care of your property and take precautions against crime, your chances of becoming a victim are small. Note that the rate of crime in Australia's cities varies considerably from suburb to suburb, and anyone coming to live in Australia would be well advised to avoid high crime areas if possible.

Further Information: Police forces, central government, local authorities and security companies, all publish information and give advice on crime prevention. Police forces have local crime prevention officers whose job is to provide free advice to individuals, homeowners and businesses. See also **Home Security** on page 139, **Car Theft** on page 262, **Legal & General Advice** on page 451 and **Police** on page 455.

ECONOMY & TRADE

Despite its relatively small population (around 18m), Australia has the world's 13th largest economy. During most of the '80s it experienced strong economic growth and real GDP rose by around 5 per cent a year between 1987 and 1989, which was followed by a severe recession in the early '90s. During the '80s, Australia's current account deficit averaged over 4.5 per cent of GDP, which was around twice the average of the previous 20 years. It has now ballooned to around $20 billion and is the Australian economy's Achilles' heel. Australia's foreign debt has increased by some 2,000 per cent since 1980 and stands at around $220 billion, some two-thirds of which is held equally by British and American investors. One silver lining on the horizon is that governments (federal and state) are set to reap a huge windfall from privatisations in the next few years.

Australia has a relatively high growth rate of 3 per cent in 1997 (much higher than the OECD average) and growth was expected to be even higher in 1998, although this has been scaled back in the light of Asia's economic crisis. Inflation has fallen from around 11 per cent in the early '80s to below 2 per cent in 1997 and actually fell below zero (month-on-month) in 1997 for the first time in 35 years. Unemployment remains a pressing problem and was 8.5 per cent in 1997, although the outlook for 1998 is a slight improvement. The country's GDP forecast for 1998 is some US$425 billion, with GDP per head at around US$22,000.

Australia has a free-market economy which is subject to extensive regulation. However, deregulation and privatisation have been the watchword in recent years (in common with most European countries) and the former monopolies of airlines, banking and telecommunications have all been opened up to competition. The country has seen huge improvements in infrastructure and communications in the last few decades. The Liberal/National coalition government (which came to power in 1996) is pledged to open up government monopoly areas of business to private sector involvement. Australia was rated the eighth least corrupt nation in a 52-country survey in 1997, while (in another survey) Sydney and Melbourne were rated two of the top five best cities in which to do business in Asia. However, the country's economic performance still leaves a lot to be desired and was rated a lowly 15th out of 17 leading industrial nations surveyed in 1995. The economy is also expected to be badly hit in the next few years by Asia's economic crisis (which erupted in 1997), with some pessimistic analysts believing that it could lead to recession in Australia. The dollar was already hit by Asia's problems in late 1997 and the knock on effect was being felt in the tourist industry, with Australian airlines slashing flights to some Asian countries. On the other hand, the lower value of the $A is expected to help exports.

The Australian economy is based on mining, agriculture (including forestry and fishing), manufacturing, services and tourism (which earns around $15 billion a year). The country has a strong service industry (such as banking and insurance) which forms the largest and fastest-growing sector of the economy, and accounts for around three-quarters of GDP and employment. Australia is a major producer of alumina, bauxite, beach-sand minerals (rutile, monazite, zircon, ilmenite), iron ore, lead, uranium and zinc. It's the world's largest producer of bauxite and alumina, the third-largest producer of aluminium, and the second-largest exporter and fourth-largest producer of iron ore. It also has large deposits of nickel, copper, coal, manganese and other minerals, plus gold, silver, diamonds, opals, sapphires, and other precious and semi-precious stones. Australia has abundant energy resources including coal, natural gas and uranium, and also has oil fields in the Bass Straits. It produces around 80 per cent of domestic energy requirements and is a net exporter of liquified natural gas. Coal is the major source of energy used for electricity production.

Agriculture has traditionally been the backbone of the economy, although its relative importance has declined over the last few decades; however, it still accounts for around 5 per cent of GDP and some 25 per cent of export earnings. Australia's most valuable agricultural exports are wool (Australia is the world's largest producer), wheat, beef, dairy products, seafood, sugar and cotton, plus veal, cereals, wine, tobacco, fruit and vegetables. Some 55 per cent of agriculture exports (worth over $10 billion) go to Asian markets, 40 per cent to Japan. Australia has the world's third-largest marine fishing grounds, although it's only 51st in terms of catch. Fish stocks in Australian waters are dwindling fast, due to over-fishing and some species are already over-fished or facing their limit. Some fish are protected by quotas such as the southern bluefin tuna. Aquaculture (the farming of fish, molluscs and crustaceans) is becoming big business and now includes salmon, trout, barramundi, tuna, oysters, abalone, mussels, lobster, scallops and shrimp.

Farming employs around 6 per cent of the workforce on some 115,000 farms, although almost 15,000 (or one in 12) disappeared between 1985 and 1995, mostly as a result of increasing competition in export markets. However, agriculture (including horticulture, fishing, forestry, horses and the service industries to agriculture and agribusiness) has also created over 20,000 jobs in the last few years. Farming in Australia is a precarious business, where poor water resources and drought are a constant threat. In recent years sheep and beef farmers have been losing money and those in some sectors such as fruit and vegetables have been hit by cheaper imported produce which has led to some producers being unable to afford to pick their fruit.

Manufacturing output has fallen consistently for a number of years (it's technically in recession) and Australia now produces fewer manufactured goods than it did some 25 years ago (it's the main reason why Australia has such high unemployment). Manufacturing employs 1.1m people and generates around 13 per cent of GDP, down from 15 per cent in 1994. Australia has seen a far greater decline in manufacturing output and employment than any other western (OECD) country in the last 25 years, during which over 500,000 manufacturing jobs have been lost. Manufacturing has been the main loser in 'downsizing' (shedding workers) in recent years and an industry report in 1997 estimated that a further 100,000 manufacturing jobs could be lost by the year 2000. Most Australian businesses are too small to compete globally and only around 200 of the country's over 50,000 businesses employ more than 500 people.

Major manufacturing sectors include automobiles; domestic durables; chemicals, textiles and clothing; complemented by a small core of high-tech companies producing computer software; aerospace; communications and electronic equipment; electrical appliances; machinery; pharmaceutical and veterinary products; and photographic, professional and scientific equipment. The country has four car manufacturers (Ford, Holden (GM), Toyota and Mitsubishi — Nissan pulled out in 1992), although the country's automotive trade deficit is still around $7 billion a year. A number of industries are protected from cheaper imports by tariffs on imported goods (arguably illegal under world trade rules), although these have been cut in recent years. Tariff cuts have cost some 45,000 jobs in the car and clothing industries in the last decade, although assistance is still worth $4 billion a year through tariffs on imports, production bounties and export incentives. Tariffs are particularly important to protect jobs in the textile, clothing and footwear (TCF) industries, where Australia has the impossible task of trying to compete with Asian countries that can produce the same products for a fraction of the price.

Australia's economy is heavily dependent on imports and exports. The country's economic performance is determined in the fields and mines, with minerals (45 per cent) and agriculture (30 per cent) making up the bulk of exports and manufactured goods accounting for just 25 per cent. This makes the economy particularly vulnerable to weak commodity prices. Australia has failed to adapt to the challenges of globalisation and is at a crossroads, facing technological changes of the magnitude of the 19th century industrial revolution. It's plagued by high production costs (particularly wages), low productivity (rated the lowest among 12 leading industrialised OECD countries surveyed in 1997) and a relatively inflexible labour market. Added to which, it has fierce competition on its doorstep and almost anything made in Australia can be produced and bought cheaper in Asia. Australia is largely dependent on trade with Japan and any downturn in the Japanese economy would hit Australia hard. Japan is Australia's largest export market, followed closely by the USA, while the UK, Italy and Germany are its most important European Union (EU) trading partners. In the last few decades, Australia's exports to the EU have declined and sales to Asian countries are now three times those to the EU. New Zealand is also an important export market.

Australia has a number of world-renowned research institutes, notably the Commonwealth Scientific and Industrial Research Organisation (CSIRO), a comprehensive program funded by the government, mainly for agriculture, manufacturing and mining. Australia also has a number of world class university research institutes. However, spending on research and development is relatively low at around 1.5 per cent of GDP and Australia languishes in 16th place on the OECD list (it also doesn't get good value for its R&D investment). Foreign investment in Australia is low and the government plans to encourage more investors by offering additional tax incentives. The federal government encourages productive foreign investment, although restrictions apply to foreign ownership in certain sectors such as banking, the media and uranium mining. *Australia's Foreign Investment Policy; A Guide for Investors* is published by the Australian Government Publishing Service. Australia is a signatory to GATT (General Agreement on Trade and Tariffs) and also to the APEC *Bogor Declaration of Common Resolve* which commits aligned Asian-Pacific nations to free trade and investment in the region by the year 2020.

GEOGRAPHY

Australia is one of the world's oldest land masses (some of its rock was formed over 3m years ago), its largest island and smallest continent, and the only continent occupied entirely by one nation. Separated from other land masses, it evolved in partial isolation, resulting in its unique flora and fauna, and the development of the primeval Aboriginal race with a civilisation stretching back 40,000 years. The country extends 3,200km/1,988mi from north to south and 4,000km/2,485mi from east to west, covering an area of 7,682,300km2 (2,966,144sq mi), including Tasmania, with a coastline of 36,738km (22,826mi). It's the world's sixth largest country (after China, Russia, Canada, the USA and Brazil) and is around the same size as the continental USA (minus Alaska), one and a half times the size of Europe (excluding Russia) and some 31 times the size of Britain. Almost 40 per cent of the country lies north of the Tropic of Capricorn.

Australia lies in the southern hemisphere southeast of Asia between the Indian and Pacific oceans. Its nearest neighbour is Papua New Guinea (PNG) which is some 200km (125mi) north of Cape York in the northwest. Bali and other Indonesian islands lie off the northwest coast and the French island of New Caledonia is situated to the northeast. New Zealand is around 1,700km (1,050mi) off the east coast and to the south lies Antarctica. Australia is surrounded by four seas (Arafura, Coral, Tasman and Timor) and three oceans (Indian, South Pacific and Southern). The Great Barrier Reef lies between 50 and 300km (31 to 186mi) off the northeast coast stretching from the Torres Strait to Gladstone. It's the largest coral reef in the world extending some 2,000km (1,260mi) and encompassing an area of around 200,000km2 (77,226sq mi). The reef is the world's largest living entity and an important marine ecosystem containing many rare life forms (it has been declared a World Heritage site).

Australia is the world's flattest continent, with an average elevation less than 500m/1,640ft (the world's average is 700m/2,296ft) and only around one-twentieth is more than 600m/1,968ft above sea level. The Great Western Plateau covers most of Western Australia, a large part of the Northern Territory and South Australia, and part of Queensland. East of the plateau are the Central Eastern Lowlands, extending from the Gulf of Carpentaria in the north to eastern South Australia and the western Victorian coast. The Great Dividing Range (or Eastern Highlands) follow the east coast southwards from northern Queensland to southern Tasmania, separating a narrow fertile strip of land on the coast from the arid inland areas. The vast flat inland plain is broken only by a few low mountain ranges such as the Flinders and Macdonnell Ranges, the Olgas and Ayers Rock (or Uluru, the largest monolith/rock on earth, 9.4km/5.8mi in circumference — if you're tempted to climb it, bear in mind that many people die of heart attacks in the attempt!). Other mountain ranges include the Hamersley Range, the Kimberleys and the Stirling Range in Western Australia. Mount Kosciusko in the Snowy Mountains (Australian Alps) is the highest point (2,230m/7,316ft) in Australia.

Australia has the lowest rainfall of any continent after Antarctica and evaporation exceeds rainfall over 70 per cent of the country. Surface water is scarce and most lakes (with memorable names such as Lake Disappointment) and rivers are dry most of the year. Most of the centre and west of the country consists of desert (some 1.5 million km2/579,195sq mi). A third is desert or arid lands, some 55 per cent semi-arid native grass and shrub lands, and only around 6 per cent is cultivated for crops or used for intensive grazing. Australia has three main deserts: the Great Sandy, the Gibson and the Great Victoria, and several smaller ones. Lush forests are found on the east coast, particularly in the far north. The country's main rivers include the Murray, Darling, Ord and Swan. The main river is the River Murray, which with the River Darling, has a catchment area covering Queensland, New South Wales and Victoria. Severe salting has occurred in recent years due to indiscriminate land clearing for agricultural use, which has reduced irrigation potential and lowered the quality of drinking water (if nothing is done, the Murray-Darling basin will be dead in 50 years' time).

Australia is divided into six states (New South Wales, Queensland, South Australia, Tasmania, Victoria and Western Australia) and two territories (the Australian Capital Territory and the Northern Territory). The island of Tasmania (also called the Apple Isle) is larger than Denmark or the Netherlands and was founded by Dutchman Abel Tasman in 1642 and originally named Van Dieman's Land (changed to Tasmania in 1856). External territories include Norfolk Island (the territory of Ashmore and Cartier Islands), Christmas Island, the Cocos (Keeling) Islands and the Australian Antarctic Territory. Macquarie Island (around 1,600km/994mi southeast of Tasmania) is administered by Tasmania.

GOVERNMENT

Australia has a three-tiered system of government: federal, state and local.

Commonwealth (Federal) Government: The Commonwealth of Australia was formed on 1st January 1901 when the states gained their independence from Britain, prior to which each state was an independent self-governing colony. Australia has a parliamentary system of government based on the British system, while the (written) constitution and federal structure is based on the US model. The powers of the Commonwealth parliament (the legislature) are laid down in the constitution, which can be amended only by a referendum carried by a majority of voters in a majority of the states, as well as an overall majority. The Australian constitution provides for a division of power between the Commonwealth and the states. The sovereign head of the Commonwealth of Australia is Queen Elizabeth II, the Queen of England, who's represented in Australia by the Governor-General and state governors (see **Republic Debate** below).

The Commonwealth government has constitutional power over Australian territories (ACT and NT) but not the states, and can overturn laws made in territories such as the controversial euthanasia law enacted in the Northern Territory in 1995. It's responsible for income and sales tax, customs and excise, defence, foreign affairs, immigration, international trade and commerce, social services, postal services and communications, currency, banking and intellectual property (copyrights, patents and trademarks). The Commonwealth government raises by far the bulk of total government spending (around 80 per cent).

Like Washington DC in the USA, Canberra is the purpose-built capital city and capital of the Australian Capital Territory (ACT). The ACT was created as a compromise when New South Wales and Victoria couldn't decide between them whether Sydney or Melbourne should be the capital of Australia. In 1911 the ACT, located roughly half way between Sydney and Melbourne, was acquired from the New South Wales government. The Northern Territory was transferred from the state of South Australia to Commonwealth administration in the same year. The Commonwealth government first convened in Canberra in 1927, prior to which Melbourne was the seat of federal government. The Australian parliament is bicameral (consisting of two houses), the House of Representatives (lower house) and the Senate (upper house). A new Parliament House was inaugurated in 1988 on Capitol Hill.

House of Representatives: The house of representatives (lower house) is elected every three years and is the premier house, whose members make up the government of the day. It comprises 148 members (MHR), roughly twice the number of senators, each of whom represents a constituency with approximately the same population. The number of members allocated to each state and territory is proportionate to the number of residents, as follows: New South Wales (50), Victoria (37), Queensland (26), Western Australia (14), South Australia (12) Tasmania (5), the Australian Capital Territory (3) and the Northern Territory (1). The principal role of the House is as legislator (the making of laws).

Senate: The senate is composed of 12 senators from each state and two from each territory, making a total of 76. Senators are elected for a six-year term (except for the Australian Capital territory and the Northern Territory, who serve for three years) by a system of proportional representation, whereby voters vote for the candidates on party tickets. In Senate elections the whole state constitutes the electorate. Half the Senate 'retires' every three years. The Senate represents state interests and reviews legislation passed by the lower house, which must pass both houses before becoming law.

Political Parties; Australia has six main political parties: the Australian Labor Party (ALP), the Liberal Party (LP), the Country Liberal Party (CLP), the National Party of Australia (NPA), the Independent Party (IND) and the Australian Democrats (AD). Some parties, such as the National Party of Australia (NPA), are regional parties and stand in one or two states only. However, Australia essentially has a 'two-party' system, comprising the Liberal and National parties (conservative, right wing), who traditionally form a coalition, and the Australian Labor Party (socialist, left wing). The party with a majority of seats in the House of Representatives generally forms the government (although if it has no overall majority and cannot find coalition partners, it could find itself in opposition). The leader of the largest party (or the largest party in a coalition) becomes the Prime Minister (currently John Howard) who presides over a cabinet of ministers.

The Labor Party held power from 1983 until 1996 and is now a much more moderate party than it was in the '60s and '70s. The Liberal/National coalition government triumphed in the 1996 general election, outing Labor after 13 years in power. In 1996 the state of the parties in the House of Representatives was Liberal Party 75, Labor Party 49, National Party 18, Independent Party 5 and Country Liberal Party 1. In the Senate the Liberal Party had 31 seats, the Labor Party 28, Australian Democrats 7, National Party 6, and the Greens and Independent Parties 2 each. Thus the Liberal/National coalition had a huge majority in the lower house, but needed support from the Australian Democrats to get legislation through the upper house. The next general election is due by March 1999 at the latest, although the government may dissolve both houses in late 1998 and call a general election. This has been prompted by the Senate's rejection of the government's Wik legislation (which reduces Aboriginal native title rights). All Australian citizens must vote in Commonwealth elections or face a fine (although there's a move to change to voluntary voting). Only Australian citizens over 18 years of age may vote or British subjects who were resident in Australia and on the electoral roll on 25th January 1984.

State Parliaments: Each state has its own parliament (with upper and lower houses, except for Queensland), a cabinet headed by the Premier, a governor (who's the Queen's representative) and its own constitution. The head of the largest party in the NT and ACT is called the Chief Minister and the Queen's representative the Administrator. The lower house is called the Legislative Assembly or the House of Assembly and is usually elected for four years, while the upper house is usually called the Legislative Council and elected for twice the period of the lower house. Queensland, the Northern Territory (self-governing since 1978) and the Australian Capital Territory have a single house (the Legislative Assembly). State parliaments are generally elected under a preferential voting system for the lower house and by a variety of other systems for the upper house. Under the preferential voting system, each candidate is ranked in order of preference, which means that the person nominated as number one on most ballot forms isn't necessarily elected.

State government was long noted for its corruption and nepotism, although this is generally considered to be no longer the case. Many state politicians do hardly anything and in some states (e.g. Victoria) the upper house rarely sits (upper houses are essentially just a rubber stamp for the lower house). The states have control over education, health, housing, community services, infrastructure, justice, police, transport, roads, water, mineral resources, forestry, conservation, Aboriginal welfare and tourism. The states receive the bulk of their funding from the Commonwealth government, although they also levy stamp duty and charges on banking and other financial transactions, plus various other duties and taxes. The states are continually in conflict with the Commonwealth government over funding for services such as health care, law enforcement and general funding assistance.

Local Government: Local councils (including city, town, municipal and shire councils) provide services to their communities and control matters that cannot be handled by larger bodies (such as real estate zoning). There are some 900 local government authorities in Australia, whose powers and responsibilities vary from state to state, consisting largely of elected representatives who usually act in an honorary unpaid capacity. Although generally well run, some councils have run up huge debts, often through building and acquisition programs. Councils are largely funded by property taxes (rates), business taxes and water rates, supplemented by state and federal funds.

Local government is responsible for a number of services including town planning; garbage collection; water and sewerage; the construction and maintenance of local roads and other infrastructure; public health; libraries; community services; weights and measures; parks and recreation grounds; swimming pools; and sport and community centres. Local government departments and officials are listed in telephone directories under 'Local Government'.

Republic Debate: There's an ongoing debate in Australia over whether the country should become a republic and replace the Queen by an elected president. The sovereign head of the Commonwealth of Australia is Queen Elizabeth II, the Queen of England, who's represented in Australia by the Governor-General (G-G) and the state governors. The G-G is nominated by the Commonwealth government and appointed by the Queen, and acts only on advice of ministers in virtually all matters. However, this system led to a major political crisis in 1975, when the G-G dismissed the elected Labor government of Gough Whitlam and called a general election after the government failed to pass the budget bill (this has in fact, occurred six times in Australia's parliamentary history). There's a huge gulf between the republicans and monarchists, although in early 1998 the majority of people were in favour of a republic, which looks a certainty. A Constitution Convention was convened in 1998 and a referendum is planned for 1999 and, if (when) the people vote in favour, a republic is expected to be created in the year 2000 or 2001.

LEGAL & GENERAL ADVICE

Australian law is based on English common law, which it resembles closely. This is divided into statute law, enacted by legislature, and common law which is developed by the courts, both of which continually evolve as a consequence of precedents set by the courts. There's also a clear distinction between criminal law (acts harmful to the community) and civil law (disputes between individuals). If there's a dispute between federal and state law, federal law takes precedence. Less serious criminal cases are heard by magistrates or justices of the peace, while serious criminal and civil cases are held before a judge and jury (e.g. in a district or county court) consisting of 12 people in criminal cases (fewer in civil cases). There's no capital punishment in Australia, which has been abolished. Note that many minor offences incur fines including topless and nude bathing (where prohibited), littering, smoking where it's prohibited, drinking under age and on trains outside the permitted hours, and taking alcohol on to Aboriginal lands (laws regarding these and other offences also differ from state to state).

Each state or territory has its own court system consisting of magistrates' courts, intermediate district or county courts and supreme courts. There are also state courts of petty sessions, children's courts, family courts (which handle divorce cases and the custody of children), small claims' courts (see page 451) and industrial courts (which hear claims concerning industrial relations law). Some disputes such as family disputes and disputes between neighbours can be resolved by mediation. Most criminal cases in Australia are heard in state or territory courts. There are huge delays in hearing cases and local courts are hugely over-burdened, with some magistrates' courts processing up to 60 cases an hour. In serious cases the accused are held in prison on remand for up to a year before their cases are heard and when the accused is on bail cases can take up to 18 months to come to court.

A federal system exists to deal with matters over which the Commonwealth government has jurisdiction. The highest court in the land is the High Court of Australia (created in 1976), which is the country's final court of appeal from the states' supreme courts. It's presided over by the Chief Justice and six other justices, all of whom are political appointees. In recent years there has been an acrimonious relationship between the High Court and politicians (at stake is the balance of power between the judiciary and the government). Other federal courts include the Federal Court of Australia and the Family Court of Australia, both of which handle specialised cases involving federal law. In 1986 Australia changed the constitution which prevented Britain making laws in Australia or having any government responsibility, which also removed the ultimate legal appeal to the British Privy Council. At federal and state levels, the office of ombudsman deals with a variety of citizens' complaints against government administration. Administrative Appeals Tribunals hear appeals in cases involving freedom of information, immigration, pensions and tax.

If you're arrested you aren't required to give your name or address and are permitted to contact a friend or lawyer (called solicitors in Australia) before answering any questions. The police will provide an interpreter if you're arrested and cannot speak English. It's advisable to say nothing until a lawyer is present and even then you have the right to remain silent (although this may change under a government review). In some states, interrogation is recorded on video. If you're charged with an offence you may be released on a surety or remanded in custody (foreigners may have their passports confiscated to prevent them leaving the country). If necessary the police will provide a duty solicitor and you may be able to obtain legal aid. Each state has a legal aid commission if you cannot afford a lawyer, although it's becoming increasingly difficult to obtain due to cutbacks (which have resulted in some people being refused help unless they are facing jail or a fine of over $1,000) and is subject to a means test. Information about legal aid can be obtained from local courts.

There are a number of legal centres in Australia staffed by volunteers where those who cannot obtain legal aid or afford to pay for a private lawyer can obtain free legal advice. Free legal advice is available in all states and territories (there's a nominal fee of $2 in Western Australia) from various organisations including community legal or justice centres, legal aid commissions and citizens' advice bureaux. Your country's consulate or embassy in Australia can usually provide you with a list of local lawyers, if necessary speaking your native language.

As in most countries, civil liberties are constantly under threat, although Australia remains one of the most free and open countries in the world. For information regarding civil liberties in Australia, contact the Australian Civil Liberties Union (ACLU, PO Box 1137, Carlton, Melbourne, VIC 3053), who publish an annual booklet (*Your Rights*) containing information about your legal rights in various situations. You can become a member of the ACLU for around $20 or send a donation. See also **Consumers' Rights** on page 434.

MARRIAGE & DIVORCE

Marriage: Like most western countries, Australia has a declining marriage rate and people are also marrying later (around 27 years of age for women and 30 for men). Many more people are choosing to remain single and there's an increasing number of single, childless women. In 1996 the lowest number of marriages per capita was recorded this century. An increasing number of marriages (around 45 per cent of the total) take place outside the traditional church. One of the reasons is that the cost of a traditional church wedding and reception costs upwards of $18,000, in stark contrast to a simple garden civil ceremony with a minister or a civil celebrant which costs less than $200.

Some 70 per cent of Australians of adult age are married, around 15 per cent are lone parents and some 8 per cent (300,000 couples) live in *de facto* marriages (an unmarried couple who live together as husband and wife). Although the law varies depending on the state, generally when a *de facto* marriage breaks up after two years, either party can apply for division of property, maintenance or custody of children as if they were formally married. Note, however, that *de facto* couples don't have the same inheritance rights as married couples and should therefore ensure that their wills reflect their wishes.

Anyone planning to marry must complete a 'Notice of Intention to Marry' form and give it to the person (e.g. a minister or civil marriage celebrant) who will be conducting the marriage. Notice must be given between one and three months before the planned date of the marriage. Both parties must provide their birth certificates and, if applicable, a divorce decree or death certificate when they have been divorced or widowed. A man must usually be 18 to marry and a woman 16, although anyone aged under 18 must have their parents' consent to marry and permission from a judge or magistrate. A marriage must be witnessed by two people aged over 18. A legal marriage that takes place overseas is almost always recognised in Australia. A woman usually takes her husband's surname when she marries; however, it isn't obligatory and she can retain her maiden name.

Divorce: Australia has the third highest divorce rate in the world, with marriages lasting an average of less than eight years (there's around one divorce for every two marriages). 1995 saw the highest number of divorces (around 50,000) for 20 years. Under the Family Law Act, the only grounds for divorce in Australia is the irretrievable breakdown of a marriage and fault (e.g. adultery, cruelty or desertion) is no longer takes into account as grounds for divorce. Under the law, a marriage has irretrievably broken down if a couple has lived apart for one year and there's no reasonable likelihood of a reconciliation. It's also possible for these conditions to be met when a couple live separately and apart in the matrimonial home, although it's difficult to prove. If a couple have been married for less than two years, they must usually have considered reconciliation with the assistance of a marriage guidance counsellor before a court will hear divorce proceedings.

The average cost of a divorce in court fees alone (plus your solicitor's fees) is around $1,700, with a fee of $460 payable just to file an application. Extra fees apply to obtaining court orders on access and custody of children and property orders. Parents seeking ancillary relief in the Family Court (which normally entails child custody or access) must pay $150 and a parent defending such an action must also pay the fee. A one-off hearing, which can be imposed by the court if parents disagree on access, costs each parent $300. If parents go to court to decide alimony, proceedings can cost up to $10,000 a day and some divorced people have little left after their assets are sold to pay legal costs.

One of the court's main duties is to protect and promote the welfare and rights of dependent children. Both parents have joint custody of a child under Australian law, although one parent can ask for and be granted sole custody, when the wishes of the child are given special consideration. Before granting maintenance applications, the age, health, income, and financial resources and obligations of each party are taken into consideration (the same applies to the division of matrimonial property). Matters concerning the division of property, maintenance and custody of children must be decided before a divorce can be granted. After one month a decree becomes absolute and parties are free to remarry.

MILITARY SERVICE

There's no conscription (draft) in Australia where all members of the armed forces are volunteers. The Australian Defence Force (ADF) is comprised of three services: the Australian Army, the Royal Australian Air Force and the Royal Australian Navy. The combined strength of the ADF (including reservists and civilians) is around 105,000 (60,000 permanent service personnel, 28,000 reservists and the remainder civilians). Some 10 per cent are women (who make up around 13 per cent of regular service personnel) who are eligible for 99 per cent of navy and air force positions and around two-thirds of army positions (women are banned from carrying combat arms). In recent years there has been an exodus from the services, with the army having a 14 per cent attrition rate (the rates for the air force and navy are slightly lower). Many army recruits don't progress beyond the initial 12-week training period and military chiefs are looking at ways to make the introduction to army life more gradual (Aussies are becoming softies).

All soldiers initially enlist for a minimum period of four years under the Open Ended Enlistment Scheme and after four years can apply for discharge by giving six months' notice. Applicants for the ADF must be Australian citizens, eligible for grant of citizenship or must undertake to apply for citizenship when they are eligible. They must be aged at least 17 and under 35 (42 if they have a particular skill) and must be at least 152cm (5ft) tall. Reservists serve a minimum of 26 days a year (14 full-time). In recent years a new form of reserve service, the Ready Reserve program, has been introduced. Members serve full-time for 12 months followed by 50 days a year training for four years. Soldiers may also transfer from the Regular Army or Army Reserve to the Ready Reserve, and are then committed to five years' part-time training.

Australia is a member of a number of defence treaties including the Five Power Defence Arrangement (FPDA) with Malaysia, Singapore, New Zealand and Britain, and the ANZUS alliance with the USA and New Zealand. The country also has a close military relationship with Indonesia, with whom it conducts combined exercises. Australia spends some $10 billion a year on defence (2 per cent of its GDP) and there are plans to modernise the defence forces over the next 10 years at a cost of $5 billion.

PETS

Pets can be imported into Australia from most countries, although there are vigorous controls and strict regulations. All imports are subject to quarantine and an import permit must be obtained prior to shipment. Applications should be made at least two months prior to the intended date of importation to the Australian Quarantine Inspection Service in the state where you will be living. The application fee is $40 and the import permit takes up to four weeks to be issued and is valid for two months. Dogs or cats must have been continuously resident for six months (or since their birth) in the country of origin immediately prior to shipment to Australia, and must *not* have been in quarantine or under quarantine restrictions during the 30-day period prior to export. Both dogs and cats must be aged at least 12 weeks at the time of export. Certain breeds of dogs which are considered dangerous aren't eligible for importation including the pitbull terrier or American pitbull, dogo Argentino, fila Brazileiro and Japanese tosa. The importation of birds and small mammals such as hamsters is also prohibited.

All imported cats and dogs must have current vaccinations. Dogs must have vaccinations for distemper, hepatitis, parvovirus and para-influenza, and must also test negative for canine brucellosis, leptospirosis and canine tropical pancytopenia, within 30 days prior to export. Cats must have vaccinations for feline enteritis, rhinotracheitis and calicivirus. Vaccinations must have been given at least 14 days prior to shipment and not more than 12 months previously. All dogs and cats must be treated for internal parasites within 14 days prior to shipment and for external parasites within 96 hours of export, and pass a clinical examination within 48 hours of shipment. Note that if dogs and cats exported to Australia don't meet all the pre-export and post-arrival testing, vaccination, health and certification requirements, they may need to be exported, treated, destroyed or remain in quarantine until any disease concerns have been resolved.

Quarantine: Dogs and cats from New Zealand, Norfolk Island and the Cocos (Keeling) Islands aren't required to undergo quarantine. Dogs and cats from approved rabies-free countries and territories including Cyprus, Hawaii, Ireland, Japan, Malta, Norway, Singapore, Sweden, Taiwan and the UK are quarantined for 30 days. Dogs and cats from countries and territories where rabies is considered to be well-controlled (including Austria, Belgium, Canada, Denmark, Finland, France, Germany, Greece, Hong Kong, Israel, Italy, Luxembourg, Malaysia, the Netherlands, Portugal, Spain, Switzerland and the USA) are quarantined for a minimum of 30 days and a maximum of 120. Pets from certain other approved rabies-free countries (mostly Pacific islands) must spend 60 days in quarantine. The importation of dogs and cats from countries and territories where dog-mediated rabies is endemic is permitted only indirectly via an approved country, where the animal must be resident for at least six months prior to export to Australia. Many pet owners decide that the cost and strain of quarantine on their pets (and themselves) is too much to bear, and find their pets new homes.

Pets must be shipped by air to Australia in an approved container available from pet shipping agents such as Par Air Services (tel. UK 01206-330332) and Airpets Oceanic (tel. UK 01753-685571) in the United Kingdom. Animals are inspected at airports prior to shipment by a veterinary surgeon. On arrival in Australia, dogs and cats are quarantined in an approved animal quarantine station at Spotswood (Victoria), Eastern Creek (NSW) or Byford (Western Australia). Quarantine costs are around $20 a day for a dog or cat. Weekly visits are permitted during the quarantine period. For further information contact the Australian Quarantine Inspection Service (AQIS), GPO Box 858, Canberra, ACT 2601 (tel. (02) 6272 3933 or freecall 1800-020504). AQIS publish a leaflet *The Importation of Dogs and cats into Australia* (AQIS information sheet 2).

Imported dogs and cats must be identified by a microchip, for which there's a one-time fee of around $35 ($15 for pensioners). Microchipping is voluntary in most states, although there are plans to make it compulsory in some states, e.g. NSW. All dogs aged over three months must be registered annually.

POLICE

Each state and the Northern Territory has its own independent police force and there's also an Australian Federal Police (AFP) force, which is the federal government's primary law enforcement agency. The AFP are responsible for protecting federal property and enforcing federal laws such as those concerning drug trafficking, organised crime, terrorism, fraud, counterfeiting, money laundering and illegal immigration. The AFP also provide community police services in the Australian Capital Territory and in Australia's external territories. The National Crime Authority (which deals with organised crime) also has a policing role. Most police forces have special squads to handle VIP protection and specific crimes such as homicide, armed robbery, illegal drug trafficking and use, and fraud. There are also water police in cities and coastal areas.

There have been numerous police corruption scandals in Australia in recent years, which if the allegations are true, has some of the most corrupt police forces in the western world. After investigations in NSW, some 200 police officers were found to have criminal records. Corruption varies from minor infringements such as accepting free food and drinks and tipping off window and other repair companies for a commission; to selling inside information to criminals; taking bribes; extortion; fabrication of evidence; stealing goods and money; assaults and sexual harassment; selling confiscated drugs; and active involvement in organised crime. Freebies and kickbacks are considered to be a legitimate perk of the job by many officers.

An almost impenetrable police culture protects crooked officers, and the authorities find it almost impossible to obtain convictions (and, in any case, don't like to wash their dirty linen in public). Whistle-blowers who shop their colleagues or don't 'play the game' are likely to be hounded out of the force or transferred to 'back of Bourke'. The anti-corruption record of the Police Integrity Commission (PIC) has been described by some politicians as a joke. Sexism and racism are widespread in Australia's police forces and female officers generally have poor promotion prospects compared with male officers. There are an increasing number of complaints by the public against the police in some states (23,000 in NSW alone in 1996/97). Not surprisingly, the police have a poor public image and are often seen as a law unto themselves.

All police in Australia are armed and in addition to guns carry other 'weapons' to pacify 'dangerous criminals', such as extendable batons and capsicum (pepper) sprays (used by NSW officers to disable armed attackers). Police officers in NSW have been issued with new semi-automatic pistols (15-shot .40 calibre) in order to confront armed gangs. There have been frequent incidents where police have shot dead unarmed assailants or even innocent bystanders (the Australian police shoot more innocent people than crooks). Since 1990, some 75 people have been shot dead by the police and around 90 others have died from their injuries. The general police policy if threatened is to shoot and ask questions afterwards, although this is changing after a number of 'accidental' deaths in recent years. Most people believe that the police ought to be able to deal with a man armed with a knife without shooting him dead, e.g. by using nets, poles, sprays and batons. The number of deaths in custody has also risen alarmingly in recent years, including many Aboriginals (blacks are around 20 times more likely to die in custody than whites).

Police in some states (e.g. Victoria) have stopped attending routine calls (such as security alarms, the vast majority of which are false) in an effort to redirect sources to fighting crime. In some areas the police have drastically reduced the number of incidents they visit in order to reduce their workload and allow more police to patrol the streets. Instead of sending a car they may ask callers to report minor incidents by phone or go to a police station.

Details of your rights regarding arrest, questioning, statements or detention by the police are explained in the ACLU publication *Your Rights* (see page 452). The police emergency number varies depending on the state — if in doubt call the operator on 1234 or the national emergency line on 000. See also **Car Theft** on page 262, **Crime** on page 442, **Home Security** on page 139 and **Legal & General Advice** on page 451.

POPULATION

The population of Australia in 1997 was around 18.4m and has increased by over 4m in the last 20 years. However, population growth has slowed in the '90s due to lower net immigration and low birth rates, and the growth rate of 1.3 per cent in 1997 is expected to fall to 0.4 per cent or less. Australia has an aging population and a declining birth rate, as more women are choosing to marry later and have less children. At the present birthrate of 1.8 births per woman (half the birth rate in 1961) and current rates of immigration, the population is expected to grow relatively slowly in the 21st century. It's expected to be 19m by the year 2000, 20m by 2010, 22m by 2020 and between 26 and 28m by 2050 (although other projections have come up with a much lower figure of 20m by 2050 if current population trends continue). In the last 20 years there has been a huge rise in the number of people aged over 65 (who accounted for 12 per cent of the population in 1997) and in particular those aged over 85. By 2020 the over 65s are expected to comprise around 20 per cent of the population. The average age in 1997 was around 34 years.

The indigenous Aboriginal and Torres Strait Islander population of Australia is around 300,000, over half of whom live in New South Wales and Queensland. The Aboriginal population was estimated at between 200,000 and 750,000 when Australia was colonised by the English in 1788, although it was reduced dramatically in the 19th and early 20th centuries, since when it has recovered. Until 1961, population estimates in Australia excluded full-blooded Aboriginal people.

Australia is a highly urbanised society with over 70 per cent of the population living in the major cities situated on or near the coast. Only some 15 per cent of Australians live in rural areas, while around 85 per cent live in urban areas (up from just over 60 per cent in 1921). Some 80 per cent of Australians live within 30km (20mi) of the coast, over 40 per cent in Sydney and Melbourne alone, and 35 per cent in New South Wales. Over 60 per cent of New South Wales' population lives in Sydney and its suburbs. Almost two-thirds of the nation's population growth is in the eight capital cities, of which Brisbane, Darwin and Perth are Australia's fastest-growing cities.

In recent years Australians have been moving to the north and west of the country, fleeing the arid interior and clinging to the coast with more enthusiasm than ever. Rapid population growth in some areas of Queensland has placed a huge burden on the infrastructure such as roads, hospitals and schools, and is also having important environmental and ecological consequences in some areas. Some environmentalists believe that Australia already has more people than its natural resources can sustain, despite the huge size of the country and the low population density, while others declare that the country can sustain a much larger population. In recent years the post-war slogan of 'populate or perish' has been changed to 'populate *and* perish' by those who would like to see immigration drastically reduced.

The long-term population shift away from the southeast to the west and the tropics has continued unabated in the '90s. Victoria has lost thousands of people to other states in the last decade or so, although by 1997 the exodus had slowed to a trickle (most people go from Victoria to Queensland). Tasmania has been losing the most people in recent years (it recorded a net loss in 1996/97) and the ACT is also losing residents at a high rate. The flood of migrants (particularly retirees) to Queensland has slowed in recent years (but showed a 30 per cent increase in the past decade). Queensland is the fastest-growing state (most new arrivals are interstate migrants, many moving there on their retirement) and it's expected to replace Victoria as the second most populous state by around 2026.

The average population density in Australia is just two people per km2 (compared with 85 people per km2 in Asia), due to vast areas which are virtually uninhabited. The capital Canberra has a density of just 20 people per km2 or around a tenth of the population density of most European cities. Victoria is the most densely populated state. The population of states and territories and their capital cities in 1995 was as follows:

State	Population	
	State	Capital
ACT	300,000	Canberra (330,000)
NSW	6.1m	Sydney (3.8m)
NT	175,000	Darwin (80,000)
QLD	3.3m	Brisbane (1.5m)
SA	1.5m	Adelaide (1.1m)

TAS	475,000	Hobart (195,000)
VIC	4.5m	Melbourne (3.2m)
WA	1.7m	Perth (1.3m)

Since the war there has also been an influx of migrants from continental Europe, including large numbers of Greeks and Italians, plus Lebanese, Turks, Yugoslavs and various others. All major cities contain suburbs with predominantly ethnic communities and atmospheres including Chinese, Greek, Italian, Lebanese and Yugoslavs. Sydney is home to more New Zealanders than most cities in New Zealand and Melbourne's Greek population is the third-largest in the world (after Athens and Thessalonica). Since the end of the official 'white-Australia' policy in 1975, Australia has admitted large numbers of Asian immigrants, including many refugees from Indochina. There are also significant numbers of immigrants from the Pacific, Middle East, southern Europe, Central and South America, and South Africa. Around 75 per cent of the population is Australian born, while the remainder are immigrants. In 1997, over 90 per cent of the population was of European descent, 5 per cent Asian and 1.5 per cent Aboriginals. However, within the next 50 years around 25 per cent of Australia's population is likely to be of Asian origin.

RELIGION

Australia has a tradition of religious tolerance and every resident has total freedom of religion without hindrance by the state or community. Australia is a secular society and has no official state religion, although around 70 per cent of the population are Christians, half of whom are Catholics. Churches, particularly the Catholic Church, play a large role in education, and many schools are partly church funded. Church attendance is low in Australia where around 20 per cent of Australians claim to have no religion. In general, Australians are fairly laid-back about religion and there are few religious zealots and bible-thumpers as are common in the USA and some other countries.

Roman Catholics (4.6m) and Anglicans (4m) are the two main religions followed by the Uniting Church (1.4m), Presbyterian (750,000), Orthodox (500,000), Baptist (280,000), Lutheran (250,000) and Pentecostal (150,000) churches. Most Protestant churches have merged to become the Uniting Church, although the Church of England has remained independent. Unlike most Christian religions, the Orthodox Church thrives in Australia, particularly in Melbourne and Sydney. There are also sizeable Buddhist, Muslim and Jewish communities in the major cities. There has been a wider tolerance of smaller religious groups in the last decade, during which mainstream Christianity (apart from Catholicism) has declined while 'nature-based' religions such as witchcraft, druidism and paganism have proliferated. Eastern and minority religions have also gained in popularity including Taoism, Japanese Mahikari and Shinto. There's no recognised Aboriginal religion, although the Aboriginal people have many sacred sites throughout the country.

Every town and city has an Anglican and a Catholic church, and Uniting churches are also common. Religious centres for all the world's major religions are found in the major cities and details of church and religious services are published in local newspapers throughout the country.

SOCIAL CUSTOMS

All countries have their own particular social customs and Australia is no exception. Australians are generally *very* informal in their relationships (unless you move in diplomatic circles) and won't be too put out if you break the rules, providing your behaviour isn't too outrageous. On the other hand, in some circles, eccentricity is much prized and you may be invited to some social functions *only* if you act disgracefully (but make sure you don't confuse the Vicar's tea party with the local wife-swapping club). However, bear in mind that Australia is a multicultural society and many people retain the same customs as their forefathers in their home country, even when their family has been in Australia for generations. As a foreigner you may be forgiven if you accidentally insult your host, but you may not be invited again. The following are a few Australian social customs:

* When introduced to someone you generally follow the cue of the person performing the introduction, e.g. if someone is introduced as Bruce you can safely call him Bruce; however, if someone is introduced as Reverend Piddleton, it might not be wise to address him as 'Piddles' (unless he asks you to). After you have been introduced to someone, you usually say something like 'Pleased to meet you', 'hello' or even 'g'day mate' and shake hands. Among friends, it's common for men to kiss ladies on the cheek (or once on either cheek). Men don't usually kiss or embrace each other in Australia (although it depends on their nationality and sexual orientation). Australians are informal and even total strangers are called mate (even women), particularly in working class circles (so don't be surprised if your plumber calls you mate). Note that 'mateship' (which roughly equates to the American term 'buddy') is a different thing altogether. It applies to men only and to be someone's life-long mate is considered an honour and a big compliment.

* Australians are a lot more casual than their British or European cousins (similar to Americans) and direct in asking questions and voicing their opinions. Don't be surprised if an Aussie gives you the third degree when you meet for the first time. It's nothing personal — they're just being curious and are genuinely interested in strangers. Australians are usually friendly and hospitable to strangers, and will often go out of their way to help you. If you're travelling around Australia don't hesitate to use your contacts to obtain a free bed (Australians you meet may offer to put you up or volunteer their friends and family). It's considered quite normal to take people up on these offers, even if they're total strangers.

* It's common for neighbours to invite newcomers around for a cup of tea (or something stronger), although in cities (where people often live next to each other and remain strangers) you may have to go out of your way to meet your neighbours. A good way to meet the locals is to hold a barbie (although difficult in an apartment) and invite all your neighbours. If you're invited to a barbie, it's common to take a bottle of wine or some beer and you may be asked to bring your own meat (or whatever else you wish to eat). Some invitations ask guests to bring along a 'plate' (of food), e.g. a buffet dish from which everyone can help themselves. Men and women tend to congregate together at social occasions such as parties or barbies. You are, however, permitted to fraternise with members of the opposite sex.

* Australians tend to dress casually, e.g. to wear shorts to the office in summer, and it isn't usual to wear a suit or tie unless you're a high-powered manager or executive or a salesperson dealing with customers. Smart casual dress is adequate for most informal

occasions, e.g. when visiting restaurants and night clubs. When going anywhere that may be formal (or particularly informal), it may be wise to ask in advance what you're expected to wear. On the rare occasions when dress is formal, such as evening dress or dinner jacket, it will be stated in the invitation and you'll be unlikely to be admitted if you turn up in the wrong attire. If you're invited to a wedding, always enquire about the dress, unless you want to stick out like a sore thumb. In Australia, black or dark dress is usually worn at funerals.

• Guests are normally expected to be punctual with the exception of certain society parties when late arrival is *de rigueur* (unless you arrive after the celebrity guest) and at weddings when the bride is always late. Anyone who arrives late for dinner (unless his house has burnt down) or horror of horrors, doesn't turn up at all, should expect to be excluded from future guest lists.

TIME DIFFERENCE

Australia has the following three time zones:

Zone	GMT +	States
Eastern Standard Time (EST)	GMT+ 10 hours	ACT, NSW, TAS, QLD, VIC
Central Standard Time (CST)	GMT+ 9.5 hours	NT, SA
Western Standard Time (WST)	GMT+ 8 hours	WA

Australia is one of the few countries in the world to use a half-hour split time zone (CST).

All states and territories except the NT, WA and QLD operate daylight saving from October to March, when clocks are advanced one hour. To add further confusion, states don't always change their clocks at the same time. In Tasmania, daylight saving starts a month earlier and ends up to a month later than in other states (it lasts for six months). In NSW, the ACT, Victoria and South Australia, the changeover takes place on the last Sunday in October and the last Sunday in March of the following year. Clocks move forward one hour at 2am. This leads to as many as five different time zones between October and March, e.g. when it's 9am in Western Australia it's 10.30am in the Northern Territory, 11am in Queensland, 11.30am in South Australia and noon in NSW, Victoria and Tasmania. Attempts are being made to rationalise summer time zones. Note that daylight saving in Australia is the opposite of daylight saving in the northern hemisphere. Time changes are announced in local newspapers and on radio and TV.

Australia hasn't converted to the 24-hour clock and times in many timetables are given using the 12-hour clock ('am' and 'pm'). In this case the practice is that times printed in light type are before noon (am) and times printed in **bold** type are after noon (pm). Note that because of the huge time difference between Australia and many other continents (e.g. there's 10 or 11 hours difference between Europe and EST), you should always check the local time when making international calls (one sure way to upset most people is to wake them at 3am). The time difference between Australia and most countries is listed at the back of the white pages under 'Telstra 0011 International and Telstra Faxstream 0015 International'. You can also obtain world time information and a time converter for over 220 countries via the internet (Telstra.com.au). The time difference between Sydney (at noon in January) and some major international cities is shown below:

SYDNEY	LONDON	CAPE TOWN	TOKYO	LOS ANGELES	NEW YORK
NOON	1AM	3AM	10AM	5PM	8PM
				(both previous day)	

TIPPING

Tipping isn't a general custom in Australia (Americans please note!), although you may wish to leave a tip when you've had exceptional service or have received good value for money. People almost never tip taxi drivers in Australia, unlike in the vast majority of other western countries. However, it's common practice to round up taxi fares to the nearest dollar, although a cab driver may round the fare down rather than give you change. Porters (who usually have set charges), hairdressers, hotel staff, cloakroom attendants and garage staff (who clean your car's windscreen or check its oil or tyre pressures) also don't expect to be tipped (but won't complain if you do). Tipping in hotels depends whether you're staying at the five-star Regent Hotel in Sydney or some back street hovel (it's unnecessary in tourist or medium class hotels, although staff in grand establishments are used to receiving tips from their wealthy clients). Note, however, that tips are regarded by some Australians as patronising or even insulting.

One of the few exceptions to the 'no tipping' rule is top class restaurants, where it's customary to tip waiters up to 10 per cent of the bill for good service. Restaurant tips can be included in cheque or credit card payments or given as cash. The total on credit card counterfoils may be left blank to encourage you to leave a tip, so don't forget to fill in the total before signing it otherwise the waiter may enter his own 'tip' (if you don't leave a tip and the waiter tips the soup in your lap on your return, you'll know why). Note that service charges aren't usually added to bills by hotels and restaurants. It isn't customary to tip a barman in a bar or pub, although many people leave their small change.

TOILETS

Public toilets in Australia are usually free, generally clean and are commonly found in parks, council and tourist offices, shopping centres, department stores, and bus and train stations. The most sanitary (even luxurious) toilets are found in hotels, restaurants and department stores, and are usually for customers only. Clean toilets are also found in public and private offices, museums and galleries, airports, car parks, petrol stations and near beaches. Pub toilets vary from 'no-go areas' to spotless.

Australians don't use the terms powder room, washroom or bathroom when referring to a toilet, but use a variety of (often colourful) names including lavatory (lav), loo, toot, dunny (an outside toilet in country areas, often consisting a wooden hut with an earth floor), bog, thunder box, public convenience, ladies or gents (room), WC (water closet), crapper (after Thomas Crapper who invented the WC), privy and ablutions (many of these are of British origin, but are in general use in Australia). Some toilets have nappy (diaper) changing facilities and facilities for nursing mothers, and there are also special toilets for the disabled at airports, bus and rail stations, and in shopping centres in major cities. Roadhouses in country areas have toilets and showers. When using a Public toilet make sure you use the correct one, as it's sometimes difficult to tell the difference between the stylish male and female signs.

20.

MOVING HOUSE OR

LEAVING AUSTRALIA

When moving house or leaving Australia there are many things to be considered and a 'million' people to be informed. The checklists contained in this chapter are designed to make the task easier and hopefully help prevent an ulcer or a nervous breakdown, providing of course you don't leave everything to the last minute (only divorce or a bereavement cause more stress than moving house). See also **Moving House** on page 137 and **Relocation Consultants** on page 115.

MOVING HOUSE

When moving house within Australia the following items should be considered:

- If you live in rented accommodation you must give your landlord notice (the period will depend on your contract). You may need to remain until a minimum period has elapsed and if you don't give your landlord sufficient notice, you'll be required to pay the rent until the end of your contract or for the full notice period. This will also apply if you have a separate contract for a garage or other rented property, e.g. a holiday home.

- Inform the following:
  - Your employer.
  - If you're a homeowner and are moving to a new council area, you should inform your present council when you move and re-register in your new council area after arrival. When moving to a new area or state you may be entitled to a refund of a portion of your property taxes (rates).
  - Your electricity, gas and water companies.
  - Your telephone company (or companies).
  - Your insurance companies (for example health, car and home); banks, building societies, credit union, post office, stockbroker and other financial institutions; credit and charge card companies; hire purchase companies; solicitor and accountant; and local businesses where you have accounts.
  - Your family doctor, dentist and other health practitioners. Health records should be transferred to your new doctor and dentist, if applicable.
  - Your children's and your schools. If applicable, arrange for schooling in your new area. Try to give a term's notice and obtain a copy of any relevant school reports or records from your children's current schools.
  - All regular correspondents, subscriptions, social and sports clubs, professional and trade journals, and friends and relatives. Give or send them your new address and telephone number. Arrange to have your mail redirected by Australia Post (see **Change of Address** on page 157).
  - If you have an Australian driving licence or an Australian registered car, give your local state traffic authority (see page 239) your new address as soon as possible after moving.
  - Your local consulate or embassy, if you're registered with them (see page 108).

- Return any library books or anything borrowed.

- Arrange removal of your furniture and belongings by booking a removalist (see page 137) well in advance. If you have only a few items of furniture to move, you may prefer to do your own move, in which case you could need to hire a van.

- Arrange for a cleaning company and/or decorating company for rented accommodation, if required.
- If you're renting, make sure that you get your bond returned.
- Cancel the milk and newspaper deliveries.
- **Ask yourself (again): 'Is it really worth all this trouble?'.**

LEAVING AUSTRALIA

Before leaving Australia permanently or for an indefinite period, the following items should be considered *in addition* to those listed above under **Moving House**:

- Give notice to your employer, if applicable.
- **Check that your family's passports aren't out of date.**
- Check whether any special requirements (e.g. visas, permits or inoculations) are necessary for entry into your country of destination by contacting the local embassy or consulate in Australia. An exit permit or visa isn't required to leave Australia.
- Book a removalist (see page 137) well in advance. International shipping companies usually provide a wealth of information and may also be able to advise you on various matters concerning your relocation. Find out the exact procedure for shipping your belongings to your country of destination from the local embassy in Australia of the country to which you're moving (don't rely entirely on your shipping company). Special forms may need to be completed before arrival. If you've been living in Australia for less than a year, you're required to export all personal effects, including furniture and vehicles that were imported tax and duty free.
- Arrange to sell anything that you won't be taking with you, e.g. house, car and furniture.
- You may qualify for a rebate on your tax payments (see page 342). If you're leaving Australia permanently and have been a member of a superannuation scheme, your super benefits won't be paid until you reach the 'preservation' age, i.e. 55 for those born before 1st July 1960 and 60 for those born after 30th June 1964. Contact your company personnel office or superannuation company for information.
- If you have an Australian-registered car which you're permanently exporting, you should ask your local state traffic authority to de-register the vehicle, and register it in your new country of residence on arrival (as necessary).
- Depending on your destination, your pets may require special inoculations or may need to go into quarantine for a period (see page 454).
- Contact your telephone and other utility companies well in advance, particularly if you need to get deposits repaid.
- Arrange health, travel and other insurance as necessary (see **Chapter 13**).
- Depending on your destination, arrange health and dental checkups for your family before leaving Australia. Obtain a copy of all your health and dental records and a statement from your health insurance company noting your present level of cover.
- Terminate any outstanding loan, lease or hire purchase contracts and pay all outstanding bills (allow plenty of time as some companies may be slow to respond).

- Check whether you're entitled to a rebate on your car and other insurance. Obtain a letter from your Australian motor insurance company stating your number of years' no-claims' discount.

- Sell your house, apartment or other property, or arrange to let it through a friend or a letting agency (see **Chapter 5**). If you sell a second home in Australia, you may need to pay capital gains tax on any profit made on the sale (see page 355).

- Check whether you need an international driving permit or a translation of your Australian or foreign driving licence for your country of destination.

- Give friends and business associates in Australia a temporary address and telephone number where you can be contacted overseas.

- If you're travelling by air, allow plenty of time to get to the airport (see page 229), register your luggage, and to clear security and immigration.

- Buy a copy of *Living and Working in* ******** before leaving Australia. If we haven't written it yet, drop us a line and we'll get started on it right away!

Have a safe journey.

APPENDICES

APPENDIX A: USEFUL ADDRESSES

Embassies and Consulates (Canberra)

A full list of embassies and consulates in Australia are contained in two booklets (*Diplomatic List* and *Consular List*) published by the Department of Foreign Affairs and Trade and available from the Australian Government Publishing Service. Note that business hours vary considerably and all embassies close on their national holidays and on Australian public holidays. Always telephone to check opening hours before visiting. A selection of embassies in Canberra are listed below:

Austria: 12 Talbot Street, Forrest, ACT 2603 (tel. (02) 6295 1533/1376).

Belgium: 19 Arkana Street, Yarralumia, ACT 2600 (tel. (02) 6272 2501/2502).

Canada: Commonwealth Avenue, Canberra, ACT 2600 (tel. (02) 6273 3844).

China: 15 Coronation Drive, Yarralumia, ACT 2600 (tel. (02) 6273 4878).

Denmark: 15 Hunter Street, Drive, Yarralumia, ACT 2600 (tel. (02) 6273 2195/2196).

Finland: 10 Darwin Avenue, Yarralumia, ACT 2600 (tel. (02) 6273 3800).

France: 6 Perth Avenue, Yarralumia, ACT 2600 (tel. (02) 6216 0100).

Germany: 119 Empire Circuit, Yarralumia, ACT 2600 (tel. (02) 6270 1911).

Greece: 9 Turrana Street, Yarralumia, ACT 2600 (tel. (02) 6273 3011).

India: 3-5 Moonah Place, Yarralumia, ACT 2600 (tel. (02) 6273 3999/3774/3875).

Indonesia: 8 Darwin Avenue, Yarralumia, ACT 2600 (tel. (02) 6250 8600).

Ireland: 20 Arkana Street, Yarralumia, ACT 2600 (tel. (02) 6273 3022/3201).

Israel: 6 Turrana Street, Yarralumia, ACT 2600 (tel. (02) 6273 1309/1300).

Italy: 12 Grey Street, Deakin, ACT 2600 (tel. (02) 6273 3333).

Japan: 112 Empire Circuit, Yarralumia, ACT 2600 (tel. (02) 6273 3244).

Korea: 113 Empire Circuit, Yarralumia, ACT 2600 (tel. (02) 6273 3044).

Malaysia: 7 Perth Avenue, Yarralumia, ACT 2600 (tel. (02) 6273 1543/1544/1545).

Netherlands: 120 Empire Circuit, Yarralumia, ACT 2600 (tel. (02) 6273 3111/3386/3089/3899).

New Zealand: Commonwealth Avenue, Canberra, ACT 2600 (tel. (02) 6270 4211).

Norway: 17 Hunter Street, Yarralumia, ACT 2600 (tel. (02) 6273 3444).

Papua New Guinea: 39-41 Forster Crescent, Yarralumia, ACT 2600 (tel. (02) 6273 3322).

Philippines: 1 Moonah Place, Yarralumia, ACT 2600 (tel. (02) 6273 2535/2536).

Portugal: 23 Culgoa Circuit, O'Malley, ACT 2606 (tel. (02) 6290 1733).

Russia: 78 Canberra Avenue, Griffith, ACT 2603 (tel. (02) 6295 9033/9474).

Singapore: 17 Forster Crescent, Yarralumia, ACT 2600 (tel. (02) 6273 3944).

South Africa: Corner State Circle and Rhodes Place, Yarralumia, ACT 2600 (tel. (02) 6273 2424-7).

Spain: 15 Arkana Street, Yarralumia, ACT 2600 (tel. (02) 6273 3555).

Sweden: Turrana Street, Yarralumia, ACT 2600 (tel. (02) 6273 3033).

Switzerland: 7 Melbourne Avenue, Forrest, ACT 2603 (tel. (02) 6273 3977).

Thailand: Optus Centre, 3rd Floor, 10 Moore Street, Canberra, ACT 2600 (tel. (02) 6230 1561).

United Kingdom: Commonwealth Avenue, Canberra, ACT 2600 (tel. (02) 6270 6666).

USA: Moonah Place, Yarralumia, ACT 2600 (tel. (02) 6270 5000).

Australian Customs Service

Australian Capital Territory: Australian Customs Service, 5 Constitution Avenue, Canberra, ACT 2601 (tel. (02) 6275 6666).

New South Wales: Regional Director of Customs, GPO Box 8, 477 Pitt Street, 1st Level North Wing, Sydney, NSW 2001 (tel. (02) 9213 2000).

Northern Territory: Regional Director of Customs, GPO Box 210, Darwin, NT 0801 (tel. (08) 8946 9999).

Queensland: Regional Director of Customs, GPO Box 1464, Brisbane, QLD 4001 (tel. (07) 3835 3444).

South Australia: Regional Director of Customs, PO Box 50, Port Adelaide, SA 5015 (tel. (08) 8847 9211).

Tasmania: Regional Director of Customs, Imports/Exports, GPO Box 148B, Hobart, TAS 7001 (tel. (002) 301201).

Victoria: Regional Director of Customs, GPO Box 2809AA, Melbourne, VIC 3001 (tel. (03) 9244 8000).

Western Australia: Regional Director of Customs, PO Box 396, Fremantle, WA 6160 (tel. (09) 9430 1444).

Motor Vehicle Registration Authorities

Australian Capital Territory: Transport Regulation, GPO Box 582, Dickson, ACT 2602 (tel. (02) 6207 7019).

New South Wales: Registrar of Motor Vehicles, Roads and Traffic Authority, GPO Box K198, Haymarket, NSW 2000 (tel. freecall 1800-624 384 or (02) 9218 6888).

Northern Territory: Motor Vehicle Registry, GPO Box 530, Darwin, NT 0801 (tel. (089) 99 3149).

Queensland: Queensland Transport, Registration Division, GPO Box 2451, Brisbane, QLD 4001 (tel. (07) 3253 4700).

South Australia: Vehicle Operations Section, Department of Transport, PO Box 96, SA 5009 (tel. (08) 8348 9500).

Tasmania: Registrar of Motor Vehicles, 1 Collins Street, Hobart, TAS 7000 (tel. (03) 6233 5201).

Victoria: Vic Roads, 60 Denmark Street, Kew, VIC 3101 (tel. (03) 9854 2651/9854 2658).

Western Australia: Department of Transport, Licensing Division, 22 Mount Street, Perth, WA 6000 (tel. (09) 9222 6229).

Motoring Organisations

Australian Automobile Association (AAA), GPO Box 1555, 212 Northbourne Avenue, Canberra, ACT 2601 (tel. (02) 6247 7311).

National Roads and Motoring Association (NRMA), 151 Clarence Street, Sydney, NSW 2000 (tel. (02) 9260 9222).

National Roads and Motoring Association (NRMA), 92 Northbourne Avenue, Canberra City, ACT 2601 (tel. (02) 6243 8800).

Royal Automobile Club of Victoria (RACV), 550 Princes Highway, Noble Park, VIC 3174 (tel. (03) 9790 2211).

Royal Automobile Club of Queensland (RACQ), 300 St. Pauls Terrace, Fortitude Valley, QLD 4006 (tel. (07) 3361 2444).

Royal Automobile Association of South Australia Inc., 41 Hindmarsh Square, Adelaide, SA 5000 (tel. (08) 8202 4500).

The Royal Automobile Club of Western Australia Inc., 228 Adelaide Terrace, Perth, WA 6000 (tel. (09) 9421 4444).

The Royal Automobile Club of Tasmania (RACT), Cnr Patrick & Murray Streets, Hobart, TAS 7000 (tel. (002) 32 6300).

Automobile Association of Northern Territories Inc. (AANT), MLC Building, 79-81 Smith Street, Darwin, NT 0800 (tel. (089) 8981 3837).

Miscellaneous

Australian American Association, 39-41 Lower Fort Street, Sydney, NSW 2000, Australia (tel. (02) 9247 1092).

Australian-Britain Society, National Office, GPO Box 551, Sydney, NSW 2001, Australia (tel. (02) 9223 5244).

Australian-British Chamber of Commerce, 314 Regent Street, London W1R 5AB, UK.

Australian Chamber of Commerce (UK), Suite 10-16, 3rd Floor, Morley House, 314-322 Regent Street, London W1R 5AJ, UK

Australian Embassy, 1601 Massachusetts Ave., NW, Washington, DC 20036, USA (tel. 202-797-3000).

Australian High Commission, Australia House, Strand, London WC2B 4LA, UK (tel. 0171-438 8818).

Australian Taxation Office, 2 Constitution Avenue, Canberra, ACT 2600, Australia.

Australian Tourist Commission, 1st Floor, Gemini House, 10-18 Putney Hill, London SW15 6AA, UK (tel. 0181-780 2227).

BDS Challenge International, Alan Allebone, 1st Floor, 240 Bay Street, Brighton, Victora 3186, Australia (tel. (03) 9596 8699). International employment agency.

Department of Business and Employment, 228 Victoria Parade, East Melbourne, Victoria 3002, Australia.

Department of Industrial Relations, Employment, Training & Further Education, 1 Oxford Street, Darlinghurst, NSW 2010, Australia.

Financial and Migrant Information Service, Commonwealth Bank of Australia, Senator House, 85 Queen Victoria Street, London EC4V 4HA, UK (tel. 0171-710 3990). Publishes a free annual booklet for prospective migrants.

Foreign Investment Review Board, Department of the Treasury, Parkes Place, Parkes, ACT 2600, Australia (tel. (02) 6263 3795). Provide information about buying property in Australia for non-residents and retirees.

United Kingdom Settlers' Association (UKSA), PO Box 707, South Yarra, Victoria 3141, Australia (tel. (03) 9866 1722).

APPENDIX B: FURTHER READING

There are many useful reference books for those seeking general information about Australia including the *Year Book Australia* published annually by the Australian Bureau of Statistics. The Australia Government Publishing Service (AGPS, GPO Box 84, Canberra, ACT 2601) publishes and distributes a wealth of useful publications for prospective migrants, businessmen and visitors, and professional publications can be obtained from Australian Professional Publications, 220 Pacific Highway, Crows Nest, NSW 2065. A selection of books about Australia are listed below (the publication title is followed by the name of the author and the publisher's name in brackets). All books prefixed with an asterisk (*) are recommended by the author. Some of the books listed are out of print, but you may still be able to find a copy in a bookshop or library.

Living & Working

The Australian Immigration Book (Made-To-Measure)
***The Cost of Living and Housing Survey Book** (Commonwealth Bank of Australia)
Get A Job in Australia, Nick Vandome (How To Books)
How To Get a Job in Australia, Nick Vandome (How To Books)
How to Live & Work in Australia, Laura Veltman (How To Books)
Live & Work In Australia & New Zealand, Fiona McGregor & Charlotte Denny (Vacation Work)
Live, Work & Play in Australia, Sharyn McCullum (Kangaroo Press)
***Universal's Job Guide** (Universal Consumer Guides)

Tourist Guides

***Australia: Lonely Planet Travel Survival Kit** (Lonely Planet)
***Australia: The Rough Guide**, Margo Daly, Anne Dehne, David Leffman & Chris Scott (The Rough Guides)
***Australia & New Zealand Travel Planner** (TNT Magazine - See **Useful Addresses**)
Australia & New Zealand, Travellers Survival Kit, Susan Griffith & Simon Calder (Vacation Work)
Australia for Women, Travel & Culture, Susan Hawthorne & Renate Klein
Berlitz Pocket Guide to Australia (Berlitz)
***Berlitz Travellers Guide Australia** (Berlitz)
Essential Australia (Automobile Association)
***Frommers Australia on $45 a Day** (Macmillan Travel)
***Insider's Australia Guide**, Harry Blutstein (MPC)
***Insight Guides: Australia** (APA Publications)
***Maverick Guide to Australia**, Robert W. Bone (Pelican)
***Sydney Time Out Guide** (Penguin)

Travel Literature

Daisy Bates in the Desert, Julia Blackburn (Minerva)
***In The Land Of Oz**, Howard Jacobson (Penguin)
Outdoor Traveller's Australia (Stewart, Tabori, Chang)
***The Ribbon and the Ragged Square**, Linda Christmas (Penguin)
***Sydney**, Jan Morris (Penguin)
Tracks, Robyn Davidson (Vintage)

The Great Outdoors

Australian Bushcraft, Richard Graves (Taylor-Type)
***Bushwalking in Australia**, John Chapman (Lonely Planet)
Bush Tucker: Australia's Wild Food, Tim Low (Angus & Robertson)
How to Survive Australia, Robert Treborlang (Major Mitchell Press)
***Outback Australia** (Lonely Planet)
Outback Australia? No Worries!, Peter Wearing Smith (Omni Travel)
***Safe Outback Travel**, Jack Absalom (Five Mile Press)
***Stay Alive, A Handbook on Survival**, Maurice Dunlevy (AGPS)

Australians

12 Edmondstone Street, David Malouf (Penguin)
The Australians, In Search of an Identity, Ross Terrill (Bantam)
***The Australian People**, Craig McGregor (Hodder & Stoughton)
Christina Stead, Hazel Rowley (William Heinemann)
***A Fortunate Life**, Albert Facey (Viking)
***From Strength to Strength**, Sara Henderson
***More Please**, Barry Humphries (Penguin)
***Patrick White: A Life**, David Marr (Vintage)
***Robert J Hawke**, Blanche D'Alpuget (Penguin)
***Unreliable Memoirs**, Clive James (Picador)
Wild Card, Dorothy Hewett (Virago)

History/Culture

Australia's Immigrants 1788-1978, Geoffrey Sherington (Allen & Unwin)
***The Fatal Shore**, Robert Hughes (Pan)
***The Lucky Country: Australia in the Sixties**, Donald Horne (Angus & Robertson)
***The Penguin History of Australia**, John Malony (Penguin)
***The Road to Botany Bay**, Paul Carter (Faber & Faber)
***A Secret Country**, John Pilger (Vintage)
A Short History of Australia, Manning Clarke (Penguin)

Aboriginal Australia

Aboriginal Art, Wally Caruana (Thames & Hudson)
Charles Perkins, Peter Read (Viking)
Mutant Message Down Under, Mario Morgan (Thorsons)
*My People, Kath Walker (Jacaranga Wiley)
*My Place, Sally Morgan (Virago)
Seeing the First Australians, Ian & Tamsin Donaldson (Allen & Unwin)
*The Songlines, Bruce Chatwin (Picador)
Triumph of the Nomads, Geoffrey Blainey (Macmillan)
*Wandering Girl, Glenys Ward (Virago)

Miscellaneous

The 100 Things Everyone Needs to Know About Australia, David Dale (Pan McMillan)
Australia (Commonwealth of Australia)
*Australia & New Zealand by Rail, Colin Taylor (Bradt)
Bicycle Touring in Australia, Leigh Hemmings (Mountaineer Books)
*The Book of Australia (Watermark Press)
*The Great Barrier Reef (Readers Digest)
How to Be Normal in Australia, Robert Treborlang (Major Mitchell Press)
The Little Aussie Fact Book, Margaret Nicholson (Penguin)
*The Penguin Australian Encyclopaedia, Sarah Dawson (Penguin)
*The Sydney Morning Herald Good Food Guide, Terry Durak & Jill Dupleix
Traditional Australian Cooking, Shirley Constantine (McPhee Gribble/Penguin)
*The Wines of Australia, Oliver Mayo (Faber & Faber)

Magazines & Newspapers

Australia News, Outbound Newspapers, 1 Commercial Road, Eastbourne, East Sussex BN21 3XQ, UK (tel. 01323-412001).
Australian Outlook, Consyl Publishing, 3 Buckhurst Road, Bexhill-on-Sea, East Sussex TN40 1QF, UK (tel. 01424-223111).
Go Australia (Go Publishing Ltd, Burlington House, 64 Chiswick High Road, London W4 1SY, UK, tel. 0181-742 2255).
Southern Cross. Free weekly newspaper for homesick Aussies (published by TNT - see below).
TNT Magazine, 14-15 Child's Place, Earls Court, London SW5 9RX, UK (tel. 0171-373 3377). Free weekly magazine for expatriate Australians.

APPENDIX C: WEIGHTS & MEASURES

Australia uses the metric system of measurement (although some goods are still sold in imperial sizes and weights). Nationals of a few countries (including the Americans and British) who are more familiar with the imperial system of measurement will find the tables on the following pages useful. Some comparisons shown are only approximate, but are close enough for most everyday uses. In addition to the variety of measurement systems used, clothes sizes often vary considerably depending on the manufacturer (as we all know only too well). Try all clothes on before buying and don't be afraid to return something if, when you try it on at home, you decide it doesn't fit (most shops will exchange goods or give a refund).

Women's clothes:

Metric	34	36	38	40	42	44	46	48	50	52
UK	8	10	12	14	16	18	20	22	24	26
USA	6	8	10	12	14	16	18	20	22	24

Pullovers:

	Women's						Mens					
Metric	40	42	44	46	48	50	44	46	48	50	52	54
UK	34	36	38	40	42	44	34	36	38	40	42	44
USA	34	36	38	40	42	44	sm	medium	large	exl		

Note: sm = small, exl = extra large

Men's Shirts

Metric	36	37	38	39	40	41	42	43	44	46
UK/USA	14	14	15	15	16	16	17	17	18	

Men's Underwear

Metric	5	6	7	8	9	10
UK	34	36	38	40	42	44
USA	small	medium	large	extra large		

Children's Clothes

Metric	92	104	116	128	140	152
UK	16/18	20/22	24/26	28/30	32/34	36/38
USA	2	4	6	8	10	12

Children's Shoes

Metric	18	19	20	21	22	23	24	25	26	27	28
UK/USA	2	3	4	4	5	6	7	7	8	9	10

Metric	29	30	31	32	33	34	35	36	37	38
UK/USA	11	11	12	13	1	2	2	3	4	5

Shoes (Women's and Men's)

Metric	35	35	36	37	37	38	39	39	40	40
UK	2	3	3	4	4	5	5	6	6	7
USA	4	4	5	5	6	6	7	7	8	8

Metric	41	42	42	43	44	44
UK	7	8	8	9	9	10
USA	9	9	10	10	11	11

Weight:

Avoirdupois	Metric	Metric	Avoirdupois
1 oz	28.35 g	1 g	0.035 oz
1 pound	454 g	100 g	3.5 oz
1 cwt	50.8 kg	250 g	9 oz
1 ton	1,016 kg	1 kg	2.2 pounds
1 tonne	2,205 pounds		

Note: g = gramme, kg = kilogramme

Length:

British/US	Metric	Metric	British/US
1 inch =	2.54 cm	1 cm =	0.39 inch
1 foot =	30.48 cm	1 m =	3.28 feet
1 yard =	91.44 cm	1 km =	0.62 mile
1 mile =	1.6 km	8 km =	5 miles

Note: cm = centimetre, m = metre, km = kilometre

Capacity:

Imperial	Metric	Metric	Imperial
1 pint (USA)	0.47 l	1 l	1.76 UK pints
1 pint (UK)	0.568 l	1 l	0.265 US gallons
1 gallon (USA)	3.78 l	1 l	0.22 UK gallons
1 gallon (UK)	4.54 l	1 l	35.211 fluid oz

Note: l = litre

Temperature:

Celsius	Fahrenheit	
0	32	freezing point of water
5	41	
10	50	
15	59	
20	68	
25	77	
30	86	
35	95	
40	104	

The Boiling point of water is 100 degrees Celsius, 212 degrees Fahrenheit.

Oven temperature:

Gas	Electric	
	F	C
-	225-250	110-120
1	275	140
2	300	150
3	325	160
4	350	180
5	375	190
6	400	200
7	425	220
8	450	230
9	475	240

For a quick conversion, the Celsius temperature is approximately half the Fahrenheit temperature.

Temperature Conversion:

Celsius to Fahrenheit: multiply by 9, divide by 5 and add 32.
Fahrenheit to Celsius: subtract 32, multiply by 5 and divide by 9.

Body Temperature:

Normal body temperature (if you're alive and well) is 98.4 degrees Fahrenheit, which equals 37 degrees Celsius.

APPENDIX D: MAP OF AUSTRALIA

The map of Australia opposite shows the states of Australia, which are listed below along with their capital cities.

State/Territory	Capital
Australian Capital Territory (ACT)	Canberra
New South Wales (NSW)	Sydney
Northern Territory (NT)	Darwin
Queensland (QLD)	Brisbane
South Australia (SA)	Adelaide
Tasmania (TAS)	Hobart
Victoria (VIC)	Melbourne
Western Australia (WA)	Perth

INDEX

N

O

P

R

S

SUGGESTIONS

Please write to us with any comments or suggestions you have regarding the contents of this book (preferably complimentary!). We are particularly interested in proposals for improvements that can be included in future editions. For example did you find any important subjects were omitted or weren't covered in sufficient detail? What difficulties or obstacles have you encountered which aren't covered here? What other subjects would you like to see included?

If your suggestions are used in the next edition of *Living and Working in Australia*, you'll receive a free copy of the Survival Book of your choice as a token of our appreciation.

NAME: _____

ADDRESS: _____

_____

_____

Send to: Survival Books, PO Box 146, Wetherby, West Yorks. LS23 6XZ, United Kingdom.

My suggestions are as follows (please use additional pages if necessary):

OTHER SURVIVAL BOOKS

There are other *Living and Working* books in this series including America, Britain, France, New Zealand (summer 1998), Spain and Switzerland, all of which represent the most comprehensive and up-to-date source of practical information available about everyday life in these countries. We also publish a best-selling series of 'Buying a Home' books including *Buying a Home Abroad* plus buying a home in Florida, France, Ireland (autumm 1998), Italy (autumn 1998), Portugal (spring 1998) and Spain.

Survival Books are available from good bookshops throughout the world or direct from Survival Books. If you aren't entirely satisfied simply return them within 14 days for a full and unconditional refund. **Order your copies today by phone, fax, mail or e-mail from:** Survival Books, PO Box 146, Wetherby, West Yorks. LS23 6XZ, United Kingdom (tel/fax:44-1937-843523). E-mail: survivalbooks@computronx .com, Internet: computronx.com/survivalbooks.

ORDER FORM

Please rush me the following Survival Books:

Qty	Title	Price*			Total
		UK	Europe	World	
	Buying a Home Abroad	£11.45	£12.95	£14.95	
	Buying a Home in Florida	£11.45	£12.95	£14.95	
	Buying a Home in France	£11.45	£12.95	£14.95	
	Buying a Home in Ireland (autumn 1998)	£11.45	£12.95	£14.95	
	Buying a Home in Italy (autumn 1998)	£11.45	£12.95	£14.95	
	Buying a Home in Portugal (spring 1998)	£11.45	£12.95	£14.95	
	Buying a Home in Spain	£11.45	£12.95	£14.95	
	Living and Working in America	£14.95	£16.95	£20.45	
	Living and Working in Australia	£14.95	£16.95	£20.45	
	Living and Working in Britain	£14.95	£16.95	£20.45	
	Living and Working in NZ (summer 1998)	£14.95	£16.95	£20.45	
	Living and Working in Spain	£14.95	£16.95	£20.45	
	Living and Working in Switzerland	£14.95	£16.95	£20.45	
	The Alien's Guide to France (summer 1998)	£5.95	£6.95	£8.45	
				TOTAL	

Cheque enclosed/Please charge my Access/Delta/Mastercard/Switch/Visa* card,

Expiry date _____ No. _ _ _ _   _ _ _ _   _ _ _ _   _ _ _ _

Issue number (Switch only) _____ Signature: _____

* Delete as applicable (price for Europe/World includea airmail postage)

NAME: _____

ADDRESS: _____

_____

_____

Send to: Survival Books, PO Box 146, Wetherby, West Yorks. LS23 6XZ, United Kingdom **or tel/fax credit card orders to 44-1937-843523.**

PUBLISHED SUMMER 1998